D0909019

THE
WALTER
SCOTT
OPERAS

BENIAMINO GIGLI as Edgardo di Ravenswood, in the Metropolitan production of *Lucia di Lammermoor*, December 17, 1920. From the collection of Dino Bontà (Rome).

CE

§

THE
WALTER
SCOTT
OPERAS

AN ANALYSIS OF OPERAS BASED ON THE
WORKS OF SIR WALTER SCOTT

§

Jerome Mitchell

The University of Alabama Press
University, Alabama

032497

ML
80
S37M6
1977

Library of Congress Cataloging in Publication Data

Mitchell, Jerome.
  The Walter Scott operas.

  1. Scott, Walter, Sir, bart., 1771-1832.
2. Opera—History and criticism. I. Title.
ML423.S494M6   782.1′3   76-7406
ISBN 0-8173-6401-3

Copyright © 1977
The University of Alabama Press
All rights reserved
Manufactured in the United States of America

in memory of

BENIAMINO GIGLI

as

Edgardo di Ravenswood

and in

many other splendid roles

CONTENTS

ILLUSTRATIONS

PREFACE

My high regard for Donizetti's *Lucia di Lammermoor* led me many years ago to read Scott's novel, *The Bride of Lammermoor,* and this in turn led me into the larger subject of the present study, which is the first serious attempt to track down the many operas based on Scott's works and the only systematic study of these operas in relation to their originals. I approach the Scott operas as a literary historian rather than as a musicologist or music critic. I am less interested in passing judgment on an opera as music and drama than in seeing what the composer and the librettist do to a given novel, story, or poem when they reshape it into an opera.

I began preliminary investigation as early as 1959, but because of other commitments could not get to work in earnest until the spring of 1963. At that time, while still a graduate student at Duke University, I compiled a bibliography of Walter Scott operas and examined two of the operas based on *Ivanhoe.* For some time I considered the possibility of writing my doctoral dissertation on the Scott operas, but difficulty in locating necessary material and many other problems that I knew would arise caused me to decide, reluctantly, to abandon the project as unfeasible for satisfying the requirements for a degree. I resumed work in the summer of 1965 while in Europe, spending several weeks going through the various card catalogues in the Département de la Musique of the Bibliothèque Nationale and the unpublished multi-volumed catalogue of printed music in the main reading room of the British Museum. Most of the obscure librettos and scores which I needed were to be found in either Paris or London. Some months later I learned that the Newberry Library had extensive holdings in nineteenth-century opera, and it was there, in the summer of 1967, that I did an important part of my research. I returned to Europe for the summer and fall of 1968, working mostly in the British Museum, but also in Paris, Copenhagen, and Amsterdam. I took home with me on microfilm or in xeroxed form all material which I did not have time to examine then. Finally, in September 1969, I was ready to begin writing the first draft. Further trips to Europe became necessary later in 1969 and in the summer of 1971.

A few words about mechanical matters. I have sometimes reduced to one staff or in other ways simplified a musical illustration for the sake of brevity and conciseness. In quoting an operatic text I have sometimes followed the libretto, sometimes the score—whichever way seemed more practicable. Since many librettos and scores were carelessly printed, I have not considered the texts sacrosanct. I have silently corrected obvious errors, supplied missing punctuation, and made other minor alterations for the sake of uniformity. I have italicized *all* stage directions which I have quoted, again for the sake of uniformity, whether or not they appeared this way in a given libretto or score; but I have normally not followed an often used printer's convention of capitalizing (rather than italicizing) each letter of every character's name that appears in a stage direction. If I have incorporated a stage direction into my own text (rather than introduced it with a colon and blocked it off), I have used quotation marks as well as italics—except in the case of short directions like *aside* and *without.* When in English we refer to a change of scene, we almost always mean a change of setting. A French *scène,* or an Italian *scena,* changes when characters either come onto or depart from the stage. I have often used the words *scène* and *scena* to avoid confusion. In referring to a particular character I have used Scott's spelling when I am talking about the character of the novel and the librettist's spelling when referring to the operatic character. This procedure avoids the constant repetition of such phrases as "Scott's Edgar," "the operatic Edgar," "the Edgar of the novel," "the Edgar of the opera." All quotations from Scott follow the Border Edition, by Andrew Lang, but chapter numbers of the novels follow the continuous numbering that is used in most editions. I have given chapter numbers rather than page numbers so that quotations and other references can easily be looked up in almost any edition—and with only a minimum of bother when chapter numbering begins anew with each volume of the novel.

This book would not have been possible without the cooperation of the various libraries in which I have worked. I would like to express my gratitude to all of them: the Newberry (Chicago), with special thanks for the summer fellowship which I was granted in 1967; the Bibliothèque de l'Opéra (Paris); the Bibliothèque Nationale (Paris), with special thanks to Mlle Simone Wallon and Mme Y. Fédoroff of the Département de la Musique; the Kongelige Bibliotek (Copenhagen)—the late Dr. Sven Lunn was most helpful; the Stichting Toonkunst-Bibliotheek (Amsterdam); the National Library of Scotland (Edinburgh); the Central Public Library of Edinburgh; and finally the British Museum (London), where I did the major part of my research. Other libraries promptly responded to my written inquiries about one thing or another.

I wish also to express thanks to Professor P. M. Mitchell (University of

Illinois), for generously giving up many hours of his 1967 Christmas holidays to help me translate two lengthy Danish librettos based on Scott; to Professor Brian Dutton (University of Illinois at Chicago Circle), Mrs. Brunella Notarmarco Dutton, Dr. Aurelia Ghezzi (University of Georgia), Mr. Pier Paolo Pisani (Georgia), and Mr. Giulio Pomponio (formerly of Georgia), for graciously taking time from their own work to help me translate several Italian Scott operas; to Professor Margaret Schlauch (University of Warsaw) and Dr. Irena Janicka (University of Lódź), for helping me obtain a microfilm of a unique operatic score in the manuscript library of the University of Wroclaw (Breslau); to Professor and Mrs. Walter F. Schirmer (University of Bonn), for their continuous interest and encouragement; to Mrs. Lionel Stevenson and the late Professor Stevenson (Duke University), also for their interest and encouragement, and especially to Professor Stevenson, for reading my work in various stages and for suggesting ways of improving it; to the Department of English and the General Research Program of the University of Georgia, for giving me large blocks of time free from teaching and for supporting my research with generous grants; to the American Council of Learned Societies, for awarding me a travel grant to fly to Edinburgh for the Sir Walter Scott Bicentenary Conference, August 15–21, 1971, at which occasion I read a paper entitled "Operatic Versions of *The Bride of Lammermoor*." (It has since been published in *Studies in Scottish Literature,* X (1973), 145–164.)

Finally, I would like to express my particular gratitude to the Gigli family, for allowing me to offer this book in memory of the beloved tenor. He has always been my favorite singer.

JEROME MITCHELL

ABBREVIATIONS AND SHORTENED REFERENCES

AMZ	*Allgemeine Musikalische Zeitung*
Baker	*Baker's Biographical Dictionary of Musicians.* Fifth Edition, revised by Nicolas Slonimsky. New York, 1958.
BM	British Museum
BN	Bibliothèque Nationale
Clément & Larousse	Clément, Félix, and Pierre Larousse. *Dictionnaire des Opéras.* Paris, 1905; reprinted by the Da Capo Press, New York, 1969.
Fétis	Fétis, François Joseph. *Biographie Universelle des Musiciens.* Second Edition. 8 vols. Paris, 1863–67. Supplément et Complément, ed. by Arthur Pougin. 2 vols. Paris, 1878–80.
Grove	*Grove's Dictionary of Music and Musicians.* Fifth Edition, ed. by Eric Blom. 9 vols. London, 1954. Supplementary Volume, 1961.
Loewenberg	Loewenberg, Alfred. *Annals of Opera: 1597–1940.* Second Edition. Geneva, 1955.
MGG	*Die Musik in Geschichte und Gegenwart.* 14 vols. Kassel, 1949–68.
Newberry	Newberry Library (Chicago)
Riemann	Riemann, Hugo. *Musiklexikon.* Twelfth Edition, ed. by Wilibald Gurlitt. 3 vols. Mainz, 1959–67.
Schmidl	Schmidl, Carlo. *Dizionario Universale dei Musicisti.* Second Edition. 2 vols. Milan, 1926–29. Supplement, 1938.
White	White, Henry Adelbert. *Sir Walter Scott's Novels on the Stage.* Yale Studies in English, LXXVI. New Haven, 1927.

THE
WALTER
SCOTT
OPERAS

Sir Walter Scott, from the portrait by Andrew Geddes. By courtesy of the Scottish National Portrait Gallery.

1

§ § §

INTRODUCTION

There is no reliable list of operas based on the works of Sir Walter Scott. The information given in scholarly articles written in 1932 by Alfredo Obertello[1] and Jacques Gabriel Prod'homme[2]—articles which mark, incidentally, the centennial of Scott's death—is far from complete. One can glean more data by looking up the entry on Scott in *Grove's Dictionary of Music and Musicians* and checking out all the cross references, but even this does not produce an adequate account. Useful bibliographical information can be found in the appendix to Henry Adelbert White's published Yale dissertation, *Sir Walter Scott's Novels on the Stage* (New Haven, 1927), but since White was mainly interested in spoken drama, he did not give exhaustive data on the operas, nor did he always separate operas from plays that have occasional musical numbers. The recent article by Elizabeth Forbes[3] is disappointing because it adds nothing to our knowledge about the subject; it simply presents the already known data in readable, paragraph-form fashion along with bits of information about the performance history of each opera mentioned, the latter apparently coming for the most part from Loewenberg's *Annals of Opera,* a standard reference work.[4]

My own list has been culled from many different sources: Obertello, Prod'homme, Grove, White, Loewenberg, Clément and Larousse's *Dictionnaire des Opéras,* Towers' *Dictionary-Catalogue of Operas and Operettas,* Fétis' *Biographie Universelle des Musiciens, Die Musik in Geschichte und Gegenwart,* the card catalogues in the Département de la Musique of the Bibliothèque Nationale, the music catalogue in the main reading room of the British Museum—and various other works too numerous to list here. Sometimes a note in a standard reference work would lead me to another work in which I might find reference to a Scott opera that I had not known about. *Die Musik in Geschichte und Gegenwart* led me, for example, to Gerhard Glaser's dissertation on Holstein,[5] where I found a brief, vague, misleading footnote referring to an opera called *Le Derout de Culloden* by one Anton Berlijn. I later found the holograph full score in an Amsterdam library. Its correct title was *Le Lutin de Culloden.* It was not based mainly on *Waverley,* as Glaser had implied, but rather on *The Heart of Mid-Lothian* (and indirectly, through an earlier French libretto). I found out about Flotow's *Alice* by chance while browsing through some of the early nineteenth-century issues of *Le Ménestrel.* And I became aware of Rieschi's *Fidanzata di Lammermoor* also by chance when I filled out a call slip one day in the Bibliothèque de l'Opéra, ordering what I thought would be the libretto to Mazzucato's *Fidanzata di Lammermoor.*

In this study I am concerned primarily with operas, and I define opera simply as that type of theatrical production in which music and song are predominant. Thus I do not list or discuss (except in a few instances, for the purpose of comparison) the numerous "musical dramas" by Sir Henry Bishop and others, because there the emphasis is more on the spoken dialogue than on the music. If all the tuneful ditties are removed, one still has a stageable dramatic work.[6] If, on the other hand, the musical numbers are removed from a French opéra comique, the spoken dialogue left over would not make good sense by itself. Despite the frequent scenes of spoken dialogue, sometimes quite lengthy, the heart of the drama is its music; and the music is generally much more sophisticated than what one finds in the English musical dramas. Sometimes the dividing line between musical drama and opera is faint. Laurent's *Quentin Durward* and Horn's *Peveril of the Peak* bear many resemblances to Bishop's works; yet I classify them as operas because they contain more music than do the usual musical dramas and because they are generally referred to as "operas" rather than "musical dramas."

In addition to genuine operas I have included the two Rossini pastiches, *Ivanhoé* and *Robert Bruce,* both of which were put together by lesser known composers who fitted a new Scott libretto to music selected from several different Rossini operas. So far as I know, no one ever fitted a Scott libretto to the music of a *single* pre-existing opera, as was actually done twice in the annals of the Shakespeare operas.[7] I have also included operas in which the relationship between opera and novel is not on a simple one-to-one basis. One of the finest and most popular of all the Scott operas, Boieldieu's *La Dame Blanche,* derives mainly from both *Guy Mannering* and *The Monastery;* others, as will be shown, contain easily recognized motifs from several different Scott novels; and in one case, *La Muette di Portici,* the librettist Scribe has borrowed a memorable character from *Peveril of the Peak* and grafted her onto a well-known story that has no connection whatever with Scott's works. Sometimes a librettist has altered his source material so drastically that the resulting opera is a virtual parody of the original story. Examples of this approach are Grisar's *Sarah,* in which a highly serious story becomes a frivolous opéra comique, and Flotow's *Alice,* in which Cavalier becomes Roundhead and vice versa, not to mention other changes. The plot of Bellini's *I Puritani,* one of the most successful Scott operas, is like *Alice* in this respect. All these operas I discuss. On the other hand I have chosen not to discuss most of the operas based on the life of Mary, Queen of Scots, because, aside from the one exception to which I have allotted a separate chapter, they apparently derive from Schiller's *Maria Stuart* and/or commonly known history rather than from Scott's *Abbot*.[8] I do not discuss Carlo Coccia's *Edoardo in Iscozia* (1831) for the same reason. It is based on the same historical background as *Waverley,* but not one element in it derives clearly and indisputably from Scott; it would be just as it is even if the Waverley Novels had not been written.[9] Another way in which I necessarily had to limit my topic was to exclude from discussion the many operas based directly on the works of writers like Hugo and Manzoni who were *influenced* by Scott.

Winton Dean remarks that "no one knows the total number of operas based on Shakespeare's plays."[10] The same could be said about Scott. I am aware of two operas based on a Scott poem, *The Lady of the Lake* (but can discuss only Rossini's, since Vesque von Püttlingen's musical setting of the same libretto no longer exists); one opera based on a story, *The Highland Widow;* one opera based on a section of one of Scott's histories; and approximately fifty operas based on the Waverley Novels, most of which I discuss (the ones I don't I failed to locate). Although my survey of the field is more complete than anything which has heretofore appeared, I do not pretend to know the titles of all the operas based on Scott's works. One cannot always know from its title alone that an opera comes from Scott. Who would ever guess, for instance, that *Ida di Danimarca* is based on *The Bride of Lammermoor?* Undoubtedly more and more titles will turn up and hopefully the words and music too.

Indeed, finding a text or score, once I knew of the opera's existence, was often a major problem. *Lucia di Lammermoor, I Puritani, La Dame Blanche,* and *La Jolie Fille de Perth* are well known and can be found, in the form of vocal scores, in most good libraries. But others, such as Marschner's *Templer und Jüdin* and Sullivan's *Ivanhoe,* are less well known and not easily accessible. Vocal scores can be found in only a handful of libraries in the United States—libraries noted for strong holdings in music, such as the Newberry, the Sibley Music Library, the New York Public Library, and the Library of Congress. Still other Scott operas are virtually unknown today. Vocal and orchestral scores and even librettos cannot be found in the United States and sometimes not even in the British Museum or the Bibliothèque Nationale, either in printed form or in manuscript. Fortunately, I discovered in the early stages of my research that the British Museum and the Bibliothèque Nationale together contained about seventy-five percent of the material I needed, and some of this was at the Newberry also. The remaining twenty-five percent proved to be a thorny problem. I found a few obscure librettos in the Bibliothèque de l'Opéra which were not available in either the British Museum or the Bibliothèque Nationale. Sometimes a letter of inquiry to the principal library of the city where the opera in question was performed produced results. In this way I located the holograph orchestral score to Bredal's *Bruden fra Lammermoor,* first performed in Copenhagen in 1832. This approach, however, was not always successful, as in the case of Thomas Sari's *Ivanoé* (Ajaccio, 1863). The obscure Italian operas have been an extremely difficult problem because there is no central depository in Italy comparable to the British Museum, the Bibliothèque Nationale, or the Kongelige Bibliotek. A letter to the Biblioteca Comunale di Milano eventually led to my locating short musical excerpts from Badia's *Conte di Leicester,* Bornaccini's *Ida di Lammermoor,* and Mazzucato's *Fidanzata di Lammermoor,* but finding the complete music seems hopeless at the present time.

Each opera I discuss is accompanied by a bibliographical note as to the whereabouts of the music and text I examined in preparing this book. Finding a vocal score did not automatically end my difficulties, since most of the French opéras comiques, in the form of either vocal or orchestral scores, do not include the spoken dialogue. If I could not find a separate complete libretto, I was out of luck. This was unfortunately the case with Flotow's *Rob Roy.* I give bibliographical data so that other persons seriously interested in the Walter Scott operas will not have to go to the trouble I did searching for necessary material. I discuss several operas on the basis of having seen only the text; the bibliographical note indicates clearly that I was unable to locate the music. Operas whose existence I know about but which I could not find in any form whatever are listed in the appropriate places. I hope that these will eventually turn up.[11]

Except for one light-weight "romantic opera" designed to be performed by teen-age students,[12] all the Scott operas are a product of the nineteenth century. They span the century from Rossini's *La Donna del Lago* (1819) to several done in the 1890's: De Koven's *Rob Roy,* De Lara's *Amy Robsart,* Klein's *Kenilworth,* MacCunn's *Jeanie Deans,* Maclean's *Quentin Durward,* and Sullivan's *Ivanhoe.* The nationalities of the various composers are for the most part Italian, French, and German, in that order, but also English (4), Belgian (2), Danish (2), Irish (2), American (1), Dutch (1), and Scottish (1). The well-known composers include Adam, Auber, Balfe, Bellini, Boieldieu, Donizetti, Flotow, Nicolai, Rossini, and Sullivan. Among the librettists are such well-known names as Cammarano, Carré, Piave, Saint-Georges, Scribe, and Tottola. The operas vary in style from typical early nineteenth-century romantic opera and opéra comique to the Wagner-influenced works of the latter part of the century.

Chapters 2 through 18 are arranged chronologically according to the publication date of the work by Scott in question. Thus the chapter on *The Lady of the Lake* comes first, since this was the earliest of Scott's works (1810) to be given operatic rendition. *The Monastery* is out of order since it must be discussed in conjunction with *Guy Mannering.* Chapter 18 too is a bit out of order. The early chapters of *Tales of a Grandfather* which are apparently the main inspiration for Rossini's *Robert Bruce* were first published approximately one year before *The Fair Maid of Perth,* but an important revised edition of the First Series of the *Tales* appeared the same year as did *The Fair Maid,* and Scott did not complete the *Tales* as a whole until 1829; moreover, the Royer-Vaëz libretto may owe something here and there to Scott's *History of Scotland* (1829–30). Also, for the sake of symmetrical organization, it seemed appropriate to begin with a Rossini opera based on a poem and to end with a Rossini opera based on an historical work, the music of the latter (a pastiche) being drawn in large part from *La Donna del Lago.* Consequently all the novels under consideration fall into place in the middle chapters, which vary in length, since some of the novels—especially *The Bride of Lammermoor, Ivanhoe,* and *Kenilworth*—inspired more operas than did others. Each discussion of an opera begins with a brief account of its performance history, but the major part of the discussion is concerned with what happens to the novel (poem, novella, or historical work) when it is turned into an opera. What does the librettist do to the original story—how does he reshape it—to make it something the operatic composer can feasibly handle?

The task of turning a novel into a libretto differs from that of doing the same with a play. Many problems of stagecraft that a librettist has in common with a dramatist have already been solved when the librettist works from a play. Of course certain changes must still be made. Minor characters, sub-plots, and episodes not conducive to opera are omitted, while elements of the play that do lend themselves to operatic treatment are often expanded, so that the composer can exploit them to the fullest. Through judicious omissions and a careful redistribution of emphasis, the skillful librettist can often produce a satisfactory vehicle for opera without having to overhaul completely his source's basic structural framework, already designed for effective two- or three-hour presentation in the theater. In reshaping a novel the librettist normally has more decisions to make regarding structure, more chances to display his own dramatic talents, and often more problems to face. While he obviously has greater opportunities for originality, at the same time he runs a greater risk of botching things up. Nevertheless in the case of Scott's novels his problems are not all that formidable. Throughout this study I shall point out time and again the theatrical quality of the Waverley Novels. They usually break down into a few big scenes. They abound in direct discourse, with characters often being given Shakespeare-like soliloquies that can easily be converted into texts for arias. Moreover, since there is nothing sacrosanct about Scott's diction and phraseology, the librettist need not have any qualms about altering things as he sees fit, perhaps drastically. The same librettist might hesitate before tampering too much with a Shakespearean text; and indeed one weakness of some Shakespeare operas is that their wordy librettos follow the play too closely, thereby imposing impossible limitations on the composer.[13] As for Scott's long passages of physical description, these are not problems for the librettist; they are rather the province of those in charge of the set, the lighting, and the costumes. The overall esthetic effect appropriate to a given scene is best handled by the composer.

Since any Scott novel provides far more than enough material for an operatic libretto, the librettist has at the outset the problem of deciding what to omit. Minor characters usually disappear, and sometimes major characters as well. Lady Ashton, for example, does not turn up in *Lucia di Lammermoor.* Since her haughty personality completely dominates the main course of events in Scott's story, this one omission by Cammarano results in the opera differing very markedly in complexion from the novel. Also omitted is Caleb Balderston, faithful old servant to the Ravenswood family, a tragi-comical figure, and a minor character in the sense that he and the episodes in which he is predominant stand apart from the novel's central conflict. Thus the intensely moving scene in which Edgar takes leave of Caleb just before riding off to fight a duel with Lucy's brother Sholto (and accidentally meeting death in the quicksand between Wolf's Crag and the spot chosen for the duel)—in context one of the great moments in Scott—does not appear in the Cammarano-Donizetti version. Even though *Lucia di Lammermoor* follows its source more closely than do most Scott operas, it is something altogether differ-ent. Another remarkable operatic treatment of *The Bride of Lammermoor* is Adam's *Caleb de Walter Scott.* As the title indicates, Caleb is retained—but virtually every other character of the novel is omitted. An alternate means at the librettist's disposal for compressing the original story is to amalga-mate two or more of its characters into one. Enrico Ashton (Lucia's brother) is a composite of Sir William Ashton (Lucy's father), Lady Ashton (her mother), and Sholto and Henry Ashton (her brothers)—and the result is a pasteboard figure, at least in comparison with Sir William and Lady Ashton. Still another means of compression is to run together two or more distinct scenes of the original. The formal accusal of Rebecca at Templestowe (chapter xxxvii of *Ivanhoe*) and the trial by combat (chap-ter xliii) become one scene in Castegnier's *Rébecca.* Just the opposite process, expansion, frequently occurs when the librettist sees some aspect of the novel which, if magnified properly, would be obviously conducive to effective musical adaptation. The most striking example of this is the famous "Mad Scene" from *Lucia,* in which a few lines of description and Lucy's one sentence—"So, you have ta'en up your bonny bride-groom?"—are blown up into a vehicle for the most celebrated musical pyrotechnics for soprano in all Italian opera. Elvira's mad scene in *I Puritani* is based on Scott's mere mention that Edith Bellenden, of *Old Mortality,* became emotionally distraught after she had by chance caught a glimpse of her long-absent friend, Henry Morton. The character Elgitha in some of the *Ivanhoe* operas is greatly enhanced from the small role she plays in the novel, because of the need for another female principal.

Frequently some aspect of the novel is altered for one reason or another. Edgar's fate is handled somewhat differently in each opera based on *The Bride of Lammermoor*. In Adam's *Caleb* Edgar does not appear as a character; in Carafa's *Nozze di Lammermoor* he stabs himself and falls by the side of Lucia, who has just succumbed from poison; in Rieschi's *Fidanzata* he remains alive, so far as I can tell from the printed libretto (the stage directions are not explicit); in Bredal's *Bruden* his death in the quicksand is told to the deranged Lucie during her mad scene (and the news hastens her death); in Mazzucato's *Fidanzata* he dies in a tidal wave; and in Donizetti's *Lucia* he stabs himself at the burial-ground of his ancestors. In almost every case, as in the novel, he dies—in one way or another. The fate of Amy Robsart, on the other hand, is sometimes not so grim as what happens to her in the book. In Auber's *Leicester* no order is ever given to do away with her; in Donizetti's *Castello di Kenilworth* a villainous attempt to poison her is thwarted by the entrance of Leicester and the Queen, and like Auber's *Leicester* the opera ends happily; in Weyse's *Festen* Varney steps into the booby trap set for her and plunges to his death in her stead. Badia, De Lara, and Klein preserve the tragic ending but in different fashion. In Badia's version Varney tells Leicester during a ball-room scene that he has done away with Amy (we are not told how); Leicester then suddenly and impetuously stabs him. In De Lara's *Amy Robsart* Amy plunges to her death, as in the novel. In Klein's *Kenilworth* she takes poison to escape Varney's lust.

The fourth and final act of MacCunn's *Jeanie Deans* reveals an alteration of Scott's narrative in the interest of good theater. Effie is led from Tolbooth Prison to the place of her execution, in view of a huge chorus obviously sympathetic with her plight. Her lover Staunton gives a signal, and the mob attacks her guards (this being suggested by the melee at the execution of Wilson, in the early chapters of the novel). More guards arrive, and the situation becomes tense. Suddenly Jeanie rushes in, just in the nick of time, with pardons for both Effie and Staunton. The act ends with everyone singing Jeanie's praises. Thus *Jeanie Deans* is an excellent example of the romantic "rescue" opera. The events that I have just recounted are based on several threads of Scott's story, but there is no one scene in *The Heart of Mid-Lothian* that corresponds in all particulars to the highly theatrical and musically effective closing scene of the opera.

I have already alluded to operas based on *two* novels and those that contain obvious motifs from Scott. There is no hard and fast rule as to which approach a librettist and composer should use in order to come up with a successful opera. Nor is there any assurance that a libretto that stays close to the novel and preserves its flavor will be more successful than one that does not. In fact three Scott operas still occasionally heard—*I Puritani*, *La Dame Blanche*, and *La Jolie Fille de Perth*—depart drastically from their originals. On the other hand Sullivan's *Ivanhoe* and MacCunn's *Jeanie Deans* stay reasonably close to Scott, and they too have had some degree of success. *Lucia di Lammermoor* is the only Scott opera that one can truly call a fixture in the standard repertoire of most major opera houses. Its libretto follows Scott closely on occasion (the Sextette, for example) but just as frequently goes its own way. Likewise there is no assurance that a composer's occasional use of Scottish or English tunes will have bearing on the success or failure of the opera. *La Dame Blanche* and *Jeanie Deans* contain Scottish melodies, but so do many totally forgotten Scott operas (and "musical dramas"). *Lucia di Lammermoor* contains no trace whatever of music with a Scottish or English flavor: neither do Carafa's *Nozze di Lammermoor,* Pacini's *Ivanhoe,* Ricci's *Prigione di Edimburgo,* and a host of other forgotten works.

For the convenience of readers who might be interested in only certain novels and their derivative operas, I have designed Chapters 2 through 18 as units in themselves, with of course many allusions and cross-references to other parts of the book. In his study of the Shakespeare operas Winton Dean could assume that his readers were familiar with Shakespeare and that no plot summary of the play was necessary. Unfortunately, in the second half of the twentieth century one cannot make such an assumption with regard to Scott. Nevertheless the novels under discussion here are not given separate, detailed plot summaries, and each chapter is written as if the reader *were* reasonably familiar with the basic plot outline of the novel in question. If summaries are needed, they are available elsewhere.[14]

My concluding chapter sums up what has evolved from the preceding chapters. It brings together for final discussion the elements in Scott's works that are conducive to good opera—the pictorial element; the theme of "opposing fanaticisms,"[15] often brought vividly to life in one or two big highly dramatic scenes; the well-drawn characters, from both high and low life; the theatrical direct discourse, including soliloquies. In addition the concluding chapter tries to determine what influence the Scott operas have had on others now in the standard repertoire. Many parallels can be observed because of the use of certain operatic conventions that are the common stock of all librettists and composers. Other parallels, however, seem to me directly traceable to the Scott operas. Wagner's conception of Telramund in *Lohengrin* owes much to Marschner's Brian de Bois-Guilbert. In its emotional core *Carmen* is a better "Scott opera" than *La Jolie Fille de Perth.*

On 31 October 1826 Scott witnessed a performance of Rossini's *Ivanhoé* in Paris. He wrote about the occasion in his *Journal:*

> In the evening at the Odéon, where we saw *Ivanhoe.* It was superbly got up, the Norman soldiers wearing pointed helmets and what resembled much hauberks of mail, which looked very well. The number of the attendants, and the skill with which they were moved and grouped on the stage, were well worthy of notice. It was an opera, and of course the story greatly mangled, and the dialogue in a great part nonsense.[16]

The passage is remarkable in that he says absolutely nothing about the music, which apparently made no impression on him. Next to Shakespeare he inspired more operas than did any other single writer. There are at least fifty, as I have already noted, not counting the numerous "musical dramas." That his name should loom so large in the history of opera seems rather ironic in view of his own rudimentary knowledge about music.[17] But life is full of ironies, not the least of which is that Scott's literary reputation, formerly so very high, has fallen to such an extent that he is now read mainly by a small group of loyal admirers and by specialists.[18] If the present study leads to a more mature appreciation of Sir Walter Scott's art and of his influence on European culture of the nineteenth century, my purpose will have been accomplished.

2

§ § §

THE LADY OF THE LAKE

*T*he *Lady of the Lake* was published in 1810, and in the same year Thomas Dibdin's *Lady of the Lake*, a play interspersed with several musical numbers, was performed at the Surrey Theatre.[1] In 1811 a genuine "musical drama" entitled *The Knight of Snowdoun*, with words by Thomas Morton and music by Henry R. Bishop, was performed at Covent Garden. Although my policy, as I indicated earlier, is not to discuss musical dramas, I have chosen to make an exception here for two reasons: first, *The Knight of Snowdoun* is not discussed by White, who was concerned with dramatic versions of only the novels, and, secondly, it contrasts interestingly with Tottola and Rossini's much celebrated *Donna del Lago* (1819), the only opera of any consequence based on the poem. A second musical setting of Tottola's libretto was composed in the late 1820's by a young Austrian, Johann Vesque von Püttlingen (who later used the pseudonym J. Hoven). The first act was performed in concert version (with piano accompaniment) by amateurs in a private house in Vienna; it was well received. Unfortunately, the score has not been preserved.[2]

The Knight of Snowdoun

Bishop's overture begins with a brief *largo*. This is followed by a rollicking *allegro a la chasse*, in which the composer says he has "endeavoured to delineate, as far as Musical expression would allow, that part of the First Canto of the celebrated Poem this Opera is founded upon which describes THE CHACE": [3]

Example 2-1

Thus *The Knight of Snowdoun,* the first significant musical version of a work by Scott, contains something which was to be a staple in almost all the Scott operas: namely, hunting music in 6/8 time—although in later operas this usually takes the form of a chorus of hunters rather than a purely musical depiction of the hunt. Bishop labels the third movement of the overture an *andantino scozzese;* it is a plaintive Scottish melody played by a solo oboe. Then comes a lively Scottish folk dance:

Example 2-2

The liberal borrowing of Scottish melodies and folk dances is very typical of all the Bishop musical dramas based on Scott that I have examined. As we shall see, Scottish music occurs in about half the genuine operas, but to a much lesser degree—just enough to give a touch of local color.

"*THIS musical Drama is founded on the Poem of the* LADY OF THE LAKE, *but as the writer's humble judgment has directed him to select, rather than to copy, he trusts the admirers of the Poem will concede to him the indulgence of making such alterations in the original story, as stage necessity has induced him to adopt.*" So reads the "advertisement" prefixed to the complete text (see fn. 3). A glance at the dramatis personae shows that there indeed are alterations. Among the male characters are the names Young Douglas and Macloon, who are not in the poem, while the list of females includes the unfamiliar names Alice and Isabel, but not Margaret or Blanche of Devon. The poem's six cantos are reorganized into three acts.

When the curtain rises after the overture, we see "*a romantic view on the Highlands—On one side, a rocky promontory, with a path leading down, which abuts upon a lake—On the other side, a cut-wood, with rocks intermingled—In the midst of the lake is an island, luxuriantly wooded—In the back-ground, a rocky mountain.*" The wild mountainous landscape is a typical setting of a Scott play, musical drama, or opera; we shall observe it again and again. "*Among the rocks, a white horse is seen dying—The Knight of Snowdoun leaning on a hunting spear, looking at him.*" The drama thus begins at section ix of the first canto. Snowdoun says farewell to his horse, as in the poem, and then blows his bugle. Ellen appears forthwith, thinking the bugle blast that of her father, or of *Roderick.* In the poem Ellen thinks it is either her father, or Malcolm; but here Roderick is her true love, while Scott's noble Malcolm is parodied almost beyond recognition in the cowardly fool Macloon. Ellen is somewhat offended by Snowdoun's openness in admiring her beauty, and he begs forgiveness. She wonders what has become of her maid Alice:

> Where can my maid have strayed? Alice! Ah, her beloved Norman lives down the glen.—Alice!—no answer.—Stranger, my poor attentions wait your acceptance. (*Harp and clarinet.*) Hark! our minstrel's notes recal [*sic*] my wandering steps, and announce our humble, but welcome cheer's prepared.

The two of them climb into her boat and push off behind a promontory. Ellen's casual reference to her minstrel is all we hear of Scott's Allan-bane, a major character in the poem.

Alice enters, followed by "red" Murdock, who has been trying for some time to thwart her plans to marry Norman, since he desires her for himself. He becomes suspicious when Alice tells him of the stranger whom she has noticed. As soon as he has gone off to look into things Alice expresses her utter dread of him. Norman enters. Alice tells him that Murdock had told her their clan was raising arms in behalf of Douglas. Norman replies that they must wed before he goes off to fight, and the two then sing a duet ("All young men and maids"), after which they leave the stage.—This episode has no parallel in the poem. Noteworthy is the added dimension to Scott's villainous Murdoch. Although there is no Alice in the poem, the romance between Alice and Norman is no doubt suggested by Scott's sober and compelling account of Norman's being called to arms, away from his newly-wed Mary (III.xx–xxiii). In the musical drama the Alice-Norman-Murdock triangle evolves into a comic subplot.

The second scene takes place in the "sylvan Bower" of Ellen and her father. "*A rustic building—In the centre, a porch formed by unbarked trees, with ivy, wild clematis, and eglantine, climbing round them. It has folding doors, leading to an apartment, and formed of wicker-work. A table, covered with skins of beasts—On each side of the porch, stags' antlers, and the skins of beasts and birds of prey are fixed—Behind, the lake and mountain are seen.*" The description follows Scott in some details (I.xxvi–xxvii) but does not mention the weapons hanging from the walls. Isabel the housekeeper (who takes the place of Scott's Lady Margaret) bewails the plight of the Douglases, who do not now have enough servants to attend properly to the stranger. She speaks of her "sweet nephew, Macloon" (Scott's Margaret is Roderick's mother): "Oh, he's an elegant creature!—has been in the South, and is so superior in dress and manners to these brawny Highland carls." Macloon is in love with Ellen, and he bemoans the fact that she is more interested in Roderick than in him. One reason Ellen does not care for him is that he was partly to blame for the capture of Young Douglas (her brother) by

Earl Mar's men. (Much of the later action of the musical drama revolves around Young Douglas, who has no counterpart whatever in the poem.) When Ellen and her unknown guest enter, she reveals apprehension at disclosing her identity to him; but he tells her at once he is the Knight of Snowdoun—"and [his] duty is, to ward the palace and person of Scotland's king." Ellen is deeply worried about having an attendant of King James as a guest under her roof. Suppose her father should come home? She calls on Macloon to guide Snowdoun to safety and to keep her identity concealed from him. She then leaves the stage for a few moments. During her absence Murdock privately coerces the cowardly Macloon into promising not to lead Snowdoun south, but rather to Goblin's Cave; Murdock being dead certain that Snowdoun is a "wheedling spy, sent by King James." Macloon and the unsuspecting Snowdoun leave.

The rest of the scene is obviously based on story-material from the poem, but woven together in different fashion and somewhat altered, especially with regard to Ellen's feelings toward Roderick. Ellen re-enters and speaks briefly with Murdock, asking him specifically about Roderick Dhu. He replies that he left him in parley with Ellen's father; that Roderick had said to Douglas, " 'Give me . . . but beauteous Ellen's hand, and the Douglas shall not hide in covert, like a hunted quarry—Each mountain clan will make your cause its own . . . .' " At this point, says Murdock, he was dismissed from Douglas' and Roderick's presence. *Exit* Murdock. Ellen, left alone on stage, broods on Roderick's "wild passions"; nevertheless she is grateful for his help to her father in times past and she will be true to him. (In the poem these are feelings Allan-bane tells Ellen she *should* have toward Roderick.) Douglas enters. He is quick to tell Ellen that he does not like Roderick's plan; that he does not want his daughter's "angel form [to] become the meed of discord." Also, he does not want people to die in his behalf. "I now can claim the proud distinction of a wronged, but loyal subject, and shall I sink to the base level of treason and revenge? No, my Ellen, we must fly this sylvan bower, to some rude shelter unknown to Roderick." When Ellen expresses regret at this, Douglas replies: "By that alone can I avert the war,—assert my loyalty and truth,—save Roderick from the vengeance of King James, and preserve the life of thy innocent, but enthrall'd brother."

The scene now changes to *"a View of an Highland Village—A rustic Bridge—On one side an old Abbey Gate."* *Enter* townsfolk, Old Norman, Norman, and Alice. The young lovers are about to go into the abbey to be married, but first Alice sings a song entitled "Hospitality"—a song with an unmistakably Scottish flavor:

Example 2-3

Thy jo-cund eye, thy friend-ly glow, can warm a-mid De-cem-ber snow.

Suddenly Murdock rushes in (rather than the Malise of the poem) and calls Norman to arms. He is delighted that he has marred the wedding. All the men present rush offstage and return almost immediately brandishing weapons. The scene ends in a rousing chorus, with Alice, as soloist:

> CHORUS: Now tramp, and tramp, o'er moss and fell,
>   The batter'd ground returns the sound;
>   While breathing chanters proudly swell,
>   Clan Alpine's cry—is "Win or die."
> ALICE: Guardian spirits of the brave,
>   Victory o'er my Norman wave!

This rather than the "Song" that Scott's Norman sings to Mary (III.xxiii).

The fourth scene takes place in *"a Defile between Mountains."* Macloon is leading Snowdoun not southward, as Ellen had wished, but to Goblin's Cave. Murdock enters; he relieves Macloon of his duties as guide and tells Snowdoun that he himself will now guide him to safety.

> SNOWDOUN: (*Apart.*) Sure, treachery and ambush are prepared.
>   Heart, hold thy steady pulse! [MURDOCK *shouts.*]
>   (*Draws.*) What meant that shout?
> MURDOCK: See, noble sir—it was to scare yon ravens from your
>   dead courser's body.
> SNOWDOUN: Well had it been for thee, my gallant steed, had'st thou
>   ne'er snuffed this Highland air, and, perhaps, well for
>   me. On, fellow! but give to these echoes one word more
>   'tis at the cost of life!

>   *(Lays hold of* MURDOCK'S *plaid.)*

This part of the scene obviously follows Canto IV, section xx, but what comes next differs markedly from the poem. A harp sounds in the distance. Snowdoun takes his eyes off Murdock for an instant, and Murdock disappears. Snowdoun is now sure he is betrayed, but, realizing that the strain from the harp signifies that Ellen is near, he says bravely: "If death must come, Ellen, I'll meet it in thy arms." (The episode involving Blanche of Devon is omitted, and Murdock, who must be retained for the comic subplot, is not killed by Snowdoun.)

Scene v opens on the entrance to Goblin's Cave. *"Douglas on a bank, asleep,—Alice playing a harp,—Ellen motions her to silence, and approaches Douglas."* Norman rushes in suddenly and asks Ellen where her father is. Douglas awakens. Norman tells him that Roderick has learned that he and Ellen have left their bower and is furious; in fact he has sent out scouts to discover their retreat. Douglas is angry that Roderick is trying to force him into joining a conflict which he prefers to avoid. He tells Ellen she must become a "bride of heaven" (i.e. go into a cloister), and he leaves the stage, ostensibly to make arrangements for Ellen. Norman leaves also, in order to keep watch from a distance on the cave, which is to be Ellen's hideout until her father returns. Snowdoun then enters unexpectedly.

Ellen shrieks. She realizes his life is in grave danger in the vicinity of Goblin's Cave. He professes ardent love for her, but she does not reciprocate:

ELLEN: Forbear.—Oh! spare me—Alas, my family are poor, and exiled! To link with this attainted hand were infamy.
SNOWDOUN: Infamy and thee!
ELLEN: Nay, then, hear, and pity me. I own a passion, nay more, an unworthy one—The death-pangs of hope now struggle in this bosom, and like a matron, that sorrows o'er her murdered infant's tomb, I can welcome here no passion but despair!—Thou hast my secret,—be generous, and leave me.

In the poem (IV.xvii) her meaning is not quite so vague as it is here (and her secret love is of course Malcolm rather than Roderick). A shrill whistle from Norman *without* signals approaching danger. As in the poem (IV.xix) Snowdoun gives Ellen the ring that will gain favor for her from King James. He bids her farewell and exits. Norman tells Ellen to hide quickly in the cave, since some of Roderick's followers are approaching to seek her out. At this point the finale to Act I ("What, ho, clansman, ho!") begins. It is an unusually elaborate ensemble for a Bishop musical drama. Norman and Ellen manage to scare the clansmen away by convincing them that the cave is haunted. During the course of the ensemble the clansmen hear a voice from the cave: "Mortals forbear!" (actually Ellen's voice), and they are certain it is that of a spook. Thus Ellen is saved.—In the poem Ellen and Douglas sequester themselves in Goblin-cave, but there is no raid on it by Roderick's followers. The ending of the first act of the musical drama curiously brings to mind the fake supernatural machinery that Scott himself was to utilize seventeen years later in *Woodstock*.

Act II begins on "*a rocky promontory—On one side of the stage a watch-fire, and wallet near it—Near it stands a Highland Warrior, his arm resting on his shield—He looks on the sky, absorbed in meditation—Enter the Knight of Snowdoun, exhausted with fatigue—The Warrior starts on seeing him, braces his targe, and advances.*" The ensuing dialogue between Snowdoun and the Warrior (who is actually Roderick) is suggested by Canto IV, section xxx. The rest of the scene has no parallel in the poem. Macloon tells Norman he knows where Young Douglas is confined and gives him a paper which shows exactly where. After Norman has exited, Macloon admits he imparted this information to Norman to keep from having to participate in the liberation attempt himself (because he is a coward). The scene closes with Macloon's air, "Do as company do." Next we see "*a mountainous Country—A Lake—Rushes—Willow—Heather and stunted Oaks form the foliage, with Rocks intermingled.*" The Warrior has led Snowdoun to safety, and their opening brief dialogue is suggested by the opening sections of Canto V. When he finally discloses himself to Snowdoun, his followers appear from behind every bush, but as in the poem he will not take advantage of the situation and break the laws of hospitality. Nevertheless he wants to fight man to man with Snowdoun, who tries in vain to avoid the needless conflict. After they go offstage to fight, Murdock (who it will be recalled was not killed by Snowdoun) views the encounter from a vantage point and relates to the audience what is going on. When Lowland troops come to rescue Snowdoun, Murdock quickly calls on the clansmen to help save Roderick. They do so, but Roderick is put out with them for stopping the fight at a point where Snowdoun had momentarily gotten the better of him. Their heated words are broken off when Norman comes in with the information as to where Young Douglas is confined. Roderick makes up with his clansmen, and together they go off to free Young Douglas. (Since Roderick is Ellen's true love in the musical drama, he is allowed to survive his encounter with Snowdoun virtually unscathed.) In the third scene, which has no parallel in Scott, we are back at "the Bower." Isabel remarks on how unhappy Ellen is because her father has not returned. She then sings an air, "What news, my pretty page?" after which Alice and Ellen enter. Against Alice's wishes Ellen goes off to seek her father. Murdock then comes on stage for a few moments and scares Alice by saying he is determined to marry her. After he has gone Isabel and Alice sing a duet ("To woo his mate").

The setting of the fourth scene is a fort occupied by the English. *"Enter the Captain of the Fort, 1st Lieutenant, and Earl Mar's banner, twelve guards through the gate."* A 2nd Lieutenant enters and informs the Captain that their troops "have just surprised a female." The Captain says he will go question her as soon as he has discharged his duty at the fort. He then speaks briefly with their prisoner, Young Douglas. Suddenly vessels are seen approaching in the distance. Young Douglas realizes that Roderick and the clansmen are coming to his rescue. The Captain orders his men to conduct Young Douglas "to the remotest tower" where they are to defend him as long as they can; if defense becomes impossible they are to execute him, rather than allow him to escape. At this point there is a big musical ensemble ("Gallant liegemen"), and as the Highlanders approach they sing the fourth stanza of Scott's "Boat Song" (II.xx). During the course of this number the Highlanders, still *without,* begin to win the battle. The Captain, Lieutenant, and guards rush off to execute their prisoner, and the Highlanders burst in.—There is no such scene in The Lady of the Lake; but it is interesting to observe how the "Boat Song," lifted from its context in the poem, is made use of. This is the only place in the musical drama where the text of a song is Scott's. Strangely enough, librettists seldom borrowed his lyrical poems, even though they abound ready-made not only in *The Lady of the Lake* but in many a Waverley Novel.[3b]

At the end of the ensemble Norman and the Highlanders rush out to rescue Young Douglas, while Roderick remains on stage. *"Enter Ellen, not seeing Roderick, nor Roderick seeing her."* But they do see one another very soon, and Ellen upbraids him for forcing her father to leave his calm retreat. They have a lover's quarrel. Ellen is convinced that her brother is dead, but Roderick, at that moment hearing a war song *without,* is certain that Young Douglas yet lives. Everyone re-enters. *"Young Douglas flies to Roderick—Roderick delivers him to Ellen—They embrace—the Captain gives up his sword to Roderick—Soldiers passing by him, and laying down their arms. Young Douglas points this out to Ellen, who, all gratitude to Roderick, falls at his feet.—Young Douglas kneeling on the other side of him."* The Captain himself, out of compassion, prevented his soldiers from executing Young Douglas, but he fears that Earl Douglas is no more. He produces a dispatch which Roderick reads aloud: " 'Earl Douglas, captured near Cambus Kenneth shrine, will this night meet the death he merits, unless a ransom of five thousand marks be paid for his release—by order of Earl Mar.' " Roderick wants to go out immediately to rescue Old Douglas, but the Captain tells him it is useless, because Mar's force is much greater than that of the Highlanders. Roderick is in a quandary:

> Is there no hope? Cannot gold, so often useless to its owner, be gained for such exalted purpose? *(After a short pause.)* It can! it breaks! it bursts upon my mind! Return in triumph to the isle—The oath I registered on high, was to preserve thy race, or perish.—Thus far heaven has been propitious to my vow—the rest shall be accomplished—Ellen, beloved, farewell—Vich Alpine will restore thy father.

The curtain falls. Roderick obviously has a plan, but in true theatrical fashion he chooses to keep everyone (audience included) in suspense as to what it is until the next act. The plot of the musical drama has gone its own way.

At the opening of Act III we are in Earl Mar's camp. The Earl is bemoaning Young Douglas' rescue, and he instructs two officers to double the reward for Roderick. He is jubilant when muffled drums *without* indicate to him that the elder Douglas is a prisoner. He makes clear to his men that he does not want Douglas to know of his son's rescue. Douglas is brought in. Mar thinks of him as a confederate of Roderick and orders the guards to take him out and execute him. Suddenly Roderick himself, disguised, rushes in. He asks Mar to repeat his promise that anyone who surrenders Roderick to the authorities will receive a reward of 6000 marks. Roderick then reveals himself, puts himself in captivity, and uses the reward money to buy Douglas' freedom. At the end of the scene (which has no counterpart in Scott) he informs Douglas that his son is alive.

In scene ii we are back in the bower with Alice and Isabel. Alice no sooner expresses her concern about Norman's not having returned than he enters. He says that the priest necessary for their wedding is not to be found, that the rascal Murdock "has purposely got him out of the way," but that he will marry Alice that very night notwithstanding. He exits, leaving Alice on stage to sing her "bravura" (coloratura) air, "When wedded joys are nigh." Murdock then enters, bringing with him a monk heavily guarded by two Highlanders. He intends to force Alice into marrying him. To stall for time, Alice says that the holy man must first absolve her of her promise to Norman. Unseen by Murdock, Norman re-enters. The upshot is that the monk marries Norman to Alice almost under Murdock's nose. The scene ends in a quartet sung by Isabel, Alice, Norman, and Murdock ("Lovely bridegroom! beauty's pride").—There is nothing comparable to this in the poem. The scene provides comic relief which the dramatist Morton evidently felt desirable; it is the high point of the subplot; and it again shows Scott's Murdoch in new garb—as the typical comic stage-villain of melodrama.

Scene iii returns in part to the poem. The setting is the armory at Stirling Castle, where Roderick has been imprisoned. After settling a dispute among the soldiers John of Brent sings a song he brought from England (*not* Scott's "Soldier's Song") and the men join him in the refrain. Macloon and Ellen enter, she with her face concealed. As in the poem John wants to make love to her, but she stops him with the dignity of her speech and bearing.

> ELLEN: Soldiers! my father was your friend; cheered, marched, bled with you—Shall the injured and defenceless suffer from the strong and brave?—shall an exile's daughter—?
>
> BRENT: An exile's daughter art thou?—that touches home—My poor Rose! thou may'st beg in vain for help. (*Wipes his brow.*) Stand back! (*Soldiers fall back.*) Can I serve you, sweet one?—Just Rose's age!

This bit of dialogue follows Scott closely, but the situation on stage is somewhat different in that in the poem Ellen is accompanied by the old minstrel Allan-bane. Ellen wants to know where she can find the Knight of Snowdoun, and Brent goes off to fetch him. In the ensuing comic dialogue between Ellen and Macloon (which departs from Scott) Macloon gets the mistaken idea that Ellen is romantically interested in him. Snowdoun enters. He is surprised when Ellen tells him that she is Earl Douglas' daughter, but he promises to lead her to the king. As she and Snowdoun leave the stage she asks Macloon to find the imprisoned Roderick and tell him that she has flown to his relief and that he is the "sole lord of her affections." Macloon's happy illusion is thus destroyed. Left alone, he says he will give up "northern lights" for "southern constellations" and ends the scene with a song.

The final scene follows loosely the last pages of the poem. The setting is the interior of King James's palace, and the entire court is present. Earl Mar leads in Roderick. The captive and Snowdoun exchange a few heated

ELIZABETH RAINFORTH as Ellen and Mrs. Alfred Shaw as Malcolm, in the English production of *La Donna del Lago* at Covent Garden, January 31, 1843. From the music cover to the song "Joyless the revel would be" and by courtesy of the Covent Garden Archives.

CESARE VALLETTI as Giacomo (Uberto), in the 1958 revival in Florence of *La Donna del Lago*. By courtesy of Mr. Valletti.

words about their earlier man-to-man fight, which had been broken off. They are about to begin the fight anew, but the nobles present interfere and insist on sending Roderick to instant death. When Ellen asks to see King James, Snowdoun reveals that he himself is the king. Ellen then asks for Roderick's freedom, telling the king about his nobility in giving up his own life to save her father, Earl Douglas. Mar confirms that what Ellen says is indeed true. James agrees to Ellen's wish (as in the poem he agrees to her wish for Malcolm's freedom). He *places a golden chain round Roderick's neck, and puts Ellen's hand on the extremity of it,*" saying: "Thus Snowdoun's Knight redeems his signet ring, and thus enthrals, with galling chains, a misguided, but noble-hearted Chieftain." The now subdued and very grateful Roderick promises to be henceforth a loyal subject to the king. Earl Douglas and his son enter, and James tells the entire assembly that he is thoroughly convinced of the Earl's loyalty. The musical drama ends with a brief finale:

> Now our Monarch's hopes are crown'd,
> Strike your harps, your trumpets sound,
> > While joyous we
> > The union see
> Of loyalty and liberty.

Additional commentary is not necessary, but one last observation seems in order. The singing parts go to Alice, Isabel, John of Brent, Macloon, Murdock, and Norman—but not to any of the major personages: Ellen, Douglas, Roderick, and Snowdown. Such procedure never occurs in genuine opera.

La Donna del Lago

Although this, the first Walter Scott opera, quickly found a place in the repertoire of most European opera houses and because of the excellence of its music proved to be one of the most successful of all the Scott operas, the première in Naples at the San Carlo (24 September 1819) was a minor fiasco.[4] The performance began smoothly enough. The famous soprano Isabella-Angela Colbran, who was singing the title role, delivered her opening aria, "Oh, mattutini albori," beyond reproach; and her duet with tenor Giovanni Davide (as the disguised king) was well received. But when Tenor Andrea Nozzari (Rodrigo) made his entrance from the rear of a very deep stage—singing slightly off pitch because he could not hear the orchestra— the audience became unruly and vociferous in their expressions of disapproval. At the first sound of the trumpets in the finale to Act I, a courtier sitting in the pit began to beat time with his cane, imitating the sound of a galloping horse. Soon the entire audience followed suit. Immediately after the performance Rossini was in Signorina Colbran's dressing-room congratulating her on her personal success—and perhaps wanting a bit of sympathy from her for his own apparent failure (two and one-half years later she became his wife). While the mingled applause, whistling, and boos were still audible, a man came to the door and informed the tense composer that the management wanted him on stage for a curtain call. Infuriated, Rossini hit the fellow—and that very night departed by coach for Milan. Along the way and in Milan he perversely told everyone-who-asked that his opera was a great success. Ironically, he told the truth, for the very next performance in Naples *was* a great success. And in the next few years *La Donna del Lago* (sometimes in translation) was performed successfully all over Europe, even in places off the beaten path, such as Malta and Ajaccio.[5] In 1829 it came to the United States, with productions in both New Orleans and New York. It was also performed in Latin America (Mexico City, 1823; Havana, 1840; Rio de Janeiro, 1843; Valparaiso, 1844). The opera indeed remained a favorite well past the middle of the century. In the twentieth century performances have been few, mainly because of the difficulty in finding singers capable of executing the demanding roles. The most recent major revivals were by the Maggio Musicale Fiorentino (9 May 1958), with Rosanna Carteri as Elena and Cesare Valletti as Uberto (Giacomo V)—Tullio Serafin conducting,[6] and at London, Camden Town Hall (6 May 1969), with Kiri Te Kanawa as Elena, Gillian Knight as Malcolm, Maurice Arthur as Uberto, John Serge as Rodrigo, and Robert Lloyd as Douglas—Gerald Gover conducting.[7]

There are only two other named characters, Albina and Serano, who are servants in the Douglas household and who usually sing only in passages of recitative, giving information necessary to one's understanding of the opera plot. In reducing the number of characters Andrea Leone Tottola made the original story much simpler and therewith more appropriate for the type of music which Rossini would write, but at the same time he lost much of what makes the story and its characters Scottish. Not that this was at all necessary; the opera's well-deserved fame proves it was not. I am saying only that the opera is quite different from the poem.

The fine overture contains a motiv played by the horns that is heard again in the first scene during both choruses of hunters:[8]

Example 2-4

When the curtain opens we are in a remote part of the Highlands. It is dawn. Hunters appear, singing a rousing chorus as they are about to go off in pursuit of game, and when they have left the stage, Elena enters. Stendhal was very much impressed with the staging at the première: "The *décor* of the opening scene showed a wild and lonely loch in the Highlands of Scotland, upon whose waters, the *Lady of the Lake,* faithful to her name, was seen gliding gracefully along, upright beside the helm of a small boat. This set was a masterpiece of the art of stage-design. The mind turned instantly towards Scotland, and waited expectantly for the magic of some Ossianic adventure" (*op. cit.,* p. 377). Elena soon begins her cavatina, "Oh, mattutini albori":

Example 2-5

Oh, mat - tu - ti - ni al — bo — ri! vi ha pre - ce - du - ti a - mor.

This is perhaps the best known melody of the opera and indeed a theme song of sorts, appearing also in the opening duet between Elena and Uberto, and elsewhere. Her mind is on her absent lover, Malcolm, and when she hears the sound of a horn in the distance, she expresses the wish that he might be among the hunters. Uberto, the disguised king, then enters, accompanied in the orchestra by a motiv fully appropriate to the noble, brave character depicted by Scott (I.xxi):

Example 2-6

Uberto is fascinated with Elena's beauty, and their opening duet, as I have just indicated, borrows the melody of Elena's cavatina. "Its outstanding features," Stendhal writes, "are its freshness and a suggestion of *emotional sincerity* which is truly charming" (p. 379). At the point where Uberto sings *aside,* "Oh Dio! Confuso appien son'io!" there is a wonderful example of Rossini's careful union of sound and sense:

Example 2-7

We begin in the key of G major. At the word "Dio" there is a surprise modulation to the altered VI chord, E-flat major. The far-away key fits the ensuing text perfectly. At the end of the *aside* we are back to the dominant of G major by way of a "German" chord—and then G major again. Elena invites Uberto to go with her and partake of her hospitality. He accepts, and they embark on the lake together. When they are out of sight the hunters re-enter, in search of Uberto. The number begins with a typical Rossini "crescendo" and develops into what is perhaps the most effective "chorus of hunters" of all the Scott operas. The scene ends as the hunters disperse, still in hopes of eventually finding their missing companion.—The chorus of hunters is of course suggested by Scott's account of the chase in the opening sections of Canto I. The encounter of Elena and Uberto is based loosely on the middle sections, the main difference being that Elena is on stage first, singing her "Oh, mattutini albori"—this rather than an "Addio, mio sfortunato destriero" that Tottola might have written for Uberto, had he chosen to follow Scott more closely.

In scene ii we are in Douglas' lodge. In the opening recitative Albina and Serano discuss Douglas' plans to marry off Elena to Rodrigo. Albina realizes how unhappy Elena will be. When the two servants have left the stage, Elena and Uberto enter, to the accompaniment of "Oh, mattutini albori" in the orchestra but now in the key of C major and with slightly different harmonization. Uberto sees the weapons that are hung on the walls and in an *aside* expresses his fear (the orchestral accompaniment reinforcing the text and contributing immeasurably to the mood, as so often in Rossini). When Elena tells him she is Douglas' daughter—and here the libretto departs from the corresponding passage in the poem— Uberto is even more apprehensive. Tottola and Rossini's exaggeration of Uberto's fear is a bit damaging to his character and tends to contradict the stalwart motiv that accompanied his first entrance (see Example 2-6), but it does heighten the dramatic intensity. One might bear in mind, however, that Scott's James Fitz-James is not so cowardly. At this point companions of Ellen, along with several villagers, enter and sing a chorus ("D'Inibaca donzella") in which they both praise her and mention Rodrigo's interest in her (not in Scott). Uberto is jealous at what he hears. Misunderstanding Ellen's reaction to the song of her companions, he gets the idea in the ensuing duet that she is interested in *him,* and he is overjoyed:

Example 2-8

The florid melodic line fits the text perfectly. (The situation is reminiscent of the ludicrous passage in the Morton-Bishop musical drama in which Macloon mistakenly thinks that Ellen loves him.) Uberto then becomes a bit forward with her, and she refuses his advances in ladylike fashion, the music again perfectly setting the text beginning with Elena's words: "Hai tu obliato che ospite sei?"[9] Nevertheless his advances have reawakened her tender feelings toward Malcolm. The passage leads into the moving final part of the duet: "Cielo! in qual'estasi," after which Elena goes into her room and Uberto, escorted by Albina and the chorus of damsels, leaves the cottage—still under the delusion that Elena loves him.

From the opposite side of the stage young Malcolm enters, wrapt in gloomy thoughts. Rossini has scored the role for a contralto.[10] In a recitative-cavatina-cabaletta he sings of his thwarted love for Elena and bemoans the difficulties about to befall them. He moves to a place where he can watch unobserved when Douglas and Elena enter. Douglas sings of his plans to have Elena marry Rodrigo, but she expresses reluctance to do so during a time of war. In the aria "Taci, lo voglio" he makes clear that he will brook no disobedience from her. Thus his personality differs significantly from that of Scott's Douglas, who has no intention of forcing his daughter into a marriage she does not want. When Douglas goes off to greet Rodrigo, Malcolm comes forth from his place of concealment and reveals himself to Elena. The two lovers repledge their love for each other in the duet, "Vivere io non potrò."—All this is based very loosely on the middle sections of Canto II.

Scene iii opens on another part of the lake, as Rodrigo advances in the company of the warriors of his clan. The text of the opening chorus owes little to Scott's "Boat Song" although no doubt was suggested by it. Upon entering, Rodrigo sings an aria in which he expresses his love for Elena. He wonders why she does not accompany Douglas, and Douglas is quick to assure him that she will soon appear. She, Albina, and the damsels then enter, the chorus singing the march that was heard in the orchestra at the very beginning of the scene:

Example 2-9

Immediately afterwards begins the highly praised finale to Act I. It is first a trio of Rodrigo, Douglas, and Elena; Rodrigo wondering why Elena is so silent and apathetic. Malcolm then enters, to the accompaniment of music of military flavor, and announces that he and his forces have come to join those of Rodrigo. When he hears Rodrigo speak of Elena as his consort, he involuntarily expresses disapproval, and Rodrigo becomes suspicious. While the passions of all still lie smouldering, Serano enters in haste to announce that the enemy is approaching. All decide to forget their private wrongs and unite against the common foe. In a highly dramatic passage beginning with the words "A voi, sacri cantori!" Rodrigo calls on the bards to "resound the warlike song,/And wake in every breast/The ardours of the fight."[11] The bards perform their sacred duty as requested, to the accompaniment of harps. Suddenly a brilliant meteor darts across the sky which they take as a propitious omen for their enterprise. Military music is heard again, now with trumpets and chorus; and the act ends with an impressive display of virtuosity on Rossini's part, as the chorus of bards commingles with the military music and both are heard simultaneously.—The closing scene has no exact counterpart in the poem but is obviously suggested by the events at the end of Canto II and beginning of Canto III.

The first scene of Act II is at the grotto where Elena is hiding until the end of the war. It opens with an aria ("O fiamma soave") for Uberto, who has come to seek his beloved Elena. When she enters, he declares his love for her. In the duet that follows she urges him to be reasonable and destroys his illusion that she loves him, although unlike Scott's Ellen (and Morton's Ellen) she does not imply that she has another lover. Uberto decides to respect her feelings, and he gives her the ring that will procure access for her to the king and whatever favor she might desire. This much of the scene is based on the poem, Canto IV, sections xvi–xix. At the end of the duet Rodrigo enters and is enraged to see Elena with another man. When he demands to know who the stranger is, Uberto boldly replies that he is a friend of the king and a foe to the foes of the king. The chance encounter very quickly leads to heated works, and when Uberto asks,

> Ov' è il tuo stuol seguace
> Che i suoi doveri oblia?
> Alla presenza mia
> Impallidir saprà!
> (Where is thy lawless band,
> Have they forgot their duty?
> Before my presence they
> Should learn to tremble here!)

Rodrigo replies:

> Dai vostri aguati uscite
> Figli di guerra!
> (Have then thy wish!—Ye sons
> Of war, from ambush rise!)

As in the poem, a great many clansmen instantly come out of concealment. Tottola bases this segment of the scene on the closing sections of Canto IV and the beginning of Canto V, but in greatly condensed form and with one major alteration that heightens the dramatic possibilities: Elena is present. When at Rodrigo's command the clansmen are about to assault Uberto, Elena intercedes and manages to prevent what would have been instant death for him. Upon reflection Rodrigo decides that he will tame Uberto's pride in single combat. An exciting trio with chorus ensues, at the end of which Rodrigo and Uberto go off to fight. Elena and the clansmen follow after them.—There are two interesting changes in characterization here. Unlike Snowdoun, Uberto makes no attempt to dissuade Rodrigo from so senseless a conflict; he is just as hot-headed as Rodrigo. Secondly, if it had not been for Elena, Rodrigo would have taken advantage of Uberto's helplessness and had him put to death. Such untoward behavior would have been unthinkable, from a moral standpoint, for Scott's Roderick, who, although misguided, is a highly respected chieftain with an innate sense of fair play.

Albina and Malcolm then enter in search of Elena. Albina wonders why her mistress has not obeyed her father's wish and stayed at the grotto. Malcolm knows that a fight is raging and that Rodrigo is engaged in single combat with an unknown champion. Serano enters, but without Elena. When asked where she might be, he replies:

> Del padre in traccia
> Un suo cenno me trasse:
> Se in questa guisa ei diose,
> Pace alla patria mia donar mi è dato;
> Dille, che il mio morir troppo è a me grato. . . .
> Tutto narrai; E già fuor di se stessa
> Corre al Reggia.
> (By her command
> I sought her sire, who said,
> "If my life my country's peace
> Can purchase, then indeed
> Will death to me most welcome be.". . .
> I told her all; and even now,
> All wild, she hastens to the king.)

Malcolm is discouraged at this unexpected turn of events, and he sings an aria in which he expresses his utter despair ("Ah, si pera"). Throughout the opera Tottola and Rossini depict Malcolm as a tearful, pessimistic young man who does little more than bemoan his hard luck. He lacks both the spirit and the personal dignity of Scott's Malcolm. At the end of the aria clansmen come in with the news that Rodrigo has fallen *estinto* and that the king has won the field. The scene ends as Albina, Serano, Malcolm, and the clansmen all lament the outcome of the day.—There is no exact parallel to all this in Scott.

The final scene takes place at the castle and begins with Giacomo (Uberto) and Douglas singing in recitative. Douglas offers to give up his life if this will end the sanguinary war that was kindled in his cause. Giacomo is piqued because Douglas had entered the tournament celebrating his victory and defeated all the champions. Douglas replies that he simply wanted to reawaken in the king the memory of the lessons he once taught him. Giacomo finds this a feeble excuse and orders the guards to take Douglas away—and then, when alone, he admits how difficult it is for him to dissemble rigor toward Douglas. This brief passage alludes to events of the second half of Canto V, but in such condensed fashion that the full meaning is virtually incomprehensible to someone not already familiar with the poem. The remainder of the scene is based on the final sections of Canto VI. Giacomo leaves the stage just before Elena enters. She has come to seek the king in the hope of saving, by means of the ring Uberto gave her, the lives of her father, Rodrigo, and Malcolm. Suddenly she hears a familiar voice from *within* singing the melody of her cavatina ("Oh, mattutini albori"). She realizes at once that it is her friend Uberto. (Tottola undoubtedly got the idea of having an offstage song here from Malcolm's "Lay of the Imprisoned Huntsman," Canto VI, section xxiv.) Uberto enters and promises to lead Elena to the king. At this point all the courtiers come in and surround the throne, and Elena soon realizes that Uberto is the king. As in the poem Giacomo calls in Douglas, whom he has fully pardoned, and unites him with his daughter; he tells of Rodrigo's death; and he says that he will put Malcolm in chains—but he is only teasing: he means the chains of wedlock. Elena sings an aria ("Tanti affetti") in which she expresses her happiness and gratitude. And at the very end she is joined by the chorus and all the principals:

Cessi di stella rea
La fiera avversità.
(The adverse stars their anger cease,
And every bosom tastes of peace.)[12]

The story of Scott's poem is obviously much simpler in the opera than in the Morton-Bishop musical drama. While the musical drama retains most of the poem's characters and adds several besides, the opera has only the barest minimum. In addition, Tottola alters the personalities of the four men in the interest of good drama. Douglas becomes a domineering father who will not abide any disobedience from his daughter. In the passage preceding their personal combat, Rodrigo behaves in a manner most unbecoming of a Scottish chieftain and Uberto makes no attempt to bring about a peaceful settlement; their uncontrolled passions, along with the presence of Elena, make for an effective situation for musical rendition. The operatic Malcolm is not very plucky, but his woeful laments inspire music that contrasts effectively in mood with what comes before and after. While the musical drama actually adds more in the way of plot to Scott's original story, the opera retains only the essentials, with a few deft alterations. Tottola apparently thought of the poem in terms of a few striking scenes: (1) the meeting of Ellen and Snowdoun, (2) the arrival of Roderick and his dislike of Malcolm, (3) the dispute between Roderick and Snowdoun, and (4) the poem's final scene in which Snowdoun reveals his true identity to Ellen and pardons her father and Malcolm. He then reconstructed the story, with these scenes as focal points, as follows:

(1) Chorus of hunters—initial meeting of Elena and Uberto—a second chorus of hunters—Elena and Uberto at the cottage. A transition, in which first Malcolm and then Douglas are introduced.

(2) Arrival of Roderick—his suspicions regarding Malcolm—chorus of bards and a call to arms.
(3) Another meeting of Uberto and Elena—dispute between Rodrigo and Uberto (with Elena present) leading to their armed conflict offstage. A transition, in which Malcolm reappears.
(4) Final scene.

The reasons for the war between the Highlanders and the forces of the king are not made clear in the libretto, and thus one of Scott's favorite themes—the conflict between two opposing cultures—does not come through. In broad outline, however, the story of the opera is relatively close to the original story. Tottola left Rossini ample room to display his ingenuity, and in the final analysis the music is responsible for the fame the opera has had. Although Rossini made no use of Scottish melodies, he well understood the essence of the story, as reworked by Tottola; and he had an uncanny knack, as I have suggested in the illustrations above, for setting a text to music effectively (the melodic line) and for creating in musical accompaniment the mood perfectly appropriate for a given text, action, and/or setting. Stendhal argues interestingly that "Rossini uses his *orchestral harmony* to prepare the way for, and to reinforce, his passages of vocal music" in the manner that Scott, in his most successful works, "prepares the way for, and reinforces, his passages of dialogue and narrative by means of *description*" (*op. cit.*, p. 57). It is too bad that *La Donna del Lago* is not performed more often. The difficulty, as I have already noted, is that Rossini's vocal demands on the principals—especially Malcolm, Rodrigo, and Uberto—are formidable, and there are few singers today who can do justice to the roles.

3

§ § §

WAVERLEY

Several of the standard reference works in music—Baker, Fétis, Grove, Riemann, Schmidl—mention an opera entitled *Waverley* by Franz von Holstein. They are all mistaken. What they apparently have in mind is *Die Gastfreunde,* an opera which Holstein completed on 1 December 1852—both text and music—when he was twenty-six years old, and which draws somewhat on *Waverley* for its historical background. In this form the work was neither performed nor published,[1] but it finally did appear, twenty-three years later, in a much revised version entitled *Die Hochländer.*[2] On the surface the changes seem significant and basic. Holstein transformed the earlier five-act "numbered" opera, with its clear division into scenes, into a four-act "continuous" opera, and he claimed that he did not take over unchanged more than a handful of verses from *Gastfreunde.* In reality, however, a great many verses (and verse-paragraphs) are exactly the same, and the division into acts is also basically the same— Holstein simply combined the third and fourth acts of *Gastfreunde* to make up the third act of *Hochländer.* It is true that he thoroughly reworked the first act; nevertheless the main thread of action is the same.[3] I have chosen to base my discussion on *Hochländer* rather than *Gastfreunde,* since the revised opera is what Holstein chose to present to the world.[4] Even though its story is quite different from Scott's *Waverley,* there is ample justification for me to examine it in the present study, and this seems the most appropriate place. Besides the historical background, there are a number of motifs and details that almost certainly derive from Scott. This is not true of Coccia's *Edoardo in Iscozia,* as I indicated in Chapter 1, which simply utilizes the same historical background as does *Waverley,* and nothing more. Two other possible candidates for inclusion in this chapter—Reginald De Koven's *Rob Roy* and A. W. Berlijn's *Lutin de Culloden*—are discussed elsewhere, in more appropriate contexts.

Die Hochländer

Holstein completed the score to *Hochländer* in the winter of 1874–75, and the work was first performed in Mannheim on 16 January 1876—

without success. In November of the following year it was given in Rotterdam (in German). The last revival was in Altenburg on 14 December 1900. Holstein had the misfortune of being overshadowed by another poet-composer, Richard Wagner. *Die Hochländer* appeared the same year that the complete Ring was first performed, and Holstein's earlier opera, *Der Haideschacht,* appeared the same year as *Die Meistersinger* (1868).

The first act takes place before the gates of Edinburgh in the summer of 1745. A force of Highlanders is about to capture the city. Scottish chieftain Fergus, Earl Arthur Macdonald, and a chorus of Highland warriors soon enter and announce to the crowd their victory. Arthur says furthermore that the prince himself, Karl Eduard Stuart, is approaching the city. At this point Magdalis, an old servant passionately sympathetic with the Stuart cause, arrives on the scene. She wants to see and greet Prinz Charlie, and she sings a song about him which she has had on her mind for some time:

Example 3-1

This of course is the well-known Scottish folk melody, "Charlie Is My Darling," which Holstein uses here and elsewhere in the opera to add a touch of local color and to accentuate the idea of the Stuart cause.[5] Magdalis is joined by the chorus. Later in the act Arthur speaks (i.e. sings) to Magdalis about her son Reginald, who disappeared many years previously. She says that if he were alive he surely would not have spared his blood in such a worthy cause. After Arthur has left the stage, the long-lost Reginald enters and reveals himself to Magdalis, who is overjoyed to see him. He tells her that ambition drove him away from home—and so did love. He does not tell her the name of the girl he loved, but he indicates that she belonged to a higher social class than he. (She is Ellen, Arthur's cousin.) Magdalis is horrified to hear that Reginald is in the English army, serving under Lord Astley Cameron, sworn enemy of Arthur Macdonald and the adherents to the Stuart cause. (She has another reason besides to be horrified, as we learn later.) She then tells him, much to his surprise, that he is not her son—that he is nobly born. She goes on to say that long ago she promised his mother, on her deathbed, to save her young son from the heretical beliefs of his father. To do so she abducted him and raised him as her own son at the castle of the Macdonald family. Since she had previously sworn an oath never to reveal the name of his father, she refuses now to tell him when he asks. Karl Eduard finally arrives and is joyfully greeted by all. But in the midst of the festivity Fergus seizes Reginald, accuses him of treason, and wants to have him put to death. Magdalis begs for mercy, and even Arthur Macdonald speaks up in his behalf. Things work out in such a way that Karl Eduard graciously offers Reginald a position in his own service. Reginald is much impressed, but he decides he must remain true to the English army. He is allowed to leave. The act ends with the chorus singing a reprise of Magdalis' song (see Example 3-1), but now in E-flat major.

Acts II, III, and IV take place the following spring, after the defeat of Karl Eduard at Culloden. The first scene of Act II reveals the interior of a Highland cottage in which English soldiers are quartered. The soldiers are drinking, shooting dice, playing cards, singing loudly, and flirting with the canteen-women. One soldier warns the others to quiet things down, since their commander, Lord Astley, despises "mit Puritaner-tugend" every pleasure of youth. But the boisterous noise continues until Astley himself enters. He gives thanks to God for the great victory at Culloden and tells the soldiers of the £30,000 reward for whoever should capture Karl Eduard alive or dead. Reginald enters and expresses to Astley his unhappiness over Scotland's sorrow. He asks permission to go apprehend Arthur Macdonald, with the ulterior purpose of protecting him from the rigor of the English law. (Also he wants to see Ellen.) After Reginald has departed, Astley sings briefly of his fondness for him. News is then brought in that Arthur has already been captured. Astley resolves to have him executed early the next morning.

The second half of the act takes place in the Macdonalds' castle. It opens with an aria by Ellen, who awaits the return of her fiancé Arthur and fears for his safety. Immediately after her aria she hears footsteps and thinks that Arthur has indeed returned. But it is Reginald. She is afraid and flees, not recognizing him after such a long time. Magdalis then enters. Upon seeing Reginald she advises him to leave the castle posthaste, lest the Highlanders avenge their defeat on him. The Highland warriors, most of them wounded, soon come on stage, along with servants of the castle and other Highlanders. The warriors sing of their grievous misfortune. When Ellen re-enters, they tell her of Arthur's having been captured. Suddenly knocking is heard at the main gate of the castle. Everyone wonders who it can be at such a late hour. Ellen says that the stranger will be received, whoever he might be. Magdalis then leaves the stage to admit him. When she returns she is distraught, because she thinks she has seen Arthur's ghost. Soon Arthur himself walks in, to the joy of everyone. It is decided that his marriage to Ellen will take place that very night, but there is something mysterious about it all, Arthur several times alluding to the necessity of his departing the next morning. Ellen suspects that something is amiss, but the festivities continue, as the act ends.

The third act opens on a terrace in front of the castle. It is night.

Reginald is discovered, staring upwards at the light coming from the
windows of the castle. He wonders what the cries of joy he has heard can
mean, and he broods over Ellen's not having recognized him. These
thoughts lead him into an aria ("Holder Jugendtraum—du bist ent-
schwunden"), after which the chorus enters, singing of the wedding:

Example 3-2

The familiar melody is "Long, Long Ago," which Holstein borrowed to
add local color to the scene. Reginald sees that Ellen is Arthur's bride, and
he is overwhelmed with sorrow. In another aria he muses on the power he
has to remove Arthur from competition by arresting him. As elsewhere in
the opera, he is torn between his love for Arthur as a friend and his duty
toward England, coupled with his desire to have Ellen for himself. Arthur
tells Ellen again that he can stay only until dawn; then he will have a duty
to perform. He sees Reginald, and the two sing a brief duet of friendship.
He explains to Reginald that his compassionate captors have freed him
for one night so that he can visit his family and friends, but the next day he
must return to prison and be executed. Reginald's first reaction is one of
delight, but his better nature soon gets hold of him. At this point Karl
Eduard, having escaped his pursuers, appears on the scene. All the
Highlanders at Arthur's castle pledge support to him, but he says he does
not want to involve them in his fate. Magdalis offers to lead him to the
shore, where a French boat is awaiting him. He sings "So leb' denn wohl,
mein Vaterland" and leaves, guided by Magdalis and accompanied by the
Highlanders. Arthur, who is left alone on stage, implores heaven to
protect the prince, and he then hurries into the castle to be with Ellen—
for the last time.

The scene now changes to Ellen's room, and Ellen, followed by Reginald, comes in hurriedly through a side-door. Reginald explains to her
that Arthur must return at dawn to the English fort to be executed. He
gives her a sleeping potion to administer to him. He does not reveal to
Ellen what his plans are, but he has decided to return to the fort to die in
Arthur's place. When Arthur enters, Reginald melodramatically bids
farewell to the newlyweds and departs. Ellen gives Arthur the sleeping
potion in a glass of wine. It does not take effect immediately, and there is

much singing as he gradually loses his faculties. Concerned about his loss of honor if he breaks his word, he attempts to leave, but sleep finally overpowers him. Ellen thanks God that he is saved, and the curtain falls.

The last act takes place at an English fort, partially in ruins, on the coast. It opens with a chorus of Highland prisoners. Reginald then appears on the scene, impersonating Arthur Macdonald. The Highlanders realize he is not Arthur, but he quietly tells them that he will save Arthur's life by dying in his place. As preparations are being made for the execution of the captive Highlanders, Astley comes in suddenly and interrupts the proceedings to ask Arthur what has happened to Reginald, whom he now knows to be his long-lost son. Reginald's ruse is soon discovered. He tells Astley that he has come to die for his friend. During the course of the large ensemble that ensues, Astley sings that Reginald can indeed save Arthur's life, but not his honor. Reginald admits that he had not thought of this. Suddenly Arthur himself appears. He asks Reginald, "O friend, did you believe I could live, robbed of honor?" Astley is horrified that Reginald and Arthur are friends. He separates them from their embrace and gives orders for the immediate execution of all the prisoners, Arthur included. Just as this is about to be done an adjutant rushes in with news that there is activity on the shore; that Highlanders have congregated and a French ship is approaching. Arthur and the Highland prisoners are overjoyed. They rush to the drawbridge and sing "Karl Stuart unser Liebling" (Magdalis' song from Act I). Then Reginald himself, having tried in vain to pacify Astley, joins Arthur and the Highlanders at the drawbridge. In the melee that develops between the prisoners and the English soldiers, Reginald is shot. Magdalis, Ellen, and other Highland women now appear on a nearby promontory, and Magdalis announces that the prince has escaped. Shortly afterwards the mortally wounded Reginald dies, as Magdalis and everyone present look on. In a fit of remorse Astley releases all the prisoners, and the act ends with a brief final ensemble of the remaining principals and the chorus. As the curtain falls we see in the far distance the prince's ship.

When Holstein was but a small boy, his grandfather used to read the Waverley Novels to him. The impressions, the story patterns, and the motifs that he then absorbed remained in his memory throughout his entire life and provided the material for his librettos—but in jumbled fashion.[6] The foregoing summary reveals how markedly different the main story-line of *Hochländer* is from that of *Waverley,* or of any other specific Waverley Novel. Nevertheless the story unquestionably sounds like something Scott might have written, and the reason for this is that it draws on *several* of his works. Because it owes more to *Waverley* than to any other single work, the best solution seemed for me to discuss it here, in a chapter to itself.

Prince Charles Edward appears in both novel and opera, and it is obvious that the historical events that lie behind the opera—the capture of

Edinburgh by forces loyal to the Stuarts and their defeat at Culloden—are the same as those in *Waverley*. In view of the existence in addition of parallels beyond the historical background, it seems safe to assume that Holstein drew on *Waverley* for the historical events of *Hochländer* rather than on some standard history of the age. But no one scene of the opera has an exact parallel in the novel. Even the capture of Edinburgh and the arrival of Karl Eduard—events so effectively brought to life in *Hochländer*—are simply referred to as having taken place in *Waverley* (chapter xxxix). Nevertheless one extra-historical detail in Act I does have a parallel in Scott. When Reginald, although much impressed with the prince, declines to enter his service, the prince graciously permits him to leave Edinburgh to join his own forces. One is reminded of Charles Edward's words to Waverley at their first encounter: ". . . I desire to gain no adherents save from affection and conviction; and if Mr. Waverley inclines to prosecute his journey to the South, or to join the forces of the Elector, he shall have my passport and free permission to do so" (chapter xl). Although Waverley is so impressed that he stays (whereas Reginald leaves), the resemblance in basic situation is certainly noticeable. Both here and elsewhere Holstein's portrayal of Reginald owes much to Edward Waverley. Just as Everard and Rachel Waverley are unhappy about their nephew Edward's becoming an officer in George II's army, so also is Magdalis displeased when Reginald tells her that he serves under the English general, Lord Astley. Like Waverley, Reginald has divided loyalties—to the Scottish people, especially the Macdonald family and his foster mother, Magdalis, and to the English, especially Lord Astley, who turns out to be his father and who is slightly reminiscent of Scott's Colonel Talbot on one hand—and of Davie Deans, of *The Heart of Mid-Lothian,* on the other (because of his disapproval of the pleasures and vices of youth). At first Reginald refuses to follow the cause of the Highlanders, but in Act IV he finally does so, only to be mortally wounded in a melee. Waverley too vacillates from the English side to the Scottish side, but then fortunately manages to get back on the English side after the Scots are defeated. The death of Reginald is perhaps more convincing than the good fortune of Waverley, who in real life might not have gotten off so easily for his mistakes. Holstein's Scottish chieftain Fergus owes a little to Scott's Fergus MacIvor, but not much more than his name. The episode in which Reginald returns to the Macdonalds' castle the night of Ellen and Arthur's wedding was probably suggested by Scott's account of Wilibert of Waverley, a tale of family tradition that Edward heard in his youth: "The deeds of Wilibert of Waverley in the Holy Land, his long absence and perilous adventures, his supposed death, and his return on the evening when the betrothed of his heart had wedded the hero who had protected her from insult and oppression during his absence; the generosity with which the Crusader relinquished his claims, and sought in a neighbouring cloister that peace which passeth not away;—to these and similar tales he would hearken till his heart glowed and his eye glistened" (chapter iv).

Works other than *Waverley* that contribute to *Hochländer* include *The Abbot, Guy Mannering, The Monastery,* and *The Highland Widow.* Old Magdalis owes her name, and in some measure her zeal in behalf of the lost Stuart cause, to the fanatical Magdalen Græme of *The Abbot.* Like Vanbeest Brown (Harry Bertram) of *Guy Mannering,* Reginald grows up not knowing who he really is, and Magdalis, like Meg Merrilies, holds the key to his identity. Almost the same thing can be said with regard to Roland Græme (Roland Avenel) and Magdalen, his grandmother. As in *The Monastery,* the story of the opera involves two young men of the same household in love with the same girl. Reginald, like Halbert Glendinning, leaves the household in order to better his condition and thus become a more acceptable suitor to the girl, who belongs to a higher social class than he.[7] The motif of a son running away from home and joining the English army and thereby displeasing his mother recalls to mind *The Highland Widow.* Like Elspat MacTavish, Magdalis is greatly perturbed when Reginald, after a long absence, returns home and tells her that he serves in the English army. Elspat is so fanatically opposed to the English that she gives Hamish Bean a sleeping potion that prevents him from returning to his regiment—an incident which doubtless lies behind the sleeping potion episode in the opera, although here the characters involved are bride and groom rather than mother and son. Magdalis' guiding Karl Eduard to the coast, where a French ship awaits him, is reminiscent of a similar episode in *Woodstock* involving Alice Lee and Charles II; it also brings to mind the true historical account of Flora Macdonald and Charles Edward— although, to be sure, Magdalis is considerably older than either Alice or Flora. Holstein's Ellen probably owes her name to Ellen Douglas, the Lady of the Lake. The motif of a man who is prepared to die in place of a friend is slightly reminiscent of Earl Douglas' voluntary placement of himself in captivity in order to forestall a war in which Roderick and countless Highlanders would be killed.[8]

It is doubtful that *Die Hochländer* will ever be revived, since Holstein's music, although quite adequate, is dated. The opera would be of no particular interest now except perhaps to musicologists and antiquarians.

4

§ § §

GUY MANNERING
(and *THE MONASTERY*)

T he only opera based on *Guy Mannering* alone to which I can find reference is an obscure work of an obscure composer.[1] About 1825, when she was but twenty, Mlle Louise-Angélique Bertin completed the score to her first opera, *Guy Mannering,* which was performed privately with success. Because she had not studied music theory and composition before tackling this job, her harmonic textures were strange and irregular, but the opera was interesting, and it showed promise of better things to come.[2] Unfortunately I have not been able to locate either the music or the text, which doubtless would exist only in manuscript, if they exist at all.[3] The main opera to be discussed here, Scribe and Boieldieu's *La Dame Blanche,* is based on both *Guy Mannering* and *The Monastery.* Following almost a half century later, *Der Erbe von Morley* draws somewhat on *Guy Mannering* and to a much lesser extent on *The Monastery*—either directly, through poet-composer Holstein's memory of the Scott novels he had heard read aloud as a child (see Chapter 3), or indirectly, through his acquaintance with the earlier opera, or both.

La Dame Blanche

Next to *Lucia di Lammermoor, La Dame Blanche* has been the most successful of all the Scott operas. It was first performed on 10 December 1825, at the Opéra-Comique, the principal roles being sung by Mme Rigaut (Anna), Ponchard (Georges Brown), Henry (Gaveston), Féréol (Dikson), Mme Boulanger (Jenny), Mme Desbrosses (Marguerite), Belnie (Gabriel), and Firmin (Mac-Irton). It was performed there for the 1000th time on 16 December 1862 (the composer's birthday) and for the 1,675th time on 12 March 1914. Throughout the nineteenth century there were innumerable productions all over Europe, and when not in the original French it was given in Czech, Danish, Dutch, English, German, Hungarian, Italian, Polish, Russian, or Swedish translation. It was first performed in the United States on 24 August 1827, in New York. There were also performances in Latin America. It was the first opera ever given in Jakarta (Batavia); the date of the memorable event was 10 October 1836. Thirty

ISABELLA PATON as the White Lady, in the English production of
Boieldieu's *La Dame Blanche* at Drury Lane, October 9, 1826. From the
Enthoven Collection, Victoria and Albert Theatre Museum.

Scenes from the 1970–71 production in Karlsruhe of *Die weisse Dame*. top: Ursula Gust (Margaret), Anton de Ridder (George Brown) and Jef Vermeersch (Gaveston). bottom: Anton de Ridder (left) as George Brown and Harald Axtner (center) as Dikson. By courtesy of the Badisches Staatstheater.

years later it was performed in Surabaya. "The success of 'La Dame blanche' was unprecedented," according to *Grove's Dictionary*. "Boieldieu modestly ascribes part of this success to the national reaction against the Rossini-worship of the preceding years, and it must have been partly due to the vogue of Walter Scott in France[4] . . . and to the pleasure derived from the Scots tunes used by Boieldieu in the opera, somewhat distorted, but not more so than in Haydn's and Beethoven's settings made for George Thomson. The delightful musical qualities of the work, however, were enough to keep it in the repertory, where it remained for many years as one of the masterpieces of the French school of comic opera." Revivals have been few since the last revival at the Opéra-Comique (7 January 1926). A concert version without the spoken dialogue was given at the Holland Festival in November 1964, starring Nicolai Gedda as Georges Brown.[5] In 1971 a bold "Neufassung" by Karlheinz Gutheim was successfully produced in Karlsruhe, with Rose Marie Freni as Anna and Anton de Ridder as Georges Brown.[6] There is a commercial recording of the complete opera on Vega.[7]

The overture contains one lively Scots tune:[8]

Example 4-1

This comes in the long *allegro* section, most of which was put together in great haste, the night before the première, by Boieldieu's protégé, Adolphe Adam, about whom more will be said in later chapters. Boieldieu has used the tune in Act I, as well as the second major theme:

Example 4-2

The conclusion comes from his own earlier opera, *Telemachus*.

Scribe's excellent libretto is an amalgamation of story patterns, motifs, and characters from both *Guy Mannering* and *The Monastery*. The first act takes place at the farm of Dikson and his wife Jenny, who are tenants to the counts of Avenel. (Dikson is slightly reminiscent of Dandie Dinmont, of *Guy Mannering,* and his name is a common Scots name. The name *Jenny* sounds a bit like *Jeanie,* as in Jeanie Deans; on the other hand Scribe might have read *Old Mortality* and thus knew of Jenny Dennison. The Avenel family is prominent in *The Monastery,* rather than *Guy Mannering.*) In the background we see the picturesque craggy and mountainous landscape that is so typical of Scott operas. In the opening "pastoral" choral music a group of Scottish peasants sing of the coming baptism, which is a festive occasion for the parents and their friends. Unfortunately Dikson and Jenny do not have anyone for the godfather. It was to have been the sheriff, but he has fallen sick; and Jenny insists that whoever is chosen for godfather must be a person of importance. A stranger then enters, introducing himself as an officer of the king and soon launching into the famous aria, "Ah! quel plaisir d'être soldat!" (which Boieldieu had composed and used two years previously). Jenny has the brainstorm of asking the attractive stranger to be godfather. He accepts graciously, and there is a reprise of the opening chorus.

In the ensuing spoken dialogue Dikson asks the stranger his name. "Georges Brown," he replies (cf. Vanbeest Brown, of *Guy Mannering*). He knows nothing for certain about his parentage and infancy, but he does vaguely remember a young girl with whom he was raised and an old woman who sang Scottish songs. At an early age he was taken aboard ship by a man named Duncan, who called himself his uncle. He was badly treated, but finally managed to escape. (All this is very reminiscent of what happens to Vanbeest Brown, alias Henry Bertram; Henry, however, has no memory of a young girl, since his sister Lucy was born after he was kidnapped; Scribe's Duncan corresponds roughly with Dirk Hatteraick.) He then tells of his service in Hanover (rather than India) as a soldier of King George. He speaks of a colonel who was like a father to him (cf. Col. Guy Mannering), but the colonel was killed in battle and Georges himself fell by his side, badly wounded. When he revived he found himself in a strange hut and under the care of a beautiful girl, who would not allow him in his weak condition to speak. After a while she discontinued her visits. He then left the hut, not knowing who his benefactress was. He has not been able to find any trace of her. (This motif is reminiscent of Rebecca's nursing Ivanhoe back to health, especially as handled in some of the *Ivanhoe* operas.) After having returned to England he ran across Duncan by chance in London. He was tempted to take revenge on him for past wrongs but could not bring himself to do so, since Duncan was old and suffering. He even shared his purse with him, demanding nothing in return. (This detail, which is a nice touch in Scribe's characterization of Georges, is not in Scott.) The spoken dialogue is followed by a trio (Jenny, Dikson, Georges) with chorus. Jenny tells her friends that it is now too late in the day to have the baptism. She invites Georges to partake of their hospitality, and he readily accepts.

When Georges asks (in spoken dialogue) what there is of interest in the vicinity to see, Dikson tells him of the château. Jenny explains that part of it is closed, but visitors may go to see the ruins. Dikson says that Georges has come at a bad time, since Gaveston, the intendant of the château, has just arrived for its sale. It belongs to the Avenels, who were on the side of the Stuarts in the late troubled times. The count fled with part of his family to France, where it is said that he died. Gaveston has messed up the finances of the family to such an extent that he must sell the whole estate to pay the creditors. It appears that he will buy the estate himself and thus become the next count. (All this is based loosely on *Guy Mannering;* Gaveston corresponds with Scott's Glossin; he perhaps owes his name to Marlowe's Earl of Cornwall.) Jenny says that their garçon Gabriel has recently seen the White Lady. Georges is curious about who this might be. Dikson explains that for four hundred years she has been the protectress of the Avenels; that whenever something either lucky or unlucky is about to happen to the family, she appears—in long white garments and with a harp. Jenny then sings a *ballade* about the White Lady, which contains a musical figure which we have already heard in the overture:

Example 4-3

La dame blan - che vous re - gar - de; la dame blan - che vous en - tend.

(The motif of the White Lady obviously comes from *The Monastery;* Gabriel owes his name, but nothing more, to the gypsy Gabriel, of *Guy Mannering,* who remembers the kidnapping of young Henry Bertram.) In the dialogue that follows, Gabriel announces that the principal farmers of the area have gathered, and we learn that they are planning to unite in order to outbid Gaveston at the auction of the estate. If any descendant of the Avenels should ever turn up at some later time, they will restore the estate to him. Georges is impressed with this story of their devotion.

Dikson then tells Jenny and Georges of his having summoned the White Lady many years previously, when he was in dire financial straits, and agreeing to give body and soul to her at some future time, if she would give him on the spot two thousand Scottish pounds. He was given the money, but some day he will have to turn himself over to her. (Scribe may have borrowed this twist in the libretto from the Faust story.) Jenny is distressed; she wonders what will become of her, and their child, should the White Lady suddenly decide to reclaim Dikson. Gabriel re-enters to inform Dikson that the farmers await him, and Dikson asks Georges to keep Jenny company during his absence. In the charming duet that follows, Jenny tells Georges that her husband has fear of lots of things, and Georges replies that *he* has fear in the presence of a pretty girl. When

Dikson re-enters he is terribly afraid, because a mysterious small man has
just given him a piece of paper signed by the White Lady which reads:
"You have sworn obedience to me. The hour is come, and I have need of
you. Be at the gate of the château this evening and demand hospitality in
the name of Julien of Avenel." At this point the finale to Act I begins. A
storm is brewing, and as the number progresses it becomes more and
more intense. Dikson and Jenny realize that the fatal moment has come.
She does not want him to go, but he is afraid of the consequences if he
refuses. Georges then offers to go in his place. He is not afraid. He
promises to return on the morrow for the baptism and even looks forward
to the adventure. Dikson and Jenny are afraid of what may happen to
him. When the storm reaches its full force, Jenny expresses the idea that
the very elements are hostile to them. At the end of the number Dikson
leads Georges out to show him the way. Jenny remains on stage alone,
following them with her eyes and raising her arms to heaven. The stage
directions in the Peters vocal score reveal a humorous aspect to the
situation: Georges kisses Jenny while Dikson is not looking just before he
and Dikson depart.—The finale has no parallel in Scott.

Act II takes place in a large Gothic room of the château. Marguerite, an
old domestic servant of the Avenels, sings a song about them as she works
at the spinning wheel. She hopes to see some of them again before she
dies, especially Julien. (She is slightly reminiscent of Scott's Meg Merrilies;
Meg is a diminutive form of *Margaret*.) Then, in a soliloquy, she speaks of
Anna, a poor, dear orphan who was brought up by the Avenels. Anna has
just returned to the château, in the company of Gaveston, her guardian.
She reminds Marguerite of Julien, since the two used to play together as
children. Marguerite then looks out and sees a light in the part of the
château that is in ruins. She thinks it might be the White Lady come to
presage the return of Julien, or his death. But Anna herself now enters
and says that *she* has just come from the ruins. When she remarks that one
building in the middle of the park was locked, Marguerite explains that it
has been locked ever since the death of the last count. Anna tells Marguerite of Julien's mysterious disappearance, of the countess' imprisonment
and subsequent death, and of her own trip to the continent with Gaveston.
She tells of an armed conflict that occurred at a time when he was away
from her and of her having saved a young wounded soldier who reminded her of Julien (see above). Marguerite says that she has often
dreamt of a marriage between Anna and Julien. Anna remarks that this
would be impossible because of the great difference in their social status.
Hearing Gaveston approaching, she quickly tells Marguerite that someone will soon come to the château to claim hospitality in the name of Julien
of Avenel. Marguerite leaves the stage as Gaveston enters.

Gaveston is skeptical of the White Lady and of Dikson's story about her.
Anna assures him that there is some truth to the story; that it was actually
the last count who gave him the money in the name of the White Lady, to

get him out of the way (the count was being pursued). Gaveston is aware of the farmers' plans to overbid him at the auction of the estate, but he is confident that he will prevail. Like Scott's Glossin he believes that the people will reverence him once he is count. He then says that the last count sold a great deal of property before his departure to France, and he wonders what he did with the money. He has reason to believe that a paper which the countess, on her deathbed, gave Anna will tell the story. Anna says that she read the paper and then destroyed it. She refuses to tell Gaveston the contents. At the beginning of the next musical number a bell is heard from *without*. Anna tells Gaveston that it must mean that a traveller seeks shelter in the château. Gaveston is reluctant to admit him, but when Marguerite re-enters she says that she has already done so. Gaveston is angry. Anna tells him that if the stranger (whom she takes to be Dikson) can stay, she will tell him on the morrow the contents of the paper bequeathed to her by the last countess. Gaveston agrees, but he insists on Anna's retiring to her apartment before the stranger enters the room they are now in. Anna departs. The stranger is of course Georges, who is very much impressed with the château and its surroundings. When he begins to talk about the White Lady, Gaveston thinks he is mentally deranged, but Georges is convinced that she exists and that he can find her in the château.

After Marguerite (who has been all eyes and ears) and Gaveston depart, Georges, left alone, summons the White Lady in his famous aria, "Viens, gentille dame":

Example 4-4

Nothing so far in the act has revealed an exact parallel in Scott. Neither does this magnificent aria, but it was no doubt suggested by Halbert Glendinning's summonings of the White Lady, in *The Monastery*. At the end of the aria a harp is heard, and Anna, disguised as the White Lady, appears. She is of course surpised to find Georges rather than Dikson. She tells him that she knows all about his being cured by the unknown girl (but does not admit that she is that very girl). Georges promises to do her bidding if she will eventually reveal to him the unknown beauty. In the ensuing duet Anna (the White Lady) tells him of the attempt Gaveston will make to get the estate. She wants Georges to help out. When he gives her his hand, both are aroused, and the music very nicely underscores the text:

Example 4-5

De l'a-mour, de sa dou-ce ma-gi - e, crai - gnons crai-gnons le pou - voir se - duc-teur.

Cet-te main, cet-te main si jo-li - e, le   plai - sir fait pal - pi - ter mon cœur.

She promises that he will see the unknown girl the next day. When she swears an oath that this will be so and gives him her hand, both again are aroused. *Exit* Anna.

Gaveston then re-enters and announces to Georges that it is daybreak. Georges tells him he has spoken with the White Lady. He says furthermore that she is angry about Gaveston's forthcoming attempt to buy the estate and that she will attempt to thwart his plans. Gaveston still thinks that Georges is mentally deranged; nevertheless he invites him to witness the auction. The musical finale to Act II involves all the principals, together with a chorus of farmers and vassals, and is known as the auction scene. Although the similarities between Scribe's libretto and Scott are few at this point, the scene does derive from chapters xi, xiii, and xiv of *Guy Mannering,* which culminate in the Ellangowan estate falling into the hands of Glossin. Dikson bids in behalf of the farmers, but Gaveston outbids him. Then Anna enters, and Georges immediately recognizes her as the unknown beauty who nursed him to health. She makes him think that the White Lady has sent her. Georges begins to bid against Gaveston and eventually outbids him. At Gaveston's request, Judge Mac-Irton reads to Georges what the law says regarding a bidder who cannot pay (he will be imprisoned), but Georges is reckless and undaunted. He tells everyone his name and rank ("Georges Brown, sous-lieutenant; / Douze cents francs / D'appointements"), and the act ends in a large ensemble. Georges does not yet know how he will pay, but he trusts in Anna and in the White Lady.

Act III takes place in a stately Gothic room of the château. A gallery is in the center background, with staircases at either end. At the foot of the staircases are four pedestals—but only three support statues. The act opens with a recitative and aria for Anna, who sings that Georges has reminded her of Julien. In the spoken dialogue that follows, she explains to Marguerite that Georges is depending on her for the money needed to purchase the estate. She is dismayed that the statue of the White Lady is missing, because it is stuffed with money (this is the secret which the dying countess imparted to her). At first Marguerite expresses surprise that it is gone, but on second thought she recalls its mysterious disappearance on the night the last count left Avenel. It must have disappeared through some secret passage. Anna wants Marguerite to find the passageway if possible. They both leave the stage when they hear footsteps.

Georges Brown, the new owner, enters, accompanied by a group of farmers, peasants, and other inhabitants of the estate. Witnessing the setting, he vaguely recalls impressions from his earliest days. When the chorus sings what is designated in the Peters vocal score as a "Schottischer Nationalgesang," Georges inexplicably recalls part of it:

Example 4-6

This episode in the opera is suggested by Henry Bertram's feelings when he returns to Ellangowan after many years (see chapter xli of *Guy Mannering*); he seems to remember the setting, but does not know who he really is. In a soliloquy Georges still marvels that he is actually beholding what he has often dreamt of. He then begins to wonder how he will pay. When Gaveston enters, Georges confesses that he has no money, but he assures him that the White Lady will provide, since he bought the estate as her agent. When Gaveston reminds him of the prison sentence that awaits him if he cannot pay, he replies that the White Lady will then certainly come to save him from such an embarrassing predicament. *Exit* Georges.

Judge Mac-Irton then comes in and tells Gaveston that he would like to speak with him in private. In the meanwhile Anna has found the secret passageway, and she sees the two men talking. She closes a panel and disappears from view, but she eavesdrops on the private conversation. Mac-Irton tells Gaveston that Julien of Avenel is in England. It seems that Duncan, on his deathbed, had signed before witnesses a statement to the effect that Georges Brown was actually Julien. He evidently gave out his information in remorse for what he had done to the boy, who was kind to him when he was in a position to get revenge (see above). Gaveston does not think that there is anything to fear, since Georges (Julien) still does not know who he really is. And what can it matter if he finds out later, but in the meantime has lost his estate to Gaveston? When Gaveston and Mac-Irton are gone, Anna emerges from hiding and in a recitative expresses her distress at what she has overheard. The man whom she has loved as Georges Brown is actually Julien of Avenel and thus beyond her reach, since she is a lowly orphan. (Her plight is reminiscent of Lucy Bertram's inferior position to Charles Hazlewood, in *Guy Mannering;* Lucy too is an orphan.) Marguerite enters and tells Anna that Julien is bound to return, for she has found the missing statue of the White Lady in a subterranean chapel where she had gone to pray for him (and the reappearance of the statue signifies to her that Julien will come back). On the night of his departure the last count had taken it there. Marguerite is overjoyed, but not Anna, who orders her to prepare for their immediate flight from the château. Marguerite does not understand what is what, but she readily agrees to do what Anna says when Anna tells her it is for Julien's sake. Anna, alone, says that she will pay back her debt to her benefactress by arranging for Julien to receive the money, without his knowledge that she had a part in it. Jenny then enters and announces that Mac-Irton and other men of law have arrived. Anna realizes that there is not a moment to lose, and she rushes off to the chapel (to procure the money hidden in the statue of the White Lady).

Upon re-entering, Georges sees Jenny and thinks momentarily that she is the White Lady. He is so intent on finding the Lady that he thinks every lady he sees is she. When he begins to flirt with Jenny, she realizes that his good fortune has not altered his personality. *Enter* Dikson. He has found out that the White Lady, according to popular belief, has given Georges the château and much money, and all this would have fallen to himself if Georges had not gone to meet her in his stead. He and Jenny argue. She says he was foolish, and he replies that she is to blame, because she did not want him to go. Georges then surprises them by saying that he will *give* them the château and that Dikson can declare himself proprietor to the gentlemen who are now arriving. The musical finale to the opera involves all the principals and a large chorus of farmers, tenants, and men of law. When Mac-Irton speaks of paying for the château, Dikson, in true form, loses his nerve (becomes afraid) and begs Georges to take the gift back. Georges agrees. He still hopes that the White Lady will appear. Suddenly a harp is herd, and the Lady (again Anna in disguise) does appear, on the pedestal that had been lacking a statue. She tells everyone that Georges is Julien of Avenel, and thus the rightful heir to the estate. She shows him the money that is his, places the coffer on the pedestal, and forbids anyone to follow her as she departs. But Gaveston dares despite her warning, and to the astonishment of all present he discovers *Anna*. Julien is overjoyed at finding his beautiful unknown savior again. Anna says that she is a penniless orphan and as such cannot possibly become his wife. Julien replies that he will renounce the rank and goods that he in fact owes to her if he must share them with someone other than her. The chorus sings that Anna is worthy to be a countess, and Julien obviously wants to marry her. Old Marguerite is overjoyed. Jenny says that the tenants have found a good master, and Dikson says that their son has found a good godfather. The opera ends with the chorus and most of the principals singing again the anthem which had stimulated Georges' memories of his childhood:

Chantez, joyeux ménestrel,
Refrains d'amour et de guerre;

Voici revenir la bannière
Des chevaliers d'Avenel.

At first glance it seems a bit ironic that Georges turns out to be Julien of Avenel (of *The Monastery*) rather than Henry Bertram (of *Guy Mannering*), in view of the evil personality of Scott's Julian. Such distortions often occur in the Scott operas, especially in those of the French and Italian schools. It may be, however, that Scribe was thinking of Roland (Græme) Avenel, Julian's son and the hero of *The Abbot,* who, incidentally, also learns during the course of events who he really is. The foregoing summary shows that despite its many departures from Scott and its own unique features Scribe's libretto still owes its essential story material to *Guy Mannering* and *The Monastery.* It is interesting to see how the two are woven into one. The skillfully wrought libretto, the "homely sweetness" of Boieldieu's melodies,[9] and the excellent characterization on the part of both librettist and composer are important factors, along with others already noted, contributing to the success of this truly outstanding example of opéra comique.

Der Erbe von Morley

Holstein's *Erbe von Morley* was first performed on 23 January 1874, in Leipzig. It was first given in Munich on 27 November 1874 and was well received, despite the very noticeable vocal limitations of the tenor who played the important role of Charles, the young naval officer.[10] Productions staged in Weimar and Rotterdam were also well applauded by the public.[11] It was revived in Frankfurt (25 January 1895) and Braunschweig (15 October 1899).

The action of the opera takes place at Morley House, in the north of England, several years after the Battle of Trafalgar. A short, tranquil orchestral introduction contains two important motivs:[12]

Example 4-7

As the opera unfolds, it is clear that both motivs are associated with Charles Morley, the missing heir to the estate. *Der Erbe von Morley* has little resemblance to *Guy Mannering* and even less to *The Monastery;* nevertheless, I have chosen to discuss it since it compares interestingly with *La Dame Blanche* and owes at least something to Scott.

The curtain rises on a park adjacent to Morley House. It is morning. The servants are demanding to be paid their wages that very day, and Allan, an old servant of the family, tries to pacify them. (He probably owes his name to Allan-bane, of *The Lady of the Lake.*) He remarks that Viscount Godolphin will be angry if he should hear their cries and says furthermore that Godolphin will be Lord of Morley House on the morrow, since the only son of the deceased lord has disappeared apparently forever. Eveline, daughter of the deceased lord, comes on stage and urges the servants not to disturb the repose of Lady Sarah, her grandmother, with their cries. She pays them out of her own purse, and they thank her profusely. Eveline too is very much aware of the fact that if her missing brother, who was in the navy, does not appear at noon the next day, he will be deprived of his inheritance. She feels that he will come, but Allan notes pessimistically that two years have passed since the Battle of Trafalgar and there has been no word of him. Suddenly they hear the sound of a hunt *without.*

Lady Sarah, who has been awakened by the hunting horns, enters. She is in a pensive mood because she is afraid that Charlie, the rightful heir, is indeed dead. The optimistic Eveline replies that she has dreamt of Charlie's return, and she feels that her dream speaks the truth. Godolphin now enters, to the orchestral accompaniment of a motiv well suited to his proud, unscrupulous character:

Example 4-8

We learn from Lady Sarah that Godolphin was responsible for encouraging the youthful Charlie to go to sea. We also learn that Sarah drove her daughter Bella away from home many years ago, because she was displeased with her choice for a husband, and that Bella died in foreign parts. When Godolphin announces his interest in marrying Eveline, Lady Sarah is shocked. We learn from her that the previous lord, shortly before his death, altered his last will and testament, but the important paper has apparently been stolen. After Eveline and Sarah have left the stage, Godolphin expresses fear that Charlie might still live and that the codicil insuring his inheritance might just turn up.

A comic interlude follows that involves Lydia Thompson, a young widow who is related to Lady Sarah, and William Seyton, advocate, who is in love with her. Lydia does not take him seriously. When Eveline re-enters, the three sing a trio about how happy they are to see one another, after which Lydia orders William to ride forth to see about her lavish wardrobe.[13] During his absence Eveline tells Lydia of her deep affection for her absent brother.[14] Something tells her that he will come back. As they are leaving, a young man in a naval uniform enters unobserved. He has come *from India* (note the parallel with *Guy Mannering*) and must bring the news of his friend Charles Morley's death to his family; but at the moment he does not know that he has arrived at the right place. He follows the ladies.

Godolphin comes back on stage and reads a letter from Justice of the Peace Blackstone, who has learned from a correspondent at the passport office in Dover about someone coming to Morley House who might be Lord Charlie. Godolphin is upset. The young naval officer (whose name also is Charles) re-enters, for the moment unobserved, and remarks how curiously an old servant (Allan) stared at him when he inadvertently disturbed him in sleep. He looks at a drawing of the Morley House in his late friend's memobook and now realizes he has arrived at his destination. Godolphin looks up and sees him, and a charming duet ensues. Bagge rightly observes that it is a piece in light conversational tone reminiscent of French models.[15] The playful motiv in which Charles evasively answers Godolphin's question as to who he might be is most attractive:

Example 4-9

Bin Ma - ri - ne - of - fi - zier

Charles does not give out much about himself, because he realizes that Godolphin must be the evil uncle about whom his late friend often spoke. At first Godolphin thinks that the young stranger may be Lord Charlie himself, but then he thinks he is mistaken, and yet he is not certain. When he shows Charles to the apartment where he can stay, Charles humorously pretends to be afraid, since this is the very apartment in which Lord Morley died.

As the finale begins, a hunting party rides up. Godolphin says that he will have to excuse himself from their merry company, but they will not hear of it. Suddenly Allan comes in, exclaiming that he has seen Lord Charlie. In a rage Godolphin orders the old man to be gone by the next day. Both Lydia and Eveline agree that strange things are going on. At the end of the finale William returns heavily laden with Lydia's wardrobe. Godolphin runs into him, causing him to spill everything. Godolphin exits with an angry gesture as William stands perplexed amidst the scattered toilette articles. The others burst into laughter.

The second act takes place in a garden-salon of the palace. Lydia sings a light, frivolous aria expressing her desire to remain single and enjoy herself. She and Eveline speak of Bella; and then together, Eveline doing the first and third stanzas and Lydia the second, they singe the "Ballade of the Laird of Callingmore," a song which Bella used to sing. It concerns a laird who is mysteriously killed when he hunts on a Sunday. Charles the naval officer, who is in the wings, sings the refrain to the third stanza. Eveline thinks that she hears the voice of her brother, and she and Lydia are terrified. When they hear someone approaching the door they both cry out, "Gott steh' uns bei!" It turns out to be no-one but William,[16] who has found the stranger's (actually Lord Charlie's) memobook. Lydia is put out with him because he thinks that Godolphin has legal right to be lord, the codicil not having turned up. She and Eveline then leave the stage for a few moments.

Charles comes in, looking for the memobook he has lost, and is mistaken by William for Lord Charlie. It seems that Charles had been locked in the guest's apartment by Godolphin, but he managed to escape. We learn that he was able to sing the refrain to the *ballade* because he remembered his mother having sung it (note the parallel with Georges Brown's recalling the Scottish anthem in *La Dame Blanche*). He promises William that he is not interested in Lydia. When they hear Lady Sarah and the other ladies approaching, William urges Charles (whom he believes to be Lord Charlie) to hide again, so that Lady Sarah will be spared the sudden shock of seeing him.

In the ensuing quintet Eveline, Lydia, Lady Sarah, William, and Allan sing about the coming of night. Sarah and Eveline, William and Lydia then play chess, during the course of which William communicates to Lydia the news that Lord Charlie has returned. William then pairs off with Lady Sarah, while Lydia plays with Eveline and tells her the news. When she says, "Charlie ist hier!" Eveline cries out, "O Gott!" and Lady Sarah naturally wonders what is the matter. Lydia tells her that a bee had caught itself in Eveline's dress. Eveline indicates to Lydia that she will see Lord Charlie after Lady Sarah has gone to bed. After another quintet ("Lasst uns nun zu Ruhe gehen"[17]) the ladies and Allan leave the stage. William tells Charles that Eveline has agreed to see him, and after the supposed lord's exit William dresses himself in his uniform, musing that

Lydia would fall for him if he were a naval officer. The memobook having indicated where the all important codicil is located, William goes into the archives in search of it.

The finale begins with a group of constables and their lackeys coming silently into the room. They are followed by Godolphin, whose intention is for them to apprehend the person whom he believes to be Lord Charlie. When William, still in Charles' uniform, re-enters bearing the codicil, which he has indeed found, the constables and lackeys seize him, thinking he is Lord Charlie. They convey him away forthwith. At this point Charles re-enters and sings a fine aria ("Nur auf ihrem leisen Flügel/Durch die Gärten rauscht die Nacht"), after which Eveline re-enters. She thinks that Charles is her brother, Lord Charlie, and the two sing a tender duet. When Lydia and Allan arrive back on the scene, Eveline introduces them to her long lost brother. Charles is now disturbed, because he realizes that Eveline's love is for her brother, not for him; and he realizes what a shock it will be to her when she learns the truth. Charles looks so melancholy that both Eveline and Allan remark about how much he has changed in the intervening years. Although they all make every effort not to awaken Lady Sarah, she does awaken, comes on stage, sees Charles, thinks in the dark that he is her son, and faints away. In the confusion that follows, Charles escapes, and the curtain falls.

Act III takes place in a grand Gothic hall. It is still night. Godolphin gloats over having found the codicil which he got from William, whom he takes to be Lord Charlie. He sings an aria about whether or not he ought to destroy it, since it stands in the way of his inheriting the estate of the late lord. He finally in fact does burn it and then sings of his joy at being about to become the new lord. Justice of the Peace Blackstone then comes in with news that Charles the naval officer is not Lord Charlie, but that the real Lord Charlie is alive and well in Paris. He reads a letter indicating that Lord Charlie not only lives but has married a Spanish lady who took care of him in prison when he was wounded (cf. the similar motif in *La Dame Blanche*); that he has not corresponded with his relatives, knowing that his wife's Catholicism would displease them. Blackstone reminds Godolphin that Paris is far away and assures him that only the codicil could prevent him from inheriting the estate. When Godolphin informs him that he has just burned it, Blackstone says *aside*, "Wie gut, dass ich die Abschrift fand!" (How fortunate that I found the copy)—a hint to the audience that Blackstone may produce this later on when an occasion presents itself. Godolphin and Blackstone then look out the window and see a crowd of people greeting someone whom they mistake for the new lord but who in fact is Charles the naval officer. Godolphin is of course surprised, because he thinks he has imprisoned him. As the people sing "Lord Morley hoch! Hoch unser Herr!" we hear in the orchestral accompaniment a Scottish folk dance:

Example 4-10

This is the only Scots tune in the entire opera; it reminds one of a similar tune in *La Dame Blanche* (cf. Example 4-1). *Exeunt* Godolphin and Blackstone.

Allan enters, noting that now that day has come, the person whom they all mistook for Lord Charlie is not he. Godolphin having ordered his departure (see above), he sings an aria about taking up his staff and being on his way. Before he leaves, however, Charles requests that he give Eveline a message. She enters, and in another long duet Charles tells her that he loves her and hopes that she will forgive him for allowing everyone to think he was Lord Charlie. She admits that she is not altogether indifferent to him, and she gives him a medallion as a token of her interest in him. As he is leaving the house Godolphin orders his men to seize him.

At the beginning of the finale the chorus is still under the impression that Charles will be made the new lord. Godolphin tells them that the man whom they took to be Lord Charlie is not Lord Charlie, and he orders the imposter to be brought out. Charles readily admits that he is not Lord Charlie and says furthermore that Lord Charlie no longer lives. Lady Sarah is distressed, as are all the other principals, except Godolphin. Charles then explains that he had known Lord Charlie; the two of them had identical forenames and even looked alike. Before the Battle of Trafalgar Lord Charlie had a premonition that things would not go well for him. He accordingly gave Charles his memobook, telling him to go to Morley House in the event of his death and to protect the members of his immediate family from the ambitious Godolphin. Charles saw Charlie hit by a bullet and fall overboard. He tried to rescue him, but he too was wounded to the point of unconsciousness, and when he awoke he found himself on a hospital ship bound for Calcutta. Godolphin sarcastically says that he does not believe Charles' story. He points to the medallion and asks him whether he has brought it with him from India. Eveline admits that she has just given it to him. When Lydia discloses that the medallion contains a picture not of Eveline but of Bella Morley, Charles immediately recognizes the name Bella as being that of his mother. Lady Sarah then embraces him as her grandson. Despite this unexpected turn of events Godolphin insists that the estate is now his, according to the late lord's will. Suddenly William breaks in with news that the real Lord Charlie lives. He explains that while still in confinement he came upon Charlie and that

Charlie, recognizing his old school companion, helped him escape. Allan rushes in with the happy news that Lord Charlie is approaching the palace. Godolphin says that he is arriving too late, but William reminds him of the codicil which Godolphin's men have taken from him. In an attempt to save Godolphin's honor, Blackstone now produces the copy of the codicil. Its legitimacy is unquestionable, and Godolphin stalks off in a rage. In the last moment of the opera Lord Charlie and his wife finally arrive. As they are being greeted, the curtain falls.

The main resemblance between *Der Erbe von Morley* and *Guy Mannering* is the motif of a young heir who is missing and presumed dead, and who consequently is about to be dispossessed of his inheritance. Arriving on the scene after many years of absence, he manages to get back what is rightfully his, despite opposition, which comes in the opera from the late lord's cousin, Viscount Godolphin, who is clearly based on Scott's evil lawyer, Glossin (not a member of the family). But the opera plot has a different twist in that a young man who has been a friend to the presumably dead heir arrives on the scene with instructions from the deceased to prevent the estate from falling into the hands of the avaricious Godolphin. The young man decides that the best course of action is for him to impersonate temporarily the rightful heir. Like Vanbeest Brown (Henry Bertram) of *Guy Mannering*, he too has been in India, and again like Brown he does not know who he really is. As we have just seen, he learns during the course of the third act that his mother Bella was the daughter of Lady Sarah Morley, and thus he and the heir, whom he still believes dead, are cousins. Finally the rightful heir appears. The faithful old servant Allan is more reminiscent of his namesake Allan-bane (*The Lady of the Lake*) or Caleb Balderstone (*The Bride of Lammermoor*) than of either Dominie Sampson or Meg Merrilies. The action takes place in the north of England rather than in Scotland, and the time is the early nineteenth century rather than the third quarter of the eighteenth century.

Despite Gerhard Glaser's implications to the contrary,[18] there are really no parallels between the opera and *The Monastery* unless one stretches a few points. The slight Gothic element perhaps owes something to the novel, especially Eveline's *ballade* about the Laird of Callingmore and his mysterious death. The second stanza recalls to mind the White Lady:

Und als er kam zum Erlenteich,
Da lag ein Weib so schön, so bleich:
"Halt' an Laird Callingmore!
Ich gab dir Jugend, Glück und Ehr',
Thu' mir's zu Lieb' und jag' nicht mehr."

Lady Sarah Morley, who is long-suffering, much respected, and fragile in health, may have been suggested to Holstein by Lady Avenel of the novel. William may owe something to Sir Piercie Shafton, but, as I remarked earlier, he also seems hewn from the same block as is Flotow's Sir Tristan.

S. Bagge denied that there is much resemblance between *Der Erbe von Morley* and *La Dame Blanche*. He noted a difference in personality between Gaveston and Godolphin. He stressed the point that Georges Brown, who is indeed the heir, returns to his ancestral home unwittingly, without anyone realizing who he is; whereas Charles the naval officer is believed by virtually everyone to be the heir, but he is not, and he knows he is not. Furthermore he claimed that *La Dame Blanche*, which he describes as "reizend" and "pikant," lacks "das gemütvolle Element" to be found in *Der Erbe;* that this typically German quality gives Holstein's music more depth and makes it of enduring worth.[19] I find his remarks unconvincing because he does not explain the difference in personality between the two villains, he glosses over the obvious fact that both Charles and Georges return to their ancestral home without knowing it, and he shows a singular lack of sensitivity for the emotional core of *La Dame Blanche*. The similarities between the two operas are striking, Bagge notwithstanding, and most of them have already been noted during the foregoing discussion. To sum up, both Godolphin and Gaveston are unscrupulous, avaricious, and most eager to get possession of an estate. Both Charles the naval officer and Georges Brown return to their ancestral homes unwittingly, after having been wounded in battle; they are very much interested in chasing after young ladies; and they begin to remember their past when they hear old songs. Both Lord Charlie and Georges Brown are nursed back to health, after having been wounded in battle, by young ladies whom they later marry. Justice of the Peace Blackstone is reminiscent of Mac-Irton, "juge de paix du canton," and Allan, faithful old servant to Lady Sarah, brings to mind Marguerite, "ancienne domestique des comtes d'Avenel." Eveline's eerie "Ballade of the Laird of Callingmore" serves the same function as does Jenny's *ballade* about the White Lady. In both operas a document that has been destroyed plays an important role in the unraveling of the plot.[20] Finally, both Holstein and Boieldieu use a Scots folk tune on occasion, and I think it no coincidence that the tunes are similar.

Der Erbe von Morley is, to my notion, a more satisfying opera than *Die Hochländer* (see Chapter 3). Holstein's modest talents were better suited to lighter subject matter. The reviewer of the first performance in Munich found the musical invention rich and natural, the harmony simple and effective. He also remarked about Holstein's success in giving the different characters music appropriate to their different personalities.[21] Bagge was equally impressed with this aspect of the work and commented in particular on Holstein's versatility in handling many different characters and situations, yet managing to create the appropriate tone, and always subordinating the manifold details, which in themselves are impressive, to the overall design.[22] Despite the modest success of the work in its own day, no mid-twentieth-century revival seems likely in view of the near total oblivion of the poet-composer and the similarity in both subject matter and musical atmosphere to Boieldieu's masterpiece.

5

§ § §

OLD MORTALITY

$\mathbf{A}$lthough *Old Mortality* (1816) is generally admitted to be one of the half dozen finest of the Waverley Novels, it has inspired only a single opera—and indirectly, through the medium of a spoken drama which differs enormously from the novel. Since this opera, *I Puritani,* is one of the few Scott operas still in standard repertoire, I have chosen to discuss it, despite its very slight resemblance to *Old Mortality* or any other Waverley Novel. The earlier Farley-Bishop musical drama, on the other hand, does follow the novel rather closely. My discussion first of it brings into sharper relief, by contrast, the divergence of the famed opera from its ultimate source.

The Battle of Bothwell Brigg

On the title page of the complete text *The Battle of Bothwell Brigg* is given the appellation "A Scottish Romance"; the author is Charles Farley.[1] The work was first performed in London, at Covent Garden, on 22 May 1820. The indefatigable Henry Bishop did the music.[2] Almost all the memorable characters of the novel are included—Lord Evandale, Claverhouse, Major Bellenden, Henry Morton, Cuddie Headrigg, Bothwell, Balfour, Lady Margaret, Edith Bellenden, Jenny Dennison, Mause Headrigg; one notable personality is omitted—Habakkuk Mucklewrath; and a few new characters of minor importance are added, such as the warder of Til-lietudlem, whose name is Douse Davie (obviously lifted by Farley from *The Heart of Mid-Lothian*). The main singing roles are for Edith (done originally by Miss Maria Tree) and Lord Evandale (Mr. Durusett).

After the potpourri overture the curtain opens and reveals the Castle of Tillietudlem, ancestral home of the Bellenden family. *"Douse Davie is seen upon the ramparts, as looking upon the valley beneath."* In the chorus "Lads and lasses, one and a' " rustics sing that now that the wappenschaw is over, they will go to the tavern to celebrate. Guydill, steward to Lady Bellenden, urges them to cause no tumult but to go with taverner Niel Blane "and drink a cup to the Capt. o' the Popinjay." (There is no exact parallel to this in Scott, but it is suggested by the events of chapters ii & iii; Farley begins the musical drama *after* the wappenschaw, which might have proved difficult to stage.) Guydill tells Davie that young Henry Morton is Captain of the Popinjay. Davie remarks that Henry (a Presbyterian) unfortunately has no chance with the beautiful Edith, since her grandmother, Lady Margaret, naturally favors the Royalist Lord Evandale. Guydill informs Davie that Lady Margaret is approaching the castle, not in the best humor; and after Davie exits Guydill muses on the impossibility of anything ever coming of the interest Edith obviously has in Henry Morton. The entrance of Lady Margaret, Edith, Jenny and other domestics follows loosely the opening pages of chapter vii. Lady Margaret is still angry about the poor figure her servant Goose Gibbie has cut at the wappenschaw. During the course of the conversation we learn that Major Bellenden was a spectator there (this is not the case in the novel) and that Mause and Cuddie Headrigg have some time previously left Tillietudlem to work for the Milnwoods (again unlike the novel: Scott's Lady Margaret *dismisses* them since Cuddie's not being on hand necessitated her having Goose Gibbie in her entourage and thus indirectly caused the ridicule she suffered). Lady Margaret is awaiting the arrival of Col. Graham of Claverhouse, and the scene ends in a chorus ("Forward, away!").

The second scene is a hall of the castle. Edith, alone, expresses her love for Morton in the song "Ah! happy day!" Jenny enters to tell her that soldiers are approaching with two prisoners (here the plot follows ch. ix of the novel). Lady Margaret receives Sergeant Bothwell, the leader of the group cordially and tells him that she is expecting Claverhouse. After Bothwell exits, Major Bellenden, who has been celebrating at Niel Blane's tavern, comes on stage. (In the novel Edith writes to him to inform him that Morton is a prisoner.) Certain French phrases which he occasionally uses make him somewhat unlike Scott's Major Bellenden, but as in the novel he cuts Lady Margaret short every time she is about to launch into an harangue about her having entertained Charles II at Tillietudlem long ago. At the end of the scene a sound of trumpets is heard in the distance, heralding the approach of Claverhouse and his entourage.

Claverhouse is well received at Tillietudlem. When he instructs Bothwell to bring in the prisoners, Edith and Jenny leave the stage. Lady Margaret and Major Bellenden are both surprised to see Henry Morton prisoner. Morton is insolent with Claverhouse because he thinks Claverhouse has had no legal right to apprehend him. (This part of the scene is based on chapter xiii; even some of the dialogue is more or less the same.) Claverhouse wants to have him immediately executed, but Lady Margaret and Major Bellenden plead for his life. (In the musical drama there is no Lord Evandale at this point to plead also for Henry's life.) Claverhouse then examines Cuddie Headrigg and his mother, Old Mause. When Mause cannot resist making known her radical religious opinions, they are both sent off, presumably with a death sentence. (Here the dialogue follows ch. viii, at the point in the story where Bothwell interrogates Cuddie and Mause at Milnwood.) Lord Evandale finally enters, bearing with him a packet from Glasgow addressed to Claverhouse. Claverhouse reads and becomes visibly agitated. He tells everyone of Balfour's foul murder of the archbishop (in the novel we know this much earlier). Morton has admitted to aiding Balfour, but he swears ignorance of the murder (as in chapter viii, at Milnwood). Evandale informs Claverhouse that ruffians are lurking on Loudon Hill. The scene closes with Claverhouse and his soldiers departing to fight the rebels.

In the next scene Edith entreats Evandale to intercede with Claverhouse in Morton's favor. (In the novel this conversation takes place *before* Claverhouse's examination of Morton.) Even though Morton is his rival in love, Evandale will try to help him. They then sing a duet, the music composed by Paer but "adapted to the English stage & arranged" by Bishop.

The fifth scene takes place at *"A Wild rocky Pass."* Morton and Cuddie, still prisoners, are under the surveillance of Bothwell and the royal troops, led by Claverhouse. Suddenly the enemy appears. Morton and Cuddie set themselves free, Balfour defeats Bothwell, and Morton saves Evandale from death at the hands of Balfour (everything based on chs. xvi & xvii of the novel). When Evandale asks, "And is it possible, Morton, you can be a traitor?" Morton replies, "No, no; believe me, I never had a thought of mixing with these misguided men; but, as it is, I may, per-chance, serve my country, and bring them back to their duty." (This departure from Scott changes Morton's character; as the musical drama evolves he is shown as a spy in the camp of the enemy.) Evandale escapes by means of a horse which Cuddie has procured. This is noticed by several rebels, who begin to fight with Morton and Cuddie. Balfour stops the melee (which is broken up by the Rev. Kettledrumle and Old Mause in the novel). He is perturbed that Evandale has escaped, but commands the rebels not to harm Morton and Cuddie. The act closes with the chorus "Loud and cheerily raise each voice!"

As Act II opens, at the camp of Balfour and the rebels, Henry Morton is bemoaning his fate. Balfour enters, followed by other members of the war council. When Balfour announces his determination to attack Tillietud-lem, Morton is horrified. He gives Cuddie (dressed in the dead Bothwell's uniform) a secret message to take Major Bellenden to inform him about the planned assault on the castle.—There is no such message in the novel. Rather, Morton agrees to Balfour's plans in hope of saving his friends' lives; he is upset when, after the first day of the assault, he is transferred to fight in Glasgow.

The second scene takes place in the *"Grand Hall of the Castle."* In the opening dialogue between Major Bellenden and Lady Margaret (drawn from chapter xix), the Major tells her that martial law supersedes all other laws. Guydill brings in the news that the rebels have won the day and that they are hastening toward Tillietudlem. The Major determines to defend the castle. All at once Jenny rushes in, screaming that one of the rebels has already entered by way of the kitchen; that she has poured scalding hot broth over his head. Cuddie reveals himself (he was in Bothwell's uniform) and conveys to the Major the message from Morton, which reads: ". . . Let not reports deceive you: I will so use the power they have given me, to serve my king against these misguided men. The cruel Balfour meditates an instant attack on the castle. . . ." Cuddie relates that Morton saved Evandale's life. Relieved that Morton is no rebel, Edith pens a message for Cuddie to take back to him. Alone on stage at the end of the scene, she sings, "Oh! never can the laddie prove/To honour false whose love is true!" (Cuddie's mishap in the kitchen comes from chapter xxv, but there he is no bearer of messages; the castle is actually being assaulted.)

In the third scene we are in a room of a hut in the rebel camp. Henry is revulsed by the rebels' leaders. He tells Balfour he will stay only if there is no slaughter and if Balfour will give over to him Lord Evandale, who has again been taken prisoner (suggested by the saving of Evandale by Morton and the Rev. Poundtext, chapter xxvii). Balfour agrees to Morton's demands, but as he leaves he instructs his man Dingwell (not in the novel) to spy on Morton. Cuddie enters, with messages to Morton from Edith and Major Bellenden. When Morton tells Evandale that he will again help him escape (in the novel he is released to go to Tillietudlem to persuade Major Bellenden to surrender), Dingwell and several rebels rush in and seize both of them. Fortunately Cuddie manages to escape. The rebels drag Evandale back into confinement and decide to murder Morton as soon as the day of fast has passed. After a while one of the party moves the dial forward, and the clock strikes twelve. Just as they are about to slaughter their victim, Claverhouse enters with a group of Royalist soldiers. Morton is saved. His plight had been told to Claverhouse by the faithful Cuddie. (This episode is based on Morton's near murder by Habakkuk Mucklewrath and other covenanters in chapter xxxiii of the novel, which takes place *after* the battle for the bridge.) Morton tells Claverhouse that Balfour and his men intend to storm the castle that night, and Claverhouse says that they must be prevented from doing so at Bothwell Brigg (in the novel the castle has already been assaulted and given up). Henry Morton will fight with the Royalists at the bridge (unlike what we have in the novel, where Henry is still on the side of the rebels).

The short fourth scene has no exact parallel in Scott. Balfour is informed of Morton's treachery and of his rescue. He learns too that Claverhouse's forces are being joined by those of Monmouth and Ross. He arouses his men to go with him to fight at Bothwell Brigg. *"They shout and follow Balfour off."*

The battle itself is based loosely on chapter xxxii of the novel. The set for this scene must have demanded ingenuity on the part of the designer, the stage directions indicating that the bridge *"occupies the whole width of the stage."* The director's talents must have been brought into play too:

> *The battle has commenced as the scene is discovered. The conflict most*
> *obstinate on both sides. Balfour, Claverhouse, Ross, Morton, Lord Evandale,*
> *very conspicuously placed among the whole. The bridge taken and retaken.*
> *The bridge is full of Balfour's troops in seeming triumph, a field piece is fired*
> *at it. The bridge bursts from the centre arch, and the troops are precipitated*
> *into the water; Balfour is seen swimming; he climbs by the help of a tree that*
> *overhangs the river, and when he is hanging by the branch, a gun-shot hits*
> *him, and he falls into the water. The royal party are grouped in various*
> *striking situations as the scene closes.*

Balfour meets his death much later in the novel, but Farley cancels the last eleven chapters.

The final scene, which has no parallel in Scott, takes place in the hall of the castle. Major Bellenden announces the victory to Lady Margaret. Cuddie relates that Balfour has fallen and that Henry Morton fought bravely. Upon the entrance of Claverhouse, Morton, and Evandale, the Major says that he hopes there will soon be a "bridal-feast" for Morton and Edith; Cuddie adds: "And Cuddie and Jenny too, I hope." (Evandale's romantic interest in Edith is forgotten about.) The act ends in a musical finale in which Edith, Cuddie, Jenny, Major Bellenden, and the chorus sing in celebration of the great victory.

In comparing the musical drama with the novel one notices occasional rearrangement in the order of events, occasional splicing together of scenes, a good bit of condensation, and in general a marked simplification of the story and its characters; nevertheless *The Battle of Bothwell Brigg* is clearly Scott's novel in musical-dramatic adaptation. The relationship between *I Puritani* and *Old Mortality* is not so conspicuous.

I Puritani

I Puritani (or *I Puritani di Scozia,* as it is sometimes called) was first performed in Paris, at the Théâtre-Italien, on 25 January 1835; the major roles were sung by Giulietta Grisi (Elvira), Rubini (Arturo), Tamburini (Riccardo), and Lablache (Giorgio). This was the last opera to come from the pen of Bellini, who died later in the same year. The libretto was done by Count Carlo Pepoli, a refugee from the Austrian occupied parts of Italy and a minor literary figure of the times. The opera has had a long, distinguished performance history extending into the third quarter of the twentieth century,[3] and it is available on discs.[4]

Count Pepoli based his libretto on the Scott-derivative play *Têtes Rondes et Cavaliers,* by François Ancelot and Xavier-Boniface Saintine, which was first performed in Paris, at the Théâtre National du Vaudeville, on 25 September 1833.[5] The cast of characters—which includes Lord Arthur Clifford, cavalier; Georges Monck, general of the Parliament; Lord Walton, governor of a fortress near Plymouth; Henri Mulgrave, captain in the army; Habacuc Pembrock, Puritan sergeant; Lucy, daughter of Walton; Henriette de France, widow of Charles I; and Sara Walker, companion to Lucy—indicates in itself that the play has little resemblance to *Old Mortality*. Nevertheless, Habacuc Pembrock owes at least his forename and some of his religious beliefs to Scott's unforgettable Cameronian fanatic, Habakkuk Mucklewrath and probably his surname to the Rev. Mr. Pembroke, chaplain at Waverley Honour (not a Puritan). Also Captain Mulgrave, one of the protagonists, has the same forename as Scott's Henry Morton. The setting is the vicinity of Plymouth, rather than Scotland, and the story occurs during the years of the Protectorate, rather than after the Restoration.

Act I takes place in the fortress over which Lord Walton is governor. Lucy anxiously awaits the arrival of her fiancé Lord Clifford, a Royalist sympathizer. Although Walton has made his peace with the Puritan regime, he too was once a Royalist and has thus given his approval to the forthcoming marriage. Henri Mulgrave, who is also in love with Lucy, is understandably jealous of Clifford. Furthermore, he is disgruntled because he feels that Walton had long ago promised Lucy to him, rather than Clifford. Like Scott's Henry Morton, Mulgrave is a Presbyterian, a moderate in his religious persuasion. He tries to dissuade Walton from allowing his daughter to marry a man of avowed Royalist sympathies, but Walton is determined to go through with the marriage contract at once. When Clifford arrives, definite plans for the wedding are made. During the course of events Clifford is introduced to a supposed French countess whom Walton has been detaining in house arrest. Later in the act Walton tells her that he must convey her to London to appear before Parliament. Realizing this would be the end for her, she reveals herself to Clifford as Henriette de France, widow of Charles I, and gets him to help her escape. As luck would have it she is wearing Lucy's bridal veil, which Lucy had playfully asked her to try on. Thus to an unwary eye she might pass as Clifford's bride-to-be. Mulgrave allows the two to leave the castle, even though he realizes that the disguised lady is the supposed countess, because the apparently off-color incident will surely spell out the end of Clifford's claim on Lucy. When the escape is discovered, Mulgrave maintains that Clifford has *eloped* with the countess. Thinking Clifford has jilted her, Lucy becomes mentally deranged.

Act II takes place at the house of Sara Walker, near the fortress. When the curtain opens, Sara and Habacuc are revealed discussing Lucy's derangement. Habacuc proposes marriage to Sara, but she puts him off when Mulgrave pays a call to inquire about Lucy. Lucy then enters, obviously under great mental stress of some sort. Somewhat later in the act Clifford bursts in. He has temporarily eluded the Roundheads who are in pursuit of him and has come at great danger to himself to see Lucy, not knowing she is ill. Sara thinks that the appearance of Clifford will perhaps cause Lucy to regain her sanity. Accordingly, Lucy and Clifford have a long conversation. At first she thinks that Clifford thinks she is the lady with whom he eloped. She regains her reason when he assures her of his undying love and tells her that the countess was really the Queen. He shows her a letter from Charles II which proves what he has told her. Lucy persuades him to let her keep the letter, since it would mean death for him if found on him. Suddenly they hear Mulgrave and the Roundhead soldiers arriving. When Clifford tries to persuade Lucy to go quickly with him, her insanity returns. Thinking that he is about to flee again with the countess, she cries out for help. Clifford is arrested, and Mulgrave announces that he will be put to death. Lucy faints.

In Act III we are back at the fortress. The hour of Clifford's execution has almost arrived. Lucy, now completely sane, has just returned from a trip to London, where she pled in behalf of Clifford at the feet of Cromwell himself. Cromwell granted her request, but word from him has not yet arrived in Plymouth, and Mulgrave is about to go through with the execution. General Monck and Clifford have a long conversation. Clifford knows well that Monck's sympathies are with the Royalists, even though he is at the moment in the service of the Commonwealth, but Clifford will not betray him, even though he himself must die. Mulgrave then comes in to escort Clifford to the scaffold. In a last minute attempt to save him Lucy says that he knows about a Royalist conspiracy and that to execute him would only deprive the Puritans of valuable information. To prove her point she produces the letter from Prince Charles and shows it to Mulgrave. The execution is postponed. In the meantime the stay of execution finally comes from Cromwell, but now Clifford has been accused of the even worse crime of conspiracy. In a *scène* with Mulgrave, Lucy implores him to consider the letter a frantic attempt on her part to save her lover and not to believe that it is true. Mulgrave replies that not only he but several soldiers saw it too, and it appeared genuine. Lucy tells him she will be his slave if only he will free Clifford. When Mulgrave replies that he must do his duty, Lucy accuses him of wanting to take ultimate vengeance on a rival in love. In the closing *scène,* fortunately, Mulgrave has a change of heart. He tells General Monck that the letter is false. Monck is at first reluctant to believe what he says. Mulgrave then reads a passage from the letter in which Prince Charles stated that he considered Monck one of his best friends near the person of Cromwell. Monck impetuously seizes the letter and crushes it in his hands. Obviously it is false, he says. So Clifford is saved, as Monck himself is almost revealed for what he really is. Lucy will go into exile with Clifford.

The story of the play is obviously quite different from *Old Mortality,* yet it does recall to mind the novel in a few respects besides the already mentioned forenames *Habacuc* and *Henri.* The satire directed toward Puritans in the person of Habacuc—their drab dress, sour dispositions, and love for long sermons—owes much to the novel. Also the proverbial abhorrence of Puritans to dancing comes out; the playwrights may have gotten this notion from Douce Davie Deans, of *The Heart of Mid-Lothian*. Habacuc is teased by Sara because he is not quite so holy as he pretends, and indeed the whole relationship between Habacuc and Sara may have been suggested by the Cuddie Headrigg-Jenny Dennison relationship of the novel. The motif of two honorable young men of opposing political and religious beliefs vying for the affection of one lady derives from the Edith Bellenden-Henry Morton-Lord Evandale triangle. Like Morton, Henri Mulgrave too saves his rival from death, but in the play the lady favors the Royalist rather than the Presbyterian. Lucy's mental derangement is based on Edith's temporary derangement in chapter xxxviii: while Evandale is pleading with her to marry him before he goes off to the Highlands to join the Royalist forces, she catches a glimpse of the long-absent Morton, who immediately disappears from view, and she becomes "dangerously ill." Ancelot and Xavier exaggerate this relatively minor incident and make a big to-do about Lucy's madness, perhaps following examples already set in one or more of the plays or operas based on *The Bride of Lammermoor,* which blow up out of all proportion Lucy's madness (but not Donizetti's *Lucia,* since it had not yet been written). Clifford's sense of honor tells him to save the Queen, even if his love affair with Lucy must suffer. In the novel Evandale's honor tells him to leave Edith, even though she implores him to stay, and join the Royalist forces. And yet the situation is rather different, since it is obvious to Evandale that Edith wants him to stay not because she loves him but because she fears for his safety. The motif of the concealed countess perhaps derives from *Peveril of the Peak* (see Chapter 12), and the brief account of Lucy's journey to London to plead for Clifford's life was almost certainly suggested by Jeanie Deans' similar journey in *The Heart of Mid-Lothian* (see Chapter 7).

In the opera Lord Arthur Clifford is called Lord Arturo Talbot,[6] Henri Mulgrave becomes Sir Riccardo Forth, and Lucy becomes Elvira. Henriette de France appears under the same name but in Italian form (Enrichetta di Francia), and Lord Walton is given the forename Gualtiero. Sara Walker and Habacuc Pembrock have no counterparts; but there are two new characters: Sir Bruno Robertson (a Puritan and Captain of the Guard) and Sir Giorgio Walton (Elvira's uncle). The latter probably owes his forename to Georges Monck and something of his personality to Scott's Major Bellenden, Edith's great uncle. As in the play the scene is laid at a fortress near Plymouth, and thus the opera's alternate title, *I Puritani di Scozia,* is absurd—absurd but interesting, in that it is further indication of the tremendous vogue that Scottish subject matter had on the continent and of the romantic yearning stimulated by just the word *Scotland.* Also, Pepoli and Bellini no doubt knew that the play was based on Scott's *Old Mortality,* which Defauconpret entitled *Les Puritains d'Écosse* in his very early translation (Paris, 1817).

Act I corresponds with Act I of the play.[7] In the opening scene, however, preparations are being made for the wedding of Elvira and Riccardo. Later Elvira learns from her uncle that "he has been able to intercede with her father on her behalf, and that her bridegroom is to be Lord Arthur Talbot."[8] Act II follows roughly the first part of Act II of the play, with the addition of Sir Giorgio imploring Riccardo to spare Arturo's life should he ever be captured: the sight of him may restore Elvira to her senses. Act III follows the remainder of Act II with one major alteration: Elvira regains her sanity when Riccardo is captured and sentenced to death; and with a deus ex machina: "Suddenly the sound of trumpets is heard and a messenger hurries in with a letter from Sir George. The Stuarts have been defeated and Cromwell has pardoned all prisoners. Amidst general rejoicing the lovers embrace and happily contemplate their future happiness."[9] The ending was no doubt suggested by Cromwell's pardon of Mulgrave in the play's third act, but the act itself has been omitted from the operatic libretto. This is nothing unusual in the conversion of play to libretto; Boito and Verdi omit the first act of Shakespeare's *Othello*. A detailed summary of *I Puritani* is unnecessary, since, with the exception of Elvira's uncle, it would not reveal any connections between the opera and *Old Mortality* besides those I have already pointed out between the play and the novel.

I Puritani aptly illustrates the remark which I made in Chapter 1 that the success of a Scott opera is not determined by close dependence on its source. Obviously the success in this case is owing primarily to Bellini's music, not to *Old Mortality*, and not to Pepoli's libretto, which some observers describe as amateurish in comparison with Romani's librettos for *Norma* and *La Sonnambula*. This is not to say that *Old Mortality* does not lend itself to operatic rendition. In some ways it does. Take, for example, Morton's long soliloquy in chapter vi, just after he has saved Balfour from falling into the hands of his enemies. The opening long paragraph, beginning with the words "Farewell, stern enthusiast," could be easily turned into the text for a formal recitative and aria. The second paragraph ("But I am no slave . . ."), with its change of mood, would make an excellent cabaletta. One might also note the possibilities for arias in Morton's brief soliloquies in chapter xxvii, when he is still in the rebel camp ("I shall fall young . . ."), and in chapter xli, while in the course of his search for information as to Balfour's whereabouts he observes a mountain brook ("Murmerer that thou art . . . why chafe with the rocks that stop thy course for a moment?"). An incident with striking operatic possibilities occurs in chapter xv, just before Claverhouse's unlucky encounter with the rebels at Loudon-hill:

> As the horsemen halted their lines on the ridge of the hill, their trumpets and kettle-drums sounded a bold and warlike flourish of menace and defiance that rang along the waste like the shrill summons of a destroying angel. The wanderers, in answer, united their

voices, and sent forth, in solemn modulation, the two first verses of the Seventy-sixth Psalm, according to the metrical version of the Scottish Kirk:—

> "In Judah's land God is well known,
>   His name's in Israel great;
> In Salem is his tabernacle,
>   In Zion is his seat.

> There arrows of the bow he brake,
>   The shield, the sword, the war.
> More glorious thou than hills of prey,
>   More excellent art far."

A shout, or rather a solemn acclamation, attended the close of the stanza; and after a dead pause, the second verse was resumed by the insurgents, who applied the destruction of the Assyrians as prophetical of the issue of their own impending contest:—

> "Those that were stout of heart are spoiled,
>   They slept their sleep outright;
> And none of those their hands did find,
>   That were the men of might.

> When thy rebuke, O Jacob's God,
>   Had forth against them past,
> Their horses and their chariots both
>   Were in a deep sleep cast."

There was another acclamation, which was followed by the most profound silence.

Also the events of chapter xxxiii—Morton's falling into the hands of Habakkuk Mucklewrath, Ephraim Macbriar and other fanatical Cameronians and their attempt to murder him—would be excellent material not only for spoken drama (see above) but for opera as well. On the other hand, the novel would present difficulties for the librettist. Unlike *Ivanhoe,* for example, it does not break down readily into a small number of picturesque scenes crucial to the story (see Chapter 9). Rather, it has many important, memorable scenes, and the necessary omission of some of them in a libretto would markedly alter the character of the story. Moreover, the intellectual content of the novel, that is, the political and religious dispute, is not conducive to opera. In the Farley-Bishop musical drama, which of course contains spoken dialogue, the leading characters are pasteboard figures, from the standpoint of intellect, in comparison with their counterparts in Scott. In an opera there is even less possibility for political and religious polemics. So despite some material undeniably conducive to good opera, there would be problems too—problems which the deft librettist and composer could solve only by making drastic alterations.

SCENE FROM the Metropolitan's new production of *I Puritani*, with Joan Sutherland as Elvira and Luciano Pavarotti as Arturo. By courtesy of the Metropolitan Opera Archives.

6

§ § §

ROB ROY

There are only two operas, to my knowledge, based on *Rob Roy* (1817),[1] and they are both the work of well-known composers. Friedrich von Flotow's *Rob-Roy* (1837) is the earlier of the two and indeed one of the first operas which Flotow composed. At about the same time he set to music a libretto based on *Woodstock* (see Chapter 15). His interest in British subject matter culminated ten years later in his most beloved opera, *Martha*. The second operatic *Rob Roy* was done in the last decade of the century by Reginald de Koven, a leading figure in the annals of American light opera from about 1890 until his death in 1920.

Flotow's *Rob-Roy*

A private performance of *Rob-Roy* in the spring of 1837 in Paris, at the Hôtel Castellane, was reviewed favorably in *Le Ménestrel*.[2] It had previously been given with success at Royaumont, the château of the Marquis of Belisson. The libretto was done by Paul Duport and Pittaud de Forges. M. Panel was well applauded for his interpretation of the title role, and Mme de Forges was "charmante" in the role of Diana Vernon. In the early days of his career Flotow had to be satisfied to see his works performed in private theaters of opera enthusiasts such as the Marquis of Belisson and Count Castellane. Normally the singers were amateurs. The reviewer for *Le Ménestrel* recognized young Flotow's talent and expressed hope that he might soon be in a position to leave the narrow confines of a theater of amateurs.

Unfortunately I cannot give this opera the thorough discussion which something by Flotow deserves, since I was unable to find either the libretto or the complete music. Apparently the libretto was not published; if it still exists in manuscript, I do not know where.[3] Like all French opéras comiques of the period, *Rob-Roy* must have had much spoken dialogue. In the absence of this, one simply cannot say what has been done with Scott's novel. As for the music, seven pieces were published: a polonaise for Diana Vernon ("Autrefois, quand du bal j'entendais le signal, quel bonheur! quelle ivresse!"), a duet for Diana and Rob-Roy ("Juste ciel! au secours!"), a duet for Arabelle[4] and Jarvie ("Eh quoi! Monsieur, votre police prétend donc s'exercer au bal?"), an aria for Rob-Roy preceded by a brief passage sung by another character ("Ecoutez, écoutez, au sommet des montagnes . . ."), an aria for Diana ("Quel noble caractère!"), a quartet made up of Diana, Arabelle, Jarvie, and Rob-Roy ("Quoi! c'est lui! quel effroi!"), and a finale involving the same four principals ("Eh bien! que faudra-t-il écrire?"). It may be that the entire opera consisted of no more than seven musical numbers, in view of Mrs. Flotow's later designation of it as a one-act opera.[5] I was able to find only the first four numbers.[6] In her polonaise Diana sings that she has given up the bustling world of dance and pleasure for an imaginary world free from regret:

Example 6-1

The music has no hint of Scottish flavor either here or in the other three pieces which I examined. At the beginning of the duet "Juste ciel!" Rob-Roy comes suddenly upon Diana and startles her. She manages so well to conceal her fear in his presence that he is impressed with what he thinks is her courage. She is strangely attracted to the man whom she looks on as a wild, untamed hero. The duet of Arabelle and Jarvie is comic in tone. It seems that Arabelle has been held three hours in captivity by Rob-Roy. When Jarvie anxiously questions her about the incident, she senses that he is suspicious of her moral conduct and accordingly punishes him by telling him nothing specific. In the fourth number Rob-Roy summons the clansmen to rally around him in support of Charles Stuart. . . .

This is all I know about Flotow's *Rob-Roy*. Like many another opéra comique based on Scott, it apparently diverged markedly from its source. So suggests the scanty information which I have been able to bring together.

De Koven's *Rob Roy*

Reginald de Koven's *Rob Roy*, with a libretto by Harry B. Smith, was first performed in 1894, in New York. Smith and De Koven had collaborated earlier in the highly successful *Robin Hood,* which contains the well-known song, "Oh, Promise Me." In her memoirs, *A Musician and His Wife,* Mrs. De Koven notes that some critics considered *Rob Roy* superior to *Robin*

Hood.[7] It held the stage four years after its première,[8] and it was revived in 1913.[9]

The story of this light opera has even less resemblance to Scott's novel than does *I Puritani* to *Old Mortality*. Here is a plot summary, as given in the Schirmer vocal score:[10]

Act I: A number of Highlanders led by Lochiel visit Perth to obtain a sum of English gold held by the Provost for expected English troops. The robbery is discovered and a fight ensues between the Highlanders and the townsfolk. Lochiel explains that the money is wanted for the cause of Prince Charles Stuart who has arrived from France and is preparing to lead the Scotch against the English. The purpose of the uprising is the restoration of the Stuarts to the English throne now occupied by George the Second. Flora MacDonald, an enthusiast for the Stuarts' cause, arrives with a hunting party and cajoles the Provost into consenting to the gathering of the clans in Perth. The Provost is anxious to be friendly with both the Scotch and the English. Hearing of the Scotch victory, he compels his daughter Janet to marry Sandy MacSherry, a town crier who claims relationship with the Stuarts. Immediately after the wedding, English soldiers enter the town and the commanding officer, Captain Sheridan, falls in love with Janet. The Provost compels Janet to declare herself the wife of the Captain, and, in order to get Sandy out of the way, accuses him of the robbery of the English gold. Janet, to save her father, declares herself the wife of Captain Sheridan. Immediately afterward Rob Roy and his Highlanders capture the town. The Provost, now eager to be rid of his English son-in-law, causes Captain Sheridan to be arrested. It now appears that when Janet went through the Scotch form of marriage with Sandy and the Captain, she was secretly married to Rob Roy. She proposes to escape her two nominal husbands by going with Rob's regiment as his Orderly. The Scotch now being victorious, the Provost and his henchmen appear as Highlanders and, in song, vow to be Scotchmen till the Scotchmen are beaten. The gathering of the clans is heralded by the music of bag-pipes; the ceremony of the "Elevation of the Standard" takes place and the act ends with a Jacobite war song.

Act II: The Highlanders led by Rob Roy are posted to guard a mountain pass. The Battle of Culloden is in progress and the Scotch expect a great victory. After a song by Janet, bag-pipes are heard in the distance. The Highlanders at first think this the signal of victory, but presently they recognize the song of defeat, the coronach. The Scotch led by the Prince and Lochiel return wounded and defeated. A chorus declaring allegiance follows, and the Prince, cheered by the fidelity of the Highlanders, vows to prey upon the "Brunswickers" as his predecessor Prince Rupert did upon the Roundheads. "The lay of the Cavaliers" is the song that follows. A reward is offered for the Prince who, disguised as a peasant, is sheltered by the

MacGregors in their mountain retreat. The Provost and his henchmen appear as wandering ballad-mongers, having fled before the
battle. They are still in Highland dress, not having heard of the rout
of the Scotch. Sandy MacSherry arrives and informs the Provost of
the English victory, and the Provost, changing Highland kilt for
English uniform, becomes an Englishman. He determines to obtain
the reward offered for the Prince, and the act is mainly devoted to
his efforts toward this end and his sudden change of nationality
according to the fortunes of war. At length the English capture the
Prince in the dress of a miller's boy and are about to lead him away
when Flora appears in the Prince's costume, declares him to be her
servant and gives herself up as the Prince. The act ends with an
ensemble as Flora is led away by the English soldiers, in spite of the
efforts made to rescue her by the Prince, Rob Roy and their followers.

Act III: The English troops are in bivouac near Stirling Castle and a
Drummer's Song begins the act. The Prince comes to rescue Flora
who is imprisoned in the Castle and is to be shot on the coming
morning. Lochiel has taken the turnkey's place and aids her escape.
Flora goes to the MacGregors' Cave, where the Prince is to join her
spying into the force and plans of the English. Flora's escape leaving
the cell empty, Lochiel replaces the prisoner with Sandy MacSherry
who has been made tipsy by the English soldiers. The Provost, now
an English Corporal, believing Flora still in the Castle, brings her a
market-woman's dress in disguise. Sandy escapes in the dress, the
Provost still supposing that he is assisting Flora. Hearing of the
Prince's danger, Rob and Janet come as Lowland rustics to aid him
with the English gold (stolen in Act Ist.), which is concealed beneath
the vegetables in their farm-wagon. The Provost sends his servants
to the MacGregors' Cave to capture the Prince; but the servants find
Flora, who is there awaiting the Prince, and bring her back to camp.
She is about to be shot when Prince Charles enters and gives himself
up. As he is about to be executed, the peasants throw off their long
Lowland coats and disclose themselves as Highlanders fully armed.
They hold the English at bay while the Prince and Flora escape to
France in a vessel which is seen sailing away as the curtain falls.

Aside from its title and the presence in it of a character named Rob Roy,
De Koven's opera has no connection with Scott's *Rob Roy*. It owes more,
but not much more, to *Waverley*. The time of the action is 1745, rather
than 1715, and the central event is the Battle of Culloden. In large part
the story is concerned with a love affair between the Prince and Flora
MacDonald. For the original of the Prince, Harry Smith might or might
not have had Scott's Young Pretender in mind. As for Flora, she perhaps
owes a slight bit to Scott's Flora MacIvor, but more to the Flora Macdonald
of history. Dugald MacWheeble, Mayor of Perth, apparently owes his
surname to Bailie Duncan MacWheeble, and Lochiel his name to Scott's

Lochiel (both characters are in *Waverley*). The ending of Act I, with the elevation of the standard and the Jacobite war song, is reminiscent in spirit of the finale to the first act of *La Donna del Lago*. The Provost's frequent changing of his loyalties is an aspect of the opera's comedy, but it also brings to mind some of Scott's typical heroes (Waverley himself, for example). The motif of the disguised prince may owe something to *Woodstock*, although in the novel the prince is Charles II. One wonders whether De Koven might have seen *Die Hochländer* (see Chapter 3) during the course of his studies in Germany and Austria and later discussed the opera with his librettist. In addition to the obvious similarities in character (the Prince) and non-dramatized incident (the Battle of Culloden), there is the dismal homecoming of the Highlanders after their defeat, which has a counterpart in Act II of Holstein's opera. Flora's disguising herself as the Prince and her willingness to die in his place, together with his last-minute arrival on the scene and disclosure of himself to prevent her death, bring to mind the similar incident in Holstein involving Reginald and his friend Arthur MacDonald (note also the name *Macdonald*). The visual aspect of the ending, with the Prince's vessel seen in the distance, is virtually the same as the ending of *Die Hochländer;* the difference is that since there is no love affair between old Magdalis and Prinz Charlie, she, unlike De Koven's Flora, does not accompany him on his voyage.

One observer, with reference to *Robin Hood,* noted that "in subject and spirit" it is a "light dramatic opera rather than a comic opera in the English sense of the term."[11] The same can be said of *Rob Roy;* and it is not surprising, in view of De Koven's rigorous training in Germany and Austria. In *Rob Roy* his harmonic structure is often as simple as Bishop's, with a preponderance of tonic, dominant, and sub-dominant chords. But on occasion he shows creditable mastery of nineteenth-century harmonic technique. He can handle chromatic progressions effectively, as well as chromatic modulations of the third-relationship type, and he is fond of seventh chords. One might recall that he ended his career with two grand operas.[12] There are many Scots tunes in *Rob Roy,* but no original tune that would compare in popularity with "Oh, Promise Me."

7

§ § §

THE HEART OF
MID-LOTHIAN

This chapter is concerned with an English musical drama by an English composer (Bishop); a French-text opera by an Italian composer (Carafa); an Italian-text opera based on the libretto of the preceding, by an Italian composer (Frederico Ricci); a French-text opera that borrows here and there from the earlier French libretto, by a Dutch composer (A. W. Berlijn); and a full-fledged English-text opera by a Scots composer (Hamish MacCunn). As usual, I am interested in the musical drama mainly as a springboard into a discussion of the operas. Although only names today in the history of opera, both Carafa and Ricci enjoyed a considerable degree of renown in their time, and their operas based on *The Heart of Mid-Lothian* were widely performed. Berlijn is totally forgotten today, and in his own day his reputation was just local; his Scott opera was never performed. MacCunn's *Jeanie Deans,* a product of the last decade of the century, is one of the last Walter Scott operas ever written; it is the only Scott opera by a Scots composer. Performances have taken place in England and Scotland, but not elsewhere.

The Heart of Mid-Lothian

The Heart of Mid-Lothian, with words by Daniel Terry[1] and music by Henry R. Bishop,[2] was first performed on 17 April 1819, at Covent Garden. The cast of characters includes David Deans, Dumbiedikes, Poinder, Ratcliff, Robertson, Saddletree, Sharpitlaw, Mrs. Balchristie, Effie and Jeanie Deans, Madge Wildfire—and two characters not in the novel: Lord Oakdale and Wilmot, his secretary. Mrs. Charles Kemble created the role of Madge Wildfire, and Miss Catherine (Kitty) Stephens sang Effie Deans.[3] Bishop borrowed a number of Scottish folk melodies for this three-act musical drama; several come in the overture.

Act I has seven scenes. The first depicts *"the High Street in Edinburgh.—A View of the Tolbooth; Door burnt down, &c.—Shouts, &c. behind the Scene, as the Curtain rises.—Several Rioters pass across, huzzaing and brandishing their Weapons, as returning from Porteus' [sic] Murder.—Saddletree looks from his*

Shop-door, but draws back as they pass.—Other Rioters rush on." (See chs. vi & vii of the novel.) Following the chorus of rioters ("Shout! comrades, shout!") Dumbiedikes, who is a composite of Scott's Dumbiedikes and Reuben Butler, *"rushes in, terrified, as if making his escape."* He asks Saddletree for protection from the mob, but the rioters soon capture him. As they are about to take him off to hang him, Robertson enters and persuades them to let him go. Robertson broods on the plight of Effie, who unlike Scott's Effie is not in prison at this point, and then leaves the stage. In the last moments of the scene Ratcliff, like his counterpart in Scott, decides to go over to the side of the law. Sharpitlaw and Poinder want him to direct them to Madge Wildfire, thinking it is she who led the Porteus mob. Scene ii depicts *"the Inside of a miserable Hut. Madge Wildfire is discovered busied with some Parts of a Child's Dress. She should have the affection of great gravity and importance,—occasionally, however, betraying in her motions the caprice of insanity. She looks at an Almanack."* During the course of her incoherent opening monologue she broods about her lost lover and child. When Sharpitlaw and Ratcliff come to examine her, she admits, at the coaxing of Ratcliff, that Robertson and she had exchanged clothes. But Sharpitlaw frightens her, and she lapses back into her usual state of mind, singing, "What did ye with your bridal ring?" (In the novel, ch. xvi, this examination takes place at the Tolbooth.) Madge agrees to take them to Muschat's Cairn, where she is supposed to carry food to Robertson at midnight. Sharpitlaw tells Ratcliff that Effie is to be arrested for alleged child-murder. Scene iii takes place at *"Saint Leonard's Craigs—A distant view of David Deans' cottage.—Robertson (in his own dress) is seen lurking among the Craigs. . . ."* He forces Dumbiedies (rather than Reuben Butler) to take a message from him to "the good man's daughter." Dumbiedikes thinks that Robertson means Jeanie, but he actually means Effie, who, as already noted, is not yet a prisoner. The fourth scene is *"a room in Deans' House.— Effie discovered; she appears overwhelmed with Grief."* At the end of Effie's opening song ("My friends and fame are from me gone") Jeanie enters. Effie refuses to tell Jeanie who her seducer was, she declares that her baby has disappeared, and she closes the scene with a second song ("I'm wearing awa', Jean"). In the brief next scene *("Before the Door of Deans' Cottage")* Dumbiedikes conveys to Jeanie the stranger's message (see chapter xii). She will go to meet the man, despite Dumbiedikes' misgivings, and she makes him promise not to tell her father. In the final scene we are back inside the cottage. Deans blames Saddletree for Effie's plight, in view of the dancing that went on at his house in Edinburgh, where she had been staying. (In the novel Effie's dancing on the sly may have helped contribute to her downfall, but this did not take place at the Saddletree house.) Sharpitlaw and several Officers of Justice then enter and arrest Effie for "the alleged murder of her infant child." Dumbiedikes offers money, but in vain. Jeanie is grief-stricken. David Deans refuses to look on his wayward daughter as she is being taken away. (All this is based on the flashback in chapter x of the novel.)

Act II begins in *"an Apartment in the Gaol."* Ratcliff upbraids Sharpitlaw for not letting Jeanie visit Effie in prison. When Sharpitlaw questions Effie about her lover, the dialogue is very close to that in the novel, chapter xvii. He feels so sorry for her that he changes his mind regarding Jeanie's wish to visit her. The scene closes with a song by Effie, the melody of which is very well known:[4]

Example 7-1

Scene ii opens on the *"Duke's walk near Holyrood-House—Moonlight—Madge sings without."* After singing a brief song to the moon,[5] Madge tells Ratcliff obscurely something about a baby that she will hide in "the vaults, under the ruined chapel, down yonder, at Holyrood." *Enter* Sharpitlaw. Madge determines that Robertson will hear her before he is seen by the officers. At the end of the scene she sings,

> I'm Madge of the Country, I'm Madge of the Town,
> And I'm Madge of the lad I am blythest to own!
> The wildfire that flashes so bright and so free
> Was never so brave or so bonnie as me!

The lyrics are Scott's, transposed from a much later part of the novel (ch. xxxi) and condensed from two four-line stanzas to one. Scene iii (*"Muschat's Cairn—in the background, the ruins of St. Anthony's Chapel"*) is based on chapters xv and xvii, but there are several changes. Dumbiedikes greets Jeanie when she arrives at the point where she is to meet the mysterious stranger. She urges him to withdraw, and indeed when Robertson arrives, he is forced to withdraw. Robertson is surprised when he discovers that the damsel is not Effie, as he had expected, but rather Jeanie. He tells her that Effie is his wife, but their marriage cannot be proven, since it was held in secret, with "no witnesses but desperate men." Jeanie tells him that Effie has been apprehended and that her judge is to be "one Lord Oakdale, sent from England, with high powers, in consequence of the late turmoils." Suddenly they hear Madge singing *without,*

> O, sleep ye sound, Sir James, she said,
>   When you should rise and ride?
> A hundred men, with bow and blade,
>   Are seeking where you hide.[6]

Thus forewarned of the impending danger, Robertson *"springs down a*

concealed path, and escapes,—Jeanie runs towards Sharpitlaw, who seizes her."
He angrily threatens to imprison her unless she gives him information
which he wants. When two officers drag in Dumbiedikes, whom they have
mistaken for Robertson, Jeanie slips away unobserved. Dumbiedikes' real
identity is soon apparent. At the end of the scene he goes off with Madge,
under the impression that she is Jeanie, Madge having donned a mantle
that Jeanie had let fall in the foregoing excitement. (None of this is in
Scott.) Scene iv takes place in *"a Garden-Walk near Holyrood Palace"* and
opens with a conversation between Lord Oakdale and Wilmot. (Oakdale is
a composite of the Duke of Argyle and the Rev. Mr. Staunton, George
"Robertson's" father; Wilmot owes something to Mr. Archibald.) When
Wilmot leaves the stage, Robertson enters, trying to escape from his
pursuers. Oakdale at first tries to bar his passage, but something about the
unhappy young man moves him, and he allows him to pass on. After he
has exited, Oakdale wonders whether he could have been his long-lost
prodigal son. At this point Ratcliff, Sharpitlaw, and a group of soldiers
cross the stage in hot pursuit of Robertson. Then Madge and Dumbiedikes enter. The Laird discovers that the damsel is not Jeanie, and he
becomes apprehensive when Madge talks of marriage and threatens to
strangle him if he does not follow her.[7] When he yells out "Murder!
murder! O Lord! O Lord! murder!" Ratcliff, Sharpitlaw, and the soldiers
re-enter. Sharpitlaw orders Madge and Dumbiedikes away to prison, and
the act's final scene, which has no parallel in Scott, ends in a musical
ensemble ("Away! away! to prison bear them!").

The first scene of Act III is a dramatization of Jeanie's visit to the house
of Dumbiedikes, which Scott relates in chapter xxvi. Her conversation
with Mrs. Balchristie follows the novel, but when she speaks with the
Laird, she asks him for money to help Effie at the trial. In the novel the
trial has already taken place and Effie has been condemned to death.
Scott's Jeanie asks Dumbiedikes for money to help her out on her journey
to London. Terry and Bishop omit the journey to London and indeed the
whole second half of the novel. When Dumbiedikes asks Jeanie to marry
her, she tells him that she loves another man—which is a surprise to us as
well as to the Laird, since there is no Reuben Butler in the musical drama.
The second scene, which takes place in the prison, is suggested by Jeanie's
visit to Effie's cell, chapter xx. At the beginning Ratcliff informs Effie that
Jeanie is coming to see her. He says furthermore that Lord Oakdale will
examine her himself before the trial. Just before he exits to fetch Jeanie,
he says *aside* that he will look into the story Madge told him earlier about
the baby she is hiding, but he will not say anything yet to the sisters, for
fear of a disappointment. While he is gone Effie sings still another song
("The linnet carroll'd not more light"[8]). After Ratcliff has ushered Jeanie
in, he explains to her that the law cannot harm Effie if Effie ever told her
about her pregnancy. But Effie has told no one, not even Jeanie, and
Jeanie cannot tell an untruth. The final scene takes place in *"a State*

Apartment in Holyrood Palace." It owes something to Scott's trial scene (chapter xxiii), but there is much additional material that has only remote connection with the novel. When the curtain opens, Lord Oakdale is talking with Wilmot about the severity of the law that will bring about the execution of Effie. When David Deans enters, Oakdale tells him that he will try to get the law to show mercy if Effie will only help the authorities get hold of Robertson. Deans is reluctant to encourage her to betray the man who has trusted her. Jeanie and Effie are brought in. Unable to tell a lie, Jeanie must say that Effie had not told her "the cause of her illness." "She has killed me," Effie moans; "she might have saved me, and would not!" Jeanie implores Oakdale to have mercy; she tells him that Effie could never have harmed the babe. At this point George Robertson bursts in and rushes to Effie. Oakdale recognizes him as his son and is extremely put out with him. George begs his father for forgiveness. He insists that he is innocent of the Porteus riot; that he mingled with the rioters to do good (like Reuben Butler of the novel), but failed. He then declares before all present that Effie is his wedded wife. Ratcliff upon entering is understandably surprised to see that George Robertson is Oakdale's son. He brings with him the good news that he has found the babe. He says furthermore that Effie could have saved herself long before, "if she had only mentioned Madge Wildfire's name, the mad nurse, who stole her child." She did not do so for fear of betraying her lover. George and Effie kneel before Oakdale, and he forgives them. So does David Deans. Robertson declares that Effie's "simple loveliness has triumphed, and restored [him] back to life, to virtue, to a father, and to friends." There is an attractive musical finale.

La Prison d'Édimbourg

This opera was first performed on 20 July 1833 in Paris, at the Opéra-Comique, the leading roles being sung by Henry (le Duc d'Argile), Révial (George), Mlle Massy (Jenny), Mme Margueron (Effie), Mme Ponchard (Sarah), Génot (Patrice), and Hébert (Tom). The libretto by Scribe and Eugène de Planard[9] was set to music by Prince Michele Enrico Francesco Vincenzo Aloisio Paolo Carafa di Colobrana,[10] who during the course of his long life wrote twenty Italian and seventeen French operas. Subsequent productions in French were done in Amsterdam, Liège, and Antwerp; in German in Vienna, Frankfurt, and Basel; in Russian in St. Petersburg; and in English (as *The Heart of Mid-Lothian*) in London, at the Princess' Theatre, on 18 April 1849. *La Prison* is rated highly by Clément and Larousse: "Indépendamment d'une facture facile et d'une instrumentation brillante et colorée, on y trouve de la sensibilité et des melodies charmantes. Les rôles d'Effie et de sa sœur Jenny Deans, celui de la folle Sara, sont traités avec un talent magistral." Commenting on Carafa's work in general, Fétis observed: "Il écrit vite et negligemment, suivant l'usage des compositeurs italiens; mais, s'il avait voulu prendre plus de soin de ses partitions, on peut juger, par les bonnes choses qui s'y trouvent, que sa réputation aurait plus d'éclat." As for *La Prison,* he felt that it deserved more success and recognition that it did achieve.

The overture is in sonata-allegro form. After an introductory *andante sostenuto* the *allegro* begins with the A-theme played by the first violins:

Example 7-2

The B-theme comes first in the clarinets:

Example 7-3

The development section is very brief. In the recapitulation there is a surprise modulation in the A-theme (abbreviated in comparison with how it is in the exposition) by way of an altered (flatted) deceptive cadence to the key of B-flat. The B-theme is introduced by the oboes and is in the key of D, in accordance with conventional sonata-allegro form. The whole overture is very much in the style of Rossini, with gradual extended crescendos and a climactic conclusion. There are no Scottish folk melodies, and none of the music is used elsewhere in the opera.

Act I takes place at the Jackins' farm (in the novel, the Deans's cottage) and derives mainly from Scott's flashback (chapter x) about Effie and the events leading up to her arrest. It begins with a chorus of harvesters, who are told by Jenny Jackins (Jeanie Deans) that her sister Effie has returned home. At first unobserved by the others, Effie comes out from one of the out-buildings. She is obviously distressed about something:

Example 7-4

Veil - lons dans l'ombre et le mys - tè - re, sur mon bien le plus pre - ci -
eux. Ca - chons a ma sœur à mon pè - re, les
pleurs qui cou - lent de mes yeux.

The modulation in the fifth measure to the related minor key very nicely underscores the text, and so does the use of a Neapolitan chord in the seventh measure. When Jenny sees Effie, she greets her and, noticing that something is wrong, asks what it might be:

Example 7-5

Mais dans tes yeux j'y vois des
Je n'ai rien, ma
lar - mes! Qu'as-tu donc? Qu'as-tu donc?
sœur.
Ta main fré - mit... quel-les a - lar - mes

Again the union of text and music is most effective, especially the ominous descending chromatic scale in the contrebasses and the mysterious-sounding third-relationship modulation to B flat in the next-to-the-last measure, at the word *frémit*. When Jenny asks her why she is weeping, she replies that she is concerned about the illness of their father. Jenny says that her very presence will help cure him. (We never see Mr. Jackins in the opera, but his presence is felt. Unlike David Deans, he suffers from ill health, and yet this may have been suggested by his original's propensity to faint when under emotional stress.) Jenny then sings an aria ("Dans notre chaumière") about the festivities and dancing that will be held in the village the next day, to which she will conduct Effie. Here and there in the number there is a suggestion of dance music in both the vocal line and the orchestral accompaniment. (Readers of Scott will no doubt find this departure from the novel amusing, since Jeanie Deans would not have dreamed of attending a dance.) Effie leaves the stage when she hears a sound which Jenny thinks is their father waking up. The harvesters re-enter, and we have a reprise of their chorus.

Alderman Patrice, who has no counterpart in Scott, arrives on the scene to inquire about Effie. He does so reluctantly, out of respect for her father, the old "sous-officier." At first Jenny thinks that he may be after Sarah, "la folle de la montagne" (Scott's Madge Wildfire). When asked about Effie, Jenny tells of her being brought up at the château d'Arondel, at the instigation of milady, who had taken a fancy to her (this is not in Scott). When, upon her homecoming, she was noticeably melancholy and sickly, their father decided to send her to Édimbourg to stay with their aunt Marguerite.[11] Jenny tells Patrice that all that was six months ago; Effie has returned that very morning. Patrice asks whether she came directly from Édimbourg, for if so it was dangerous for her to have travelled all night. (In the novel the Deans cottage at St. Leonard's is only a 45-minute walk from the heart of the city.) Jenny allays his suspicion by telling him that Effie said she was conveyed home in the carriage of Robin the Miller (not in Scott). Patrice decides to seek out Robin. As he exits he expresses the hope *aside* that this story is true, so that he will not have to arrest Effie. Sarah enters, singing evidently about the baby she has found, who reminds her of her former lover, but her meaning is not clear to either Jenny or the audience at this point. She tells Jenny of the death of her mother, who used to beat her, and of having buried her the previous night. But she is not alone, she insists, for the image of her lover George is still with her. She and her mother had once concealed him in their hut from officers of the law. She lost her reason when he departed. (The material is from Scott, but distorted. Since she is already dead we obviously never see Sarah's mother, who is suggested by Scott's Meg Murdockson. No mention is made here or elsewhere of George getting Sarah pregnant and of her having a baby which the mother kills.) When Jenny leaves the stage, Sarah expresses apprehension at having left the baby all night alone (presumably while she was burying her mother). She wonders who could have left it near her mother's body. (Evidently Sarah had entered the hut while Effie was away trying to get help for the dying woman; all this comes out later.) Suddenly she hears a child's familiar cries from the out-building, which she forthwith enters. At this point the sailor-smuggler Tom makes his first appearance on stage and sings an aria about his life on the high seas. The music has a military flavor:

Example 7-6

In the middle of the aria we see Sarah escaping to the mountains with something under her mantle—Effie's baby, we learn later.

George enters as evening begins to fall. Tom tells him that he left the ship because he was bored and because he wanted to find him. He has come to the Jackins farm to try to sell gin! He urges George to flee with him back to the ship, but George is unwilling to do so, because, as we soon learn, he must see Effie, whom Tom knows nothing about. When Tom departs, Effie comes on stage. In the ensuing duet she tells George she has just spent ten days in the mountains in the hut of the old woman who had once given him asylum. She tells him of the birth of his son. (Having been away for some time, George, unlike his counterpart in the novel, had no inkling of her plight.) Effie wants to bring their relationship out into the open. She is about to take him to see the baby when Tom re-enters. Tom explains hastily that he and George are being pursued by English soldiers, led by the Duke of Argyle (who we learn later is George's father). The Rossini-like finale to the act begins with a trio of these principals, at the end of which Tom and George leave. Patrice then re-enters with soldiers and arrests Effie in the name of the law. When Jenny tries to stop him, he explains that Effie's story about Robin the Miller transporting her home was a lie. He then tells of the rumor about her bringing forth a child and covering up the sin by one far worse. Effie insists that her infant is in the out-building. She runs to fetch proof but returns distraught, the infant having disappeared. Patrice must now perform his painful duty. At the very end of the act Jenny, perceiving that her awakened father is about to come out from the farmhouse, falls against the door to prevent his egress, so that he will be spared seeing his daughter being carried away to prison.

Act II takes place in a room of the royal palace, in Édimbourg. The Duke of Argyle (a composite of Scott's Argyle and the Rev. Mr. Staunton) sings an aria in which he expresses concern for Scotland, the country where he was born. He has returned to help. (The sentiment is suggested by Scott's description of Argyle in chapter xxxv.) After the aria Patrice informs Argyle that a revolt of the prisoners has been put down but that a good jailor, who will be hard to replace, was killed in the process. He also tells Argyle that a former follower of the young prince who was defeated at Culloden wants to see him and claims that his father is a prop of the English crown. The man turns out to be George, who throws himself on the mercy of the Duke, his father. He says he was unfortunate in having served the prince. His father forgives him and requests that he leave to put on a better garment, more suited to his rank. (No mention is made here of the other illegal activities in which he is engaged; the idea of serving the Young Pretender comes from *Waverley*.) Patrice then ushers in Jenny and Effie, who have been granted a private interview with the Duke. Argyle speaks of having once given their father a tract of land (suggested by the events of chapter xlii). Effie tells him that the person who got her pregnant does not know of her arrest. She tells him in detail the complicated circumstances of the birth of her child, the old mid-wife's (Sarah's mother's) death-bed agonies, her attempt to procure help, her return to the hut only to find the body gone, her departure from the hut, her concealment of the infant in an out-building belonging to her father's farm, and the infant's inexplicable disappearance. George then comes in, reveals to Effie and Jenny his true identity, and admits to Argyle that he is Effie's lover and the father of the child. Patrice re-enters, informs Argyle that the judges are waiting, and leads the two sisters off. Argyle advises George not to discover himself to the tribunal, for if he should do so, he might be seized and condemned to death.

Patrice re-enters with news that a mad woman has led his men to the capture of the chief of the smugglers. George realizes that the captive must be his friend Tom. Patrice wants to talk with the Duke again about replacing the jailor, but the Duke must leave immediately to attend the trial. George suggests to Patrice that the jailor might be replaced with the smuggler, but Patrice is averse to this idea. (The opera plot is based here on the career of Scott's Ratcliffe, who chose not to escape from the Tolbooth during the Porteous riot and was accordingly offered a post of assistant jailor.) When Tom is brought in, George manages to make a sign to his friend not to recognize him. He asks Patrice to let him speak with the prisoner in private, and during the ensuing duet he reveals to Tom his true identity and asks him if he would be interested in the post of jailor. He then tells Patrice that he has found the prisoner worthy of the post.

This Evening, **WEDNESDAY**, April 18th, **1849**,

Will be performed (for the **First Time**) a NEW OPERA, in Three Acts, freely adapted from SCRIBE and PLANARD's celebrated Opera, "**Le Prison d' Edimbourg**" founded on SIR WALTER SCOTT's renowned Work, The

HEART OF MID-LOTHIAN

The OVERTURE and MUSIC, by CARAFA.

Director of the Music and Conductor, Mr LODER

Leader, - Mr. THOMAS.   Chorus Master, - Mr. SMYTHSON.

John, Duke of Argyll,   **HERR MENGIS,**
George, - - - **Mr CHARLES BRAHAM,**
Sharpitlaw. *(Sheriff of Edinburgh)* Mr H. HORNCASTLE,
Ratcliff, *(Captain of Smugglers)* **Mr WEISS**
Tyburn Tam, Mr HONEY   **Black Frank,** Mr WYNN
Captain of the Guard, Mr ARTHUR   Sergeant, Mr BROWN   Turnkey, Mr T. HILL
Officers of the Sheriff,—Messrs Ellar, Lebarr, Driver and Rivers.
Nobles, Burgesses, Citizens, &c—Messrs Foster, Payne, Murray, Skelton, House, May, Roberts, Gould, Shaw, Ryalls, Mainette, Morris, Grundy, Thompson, &c.
Prisoners—Messrs Taverner, Fielding, Graham, Sparks, Haywaid, Green, Price, Harcourt, Newton, Bardell, Hunt, Freeman, Gadsby, Price, &c.

Jeanie Deans, - - - - **Miss POOLE,**
Effie Deans, - - **Miss LANZA,**
AND
Madge Wildfire, by Madlle. NAU.

Burgesses Wives, Reapers, &c—Misses Coxe, Weymouth, Bennett, Charlton, Beaumont, Ebell, Walker, A. Walker, Barratt, Edmunds, M'Lewe, Ives, Meeves, Clifford, Lacey, E. Lacey Healey, Crowther, Lee, Mitchenson, Brown, &c.

The following Scenes have been painted by Mr CUTHBERT and Mr NICHOLLS.

THE FARM of DAVID DEANS.

RECEPTION CHAMBER OF THE DUKE OF ARGYLL

AND AVENUE LEADING TO THE COURT OF JUSTICE.

THE TOLBOOTH—CANONGATE,

WITH A PART OF THE

CITY of EDINBURGH in FLAMES

The Music is Published by CHARLES JEFFERY's, 21, Soho Square.
Books of the Opera may be had in the Theatre.   Price One Shilling.

PLAYBILL for the first English production of Carafa's *La Prison d'Édimbourg,* Princess' Theatre, April 18, 1849. From the Enthoven Collection, Victoria and Albert Theatre Museum.

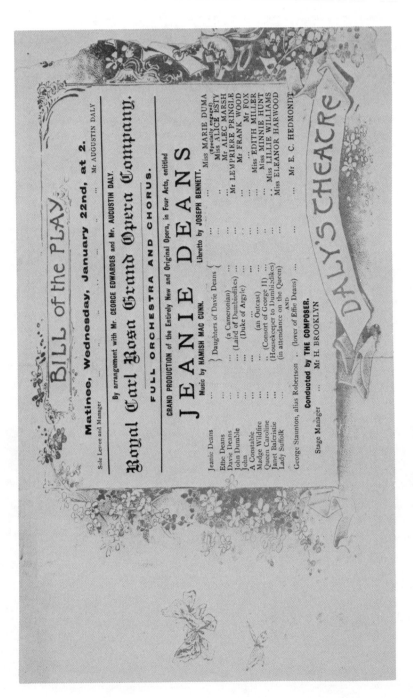

PLAYBILL for *Jeanie Deans*. From the Enthoven Collection, Victoria and Albert Theatre Museum.

Patrice retorts that the testimony of the mad woman will undeceive him. Sarah is brought in. She tells of concealing smuggled merchandise for Tom and reveals where it can be found. Thus it looks as if Tom is guilty, as Patrice thought. Sarah's mind wanders as she speaks. She mentions a man whom she loved, but her mother warned her that he loved another girl (namely Effie). She refuses to tell Patrice the man's name.

The elaborate finale, which vies with the best work of Donizetti and Rossini, begins with a trio (Sarah, Tom, Patrice) during the course of which we hear offstage trumpets that pertain to the trial. Trembling with anxiety Jenny comes in with news that the judges are deliberating Effie's fate. Sarah recognizes her as Effie's sister, and Patrice tries to explain to her that Effie is being tried for the murder of her infant son. When Sarah appears not to comprehend, Tom calls her a madwoman. "Ah! je suis folle! je suis folle!" she replies. "Fort bien! c'est ce que l'on verra." Argyle now enters and informs everyone that Effie has been sentenced to death. Sarah tells Jenny that she is happy with the outcome of the trial, because George loved her first and will love her again after Effie's execution. Jenny is horrified, and Patrice exclaims, "Tais-toi, folle, tais-toi, silence!" "Ah! je suis folle!" she says again; "eh bien! c'est ce que l'on verra." There is general grief as the finale concludes, everyone (except Sarah) singing, "O sort fatal! arrêt terrible!"—Interestingly, the trial scene is conducted offstage, as in *Aida,* Act IV, scene i. This is not the case in the novel: Scott brings his readers into the court room. Also, no mention is made of the legal matter that plays such a prominent part in the novel, namely, that an expectant mother must communicate to at least one person her pregnancy or run the risk of being accused of child-murder, if the child should die or disappear and its birth be afterwards ascertained. Thus Carafa's Jenny is not put in the moral predicament of having to decide whether to tell a lie (that she knew of the pregnancy) and thereby remove Effie's case from under the statute, or tell the truth (that she did not know) and thereby bring about an inevitable death-sentence for her.

The third act takes place in a room of the prison and begins with a chorus of prisoners, followed by a drinking song in which two prisoners, Altrec and Gilby (Jibby in the orchestral score), are prominent. They are all surprised to find that Tom is their jailor. When they ask him to help them escape, he refuses, in the aria "Anciens camarades." (I have already noted that Tom owes much to Scott's Ratcliffe. The idea of a criminal being hired by the law as jailor evidently caught the special attention of the librettists. Since so much of the novel is omitted, the Tom/Ratcliffe story-line is emphasized much beyond what it is in Scott.) When the prisoners leave, Effie enters. Tom cannot bring himself around to telling Effie that she has only one more hour to live. (His sympathy is suggested by Ratcliffe's, in chapter xxv, but Effie's execution has been stepped up from six weeks to one hour, in the interest of good theater.) The people who have condemned Effie are eager to see her hanged. (The idea is Scott's, but it is transferred from the scene of the Porteous mob.) Tom mentions that Sarah has built a "nest" under the grand clock in the belfry that adjoins the prison, but to reach it would be next to impossible. Effie does not want to try to escape anyway; she is optimistic that good news will come. When Tom leaves, she muses briefly on her past life. Jenny then enters, tells her gently that her fate cannot be avoided, the child not having been found, and brings her a blessing from their father. Effie bravely resigns herself to the inevitable. (There is no brainstorm on Jenny's part to go to London to see the Queen. Like Terry, Scribe and De Planard omit the entire second half of the novel.) Tom, dragging Sarah along with him, rejoins the sisters. It seems that during the last twenty-four hours Sarah has for some reason stolen straw, milk, a basket, and a silken cloth. She tells Tom that he cannot detain her, because she stole everything not for herself but for someone else, in preparation for a ceremony. Your marriage? Tom asks. No, she replies; her marriage will come later, when George returns; this is to be another ceremony (baptism, we soon learn). Jenny and Effie retreat to Effie's cell, and Tom leaves, so that he will not be on hand to witness Effie being taken to her execution. Left alone on stage, Sarah sings a *rondeau*.

George surprises her, but she does not recognize him as the one-time smuggler whom she loved. She wants to take him to the baptism of her child. She becomes afraid when he becomes overly eager, and she stops for a moment the prattle about baptism. As he starts to enter Effie's cell, however, Sarah says that the child is not there. In desperation George decides to grasp at this last straw of hope. He tells her who he is, but she does not believe him. During the course of their duet, which begins the finale, we the audience see officers entering Effie's cell. Finally Sarah recognizes George and falls into his arms. At that moment the officers, unnoticed by George and Sarah, lead Effie and Jenny out from the cell. Effie sees Sarah in George's arms and makes a melodramatic gesture of despair. As George tries to induce Sarah to talk again about the infant, we hear cries of people *without* who are awaiting the execution. Sarah is afraid they are coming to take her infant away. Suddenly Tom rushes in and says that the prisoners have set fire to the building. George thinks of Effie, but Tom informs him that she is already at the place of execution. When he tells Sarah that her belfry is in flames, she becomes agitated and rushes out. Altrec, Gilby, and the other prisoners enter, singing a chorus in celebration of their escape. (Both the fire and the escape of the prisoners obviously derive from the Porteous incident of the novel, chapters vi-vii.) At this point, with no pause in the music, there is a rapid change of scenery to the outside of the burning building-complex. Sarah, up in her belfry, lets the whole crowd know that the infant she is holding in her arms is George and Effie's son. She cuts a rope attached to the clock, ties it to the infant's cradle, and lets the cradle with its precious burden descend, carefully keeping it from the flames. The music reinforces the action in a conventional way:

Example 7-7

The infant is saved and all present are overjoyed. The Duke of Argyle holds the hand of his son and extends his other arm to Effie. Jenny, with her eyes directed toward heaven in thanksgiving, forms a part of the tableau. Like the old Saxon princess Ulrica (see Chapter 9), Sarah resigns herself to death in the flames—and no one seems much concerned.

Like the Terry-Bishop musical drama, *La Prison d'Édimbourg* is based on just the first half of the novel. It departs most remarkably from Scott in the exclusion of Davie Deans, Dumbiedikes, and Reuben Butler from the dramatis personae and in the reduction of the importance of Jeanie. Her role is even further de-emphasized in Ricci's opera, to which we must now turn.

La Prigione d'Edimburgo

La Prigione d'Edimburgo was one of the most successful of Federico Ricci's nineteen operas.[12] The libretto was adapted from Scribe and De Planard by Gaetano Rossi.[13] First performed on 13 March 1838 in Trieste, when the composer was twenty-nine, the opera soon reached virtually all the theaters in Italy, and during the course of the next few years productions in Italian were staged in Cagliari (1840), Vienna (1840), Barcelona (1840), Nice (1840), Malta (1841), Odessa (1841), Copenhagen (1841), Lisbon (1841), Mexico City (1842), Prague (1843), Warsaw (1844), and Buenos Aires (1853). It was produced in German in Hamburg (27 April 1842) and Budapest (15 October 1842). A Spanish version with the title *Susana* was given in Madrid on 23 May 1867.[14] Grove notes that "the *barcarola* in this opera, 'Sulla poppa del mio brick,' was for long one of the most popular melodies of Italy." It is sung by Tom. The other principals are the Duke of Argyle, his son Giorgio, Fanny (Scribe's Jenny), Ida (Effie), Giovanna (Sarah), and Patrizio. Rossi omits the bit roles of Altrec and Gilby, which are not in Scott anyway. Since the story of the opera follows the Scribe-De Planard text in many particulars as well as in main outline, a detailed summary will not be necessary here. Instead, I shall concentrate on the interesting differences.

The opening chorus of harvesters, which sounds very much like Donizetti, corresponds to the opening chorus in *La Prison d'Édimbourg*.

However, when Ida enters they too notice her sadness and remark about it, whereas in Scribe they have already exited and we have only Jenny and Effie on stage. Also, the harvesters' invitation to Ida to dance is suggested by Jenny's aria, "Dans notre chaumière." The mention of the father's blessing by Fanny and the harvesters is not in Scribe at this point: it comes later, in Act III, when Jenny visits Effie in prison and imparts to her their father's blessing shortly before she is to be executed. This whole section of *La Prigione* is structured basically as a conventional recitative, cavatina, and cabaletta for Ida, with the remarks of Fanny and the harvesters coming between the cavatina ("Dei felici miei prim' anni") and the early-Verdi-like cabaletta ("Ah! rinasce nel mio petto"). In a brief passage of recitative between Fanny and Ida, we are filled in on past events: Ida was sent to Edimburgo by their father six months hence because she was depressed, but to Fanny she seems more depressed now than then. Some of what is said is based on the spoken dialogue between Scribe's Jenny and Patrice, but Rossi delays the entrance of his Patrizio until later in the act. Giovanna's first appearance follows the corresponding passage in *La Prison* with the exception that the chorus is present. Like Sarah, Giovanna is a coloratura soprano. Her cavatina, "Oh, come è vago, amabile," parallels Scribe and Carafa's "Ah! comme il lui ressemble." Between the cavatina and the cabaletta she refers obscurely to someone's death, the chorus noticing her agitation and the music underscoring the words and action in effective, if conventional, fashion. Her counterpart Sarah comes right out and says that her mother has died and that she has buried her the night before, but Rossi delays this information until later. In the cabaletta, "Chi di voi conosce amore," she sings of the joy that will be hers when her lover returns. The passages involving Tom are quite similar to those in Scribe. In place of the military-sounding "Assis dans ma barque" we have the famous barcarola:

Example 7-8

The duet for Ida and Giorgio and the trio of Ida, Giorgio, and Tom offer no noteworthy departures from Scribe, but in the exciting finale one notices, in addition to the initial appearance of Patrizio, a vengeful attitude on the part of the soldiers toward Ida. This may have been suggested by the vengeful attitude that the people in the third act of *La Prison* take toward Effie while they are eagerly awaiting her execution. As often in *La Prigione,* Ricci's music could be mistaken for the work of

Donizetti or the early Verdi.

Act II opens with an aria for the Duke of Argyle (omitted in the Mayand vocal score) that parallels the aria in Scribe and Carafa. In the ensuing recitative, however, Patrizio does not say anything about the necessity of replacing a jailor killed in a revolt of the prisoners. Thus the prisoners' revolt that does come, at the end of the opera, is not quite so well prepared for as in *La Prison*. When Giorgio enters, the conversation among the three men is in recitative, whereas Carafa has a formal trio. Then comes a significant change. Skipping to the end of Scribe's act for the idea, Rossi has Patrizio tell in a brief recitative, Giorgio and the Duke having exited, how Giovanna has led the soldiers to the capture of Tom and his gang of smugglers. She then enters, singing about the child, but so incoherently that Patrizio does not understand. When he sees Ida coming he leaves, because he does not have the heart to see her or speak with her (here Rossi borrows Tom's words in reference to Effie in Act III, just before she is to be executed). Giovanna and Ida are now left on stage together; and in place of Effie pleading her case before the Duke, telling him the details of her unfortunate situation, encountering George and learning his true identity, and George admitting to his father that he is Effie's lover—in place of all this Rossi and Ricci have a formal "scena e duetto" for the madwoman and the alleged child-murderess (which, I might add, has no counterpart in the novel). Not realizing with whom she is speaking, Giovanna says that she once had a boyfriend named Giorgio. Ida is of course interested. Giovanna further declares that her mother used to beat her and call her a fool, since it was obvious that Giorgio loved another, namely Ida (in *La Prison* Sarah tells this in the presence of Tom, George, and Patrice). She says she would like to find her rival and take revenge on her (again the idea is borrowed from Scribe but put in different context). Ida replies that Giovanna would not be so cruel; that she would feel pity for Ida. When Giovanna says she has heard that Ida has done away with her child, Ida insists that this is not true, and indeed Giovanna finds such a horrible deed difficult to believe. Then comes a *largo* ("Un figlio, il cui sorriso") which the two sing for the most part at intervals of thirds and sixths and which brings to mind some of the duets of Bellini, who was one of Ricci's teachers. Immediately afterwards Giovanna says something only half coherent about a pretty son and Giorgio, but it is enough to cause Ida to fear that Giorgio has been unfaithful to her (in Scribe she has no suspicions until near the end of Act III). Suddenly Patrizio enters and exclaims, "Ida, ai guidici!" Now Giovanna realizes with whom she has been speaking. She tells Ida that Giorgio will be so appalled by her having murdered the child that he will abandon her. "Mio Giorgio alfin sarà!" she exclaims, and then, pointing to Ida: "La pazza è quella là." At the same time Ida laments that everything has gone amiss, yet she thinks that Giorgio will not believe she has done so cruel a deed. Nor can she believe that Giorgio has been unfaithful to her. After expressing the desire to be alone, she points toward heaven and sings, "Là troverò pietà."

As the act progresses, Patrizio proposes to Giorgio, whom the Duke has entrusted with the task of choosing a new jailor, that he choose Tom. In Scribe's libretto we have just the opposite: Patrice is skeptical of George's suggestion that Tom be given the post. Tom is surprised to learn that his fellow smuggler Giorgio is the Duke's son, and the two friends sing a duet that has a counterpart in *La Prison*, after which, however, Patrizio informs Tom that there will be no further legal proceedings against him since he has been named jailor by Lord Giorgio. Giovanna then enters and tells Tom that she wants to show Giorgio his son. She is certain that Giorgio must be with Tom, and she will await him. Tom is amused to learn that Giorgio has another son. (In Scribe's libretto Sarah says nothing specific at this point about the child.) Giovanna continues to sing about the child in her touching lullaby, "Dormi, dormi, bel bambino,"[15] after which Tom expresses deep concern about the trial of Ida now in progress. (Scribe and Carafa begin their finale here with a trio involving Tom, Sarah, and Patrice.) The chorus then sings about the trial, the women feeling pity for Ida but not so the men. (This is quite different from the corresponding passage in *La Prison*, where Jenny comes in to announce that the court is in the process of reaching a decision about Effie.) Tom explains to the chorus that Giovanna is a madwoman, and she replies, "Ah! Io pazza!—si vedrà" (this idea does follow Scribe). The elaborate finale, which interestingly does not include Fanny, now begins. The Duke informs everyone that Ida has been condemned to death. When she is brought in and sees Giorgio present in fine clothes, she is surprised—Rossi, as noted above, having omitted the scene in Scribe's libretto in which Effie and George see each other in the presence of the Duke. Thus the basic situation in the finale here is made somewhat more theatrical. Remembering her conversation with Giovanna earlier, Ida is once more afraid that Giorgio has betrayed her. He protests his innocence in the *largo* "In quest'ora tremenda, suprema," and she believes him. As the guards are about to drag Ida away, Giovanna suddenly feels great pity for her. She embraces her and absolutely refuses to leave her. The Duke tries to have the two separated, but in vain. Finally Ida says, "Vanne infelice, lasciami." (This again is quite a departure from *La Prison*, where in fact we have almost the opposite: Sarah seems pleased that Effie will die, because now George will love *her*. She expresses this sentiment to Jenny, which causes Jenny to say, "Laisse-moi, malheureux.") The finale concludes in a huge ensemble ("Oh Dio possente") composed of Ida, Giovanna, Giorgio, Patrizio, Argyle, Tom, and the chorus—but not Fanny.

The chorus of prisoners at the beginning of Act III parallels *La Prison*, but without Altrec and Gilby, and their new jailor Tom soon enters and sings with them. Rossi omits the spoken dialogue between Tom and Effie, her brief soliloquy, and her scene with Jenny. The opera continues with a recitative in which Tom accuses Giovanna of stealing several items. This is based on a scene of spoken dialogue in Scribe, which is followed by a *rondeau* for Sarah that Rossi omits. Then comes the long duet between Giovanna and Giorgio, which has its counterpart in *La Prison.* But during the course of it Ida is not removed from her cell and does not see Giovanna in Giorgio's arms; Rossi has already used the jealosy motif. The finale begins with Tom bursting in with the news that the prisoners have set fire to the building. There is no chorus of prisoners, but the rest of the action is the same as in *La Prison,* albeit briefer and without Fanny in the final tableau. This finale is not interesting from a musical standpoint: it is hastily thrown-together hackwork.

In conclusion, the plot of *La Prigione* is on the whole simpler than that of *La Prison;* much detail and several whole scenes have been omitted. The boldest innovation is the added scene with Ida (Scott's Effie) and Giovanna (Madge Wildfire), which might be compared to Dryden's departure from Shakespeare and Plutarch in *All for Love* in bringing together Octavia and Cleopatra. The most remarkable alteration is with regard to the role of Fanny (Scott's Jeanie Deans). She is the least important of the seven principals, and thus the opera's center of interest is obviously not that of the novel.

Le Lutin de Culloden

This virtually unknown two-act opera, with words by Charles Lavry and music by A. W. Berlijn, exits only in manuscript.[16] It was never performed. Berlijn submitted his partially completed score to the Royal Theater of The Hague for consideration, but it was turned down. In a politely worded letter dated 12 January 1848, the director of the Royal Theater explained to the composer that in view of other operas written in the same spirit and already performed, it would not be desirable to have still another "fantastique opéra."[17] Moreover, he continued, no singers were at present available who could sing the music as it then appeared—meaning that it was too difficult.[18] No doubt disappointed at this rejection of his efforts, Berlijn put the work aside and never did anything more with it.[19]

The libretto is an amalgamation of characters and motifs from Charles Nodier's *nouvelle,* "Trilby, ou le Lutin d'Argail," and from several different Scott novels or Scott-derivative librettos. Since it perhaps owes most to *La Prison d'Édimbourg,* I have chosen to discuss it here, even though its plot is obviously quite different from that of *The Heart of Mid-Lothian.* The six principals are the Chevalier, French officer in the service of the Young Pretender; Bolbury, sergeant; Tom Crist, Scottish farmer; Patrice, fiancé of Jeannie; Jeannie, daughter of Tom Crist; and Sara, her cousin. Lavry has borrowed the names *Tom, Patrice,* and *Sara* from Scribe, and *Jeannie* from both Scribe and Nodier, but the four characters of *Le Lutin de Culloden* stand in a relationship to one another that is quite different from what we have in *La Prison d'Édimbourg*. The action occurs in Scotland at the village of Culloden—the first act on 17 April 1746, the second two years afterwards.

When the curtain rises on the farm of Tom Crist, the villagers sing in chorus of the repose that they are enjoying despite the civil war. Sara asks Jeannie why she is so melancholy at a time when she is about to be married. The villagers believe that her frame of mind can be explained by the defeat which the army of the Pretender has suffered. (At the beginning of *La Prison* Jenny asks Effie what is amiss, and she replies that she is worried about their father's health. Lavry has amalgamated material from *The Heart of Mid-Lothian* with the historical background of *Waverley*.) Several young maidens then ask Sara to recount to them "la légende/De Trilby le gentil Lutin"[20]—Jeannie observing *aside* and mysteriously, "En mon cœur, à ce nom, Dieu! quel trouble soudain." Sara agrees to do so and launches forthwith into a *ballade;*

> Lorsque la blanche Lune
> Fait pleuvoir ses lueurs
> Sur les monts, sur la dune,
> Sur les genets en fleurs;
> Si vous voyez, dans l'âtre,
> Une vapeur folâtre
> Danser légèrement,
> Rassurez-vous, fillettes,
> Et souriez, discrètes
> A ce timide amant:
>   Car c'est lui,
>   C'est Trilby,
>   Le Lutin joli:
>   Car c'est lui,
>   C'est Trilby,
>   Le Lutin cheri.
> Et dans les nuits obscures,
> Si vous croyez sentir
> L'or de vos chevelures
> S'agiter et frémir;
> Si les parfums de l'ambre
> Embaument votre chambre,
> Laissez vous appaiser;
> Sans craindre ses caresses
> Livrez vox blondes tresses
> A son chaste baiser:
>   Car c'est lui, etc.

[Sara's refrain is repeated both times by the chorus.]

The sentiment here is suggested by Nodier's story, and as the opera progresses the "lutin" brings more and more to mind Scribe's "dame blanche" (see Chapter 4). After the villagers have left, Sara asks Jeannie again the cause of her sadness, and she replies that the political circumstances are such that a marriage, which ought to be a time of joy, would be out of place. Sara wonders how politics can possibly affect the lives of a young married couple, and Jeannie wonders in turn how Sara can say such things when politics involve their unfortunate prince, Charles Édouard. Sara then voices the thought that Jeannie perhaps has another sweetheart. Jeannie is a bit rattled at this, but regaining her composure she assures her cousin that she will marry Patrice, the man whom her father has destined for her.

After the two women have departed for the crags of Clare-loch, the Chevalier and Bolbury enter, both of them worn out in fleeing from their pursuers. All their months of sacrifice have been lost in a mere two hours. At first they beat Hawley and Sir John Cope, but then they were thoroughly routed by the greenhorn Cumberland. In his aria "Sur le champ de bataille" the Chevalier sings that even though Fortune this time has turned against them, they will some day be triumphant. But his optimism does not last long. He goes on to say that the Pretender's entire army has been beaten. "Et lui-meme, somme nous bien certains que ses jours soient en sûreté? Sa tête n'est elle pas mise à prix?" "Ah! mille mousquetades!" replies Bolbury, using a favorite oath of Scribe's Tom. "S'il y avait un écossais assez lâche..." The Chevalier wants Bolbury to go join the Pretender. At first Bolbury is hesitant about leaving his friend, but after some discussion he does go, and the exhausted Chevalier remains. After a brief spoken soliloquy he notices someone approaching. Not knowing whether the person is friend or foe, he hides in an outbuilding. It is Jeannie. She is worried about the marriage which her father is arranging for her, and in an elaborate aria no doubt inspired by Georges Brown's "Viens, gentille dame" (see Chapter 4) she summons her secret lover, the lutin. But the lutin does not appear, and Jeannie sits down in dejection. The Chevalier then re-enters. When Jeannie sees him, she thinks he is the lutin (just as Georges thinks that Anna is the White Lady). She believes that his military uniform is necessary, since he could hardly appear before her in his infernal garb. They sing a long duet with florid coloratura cadenzas. Jeannie trembles; he tells her to calm herself; she says she is not surprised to see him; he expresses surprise at this; and of course he does not understnd what is what.

> JEANNIE: A mes désirs puisque tu viens te rendre,
>   Ecoute-moi, gentil Lutin.
> CHEVALIER, *riant à part:*   Un lutin? un lutin?
>   Moi!... le tour est badin!

Jeannie impresses upon her otherworldly lover the emergency of her situation, in view of her forthcoming marriage to Patrice. The Chevalier, deciding to play along with her in this strange business which he does not understand, promises his aid. The duet continues. Both are impressed with the charms of each other. Presently, when they see two people approaching and Jeannie recognizes her father and Patrice, the Chevalier makes a quick exit—so quick that Jeannie thinks he has vanished. She wonders where he has gone, but she soon convinces herself that he has gone away just temporarily rather than frighten Tom Crist and Patrice. Father, daughter, and suitor then sing an attractive trio. Tom Crist has just returned home from a long voyage, and he is glad to be back. He drinks to the happiness in marriage of Jeannie and Patrice. He urges his future son-in-law to embrace Jeannie, but timid Patrice does not dare. Even Jeannie, thinking Trilby will surely appear, asks him why he shies away from her. But Trilby does not appear. Tom Crist is amused at the shyness of Patrice, who finally does manage to muster up enough courage to embrace her. Still Trilby does not appear. The trio concludes with Tom expressing his amusement, Patrice singing of his "ivresse," and Jeannie of her grief. After a bit of spoken dialogue about the coming festivities, Tom and Jeannie leave, Jeannie remarking *aside:* "Oh! qui me sauvera si Trilby lui-meme m'abandonne?" (reminiscent of Georges Brown's feelings when the White Lady is slow in reappearing with the necessary money to save him from his creditors).

The finale begins with Patrice, alone on stage, singing of his love for Jeannie, after which he falls asleep. The Chevalier re-enters, and seeing food on the table he sits in front of the sleeping Patrice and begins to eat greedily. In a few moments Patrice awakens, cries out in fright, and flees to the opposite side of the stage. The two sing a "duo bouffe"; Patrice is terrified, and the Chevalier is amused. During the course of the number the Chevalier hears in the distance the sound of a horn: "Je ne me trompe pas.... c'est bien le chant sauvage/Des fiers enfants de Loch-Aber./ C'est Édouard.... il m'appelle." In the meantime Patrice has noticed the large bell that is normally used to summon the farmhands to work. He begins to ring it vehemently. The Chevalier goes quickly into the out-building to pick up his belongings before rejoining Édouard, and Patrice, seeing him do so, believes that the bell has frightened him. When Patrice turns his back to the out-building to ring the bell again, the Chevalier leaves quickly through a window. The sound of the bell soon brings in Tom, Jeannie, Sara, and the villagers. They all want to know what the noise is all about. Patrice replies that a strange man suddenly appeared before him. He immediately sensed that he was a lutin and then, in addition, that he had the demeanor of an embarrassed lover. Tom Crist and the villagers are horrified to think that Jeannie has a lover. As the villagers move away from her Sara alone stands by her. Tom is relentless:

> Fille coupable;
> Que le remords enfin l'accable!
> Crains ma vengeance et ma juste fureur!
> Mais cet amant, ce lâche suborneur,

Où donc est-il?

The idea of Jeannie having a lover and Tom Crist's attitude toward her bring to mind Effie's arrest in *The Heart of Mid-Lothian*, chapter x, and David Deans's despair and anger at what his daughter has done. Here the librettist was probably influenced by the novel rather than *La Prison*, in view of the fact that Scribe never brings Jenny and Effie's father on stage. Pointing to the out-building, Patrice tells everyone that that is where Jeannie's lover is hiding. When the villagers cry out for vengeance, Patrice and several farmers storm the building. But they soon return, having found no one there. (The incident recalls to mind Scribe's Effie rushing into the out-building to fetch her child, but returning empty-handed, the child having disappeared.) The finale ends in an elaborate ensemble composed of Tom, Patrice, Jeannie, Sara, and the villagers. The men want to track down Jeannie's lover and punish him. Just before the curtain falls, we the audience catch a glimpse of the Chevalier traversing the mountain in the distance.

Two years have passed when the second act begins. The villagers sing a chorus in celebration of the peace, after which Patrice sings a *ronde*. Although he maintains that the life of a soldier has its pleasures, he has no regrets when peace finally comes. Sara then enters, bemoaning the state of Jeannie, who has become mentally deranged. She asks the villagers to leave so that she can be alone for a moment with her melancholy thoughts. After a while Tom Crist enters. He is repentant of his unkind words to Jeannie in the preceding act. Directing his thoughts to her in an aria,[21] he sings:

Ô ma fille si chère,
Pardonne à ton vieux père
Un instant de colère,
Qui te mène au tombeau!

He then tells Sara how unfortunate everything has turned out, and just when he is about to reassume the titles of his ancestors. He explains that through an unlucky incident he had been accused of treason by King George. He then left the court, determined not to appear there again, and settled incognito at Culloden. (Scott's David Deans has no such past history.) He wanted Jeannie to marry Patrice because he is the son of one of their neighbors. But heaven prevented that, and indeed if heaven had done so, but not in this cruel manner, he would have offered songs of thanksgiving, for he has received this very day letters from London indicating that the king, now aware of his error in believing Tom a traitor, wants to make amends. But what is the point now of appearing at court with Jeannie the way she is; she would be completely out of place. Looking up and seeing her approaching, he says to Sara: "Elle! ah! eloignons-nous. Sa présence me ferait trop souffrir" (reminiscent of jailor Tom's feelings toward Effie in *La Prison*, Act III). Jeannie enters, and we have a typical "mad scene."[22] She is pale, her hair is in disarray, and as she sings she recalls the events of two years hence, but in somewhat confused fashion. (This number was very likely inspired by the famous mad scene in *Lucia di Lammermoor;*[23] it may also owe something to Elvira's mad scene in *I Puritani,* and as the story evolves Jeannie, like Elvira, regains her sanity at the return of her lover.) When Sara re-enters, Jeannie asks her if she has perchance seen the lutin. "Encore cette pensée!" says Sara *aside.* Jeannie is upset that everyone thinks she is a madwoman, and like Scribe's Sarah she does not believe that she is mad. They both depart when they hear approaching the cortège of ambassadors who are on their way to London to work out the last details of a peace treaty.

Bolbury and soldiers of his regiment enter, the soldiers extolling the joys of soldierhood and war. Bolbury tells them they can stop a few moments for refreshments, but he warns them not to overindulge, since their chief does not approve of boisterous behavior. When the soldiers have departed, he muses on his having taken leave of the Chevalier at this very farm, and now, two years later, he and his friend have stopped there again enroute to London to negotiate the peace. The Chevalier enters and says that he wants to stay for a while in the neighborhood. Bolbury wonders why. "Quel intérêt!" the Chevalier replies; "c'est juste; tu ne peux pas savoir, tu ne peux pas deviner..." (recalling vaguely George's words to Tom in *La Prison,* Act I, when George wants to remain at the Jackins' farm rather than return with his comrade to their ship: "Par grace! par pitié! fais ce que je te dis! un instant! un seul instant!... tu ne sais pas ce que je souffre!..."). Bolbury soon guesses that his friend has a sweetheart. In an elaborate aria[24] the Chevalier recalls to mind the incident of two years ago. He has often thought about the maiden, but how can he expect her to remember a chance encounter with a stranger? Patrice then enters, beholds the Chevalier, and becomes frightened, thinking that he is seeing the lutin again. Of course the Chevalier does not understand what is the matter.[25] When Tom Crist and the villagers enter, all are amused at Patrice, who is so frightened that he cannot speak. (Patrice owes much to Dikson of *La Dame Blanche.* Both are comic figures and both are easily frightened. Moreover, Dikson's wife, whose name is Jenny, engages for a while the amorous attentions of the hero.)

Shortly afterwards the Chevalier, left alone on stage, muses on the touching simplicity and naive sentiments of the country people. Jeannie enters, and he observes her bewilderment. They are soon joined by Tom and Patrice—Patrice having finally explained the cause of his fear. Tom thinks that Patrice must be off his rocker to believe that the highly respected Chevalier is a lutin. When Jeannie finally notices the Chevalier, she throws herself into his arms, as Tom and Patrice look on, thoroughly stupified. During the ensuing quartet the Chevalier begins to realize that Jeannie thinks he is the lutin Trilby, and he realizes too that she has refused Patrice to wait for him. He voices the opinion *aside* that if he humors her, perhaps her reason will return, and accordingly he pretends that he *is* Trilby. Suddenly Bolbury comes in and addresses the Chevalier with the words "mon capitaine." Jeannie is perplexed, but finally reason dawns on her: "O mon Dieu! mon Dieu! c'était un rêve!" Bolbury tells the Chevalier that several dignitaries have just arrived from London and are seeking the proprietor of the farm. He has reason to believe that Tom Crist is a grand personage in disguise. The finale begins with a chorus of soldiers singing that they must be on their way to London. The Chevalier, announcing that he must first repair an error which he made two years ago, asks for silence so that he may speak. On his knees he asks Jeannie for her hand in marriage. After a brief initial surprise Tom accepts him as his future son-in-law and reveals to all present Jeannie's pedigree. With the exception of Patrice all are overjoyed. It then comes out that Bolbury is in love with Sara, who readily accepts him and gives him her hand. The Chevalier tells Tom that he and his entourage must now leave for London, but upon their return two weddings will take place. The opera ends in a trite *chœur général:*

Plus de sombres nuages!
Nous revoyons ⎫
             ⎬ enfin,
Ils retrouvent ⎭
Après de longs orages,
L'azur d'un Ciel serein.

The kaleidoscopic weaving together in *Le Lutin* of characters, motifs, and story patterns from various Scott novels and operas reminds one of Holstein's worksmanship in two operas discussed earlier, *Die Hochländer* and *Der Erbe von Morley.*

Jeanie Deans

When he was but twenty-six years old, the Scottish composer Hamish MacCunn wrote a four-act opera based on *The Heart of Mid-Lothian.* The work was commissioned by the Royal Carl Rosa Opera Company. Joseph Bennett did the libretto, which incorporates very little of Scott's Scots dialect but which follows the story of the novel more closely than do the other operas discussed in this chapter. *Jeanie Deans* was first performed in Edinburgh, at the Royal Lyceum Theatre, on 15 November 1894. It was enthusiastically received by an audience which "included much of the culture, fashion, and wealth of the city."[26] The composer himself was the conductor for the occasion, and the cast included Mlle Marie Duma (Jeanie), Miss Alice Esty (Effie), Alec Marsh (Davie Deans), L. Pringle (Dumbiedykes), Frank Wood (Duke of Argyle), Miss Meisslinger (Madge Wildfire), Miss Minnie Hunt (Queen Caroline), Mme Barth (Janet Balcristie), Miss Eleanor Harwood (Lady Suffolk), and E. C. Hedmondt (George Staunton). It was produced in London on 22 January 1896, and according to Grove "it held the operatic stage until after the first world war and the advent of Puccini on the British opera stage." It was successfully revived under the baton of Ian Whyte in Edinburgh, at the King's Theatre, on 10 April 1934.[27] It was revived for broadcast over the Scottish B. B. C. on 26 April 1968.[27b]

The opera begins with an orchestral introduction that leads presently into dance music (the modal melody "Rattlin', roarin' Willie"), and when the curtain rises we see young men and women dancing in an open space in front of Davie Deans's cottage.[28] When they notice Dumbiedykes in the distance, they comment on his interest in Jeanie, and upon his entrance they politely greet him with a "Good even, Laird!" He warns them to beware of Davie Deans, "who liketh not the dance." (In the novel no one would have dared to dance in the very dooryard of Deans's cottage. Moreover, Effie's secret visits to the forest to dance are simply related to us as having occurred: we are not taken to the scene of her escapades. In opera, however, it is often desirable to have dance music, so here the "sin" that led to Effie's downfall is acted out.) When the dancers ask Dumbiedykes to sing, he hesitates, *"looking significantly towards the Cottage,"* but they allay his inhibitions with the observation, "Safe, 'tis milking time." He accordingly entertains them with an engaging, wistful song that begins, "I love a lass that's fair to see,/But much I doubt if she loves me." Afterwards the dancing resumes, now to the tune of "Tullochgorum." It *"has not proceeded far when Davie Deans enters . . . and advances into the middle of the group. All fall back from him. The dance stops abruptly."*

> DEANS: Say, who are ye that with your heathen dance
>   Invade the threshold of a godly home?
>   Have I or mine an ear for lilting tunes?
>   When did we smile upon your wanton jigs,
>   That ye should choose this place for deeds of shame?
> CHORUS: No deeds of shame, but just an honest dance.
>   Aye! honest, such as Effie Deans well knows!
> DEANS: Take not a stainless name on lying lips!
>   My Effie hath nor part nor lot with you,
>   But lives, 'fore Heav'n, a life of faith and fear—
>   So get ye gone—pollute this place no more.

(There is no such incident in the novel, but one might well have occurred, in view of Deans's uncompromisingly negative attitude toward dancing. In ch. x, on which Act I is largely based, he launches into a tirade directed toward Jeanie and Effie at the mere mention of the word "dance.") The dancers depart, while Dumbiedykes, seated on a bench outside the cottage, remains and gently chastises Deans for being too hard. In reply to the Laird's words Deans reveals his deepseated religious convictions, which admit no place for frivolous dancing. He then goes back into the cottage. *"Dumbiedykes remains seated on the bench, and is shaking with suppressed laughter as Jeanie enters . . . bearing a milk-pail."* The two discuss briefly the subject of dancing, the Laird soon learning that Jeanie agrees with her father. When he approaches her *"with a comically mysterious air"* and begins to make love in his shy way, she *"looks at him in astonishment, then stoops to take up her pail."* He gives up in embarrassment, and, calling out to Deans, he enters the cottage. *"Jeanie, coming forward, bursts into a passion of tears. Sounds of a fiddle and the cries of dancers are heard from a distance."* In a monologue she sings that something she cannot explain is weighing heavily on her spirit. She somehow senses that Effie is in trouble.

Her premonition turns out to be fact. *"Effie, looking wan and miserable, is seen at back, supporting her steps by clutching at the trees as she passes them."* In the orchestra we hear an ominous sounding motiv that comes to be associated with Effie:

Example 7-9

She sings softly, "Jeanie! Jeanie!" A crashing chord is heard in the orchestra, and Jeanie replies, "Effie! my poor bairn!" *"The sisters fall into each other's arms and remain in close embrace,"* during which time there is a long pause in the music. In the ensuing conversation Effie says she has been ill. Jeanie suspects that more is wrong, and finally the painful truth comes out. As in the novel, Effie refuses to reveal the name of her lover, but she assures Jeanie that he is no villain. When Jeanie asks where the babe is, Effie replies that she does not know. At this point two constables enter to arrest Euphemia Deans, the alleged child murderess. "O Jeanie, save me! save me!" Effie exclaims (words that Bennett has borrowed from the trial scene, chapter xxiii). *"With a shriek she falls senseless into Jeanie's arms,"* as Deans, Dumbiedykes, and the dancers re-enter. When Deans finally understands the reasons for Effie's arrest, he does not fall "extended and senseless upon his own hearth," like his counterpart in Scott, but rather he steadies himself, turns to the dancers, and says,

> O friends, I said but now,
> "My Effie hath no part nor lot with you!"
> I take not back the words. Ye are not charged
> With murder; nor on those that love you falls
> The curse of a dishonored name.

They urge him not to take things so hard. Moreover they doubt that Effie could have done so dreadful a deed. Dumbiedykes reaches for his purse and offers to give Deans gold ("siller" in the novel) to buy off the constables, but Deans commands the Laird to stand aside and not come between "this wanton" and his curse. The dancers plead with him to spare her, but he waves them off too. At this point Effie, having revived from her swoon, comes forward and kneels at his feet. She tells him that she did commit one grave sin, but insists that she is guiltless of child murder. Unmoved by her plea, Deans *speaks* one word: "Accursed!"—and all present are horrified. Then, in the typical fashion of operatic curses, he solemnly continues:

> Thou hast shamed our honest blood!
> Here is no place for thee since foul with sin
> Thou comest like the Evil One where dwell
> The just in saintly purity. Go! Go!
> The hearth and home that once held thee so dear
> Shall know thee never more.

Jeanie, Dumbiedykes, and the dancers implore him to take back the curse, "for vengeance is of Heav'n"; but Deans replies, "And mine its voice." Effie falls down unconscious, the constables move forward to apprehend her, and the curtain falls as the orchestra plays agitated music based on the motiv first heard at Effie's entrance (Example 7-9).—The most interesting change in characterization in Act I is with regard to Dumbiedykes, who is not the awkward nincompoop of the novel. Scott's Laird would not have been popular with dancers, nor would he ever have been requested to sing a song. Nor would he ever have laughed at Deans's religious fervor, even behind his back. The operatic Dumbiedykes does have some of the speech patterns of Scott's Laird, especially noticeable when he says, "Jeanie, woman"; but we have real sympathy for him in his unsuccessful affair of the heart—which, I might add, is unsuccessful for no good reason, since there is no Reuben Butler nor mention of him. The most interesting change in plot is the insertion of Deans's formal curse, which is suggested by his words to Jeanie at the end of chapter x, after Effie has already been taken away: "Where is the vile harlot, that has disgraced the blood of an honest man?—Where is she, that has no place among us, but has come foul with her sins, like the Evil One, among the children of God?—Where is she, Jeanie?—Bring her before me, that I may kill her with a word and a look!" Cursing scenes are a staple in successful opera, as Bennett and MacCunn no doubt knew.[29]

The first scene of Act II takes place at Muschat's Cairn. It is based on chapters xv and xvii, but with several changes, the first remarkable one being that Jeanie is led to the awesome place by Madge Wildfire. When the curtain rises the stage is empty, and we hear from *without* Madge singing a stanza borrowed from chapter xvi:

> I glance like the wild-fire, through country and town;
> I'm seen on the causeway, I'm seen on the down.
> The lightning that flashes so bright and so free

Is scarcely so blithe or so bonny as me.

Madge enters first, singing about the murderer Nick Muschat (whom Scott discusses earlier, in connection with Reuben Butler's chance encounter with Robertson at the same place). She continues with her account when Jeanie enters, but soon her mind wanders off to the question of who killed the child. She asks, "Was it Effie that killed the bairn?" We hear thunder and wind, and suddenly she says to Jeanie, "Find out what they mean. I must leave thee alone." We then hear her singing again from *without:*

I'm Queen of the wake and the Lady of May,
I lead the blithe ring round the Maypole today.
The wild-fire that flashes so fair and so free
Was never lithe or so bonny as me!

(With a few minor changes the stanza is Scott's but transposed from the passage in ch. xxxi that leads up to the memorable church scene, which, strangely enough, is not utilized in any of the operas.) Jeanie prays that God may watch over her, the sentiment of this brief musical passage being based on Scott's remark that Jeanie recurred frequently "in mental prayer to the protection of that Being to whom night is as noon-day." Suddenly Staunton appears, *"as though from the Cairn. A flash of lightning momentarily illuminates his figure. Jeanie utters a cry of terror."* He asks, "Art thou the sister of Euphemia Deans?" and she replies, "I am! If aught thou know'st can save her life,/By thine own hope of sweet salvation, speak!" The ensuing conversation and action follow Scott closely, with occasional remarks by Staunton, in reference to his relationship with Madge, deriving from his long sick-bed confession to Jeanie in England (chapter xxxiii). Instead of threatening her with a pistol when she does not agree to obey him in whatever he might request, he produces the pistol when she says that she cannot tell a lie to save Effie. This is certainly not very gracious conduct on his part, but it is an understandable, natural human reaction. Somehow the operatic Staunton does not seem quite so bad as his original. As the opera unfolds, it is clear that Bennett is making a conscious effort to upgrade his hero's character. Moreover his producing the pistol at this point rather than earlier makes Madge's ensuing offstage song ("When the glede's on the blue cloud," etc.) theatrically more effective. When Madge's voice becomes louder, Staunton exits, with the solemn admonition to Jeanie that "on [her] head lies Effie's guiltless blood." A storm (not in the novel) which has been brewing throughout the scene now reaches its height. The addition of it opens up all sorts of possibilities for the composer. Like formal curses, the storm is a staple of nineteenth-century opera. Examples are countless. When the loud, agitated, chromatic music in the orchestra subsides somewhat, Madge re-enters, dressed in Staunton's cloak and hat. (Her appearance in Staunton's clothes prepares us for his appearance in hers in the next scene, the assault on the Tolbooth. The clothes-swapping idea is Scott's, but altered to suit the reversal in the order of events: the operatic episode at Muschat's Cairn comes *before* the Porteous riot.) Two constables thinking she is Staunton start to arrest her, but she reveals her true identity and laughs at them. Storm music is again heard in the orchestra, but when the curtain is lowered for the change of scenery, it gradually dies away and is replaced by a motiv associated with Effie's imprisonment:

Example 7-10

When the curtain rises again, a common room inside the Tolbooth is revealed.

The action of the second scene is suggested by events that occur in chapters vi and vii; but whereas in Scott we view the riot from the perspective of the rioters, that is, mainly from *outside* the prison, in the opera we view everything from *inside*. This change results in much more prominence given to Effie and to her conversation with Staunton. The scene begins with an aria for Effie, who thinks about the peaceful cottage and surroundings where she spent her life, which now seem to her like a dream. There is then a chorus of prisoners ("Banish care and sorrow, boys") after which the prisoners are ordered to return to their individual cells. Effie remains behind, oblivious to everything that is going on about her and even to the noise of the rioters *without,* which becomes more and more noticeable. At the end of her song "Sleep, for the day is done" we hear the rioters singing, still *without:*

> We'll hang Jack Porteous on a tree
> That beareth better fruit than he.

And then we hear Staunton's voice, which Effie immediately recognizes and which rouses her from her reverie. Staunton, who is disguised as Madge, and the rioters soon break into the common room. He throws off his disguise and rushes to Effie. *"As they embrace, the rioters open the doors, right and left, and go out. A tumultuous chorus on all sides."* Left alone together they sing a love duet, toward the end of which Effie's mind begins to wander back to the words of her opening aria. (The duet is pure operatic convention; in the novel Staunton has no time to dally with her.) Shouts from *without* indicate to Staunton that the rioters have found their victim. As in Scott, he desperately tries to persuade her to leave the prison with him, but she refuses. The offstage rioters call out "Madge Wildfire!

Where art thou?" and Staunton must finally depart without her. The act ends.—Particularly effective in this second scene are the offstage voices and choruses, which make us very much aware of the exciting events. From an operatic standpoint this procedure is usually preferable to having a lot of movement and action on stage. There is a similar scene in several of the *Ivanhoe* operas. During the storming of Torquilstone Rebecca looks out from a window and reports to the wounded hero what is going on. We hear the noise of combat and the voices of soldiers *without*. Little ingenuity is required here of the librettist, since the scene as conceived by Scott is already ready-made for operatic rendition (see Chapter 9).

The first scene of Act III is Effie's cell in the Tolbooth. It is based on chapter xxv. When the curtain opens, Effie *"is discovered seated upon a pallet bed, motionless and with an unchanging expression of despair."* During the musical introduction a warder (not specified as Ratcliffe) admits Jeanie to the cell. As in the novel, Effie holds Jeanie responsible for the outcome of the trial, but when Jeanie says that she will go to London to plead before the throne, Effie asks forgiveness for her harsh words. Much of the dialogue follows Scott closely. However, some of Jeanie's lines addressed to Effie are addressed actually to Ratcliffe in the novel, and some of Ratcliffe's lines about the Duke of Argyle are assigned to Staunton, who now enters the cell disguised as a clergyman. (This is a departure from the novel. Scott's Staunton does not visit Effie in her cell after the trial.) When the warder has departed, Staunton reveals his identity. He and Effie sing another love duet, during the course of which he reminds her of her words in the duet of the preceding scene:

"Ourselves our world, where love shall be supreme,
And we shall know nor sin, nor shame, nor tears."

He tells her there is still hope, for the men who stormed the prison before could do so again. Effie again refuses to leave by an unlawful means. Jeanie then tells Staunton her plans. "Jeanie!" he replies; "brave at Muschat's cairn, in storm and tempest [and under threat of pistol, one might add]; braver now, by far!" He advises her to see the Duke of Argyle first; and when he makes clear that the present duke is the son or grandson of the Argyle who suffered during the persecution of the Cameronians (the religious sect to which the Deans family belongs), Jeanie cries out *"with exultation"*:

Thank God—thank God! to him I can appeal,
Invoking gratitude and pity both.
Argyle will hear me. At his word the fences
Round the throne will fall and let me pass.
Thank God! Thank God! Dear Effie, all is well!

As the scene draws to a close, a mood of optimism prevails that is not in the novel at this time. After Staunton and Jeanie have departed, Effie *"falls upon her knees, with eyes and hands raised toward heaven."* "Saved!" she exclaims; "at ev'ning time it shall be light!"

The second scene follows closely chapter xxvi and is a depiction of Jeanie's visit to Dumbiedykes' house, her encounter with the cross old housekeeper Mrs. Balcristie, and her words with the Laird, who asks her to marry him. The musical introduction begins with a motiv associated with Dumbiedykes and repeated with variation often during the course of the scene:

Example 7-11

When the curtain rises, Jeanie enters and is surprised to find no one stirring, even though "the day is two hours old." While she is tending to a cow, a young girl sees her, is frightened, and runs away screaming. Mrs. Balcristie then enters with an angry look on her face and rudely asks Jeanie what her business might be. The action throughout follows Scott closely, and the dialogue is condensed (and Englished) from the corresponding dialogue in the novel. *"Dumbiedykes, wearing a laced coat and hat over his night gear, appears at the window of his bedroom."* He calls out to Mrs. Balcristie in a variaton of the opening orchestral figure:

Example 7-12

Mrs. Balcristie is tamed, and Jeanie is well received by the Laird. When he asks her to be his wife, she first offers her sister's fate as an excuse but then says frankly that she does not love him. (There is no mention of Reuben Butler here or elsewhere in the opera.) He refuses to give her the money she needs for her journey to London, and she departs. In a few moments, however, he has a change of heart, runs to the gate, and calls her back—this rather than mounting his stubborn pony, Rory Bean, and riding to catch up with her, which obviously would not work well on the operatic stage. When she returns, he gives her the money—and, as in the novel, with no strings attached. She thanks him warmly and sets out on her way. In the last part of the scene Dumbiedykes has a burst of passion against Mrs. Balcristie (he throws a money-bag at her). There is no parallel to this in chapter xxvi, but it is suggested by Scott's mention later in the novel that the Laird had gotten rid of Mrs. Balchristie and taken a wife.—*Jeanie Deans* is the only full-fledged opera based on *The Heart of Mid-Lothian* to depict Jeanie's visit to the Laird's house. It is questionable whether the prominence given this material as a result of its inclusion can be justified in the overall dramatic structure of the opera, but it is easy to see why Bennett and MacCunn wanted to include it; the chapter contains some of Scott's most engaging work. Unfortunately his special, hard-to-put-into-words quality that makes one want to laugh and cry at the same time does not come through in the operatic rendition. The alteration of Dumbiedykes' personality, to which I have already referred, is one reason. Even more damaging to Scott's artistry is the condensation and Englishing of the dialogue. Two illustrations will show what I mean. When Dumbiedykes of the opera commands Mrs. Balcristie to be hospitable to Jeanie, she opens the door and says simply, "Will't please you, Jeanie Deans, to enter now?" Omitted is her question, delightfully hypocritical in view of what has just gone on, "And how's that douce honest man, your father?" Later, when Dumbiedykes gives Jeanie the money, she asks, "Is aught expected save its just return?" He replies, " 'Tis freely giv'n. Go where you like and do as e'en you please. Good luck will sure attend." Completely gone is the charm of the original:

> "But, Laird," said Jeanie, "though I ken my father will satisfy every penny of this siller, whatever there's o't, yet I wadna like to borrow it frae ane that maybe thinks of something mair than the paying o't back again."
>
> "There's just twenty-five guineas o't," said Dumbiedikes, with a gentle sigh, "and whether your father pays or disna pay, I make ye free till't without another word. Gang where ye like—do what ye like—and marry a' the Butlers in the country gin ye like—and sae, gude morning to you, Jeanie."

MacCunn's music does not compensate for this loss. Nor would the music of a better composer.

The first scene of Act IV is laid in Richmond Park. It is based mainly on Jeanie's interview with Queen Caroline, which Scott relates in chapter xxxvii. The orchestral introduction begins with a calm, pastoral theme:

Example 7-13

The ladies of the court sing a four-part madrigal, after which the Queen and Lady Suffolk *talk* while a concealed orchestra plays the Minuet from Handel's *Water Music*. Lady Suffolk says that the King pardoned Handel

BIBLIOTHECA Ottaviensis

for an earlier transgression because he was so moved by the lovely music.
The Duke of Argyle and Jeanie soon enter, and the ladies of the court
(with the exception of Lady Suffolk) exeunt. (In the novel we first see
Argyle and Jeanie in the park; they are approached by the Queen and
Lady Suffolk, without an entourage of ladies. Bennett and MacCunn have
shifted the perspective and introduced the ladies in the interest of good
opera. There is now occasion for the madrigal and the *Water Music*, both
of which create an atmosphere altogether different from that of the
preceding scenes.) The opening words of Argyle to the Queen are
abridged from Scott. The Duke tells her about Jeanie, who comes forward
slowly and kneels at her feet, not realizing at this point that she is the
Queen. As in the novel, when she begins to talk with the great ladies, she
inadvertently makes two faux pas (which, incidentally, probably go unap-
preciated by an operatic audience not familiar with the novel, since Scott's
paragraphs of explanation are lacking), but she waxes eloquent when she
pleads for her sister's life. The text of her aria follows the long speech
Scott gives her toward the end of the chapter. The Queen is moved by her
plea and promises to do what she can to help. She and Lady Suffolk then
leave. (In the novel Jeanie and Argyle leave, and what follows transpires
in the Duke's carriage. Bennett's modification avoids a change of scenery
and the obvious problem that the carriage would present.) Argyle says,
"Jeanie, your words have made the Queen a friend." Jeanie is surprised:
"The Queen! the Queen! and have I seen the Queen?" Argyle: "In very
truth, and saved your sister's life!" The musical and dramatic high point
of the scene has now arrived. In ecstasy Jeanie exclaims:

Example 7-14

This is followed by a brief passage of excited orchestral music as Jeanie *"falls fainting into the Duke's arms."* The curtain falls. MacCunn's "fundamental dependence on the German tradition" which Grove thinks "prevented him from achieving the status of a significant national Scots composer" has obviously stood him in good stead here. Musical Example 7-14 brings to mind the ending of Sieglinde's monologue in *Die Walküre*, Act I:

Example 7-15

The changes from Scott that Bennett and MacCunn make in the Richmond Park scene of Act IV are in the realm of modifications. The entire final scene, however, represents a radical reshaping of the original. It takes place in *"an Open Space Before the Tolbooth Prison"* and dramatizes what might have happened if Effie's pardon had been late in arriving. The working out of the plot owes a little to the events in the novel surrounding the execution of Wilson. The orchestra has a twelve-measure introduction, the theme of which recurs during the excitement later in the scene:

Example 7-16

"A turbulent crowd awaits the procession conducting Effie Deans to execution. As the curtain rises Madge Wildfire is discovered in the midst of the throng, some of whom are wildly dancing around her." They call on her for a song, and she readily agrees:

There is a tree, and a bonny bonny tree,
Though its limbs are of green leaves bare,
Its fruit, oh its fruit, is goodly for to see,
But to gather it will no man dare.
                    Not one, I wot.
You gape, and let it hang!

This is not in Scott. The words obviously have an underlying meaning in the context of the present scene. The people reply, "Come, Madge, a song! the fruit is not yet ripe." Staunton enters unnoticed and mingles with the crowd. Madge continues:

She's gane back to her father's ha',
O well-a-day! and well-a-day!
She's counted the lealest maid o' them a',
Ten thousand times good night, and joy be wi' thee!

At this point we hear in the orchestra the prinicpal motiv associated with Effie:

Example 7-17

Interrupting her song Madge asks, "Where is her father?" and immediately answers her own question: "Patience, he will come, and bonnie Jeanie." The final part of her song, which alludes obliquely to Jeanie's interview with the Queen, has a familiar melody:

Example 7-18

Staunton is recognized by Madge and the crowd, but he motions them to be silent. When Madge's mind wanders back to the "bonny tree," Staunton says, "O Madge! be calm! How know you this?" She replies: "The winds bear news to Madge,/And swifter lightnings, far out running time,/Do show her what shall come!" Staunton then motions for the people to gather about him and instructs them to attack the guards at his signal; by this action Effie's execution will be stayed, and in the meanwhile, hopefully, Jeanie will arrive with the pardon.

"*The Prison doors open. Guards appear, followed by Magistrates and officers of the law, amidst whom is Effie. Other guards bring up the rear.*" The people cry out in anger to the captors, but when they behold Effie they "*become silent and fall back instinctively, with murmers of compassion.*" When Deans and Dumbiedykes enter, they "*respectfully make way for Deans to approach his daughter*" (suggested by the polite conduct of the people at Effie's trial; chapter xxi of the novel). Addressing her father, Effie asks forgiveness for the shame which she has brought on him ("O father! though my hands be free from blood,/Yet am I worthy death," etc.).[30] Deans replies:

Dear child, be strong, endure; we soon shall meet
Where enters sin nor sorrow. Take with thee
A father's blessing and await him there.

"*He points reverently upward.*" (This abrupt, unprepared-for about-face on the part of Deans strikes me as utterly absurd; it is a flaw in an otherwise skillfully put-together scene.) Staunton then gives the signal, and the crowd attacks the guards. "*Effie, Deans, and Dumbiedykes are forced to the front of the stage, guarded by some of Staunton's followers. The fight sways backward and forward.*" All during the melee we hear variations of the orchestral introduction to the scene (see Example 7-16). Soldiers then enter from the prison and prepare themselves to attack the mob with fixed bayonets, as the orchestra works up to a shattering dominant seventh chord to E. At this climactic moment, "*a waving of caps and cries of joy suspend the fight. Jeanie appears, seated on a pillion behind a mounted retainer who wears the colours of Argyle. Two other men follow as escort. The soldiers and mob fall back on either side.*" All the while the orchestra is playing agitated runs based on the same dominant seventh chord. "*Jeanie dismounts, assisted by Staunton, and gives a paper to the presiding magistrate.*" The orchestra resolves itself to a crashing E-major chord, as Jeanie exclaims, "A pardon, Sir! for Effie Deans." [31] The people shout, "Hurrah! Hurrah! Hurrah! God save the King!" "*Jeanie embraces Effie and her father, shakes hands with Dumbiedykes, who tries to press upon her the contents of a heavy purse. Effie recognizes Staunton and rushes into his arms.*" When a constable lays hands on Staunton and attempts to arrest him "on a charge of riot and of murder," Jeanie produces a second pardon (not in the novel). Moreover, since his father has just died, Staunton is now the Baronet of Willingham. Asking Effie to share his lot with him, he "*leads her to her father, who lifts his hands in blessing.*" (Staunton's good fortune is not unconvincing, since, as I have already observed, Bennett and MacCunn have consciously upgraded his moral fibre throughout.) Next, turning to Jeanie and leading her to the center of the stage, he sings the following melody, which is accompanied by rapid triplet chords in the orchestra (the "German tradition" again):

Example 7-19

The chorus then takes this up, with the melody in the soprano part, and a few measures later Effie, Staunton, and Dumbiedykes join in. The opera ends as all present sing, "Fame undying, love and thanks and praise to Jeanie Deans!"

With Bennett and MacCunn we have come full circle. Jeanie is clearly the center of attention in the novel. In the Terry-Bishop musical drama she shares honors with Effie, who gets all the songs. In *La Prison d'Édimbourg* she plays second fiddle to Effie, and in *La Prigione d'Edimburgo* she is a character of no importance. The Jeannie of *Le Lutin de Culloden* has almost no resemblance to Scott's Jeanie. Bennett and MacCunn have restored her to her rightful place. *Jeanie Deans* is easily the most sophisticated, musically and dramatically, of the operas based on *The Heart of Mid-Lothian.* Moreover, I would rate it among the half dozen best Walter Scott operas. In this group it has the distinction of being the only opera with genuinely Scottish atmosphere.

HAMISH MACCUNN. From the Enthoven Collection, Victoria and Albert Theatre Museum.

8

§ § §

THE BRIDE OF LAMMERMOOR

T he operas based on *The Bride of Lammermoor, Ivanhoe,* and *Kenilworth* make up almost half the total number of Scott operas. While *Ivanhoe* and *Kenilworth* inspired librettists and composers from shortly after the time they were written until the end of the century, the *Bride of Lammermoor* operas were all written within a period of eight years—from Adam's *Caleb de Walter Scott* (1827) to Donizetti's *Lucia di Lammermoor* (1835). Since everyone is familiar with *Lucia,* the emphasis of this chapter falls on its precursors. Some of them are occasionally cited in discussions of *Lucia,* but I have yet to see an article in which the author shows even the slightest degree of familiarity with the three or four works he lists; each critic immediately dismisses them with the not so profound observation that they are now properly forgotten.[1]

Le Caleb de Walter Scott

Le Caleb was first performed in Paris, at the Théâtre des Nouveautés, on 12 December 1827. It is better described as "vaudeville" or "operetta" or, as the title-page of the libretto says, "comédie . . . mêlée de couplets," but for the sake of convenience I shall continue to call it an opera. The text is by Achile d'Artois (i.e. Louis Charles Achile d'Artois de Bournonville) and Eugène (i.e. François Antoine Eugène de Planard),[2] and approximately one-third of the music is by Adolphe Adam (who incidentally is most widely known today for his beloved Christmas carol, "O Holy Night"). The rest of the music has been borrowed from the works of such composers as Boieldieu, Méhul, and Rossini. Thus *Le Caleb* is in part a pastiche.[3] As the title would lead one to suspect, the story of the opera is not the love-story of Lucy and Edgar. In fact Caleb is the only character in the dramatis personae that has an exact counterpart in the novel. The other characters are Henri, the Count of Douglas, young officer; Édouard, his friend, young officer; Clara, sister of Édouard; Jaket, carpenter of the village; Krik, innkeeper; Emmy, shepherdess ("très jeune fille gardant les troupeaux du village"); and the Registrar ("Greffier") to the Justice of the Peace.[4] The opera has only one act, and the setting remains the same throughout—in front of the house of Jaket, with the Scottish Highlands in the background. There are twenty-eight *scènes*.

Scène i: The orchestral score has no overture. In the opening chorus, which is the work of Adam (folios 1–8), the villagers sing that daybreak calls them to work. *Scène* ii: Having gotten away from his wife, Krik comes to his friend Jaket's house and expresses the desire to have lunch with him. They celebrate by drinking a bottle of wine, which Jaket had bought from the château when the wine cellar was put on sale, and they sing a drinking song (borrowed from Méhul). They both look forward to profiting when the Registrar comes to make arrangements for the final dissolution of the Douglas estate. (This motif could have come from *The Bride of Lammermoor,* but it also calls to mind the selling of the Ellangowan estate, in *Guy Mannering,* and the auction scene of *La Dame Blanche.*) A carpenter by trade, Jaket wants to get hold of the rights to cutting the forest, and Krik hopes to obtain a license to sell gin and other spirits. Accordingly, they decide to ask the Registrar to dinner in hope that the hospitality which they extend to him will help further their cause. (Scott's cooper, John Girder, wines and dines the Marquis of A— and Edgar of Ravenswood for comparable ulterior reasons.) They decide to ask Emmy to take care of the necessary arrangements. *Scène* iii: When she enters, they ask her if she knows how to turn a spit. She replies that she does so every Sunday at the Justice's house. She then sings a song (not by Adam) about her duties there, in which the Justice's dishonesty (he will accept bribes) and his amorous interest in her are highlighted in a humorously satirical fashion. *Scène* iv: Alone on stage for a few moments, Krik speaks of Caleb, the major-domo of the château, who uses all sorts of stories to cover up the fall in fortune and power of the family he has served for sixty years. Seeing Caleb coming, he decides to spy on him to find out what makes him tick. *Scène* v: Caleb enters, wearing a tattered coat, and sings about how cold he is ("Qu'il fait frais!").[5] At the conclusion of the song Krik comes out from hiding. In the ensuing duologue Caleb, as might be predicted, tries to cover up the misfortunes of the Douglas family. Krik wonders why he is so attached to the Douglases, and Caleb explains why in another song.[6] *Scène* vi: Jaket invites Caleb to dinner, but, as both Krik and Jaket foresaw, he refuses out of a sense of dignity. He gives the excuse found here and there in the novel that he has already eaten, like a prince, in the château. Krik and Jaket tease him during the course of the next musical number.[7]

Scène vii: After the two villagers have gone, Caleb takes from his pocket a piece of bread and one sardine wrapped in paper. He speaks of the hard times. Nevertheless, he muses, a bed of straw is not so bad. He has no other servants to fuss about, and when his master returns he alone will receive his regards. He then sings that things are not so bad after all; the frugal person lives easily, whereas the affluent always desire more and more. *Scène* viii: Clara enters. She has been eight days in the village at the house of a relative. Although never having seen Caleb before, she recognizes him immediately because she has heard so much about him while in Ireland. She tells him that a young, wounded, shipwrecked officer, whom she had saved and then nursed back to health, had shown her a miniature portrait of him and had referred to him as his best friend. Furthermore, she tells him that her brother, who serves in the same corps, wrote her recently that the two would soon be discharged. Thus Caleb's master is no doubt on his way home. In the ensuing duet she tells him that her mother was cousin to the detestable Edinburgh solicitor who, through the Justice of the Peace and the Registrar, has caused so much trouble for Henri de Douglas and his estate. She explains that inasmuch as the old solicitor does not like her or her brother, who are his only next-of-kin, he will probably bequeath everything he owns to an old governess. *Scène* ix: Édouard arrives, and we have a trio, which is borrowed from the finale to the first act of *La Dame Blanche*.[8] Édouard and Clara sing of their joy at seeing one another again, while Caleb sings in joyful expectation of his master's arrival. Édouard cannot understand why Henri has not yet arrived, but he is certain that his arrival is imminent. Caleb is worried that he is not properly dressed to receive his master. He goes back to the château to put on his outfit of major-domo, which he managed to keep from the solicitor. *Scène* x: Édouard teases Clara about the possibility of a marriage between her and Henri. She insists that Henri has never given her reason to believe that he loves her. Édouard replies that he often noticed a gleam in Henri's eyes, during the period of his convalescence. Seeing Henri approaching, they hide in the bushes to eavesdrop on him.

Scène xi: Henri sings a song (borrowed from Madame Duchambge) in which he reminisces about the joys of his youth. Now all is changed. The clan used always to greet him upon his homecoming, but not any more. "Mais," he concludes, "il m'y reste un ami véritable,/Et c'est un bien que j'ai voulu revoir!" *Scène* xii: Caleb re-enters, sees Henri, and greets him joyfully. Clara and Édouard, still hiding in the bushes, are touched at the reunion of Henri and the faithful old servant. In a duet (borrowed from Rodolphe Kreutzer's opera, *Aristippe*) Henri asks Caleb whether his travels have altered his appearance; Caleb replies that his tears prevent him from seeing. Next, in spoken dialogue, Henri tells Caleb that he suspects he has tried to conceal, when writing to him, the misfortunes that have befallen the family estate. "Impossible!" Caleb replies; "impossible! monseigneur! jour de Dieu! un château où a soupé le roi Jacques II." (Caleb refers more than once to James II's visit. The librettists apparently borrowed the idea from Lady Bellenden's frequent references, in *Old Mortality*, to Charles II's having once dined at Tillietudlem.) Caleb informs Henri that Clara and Édouard are in the neighborhood. Henri expresses the wish that he were in a position to marry Clara. At this point begins a quartet, with music by Adam—Henri singing of his love for

Clara, who saved his life; Caleb assuring Henri that she loves him; Édouard singing *à part* of his pleasure in learning that Henri loves her; and Clara expressing *à part* her pleasure in knowing that Henri's feelings are the same as hers. In the second *couplet* Henri sings that he has now only himself to offer her inasmuch as his estate has been taken from him. In the spoken dialogue that follows the quartet he tells Caleb that marriage is now utterly out of the question; that he will leave Scotland and seek his fortune elsewhere. Upon hearing these words Clara, still in hiding, exclaims, "O ciel!"; Édouard, also still in hiding, presses her hand and says, "sois tranquille, il n'est pas encore parti"; the two then depart unobtrusively.

Scène xiii: Henri announces to Caleb that he wants to invite Édouard to dinner. Realizing the lack of provisions in the château, Caleb is noticeably bewildered, but he does not let Henri know why. Moreover, Henri wants the old servant to find fifty crowns so that he can pay back a long-standing debt to Édouard. *Scène* xiv: Caleb, alone on stage and very distressed, wonders how he can manage the dinner and raise the fifty crowns. He has no money, and he has no credit in the village. He then sings a song about the vicissitudes of Fortune. The times are not always pretty; nevertheless he will continue to serve Henri and do everything possible to please him. *Scène* xv: Looking into Jaket's kitchen and observing Emmy turning a spit, he tells her that she is burning her roast. She does not think so. He enters, unhooks the spit, holds it, and paces up and down. In the ensuing duet he expresses his joy at having found a dinner for his master; Emmy, who is a bit naive, maybe even feeble-minded, and certainly stupid, thinks that he is supposed to be helping her. He asks her to help him set up a table "sous cet épais feuillage," and she does so, thinking that Jaket and Krik will soon arrive and not suspecting that anything is amiss. (The action here is suggested by Scott's account of how Caleb stole the wild-fowl from the Girders' hearth, chapters xii-xiii.) *Scène* xvi: Emmy is of course surprised when Édouard, Henri, and Clara arrive for dinner rather than Jaket and Krik, but Caleb manages to silence her. When the conversation turns to the armorial design on one of the forks—a cavalier and his steed engulfed in sand—Clara is reminded of the *ballade* about the bride of Lammermoor. Caleb remarks that the cavalier was *an ancestor* of the family and then asks Emmy to sing the *ballade* for the guests. She does so gladly:

Example 8-1

Un peu louré

Un beau jeune homme é - tait Qu'Hen - ri l'on ap - pe - lait; É -

tait fil - le jo - li - e Que l'on nom-mait Lu - ci - e. Le sort les rap - pro -

cha, Et leur cœur s'al - lu - ma. Ah! _____

ppp Jeu - ne fil - le pres - sé - e D'être à l'a - mour, Songe

à la fi - an - cé - e De lam Mer - mour! Jeu - ne fil - le pres -

sé - e D'être à l'a - mour, Songe à la fi - an - cé - e De

ppp lam Mer - mour! La fi - an - cé - e De lam Mer -

ff mour! La fi - an - cé - e De lam Mer - mour.

DEUXIÈME COUPLET	TROISIÈME COUPLET
D'être bientôt unis,	Contre un cruel rival
Tous deux s'étaient promis;	Henri court à cheval;
Ce jour qu'ils devaient l'être,	Tout brûlant de vengeance,
Refusa de paraître;	Sur le sable il s'élance!...
Mais le jour arriva	Mais un gouffre était là;
Où l'on les sépara...	Son cheval s'enfonça...
Ah!...	Ah!...
Jeune fille pressée, etc.	Jeune fille pressée, etc.

(I have quoted the entire *ballade* because it is the only part of the opera that touches on the novel's main concern. Interestingly the cavalier's name is Henri, who in the novel is Lucy's likeable younger brother, not her lover. The music is Adam's, and in atmosphere it is reminiscent of the *ballade* of Boieldieu's Jenny about "la dame blanche.") Emmy is praised for her singing. Édouard then announces that he must see the Justice of the Peace about a business matter, and the *scène* closes with an ensemble for the five principals who are on stage.

Scènes xvii–xviii: After a very brief dialogue with Emmy, Caleb retreats to the tower of the castle, while Emmy, left alone on stage, sings her engaging song to the ducks. The music is Adam's:

Example 8-2

Lors - que j'en - tends di - re du mal des bê - tes, Au me - me in - stant ça m'don - ne à ré - flé - chir.

Scènes xix–xx: Krik and Jaket re-enter and sing a duet in expectation of their dinner. When Emmy informs them that the dinner has already been eaten up by M. Caleb and his guests, they are understandably very angry. Determined to rouse Caleb, they beat on the door to the tower. At this point comes an ensemble (borrowed from the first act of *La Dame Blanche*) in which Krik, Jaket, and Emmy express their exasperation with Caleb, while he sings of his joy in having tricked them. After the ensemble he tells the two men that they ought to be thankful for having had the opportunity to serve the young master. He speaks furthermore of a grand marriage which will result in the payment of the family's manifold debts. Afterwards he will have both Krik and Jaket hanged for their misdeeds, but he will make Emmy "femme de chambre." *Scène* xxi: Caleb acts surprised at the men's insolence, especially in view of certain services he says he had intended to render them. He says that he was about to entrust carpenter Jaket with redoubling "tous nos baux à ferme" and that Krik was to be licensed to sell "eaux-de-vie." Jaket and Krik immediately change their tune. Sensing his advantage, Caleb instructs them to go find the Registrar and ask him to draw up two official licenses. As they are about to leave, he reminds them of "le pot-de-vin d'usage" which they owe (cf. the duty-eggs and butter of the novel, ch. xi), and he manages to extract from them twenty-five crowns apiece, threatening to give the licenses to other people if they do not pay up immediately. The trio at the end of the *scène* is borrowed from Rossini. (Krik's and Jaket's change of tune when they hear of the approaching good fortune of Henri reminds one of Girder's about-face, in chapter xiii, when he hears that Ashton and Ravenswood are friends and thinks that Caleb might be able to help him get the position of cooper to the Queen's stores, which has just been left vacant owing to the death of Peter Puncheon.)

Scène xxii: Caleb, alone for a few moments, trembles at the thought of explaining all the ruses which he has used this day. *Scène* xxiii: Upon the entrance of Clara and Henri, he gives Henri the fifty crowns and then exits. *Scène* xxv: Henri tells Clara that since his estate has been lost, he must depart. She replies, singing the same melody, that he may possess more than he thinks. *Scène* xxv: Emmy and Caleb re-enter with the news that the whole clan has arrived to pay homage to Henri. *Scènes* xxvi–xxviii: The final ensemble is by Adam. Here is the principal melody, as it appears in the violins:

Example 8-3

Everyone sings "honneur" to Henri, even the Registrar, who has brought with him a marriage contract. Krik and Jaket are delighted to receive their coveted licenses. They all say that they have been authorized to do as they do by the proprietor of the château. Henri is dumbfounded. Finally Édouard arrives, with an explanation. It seems that the avaricious old solicitor has died intestate, and thus his next of kin, Édouard and Clara, have automatically inherited the vast estate which he had wrested from Henri. Édouard has ceded the château and land surrounding it to his sister, so that in marrying Henri she can give back to him what had been wrongfully taken from him. Henri is overjoyed. The opera ends with a reprise of the chorus:

> Honneur, honneur,
> A monseigneur!
> Pour le fêter chantons en chœur:
> Vive à jamais notre bon seigneur![9]

The opera is interesting because of its excellent depiction of a character who does not figure at all in *Lucia di Lammermoor.* Adam's Caleb does not have quite the tragic dignity that he has in the novel, but his genuine affection for Henri and his loyalty to the Douglas family are brought out convincingly throughout, especially in *scène* viii, when he learns from Clara that his young master is on his way home. Interesting too is that the opera's main event—Caleb's stealing of the roasted wild-fowl—is something that Scott, in a later edition of the novel, felt necessary to justify in a long footnote because of adverse criticism which the passage had received. The memorable incident does not occur in any of the other operas based on *The Bride,* but, as Hans Christian Andersen explains in his foreword to *Bruden fra Lammermoor* (see below), it would be out of place in a tragic opera—and all the other operas are tragic.

Le Nozze di Lammermoor

Le Nozze di Lammermoor was Michele Carafa's first venture into the realm of the Waverley Novels. Giuseppe Luigi Balochi wrote the libretto.[10] The première took place in Paris, on 12 December 1829, at the Royal Italian Theater. Whereas Carafa's later *Prison d'Édimbourg* (see Chapter 7) is outwardly in the form of an opéra comique and thus has long passages of spoken dialogue, *Le Nozze di Lammermoor* presumably has sung, cembalo-accompanied recitatives rather than spoken dialogue.[11] The cast of characters includes Lord William Ashton, Lady Ashton, Lucia, Elisa (young widow, friend of Lucia), Edgardo, "Colonel" Bucklaw, Caleb Balderston, Misia, Bidebent, and Donaldo (confidant and secretary to Lord William).[12] Donaldo has little resemblance to Scott's Lockhard, and Elisa has no resemblance besides her name to Alice, but the other characters are fairly close to their originals. (In the novel Lucy's brother Sholto holds the rank of colonel, not Bucklaw.)

The sombre opening measures of the opera bring to mind the opening of *Lucia di Lammermoor,* but unlike what we have in *Lucia* they lead into a formal overture. The restless A-theme of the sonata-allegro suggests the tragic events that will unfold:

Example 8-4

We hear it again in the last scene of the opera, at the point where Edgardo voices the belief that Lucia has betrayed him. The rather trite B-theme—

Example 8-5

—is the melody of the final part of the love-duet (Act I). Carafa's overture differs, then, from his overture to *La Prison d'Édimbourg,* which has no thematic connection with the opera proper. Neither has the slightest trace of Scottish folk music.

The curtain opens on a wild Scottish landscape, with the Tower of Wolfcrag (*sic*) to one side. As in many a Walter Scott opera, including *Lucia,* the opening number is a rousing chorus of hunters in 6/8 time. Donaldo and the hunters are in pursuit of a wild bull. As soon as they have departed, Caleb Balderston and Misia come out from the tower. Caleb is glad that they have gone, for if they had stopped to refresh themselves he could not have provided for them and thus could not have upheld the honor of the family. Misia tells him that he is a bit silly on the subject of "the honor of the family." The hunters return seeking Edgardo, who they say has valiantly saved a young lady from the wild bull. They call out "Edgardo! Edgardo!"—and receiving no answer they ride off to continue their search. (Musically and dramatically the number owes much to Rossini's chorus of hunters in *La Donna del Lago*.) In a passage of recitative Donaldo relates to Caleb the details of Edgardo's slaying of the bull. It seems that Lord William's life was also in danger, and Lord William is therefore anxious to locate Edgardo so that he can thank him in proper fashion. (One might note that Balochi has compressed Scott's story by amalgamating the events of chapter v (the slaying of the bull) with those of chapter ix (the hunt near Wolf's Crag).) When Donaldo and Caleb have departed, Edgardo enters in an agitated condition. In orchestra-accompanied recitative he tells of having sworn vengeance at the tomb of his father against the Ashtons; he realizes, however, that he is procrastinating because of his love for Lucia. In the aria that follows he implores the shades of his ancestors to blot out this culpable emotion and make the desire for revenge reign in his soul.

The scene changes to a Gothic room in Wolfcrag. On the wall over the main door is a portrait of Sir Maliso di Ravenswood, which bears the caption "L'istante attendo." (In the novel this portrait is at Ravenswood Castle. When Edgar visits Ravenswood in chapter xviii, young Henry Ashton is frightened at his resemblance to the portrait of his renowned ancestor, who had patiently bided his time and then slaughtered his enemies in the very castle which they had usurped from him.) Outside a fierce storm is raging. Suddenly Caleb and Misia hear knocking at the door. Caleb looks out and sees a charming young lady accompanied by a gentleman. The honor of the family demands that he let them in. They turn out to be Lord William and Lucia, who seek protection from the storm. When Lucia expresses fear of the tower's unfriendly aspect, her father tries to calm her. Edgardo enters and is both surprised and angry at seeing Lord William and Lucia at Wolfcrag. We now have an elaborate quintet: Edgardo giving vent to his fury, Lucia expressing her fear, William singing that love will calm Edgardo, and Caleb and Misia singing that Edgardo will not be able to contain the fury that agitates him. When Edgardo becomes extremely rude to Lord William, Lucia tries to pacify him and succeeds temporarily in doing so. (All this is based on chapter x, with the omission of Bucklaw's attempt to gain admission to the tower; Bucklaw is not introduced until later, and then not in the company of Craigengelt, who is omitted altogether from the dramatis personae.) In a passage of recitative based loosely on material from chapters xiv and xv, Lord William tries to convince Edgardo that he is not his enemy. He shows him certain papers as proof—but remarks *aside* that the party of Sir Athol (Scott's Marquis of A—) may triumph and that there may be a new inquiry into the legal dispute between the heir of Ravenswood and the Ashton family. When Lord William sees that Edgardo is convinced of his feigned good will, he invites him to come for a visit at Lammermoor.[13] He then sings an aria ("Di sospirata calma/O lieto ameno dì") in which he outwardly expresses his joy at the reconciliation, but in an *aside* praises himself for his political skill.

The scene changes to the grand park at Lammermoor, with the "fontana della Sirena" near by, and begins with a chorus of cavaliers, who sing in anticipation of Lady Ashton's return. (From here until the end of the act the libretto is based loosely on chapters xx–xxii.) Colonel Bucklaw enters and sings an aria in which he boasts of his good fortune; he has inherited a great deal of money from his late lamented aunt. When he and the cavaliers depart, Edgardo enters. He is agitated at being at Lammermoor, since he feels that he is forgetting his oath of vengeance. Just when he has convinced himself that he ought to leave, Lucia enters—and of course he stays. He tells her it is said that this place has always been fatal to the Ravenswoods, and he reminds her that it was here that he first saw her. (Note that the librettist has moved Scott's fountain from the forest to the castle grounds, but not much is made of it.) When he is again on the point of leaving, she tells him, for the first time, that she loves him. Departure now is out of the question. They pledge their troths, despite Lucia's momentary hesitation about doing so away from the altar. Edgardo solemnly breaks a ring (instead of a coin), giving half of it to her and keeping the other half for himself. As the duet ends, they both ecstatically express the hope that heaven will vouchsafe to favor their vows. (This meeting of Lucia and Edgardo is Carafa's equivalent of Donzetti's fountain-scene duet, which concludes the first act of *Lucia di Lammermoor*.)

The scene changes to a magnificent gallery in Ravenswood Castle. The chorus sings in celebration of the arrival of Lady Ashton, who soon enters along with Bucklaw, Donaldo, and others in her entourage. She sings a difficult, florid aria for contralto in which she tells of the victory that has come to her party. Her fearless, domineering personality is reflected in the orchestral accompaniment, which has the same rhythm Verdi was to use in his "Di quella pira":

Example 8-6

po - co av - ver - so il fa - to

Before leaving the stage for a few moments, she instructs Lord William to remain where he is until she returns, because she has something important to discuss with him. He suspects what it is—namely, that he has been to see Edgardo at Wolfcrag. In the meanwhile Bucklaw begins to suspect Lord William of trickery when he learns from Donaldo that Edgardo is a guest at the castle. Lady Ashton returns and severely upbraids Lord William for going to Wolfcrag. He replies that he did so in the best interests of their family and tries to prove his point by showing dispatches to her that refer to impending danger for their party. She is not convinced. She says furthermore she has heard that Edgardo is at the castle, and she wants him to leave immediately. William tries to pacify her, but to no avail. During most of their duet they argue about whether or not Edgardo may remain. The duet leads into the finale to the act. Bucklaw and Donaldo, who had left the stage for a few moments, re-enter— Donaldo announcing to Lady Ashton that Edgardo wants to offer homage to her. In high dudgeon she says that she will not receive him, but William countermands her desire and says that he may indeed enter. After a brief trio of Lady Ashton, Bucklaw, and Lord William, Donaldo leads Edgardo in, and in the quintet that ensues Lady Ashton becomes extremely angry. Suddenly Caleb bursts in (a departure from the novel) with an important message for Edgardo: his noble cousin Sir Athol has arrived at Wolfcrag and awaits him. Lady Ashton sarcastically tells Edgardo to fly to his cousin—to go ahead and betray his fatherland, his faith, his honor. Edgardo seethes with rage. As the chorus menacingly orders him to depart, Lucia and Elisa enter. Lucia announces to all present that she is Edgardo's fiancée (another departure from the novel). The ensemble soon develops into an elaborate octet with chorus, everyone giving vent to emotions appropriate to the situation. Afterwards the tempo changes from *andante* to *vivace*. Lady Ashton asks Edgardo how he could have dared to hope that she, Lucia's mother, would consent to such a union. Edgardo replies that Lucia has sworn an oath. Lucia is agitated; indeed, all are. The act ends in another huge ensemble, all singing that the air holds nothing but horrible cries of rage and dolor. (Lady Ashton's homecoming, along with its immediate aftermath, is one of the most memorable scenes of the novel; it is the turning point in the plot; it obviously is perfect source material for a typical early nineteenth-century

Italian operatic finale, as Balochi and Carafa have proven. Yet, interestingly, it does not figure at all in Donizetti's masterpiece.)

There is an interval of two months between the first and second acts. A note in the libretto assures us that this small infraction of theatrical rules by which the librettist was able to preserve the principal situations of the novel does not in any way harm the unity of action. The curtain rises on the burial-ground of the Ravenswood family. Caleb, Misia, and a chorus of retainers tell the shade of Sir Allano, Edgardo's late father, to rest in peace. They assure him that the sword of vengeance is suspended above the heads of his enemies. (There is no parallel to this in the novel, but it was no doubt suggested by the account of Allan Lord Ravenswood's funeral, ch. ii.) Bidebent, the Presbyterian minister, enters from his nearby house. He deplores the secret rites for Sir Allano because of the hate evident in the words of the retainers. He pleads with all of them to end their culpable fury. Then, in a short passage of recitative, he asks Caleb whether he had had word from his master. Caleb's answer is No. Bidebent replies that he has himself sent a message to Edgardo and is sure he has received it, yet Edgardo has not responded. He implores Caleb to let him know as soon as Edgardo has returned. (This duologue, which is not in the vocal score, has no exact parallel in the novel.) Alone on stage for a few moments, Caleb wonders why Edgardo has not arrived in time to commemorate the anniversary of his father's death. Suddenly he does arrive, and Caleb is beside himself with bliss. Edgardo, however, is in a doleful mood; he tells Caleb that he must return to Ravenswood Castle. Horrified, Caleb asks him if he has not perhaps forgotten the old prophecy:

"Dè Ravenswood se l'ultimo
Inclito augusto Erede
Nell'usurpata sede
Incauto inoltra il piè,
Feral sterile vincolo
Ei quivi stringerà,
E l'almo augusto stipite
Seco si spengerà."

(Notice that this version of the prophecy does not specify that the last lord will die in the Kelpie's flow.) Edgardo replies that one cannot appease the fury of inexorable destiny. In the remainder of the duet he sings that his spirit loses its way, all his efforts are futile, nothing can save him, an invincible power draws him despite himself into an abyss, nothing equals his despair and bad luck; Caleb's words are more or less the same. (This is one of the most effective numbers in the opera. It is based mainly on a conversation between Edgar and Caleb in chapter xviii, which, incidentally, takes place *before* Edgar's first visit to Ravenswood, i.e. the visit which Balochi and Carafa have dramatized in Act I. It may also owe something to the unforgettable parting of Edgar and Caleb in the last chapter of the novel.)

The scene changes to a garden at Ravenswood Castle. Lucia is upset that her lover has not returned. In a *romanza* she calls on sweet hope to descend to her from heaven. Afterwards, in recitative, Elisa informs her that she has no news of Edgardo; she has seen Caleb, who has told her that he does not know what has become of his master. Lucia is afraid that he has died. Elisa tells her that there is a possibility that his letters have been intercepted. Lucia replies that she entrusted her last letter to the minister, who sent it by a faithful messenger (as in the novel). Bidebent enters. He tells Lucia that Edgardo has not responded to the letter, that the allotted time having expired she can no longer oppose marriage to Bucklaw, and furthermore that rumor has it Edgardo has married a young French lady of illustrious family. "O Dio!" Lucia exclaims. Bidebent advises her to respect the will of heaven. Alone on stage Lucia sings a recitative and aria. In the former she expresses her dismay at Edgardo's faithlessness; her spirit loses its way; she realizes that the altar is being prepared for her marriage to Bucklaw. She then mentions poison which one Alisia has left her as a means of ending her difficulties. It seems that Alisia had been employed by Lady Ashton to watch over Lucia, and to spy on her, but was then suddenly dismissed. To get revenge on Lady Ashton she has left Lucia a vial of poison. (This complication is suggested by Ailsie Gourlay's machinations, chapter xxxi, but in the novel no poison is involved.) In the aria Lucia declares that she will never become the spouse of another man; she will not betray her oath to Edgardo. While she is singing, cavaliers and ladies enter and announce to her that Bucklaw has come. They wonder why she is so sad.

The scene moves to a room in the castle. Bucklaw tells Lord William that he is sick and tired of waiting for a response from Edgardo. He wants to have the marriage contract signed that very day. Moreover, he blames Lord William for the delay. As for Edgardo's shooting of the wild bull, Bucklaw says that the shot was actually intended for William, but a billy-goat got in the way and thus William was saved. (Cf. Lady Ashton's words in the novel, chapter xxii: "Saved your life! I have heard of that story . . . the Lord Keeper was scared by a dun cow, and he takes the young fellow who killed her for Guy of Warwick—any butcher from Haddington may soon have an equal claim on your hospitality.") In the ensuing duet, which is not an especially interesting number, Bucklaw insists on having the marriage contract drawn up, and Lord William as always gives in, thinking he is acting diplomatically rather than showing the weakness of his personality. The duet is followed by a short passage of recitative in which Lady Ashton also upbraids William for unduly postponing the drawing-up of the marriage contract. She then encounters Lucia and reminds her that the agreed-upon time has expired without any reply from Edgardo and that it seems Edgardo has married abroad anyway. In an elaborate, florid duet Lucia tells her mother that she will succumb to inexorable destiny, but she indicates *aside* that she will keep her oath to Edgardo even if she must commit suicide. Lady Ashton pretends to offer consolation, but she gloats *aside* over her triumph.

For the finale the scene changes to a grand salon in the castle. It begins with fine festive music in the orchestra, and soon a chorus of cavaliers and ladies sing in joyful anticipation of the occasion. They greet Bucklaw warmly when he enters, in the company of Lord William, Bidebent, Donaldo, and a notary. (In the novel there are no well-wishers at the signing of the contract.) Lucia then enters, in the company of her mother and Elisa. She is so emotionally upset that she does not realize when Bucklaw addresses her. He tells her that if she does not want him she must speak freely. She replies that she will obey her mother. After Bidebent has pronounced a few words appropriate to the occasion and all have prayed for God's blessing on the young couple, the principal personages approach the grand table for the final signing. Lord William signs, then Lady Ashton (rather than Sholto), then Bucklaw. When Lucia's turn comes, she signs without first dipping the pen in the ink. Lady Ashton does this for her and returns the pen to her. She signs, singing *aside* to Elisa, "Ah! mancando il cor mi va!" At this moment Edgardo forces his way into the salon. A large ensemble develops (Lucia, Elisa, Lady Ashton, Edgardo, Bucklaw, Lord William, Bidebent, and the chorus, including Donaldo), all singing *aside* words appropriate to the situation. (This is Carafa's equivalent of Donizetti's famous Sextet.) Afterwards Bucklaw cries out for vengeance. Edgardo holds up a letter and tries to find out whether Lucia wrote it of her own free will. (In the opera the letter's contents are not made explicit; Scott's Lucy questioned the wisdom of her relationship with Edgar in this letter.) Bidebent tries to calm things down. It is agreed that Edgardo may speak with Lucia in the presence of only Bidebent and Lady Ashton. Accordingly, everyone exits except these four principals. At first Lucia is silent when Edgardo addresses her, but finally, *"con sentimento di dolore,"* she sings, "Mia madre! mia madre!" Both Lady Ashton and Bidebent insist that Lucia's decision was not forced upon her. When they show Edgardo the signed contract, he believes that Lucia has betrayed him. He takes from his pocket their signed promise of marriage and the half of the broken ring from a ribbon around his neck, and he places both on the table, saying in bitter irony that he renders them back to her:

> Ecco a te i pegni rendo
> D'un puro eterno amore...
> Forse al secondo vincolo
> Il tuo barbaro core
> Più fido almen sarà.

We hear in the orchestral accompaniment the restless minor theme of the overture (see Example 8-4). Lucia says that she deserves his pity, but he demands her half of the ring. As in the novel, he is astonished when he sees that she still wears it next to her heart.

Up to this point the finale has followed Scott's events of chapters xxxii –xxxiii rather closely. But now comes a radical departure: Lucia suddenly announces that she has taken poison! Lady Ashton, Edgardo, and Bidebent are thunderstruck. Lady Ashton cries out for help. In a few seconds Elisa, Donaldo, Bucklaw, Lord William, and even Caleb, together with the numerous cavaliers, ladies, and servants, are back on stage. Addressing her mother, Lucia explains that the poison was given to her by Alisia. Edgardo furiously upbraids Lady Ashton, and Bucklaw challenges him to a duel. They are about to rush out to fight when Lucia cries out for both of them to stop. She tells Bucklaw that she could never have made him happy, and she tells Edgardo that she has ever remained faithful to him. She implores them both to live in peace. Everyone present is deeply moved by her nobility of character. She slowly succumbs to the poison, pressing Edgardo's hand to her heart: "Addio! ah! senti.../ Del mio cor gli estremi palpiti.../ Per te solo... io moro... ahimè!..." Unable to contain his grief, Edgardo stabs himself and falls down next to her. The remaining principals and the chorus solemnly sing, "O funesto orrendo evento!/O spectacolo d'orror!" and the curtain falls.

Following the signing of the contract there is no marriage night during which Lucia stabs Bucklaw; he is alive and well at the end and sings in the final brief ensemble. There is no mad scene. Edgardo neither meets death in the quicksand near Wolf's Crag nor stabs himself fatally at the burial-ground of his ancestors. Thus the ending of *Le Nozze di Lammermoor* differs markedly from the novel and from Donizetti as well. Although Caleb Balderston is retained, he is not at all the dominant figure that he is in Adam's opera, nor the tragi-comic old retainer of the novel (Balochi and Carafa virtually do away with the comic side of his personality). Despite the many changes, a great deal of the novel is retained—more of it than in any other *Bride of Lammermoor* opera except Andersen and Bredal's *Bruden fra Lammermoor*. There are no Scottish folk melodies anywhere in the score.

Rieschi's *La Fidanzata di Lammermoor*

Luigi Rieschi's *Fidanzata di Lammermoor*, with words by Calisto Bassi (who did the libretto for Rossini's *William Tell* and who translated into Italian Royer and Vaëz's libretto for the Rossini pastiche *Robert Bruce*), was first performed in Trieste, in the autumn of 1831. The libretto was published (by Michele Weis),[14] but the score apparently not. I have not been able to find any trace whatever of the music.[15] The same libretto was set also to music by Giuseppe Bornaccini and performed in Venice, at the Teatro di Apollo, in the autumn of 1833. It bears the title *Ida,* after the heroine in Bassi's version of the story.[16] I do not know whether the complete score still exists. One printed excerpt, an aria for Ida, can be found in the Biblioteca del Conservatorio "Giuseppe Verdi."[17] A revised version of Rieschi's work entitled *Ida di Danimarca* was presented as if it were a new opera in Milan, at the Carcano, in the summer of 1854. It seems not to have been successful.[18] My discussion in the following paragraphs is based on the libretto to *La Fidanzata di Lammermoor*, which in conclusion I compare and contrast with the revised libretto, *Ida di Danimarca*. I have not seen any of Rieschi's music.

The cast of characters includes only six principals: Guglielmo Ashton, Ida (Scott's Lucy), Edgardo, Lord Hayston di Bucklaw, Gualtiero (friend of Guglielmo; has little resemblance to Scott's Lockhard), and Alina (friend of Ida; has no resemblance to Alice).[19] *Scena* i: The curtain rises, revealing a pleasant spot in the vicinity of Ravenswood Castle. We see the ruins of a Gothic building which shelters the "Fontana della Sirena." It is dawn. As often in Walter Scott operas, the first number is a chorus of hunters ("Campo ai veltri"), after which Guglielmo expresses to Gualtiero his displeasure at the relationship between Ida and Edgardo. Guglielmo says that he will pretend to be friendly with Edgardo, but in reality he will seek vengeance. Instead of killing him outright, he will try to work things out in such a way that he will die from the palpitations of love. *Scena* ii: When they have departed, Edgardo enters. In a pensive mood he observes that this is the very place where he first became attached to Ida. He realizes the moral dilemma he is in: he ought to hate her whom he loves. Guglielmo re-enters and pretends to extend friendship to Edgardo, who, however, is suspicious. In the ensuing duet Edgardo sings of having sworn at the deathbed of his father to kill Guglielmo, yet he finds himself unable to do so. When Edgardo does not respond to Guglielmo's specious words, Guglielmo suddenly announces that he intends to join Ida to another man in matrimony later that very day. In the final part of the duet Edgardo sings of his anger and fury, while Guglielmo declares that heaven will shackle Edgardo with a long life of remorse. *Scena* iii: Having killed a stag, the hunters return. They sing a drinking song in celebration of joy and pleasure. Their vigorous life in the forest may be uncomfortable and even brief, but it is preferable to the life of the wealthy man who has won his fortune through dishonesty and fraud. They depart, singing. *Scena* iv: Guglielmo tells Gualtiero of his encounter with Edgardo, and he begins to plan the vengeance which he will take. He will send a message to Bucklaw, who does not live far away. He believes that Ida's large dowry will make him an eager bridegroom, even though he has not heretofore shown any especial interest in her. Gualtiero pointedly observes that if Ida loves Edgardo, a forced marriage to another man will cause her to suffer. Guglielmo replies that for all he cares she may die, as long as he can have his revenge. (Scott's William Ashton is also a man of intrigue, but, unlike Guglielmo, he is mild in temperament and easily manipulated by people having more forceful personalities. Bassi's ruthless Guglielmo Ashton obviously embodies much of the personality of Scott's Lady Asthon, who is not included in the dramatis personae.)

Scena v: We have now a chorus of maidens ("È la luce il don più vago"), after which Ida, terribly depressed in spirit, confides to Alina in an aria ("Sognai ch'errante e profuga") a strange dream which she has had. She dreamt that she was about to marry. Edgardo smiled on her; the sacred incense burned; the altar was beflowered. But suddenly things changed. She beheld a man who for her sake had been grievously wounded lying on the ground, dying, and screaming desperately. When he threw into her face the blood that he had collected in his hands, she woke up in terror, but in her memory the dying man and his blood are ever present. Alina tries to pacify her, but in vain. (The dream foreshadows the ending of the opera. It was no doubt suggested by Scott's account of the legend of the fountain, but the details are quite different.) *Scena* vi: Edgardo enters, notices Ida, meditates on his love for her, and is soon seen by her. Unbeknownst to either of them, Guglielmo and Gualtiero are hiding in the bushes, watching their actions and eavesdropping on their duet (a significant departure from the novel). Edgardo tells her that this is the last time he can see her, for he must leave at once. She implores him to stay. He expresses the wish that he might have known her in another age, when he would not have been driven by the desire to kill her father. She then declares in no uncertain terms her love for him. He in turn eloquently expresses his love for her, but he observes also that the place they are at has always been unlucky to his ancestors. When he speaks of vengeance again, she tells him to kill her along with her father; let him rip open her breast with the sword, and he will see how every fibre of her being palpitates with love for him. They settle their agitations in the remainder of the duet, and then Edgardo breaks a coin in two, giving half to her and telling her it is to be a pledge of eternal and firm faith. He requests that she return it to him if she should ever change lovers. She says she would sooner die than betray him. *Scena* vii: Gualtiero reveals himself and tells Ida that her father is calling for her. Edgardo is reluctant to accompany her. As they are about to part, their eyes meet, and drawn by like sentiments they reunite in duet, singing, "Ogni affanno ed ogni brama/Teco il cor dividerà." *Scena* viii: When the lovers have departed, Guglielmo comes out from hiding and tells Gualtiero that necessity forced him to court Edgardo's favor when Edgardo's fortune was high. Subsequently he discovered that he was an enemy to the king. He broke off from him at once, and shortly thereafter Edgardo and his faction lost their power. Guglielmo considers Edgardo's wanting Ida another great outrage. He assures Gualtiero that Bucklaw will marry her.

Scena ix: The action now moves to a gallery of the castle, where Ida and Edgardo are deep in conversation. Edgardo looks at a portrait of his father, who seems to stare threateningly at him in reminder of his oath. (In the novel the portrait is that of Edgardo's thirteenth-century ancestor, Malisius de Ravenswood. Young Henry Ashton notices Edgar's likeness to

the portrait and is frightened; see chapter xviii.) Edgardo and Ida rede-
clare their love for one another. *Scena* x: Guglielmo comes in, again
pretending friendship. He admits that Bucklaw is on his way to the castle
to marry Ida. He says that he had really wanted Ida to marry Edgardo, but
Edgardo had not been willing—and there is some truth in this contention,
Edgardo having refused Guglielmo's overtures at an earlier time because
of the oath he swore at his father's tomb. Edgardo and Ida kneel at
Guglielmo's feet and express their love for one another. He pretends to be
both moved and grieved at their sadness. Unfortunately, he says, Ida is
tied to Bucklaw by an oath, which if broken would render her infamous.
But he has a solution—flight. When Edgardo expresses concern for his
honor, Guglielmo replies, "L'onor?... che monta!/Te con lei felice io
bramo." Suddenly from *within* shouts of "Viva! viva!" are heard. *Scena* xi:
Gualtiero bursts in with the news that Bucklaw is now arriving. Ida and
Edgardo, who are about to flee at Guglielmo's hypocritical instigation,
run into Bucklaw as he enters. Guglielmo greets the bridegroom warmly
and thereby angers Edgardo, who reminds him that he has just promised
Ida to him. A large ensemble commences: Guglielmo asking Edgardo to
restrain his fury for Ida's sake; Ida asking him to restrain his fury;
Edgardo saying that he *will* restrain himself for her sake; Bucklaw lamenting that if she is taken from him (Bucklaw) his days will be sorrowful;
Gualtiero observing that Bucklaw indeed will live in sorrow if he does not
get Ida; and Alina imploring heaven to recompense Edgardo for his faith.
Suddenly Guglielmo peremptorily orders Edgardo to depart from the
castle. (This is no doubt suggested by Lady Ashton's similar action against
Edgar when she arrives home after a long absence and finds him there as a
guest and suitor; see chapter xxii.) In the final sextet Ida and Edgardo
sing of their anguish; Guglielmo, of the joy he has in hurting Edgardo;
Bucklaw, of his rising hopes; Alina, of Ida's plight; Gualtiero, that the
impious one (meaning Edgardo) will have no hope of calm; and the
chorus expresses the hope that discord may remove its terrifying torch.

The first half of the second act takes place in an "appartamento
superiore" of the castle. *Scena* i: Guglielmo, in a pensive mood, is seated
at a table. He asks Gualtiero to go find Edgardo and bring him back,
because he wants to speak with him again. He feels some degree of
revulsion at what he must do, since it is obvious to him that Ida adores
Edgardo, but necessity demands it. He asks himself why he hates Edgardo
so intensely, and he must admit that he has no good reason (note that this
contradicts what he said in I. viii). *Scena* ii: Ida enters. In an elaborate duet
Guglielmo convinces her that Bucklaw was an accomplice in the murder
of Edgardo's father, in which he himself had a part, and if she should
reject Bucklaw he might bring everything out into the open and thereby
ruin both father and daughter. He wants her to forget Edgardo. At first
she says that the sacrifice is too great, but ultimately she gives in. She is
terribly depressed. *Scena* iii: Back in the gallery of Act I, Edgardo won-

ders why Guglielmo has sent for him. *Scena* iv: Ida and Guglielmo come in. Guglielmo deceitfully tells Edgardo that even though he seems to favor Bucklaw, in reality he does not. However, before Edgardo can marry Ida, he must first undergo a period of exile. Edgardo wonders (with good reason) whether or not Guglielmo is telling the truth. When Ida begins to cry, Edgardo is made to believe that her tears are due to the necessary absence he must undergo. In an aria he declares that upon his return he will love her even more, if being away from her does not kill him. The situation is dramatically ironic, since Ida and we in the audience are aware of Guglielmo's trickery. *Scena* v: The chorus announces that Bucklaw is arriving for the wedding. Guglielmo convinces Edgardo that he must depart, telling him that his presence might botch up complicated plans. Edgardo apparently does not believe that Bucklaw will really marry Ida, after what Guglielmo has just told him. Edgardo and Ida take tearful leave of one another. Even Guglielmo says that he feels the weight of her suffering on his own heart.[20]

In the first half of Act III the setting is once more the "appartamento superiore." *Scena* i: Everyone is congregated for the signing of the marriage contract, and the chorus sings of the joy of the occasion. As the concerned personages sit at the table and prepare to sign, Alina fixes her eyes on the door, as if she were awaiting someone. Bucklaw notices Ida's extreme dejection and says something about it to Guglielmo. As Ida is in the very act of signing, a commotion is heard from *without*. *Scena* ii: Edgardo bursts in, sees Ida with pen in hand, and cries out "T'arresta!" Furious that Edgardo has come, Guglielmo gives an order for him to be dragged forcibly from the room. At this Edgardo whips out a dagger and a pistol and threatens immediate death to anyone who lays hands on him. A large ensemble involving Ida, Alina, Edgardo, Guglielmo, Bucklaw, and the chorus then begins with the words "Oh! qual gelo al cor me piomba!" All express emotions appropriate to the situation. (This is Bassi and Rieschi's equivalent of Donizetti's Sextet.) After the ensemble Edgardo asks Ida whether she has indeed betrayed him. At first speechless, she finally admits that she has signed the contract. Edgardo is beside himself with rage. He demands the pledge of their faith (i.e. the broken coin) which she is still wearing. Guglielmo (assuming a function of Scott's Lady Ashton) assists her in removing it and hands it over to Edgardo. When Ida begs for his pity, he scorns her in the utmost rage. Again Guglielmo orders Edgardo out. He says he will leave, but adds the wish that the wedding may surge with a thousand pains. There is another large ensemble, after which Ida is led out by Guglielmo and Bucklaw, who look at Edgardo with an air of triumph. Alina holds him back to speak with him in private. *Scena* iii: Alina tells Edgardo that as soon as she learned that there would be a forced wedding, she sent word to him to make him cognizant of it; unfortunately she found herself unable to inform Ida of what she had done, because after Edgardo had departed (at the end of Act

II), Guglielmo never left Ida's side. Alina's words are in vain. Edgardo still believes that Ida has betrayed him and swears vengeance.

The remainder of the opera takes place in a beautifully adorned and illuminated salon of the castle. A staircase leads up to a loge and other rooms. *Scena* iv: A full chorus is on stage, singing in celebration of the wedding of Ida and Bucklaw. Suddenly a prolonged groan is heard from one of the upper rooms. In a few moments Ida appears, holding a bloody dagger in her hands. It is obvious to all that she is mentally deranged. *Scena* v: She slowly descends the stairs. In broken phrases she asks her father to go upstairs and find out whether Bucklaw is still alive. He does so, soon returning with the news that Bucklaw is dead. Ida seems relieved. She sings that now Edgardo will be her husband, but when her mind wanders to the subject of their love-token (see *scena* ii) she becomes distressed, realizing that she no longer has it. *Scena ultima;* Edgardo bursts in, not knowing, of course, what has just occurred. He has come, he says, to avenge himself and then die. Ida tells him that the monster who took her from him is dead—and that she herself killed him! Everyone present is astonished. She sings to Edgardo of the fountain which brought sorrowful memories to him and asks whether it still makes him sad, now that it smiles beneficently at their love. The chorus laments her derangement, and Edgardo blames Guglielmo for what has happened. When Ida again becomes aware of her misery, Guglielmo tries to console her, but she will not allow him to approach her inasmuch as she is tainted with crime. Yet, she says, heaven has given her a just penalty: she has taken poison. She asks her father and Edgardo to forgive her and to live henceforth in peace with one another. They agree to do so. "Ah!..." she replies, "son... felice... ancor./Edgardo.... io.... mo.... ro...." She dies. Edgardo swoons over her lifeless body, Guglielmo is grief-stricken, and the chorus sings "Ahi!... qual terror!!—" as the curtain falls.

Ida's suicide by means of poison probably owes something to *Le Nozze di Lammermoor*. Also, her dying wish that Edgardo and her father be reconciled reminds one of the similar wish of Carafa's Lucia with respect to Edgardo and Bucklaw. Ida's stabbing of Bucklaw on her wedding night comes from Scott, but unlike what we have in the novel the stabbing is fatal (as it is in Donizetti). Bassi and Rieschi's *Fidanzata* is the first *Bride of Lammermoor* opera to have a mad scene, which is suggested by the discovery of Lucy Ashton, in a deranged state of mind, hiding in a corner of the chimney in the room where she stabbed Bucklaw—she does not descend the stairs in the novel and display her madness before the wedding guests. Interestingly, Edgardo is apparently alive at the end, although unconscious. With the omission of Caleb Balderston, Bassi completely does away with the comic aspect of the story. Guglielmo takes on much of Lady Ashton's personality and performs some of the functions which Scott assigns to her. He also resembles Lucy's older brother, Sholto. His refined, subtle way of getting revenge on Edgardo by pretending friendship and then doublecrossing him, his deepseated hatred for him, and his disregard for his daughter's feelings make him a quite different person from weak-willed, vacillating William Ashton of the novel and of *Le Nozze di Lammermoor*. Despite Bassi's drastic reduction in the number of characters, the plot seems unduly complicated and is sometimes contradictory. The events prior to the time of the opera which caused the enmity between Edgardo and Guglielmo are not well explained. The forcing of Scott's narrative to conform to the unities of time and place adds to, rather than detracts from, the confusion, and it makes some of the incidents seem rather incredible.

Some of these and other structural problems have been partially solved in the revised version, *Ida di Danimarca*. As the title indicates, the setting has been moved from Scotland to Denmark. The names of the six principals are now Gustavo Jutland (Guglielmo Ashton); Ida; Olvardo, sere di Nordemberg (Edgardo); Arturo, conte di Alsen (Bucklaw); Roggiero (Gualtiero); and Alvina (Alina).[21] *Ida* is divided into four acts rather than three. Several *scenae* are abridged in comparison with their counterparts in *Fidanzata*, and several are altered; three are omitted. I can most clearly show what has happened in an annotated table:[22]

Ida I.i = *Fidanzata* I.i.

I.ii corresponds to *Fidanzata* I.ii, but at the beginning and ending of the *scena* the words to the duet (Olvardo and Gustavo) differ slightly and insignificantly.

I.iii = *Fidanzata* I.iii.

Fidanzata I.iv has no counterpart in *Ida*.

Ida II.i corresponds to *Fidanzata* I.v, but Ida's account of her nightmare has been replaced with a general account on her part of her inability to be joyful.

II.ii corresponds to *Fidanzata* I.vi, but cut here and there.

II.iii = *Fidanzata* I.vii.

II.iv corresponds to *Fidanzata* I.viii, but much cut. In *Fidanzata* Guglielmo explains his reasons for not liking Edgardo; these remarks contradict what he says in *Fidanzata* II.i. The contradiction has perhaps intentionally been removed.

II.v = *Fidanzata* I.ix.

II.vi corresponds to *Fidanzata* I.x, but with a cut at the end.

II.vii = *Fidanzata* I.xi.

II.viii corresponds to *Fidanzata* I.xii, but with the recitative portions somewhat cut.

Ida III.i = *Fidanzata* II.iii.

III.ii corresponds roughly to *Fidanzata* II.iv, but without Ida.

III.iii corresponds roughly to *Fidanzata* II.v, but without Ida.

III.iv corresponds roughly to *Fidanzata* II.i –ii, with the final duet at the end changed. In *Ida* this scene between father and daughter comes *after* the father has gotten rid of the lover. Why the scenes of *Fidanzata* have been rearranged, and why Ida is omitted from two scenes in which she appears in *Fidanzata* are questions not easily answered. I prefer the dramatically ironic situation in the earlier version, with Ida on stage fully realizing that her father is deceiving Edgardo and being powerless to do anything about it, but perhaps this kind of thing is unconvincing in an operatic plot because it is too complicated. Also, the fact that she allows her father to deceive Edgardo might be looked on by some as damaging to her character. Moreover, since she cries during the trio, one wonders why Edgardo does not sense that something is rotten in Lammermoor. The complicated relationship between characters is done away with in *Ida*. As a final note, Guglielmo's words in *Fidanzata* II.i to the effect that he has no good reason for hating Edgardo are cut. I have already observed that these words are unconvincing and tend to contradict what Guglielmo said earlier, in I.viii.

III.v   is a *scena* for Alvina alone, which has no exact counterpart in *Fidanzata*. It takes the place of *Fidanzata* III.iii (the *scena* for Alina and Edgardo immediately following the big *scena* in which Edgardo discovers Ida's supposed faithlessness). In *Ida* III.v Alvina hopes that her messenger reaches Olvardo so that he will return and do something about the marriage which Ida is being forced into. This short *scena* makes possible the omission of anti-climactic *Fidanzata* III.iii.

III.vi   =   *Fidanzata* III.i.

III.vii   =   *Fidanzata* III.ii.

        Fidanzata III.iii is omitted from *Ida;* cf. *Ida* III.v.

Ida IV.i   =   *Fidanzata* III.iv.

IV.ii   corresponds to *Fidanzata* III.v, with a few minor changes, the main one being that Ida's father does not go up and actually investigate what has happened to Arturo (Bucklaw) and then come back with the news that he is dead. Apparently it is assumed that Arturo is dead from what Ida says. The action in the earlier opera is really not necessary; moreover, it might prove cumbersome for the father to run all the way up the stairs, go into the bridal chamber, and return with the bad news—all this in a very short time.

IV.iii   corresponds with the *scena ultima* of *Fidanzata*, with a few omissions. The lines in which Ida comes out and says that she killed Bucklaw are omitted, perhaps because what has happened is self-evident. Also omitted is her final wish to have her father and lover reconciled, perhaps because it is unconvincing, too sentimental, and a bit ludicrous.

The appended extra *scena* for Bucklaw in *Fidanzata* is omitted from *Ida*.

Bruden fra Lammermoor

Bruden fra Lammermoor was first performed on 5 May 1832, in Copenhagen. The lengthy text, which has much spoken dialogue, is the work of Hans Christian Andersen, and the music is by the Danish composer, Ivar Frederik Bredal. Andersen categorizes the work as "et romantisk Syngestykke," to borrow a phrase from his foreword to the separately printed text.[23] Although several individual musical numbers were published with piano or guitar accompaniment,[24] there is no complete vocal score. The orchestral score exists only in manuscript.[25] The opera seems to have had a fairly satisfactory critical reception,[26] but it was not produced outside Denmark. Nor was it ever revived, to my knowledge.

The overture contains material heard later, such as this, the melody of Edgar's *romance* ("Du som kjender hver en Tanke"):[27]

Example 8-7

More important to the musical structure of the opera is a familiar Scottish tune:

Example 8-8

All of us know this as "Charlie Is My Darling."[28] We hear it again in Act I, sung by the witch Ailsie and beginning with the words "Et Dyb og dog Guds Himmel"; in the second stanza the last eight measures bear ominous words:

Naar sidste Laird til Ravenswood

Faaer sig en Død til Brud,
Den Havfrue fanger ham paa Stand
I Strandens Flyvesand.[29]

Sometimes sung and sometimes in the orchestra, this half of the tune recurs, functioning as a leitmotiv having to do with Edgar's ultimate fate. The following restless passage from the overture—

Example 8-9

—is heard again in Act I, when the imminent storm forces Edgar to offer hospitality to Lucie and Sir William (see below).

The first scene of Act I takes place in the forest near Wolf's Crag and opens in predictable fashion, with a chorus of hunters ("Glade Lyst! hør Hornet toner!"). This is followed by a "Hexesang" for Annie and Ailsie. For some reason Andersen and Bredal omit Maggie, the third member of Scott's trio of beldams, but their retention of even two makes *Bruden* unique among the operas based on *The Bride of Lammermoor*. (Ailsie, or rather Alisia, is *mentioned* by Lucia in *Le Nozze di Lammermoor*, but she does not appear as a character.) After the "Hexesang" there is a reprise of the chorus of hunters. When the hunters have departed, Annie and Ailsie discuss in spoken dialogue the Ravenswood family and in particular the funeral of the old laird, Edgar's father. (The conversation has no exact parallel in the novel. Some of it is drawn from the conversations of Annie, Ailsie, and Maggie as they observe first Lucy's wedding (chapter xxxiii) and shortly thereafter her funeral (chapter xxxiv), but most of it is based on Scott's description of the former laird's funeral in chapter ii, with the insolent attempt on the part of the established Presbytery to stop the Scottish Episcopal ceremony and Edgar's vowing vengeance on Sir William Ashton, who issued the warrant that empowered the officers of the law to act as they did.) When the two old women have gone, Edgar enters. In an opening recitative he expresses the desire for revenge, but in the ensuing cavatina he becomes pensive and broods on the grievous misfortune that has befallen his family:

Example 8-10

Man - dens dy - be bit - tre Sorg   knu - ste al - le Bar - nets Drøm - me; i Ru -

i - ner staaer min Borg,   ved det bar - ske Nord-havs Strøm - me.

In the final part of the aria (the cabaletta) his thoughts again turn to revenge. Hearing cries for help, he looks into the wings and sees a young lady and an older man threatened by a wild beast with instant death. He quickly raises his weapon, takes aim, shoots, and kills the beast. Lord Ashton enters, holding Lucie in his arms, and asks the young man for assistance. Just as she begins to revive, a storm bursts forth. Not realizing who their savior is, father and daughter ask for his hospitality. He then announces that he is a Ravenswood. "O milde Gud!" they exclaim, but the storm admits of no further delay. With mixed feelings of pity, hatred, and revenge, Edgar leads his sworn enemies to shelter. (In constructing this part of the scene Andersen has amalgamated two separate incidents of the novel: Edgar's slaying of the bull (chapter v) and the hunt that is interrupted by a storm (chapter ix), forcing Lucy and her father to seek shelter and hospitality at Wolf's Crag; cf. Balochi's similar technique in *Le Nozze di Lammermoor*.)—The scene now moves to the common room of an inn (the Tod's Den of the novel). Bucklaw and Craigengelt are discussing Ravenswood and speculating on what might be the outcome of his encounter with Ashton. With few changes the dialogue is a rendition in Danish blank verse of Scott's dialogue in the first half of chapter vi. Then comes a departure from the novel: Annie and Ailsie come in and inform the two men that Edgar of Ravenswood is entertaining Lord Ashton and his daughter at Wolf's Crag. They tell about Edgar's having saved the Ashtons from the wild beast and observe that he might have taken advantage of the situation and gotten his revenge. They then tell the old story of the mysterious maiden of the fountain and her Ravenswood lover (which Scott relates in chapter v), and immediately afterwards they sing their song that alludes to the fate that will befall the last Laird of Ravenswood (see above). Suddenly hearing the hunters *without,* Bucklaw cannot resist the temptation to join them. (In the novel he is hiding at Wolf's Crag and languishing in boredom when he hears the sounds of a hunt.) Before leaving, however, he has just time for a long aria. Craigengelt has urged him to stay under cover, but he is young, and he explains in the recitative that he cannot while away his whole life in hiding. In the aria he asks what can the heart of youth fear. "He, he, he, he!" cackle Annie and Ailsie; "En lystig Unger-Svend!"—The scene changes again, this time to Wolf's Crag. It opens with a duet in which Caleb and Mysie sing about the fierce storm that is raging. Then, in spoken dialogue, they discuss the fallen fortune of the Ravenswood family. When Caleb becomes aware that Edgar is returning with guests, he is terribly flustered, because he knows that there is virtually no provision on hand. As the three come in from the storm, Caleb, in true form, apologizes for the absence of the imaginary other servants, who he says have gone to witness the hunt. The finale begins with Caleb singing of the storm's having destroyed the plates and glasses and food. Lucy, Edgar, and Ashton express emotions appropriate to the strange situation in which they find themselves. During the course of the finale the scene shifts to outside the tower. We hear again the chorus of hunters. Bucklaw is among them, and they all seek shelter from the storm. Caleb, however, will not admit them, and the act ends as they clamorously express their anger and frustration. (The two scenes at Wolf's Crag are based on the events of chapters x–xi.)

Act II begins outside an inn, where Craigengelt and Bucklaw are sitting with a group of hunters. Bucklaw tells his friend of being turned away from Wolf's Crag. Then, as they discuss the feasibility of his fighting a duel with Edgar, the dialogue is a near word-for-word translation into Danish prose of Scott's dialogue in chapter xxi. (In the novel, however, the setting is at Girnington, some time after Lady Girnington's timely demise and Bucklaw's consequent good fortune.) Presently a messenger arrives with a letter for Bucklaw from London which indicates that Turntip (Scott's "old driveller Turntippet") is dead and thus Bucklaw's inheritance of his late aunt's (in the novel, great-aunt's) estate is certain. Joyfully he sings a song about money ("Penge, Penge!"), and the hunters congratulate him. At the end of the scene we have *again* the chorus of hunters ("Glade Lyst! hør Hornet toner")—and it begins to grow a bit wearisome. The scene now shifts back to Wolf's Crag. Edgar, alone on stage, broods in spoken blank verse about his desire for revenge on one hand, and on the other his deep regard for Lucie. In his ensuing *Romance* (see the melody of the overture, Example 8-7) he expresses the desire for peace. Lucie enters, and we have spoken duologue followed by a duet and then more spoken duologue. The duet is the counterpart of Donizetti's fountain-scene duet, but the setting is Wolf's Crag, *before* Edgar's visit to Ravenswood. Much of what is said and sung comes from Lucy and Edgar's conversation at the fountain, in chapter xx. They declare their love for one another; Lucie mentions her fear of her mother; and as an emblem of their troth-plighting they exchange rings (rather than break a gold coin in two). Brother Henry's shooting of a raven which drops ominously at the lovers' feet obviously cannot happen in the operatic version because of Andersen's change in setting and his rearrangement of the order of events (Henrik is introduced later). When Lucie has exited, Caleb enters and warns Edgar not to go to Ravenswood Castle (as in chapter xviii). In the Duettino we hear again the ominous prophecy, now sung by Caleb:[30]

Example 8-11

The act ends in an ensemble composed of Lucie, Edgar, Lord Ashton, Caleb, and Mysie. Caleb gives Edgar a purse filled with money (as in chapter xviii), and he and Mysie both express the fear that they will not see him again. Their last words are a warning to him to beware the quicksand: "Herre, tænk paa Flyvesandet, / Og den blege, døde Brud!" At the very end of the act we hear in the flutes and oboes the above-quoted melody, now in the key of d minor. (In the novel Misie is not present as Edgar leaves Wolf's Crag in the company of Lucy and her father; the slight alteration makes possible the inclusion of a second female voice in the final ensemble.)

Act III takes place at Ravenswood Castle, and as the curtain rises, two servants, Dich and John, are talking. They express the fear that when Lady Ashton arrives home she will be highly displeased with Edgar's visit. (This opening conversation has no exact parallel in the novel, but something like it might well have occurred in view of the situation that Scott presents. The act is based mainly on Scott's account of Edgar's arrival at Ravenswood (chapter xviii) and of the events surrounding the homecoming of Lady Ashton (chapter xxii), with the omission of the Marquis of A—.) The first musical number is a chorus of hunters and servants who are in Lord Ashton's entourage. Edgar is pensive when he looks around him and remembers scenes from his boyhood:

Min Barndoms Lege-Plads!—O bittre Qval!
Her leged' jeg, som Barn, i denne Hal—
Hist hang mit lille Jagtspyd og min Bue—

(Cf. the words of Scott's Edgar to Lord William: ". . . there, in yonder corner, under that handsome silver sconce, I kept my fishing-rods, and hunting poles, bows, and arrows.") Lord Ashton's introduction of Edgar to his young son Henrik, who is afraid of him, follows the novel closely; their conversation is in spoken blank verse. The next choral number is sung to the old Scots tune, "My Lodging Is on the Cold Ground," as Andersen indicates in his foreword:[31]

Example 8-12

This is followed by a lively "Skotsk Reel":

Example 8-13

Then, as Edgar sings "De gamle Melodier,/Hvor smelte de mit Bryst!" we have a melody in the first violins that begins thus:

Example 8-14

Toward the end of this plaintive number Lucie sings to Edgar, "Lad Dig mit Haandtryk sige,/Hvad Læben dølge maa!" and then we have two additional lively dance tunes:

Examples 8-15 & 8-16

Suddenly Dich and John burst in with the news that Lady Ashton has just arrived. Lucie and Lord Ashton are distraught. As the chorus sings "Gamle Minstrel, dine Sange/Tør ei længer tone her!" we hear again, not in the vocal line but in the first violins, a fragment of the melody "My Lodging Is on the Cold Ground" (see Example 8-12). The long expected Lady Ashton finally enters, accompanied by an entourage of followers among whom are Bucklaw and Craigengelt. She is very much put out with Lord Ashton for having Edgar as a guest, and the ensuing duologue in blank verse follows the novel closely. She then sings a dramatic aria ("Der rinder Helteblod i disse Aarer!"), after which she hands Dich and John a message to give to Edgar which requests his immediate withdrawal from the castle. She tells Ashton that she is determined that Lucie shall marry Bucklaw. (In the novel there is no talk at this point of a marriage between Bucklaw and Lucy. However, Lady Ashton has plans for such in the back of her mind, and she is expecting Bucklaw, who arrives, not when she does, but later, at the end of the chapter.) In the ensuing duet Lady Ashton again expresses her determination to go through with the marriage plans, while Ashton expresses deep concern for the effect these plans may have on the tender Lucie. After the duet Ashton leaves the stage. Lucie enters and greets her mother, who tells her forthwith that she is to marry Bucklaw. Lucie is horrified. Angered at her reaction, Lady Ashton tells her she suspects that she is in love with Edgar. She then orders preparations to be made at once so that the wedding of Lucie and Bucklaw can take place that very night. (Andersen has telescoped the action of the novel in the interest of effective theater.) The act ends with another dramatic aria for Lady Ashton ("Man tør mig trodse her,/Min Villie glemme!"), which requires a voice that is large, high, and mature, but flexible; the vocal line is studded with high C's.

Act IV opens in a garden outside Ravenswood Castle. It is evening. Wedding music and the noise of celebration are heard in the distance. The two old beldams, Annie and Ailsie, are sitting on a stone (the "through-stane" of the novel) and observing what they can. Ailsie begins the scene by singing the well-known gruesome "Ballad of the Two Ravens," which Andersen found in Scott's *Minstrelsy of the Scottish Border*. The tune is that of "Auld Robin Gray":[32]

Example 8-17

Der sid - de to Rav - ne paa Træ - et hist, saa sor - te man al - drig

saae dem for vist! de skri - ge hæst o - ver Sko - vens Krat: "hvad

faae vi at spi - se i den - ne Nat!

Afterwards the two discuss the wedding in spoken dialogue that is very close to the diabolic conversation of Annie, Ailsie, and Maggie in chapter xxxiv. Ailsie predicts that the bride will soon be dead.—The scene now shifts to the grand hall of the castle. The chorus sings in celebration of the occasion, and Bidethebent brings forth the marriage contract which is to be signed. When Bucklaw wonders why Lucie is so pale and silent, Lady Ashton tells him that she is afraid of even the name *bride*. Lucie sits at the table, signs the document, but suddenly utters a cry and drops the pen. "Han kommer!" she says; "ham det er." Edgar bursts in. The music stops, and there are several moments of silence, as in the novel. The spoken dialogue (rather than a musical ensemble) that follows is very close to Scott's dialogue in chapter xxxiii. The main difference is that the role of Bucklaw is enhanced as a result of Andersen's omission of Sholto Ashton from his dramatis personae. When Edgar insists on hearing from Lucie's lips what has occurred, all the wedding guests except Lady Ashton and Bidethebent retire temporarily from the room. To Edgar's questions Lucie can only reply, "Min Moder—!" Bidethebent tells Edgar that she signed the contract of her own free will. Upon hearing this, Edgar returns to Lucie her ring, while her mother clips the ribbon she wears that bears Edgar's ring and returns it to him, saying, "Alt er nu til Ende!" At this point Edgar sings a short poignant aria—the first music we have had since before his entrance. It begins thus:[33]

Example 8-18

Du var min Tan - ke, var min Drøm! Jeg hang ved dig med Sjael og

Hjer - te; Ej Dø - dens kol - de, stær - ke Strøm ud-sluk - ke vil min dy - be Smer - te!

Afterwards he leaves the room abruptly, and Lucie sinks down unconscious. With the re-entrance of the wedding guests, the finale begins. They sing of the approaching duel between Edgar and Bucklaw, and they notice how pale Lucie is, lying on the floor. When she revives, her reason has completely left her, and a mad scene begins. It is made up of sung and spoken fragments of earlier passages in the opera. The spoken fragments usually are accompanied, in "melodramatic" fashion, by diminished seventh tremolos in the strings. The music which Lucie recalls includes the first eight measures of "Et Dyb og dog Guds Himmel" (the tune "Charlie Is My Darling") and two fragments from the love-duet of Act II:[34]

Examples 8-19 & 8-20

Finally, she sings the third stanza from the "Ballad of the Two Ravens," which we heard at the very beginning of the act:

> Hans Hund drager atter paa Jagten hen,
> Hans Falk faaer sig snart en Herre igjen,
> Og Bruden finder en Hjertenskjær,
> Men vi faae et kosteligt Maaltid her!

These words indicate that Lucie has had a mysterious, inexplicable premonition of her lover's fate, for Bucklaw now re-enters with news of Edgar's death. He explains that he arrived first at the place where he and

Edgar were going to fight their duel. (In the novel Edgar is to fight against Sholto Ashton.) He saw Edgar approaching on horseback, but the next moment both horse and rider were swallowed up by quicksand. He went up to the spot where he had last seen him but could find no trace of him other than a black feather from his cap. Upon hearing Bucklaw's words Lucie cries out, "Edgar af Ravenswood!" and falls down dead. Everyone on stage is horror-stricken. In the final pages of the score Annie and Ailsie move forward from amidst the servants and sing the opera's chief leit-motiv in a low register (see Example 8-11). Bidethebent and the chorus sing a few appropriate last words as the orchestra plays a solemn *andante maestoso*. The curtain falls.—The closing scene differs interestingly from the novel in that Lucie does not stab Bucklaw, and her death comes *after* Edgar's death. The main events of the novel's final chapters—the signing of the contract, the wedding, Lucy's madness, her death, Edgar's death—are telescoped into a single operatic scene.

Much of the novel is retained in *Bruden fra Lammermoor*. The only noteworthy characters that do not appear are Sholto Ashton, the Marquis of A—, and the Girders. Like Carafa's librettist, Andersen has toned down the comic side of Caleb's personality. The retention of Scott's domineering Lady Ashton is welcome on one hand, but at the same time it presents something of a problem for the composer. A second equally important female principal must of course have music in keeping with her importance. The result is that her two arias detract from the impact of Lucie's mad scene. Thus Lucie must share the honors of the evening with her mother, who is also a soprano. Carafa was wiser than Bredal on this last point: his Lady Ashton is a contralto. A unique feature of the Andersen-Bredal opera in comparison with other *Bride of Lammermoor* operas is the retention of two of Scott's three beldams. Their very presence in a three-hour opera would give them a position more emphatic than what they have in the novel, and here, in addition, they are assigned new material. Thus the Gothic aspect of the novel, which Scott is careful to keep in the background, becomes prominent in the opera. Of the *Bride of Lammermoor* scores that I have been able to examine, Bredal's alone contains Scottish folk melodies.

Mazzucato's *La Fidanzata di Lammermoor*

This second opera bearing the title *La Fidanzata di Lammermoor* was first performed in Padova, at the Nuovissimo, on 24 February 1834. Its composer, Alberto Mazzucato, was only twenty-one years old, yet he was four years older than librettist Pietro Beltrame. The opera had a satisfactory reception, and in the autumn of the next year it was performed in Milan, at the Carcano, "con successo equale." [35] I have no records of subsequent productions, despite the fact that Mazzucato was active in the musical life of Milan until the 1870's, both as editor of the *Gazzeta Musicale di Milano* and as concertmaster of the orchestra at la Scala. A libretto was published concurrently with the production at the Carcano.[36] Unfortunately, aside from a single number, I have not been able to locate the music.[37]

The opera has only five principals: Guglielmo, Lord Ashton; Malvina, his daughter; Ernesto, Lord Bucklaw; Edoardo, sere di Ravenswood (a mezzo-soprano); and Adele, companion to Malvina.[38] This is the same line-up as in Rieschi's *Fidanzata,* with the omission of the uninteresting Gualtiero. Also as in Rieschi, the unities of time and place are strictly observed. The curtain rises, revealing a "galleria terrena" of Ravenswood Castle. The opening number is a chorus of Guglielmo's followers, who comment upon the noticeable sadness of Malvina: she has her eyes continually fixed on the ground. Guglielmo enters and sings of the forthcoming marriage (that very day) of Malvina and Ernesto. He also informs the chorus of the rumor that "the last son of the traitor" has returned recently from foreign parts; thus they will all have an opportunity to fight against him. When Guglielmo and the chorus have departed, Malvina enters, accompanied by Adele, who begins the *scena* by asking her why she is so dejected. Malvina replies that she has no other choice but to obey her father's command to marry Ernesto. She laments that when Edoardo returns he will find her the wife of another man. Adele urges her to calm herself, but to no avail. Suddenly they hear an offstage chorus greeting Ernesto, who has just arrived. Malvina believes that the joyful cries she hears have in effect decreed her death; that the splendor of the wedding festivities will soon change to the dim light of the sepulchre. (There is a similar incident in the second act of Donizetti's *Lucia.* When Lucia and Enrico hear festive music in the distance, Lucia asks what this might mean. Enrico tells her that her husband-to-be has arrived. "A te s'appresta il talamo," he adds. Lucia replies: "La tomba, la tomba a me s'appresta!") Adele leaves as Guglielmo re-enters. He asks Malvina why she is so distressed and why she weeps so much. She replies that she is still lamenting the death of her late mother. (To devotees of the novel this is an ironic detail; interestingly, it occurs also in Donizetti.) Guglielmo tells her that marriage with Ernesto will compensate her for the loss of her mother; it will cheer her up. He reminds her that he is indebted to Ernesto in view of Ernesto's having once saved his life by risking his own life. (No mention is made of a wild bull. In the novel Edgar, not Bucklaw, saves both William and Lucy from being gored to death.) He urges her to assume a cheerful countenance inasmuch as she is about to become a bride. When she asks whether he still insists on her marriage, he becomes angry. She exclaims that he can indeed force her to marry Ernesto, but that no human power can command her heart. He then asks her whether she has perchance fallen in love with someone else, and she admits that she has—that heaven has joined her heart with that of another man. He in turn calls her ungrateful and reminds her of her mother's dying wish. She laments and regrets that she must go against her mother's wish, and she begs his forgiveness. When he demands to know who her lover is, she will not say. He then tries another tactic. He tells her that a refusal on her part to marry Ernesto would assuredly bring death upon himself. In the final part of the duet he explains that Ernesto would become a dangerous, implacable enemy if the proposed marriage should be thwarted. Deeply moved by these words, she agrees to sacrifice her wishes to his. (The duet between father and daughter ends similarly in Rieschi's *Fidanzata*, II.ii.Cf. Enrico's similar tactic in the second act of *Lucia*.)

The scene changes to a pleasant park near the castle and begins with a chorus of retainers singing joyfully about the forthcoming marriage. When they have departed, Ernesto expresses concern to Guglielmo about Malvina's lack of interest in him. She is always melancholy, he says, and sometimes she even seems to regard him with horror. Guglielmo explains that all this is a result of her mother's death; that marriage will bring comfort to her. The chorus returns with news that enemies have arrived in the vicinity. Ernesto expresses the hope that they may be quickly dispersed and punished. All then sing in anticipation of the sacred rites to be celebrated in the castle, and as the number ends they leave for the castle. Edoardo now arrives. In a long aria he comments on the hill, the river bank, the fir trees—all of which bring back fond memories. He thinks of Malvina and deplores that he has had to be away from her. She then enters, not knowing that he has returned, and she is of course surprised to see him. He thinks that her tears are due to her joy in seeing him again, but it soon comes out that she is to be married that very day. She explains that she was forced into this unhappy situation and implores him to flee and save himself. Angry at first, he shows her the "monile" which she once gave him as a pledge of her fidelity. She replies that she has never ceased to love him, and when she says that she wears next to her heart the "monile" that he gave her, he is fully convinced that she has not betrayed him. He wants her to flee with him, but she says that such recourse would be mad. Evidently believing that she can somehow delay things, she says that at length they will be united. (There is no exact parallel to this meeting of the lovers in Scott. It presumably occurs after a meeting, not dramatized, in which they plighted their troths, but *before* Edoardo disrupts the wedding. Nevertheless it owes something to Scott's account of Lucy's and Edgar's initial declaration of love, chapter xx, and to the tense private meeting of Lucy, Edgar, Lady Ashton, and Bide-the-bent in which both lovers bring forth their halves of the broken gold coin—this occurring in chapter xxxiii, immediately *after* Edgar has burst into the castle and disrupted the signing of the marriage contract.)

The scene now changes to a grand, festively decorated room of the castle, and the chorus sings of the joy of the occasion. Suddenly the festivities are interrupted by the entrance of Edoardo. (What has been going on is simply a part of the wedding; the signing of a marriage contract is not specified.) When he says that he has come to defend his rights, there is great consternation and surprise. He announces that Malvina is his in the eyes of heaven. Guglielmo thinks that he is mad; he tells him that she is about to marry Ernesto. Edoardo replies that if this should happen, a holy oath would be broken. Guglielmo, who is still unaware of the intruder's identity, cannot believe that Malvina could have engaged in such an oath. At this point we have an elaborate ensemble: Edoardo telling Ernesto he has betrayed him; Ernesto declaring that he thought Edoardo was dead, that he has not been faithless; Guglielmo expressing to Malvina his anger and urging her to reveal her lover's name; Malvina begging her father's pardon and singing that she meant no offense in loving the young man; and Adele and the chorus noticing the wrath of Guglielmo and hoping that he can be calmed down. This is Mazzucato's equivalent of Donizetti's Sextet (see fn. 37). Immediately following the ensemble Guglielmo demands that the intruder reveal his identity. All are shocked when he replies that he is the last scion of the Ravenswood family. (In the novel and in Donizetti it is clear who the intruder is when he first enters.) When Guglielmo asks him what could possibly have brought him to these parts, he replies that it was love. Guglielmo menacingly tells him that he will find certain death. At this point Ernesto breaks in and defends Edoardo from the wrath of Guglielmo, who can scarcely believe what Ernesto is doing. The final ensemble now begins. Ernesto explains that Edoardo once saved him from inevitable death and believes that fate will be propitious to him if he saves Edoardo in return. (Early in the novel Bucklaw is grateful to Edgar for letting him off lightly after having defeated him in an armed encounter that Bucklaw himself had hot-headedly forced upon him.) Malvina tries to pacify her relentless father. Ernesto then sings *aside* that he is saving Edoardo now so that he can take proper revenge at some later time. Edoardo sings *aside* that he wants vengeance but that he must restrain his fury for Malvina's sake. Adele observes *aside* that the days of joy are gone. As the act closes, Guglielmo and the chorus express their unalterable determination to have bloody vengeance.

At the beginning of Act II we are back in the "galleria terrena." Adele and the chorus comment on Malvina's profound sadness. When they have departed, Guglielmo upbraids Malvina, in the presence of Ernesto, for her relationship with Edoardo. He tells her that Edoardo is in his power and that the only way for him to be saved is for her to marry Ernesto. Malvina meditates *aside* on whether Ernesto has betrayed Edoardo. If so, and if she must marry him, she will be marrying a sinful husband. And if she should murder him, how cruel it would be that she had married him. Ernesto sings *aside* that Guglielmo is faking; that Edoardo is not in his power. Finally Malvina agrees to the marriage, but she give Ernesto stern warning that he will suffer as a result. Guglielmo explains away her passion as typical of ever-changing women. As the trio ends, Ernesto re-declares his love for Malvina despite her hatred for him.—The scene now moves to outside the castle; it is night. A chorus of armed men sing that Edoardo will be found no matter where he is hiding; that the sword of vengeance will fall on him. When they are gone, Edoardo enters. Seeing the festive torches, he wonders what is happening in the castle. He finds himself unable to leave the vicinity despite the danger for him in remaining. He wonders whether Malvina has been forced to undergo an undesired marriage, and he is vexed by the uncertainty of it all. Hearing a chorus *within* singing of joy and love, he becomes extremely agitated and decides to enter the castle. Ernesto meets him at the atrium, prevents him from entering, and tells him that Malvina is now *his* wife. "Yours?" Edoardo asks; "what do I hear?... And I am not killing you?..." Ernesto reminds him that he (Edoardo) owes his life to him (see the ending of Act I). A duet begins. Ernesto declares that a bond no longer exists between them; that neither is beholden to the other any more. They both express the desire to fight. Edoardo in fact draws his sword and wants to settle the issue on the spot. Ernesto says that the time and place are not right—that Guglielmo might come and interrupt them. He tells Edoardo to meet him early the next morning at the dunes. Finally, each expresses the hope that his desire to do away with his rival may be fulfilled. (The normally omitted scene at Edgardo's castle in Donizetti's *Lucia* involves a similar encounter, but it is between lover and brother rather than lover and rival. Both opera librettos owe something to the conversation of Sholto Ashton and Edgar at Lucy's funeral.)

Act III takes place at the dunes by the sea. The tower of Ravenswood Castle, which the librettist places at the seacoast, is at one side of the stage. A storm is about to break forth and the sea is very agitated. It is dawn. The opening number is a chorus of fishermen, who sing of the approaching storm and notice that the birds are flying toward the left (a bad omen). Ernesto arrives at the place decided on for his duel with Edoardo. He observes that the very elements are conspiring against them. Perhaps he waits for Edoardo in vain, for he sees that a beach divides Edoardo's castle from their place of rendezvous and that it is covered with swollen surge. He thinks of Malvina and of her great grief at the altar. Hearing a bell toll from somewhere in the castle, he asks the fishermen what this signifies. They reply that a boat has been wrecked in the surging waters. They urge everyone to lend a hand in saving whoever may be in it. Some of them look out at the sea and in fact witness someone struggling and soon being overcome. Ernesto looks out from a height and realizes that the victim must be Edoardo. The chorus observes that he is now hidden from their view; that he has found death in the surging waters. At this point Malvina comes out from the castle, followed by Guglielmo, Adele, and guards. Quickly grasping the fact that Edoardo is dead, she falls into Adele's arms. When she frees herself and begins to sing, it is immediately obvious to all that she is emotionally disturbed. She does not fully understand where she is, and she is hot and cold at the same time. She thinks that she sees

Edoardo smiling lugubriously on her. She wants to go to him. Guglielmo urges her to calm herself, but to no avail. She sees Edoardo again and believes that he has prepared an angelic dwelling for her. She longs for death. Suddenly she seizes a dagger from Ernesto and kills herself. All present cry out in horror, and the curtain falls.

Edoardo's death scene is close to what it is in Scott, and it gives Mazzucato the opportunity to work in a chorus of fishermen, which is unique among the operas based on *The Bride of Lammermoor*. In *Bruden fra Lammermoor* Edgar meets his death exactly as in Scott, but we are not present at the scene: Bucklaw merely tells us, along with the wedding guests, what has happened. As in *Bruden*, Edoardo dies *before* Malvina. The mad scenes, on the other hand, are put in different postions. In *Bruden* Lucie becomes deranged just after Edgar has returned her pledge, convinced of her bad faith. In *Fidanzata* Malvina has her mad scene just after she realizes that Edoardo is dead. In *Bruden* Lucie dies of natural causes when Bucklaw brings in the news of Edgar's death; in *Fidanzata* Malvina fatally stabs herself. One wonders whether the final scene of *Fidanzata* might have had some influence on Cammarano and Donizetti in the working out of their final scene, even though the basic situations are totally different. Nevertheless Edgardo, like Malvina, fatally stabs himself shortly after he learns of the death of his beloved. Moreover, both final scenes involve the tolling of a bell from the castle. In Mazzucato it signifies that some poor wretch is being drowned in the storm; in Donizetti, that Lucia is dead. To sum up, Beltrame and Mazzucato's *Fidanzata di Lammermoor* represents a greatly simplified version of Scott's story. The cast of characters is cut to the bone. Both Lady Ashton and Caleb Balderston are omitted. In comparison with other *Bride of Lammermoor* operas, the most interesting and remarkable feature about *Fidanzata* is that it comes closest to depicting Edgar's death as Scott conceived it.

Lucia di Lammermoor

Lucia was first performed in Naples, at the Teatro San Carlo, on 26 September 1835, and was enthusiastically received. Sig[ra] Fanny Tacchinardi-Persiani sang the title-role, and Luigi Duprez, Edgardo; others in the cast were Domenico Cosselli (Enrico Ashton), Gioacchini (Arturo Bucklaw), Porto (Bidebent), Sig[ra] Zapucci (Alisa), and Teofilo Rossi (Normanno). I shall not attempt here to relate *Lucia*'s extensive performance history. Because, unlike other Scott operas, it has held its immense popularity until the present day, it conceivably has been performed more times than all the others put together. Complete recordings have been numerous, and recordings of individual numbers are countless.

Since everyone is familiar with the story of the opera, I shall focus my attention on aspects of it that compare or contrast interestingly with the novel and with the other *Bride of Lammermoor* operas. Since most of my points have already evolved during the course of the preceding discussion, what follows serves mainly as a final bringing-together and summary. The cast of characters shows that Cammarano has taken a middle-ground approach to his subject matter.[39] More of Scott's characters are to be found in *Lucia* than in Rieschi, Bornaccini, or Mazzucato, but fewer than in Carafa and Bredal. Lord Enrico Ashton is a composite of four Ashtons: the Lord Keeper, Lady Ashton, and their two sons, Sholto and Henry. He owes his chief personality traits to Lady Ashton and Sholto, and only his name to young Henry. Lucia is Scott's Lucy, but more passionate in temperament and not so easily manipulated by others. Edgardo resembles Edgar in almost every way except in Edgar's brooding, unspoken discontent: the operatic protagonist is all too ready to display his emotions when an occasion presents itself. Lord Arturo Bucklaw is a pasteboard replica of Scott's hot-headed, rather stupid, but likeable, Hayston of Bucklaw. Raimondo Bidebent, "tutor and confidant of Lucia," is mainly the Reverend Mr. Bide-the-bent of the novel, but he owes something in Edgardo's death-scene to Caleb Balderston. Alisa, Lucia's companion, has no resemblance other than in name to Scott's blind Alice; her function is the same as that of Elisa in *Le Nozze di Lammermoor*, Alina in Rieschi's *Fidanzata di Lammermoor*, and Adele in Mazzucato's *Fidanzata*.[40] Normanno, "Captain of the Guard at Ravenswood," owes at least his name to Norman the park-keeper, who figures briefly in an early chapter of the novel.

An opening chorus of hunters in 6/8 time is a staple of the Walter Scott operas, and *Lucia* is no exception. Moreover, models exist in the earlier *Bride of Lammermoor* operas. Cammarano and Donizetti were almost certainly unacquainted with *Bruden fra Lammermoor,* but they probably did know *Le Nozze di Lammermoor,* and they could easily have seen the printed libretto, if not the music, to Rieschi's *Fidanzata di Lammermoor* (Bornaccini's *Ida*), which all open in this way. In the accompanied recitative following the chorus of hunters Bidebent attempts to excuse Lucia's reluctance to marry on the grounds that she is still mourning the death of her mother. As we have already observed, this singularly ironic twist in Scott's story appears first in Mazzucato's *Fidanzata*, the libretto to which would have been easily accessible to Cammarano. In view of a number of parallels that can be pointed out, I believe that he knew and was influenced by all three of the earlier Italian librettos. Enrico's concern in the opening scene and elsewhere about the ruin that will necessarily come upon the Ashton family unless Lucia marries Bucklaw is much closer to what we have observed in Rieschi and Mazzucato than to the apparent source of the idea: William's premature plans to have Lucy marry *Edgar* and thereby avoid the disaster that might fall on the Ashton family if the Tory party should prove ascendant, as seemed likely.

The famous Sextet (which involves Lucia, Alisa, Edgardo, Bucklaw,

LilyPons as Lucia. By courtesy of the Metropolitan Opera Archives.

LUCIE DE LAMMERMOOR

Grand Opéra en 4 Actes

Paroles de Mʳˢ ALPHONSE - ROYER et Gustave VAËZ

MUSIQUE DE

G. DONIZETTI.

Partition, Chant et Piano.   Prix 10 ᶠ net.

Paris, chez Bernard-Latte, 2. Boulevard des Italiens.
Passage de l'Opéra.
Naples.   Girard & Cⁱᵉ.

TITLE-PAGE of the French vocal score of Donizetti's opera.

Enrico, and Bidebent) follows closely the parallel material in the novel. There is even a complete pause for a few moments before it begins. All the other Italian operas that I have examined include this dramatic scene of confrontation and use it as the basis for a large ensemble. (Andersen and Bredal include the scene, but they have spoken dialogue until much later, when Edgar is about to depart, and then there is a short aria for him rather than an ensemble.) Of the Italians Carafa follows Scott most closely in having all the wedding guests leave the room so that Edgardo can speak with Lucia in the presence of only Lady Ashton and Bidebent. Rieschi, Mazzucato, and Donizetti keep everyone on stage during Ravenswood's questioning. Everyone observes the heroine's shame and her lover's anger when he is convinced that she has been faithless. Scott's Edgar does not end his remarks by cursing Lucy, but a conventional operatic cursing scene can convincingly be added in light of the situation that has developed. We have this in *Lucia,* but the model was already present in Rieschi's *Fidanzata.* The usually omitted scene at Wolf's Crag, in which Enrico visits Edgardo and challenges him to a duel, may owe something to the similar scene in Mazzucato's *Fidanzata;* it is much closer to Mazzucato than to the brief episode in the novel that suggested it (see above). There are models for the celebrated mad scene in Rieschi and Mazzucato (and Bredal). Moreover, in Rieschi's *Fidanzata* Ida stabs Bucklaw to death, and this is exactly what we have in *Lucia,* whereas in the novel Bucklaw survives the ordeal. The last scene of Lucia is the most radical departure from the novel, but Cammarano and Donizetti's conception of it is not altogether original. I think that they got the idea for the setting—the burial-ground of the Ravenswood family—from the opening scene of the second act of *Le Nozze di Lammermoor,* in which the principals involved are Caleb, Bidebent, and Edgardo; in *Lucia* we have Edgardo and Bidebent. Edgardo commits suicide by stabbing himself, as in Carafa—and like Malvina in the Mazzucato opera. The ominous tolling of the bell which signifies that Lucia is dead is reminiscent of bell-tolling for a different purpose in Mazzucato (see above).

There are several interesting minor deviations from the novel. When Normanno tells Enrico and Bidebent about the wild bull incident, it seems that Edgardo had saved Lucia from certain death, but she was alone. Lucia's account of her mysterious experience at the fountain does not follow the old legend about a former Lord of Ravenswood and his demon lady-love so much as it does Edgar's experience of seeing an apparition of the recently deceased Alice, when he passes by the fountain after having been evicted by Lady Ashton from Ravenswood (chapter xxiii). During the course of the fountain-scene duet Lucia and Edgardo exchange rings rather than divide a gold coin. These and other minor alterations I could mention do not make the general character of the opera markedly different from that of the novel. Other alterations do, especially the omission of Caleb Balderston and Lady Ashton from the dramatis personae, and even of the Lord Keeper, who, although weak in personality, is an excellent portrait on Scott's part. Moreover the omission of Alice and the three beldams pretty much does away with Scott's carefully handled Gothic atmosphere, of which there is only a trace in Lucia's cavatina at the fountain ("Regnava nel silenzio"). What Cammarano and Donizetti have done instead is to concentrate on the love-story of Edgar and Lucy and to omit everything in the novel that is not obviously related to it. They capitalize on effective scenes already in the novel—the picturesque, quiet scene at the fountain where Edgar and Lucy plight their troths and the dramatic confrontation between Edgar and the signers of the marriage contract—and they create effective scenes from material that Scott does not fully develop: the meeting of Edgardo and Enrico at Wolf's Crag and especially the celebrated mad scene. Finally, in the circumstances of Edgardo's death they have created something altogether different from what we have in Scott, but very effective in the musical idiom in which Donizetti worked.

To Cammarano and Donizetti the love-story was the emotional core of the novel. They knew that this was conducive to good, effective opera as it had evolved in Italy in the 1830's. They borrowed ideas from earlier *Bride of Lammermoor* operas and avoided their weaknesses. No Scottish local color is manifest in either text or music. For all the disparaging things that have been said about the way Scott's story and its characters turn out in the operatic rendition, the test of time has proven that Cammarano and Donizetti knew what they were about.

9

§ § §

*IVANHOE**

Ⅰn this chapter full discussion is given to seven operas that range from a Rossini pasticcio of 1826 to Sir Arthur Sullivan's *Ivanhoe,* 1891. I have chosen not to include the musical drama *Ivanhoe; or, The Knight Templar,* that was first performed at Covent Garden on 2 March 1820. Nevertheless a few points about it deserve brief mention. The text is by Samuel Beazley,[1] and the music, selected from the works of Stephen Storace by William Kitchiner and arranged by John Parry, was published in 1820 in the form of a vocal score, a copy of which can be found in the British Museum. An interesting preface, written apparently by Dr. Kitchiner, consists of observations on vocal music, with emphasis on the importance of the text and on the difficulty of singing correctly a simple English ballad.[2] There are singing parts for Robin Hood and other members of his band of outlaws, and for Rowena, De Bracy, Wamba, and Elgitha, Rowena's lady-in-waiting. The mere fact that Elgitha is included greatly enhances the very small role she plays in the novel, where Rebecca, Rowena, and Ulrica are the only women of any consequence. One of the musical numbers is a comic love-duet for her and her friend Wamba, which has no parallel in the novel. The song "Barefooted Friar," however, owes even its text to Scott. The plot as reflected in the musical numbers includes the capture of Rowena by De Bracy, her refusal of his amorous overtures, and her eventual rescue from captivity.[3]

There are two *Ivanhoe* operas which I know about but unfortunately cannot discuss, since I was unable to locate either the text or the music. *Ivanoé,* a three-act opera by the Corsican composer Thomas Sari, was first performed about 1863, in Ajaccio. According to the Fétis Supplément it was given several times during the following two years by an Italian troup. After having learned that neither text nor music was in the Bibliothèque

---

*The reader should be warned that the numbering of the chapters in the Border Edition is faulty. The chapter (in the first volume) which should be chapter vii is mistakenly numbered viii, and thus all the remaining chapters are off by one. My references to chapters of the novel reflect the correct numbering found in other editions.

Municipale d'Ajaccio, I wrote to the composer's son, a former commissioner of mortgages who is now living in retirement in Campo, for whatever information he might have. He replied that the opera was performed only in Ajaccio, where it was warmly received by the public; it was not published in any form. Unfortunately, M. Sari's kind efforts to locate manuscripts have thus far proved unsuccessful. Another opera based on *Ivanhoe* and entitled *Ivanhoe,* with music by Attilio Ciardi and words by Cesare Bordiga, was first performed in Prato, on 8 September 1888, at the Metastasio Theater. According to Schmidl, it was well received. More than this I am unable to say.

I have chosen not to discuss the school operetta *Ivanhoe,* which was published by J. Curwen & Sons in 1907. The text was "adapted from Sir Walter Scott's novel" by May Byron and the music composed by C. Hutchins Lewis. I examined the copy in the British Museum. I found the text silly and the music insipid, and I have great sympathy for the unfortunate young people who were forced to learn and perform this work.

Rossini's Ivanhoé

Ivanhoé was first performed in Paris, 15 September 1826, at the Odéon. Émile Deschamps and Gustave de Wailly collaborated in doing the libretto,[4] while the music was selected from four Rossini operas— *Semiramide, Mosè, Tancredi,* and *La Gazza Ladra*—and arranged by Antonio Pacini (not to be confused with Giovanni Pacini; see below). *Ivanhoé* is thus a pasticcio.[5] Scott himself was in the audience for the performance of October 31st, and he wrote about it briefly in his *Journal* (see Chapter 1). The opera was successful. It was performed in the original French in Ghent (10 January 1827), in Lille (20 February 1827); in a much revised English version by Michael Rophino Lacy, entitled *The Maid of Judah; or, The Knights Templars,*[6] in London, at Covent Garden (7 March 1829), in Dublin (30 June 1830), in New York (27 February 1832), in Philadelphia (6 March 1834); in German translation in Coburg (1833).

The cast of characters includes Ivanhoé (sung at the première by Lecomte), Cédric (sung by Adolphe), Brian de Boisguilbert (Leclere), Albert de Malvoisin (Peyronnet), Marquis Lucas de Beaumanoir, top general in the Norman army (Charles), Ismael, a Mohammedan, treasurer to the Normans (Léon), Léila, his daughter (Mlle Lemoule), Thierry, mute servant of the Normans, and a herald. Thierry has no exact counterpart in the novel, but Ismael is Scott's Isaac of York and Léila, Rebecca. Not only are their names changed but also their religion, perhaps because the librettists hesitated to portray strong anti-Semitic feeling on stage.[7] De Bracy is not among the dramatis personae, but he is mentioned once as being an enemy of Boisguilbert. There is no Athelstane the Unready, but Cédric speaks several times of one Olric, his devoted Saxon comrade-in-arms who fell by his side while fighting in the Holy Land. Notable

Painted & Engraved by T.L. Busby, for the Dramatic Magazine.

MRS. JOSEPH WOOD (Mary Ann Paton) as Rebecca, in the production of Rossini's *Ivanhoé (The Maid of Judah)* at Covent Garden, March 7, 1829. From the Enthoven Collection, Victoria and Albert Theatre Museum.

HENRY PHILLIPS as Cedric, in the production of Rossini's *Ivanhoé (The Maid of Judah)* at Covent Garden, March 7, 1829. From the Enthoven Collection, Victoria and Albert Theatre Museum.

omissions include Rowena, Ulrica, Richard the Lion-hearted, Robin Hood and his band of outlaws, Prince John, Waldemar Fitzurse, Front-de-Bœuf, Wamba, and Gurth.

The overture is the brilliant overture to *Semiramide;* none of the musical material is heard elsewhere in the opera. When the curtain rises, we are in a large Gothic room in Rotherwood, Cédric's château. Cédric and a chorus of Saxons are singing. Presently they are interrupted by Léila and Ismael, who knock at the door and beg asylum. The chorus is angry that Moslems should have the audacity to come to the castle of a Saxon nobleman, but a pilgrim who has recently returned from the Holy Land (Ivanhoé in disguise) tells Léila to go ahead and be seated and not pay any attention to the rude people. She expresses gratitude to him for his thoughtfulness. Despite the wishes of the Saxon retainers, Cédric decides to extend hospitality to the Moslems. The musical number ends in a large, conventional ensemble that involves Cédric, the Pilgrim, Léila, Ismael, and the chorus. Next, in spoken dialogue, Cédric remarks that the treaty between England and King Philippe of France will expire the next day. Perhaps he will no longer be in a position to offer hospitality. He says that Léila and Ismael may stay, and yet their presence brings back dolorous memories to him. While fighting in the Holy Land fifteen years ago he had the misfortune to see his friend Olric, the last male descendant of King Alfred, perish in battle. Olric's young daughter Édith fell into the hands of the enemy, and Cédric does not know what became of her. (Scott's Cedric has never been in the Holy Land; however, the allusion to Olric is based on Cedric's grief at the supposed death of Athelstane at Torquilstone. Athelstane has no daughter; his mother's name is Edith.) Cédric wants to drink a toast to the most valiant of the crusaders, and he asks the Pilgrim to name him. The Pilgrim replies enthusiastically, "Au roi Richard!" (The incident is based on a similar incident in chapter xiv. During the course of the dinner at Ashby, Cedric and his party are insulted by Prince John and the Normans. Cedric accordingly embarrasses his rude hosts by quaffing a goblet to the health of Richard the Lion-hearted.) Cédric thinks of Richard as someone who has drawn his only son Ivanhoé away from him, but he will not refuse to drink the toast. (There is nowhere a clear explanation as to why Cédric has fallen out with Ivanhoé. It cannot be owing to his affection for Rowena, inasmuch as she is totally omitted from the story of the opera.) As the dialogue progresses Ismael explains how on returning home from the lists of Ashby, he and his daughter were pursued by a band of archers led by the notorious Boisguilbert. Ismael had observed during the course of the tournament that Boisguilbert was eyeing Léila with obvious interest. In an aria ("Bois-guilbert, dont la vengeance / Fut toujours l'unique loi!") Ismael gives further detail about the unpleasant encounter. Aided by the darkness of a storm, he and Léila managed to escape their pursuer in the wooded area surrounding Cédric's château. (In the early chapters of the novel Isaac, not accompanied by Rebecca, seeks shelter at Rotherwood from a storm, but he is not being pursued by Bois-Guilbert. The tournament at Ashby and its aftermath occur *after* the scene at Rotherwood.) In a bit of spoken dialogue Cédric says that he must prepare the château for a possible attack from Boisguilbert. He and his retainers depart, and Léila retires for the night, the Pilgrim and Ismael remaining on stage.

The Pilgrim recognizes Ismael as being the treasurer to the King of France and expresses surprise *à part* that he should be in Cédric's château. When he suddenly addresses Ismael by his name, Ismael is surprised that the Pilgrim knows who he is. The Pilgrim asks him if it was really the fear of Boisguilbert that brought him to the château. Ismael says that even though he is the French king's treasurer, he has nothing to do with politics; moreover, he is not so rich as most people assume. The Pilgrim replies that he happens to know about the stone at the foot of the palm-tree in Ismael's garden in Jerusalem which conceals a staircase that leads into a treasure-laden vault. (The spoken dialogue here is suggested by Locksley's remarks to Isaac in chapter xxxiii, but in the novel we have an apple-tree, and the site is York rather than Jerusalem.) He then asks Ismael if he remembers the wounded chevalier whom Léila had graciously received at a time while he was away and whom he peremptorily dismissed from the house upon his return. Ismael replies that he was afraid to expose the heart of his daughter to the young man. Ismael leaves the stage after the Pilgrim has promised not to tell the secret of his treasure-vault, nor of his connection with King Philippe. The Pilgrim, alone, speaks of Léila's having nursed him back to health in the Holy Land. (This motif is suggested by Rebecca's care of Ivanhoe after his having been grievously wounded in the lists of Ashby.) In the first half of a formal aria he sings that he owes his life to Léila, and in the ensuing cabaletta he expresses his determination to succor her in her hour of trouble. After the aria Cédric re-enters and questions the Pilgrim about the war in the Holy Land. The Pilgrim replies that things are going rather badly. He then tells of a tournament in which Brian de Boisguilbert, Albert de Malvoisin, and Lucas de Beaumanoir were defeated by King Richard, Sir Henri Douglas (not mentioned in the novel), and a knight responsible for Brian's defeat whom he finally names as Wilfrid d'Ivanhoé. (In the novel Brian himself, before the entire assembled company, names Ivanhoe as his vanquisher.) Cédric remarks gruffly that the destiny of his disobedient son is as indifferent to him as that of the vilest of the Normans.

Suddenly the ominous sound of a horn is heard from outside the château—this being suggested by the horn heard by the defenders of Torquilstone just prior to their receiving a message from the Saxon assailants. Léila and Ismael re-enter in fear and distress. A quartet begins with the Pilgrim telling father and daughter that they need not fear:

Example 9-1

Ah! point d'a - lar - mes,   Sé - chez vos lar - mes, Comp - tez   sur   nous.

Afterwards Boisguilbert's herald comes in and announces that his master demands Léila and Ismael; if they are not given over to him immediately, he will attack the château. The Pilgrim defies both the herald and his master, and Cédric now realizes who his guest really is. (In the novel the recognition occurs at the end of the second day of the tournament at Ashby, when the wounded Disinherited Knight's helmet is removed.) Léila is overjoyed that Ivanhoé will be her champion:

Example 9-2

Vo - lez à ma dé - fen - se, Mon no - ble che - va - lier.

The Saxon retainers sing "Aux armes! victoire!" and they rush out with Cédric and Ivanhoé to help defend the château. For a few moments Léila and Ismael are left alone on stage. Léila tells her father he should be grateful for the services of the young chevalier. As they begin to hear sounds of combat, they are joined by a chorus of Saxon women, who enter hurriedly and in great distraction. Suddenly Ivanhoé is brought in, sustained by two soldiers. He is badly wounded. In spoken dialogue he implores Léila to try to flee from the Normans, since he is now obviously incapable of defending her, but she refuses to abandon him and insists on dressing his wound. When he expresses the desire to look out the window to see what is going on, she replies that any exertion on his part would tend to aggravate his symptoms. She says that she herself will go to the window and give him an account of all that is happening. He insists that she protect herself from the arrows with "cet ancien bouclier." She does so, looks out the window, and exclaims, "O spectacle horrible!" She sees that the château is taken and that Boisguilbert is on the ramparts; Cédric's vassals are fleeing. (The dialogue and the situation are based on the similar material in chapter xxix, during the storming of Torquilstone.) At this point begins the finale. "Hélas!" Léila exclaims; "ô douleur!/ O jour funeste!" Ivanhoé declares that he will either save her or die in the attempt. The Norman soldiers, who have now entered, reply menacingly: "Craignez notre vengeance:/ Oui, vous allez périr." In a quartet Léila, Ivanhoé, Ismael, and Cédric lament their ill-luck; here is Léila's melodic line:

Example 9-3

O sort in - fi -dè - le,   Tu trom - pes mon   zè   -   le.

At the beginning of the *allegro vivace* she implores Ivanhoé not to abandon her:

Example 9-4

Mon pè - re, craig-nons leur ven - gean-ce.   Sei - gneur, ne m'a - ban - don - nez pas.

Boisguilbert orders her to follow him. As the finale reaches its climax two additional melodies, typical of Rossini, are introduced; they appear first in the orchestra:

Examples 9-5 and 9-6

And the act closes as the relentless Boisguilbert forcibly takes Léila away, despite her protests. (The librettists have boldly amalgamated Scott's scene at Rotherwood with the storming of Torquilstone. As in the novel, a castle is taken, but here the Saxon defenders lose out to Boisguilbert and his Norman lackeys.)

The first part of Act II takes place in a room high up in the château de Saint-Edmond. (This is the Templestowe of the novel.) Boisguilbert is in command of the château during the absence of Beaumanoir, who is expected back very soon. When the curtain rises we see Léila alone on stage. Looking out the window she sees her father, who has come to the château in search of her. She signals him and quickly pens a letter for him to take to Ivanhoé. In it she implores Ivanhoé to aid her, but then recalling that he is wounded, she advises him to inform King Philippe of her captivity; his army is only a half-day's march from Rotherwood. (There is no parallel to this in Scott.) In an aria she sings of her strong feelings for Ivanhoé. She asks the god of her father to pardon her for this transgression, but she cannot help it: love reigns in her soul and triumphs over duty. Her heart burns to see him; his very presence will relieve her suffering. After the aria Boisguilbert enters and expresses his love for her. (The spoken dialogue and the duet that follows are based on the scene between Rebecca and Bois-Guilbert that takes place in the novel at Torquilstone, ch. xxiv. The librettists have removed the well-known material from its original context and grafted it onto the events that occur at Templestowe.) Léila tells her would-be ravisher that her father will pay whatever ransom he desires. He replies that he is not interested in money. When he tells her that as his prisoner she must submit to all his wishes, she threatens to proclaim his misdeeds all over Europe. He then declares that in order to leave the château she must agree to be his mistress. At this point she runs to a "plateforme d'ou elle est prête à s'élancer," and we have an elaborate duet. He swears that he will not harm her; she threatens to jump. At the end of the duet he hears someone coming. When he moves toward her she again threatens to jump. Afraid that she may indeed do so, he moves to the opposite side of the stage, tells her not to fear, opens a secret door, and tells her to conceal herself in the adjoining room. "Fasse le ciel," exclaims Léila, "que je n'aie point à me repentir de ma confiance!"

Malvoisin enters and upbraids Boisguilbert in spoken dialogue for persisting in his dangerous enterprise. He tells him that all the chevaliers, spurred on by his enemy Maurice de Bracy, are murmuring against him. They question the motive he had in attacking Cédric's château when he ought to have thought about repulsing King Philippe of France. Moreover, a man of arms in De Bracy's service intercepted the letter which Léila dropped from the window of her place of confinement. Malvoisin tells Brian that he tried to justify his (Brian's) actions by telling the murmurers that the girl was apprehended because she was thought to be an agent of the French king sent on a mission to procure the help of the Saxons in the forthcoming conflict. Up to this point the *scène* has no parallel in the novel, but the next bit of dialogue is apparently suggested by part of the conversation in chapter xxxiv between Prince John and Waldemar Fitzurse, who are not included among the dramatis personae of the opera:

BOISGUILBERT: Qu'avez-vous fait, Malvoisin? Quoi! sans me con-
          sulter...

MALVOISIN: Le pèril était pressant, il fallait vous disculper. . . .

"By the face of God!" he [John] said, "Waldemar Fitzurse, much

hast thou taken upon thee! and over malapert thou wert to cause
trumpet to blow, or banner to be raised, in a town where ourselves
were in presence, without our express command."

"I crave your Grace's pardon," said Fitzurse, internally cursing the
idle vanity of his patron; "but when time pressed, and even the loss
of minutes might be fatal, I judged it best to take this much burden
upon me, in a matter of such importance to your Grace's interest."

And then the dialogue skips to the conversation between Bois-Guilbert
and Malvoisin in chapter xxxvi:

BOISGUILBERT Je la laisserais périr! Malvoisin, ce conseil est celui
              d'un...

MALVOISIN: D'un ami qui vous rend un service dont vous sentirez
             plus tard l'importance.

"Malvoisin," said Bois-Guilbert, "thou art a cold-blooded—"
"Friend," said the Preceptor, hastening to fill up the blank, in
which Bois-Guilbert would probably have placed a worse word,— "a
cold-blooded friend I am, and therefore more fit to give thee advice."

Suddenly hearing a clarion from *without*, they both realize that
Beaumanoir has returned to the château. Malvoisin exits. Boisguilbert
then calls Léila from the chamber where she has been concealed: "Léila!
Léila! un danger terrible vous menace!" He tells her about the intercep-
tion of her letter and the accusations that have been made against her. He
says that he alone can save her; that he will give up his honor if she will
consent to be his mistress. (The dialogue here is drawn from the conversation between Brian and Rebecca in chapter xxxix, which takes place *after*
the trial.) Malvoisin re-enters. He tells Léila and Boisguilbert that the
council has assembled and that the ill-advised letter is before the eyes of
the judges. They then sing a trio ("Souffrance cruelle"), during the course
of which a chevalier comes in to tell Léila she must go immediately to the
room where she is to be tried. When she has gone, Boisguilbert tells
Malvoisin that he will be Léila's champion. Malvoisin replies that he
cannot appear in the lists without Beaumanoir's authorization, and surely
Beaumanoir would never permit him to fight against one of his comrades.
(The dialogue follows loosely the conversation between Brian and Malvoisin at the end of chapter xxxix—which takes place *after* Rebecca's trial.)
Unlike his counterpart in the novel, Malvoisin suggests that Boisguilbert
enter the lists with "la visière baissée" (i.e. incognito). Both here and
during the trial the operatic Malvoisin makes something of an attempt to
help his friend.

The scene now changes to the grand hall of the château, where
Beaumanoir is presiding over a panel of judges. From the words of the
awesome opening chorus, it is clear that all the chevaliers present are very
much down on infidels:

Example 9-7

Beaumanoir then makes a sign for the accused person to be brought in to stand before her judges. Léila enters, and in a few moments Boisguilbert and Malvoisin also appear. Beaumanoir charges her with carrying messages from King Philippe to Cédric, with the intention of inciting the Saxons against the Normans, and he condemns her to be burned alive. All this is *spoken* in "melodramatic" fashion to the accompaniment of a long sustained A-flat chord in the strings. The chord changes to a D-flat triad as he says, "L'arrêt sera exécuté demain avant la sixième heure du jour." Then we have a dominant seventh chord built on E flat, which leads into one of the most impressive ensembles to be found in any Walter Scott opera. It begins with Léila lamenting her cruel fate:

Example 9-8

As the chorus sings "Point de clémence!/Plus d'espérance!/La mort s'avance!/Tu vas périr!" Léila reads unobserved a message that has been given to her from Boisguilbert. Then, as in the novel, she throws down her glove and exclaims, "Dieu, j'en appelle à ta sentence!" The atmosphere of unexpected hope is emphasized in the score by a change from A-flat minor (see Example 9-8) to A-flat major. Suddenly Ismael manages to force his way into the august assembly (there is no parallel to this in the novel). Léila urges him to flee; he demands that the barbarians give his daughter back to him. As in the novel, Beaumanoir calls on Boisguilbert to be the defender of the court's judgment. The act ends in a huge ensemble composed of Léila, Ismael, Beaumanoir, Boisguilbert, Malvoisin, and the chorus. The note of hope is now gone. As the curtain falls, Léila sings, "Je vais périr!"

The whole third act takes place beside the lists in front of the château de Saint-Edmond. Before the curtain rises, we hear a *marche militaire*. When it does rise, Malvoisin, in spoken dialogue, orders his men to occupy all roads that lead to the lists and to drive back any Saxons who might want to approach and, above all, Ismael, whom they let slip into the hall of judgment through negligence. After he has gone to enter the lists, the men sing a brief choral number ("Faisons silence") and then depart. Ivanhoé, *"enveloppé dans un manteau,"* enters. He wonders how he can possibly wrest Léila from her captors in view of his being without armor. Ismael enters and informs him that the barbarians have condemned Léila to death. He explains that she must have a champion, tells Ivanhoé that he is their only hope, and indicates that the needed armor can be procured. (The last detail is a throwback to chapter vi; Isaac agrees to procure arms for the Pilgrim to fight in the tournament at Ashby.) They quickly leave the stage as Malvoisin, Thierry, and several men of arms enter. Malvoisin commands the men to go after the two fugitives, one of whom he thinks may be Ivanhoé. Boisguilbert then enters and asks Malvoisin to help him bring about Léila's escape. Malvoisin replies that escape is impossible, for the château is guarded by men faithful to Beaumanoir. He urges his friend not to sacrifice everything to a foolish passion. When Boisguilbert asks who will protect Léila, Malvoisin replies that if no one appears she must die, but that Boisguilbert will not have contributed to her death. As in the novel, Boisguilbert admits that Léila despises him and decides for the moment not to sacrifice everything for her. (Much of the duologue follows the conversation between Bois-Guilbert and Malvoisin at the end of chapter xxxix.) Hearing a bell that indicates that the *cortége funèbre* is about to begin, Malvoisin enters the château. In an aria Boisguilbert changes his mind about Léila and decides that he cannot abandon her to so cruel a destiny. His sword will acquit her. And yet he is in quite a predicament: if he wins in the lists, he sends her to her doom; if he loses, he is forevermore dishonored. Nevertheless his loss of honor is of no matter if he can win her love. If she agrees to yield to him, his arm will lift her from the fury of her captors. When the chevaliers come in to escort their champion to the lists, Boisguilbert expresses again, *à part,* his desire to save Léila: "Injuste puissance,/Ma terrible lance/De votre vengeance/ Saura la sauver!"

Malvoisin, Beaumanoir, Léila, chevaliers, and peasants now enter in a *cortége funèbre,* as the orchestra plays a march:

Example 9-9

Tempo di marcia sostenuto

Violins

The melody brings to mind the ensemble of the trial scene (see Example 9-8). Next comes a choral number in which the women implore God to protect innocence while the men say that He will confirm the just sentence.[8] Afterwards, in spoken dialogue, Malvoisin tries to keep Boisguilbert from approaching Léila. As in the novel, Beaumanoir says, "Laissez-le, Malvoisin. Dans un appel au jugement de Dieu, tout ce qui peut faire connaître la vérité, doit être permis." Again as in the novel Boisguilbert tries once more to win Léila over, but she refuses. She motions to the guards and says, "Qu'on me mene au supplice." The march recommences, and Léila is about to be led off. Suddenly cries are heard. A chevalier, with his *"visière braissée,"* enters and says that he is come to be Léila's champion. He then discloses that he is Wilfrid d'Ivanhoé. The ensuing spoken dialogue follows Scott closely. Boisguilbert at first refuses to fight the recently wounded Ivanhoé, but when Ivanhoé insists, Boisguilbert agrees. Beaumanoir gives his sanction to the enterprise, and all present leave the stage for the lists. Ismael enters. Hearing fanfares emanating from the lists, he realizes that the combat is taking place and he wonders how Ivanhoé is making out. He has something apparently of some consequence on his mind. Addressing Léila as if she were present, he says, "Pas une personne à qui dévoiler ce fatal secret dont la revelation peut te sauver!" Of course we in the audience wonder what this is all about, and it soon comes out. Cédric enters. He has come to try to prevent the unequal combat. When he and Ismael suddenly hear cries of "Victoire!" from the lists, Ismael implores him to save the daughter of his friend! He explains that Léila is actually Édith, the daughter of the Saxon nobleman Olric, who had entrusted her to his care just before his untimely death in combat in the Holy Land. Cédric is overjoyed: "O bonheur! la fille d'Alfred-le-Grand! courons, amis!" At this point begins the finale to the act. Cries of "Victoire!" are again heard from the wings, and for a few uncertain moments Cédric and Ismael are afraid that Ivanhoé has been defeated. Soon everyone re-enters. Ivanhoé has won. No mention is made of Boisguilbert's having died "a victim to the violence of his own contending passions." Cédric tells Ivanhoé who Léila really is, and Ivanhoé forthwith asks her to be his spouse. As in the novel, Beaumanoir declares that Heaven has decided the issue: "Le ciel se déclare!/Respectons ses arrêts." The chorus repeats his words. Ivanhoé urges that the Saxons and Normans forget their enmities, because, after all, they are all English. Suddenly Malvoisin rushes in with news that the enemy is advancing (presumably the French, under King Philippe). "Aux armes, chevaliers!" he cries. The opera ends with everyone present joining Malvoisin in his call to arms and expressing the desire for vengeance against the enemy.

There is no mention anywhere in the novel of a French army encamped near Rotherwood nor of a truce between England and France that is coming to an end. Many bold changes have been made in the original story, as the foregoing discussion reveals. Léila's turning out to be Christian and thus eligible to marry Ivanhoé fulfills the wishes of many readers of the novel, who find Rebecca a much more attractive character than Rowena. There are no English folk melodies in the score. As in the next opera we shall examine, the high point musically and dramatically is the trial scene.

Der Templer und die Jüdin

Heinrich Marschner's highly successful *Templer und Jüdin* was first performed on 22 December 1829, in Leipzig. His third wife's brother, Wilhelm August Wohlbrück, wrote the text. During the next twenty years productions in the original German were staged all over Europe north of the Alps—Berlin (1831), Budapest (1832), Amsterdam (1838), Prague (1839), Riga (1839-40), St. Petersburg (1840), London (1840), Graz (1846), Basel (1846), Vienna (1849). The opera reached New York in 1872. It was done in Danish in Copenhagen (1834); in Hungarian in Budapest (1890). Performances have extended into the twentieth century. There were revivals in Strasbourg on 20 April 1912; in Cologne, in the modernized version by Hans Pfitzner, on 25 September 1913—the latter being quite favorably reviewed the next day in the *Kölnische Zeitung* (Mittags-Ausgabe).

The cast of characters includes two sopranos: Rebecca and Rowena; three tenors: Ivanhoe, Bracy, and Wamba; three baritones: Guilbert, Lokslei, and Oswald; and four basses: Beaumanoir, Cedric, Tuck, and the Black Knight.[9] Adelstane (or Athelstane) and Isaak are listed among the dramatis personae in the libretto, but not in the vocal score, since neither role involves any singing beyond what is in a choral part. Notable omissions include Front-de-Bœuf, Gurth, Prince John, and Ulrica. The opera's title comes from the words of Scott's Earl of Essex to Ivanhoe, in the last chapter: "I was drawing towards York, having heard that Prince John was making head there, when I met King Richard, like a true knight-errant, galloping hither to achieve in his own person this adventure of the Templar and the Jewess, with his own single arm." As the title indicates, the emphasis here falls on Bois-Guilbert and Rebecca; Ivanhoe and Rowena are of secondary importance.

After an exciting overture typical of German romantic grand opera of the early nineteenth century, the curtain rises on a scene that comes almost at the mid-point of the novel. Bracy and a group of his soldiers are about to ambush Cedric, Rowena, and their retinue as they are returning home from the lists of Ashby:

> BRACY: Ihr lagert still euch dort im Wald.
> CHORUS: Wir lagern still uns dort im Wald,
> Der Zug muss hier vorbei.
> BRACY: Er ist nicht fern, er nahet bald
> Und glaubt die Strasse frei.

The number is in 6/8 time and resembles in spirit the choruses of hunters that open many a Walter Scott opera. Guilbert arrives on the scene and is at first not recognized, nor does he recognize Bracy and his followers. A fight immediately ensues, but soon Bracy and Guilbert recognize each other's voice, and the fighting stops. Each wonders what the other is doing in the forest. Finally Bracy declares that he has come to woo a wife through force, and for a moment it appears that both men have the same purpose. Guilbert, however, is seeking to waylay not Rowena but Rebecca, "die schöne Jüdin." He and Bracy decide to help each other.—The opera does not follow Scott exactly. In the novel De Bracy and Bois-Guilbert, along with Front-de-Bœuf, had planned *together* in advance to ambush Cedric's train. Their unexpected encounter in the opera and their failure at first to recognize one another make the situation more tense dramatically than it would have been if Wohlbrück and Marschner had followed Scott to the letter.

Bracy, Guilbert, and their men depart as Cedric and his entourage draw near. The music accompanying their entrance is often repeated during the course of the opera and is always associated with the Saxons:

Example 9-10

Cedric curses the foolery that prompted him to take Rowena with him to the tournament. In orchestra-accompanied recitative Rowena upbraids him for allowing his only son, who had been severely wounded, to be looked after by complete strangers. Fully realizing why Rowena is so concerned about Ivanhoe, Cedric reminds her of the royal blood that flows through her veins. She replies that all hope of restoring the Saxon monarchy is in vain, for Richard is very much in command, and she urges him to make peace with the world and with his noble son. He says he will refuse as long as Ivanhoe continues to aspire to her affection. (The recitative brings out in concise fashion information that Scott develops in the early chapters.) At this point Wamba interrupts and sings a song in which he advises Rowena to let things take their course (" 's wird besser geh'n! 's wird besser geh'n!/ Die Welt ist rund und muss sich dreh'n"). This is the first of several songs that do not contribute much to the furthering of the plot. Suddenly Oswald, Cedric's steward, enters and warns his master that suspicious people are lurking in the forest; that they have already taken as prisoners Isaak von York and his beautiful daughter. (In the novel Isaac, Rebecca, and, unbeknownst to the Saxons, the wounded Ivanhoe are a part of Cedric's entourage when the attack comes.) The scene closes with a "Schlachtlied der Sachsen," the melody of which we have already heard (see Example 9-10).

The action now shifts to the hut of Friar Tuck. The whole scene consists of his "Song of the Barefoot Monk," in which he is joined by the Black Knight and a chorus. This was undoubtedly suggested by "The Barefoot Friar" of the novel (chapter xvii), but the German text does not follow Scott's poem. The piece is one of the most engaging in the entire score. Especially delightful is the mock-serious Latin refrain:

Example 9-11

The comic gaiety of this brief scene is in contrast with the serious atmosphere of the rest of the act. Wohlbrück and Marschner have omitted the long conversation between Tuck and the Black Knight which takes place in the novel.

The scene now changes to a tower room of the castle where the Normans have taken their captives. Rebecca is pushed rudely by a servant into the room. She soon discovers the window from which she can plunge to her death, if necessary. (In the novel the window is not mentioned until she actually does threaten to jump out.) Guilbert enters, and much of the ensuing "Grosse Scene und Duett" follows closely Scott's dialogue of chapter xxiv. Many parallels could be pointed out. During the course of the duet Rebecca moves toward the window:

> Ein Sprung und ich bin frei!
> Zurück! Nah'st du nur einen Schritt,
> Stürz' ich hinab von dieses Thurmes Zinnen!
> Zerschmettert soll mein Leib an jenem Felsen liegen,
> Eh' ich mich deiner freveln Lust will fügen.

> "Remain where thou art, proud Templar, or at thy choice advance!—one foot nearer, and I plunge myself from the precipice; my body shall be crushed out of the very form of humanity upon the stones of that court-yard, ere it become the victim of thy brutality!"

And as the duet ends we hear Saxons *without* singing the by-this-time familiar "Schlachtlied." (They are Saxon forces come to rescue Cedric and his followers, who have now been captured. Unless there is more to the text than appears in the vocal score and the librettos which I used, the action at this point would be difficult for anyone to grasp who was not already familiar with the novel.) Norman soldiers *without* sing in reply, Guilbert joining in. After he has departed, the offstage chorus of Saxons is again heard, and at the same time Rebecca exuberantly sings praises to the God of Israel. Then, in a quieter mood, she sings a moving arioso in which she beseeches God to help Ivanhoe and her father.

Ivanhoe now enters. He sees the unknown beauty who has saved his life and addresses her in tender words. When Rebecca tells him that she is a Jewess, his reaction is more emotional than that of Scott's hero: "Du eine Jüdin? Was muss ich hören!" (Dramatic compression of the plot is evident here. The parallel incident in the novel occurs *before* Ivanhoe and Rebecca are in captivity; Scott tells us about it in a flashback.) The following dialogue also differs from the novel in that Scott's Cedric does not know until later that Ivanhoe is a prisoner:

IVANHOE:	Sprich, Mädchen, wo mag Ritter Cedric sein?
	Hält ihn ein gleich Geschick an diesem Orte?
REBECCA:	Gefangen sah er Euch, und laut rief er:
	Mein Sohn! mein Sohn! so sehe ich dich wieder!
	Auch Lady Row'nas Herz erbangte schwer—
IVANHOE:	Auch sie!—O theures Mädchen, Segen auf dich nieder!

At this point the audience might well wonder whether Ivanhoe means Rowena or Rebecca. Rebecca also wonders ("Theures Mädchen, sagt' er—wem?"), but in the following duet she soon learns, to her disappointment, that he means Rowena. They hear the noise of strife *without*. Rebecca goes to the window, but she cannot see anything: "Von diesem Thurme kann man nichts erspähen." She then goes out to try to obtain precise information on what is happening. (In the novel Rebecca *does* see the fighting from the window, and she relates what she sees to Ivanhoe, who has not recovered sufficiently from his wounds to take part himself in the combat. Wohlbrück and Marschner have missed an opportunity for an effective operatic number.) While she is gone the Black Knight enters and saves Ivanhoe from the fire that is beginning to engulf the castle. Agitated musical figures built on diminished seventh chords are heard in the orchestra. Rebecca re-enters and finds herself in a dangerous predicament, because the flames are becoming more pronounced. She expresses her dread of what may happen to her father, while at the same time we hear in the background the choruses of Normans and Saxons. In the midst of the excitement Guilbert enters. His first words to Rebecca follow the novel very closely:

Hab' ich endlich Dich getroffen!
Noch ein Rettungsweg ist offen;
Dir und mir ihn zu bewachen,
Ringsumgeben von Gefahren,
Bahnt' ich mir den Weg zu dir.
Auf denn! rasch und folge mir!

"I have found thee," said he to Rebecca; "thou shalt prove I will keep
my word to share weal and woe with thee—There is but one path to
safety, I have cut my way through fifty dangers to point it to thee—
up, and instantly follow me!"

In a highly dramatic passage in the score he forces Rebecca to go with him
despite her unwillingness and her cries for help. (Note that in the opera
this incident occurs *after* Ivanhoe has been rescued and thereby receives
greater emphasis.) The fighting backstage now moves on stage. We hear
the Saxon leitmotiv in the orchestra as Cedric fights against Bracy, defeats
him, and takes him as a prisoner. (In the novel the Black Knight has this
honor.) Rowena, Cedric, and Wamba thank Lokslei for his help in rescuing them, and the act closes with an impressive ensemble composed of
Rowena, Wamba, Lokslei, Cedric, and a full chorus. All sing of joy except
Cedric, who broods on the death of his friend Athelstane—and this is the
last we hear of Athelstane the Unready in the opera. (The action, words,
and tableau for the last portion of the finale are borrowed with alterations
from the meeting in the forest which occurs, in the novel, immediately
after the fall of Torquilstone.)

For the opening scene of Act II we move to the forest. The ensemble
which develops is similar in make-up to that at the end of Act I. Rowena,
Wamba, and Cedric thank the outlaws for their help and remark that they
are on their way home. Next we have a "Lied des Bruder Tuck mit Chor,"
the text of which is not based on any poem in the novel. Immediately
afterwards Ivanhoe comes in, interrupts the merriment, and identifies
the Black Knight, who all the while has been carousing with the outlaws, as
Richard Löwenherz. Lokslei explains to the King that his wicked brother's
injustice compelled him and his followers to break the law of the land. The
outlaws swear allegiance to Richard, and the scene closes as Ivanhoe and
the chorus sing in praise of him. (In the novel the identity of the Black
Knight is revealed under different circumstances. Hard pressed by
would-be assassins, he is saved in the nick of time by Locksley and his men.
At this point he reveals that he is King Richard. See chapter xl.)

The next number is a long "Scene und Arie" for Guilbert, who is now
presumably back at Templestowe. (Stage directions are inadequate in the
vocal score and non-existent in the librettos which I used.) He is frustrated
by Rebecca's unwillingness to become his mistress, and he thinks that she
is ungrateful to him for having saved her from the flames. He maintains
that if she really knew his feelings, she would be more compassionate
toward him. In the ensuing *allegretto* he tells about his ill-fated love for
Adelheid von Montemar (as in his conversation with Rebecca, in the
novel, at Torquilstone). Having been betrayed, he killed both Adelheid
and her bridegroom at their wedding: "Beim Hochzeitsmahl durchstösst

mein Stahl den Buben, die Verrätherin!" (In the novel the nature of his revenge is not specified: "Truly did I love her," Brian says, "and bitterly did I revenge me of her broken faith!") After this disappointment he became a Templar, but he has found no happiness. He is lonely, and his life has no meaning. Through Rebecca's love, however, he thinks he can be saved. The aria ends in a joyful mood of hope. (This scene, which has no exact parallel in Scott, figures significantly in Wohlbrück and Marschner's portrayal of Guilbert, who is no pasteboard operatic villain. It is the longest scene given to any single character.)

The final scene of Act II, easily the most impressive part of the opera, is a musical adaptation of Rebecca's trial at the Preceptory of Templestowe (chapters xxxvii–xxxviii). When the curtain rises we see a stage full of people. The opening "Chor des Volks" is followed by stately music sung by Beaumanoir and the Chorus of Templars. As in the novel, Beaumanoir glances at Guilbert and remarks about his disturbed emotional state. He says that she who has bewitched the knight must pay for her sin. At this point Rebecca is brought in, while both the Chorus of People and the Chorus of Templars sing, "Fluch der Jüdin! Fluch der Zauberin! . . . Sie sterbe! Sie sterbe!" Beaumanoir finds it necessary to order the guards to protect Rebecca from the fury of the crowd. (The dramatic situation implicit in Scott is greatly heightened.) Guilbert stealthily hands Rebecca a piece of paper which later becomes significant in the working out of the plot. Beaumanoir then accuses Rebecca of witchcraft, and when he asks Guilbert for his feeling in the matter, Guilbert replies in words closely paralleling the original:

Guilbert hält solch ein thörichtes Beschulden
Nicht einer Antwort werth.
Doch wird sein tapfres Schwert
Keine Beleid'gung seiner Ehre dulden!

"Brian de Bois-Guilbert," he answered, "replies not, most Reverend Father, to such wild and vague charges. If his honour be impeached, he will defend it with his body, and with that sword which has often fought for Christendom."

In reply Beaumanoir forgives the Templar for his rudeness, which he believes is a result of his being under the power of a witch. He then demands that Rebecca remove her veil. She hesitates:

Example 9-12

And as she continues singing she begs her judges for compassion:

Ach, um Eurer Töchter willen—
Doch, Ihr seid ja kinderlos,
Rauhe Männer seid Ihr bloss;
Nun denn, bei dem Angedenken
Eurer Mütter, Eurer Schwestern!
Woll't Barmherzigkeit mir schenken,
Lasst von roher Männer Händen,
Zucht und Sitte zu verlästern,
Nicht den Schleier mir entwenden.
Wenn   I h r   wollt, dass ich es   s o l l,—
Ihr seid alt und würdevoll,—
Will ich dem Gebot mich fügen,
Und das schamerglüht' Gesicht
Einer Unglücksel'gen zeigen,
Das um Mitleid zu Euch spricht.

Throughout this highly effective portion of the trial scene, which follows Scott closely, there is chromatic movement in both the melodic line and the harmonic structure, as if Marschner were consciously trying to give his music a flavor appropriate to Rebecca and her race. After she does remove her veil Beaumanoir repeats the charges against her and forthwith sentences her to death: "Drum, Brüder, auf! lasst uns das Urtheil sprechen:/ Sie sterbe in des Scheiterhaufens Gluth." His sentence is backed up by the Templars, who sing in unison, "Sie sterbe! Sie sterbe!" (The cruelty of the Christian judges is much increased from what it is in Scott.) As in the novel, Rebecca says that she knows it would be in vain to ask for pity, and then she dramatically turns her remarks toward Guilbert:

Nur auf dich allein, auf dich,
Hier wie dort beruf' ich mich:
Ist die Wahrheit hier gesagt,
Wess' man mich jetzt angeklagt?
Bin ich schuldig dessen? Sprich!

After a moment of silence the chorus observes that an evil, supernatural force must be present. Again as in the novel Rebecca calls on Guilbert to answer her question. After another slight pause, he excitedly exclaims in his speaking voice, "Das Blatt! Das Blatt!" (Again Wohlbrück and Marschner have heightened the dramatic intensity implicit in the novel.) The chorus comments on the peculiar situation that has arisen, and then Rebecca reads aloud, in her speaking voice, the writing on the paper: "Einen Kämpfer ford're dir!" She forthwith demands a champion in words paralleling Scott very closely and throws her glove down in front of Beaumanoir and the Templars. In the ensuing ensemble, which is composed of Rebecca, Guilbert, Beaumanoir, and the entire chorus, Rebecca sings that the brave knight whom she nursed back to health will come to her rescue, while Guilbert sings that now *he* can be her champion. After the ensemble Beaumanoir turns to the Templars and asks them who shall be the champion of their order. They reply, "Bois Guilbert soll der Kämpe sein." Guilbert's reaction—"Wer? Ich? Ha! nimmermehr!"—is not expressed in the novel. Instead of being given three days to find her brave knight, Rebecca is given only until sunset of the day of the trial (cf. the Rossini pasticcio). In the final ensemble (Rebecca, Guilbert, Beaumanoir, and chorus) Guilbert laments that he can no longer help her. So ends the magnificent trial scene.

The first scene of Act III has no parallel in the novel. Its primary function is to provide us with a few minutes of emotional relief between the trial scene and the remainder of the opera. In the opening dance music the chorus sings in praise of King Richard. This is followed by a "Romance" for Ivanhoe, who also sings Richard's praises, as the chorus joins him in the refrain. Finally, we have a song for Wamba ("Es ist doch gar köstlich, ein König zu sein"). —The second scene is based on the meeting of Rebecca and Bois-Guilbert in her cell at Templestowe, after the trial (chapter xxxix). When the curtain rises, Rebecca, alone on stage, sings a moving prayer (the text does not follow Scott's "hymn"). Afterwards Guilbert enters. As in the novel, he tells Rebecca that his name will be forevermore ruined if he does not appear in the lists, yet he will give up all if she will become his mistress. The rest of the scene departs from Scott. When Rebecca says that she will not have him, he angrily vows revenge: "Du verschmähest meine Liebe?/ Stolze Spröde! Nun wohlan!/ Nur der Rache süssem Triebe / Weih' ich meine Seele dann." As the duet develops, Rebecca sings that she will thank God even at the stake that she resisted Guilbert's temptation; he maintains that when she is burning she will regret her choice. Near the end, ominous-sounding trumpets announce that the time for Rebecca's fate to be decided is drawing nigh.

The final scene is based on the two concluding chapters of the novel. It begins with a stately "Marsch der Templer." At Beaumanoir's request the trumpets sound a summons, as in the novel, but no champion appears. When Beaumanoir asks Rebecca if she will accept her punishment, she redeclares her innocence in a moving arioso. (In the novel a herald asks Rebecca the question and conveys her message back to Beaumanoir.) He replies, "Wir harren bis zum spät'sten Abendroth." (Scott's justices are willing to wait only "until the shadows be cast from the west to the eastward," but, as I indicated above, the trial by combat takes place three days after the preliminary trial; in the opera it takes place the same day.) Then, as in the novel, Guilbert makes one last attempt to seduce Rebecca. After she has once more rejected him, he murmurs, "Ein kalter Frost durchschauert mein Gebein,/Und Wahnsinn stürmt, ich fühl' es, auf mich ein." (These words are not in the novel.) When Beaumanoir asks him if Rebecca is still firm in her conviction, he replies *in immer grösserer Geistes-verwirrung*:

> Ja, sie ist fest, die holde Zauberin;
> Sie springt vom höchsten Thurm hinab,
> Kalt blickt sie in das off'ne Grab,
> Sie scheut selbst nicht den Flammentodt.
> Der endet freilich alle Noth!
> Mir wird das wenig frommen—
> Halloh! halloh! will denn kein Kämpe kommen?

A stage direction indicates that he sinks into deep brooding. (The whole incident is greatly exaggerated from what is only suggested in Scott.) When it looks as if no champion is going to come, Beaumanoir orders the wood to be lit. But finally, in the nick of time, the champion does arrive, and after a short exciting ensemble (Rebecca, Guilbert, and chorus) he raises his visor and dramatically announces that he is Wilfried von Ivanhoe. Rebecca readily accepts him as her champion, the combat takes place (on stage). and in the second round *"holt Guilbert zu einem fürchter-lichen Hiebe aus, stürzt aber mit diesem Schlage in sich selbst zusammen."* Ivanhoe releases Rebecca, and the chorus announces that the King has arrived. As in the novel, Richard upbraids Ivanhoe for fighting with his wounds not fully healed. Then Rowena, who unlike Scott's Rowena has come with the King to Templestowe, embraces her favored suitor; she has at long last received Cedric's permission to marry him. When Richard asks Rebecca if she has any desire, she replies that she has received reward enough in having Ivanhoe fight for her. (In the novel Rebecca, together with her father, retires from the scene unobserved.) Richard upbraids the Temp-lars, as in the novel, and the opera closes with a large choral ensemble that sounds very much like early Wagner.[10] Once more the King is lauded:

> Lasst lauten Jubelruf erschallen,

Dass Berg' und Thäler wiederhallen,
Und freudig jauchz' es himmelwärts:
Hoch lebe Richard Löwenherz!

To sum up, Wohlbrück and Marschner have taken one central aspect of
the novel, the relationship between Rebecca and Brian de Bois-Guilbert,
and have constructed the opera with this in the forefront. Except for the
short scenes of comic relief, everything included relates to what they
considered to be the novel's emotional core. They often follow Scott
closely. When they alter or expand the original in any way, they do so with
the idea of heightening the musical and dramatic possibilities already
implicit in the scene or incident in question. The trial scene is excellent.
The opera well deserves the success which it had for a long time in
German and Austrian opera houses.

Pacini's *Ivanhoe*

Giovanni Pacini's two-act opera *Ivanhoe* was first performed in Venice,
on 19 March 1832, at the Fenice.[11] Gaetano Rossi wrote the libretto, which
owes much to Deschamps and De Wailly's libretto for the Rossini
pasticcio. Pacini writes in his memoirs that the opera "consequi successo di
pieno entusiasmo." He continues: "Ascrivo a mia gloria il poter dire, che
ebbi ad interpreti le famose Carradori [as Rebecca] e Giuditta Grisi [as
Wilfredo], il tenore Reina [as Briano di Boiguilbert], cantante pieno
d'anima ed attore perfetto, ed il celebre Coselli [as Cedrico]. Un *coro* della
precitata opera si rese talmente popolare nell' incantevole città, che anco
di presente vien ripetuto nei giorni carnevaleschi dai figli della Laguna."[12]
During the carnival of 1833-34 *Ivanhoe* was produced at la Scala.[13] The
singers included Ignazio Marini (Cedrico), Brigida Lorenzani (Wilfredo),
Felicita Bayllou (Editta), Giuseppe Vaschetti (Alberto di Malvoisin),
Berardo Winter (Briano di Boiguilbert), Domenico Spiaggi (Ismaele),
and Giuseppina Demerì (Rebecca). One can readily see that the cast of
characters is basically the same as in the Rossini pasticcio except for the
addition of Editta, who is Cedrico's daughter and Wilfredo's sister.

Act I takes place at Rotherwood. After a formal overture the curtain
rises on a ground-floor room of the castle. Through the rear door and
windows one can see a grove that leads to the family burial-ground on one
side, and on the other to an arcade. The first vocal number is a rousing
drinking song for a chorus of Saxons. They wish for the annihilation of
the Normans, whom they believe to be the source of all their anguish. A
minstrel who says he is a pilgrim from Palestine begs shelter from the
storm that is raging outside. The Saxons permit him to advance and
promise that he will find asylum and love at Rotherwood. The pilgrim-
minstrel (who is of course Ivanhoe in disguise) is deeply moved at being
home again. When the Saxons tell him that Editta, the mistress of the
castle, is about to come in, he can hardly conceal his emotions. Something

about the pilgrim-minstrel's appearance stimulates Editta's memory. She tells him that she heard him singing while she was tending to Cedrico, her father, who is suffering from a slight indisposition. She then anxiously asks him for whatever news he might have about Palestine. Her beloved brother, Ivanhoe, departed thither when she was a young girl, and all this time she has prayed to heaven for his safe return. The minstrel-pilgrim is so deeply moved by what she says that he almost gives himself away. He does say that Ivanhoe lives and will return. Cedrico enters, somewhat perturbed that the forbidden name has been spoken. He says that he no longer has a son, in view of the fact that the misguided young man left home to serve under Richard, the Norman king. (Cf. the Rossini pasticcio. In the novel Cedric had disowned Ivanhoe because of his love for Rowena, whom Cedric intended for Athelstane.) All present try to make Cedrico relent in his unnatural attitude toward his son, but in vain. At the close of the ensemble, everyone leaves the stage except Ivanhoe, who after a brief recitative also departs.

Rebecca now enters and sings a recitative and aria. She has finally arrived in England, after having travelled all over Europe in search of the brave knight who saved her from the brutal fury of Briano at Acri. He was severely wounded, but she had cured him. If only she could now be near the one whom she adores! Afterwards, in a passage of accompanied recitative, she thanks Editta for her part in saving her and her father the day before, when they were being pursued in the forest by iniquious brigands. Editta tells Rebecca that her native dress will bring back sad memories to Cedrico, who had once been in Palestine himself on a crusade. His friend Olderico, the last scion of Alfred the Great, was killed there, and Olderico's daughter, who was then only a child, was lost. Nevertheless Editta assures Rebecca that she will enjoy Cedrico's hospitality despite any sad memories which her presence may stimulate. (Cedrico's presence in Palestine with Olderico, which has no parallel in Scott, is borrowed from Deschamps and De Wailly's libretto.) Editta exits, and we then behold the pilgrim-minstrel (Ivanhoe) lamenting at the tomb of his mother, which is located in a far-away recess of the stage-setting. He wishes that she had lived, for she would have known how to placate Cedrico. He says that he will reveal himself to his dear sister and then bid her farewell. (Scott makes no mention anywhere of Ivanhoe's mother.) When he comes forward, he and Rebecca see each other, and an elaborate love-duet ensues. She has never forgotten his having saved her. Unlike what we have in either the novel or the Rossini pasticcio, they ardently express their love for one another—a love ill-fated. "Il tuo culto!" Ivanhoe says; "la mia fè!/ Che sarà di te... di me!" Duty precluding the possibility of their uniting in marriage, they must part, never to see each other again. As the duet closes they both express the sorrowful thought that they will not be able to be together even in heaven.

The scene now changes to the "piazzale del castello." The Saxon retainers notice a Norman herald approaching the castle, and they recognize him to be a messenger from Briano. They are apprehensive as to what his business might be, because they know well of Briano's evil deeds, especially to innocent maidens. Cedrico orders the gate to be opened; he will hear what the herald has to say. The herald enters. (We soon learn that he is Briano himself in disguise; this is not the case in the Rossini pasticcio.) He says that a female slave and her father, who both belong to Briano, have found asylum at Rotherwood; they must be returned to their owner. Cedrico refuses to give them up. The herald states Briano's demand again and tells Cedrico and the Saxons that they can expect great slaughter if the demand is not immediately fulfilled. As Cedrico again refuses, the duet leads into the elaborate finale. He requests that Rebecca be brought in. She enters, along with Ismaele, Editta, and a group of ladies. Prostrating herself before Cedrico, she implores him to defend her from Briano. When he asks her whether she is Briano's slave, she declares that she is not. Cedrico then orders the herald to depart. He replies, "Ma con lei.—Mia schiava è questa." Rebecca suddenly realizes that the herald is actually Briano himself, and she calls out for help. At this point the pilgrim-minstrel enters. He immediately recognizes Briano, and Briano in turn sees through *his* disguise and calls him by name. All present are now aware of the real identities of the herald and the pilgrim-minstrel. A quintet ensues: Cedrico expresses surprise that his son is before him, and he admits that natural, parental affection is triumphing in his bosom; Ivanhoe observes that both his father and his rival stand before him—he admits that he is greatly agitated; Rebecca expresses delight that her lover has come to her aid; Briano observes that his rival stands before him—he is furious; Editta sings that her brother is back and stands before their father—she too admits that she is greatly agitated. When the quintet has ended, Ivanhoe accuses Briano of breaking his word, for he had sworn not to harass Rebecca and her father after he (Ivanhoe) had defeated him in Palestine. Briano is not impressed when Ivanhoe hotly tells him to "be afraid" and "save himself" because he knows that his Norman soldiers are getting ready to storm the castle. Ivanhoe hastily calls the Saxons to arms, but Briano observes *con feroce gioja* that it is too late. Suddenly he disarms Cedrico and threatens to kill him. He warns Ivanhoe that if he advances one step toward him, Cedrico dies. He then demands that Ivanhoe yield Rebecca to him and promise to allow the two of them to depart. If he refuses, Cedrico dies. Ivanhoe has no choice but to give in. There are a few moments of dreadful suspense before the impressive final ensemble, which Ivanhoe himself begins with the words, "Vincesti alfine, o perfido,/Ma vivo a tuo periglio." He is soon joined by Rebecca, Editta, and Briano, then Cedrico, and finally Ismaele and the chorus. Pacini's use of sustained syncopated notes in some of the vocal lines brings to mind the Sextet from *Lucia*. The Saxons tell the barbarian Normans to tremble, for there is a God who will come to their aid. As the act closes, the triumphant Normans set fire to the castle and Briano takes Rebecca away. The Saxons swear vengeance. (Rossi and Pacini's handling of this *scena* differs from the Rossini pasticcio mainly in that there is no actual fighting between Normans and Saxons. Briano effectively accomplishes his goal by taking Cedrico as hostage and threatening to kill him if Ivanhoe does not meet his demands at once.)

The first part of Act II takes place in a room of the Castello di S. Edemondo. When the curtain rises, Rebecca is disclosed, lamenting her fate. Soon Editta appears, dressed in the costume of a Norman page. During the confusion of Act I, it seems that a Norman page was taken prisoner by the Saxons, and thus Editta managed to obtain appropriate dress for her bold venture into the castello to see about Rebecca. (There is no close relationship between Rowena and Rebecca in the novel. They do not even speak with each other until the very end, after Rowena and Ivanhoe have married. Editta's gaining access to the castello by means of a disguise probably was suggested by Wamba's disguising himself as a friar so that he can gain access to Torquilstone.) Editta informs Rebecca that Ismaele is at the foot of the tower, and she urges her to drop him a letter. Rebecca accordingly pens a note to Ivanhoe, in which she advises him, if he should have qualms about aiding her himself in view of the promise Briano extorted from him, to have Cedrico arm the Saxons and also to inform Re Filippo of her capture (cf. the Rossini pasticcio). She tosses the letter to her father, and Editta sees him carry it off. They then sing a duet in which they implore God to help them in their plight. Editta withdraws when they hear Briano coming. He enters. When he urges Rebecca to yield to his love for her, she says that she will sooner fall to her death (and presumably threatens to jump from the tower window—there are no stage directions at this point in either the libretto or the vocal score). Suddenly Editta comes out from her hiding-place. She tells Briano that she is prepared to proclaim his guilt all over Europe (in words spoken by Rebecca in the novel); moreover, she is Ivanhoe's sister. We then have a trio: Editta repeats her intention to proclaim Briano's infamy to the world; Briano expresses his surprise at the presence of Editta and calls on his heart to resume its former vigor; Rebecca implores heaven for aid. Hearing the sound of a march in the distance, Briano realizes that the Commendatore has returned. He is worried about his superior's finding out what has been going on in the castello during his absence. When he demands that the two ladies withdraw into separate rooms, they stubbornly insist on staying together, but as the number closes, his guards force them to separate. The Commendatore, Alberto di Malvoisin, now enters. (He is an amalgamation of the Malvoisin and Beaumanoir of the novel, and of the Rossini pasticcio.) In a passage of recitative, he expresses concern about Briano's rash actions and says that the only way his honor can be saved is for Rebecca to be tried as an agent of the French king.

The scene changes to a mountainous wooded place, with the remnants of the recently burned Castello di Rotherwood in the distance. Saxon *montanari* (Highlanders!) sing of their desire to triumph over the Normans; they are convinced that the star of the Saxons will rise again. Cedrico expresses his concern to Ivanhoe about the fate of Editta, whom he knows to be at the Castello di S. Edemondo. He is also unhappy about her friendship with Rebecca. When Ivanhoe says that the Saxons under his leadership will rescue *both* ladies, Cedrico wonders why he is so interested in the welfare of an infidel. He suspects that Ivanhoe loves her, and finally the truth comes out: Ivanhoe admits his love for her. (There is no parallel to this in either the novel or the Rossini pasticcio.) Cedrico is perturbed. Father and son then sing a duet, after which Ivanhoe promises Cedrico that when Rebecca is freed she will return to Asia and that he will devote his life to the pursuit of glory (i.e. he will not seek to marry her). Cedrico is relieved: "Ti benedica il Ciel!" In the second half of the duet Cedrico tells Ivanhoe to return triumphant ("E ritorna vincitor"), and Ivanhoe promises to do so ("Tornerò trïonfator").[14]

The scene now moves back to the room in the castello. The time for Rebecca's judgment has arrived. The Templars enter solemnly, as the orchestra plays a march appropriate to the occasion. Presently Rebecca is brought in by two guards. To the accompaniment of a tremolo in the strings, Alberto reads her sentence in "melodramatic" fashion: she is condemned to be burned at the stake. When he asks whether she has anything to say about the sentence, she protests her innocence, throws down her glove, and sings ecstatically that God will provide her with a champion. She then sings a cavatina ("Nel bel suolo degli eroi"), after which the Templars call on Briano to defend their order. Alberto orders a trial by combat to be proclaimed far and wide. If Rebecca's champion does not appear "al cader del nuovo giorno," she must die. Rebecca repeats her belief that a champion will come from heaven to defend her. She then launches into the cabaletta ("Dal Cielo a me scende/La fè che m'accende") which concludes the scene. (This is a good scene, but not ambitious from a musical standpoint and therefore not nearly so impressive as the parallel material in Rossini and Marschner.)

The remainder of the opera takes place outside the castle. The women of the chorus feel pity for Rebecca, who is about to be burned at the stake, her champion not having appeared. The men celebrate the glory and valor of Briano, whom no one dares to oppose. When after a trumpet fanfare the champion does not appear, Alberto orders two negro slaves to conduct Rebecca to the funeral pyre. Suddenly Ivanhoe rushes in, and a quintet develops: Ivanhoe announces himself as Rebecca's champion; Briano sings *aside* of his fear and to Ivanhoe, "Ti vincerò"; Rebecca, Cedrico, and Editta declare that God will protect the innocent. Afterwards Briano, Ivanhoe, and the spectators enter the offstage arena where the combat will take place. Cedrico and a group of Saxons are left behind. Ismaele then enters and, as in the Rossini pasticcio, informs Cedrico that

Rebecca is actually the daughter of Olderico, Cedrico's beloved friend who was killed in Palestine. He presents indisputable proof that what he says is true. Cries of "Vittoria" are heard from the arena, and for a few uncertain moments Cedrico thinks that Ivanhoe may have fallen. But when he hears the people shout "Viva Ivanhoe!" he exclaims exultantly, "Ah! il figlio mio!" Everyone re-enters, the chorus singing of Ivanhoe's great triumph. Next, in a recitative and melancholy cantabile, Ivanhoe advises Rebecca to return to Jordan, but he expresses also the hope that from time to time she will think about her champion, just as indeed he will think about her. The chorus notices the understated poignancy of his remarks. When he says "Ma basta, addio./E per sempre!" Cedrico breaks in and tells him that he can marry Rebecca, for she is not an infidel but the daughter of Olderico. The chorus observes that virtue has been rewarded. The opera concludes with Ivanhoe's florid cabaletta, "Ah! di gioje aprirsi un cielo."[15] At the very end the chorus joins in, addressing both lovers with the words, "Come un segno lusinghiero vostra vita scorrerà." The curtain falls.

In the final *scena* there is no call to arms for everyone to go out and fight the French. Thus it differs from the parallel *scène* in Rossini. There are other interesting differences between the two librettos which I have pointed out during the course of this discussion. Yet Rossi's indebtedness to Deschamps and De Wailly is obviously very great. Even though he introduces the character Editta, who is the counterpart of Scott's Rowena, there are no problems in the final resolution of the plot. Although she loves Ivanhoe deeply, she is, after all, his *sister,* and as such she does not stand in the way of his marrying his true-love, the supposed infidel Rebecca, who conveniently turns out to be of good Saxon stock.

Il Templario

Otto Nicolai's *Il Templario,* with a libretto by Girolamo Maria Marini, was first performed in Turin, at the Teatro Regio, on 11 February 1840. Next to *Die lustigen Weiber von Windsor,* which still holds the stage despite Verdi's *Falstaff,* it proved to be Nicolai's most successful opera. It was performed in the original Italian all over Europe, from Barcelona to St. Petersburg and even Constantinople. According to Loewenberg, its last revival in Italy took place in Leghorn in 1879. It was first performed in the Western Hemisphere in Mexico City (1842) and in Buenos Aires (1851). It was given in Hungarian in Budapest (1842), in German in Vienna (1845), and in a French translation by Louis Danglas in Antwerp (1861), Brussels (1862), and Bordeaux (1864).[16] The cast of characters includes Cedrico, Vilfredo d'Ivanhoe, Rovena, Luca di Beaumanoir, Briano di Bois-Guilbert, Isacco d'York, and Rebecca. As in the novel, Rovena is Cedrico's ward rather than his daughter (cf. Pacini's Editta). The opera is divided into three acts.[17]

The overture (or "sinfonia," as it is designated in the vocal score) includes material which is heard during the course of the opera, such as the *marcia funebre* of Act III:

Example 9-13

At the completion of the overture the curtain rises on a grand salon where everything has been prepared for the coronation of the victor of the tournament at Ashby. Cedrico, Rovena, and a chorus of Saxons and Normans await the arrival of the hero. The importance of the occasion is effectively portrayed in the stately, festive music:

Example 9-14

Ivanhoe, the Disinherited Knight, enters, but he is not recognized by anyone because the visor of his helmet is lowered. He sings a cavatina ("Sia meco avverso il fato,/Solo il valor mi basta"), after which he chooses Rovena as the one who shall crown him. She does so as he kneels before her. (Unlike Scott's Ivanhoe, he does not swoon from loss of blood.) This ritual is followed by more festive music, which leads eventually into Ivanhoe's cabaletta ("Per quella dolce immagine"). (Marini has compressed the events of the novel in having the selection of the Queen of Beauty and Love and the presentation of the Chaplet of Honor both occur in the same ceremony. Moreover, everything takes place in a grand salon rather than in the lists. The fighting itself, which is often awkward in operatic rendition, is already over with.)

The scene now changes to the camp of Briano di Bois-Guilbert, the principal loser of the tournament. The sombre music of the orchestral introduction sets the tone for Briano's opening recitative, in which he sings of the great shame that has befallen him in having been defeated by an unknown knight—and before the eyes of the beautiful Jewess, whom he did not know to be in England and whom he passionately adores. "Più del mio onore, più di me stesso io t'amo!" he exclaims at the end of the recitative, after which he gives vent to his feelings of love in a cavatina ("Io per te nel cor talora"). Several of his Norman friends then enter and suggest to him that they abduct the Jewess and her father. Briano's spirits rise. The scene closes as he sings a rousing cabaletta: "Se in mio poter la rende") in which he is joined by his friends, who assure him that the wandering beauty will not be able to escape them.[18] (Briano's attempt to abduct Rebecca is not to be made concurrently with an attempt on Rovena; there is no De Bracy in the opera. Moreover, unlike the parallel incident of the novel, the attempt does not succeed, as we learn later.)

The rest of the act takes place in the grand vestibule of Cedrico's castle. The first number is a conventional chorus of women ("Del cielo britanno/Rovena e la stella"). (In Danglas' *Il Templier* this is immediately followed by ballet music. Interestingly, Wamba, who does not figure at all in the original Italian version, appears here as the premier danseur.) Rovena enters, absorbed in thought. She requests that the Saxon women leave her to herself for a while. When they have departed, she sings a *romanza* ("Oh! bel sogno lusinghier!") in which she muses on the victorious knight whom she crowned and wonders whether he could possibly be her beloved Ivanhoe. Suddenly Rebecca and Isacco appear, to the accompaniment of an agitated figure in the orchestra that comes also in the overture:

Example 9-15

They seek aid. Rebecca tells how she and her father were attacked by evil aggressors who fortunately were scared off when they heard another band of men approaching. She then sings a cavatina addressed to Rovena: "Ah! quel guardo non celar,/Se ti muove il mio dolor." Rovena is so deeply moved by Rebecca's plight that she says Rebecca may stay at the castle. She says furthermore that the victor at Ashby is also a guest. To this Rebecca remarks *aside,* "Oh gioja! alle armi note/Seppe il mio cor distinguerlo." In her cabaletta, "Per te vegg' io sorridere," she thanks Rovena for her goodness and hospitality, after which everyone goes into the castle. Briano now enters, stealthily and quietly, along with a band of armed Normans, while we hear in the orchestra strains of the music from his previous scene. He orders the men to disperse and conceal themselves, and when they have done so he tells a squier to announce to Cedrico his arrival.[19] Cedrico enters and asks Briano what brings him, a Norman, to the castle of a Saxon. Briano replies that he has come to demand his female slave, to whom Cedrico has granted illegal sanctuary. Cedrico says that Rebecca is Rovena's guest; nevertheless he orders a domestic to summon both of them to his presence. At this point the finale begins:

Example 9-16

Rebecca, Rovena, Isacco, and the chorus of women re-enter. Rebecca is understandably distressed when she sees Briano, and she vehemently denies that she is his slave. As he is about to take her away by force, the victor of Ashby enters and prevents him from doing so. All now recognize him as Vilfredo d'Ivanhoe. A sextet develops: Vilfredo and Briano singing of their pent-up wrath; Cedrico singing that his indignation against his son has now ceased; Rebecca, Rovena, Isacco, and the chorus of women imploring God to come to Rebecca's aid. Suddenly Briano calls for his men. They appear and immediately overpower Cedrico and his few domestics. Rebecca is taken. When Ivanhoe puts his hand to his sword, Briano tells him that if he dares to draw it, Rebecca will die. A huge ensemble develops. Rebecca is dragged off, as the Saxon damsels sing that heaven's vengeance will fall on her ravisher. (This scene has no exact parallel in the novel. Nicolai's librettist obviously patterned it after the very similar material in either the Rossini pasticcio or Pacini's *Ivanhoe* or both.)

Most of Act II takes place within the walls of the Templars' castle. First, we are in a chamber high up in the tower where Rebecca has been confined. Her mind still on Vilfredo, she sings of having once saved him from death after he had been severely wounded, but she in turn was wounded in her soul: she loves him. Briano enters and tells her she has no hope for safety unless she puts her trust in him. He explains that if she is found inside the castle, she will be in trouble. When he expresses his love for her, she tells him in no uncertain terms that his hopes are in vain. He replies that she *must* yield to him, for the Grand Master, who has been away, is expected back any moment, and if he should find her in the castle, her fate will be dreadful. Undaunted, she runs to the balcony and threatens to jump. At this climactic moment a trumpet fanfare is heard announcing the return of the Grand Master. Briano says that now all is lost. Rebecca returns from the balcony, exclaiming joyfully, "Al rigor di sorte irata/Io non palpito, non tremo:/La virtù nel fato estremo/Paventar, cader non sa." (As in the Rossini pasticcio and Pacini's *Ivanhoe*, this well-known incident occurs at the Templars' castle rather than at Torquilstone.)

The scene changes to the "gran sala d'armi." It opens with a stately (but rather trite) march and chorus of Templars. Luca di Beaumanoir, the Grand Master, enters and acknowledges the respectful greeting that the Templars have given him. Suddenly Isacco bursts in. He asks that pity be shown to his daughter, whom Briano unlawfully abducted. Beaumanoir gives order for Briano to be called in. In the meantime he asks Isacco who instructed his daughter in the occult arts, and Isacco replies that it was Miriam—much to the damage of any chance Rebecca might have had in her trial, since the Templars consider Miriam an evil sorceress (see chapter xxxv). When Briano enters, he is obviously distraught. All now go into the judgment room except him. He is upset because he knows that he alone is to blame for Rebecca's plight. He wants to save her, but as she is being led by two guards to the judgment room, she tells him that it is too late. In the ensuing cavatina he implores heaven to save her, and he expresses great remorse for what he has done. The Templars now return from the judgment room along with a herald, who brings in a glove on a silver platter. They inform Briano that Rebecca has demanded a trial by combat, and they want him to be the champion of their order. At first he refuses, but when they say that a refusal will forevermore stigmatize him as a coward, he picks up the glove with fury and accepts the challenge. In the cabaletta that closes the scene, Briano sings that he will follow his fate; that if Rebecca must die, he will die with her. (Interestingly, the trial has been moved offstage, as is Effie's trial in Scribe's reshaping of *The Heart of Mid-Lothian;* see Chapter 7.)

The next scene takes place in a room of Cedrico's castle. Cedrico is very much put out with Vilfredo for having followed the flag of Richard, a Norman. (No mention is made of his love for Rovena; the operatic Cedrico has no plans to marry her off to a scion of Saxon royalty.) Vilfredo begs forgiveness. When Rovena enters and declares that she cannot live without him, Cedrico gives in. Musically, the scene is structured as a duet followed by a trio. It has no parallel in the novel.[20]

The setting for the third act is an open space outside the Templars' castle. When the curtain rises, the Templars are revealed impatiently awaiting the entrance of Rebecca, whose hour is come. Presently she arrives on stage, heavily guarded and in chains. A trumpet fanfare is sounded, but no champion for her appears. She is then led to the pyre, as the choruses of women and Templars sing a *marcia funebre* (see Example 9-13). Beaumanoir requests that the trumpet fanfare be sounded again. Still no champion appears. He tells Rebecca that her heaven has abandoned her, and he orders the slaves to light the fire. Just as she is about to be put to death, the galloping of a horse is heard and the women cry out, "V'arrestate: qui giunge un cavaliero." Rebecca knows immediately that he is Ivanhoe. He enters and announces before all present that he will defend the unfortunate one. He then begins a large ensemble ("Tentasti, o folle, invano . . .") which eventually includes Rebecca, Isacco, Briano, Cedrico, Luca, and both choruses. He believes that he has been sent by heaven to humiliate Briano again. In the exciting closing measures both choruses sing that heaven will decide the issue. Most of the people then enter the arena (out of the audience's sight) where the combat is to take place, while Rebecca, Isacco, and the chorus of women remain on stage. Rebecca sings a prayer ("Signor de' padri miei") in which she is joined by Isacco and the women. (It is musically effective, but there is nothing Jewish about it; it sounds like a Christian hymn.) Hearing cries of "Vittoria! Vittoria!" from *within* they anxiously ask who won. The people reply, still from *within,* "Trionfa Vilfredo, è a terra Briano./Non la spada, il ciel lo estinse." Everyone re-enters. Rebecca falls on her knees before her savior. When he bids her to rise, she replies that she cannot, for her soul is troubled and her heart palpitates. The chorus believes that she has lost her reason. Before all present she then confesses to Vilfredo her love for him. She declares that heaven has condemned her to suffer, and she is certain that love and anguish will cause her to die very soon. The chorus calls on God to sustain her in this cruel crisis. Vilfredo tells her that if she really loves him, she must be silent. "Prendi un addio," he says; "mi lascia. Scordarmi tu potrai." He promises that he will always remember that she once saved his life, and he tells her that she can console herself with the thought that he wept in parting from her. When he bids her a final "Addio," she falls senseless into the arms of her father. The chorus sings "Al prode gloria/Che il perfido svenò," and the curtain falls.

The ending departs markedly from the novel. Scott's Rebecca does not openly reveal her love for Ivanhoe. Her deep sense of pride precludes any chance of her displaying her emotions indecorously. And indeed, fearing that she just might lose control of herself, she convinces her father that they should depart quietly and unobserved. Despite the musical charm of Vilfredo's final remarks, the words make him seem a heartless, ungrateful scoundrel, very unlike Scott's Ivanhoe. In general, Marini's libretto shows a total lack of anything approaching subtle characterization. Thus the dramatic and musical possibilities inherent in some of the novel's characters, especially Rebecca and Brian de Bois-Guilbert, are not fully realized in *Il Templario.* Nevertheless the opera has its share of attractive arias, impressive ensembles, colorful pageantry, and suspenseful situations. No wonder that it was widely and frequently performed.

Pisani's *Rebecca*

Born in Constantinople in 1811 of Italian parents, Bartolomeo Pisani was the composer of five operas. His *Rebecca,* with a libretto by F. M. Piave (who wrote the librettos for several of Verdi's operas), was given one performance at la Scala, on 5 November 1865. The concert-master for the occasion was Alberto Mazzucato, who himself had composed a Walter

Scott opera some thirty years previously (see Chapter 8). According to a handwritten note on the blank page facing the title page of the libretto which I used,[21] the evening was a "fiasco completo per tutti." I have not seen any of the music, and I do not know whether it still exists; if so, it would certainly be in manuscript. The cast of characters is larger than in Rossini, Pacini, and Nicolai. It includes Rebecca (sung by Teresina Stolz), Isacco (Eraclito Bagaggiolo), Nathano, Isacco's confidant (Luigi Man- fredi), Cedrico (Pietro Bertoni), Guilfredo (Tommaso de Azula), Rovena (Marietta Butti), the Grand Master of the Templars (Luigi Alessandrini), Malvoasen (Giacomo Redaelli), Briano (Alessandro de Antoni), Editta, Rovena's handmaiden (Carlotta Pollastri), a valet of Cedrico (Gaetano Galli), and a herald of the Templars (Luigi Turco). Editta corresponds with Scott's Elgitha, and Nathano owes at least his name to the Rabbi- physician Nathan Ben Israel, who helps Isaac during the time that Re- becca is in captivity at Templestowe. The opera is divided into four acts.

The first act, which has no parallel in the novel, takes place in a pleasant valley of Palestine. It is about sunset when Isacco and Nathano enter, engrossed in conversation. Nathano has helped Isacco make the neces- sary preparations to leave Palestine for England. The way will be danger- ous, but Isacco believes that to remain is even more dangerous in view of the trouble he has had recently with a Templar, who tried to seduce his daughter. When he is back on his native soil, he will be able to breathe calmly again. Shepherds, mowers, and Hebrew peasants of both sexes now enter and unite with Isacco in prayer. When night falls, they all disperse. Guilfredo enters. He overhears Rebecca singing from within her house. He knows that she loves him, but her faith is different from his, and besides he has already given his heart to Rovena. Rebecca comes out from the house. She tells Guilfredo that she is seeing him perhaps for the last time, for on the morrow she will depart with her father for other regions. She mentions his having saved her from the bold Templar, at the cost of being severely wounded. He replies that he owes his life to her knowledge of medicine. When she laments that her destiny is unlucky, he assures her that if she is ever again in danger, he will protect her:

> Parti, se te in periglio
> Un giorno mai saprò...
> Pel Dio di tutti gli uomini
> Tuo difensor sarò!

(These words recur in the final scene of the opera.) In the last part of their duet Rebecca sings *aside* that she can hardly conceal her emotional tur- moil, and then to Guilfredo that their parting is a bitter torment to her; Guilfredo calls on Rovena *aside* to help bolster up his constancy, and then tells Rebecca that their parting is bitter not only to her. After the duet Isacco re-enters and informs Rebecca that it is almost time to depart. She exits. Isacco thanks Guilfredo again for having saved his daughter's

honor and offers him his tent until he has fully recovered from his
wounds. Nathano returns to let Isacco know that the camels are prepared
for departure. He says furthermore that Rebecca has asked to be excused
from leave-taking (a detail perhaps suggested by Scott's last chapter; see
the concluding paragraph of my discussion of *Il Templario*). Isacco,
Nathano, and Guilfredo then bid one another a fond farewell, in which
they are joined by a chorus of camel-drivers. Observing the caravan slowly
depart, Guilfredo hears Rebecca singing the same song which he overheard earlier:

> Addio deserta Solima,
> Giordano, un vale a te,
> Vivrà di voi memoria
> Soave sempre in me!

The voices of Rebecca and the camel-drivers get farther and farther away.
As the act closes, Guilfredo sings one last "Addio" and then turns his
thoughts to Rovena: "Rovena aïtami./Non vivo che per te!"

Act II opens in an English forest near Ashby. Briano, dressed as a
hunter, is chagrined that he was put down in the tournament at Ashby by
an unknown knight. And to make matters more embarrassing, the beautiful Jewess was there to behold his defeat. (So far what he says parallels the
remarks of Nicolai's Briano, *Il Templario,* Act I, scene ii.) He then vows to
make her his slave. At the end of his aria several Norman desperados, also
dressed as hunters, enter. They say that they fell upon Isacco and his
daughter, but the two were rescued by Cedrico and his followers, who
were returning from Ashby to Rotherwood. (In the novel Isaac and
Rebecca are a part of Cedric's entourage when the assault comes, and they
are all captured.) The Norman desperados agree to help Briano attack
Rotherwood, which they know is poorly fortified.—The scene changes to
an apartment at Rotherwood. Editta tells Rovena that the Jew and his
daughter are grateful to Rovena for having persuaded Cedrico to rescue
them. Rovena sends Editta out to bring in Rebecca, with whom she wishes
to speak. Alone on stage, Rovena thinks about her beloved Guilfredo. She
knows that the Jew and his daughter have just come from Palestine, where
she believes Guilfredo to be. He was forced to leave home because his
father considered his love for her a crime, and yet their oath is written in
heaven. (No mention is made of any plans on the part of Cedrico to marry
off Rovena to a descendant of Alfred the Great.) Rebecca enters. Rovena
remarks that the citation for beauty that she has just received at Ashby is
rather pointless, inasmuch as her lover is far away. Rebecca replies that *she*
is even less fortunate, because she loves someone who does not return her
love. She tells of having been saved from the lascivious Templar by a
young knight who was wounded in protecting her; she nursed him back to
health, but in so doing she herself was wounded in the heart. As the
conversation develops, Rovena becomes pale, strongly suspecting who the

young knight was. Rebecca says that his heart was promised to another lady. Both confide to each other in a duet that their conversation has brought back deep-seated memories, yet to share one's sorrow with a kindred spirit is sweet comfort. At the conclusion of the duet festive music is heard from *without*. Cedrico comes on stage for a few moments and tells Rovena that the people of Rotherwood want to pay their respects to her for having been crowned Queen of Beauty. In a final duet Rovena and Rebecca vow to keep their sorrows secret.

The scene changes to the grand vestibule of the castle, where the Saxons are singing of the recent events at Ashby. The unknown Brown Warrior defeated the Templar and then chose their own Rovena to be Queen of the tournament. (This choral number has no parallel in the novel.) The Saxons do not realize that the Brown Warrior is actually in their presence. Disguised as a pilgrim, he asks Cedrico to extend hospitality to him. A valet then enters to inform Cedrico that a Norman herald seeks an audience with him. The herald enters (he is really Briano in disguise, as in Pacini's *Ivanhoe*), accompanied by two squiers. When he announces that his master wants to have his two slaves back, Cedrico refuses to honor the arrogant request. Suddenly the supposed herald seizes Rebecca, says that she belongs to him, and orders her to follow him. Rebecca and Isacco cry out for help. Moving quickly and unexpectedly the Pilgrim frees Rebecca and at the same time informs everyone present that the herald is none other than Briano himself. He in turn is immediately recognized as Guilfredo. A large ensemble develops (Guilfredo, Briano, Rebecca, Isacco, Rovena, Cedrico, and the chorus), after which Briano declares that he fears no threats, that Rebecca is his slave. Cedrico calls the Saxons to arms. Briano calls the Normans. He then rapidly falls on Cedrico and disarms him, while the two squiers fall on Guilfredo. The other Normans rush in and very quickly subdue all the Saxons. Briano seizes Rebecca again and drags her off. The helpless Saxons vow revenge. (This is essentially the same scene we have already observed in Rossini, Pacini, and Nicolai; it has no exact parallel in the novel.)

Most of Act III takes place at Templestona (*sic*). First, we are in a small room just off the grand hall where Rebecca's trial is to be held. Malvoasen tells Briano in a passage of recitative that a herald from Cedrico tried to gain an audience at Templestona, but he was refused admission. He says furthermore that the Grand Master is fully convinced that Rebecca bewitched Briano and will therefore assuredly sentence her to be burned at the stake. Malvoasen thinks that this is perhaps the best solution to the problem, all things considered. Briano is distressed.—We now move to the grand hall for what appears to be the most ambitious scene of the opera. The Grand Master formally charges Rebecca with witchcraft and sentences her to death. When he asks if she has anything to say in her defense, she replies, "La mia innocenza." "E chi provarla puote?" he asks.

"Il giudizio di Dio," she replies, throwing down a glove in front of the tribunal. In an aria ("L'onnipossente Jeova") she declares that God will find a champion for her. The chorus is impressed with her nobility of spirit. Malvoasen then recommends to the Grand Master that Briano be selected as the champion to defend their order. The Grand Master gives Rebecca until sunset of the third day hence to bring forth a champion for herself. Cedrico's herald, who has managed to slip into the room unrecognized, tells Rebecca not to fear, for she will have a champion. He then loses himself in the crowd. As the scene closes, Rebecca sings *aside* that even though Guilfredo does not love her, he will come to her aid.

The scene shifts to a room at Rotherwood, where Guilfredo, alone on stage, sings a recitative and aria. He wonders why the Templars are delaying reply to Cedrico's herald. They must either give back Rebecca or be destroyed by the Saxons. His thoughts then turn to his beloved Rovena. At the end of the aria he sees that the herald has returned. —Meanwhile, back at Templestona, Rebecca is praying to her God in the tower-room where she has been confined. Briano enters. He expresses his love for her. He offers to be her champion, to save her, and even to conquer a kingdom for her if she will accept him as her lover. She refuses. When he lays hands on her, she frees herself *"con sublime conato,"* rushes to the balcony, and threatens to jump. (As in Rossini, Pacini, and Nicolai, this well-known incident occurs at the Templars' castle rather than at Torquilstone.) At the end of their duet, she orders him away, and he obeys mechanically. Left alone, she falls on her knees and lifts her hands toward heaven in a gesture of gratitude.

Act IV takes place outside Templestona. Her champion not having arrived, Rebecca is about to be burned at the stake. Four black African slaves are the custodians of the pyre that will be lit when the fatal moment comes. The people who have amassed for the spectacle seem sympathetic toward the beautiful witch. The trumpets sound. The Grand Master tells Rebecca that if her champion does not appear after the third trumpet-fanfare, she must die. Just when all seems lost, a trumpet-call is heard from the wings and the champion finally arrives, accompanied by Isacco. When he lifts his visor, all recognize him to be Guilfredo. A large ensemble develops—Guilfredo, Briano, and the chorus all singing that God will decide the issue. They then enter the arena, leaving Rebecca, Isacco, and the four African slaves behind. Isacco and Rebecca implore the God of Israel for help. They hear sounds of combat from the arena and presently shouts of "Vittoria! vittoria!" "Chi vinse?" Isacco asks anxiously. "Chi è spento?" asks Rebecca. The people, returning from the arena, reply, "Vittoria, sei salva!" Rebecca faints. Everyone now re-enters, including the victorious Guilfredo. He approaches Rebecca, who is still in a swoon, and sings,

Parti, se te in periglio

Un giorno mai saprò,
Pel Dio di tutti gli uomini
Tuo difensor sarò!

These are the words he sang when he parted from her in Palestine, in Act
I. She revives. She says that life has been severe to her and that further life
will be only painful. She talks as if she is about to die. Guilfredo tells her
that the storm is over; Isacco implores God to save her. Hardly able to
stand, she embraces her father and Guilfredo for the last time. She dies.
Abandoning himself deliriously on her corpse, Isacco cries out, "Ah! più
viver non poss' io!" (It is not clear whether or not he dies too; the stage
directions do not specify.) All present sing "Sventurato genitor!" as the
curtain falls.

The ending obviously differs from Scott, but it is not markedly different from the ending of *Il Templario,* where Rebecca falls senseless into her
father's arms. Piave and Pisani took their cue from *Il Templario* but carried
things to the ultimate extreme in the interest of effective tragic opera.
Their boldest innovation, however, comes at the beginning—the insertion of an entire act that takes place in Palestine. There is no parallel to this
in the novel and only the mention in Rossini, Pacini, and Nicolai that
Ivanhoe had been wounded while fighting in Rebecca's behalf in Palestine
and that she in turn had nursed him back to health. Nevertheless this
motif of the earlier operas probably derives from Scott's account of
Rebecca's tending to Ivanhoe after he has been wounded at Ashby. So
Piave and Pisani's innovation is not, after all, a total departure from the
novel.

Castegnier's *Rébecca*

I have been unable to find information about the poet-composer A.
Castegnier and the performance history of his five-act grand opera,
Rébecca. The British Museum has a copy of the French-Italian vocal score,
which was published in London [1884]; the Italian translation is by C. D.
Pavarino. A complete libretto in the original French was published in
London [1882] by Wertheimer, Lea et Cie; this too is in the British
Museum. The text differs somewhat from that of the vocal score. Another
edition *Les Normands,* was published in Trouville [1886]; the British
Museum has a copy. The text is virtually the same as that of the vocal
score.[22] White thinks that the opera was probably performed in Trouville,
but he offers no evidence.

The cast of characters is elaborate. It includes Richard, le Prince Jean (a
soprano!), Brian de Bois-Guilbert, Cédric, Wilfred d'Ivanhoe, Lady Rowena, Isaac d'York, Rébecca, Wamba, Lucas de Beaumanoir, Waldemar,
De Bracy, Malvoisin, Bohun, Oswald, and Elgitha. The vocal score indicates that Richard and Bois-Guilbert, both of whom are baritones, can be

done by the same singer; so also the roles of Cédric and Beaumanoir (1st bass), Wamba and Malvoisin (2nd bass), Waldemar and Oswald (baritone), Bohun and De Bracy (baritone), and le Prince Jean and Rowena (soprano). A *coryphée* is to represent Lady Rowena at the tournament, since the singer involved is portraying the Prince during this scene; the *coryphée* and Elgitha are to be played by the same *artiste*. Also at the tournament, the Chevalier Noir (Richard) is represented by a *coryphé*, since the singer who does Richard must do Bois-Guilbert here.

The opera begins differently from any of the other *Ivanhoe* operas. There is a brief overture followed by a prologue sung by a chorus of soldiers from behind the curtain. They are about to leave England for Palestine with Richard Cœur de Lion. The prologue is followed by music descriptive of a storm, and when the curtain rises, we are in the grand hall of the Manoir de Rotherwood.[23] The entire first act takes place here and follows chapters iii-vi of the novel. Cédric makes comments to Oswald, Elgitha, and other domestics on the fierceness of the storm. When he asks why Rowena is not present, Elgitha replies, as in the novel, that the storm surprised her mistress just as she was leaving the church, and thus she is still in her room preparing herself for supper. As the *scène* progresses, Cédric learns from Oswald that Wamba has not returned to the manoir. He is angered. He then laments briefly on his having been forced to banish his son Wilfred because of his growing attachment for Rowena, the daughter of a king. (The dialogue follows the novel rather closely.) Suddenly they all hear the sound of a horn from *without*. Oswald announces that a chevalier, his entourage, and a poor pilgrim seek shelter from the storm. Cédric is not especially happy when Oswald tells him that the chevalier is Brian de Bois-Guilbert, but he will receive him hospitably anyway. (There is no Prior Aymer among the dramatis personae.) He even orders his best wine to be brought forth. In the meanwhile Elgitha goes off to inform Rowena about the Pilgrim, who might have news of interest for her. Cédric receives Bois-Guilbert cordially, notices Wamba come in, and then sings a conventional drinking-song, after which Oswald announces the entrance of Lady Rowena. As she walks over to take her place next to Cédric, we hear a dulcet melody in the orchestra:

Example 9-17

Arpeggiated chords are in the bass clef. I have reproduced the melody because it is a leitmotiv associated with Rowena. Also, it is stylistically characteristic of Castegnier, who has a propensity to modulate to far-away keys, in this instance by way of a 3rd relationship (D flat to F, and then back to D flat). As in the novel, Cédric upbraids Brian for gazing too intently at Rowena. He refuses Brian's offer to act as escort when he, Rowena, and their party go to Ashby for the tournament; he prefers to rely on his own people. When Oswald announces that Isaac d'York seeks shelter, Cédric without hesitation orders that the door be opened to him, even though he is a Jew. Brian is chagrined.

In a short aria Isaac thanks Cédric for allowing him to be admitted into the manoir. As in Scott, no one wants the Jew to sit next to him; the Pilgrim then obligingly offers him his own place. When Cédric asks Brian whom they should toast as the best among the English knights in Palestine, he replies, "C'est le Roi, puis Guilbert, le chevalier du temple." He tells Rowena that the Saxons do not compare in valor with the Templars. At this point the Pilgrim interrupts. He reminds Brian of the tournament of Acre, at which several Saxons distinguished themselves and Brian himself was beaten. As in the novel, he names the victorious knights, but he hesitates about naming himself; and, again as in the novel, Brian himself names Ivanhoe as the one who toppled him. When he expresses his determination to have vengeance, Cédric takes his words as an insult. In the ensuing ensemble the Pilgrim, Rowena, and Cedric all give vent to their feelings of enmity toward Brian. The Pilgrim places a *relique* (Scott's "reliquary") on the table as a pledge that Ivanhoe will some day avenge the insult; next, Rowena puts down a bracelet (this is not in the novel); and, finally, Brian throws down a chain of gold. At the conclusion of the ensemble Cédric and Rowena leave the room in high dudgeon. (All this has been greatly magnified from the parallel material in Scott.) Brian then speaks briefly with Isaac. He wants money. Isaac says that he has no money to lend him. Not realizing that the Pilgrim overhears him, Brian takes his Saracens aside and instructs them to attack Isaac upon his departure the next day.

When the conspirators have departed, the Pilgrim informs Isaac of the danger he is in and offers to lead him through the forest safely to Sheffield. As in the novel, Isaac suspects that the so-called Pilgrim is in need of armor, and he offers to help him. Their duet, "De ces bois," illustrates another feature of Castegnier's musical style—his fondness for canonic patterns:

Example 9-18

He uses this device often, not just in vocal lines, but sometimes in the
orchestra. After the duet Elgitha enters to tell the Pilgrim that her mistress is coming to speak a few words with him. Isaac leaves, and when
Rowena enters, Elgitha leaves also. The last number of Act I, then, is a
duet for Rowena and the Pilgrim. She strongly suspects that he is her
beloved Wilfred in disguise—this idea being somewhat exaggerated from
the corresponding material in the novel. (Note that the *scène* takes place in
the banquet-hall rather than in Rowena's bedchamber. Castegnier has
made this minor alteration in order to avoid a change of scenery, just as in
the preceding *scène* the Pilgrim and Isaac discuss their plans also in the
banquet-hall, rather than in the sleeping quarters assigned to Scott's
Isaac. Castegnier has inverted the sequence of the two episodes probably
so that the act may end conventionally, and effectively, with a duet for
hero and heroine.)

Act II takes place at the lists of Ashby. It is based on chapters vii-ix, but
with much omitted and the two days of Scott's tournament compressed, as
in other *Ivanhoe* operas, into one. The brief orchestral introduction begins
with a canonic Wagnerian-sounding trumpet fanfare:

Example 9-19

The opening number, a "Chœur des Bourgeois," illustrates again Castegnier's fondness for modulations to far-away keys, this time by way of enharmonic modulation (D to G flat, and then back to D). The chorus greets Prince Jean, who, as in the novel, is much impressed with the beauty of Rébecca. He seriously considers naming her the Queen of Beauty and Love, but is dissuaded from doing so by his Norman followers. The ensemble that develops (Jean, the courtiers, Rébecca, Isaac, Guilbert, and the people) is greatly enhanced from the parallel material in Scott. When Jean tries to seat Rébecca in the place of Cédric (there is no Athelstane in the opera), Wamba prevents the incident from becoming unpleasant. Finally Jean orders the tournament to begin. The main event is a combat between Guilbert and the Deshérité, which takes place on stage. Guilbert is defeated. When the Deshérité is about to kill him, Jean stops the affair and awards the Deshérité the palm of victory. The as yet unknown winner selects Lady Rowena as Queen of Beauty and Love. When it becomes clear that he is wounded, he is unhelmeted and immediately recognized by all as Wilfred d'Ivanhoe. He faints—and so does Lady Rowena, unlike her counterpart in the novel. When Jean, his entourage, and all the spectators have departed, Wamba tries to persuade Cédric to forget his grudge against his son and help him, but Cédric is relentless. A bit later Rébecca manages to convince Isaac that the two of them must help Ivanhoe, since his own father has abandoned him. (The drift of the action here is drawn from chapter xxviii, a flashback in which Scott explains how Ivanhoe came into Rebecca's care.) Lady Rowena, having now revived from her swoon, implores Rébecca to save Ivanhoe. Rébecca promises to do so. The act ends in a "chœur burlesque"—a song of mirth, drink, and festivity.

   The third act takes place at the manoir d'Ashby and is based mainly on the material of chapter xiv. Prince Jean, Cédric, Waldemar, De Bracy, and Malvoisin are the principals present, and there is a large chorus of Normans and Saxons. The opening number is a drinking-song (the second in the opera); first the Normans sing, then Cédric and the Saxons, and finally Prince Jean. This is followed by a rather lengthy "Grand Ballet à la Paix," in which the future glory of England is depicted. When Lord Nelson is revealed on his ship of war, we hear "God Save the King." Afterwards, the Saxons are insulted by their Norman hosts, as in the novel. Cédric accordingly drinks a toast to Richard Cœur de Lion and then leaves the stage together with all his Saxon followers. At this point a squier brings in a letter for Jean which reads, "Prenez bien garde à vous le diable est déchaîné." (In the novel this incident occurs during the tournament, just before the archery contest.) A large ensemble develops (Jean and the Norman lords); Jean is not able to conceal his fear. The remainder of the act differs somewhat from the novel, but it is suggested by Scott's account of John's conspiracy at York to have his brother murdered (chapter xxxiv). Jean plans the murder of Richard in the company of Waldemar, Malvoisin, Guilbert, and De Bracy—and, interestingly, the whole conversation is overheard by Cédric from the wings. Guilbert and De Bracy are reluctant to take part in the affair. (In the novel John speaks with only Waldemar and De Bracy. The latter will have no part of the affair because Richard granted him his life at the recent storming of Torquilstone.) The act ends with a reprise of the drinking-song heard earlier.

The first tableau of Act IV is based on material of chapter xl: "In the meantime, the Black Champion and his guide [Wamba] were pacing at their leisure through the recesses of the forest; the good Knight whiles humming to himself the lay of some enamoured troubadour, sometimes encouraging by questions the prating disposition of his attendant, so that their dialogue formed a whimsical mixture of song and jest, of which we would fain give our readers some idea." The Chevalier Noir sings a *ballade* translated loosely from Scott's "virelai." He sings alone (Wamba does not bear him "a mellow burden"), and Anna-Marie's name is now Ophélie. The duet that comes later (Wamba: "Je ne suis pas poltron"; the Chevalier Noir: "Cet homme est un poltron") is not based on any song in the novel. As the action unfolds, the Chevalier Noir shows Wamba a horn and explains that it will bring aid in a pinch. Suddenly Cédric rushes in and informs the Chevalier Noir of the plot to assassinate him. (There is no such incident in the novel. Cédric must already know who the Chevalier Noir is, having overheard Jean plotting with his cohorts in Act III; yet he gives no indication that he knows.) The attack soon follows. When Wamba sees the assailants tying the overpowered Cédric to a tree, he blows the horn. Friendly archers appear immediately and save the day, as in the novel. (We are unprepared for the appearance of the archers, since up to this point archers have not once been mentioned; Locksley is not included in the dramatis personae.) The Chevalier Noir discovers that Waldemar was one of the would-be assassins, and his conversation with him follows the novel up to the point where he commands him to leave England *with* Prince Jean. (In the novel he tells him to leave and makes him solemnly promise never to mention John's name in connection with the assassination attempt.) The Chevalier Noir then reveals himself as Richard Cœur de Lion (and since there is no Locksley, there is no double revelation). The rest of the scene departs from the novel. A warlike trumpet fanfare heard in the distance is interpreted by Cédric as certain indication that Albert de Malvoisin is nearby. "Un nouvel assassin!" Richard exclaims, and the scene closes as Cédric, Richard, Wamba, and the archers sing an "Appel aux Armes."

The second half of the act takes place in Rébecca's cell in the Preceptory of Templestowe, and the action is based on Scott's account of her captivity at both Templestowe (chapter xxxix) and Torquilstone (chapter xxiv). First comes an important aria for Rébecca (*not* a translation of her hymn at the beginning of chapter xxxix). She wonders why she has been imprisoned. (And so do we, since Castegnier does not include the storming of

Torquilstone, during the course of which Rebecca is "rescued" by Bois-Guilbert, nor does he follow Rossini, Pacini, Nicolai, and Pisani in having Brian storm Rotherwood and drag his "slave" away by force.) If only Wilfred were around to help her! She feels love for him, but she is determined to be in control of her emotions. "Adieu, Wilfred, tu ne sauras jamais/Combien je t'aimais" (suggested perhaps by Rebecca's monologue at Torquilstone at the end of chapter xxix while the wounded Ivanhoe is sleeping, just after she has reported to him the fighting she has observed from the window). After the aria Guilbert enters, and the words of the ensuing duet follow chapter xxiv closely. When Rébecca threatens to jump from the window, he admires her spirit. At the end of the duet they hear knocking at the door. It is Malvoisin, who enters and announces that all is discovered. (In the novel Malvoisin does not interrupt any meeting between Rebecca and Brian, at either Torquilstone or Templestowe.) He says that Isaac has come to claim his daughter, that Beaumanoir believes Guilbert to be a "victime d'un sortilège," and that Guilbert can get out of his predicament only by delivering Rébecca over to Beaumanoir to be tried. Guilbert seizes Rebecca (who is still present) and says to Malvoisin, "De par le ciel cela ne sera pas!/Je l'aime..." Malvoisin replies, "C'est folie!" (The words are based on the conversation between Bois-Guilbert and Malvoisin in chapter xxxvi—not in the presence of Rebecca.) In the ensuing trio, which has no parallel in either the novel or the other *Ivanhoe* operas, Rébecca and Guilbert call Malvoisin a coward; he sings *"avec ironie"* that he is about to go out and make preparations for the trial and execution. When he has departed, Rébecca and Guilbert sing another duet. Guilbert vows that he can save her if only she will agree to be his mistress. She refuses. (Their words are drawn from chapter xxxix, which *follows* Rebecca's trial, but from the foregoing trio it is clear that her death is already predetermined and that the forthcoming trial will be a mere formality.) When Guilbert has departed, Rébecca sings a musically effective prayer ("Dieu puissant, à cette âme altière"), after which Malvoisin re-enters with four guards and rudely tells her that she must appear forthwith before the tribunal. The act closes as the orchestra repeats *maestoso* and *fortissimo* the music to her prayer.

In Act V we have the preliminary trial of Rébecca, greatly abridged from what it is in chapters xxxvii-xxxviii; the trial by combat, taking place the same day as the former; and the aftermath—all this in one tableau. The act begins with a "Marche Funèbre et Chœur." The chorus wants to see Rébecca die. Presently the Grand Master announces that she is condemned to death for practicing witchcraft in the precincts of the temple. Unprompted by a message from Brian, Rébecca throws down one of her gloves and demands a champion. The Grand Master immediately calls on Guilbert to defend the order of Templars, and he tells Rébecca that if her champion does not show up before evening, she will perish without delay. Guilbert approaches her and tempts her once more, as in the novel (but much abridged), and she again refuses him. Malvoisin then observes that time is passing rapidly and tells the Grand Master that there can be no longer a delay, that Rébecca must face her sentence. (Notice how quickly the time does pass—perhaps too quickly.) Next, Brian tries desperately to prevent the execution: he lays hold of Rébecca and attempts to lead her out from the lists. (There is no exact parallel to this in the novel.) Suddenly the crowd cries out, "Un libérateur!" Ivanhoe enters, announces who he is, and is accepted by Rébecca as her champion—with hesitation on her part, not due to concern for his weakened condition but because she realizes how great the risk is. (Unlike Scott's Rebecca, she has not requested his help, there having been no time for letter-writing; he simply arrives on the scene at a most convenient moment.) A large ensemble develops, which is composed of Rébecca, Ivanhoe, Guilbert (who, interestingly, wishes for his own defeat), Isaac, Malvoisin, the Grand Master, and, in the vocal score (but not the 1882 libretto), Rowena. (Castegnier gives no explanation for Rowena's presence; apparently he has her on stage so that the ensemble can have two female voices.) When the combat has scarcely gotten under way, Bois-Guilbert falls dead. Rébecca is set free, and in another ensemble she, Ivanhoe, Isaac, and even the Grand Master return thanks to God. Richard and his followers then enter. As in the novel, Bohun arrests Malvoisin for high treason. The Grand Master is displeased, but to no avail. Richard orders him and his Templars to depart that very instant, and as they march sullenly away he cannot help admiring their discipline. In the closing pages of the score Ivanhoe and Rowena try to persuade Rébecca to stay in England, but she is determined to leave. (This brief, remarkably effective passage derives from the poignant meeting between Rowena and Rebecca that takes place, in the novel, some time after the marriage of Rowena and Ivanhoe. Castegnier achieves his effect through understatement both in the text—this is also Scott's technique here—and, as often in French opera, in the music itself.) When Ivanhoe asks her, "Vous reverrai-je un jour?" she replies simply, "Non, adieu, monseigneur." (How completely different this is from what we have observed in *Il Templario* and in Pisani's *Rebecca!*) The opera closes with a "Chœur Final"; everyone sings, "Honneur, honneur et gloire au vaillant roi Richard!"

Rébecca is a through-composed opera; that is, there are no passages of spoken or cembalo-accompanied recitative. Castegnier makes some use of the leitmotiv, but not so extensively as does Sullivan in the last *Ivanhoe* opera to be discussed here. In addition to the melody associated with Rowena (see Example 9-17), there is a restless musical figure sometimes assigned to Guilbert. Here it is as it appears when Oswald informs Cédric that the knight who seeks hospitality at Rotherwood is none other than Guilbert:

Example 9-20

Also, there is a placid-sounding motiv sometimes used in connection with Isaac, as, for example, at the beginning of his short aria in Act I:

Example 9-21

I have already commented on Castegnier's frequent chromatic and enharmonic modulations to far-away keys and his fondness for canonic patterns. These features contribute much to the musical interest of the opera. Uninteresting, however, are some of the tediously lengthy passages of orchestra-accompanied recitative. In general, the opera is a bit too long. The music is melodic, but not memorable. Despite the operatic convention of having women occasionally sing roles of young men, Castegnier's assigning wicked Prince Jean to a soprano strikes me as a bad mistake. Also Wamba, who is a young man in the novel, should be scored for a tenor (or even a soprano)—not a 2nd bass.[24] (In the other *Ivanhoe* operas in which he is included, he is a tenor.) There are many fine things about Castegnier's *Rébecca,* but the problems and weaknesses do detract from the impact of the work as a whole.

Sullivan's *Ivanhoe*

Sir Arthur Sullivan's only full-fledged opera, *Ivanhoe,* with a libretto by Julian Sturgis, opened the new Royal English Opera House (now the Palace Theatre) built by D'Oyly Carte in Cambridge Circus. It was given inaugural performances on January 31st, February 2nd, and February 4th, 1891, with the composer conducting, and it was enthusiastically received by the public and by most critics (but not George Bernard Shaw). Repeated nightly, it then ran for over 150 consecutive performances. In 1910 it was revived for two gala evenings at Covent Garden—but more of this later. Sullivan dedicated the opera "by special permission/to/Her Most Gracious Majesty/THE QUEEN,/at whose suggestion this work was written,/in grateful acknowledgment/of Her Majesty's kindly encouragement."[25] The dramatis personae together with the names of their interpreters at the three inaugural performances are as follows:

SOPRANOS:	Rowena (Esther Palliser, 1/31 & 2/4; Lucille Hill, 2/2)
	Rebecca (Margaret MacIntyre, 1/31 & 2/4; Charlotte Thudichum, 2/2)
CONTRALTO:	Ulrica (Marie Groebl)
TENORS:	Ivanhoe (Ben Davies, 1/31 & 2/2; Joseph O'Mara, 2/4)
	De Bracy (Charles Kenningham)
BARITONE:	Brian de Bois-Guilbert (Eugene Oudin, 1/31 & 2/2; François Noijé, 2/4)
BASS-BARITONES:	Cedric (Frangcon Davies, 1/31 & 2/2; W. H. Burgon, 2/4)
	Tuck (Avon Saxon)
	Locksley (W. H. Stephens)
	Prince John (Richard Green)
	The Grand Master (Adams Owen)
	Isaac (Charles Copland)
BASS:	Richard (Norman Salmond, 1/31 & 2/4; Franklin Clive, 2/2)

The most notable omissions from the roster are Athelstane the Unready, Wamba, Gurth, and Reginald Front-de-Bœuf. Indeed, the two that I have named last do not appear in any of the *Ivanhoe* operas, and Athelstane figures briefly and unimportantly, as a very minor character, only in Marschner. Anyone can see that there is nothing strikingly operatic about Scott's sullen Gurth and his dull-witted Athelstane, and there are usually Normans enough in each opera without the relatively uninteresting Front-de-Bœuf. Unlike Marschner and Wohlbrück, Sullivan and Sturgis have not concentrated on any single aspect of the novel. Instead, they follow rather faithfully the main outline of the story, maintain in large part Scott's conception of the characters and their relative significance, and attempt to capture something of the novel's colorful pageantry.

The first scene of Act I takes place at Rotherwood and is based on chapters iii-v. In the first few measures of the orchestral introduction we hear a motiv that is associated throughout the opera with Cedric and the Saxons:

Example 9-22

When the curtain rises, we find Cedric brooding on the suppression of Saxons that has come as a result of the Norman Conquest. When he

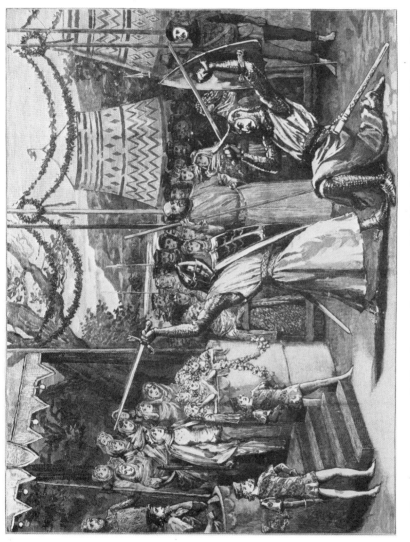

THE TOURNAMENT at Ashby. A scene from the original London production of Sullivan's *Ivanhoe*. From the Enthoven Collection, Victoria and Albert Theatre Museum.

REBECCA DEFIES THE TEMPLAR. A scene from the original London production of Sullivan's *Ivanhoe*. From *The Illustrated London News,* vol. XCVIII, March 21, 1891, p. 385, and by courtesy of the Victoria and Albert Theatre Museum (Enthoven Collection).

mentions the Normans, we hear for the first time in the orchestra a motiv associated with them:

Example 9-23

Unlike what we have in the novel, Isaac comes in to seek Cedric's hospitality *before* the Normans. When they do enter, they take their places in the hall to the accompaniment of a variation of their leitmotiv. De Bracy tells Bois-Guilbert of the beauty of Cedric's ward Rowena, while Bois-Guilbert remarks about the beauty of a Jewess whom he has recently seen. (In the novel Prior Aymer, rather than De Bracy, is with Bois-Guilbert at Rotherwood, and at this early point in the story Bois-Guilbert has not yet seen the beautiful Jewess.) When Rowena enters, Brian addresses her with flattering language, but, as in the novel, she is not impressed. By degrees an ensemble develops in which the principals and chorus sing in praise of those who fight for the Holy Cross. When Rowena asks,

> Were there no English knights in Palestine,
> No children of our happy woods and hills,
> Who might compare even with the Temple Knights?

Brian replies:

> Fair lady, with King Richard throve
> Full many a gallant knight and strong,
> Well worthy minstrels' song
> And lady's love,
> And second only to our Temple Knights.

At this point the Palmer (Ivanhoe) cries out, "Second to none!" After a brief silence he tells of the glory which the English knights have won in battle. Cedric wants to know their names. As in the novel, the Palmer tells who several of the knights were, and when he comes to the last and bravest one, he pretends that he cannot recall his name:

> The last I cannot call to mind.
> Perchance he was of lesser fame—
> Some nameless knight whom happy chance
> Made one of that high company.

The music becomes more and more agitated as Brian interrupts:

> Not so, by Heaven!

Before no nameless knight I fell.
'Twas my horse's fault—he is food for dogs ere this—
And yet I fell before as stout a lance
As Richard led.

Cedric and the chorus demand to know his name, and Brian replies, "Wilfred of Ivanhoe!" At this tense moment, according to a stage direction in the libretto, there is *"a movement in [the] hall. The clash of steel is heard as men spring to their feet. Cedric throws up his arm, and there is silence."* When Brian says that he will fight with Ivanhoe whenever he returns to England, the Palmer pledges that Ivanhoe will meet the challenge. (The opera follows the novel rather closely here, but a careful comparison of Sturgis' text here and elsewhere with the parallel material in the original shows that a certain amount of stilted "poetic" diction has crept its way into or has been substituted for Scott's vigorous rhetorical direct discourse.) Cedric offers his Norman guests more drink, but they refuse. De Bracy (rather than Prior Aymer) says, "I'll drink no more./Thy Saxon cups are potent, and tomorrow/We must be stirring with the birds' first song." As the knights are leaving the stage to go to their sleeping quarters, De Bracy suggests to Brian in a recitative that they capture the rich and beautiful Rowena when she, Cedric, and their friends are returning home from the lists at Ashby. In the novel De Bracy and Brian plot with Front-de-Bœuf to execute this crime; their conversation occurs just after the Festival at Ashby; see chapter xv.) All now go to bed, to the accompaniment of music in the orchestra suggestive of sleep.

The second scene is based on Scott's account of the meeting of Rowena and the Palmer in chapter vi, but it takes place in an ante-room rather than in Rowena's bedchamber. When the curtain rises we see Rowena alone on stage. She sings an aria in which she expresses concern for her absent lover. As soon as the Palmer enters she questions him about Ivanhoe. When she asks, "Is he not happy, then?" the Palmer replies:

Ah, what know I?
Perchance—forgive me, if I speak too bold—
Thou knowest best his chance of happiness.

(The idea is taken directly from the novel—". . . you, lady, must know better than I, what is his chance of happiness"—and again one notices stilted diction in Sturgis' rendition: "Perchance"; "knowest.") A duet develops. When the Palmer asks, "And shall I bid him [Ivanhoe] hope?" she replies, "Hope is for all the world"—a line often repeated. At the conclusion of the duet Rowena exits, and the Palmer left on stage, sings an aria ("Like mountain lark my spirit upward springs") which has no parallel in the novel. Isaac then enters, and the Palmer tells him that he heard Bois-Guilbert order his slaves to seize him and take him to Torquilstone. The terrified Isaac, seeing through the Palmer's disguise, offers him a horse and armor for the forthcoming tournament at Ashby in exchange for his help. (Notice the compression of the plot in the interest of good theater. In the novel the Palmer and Isaac travel together in the forest for some time before Isaac makes mention of horse and armor.) The scene closes as the Palmer exclaims, "On to the lists at Ashby with good cheer!"

When the curtain rises on the third scene, we are at the lists of Ashby. In the novel, one will recall, the tournament is held for two days. On the first day the Disinherited Knight (Ivanhoe) unhorses Bois-Guilbert. On the second he has tough going until he is aided by the Black Knight. He is sorely wounded in the fray, and when his helmet is removed, his true identity is revealed to all present. Later in the day the archery contest takes place. In the opera Sturgis and Sullivan omit the archery contest and compress the action of two days into one. They have followed, then, the example set in all previous *Ivanhoe* operas that include the tournament. After a few measures of restless music depicting the excitement of the tournament, we hear the chorus commenting on the prowess of the mysterious Black Knight who fought the day before. (Thus, in contrast to the novel, the Black Knight has made his appearance before Ivanhoe does.) Shortly afterwards Friar Tuck is introduced—at this point rather than later. In a comic interlude he chides the Black Knight and dubs him Sir Sluggard. The two agree to have a test of strength in the near future. The chorus sings again as Prince John and his retinue enter and take their places. As in the novel, John attempts to have Isaac and Rebecca seated in a desirable place. When Cedric objects, De Bracy advises the prince not to antagonize the angry Saxon. But it is Rebecca who succeeds in persuading him to let her father and herself keep their lowly places: "Most gracious Prince,/Nearest the earth best fits our hapless race." These are her first words in the opera. John then receives an alarming message from Louis of France—*"Look to thyself! The devil has broken loose!"*—but ignoring it for the time being he asks whether there is anyone present to challenge any of his brave Normans. Trumpet fanfares are sounded both on- and offstage. The Disinherited Knight now arrives, as a motiv associated with him is heard in the orchestra:

Example 9-24

As in the novel, the chorus does not realize the excellence of the new-comer. He forthwith challenges Bois-Guilbert, and the two fight (but not on horseback; cf. the 1910 revival). When it appears that the

Templar will be slain, Prince John, as in the novel, cries out, "Stop the combat!" and he proclaims the Disinherited Knight the victor. The knight then doffs his helmet to receive the garland of victory from Rowena, who on the preceding day had been named the Pageant's Queen (but evidently not by him, since he was not present). His true identity is dramatically revealed, and the act closes in a choral ensemble.

The first scene of Act II is set at Copmanhurst, Friar Tuck's hut in the middle of the forest. After an opening recitative by the Black Knight, who comments on his mean lodging and thievish host, Tuck comes in with water from St. Dunstan's well—something made much of in both the novel and the opera. Sturgis' libretto follows Scott closely in many parts of this scene of comic relief. However, the song that the Black Knight sings is not the one found in the novel. Neither is Tuck's rollicking song. The Black Knight and Tuck then exchange buffets—here rather than after the fall of Torquilstone. Suddenly Locksley rushes in, interrupting the horseplay with news that Cedric and his entourage have been waylaid and taken as captives to Torquilstone. The Black Knight offers his aid immediately, and he adds, "On my soul,/If but a hair be harmed of Wilfred's head,/I'll tear their castle piecemeal with my hands/And give their bodies to the kite." Locksley's archers sing, "To Torquilstone, to Torquilstone!" as the scene ends.[26] —In the novel it is not known at this point that Ivanhoe is a captive at Torquilstone. The Black Knight (Richard) learns of it from De Bracy during the course of the assault on the castle.

The scene now changes to a passageway in Torquilstone. De Bracy welcomes his prisoners. He tells Cedric and Rowena that Ivanhoe is a prisoner in the castle, and he promises them that Ivanhoe will live *if* Rowena will agree to be his (De Bracy's) bride. (This episode differs from the parallel passage in the novel in that De Bracy speaks while Cedric is present.) Cedric will not allow Rowena to save his son in this foul way. In the ensuing trio Rowena implores De Bracy to save Ivanhoe; he says that all lies in her hands; and Cedric orders her not to kneel to De Bracy, who he maintains is no whit better than a highway robber. After the three have left the stage, Bois-Guilbert enters and sings an aria about the charms of Rebecca. The text is not drawn from any particular passage of the novel. The words "I will woo and win her, as the lion woos and wins" are singularly inappropriate in view of the fact that the Templars are inimical toward Richard the Lion-hearted.

The third scene takes place in a turret-chamber, and the first voice we hear is that of Ulrica: "Whet the keen axes,/Sons of the Dragon!/Kindle the torches,/Daughters of Hengist!" etc. The text of the song is an adaptation of the war-song which Scott's Ulrica chants from a high turret during the burning of the castle. Her ensuing conversation with Rebecca is very close to Scott's dialogue of chapter xxiv. When she departs, Rebecca sings a compelling aria ("O awful depth below the castle wall! . . . Lord of our chosen race," etc.); its haunting final measures recur later in the scene:

Example 9-25

Next there is an important duet for Rebecca and Bois-Guilbert, the libretto again following the novel's dialogue closely. The musical and dramatic highpoint comes when Rebecca threatens to jump from the window. Near the end of the scene Bois-Guilbert hears an offstage trumpet summoning him to combat. Just before the curtain falls, Rebecca sings once more the closing measures of her aria. (In one way or another, a duet for Rebecca and Bois-Guilbert in conjunction with her threat to jump from the tower window, whether it be at Torquilstone or Templestowe, occurs in *all* the *Ivanhoe* operas.[27]

The events of the first scene of Act III, a room in Torquilstone, are drawn from chapters xxix-xxxi. Sturgis and Sullivan have handled the story in such a way that action which lasts several hours in the novel is compressed into a time span of only some thirty minutes. When the curtain rises, we see Ivanhoe alone on stage. *"He leans on his bed, pale and weak from his wound."* The insipid text of the aria which he sings—"Happy with winged feet/Comes the morning softly stealing in," etc.—is not based on anything in Scott. After singing, he falls asleep. Rebecca and Ulrica now enter, Ulrica telling Rebecca, "Tend thou the knight thou lovest:/ Another and a nobler work be mine!" Ulrica exits, and Rebecca sings a pastoral-like aria in which she expresses her love for Ivanhoe: "Ah, would that thou and I might lead our sheep/Among the folded hills!" When

Ivanhoe awakens, he addresses Rebecca with words that echo Scott:"And is it thou, dear maiden?/My gentle nurse!/Now all is well with me since thou art near." Then begins a musical setting of that part of chapter xxix in which Rebecca looks out on the battle from a turret window and relates the events to the bedridden Ivanhoe. The situation as Scott presents it is perfectly designed for opera. Again Sturgis follows the dialogue of the novel rather closely. The music is restless, with offstage trumpets and offstage choruses adding to the excitement. Sullivan's Rebecca protects herself at the window with "the glorious shield of Ivanhoe" rather than with "yonder ancient buckler." Then Ivanhoe and Rebecca sing a duet, accompanied by an offstage chorus of soldiers. Ivanhoe expresses his frustration at having to be idle while a battle is raging outside. Although Rebecca censures Christian chivalry, she is anything but a coward:

> And yet be witness, heav'n, with what delight,
> What rapture would I give
> My lifeblood drop by drop, so I might live
> But for one hour to see
> Judah redeemed from her captivity.

(The sentiment is slightly expanded from the parallel passage in the novel: "Would to heaven that the shedding of mine own blood, drop by drop, could redeem the captivity of Judah!") The castle now begins to burn. Bois-Guilbert comes in, as in the novel, and carries Rebecca away with him. As the music reaches a shattering climax the Black Knight enters, reveals himself as King Richard, and rescues Ivanhoe from the conflagration. (In the novel he does not reveal who he is until much later, when he is saved by Locksley and his followers from an attempt on his life; see chapter xl.) Sturgis and Sullivan could hardly have selected a more exciting place in the opera for the revelation. The warriors are duly amazed: "The King! It is the King! The Black Knight! Pardon! Pardon! Long live the King!" As the castle is succumbing to the flames, we hear Ulrica chanting for the last time her ancient war-song.

The second scene provides more occasion for comic relief, but the original story has been somewhat altered. The action takes place in the forest. In the presence of Locksley and his men, Richard frees his prisoner, De Bracy, who, unlike Scott's De Bracy, is grateful from the outset. At this time Richard asks Cedric to forgive Wilfred and to accept him again in his household. (In the novel the King's intercession takes place at Coningsburgh Castle and is followed by the absurd resuscitation of Athelstane.) Sullivan's Cedric is reluctant to allow Rowena to marry Ivanhoe because of his high respect for her pedigree—she is of the sacred race of Harold. Rowena, Ivanhoe, Richard, and Cedric now join their voices in an effective quartet, Cedric finally pardoning his son. (Since there is no Athelstane in the opera, Cedric's antagonism toward his son is not well motivated; this is a problem in some of the other *Ivanhoe* operas too, as we have already seen.) After a duet for Rowena and Ivanhoe that is not based on anything in the novel, Isaac rushes in and tells of Rebecca's plight. In contrast to the novel, Rowena hears all. At first she begs Ivanhoe not to engage in a dangerous undertaking because of his weakened condition, but on second thought she realizes that he indeed must save Rebecca if he is to preserve his own honor. Rowena, Ivanhoe, and Isaac sing a brief trio at the close of the scene.—Many people have felt the weakness of Scott's Rowena as a character. Thackeray corrected the difficulty by writing a sequel to *Ivanhoe* (entitled *Rebecca and Rowena*) in which Rowena conveniently dies so that Ivanhoe can finally marry Rebecca, who in the meantime has become a Christian. In the Rossini pasticcio Rowena is omitted altogether from the dramatis personae; in Pacini's *Ivanhoe* she (Editta) is Ivanhoe's sister. Sturgis and Sullivan have corrected the problem by assigning additional material to her and thereby enhancing her position in the story of the opera. Their Rowena is more credible than the pale, soft-spoken beauty of the novel.

The final scene is a musical setting of the final two chapters of the novel, with a few minor changes and with much omitted. Rebecca is anxiously awaiting a champion who can save her from death at the stake. At first we hear an impressive Chorus of Templars sung in Latin. The ensuing dialogue between Rebecca and the Grand Master owes something to the trial scene of chapter xxxvii. The trumpets sound, but no champion appears. When the Grand Master orders Rebecca to be bound to the stake (a detail not in the novel), Bois-Guilbert objects violently. Then, as in the novel, he tries once more to persuade Rebecca to flee with him. She refuses. During this encounter we hear strains in the orchestra of the arias which Brian and Rebecca sang in Act II. Finally a champion does appear. As he announces his name the Ivanhoe motiv is sounded with great dignity in the orchestra (see Example 9-24). Rebecca is at first unwilling to accept him as her champion because she knows that he has not fully recovered from his wounds. Brian's reaction to the champion's arrival departs somewhat from the novel. "This is the man you love!" he says to Rebecca. "Now is the hour,/Death-hour for him or me./Look to thy life, thou wretch of Ivanhoe!"[28] The combat ensues and Brian falls, as in the novel, a victim of his own passions. Rebecca is now unbound. *"She moves towards Ivanhoe,"* the stage directions read, *"but stops. Ivanhoe goes toward Rowena. Isaac goes timidly and touches the hand of Rebecca, who is gazing at Ivanhoe and Rowena; at this touch she turns and takes his hand in hers."* (This bit of action is not in the novel, but it is wholly in keeping with Scott's conception of Rebecca.) Richard now enters and forthwith banishes the Grand Master from England. When the mortified Templars threaten to appeal to Rome, Richard solemnly warns them that if the Grand Master should attempt to stay on English soil he will assuredly regret his indiscretion. The opera closes with a large ensemble composed of all the principals and the full chorus:

O Love, that hold'st the world in fee,

And strongest knights in thrall,
Our joyous hymn we raise to thee,
And hail thee lord of all.

When Sir Thomas Beecham decided to revive *Ivanhoe* as part of his 1910 Spring Season at Covent Garden, the opening night was eagerly awaited.[29] The *Evening Standard and St. James's Gazette* looked back nostalgically on the original production:

> Great interest has not unnaturally been aroused in regard to the revival of "Ivanhoe." Although it can scarcely be said that the magnificent theatre in Cambridge Circus was built solely for its production, it is unquestionable that, had there been no Sir Arthur Sullivan, there would have been no English Opera House. Never has a first night provoked a scene of greater excitement than that which saw the first performance of the composer's lyric opera, with its double cast and beautiful mise en scene. And, to judge by the pleasure with which the news of its revival has been received, its drawing capacity is still by no means a negotiable quantity. . . . It is not, however, to be expected that the music will have preserved its freshness untarnished, seeing that eighteen years is a long time in operatic history. . . . (1 January 1910)

The *Daily News* was impressed with the cost of the new production:

> One of the costliest productions from a spectacular point of view ever staged at Covent Garden will be the great revival of Sullivan's "Ivanhoe" next Tuesday. When the opera was first staged at the Palace Theatre the scenic mounting was regarded as something to be wondered at, but the spectacular display then will be as nothing compared to what the Covent Garden management intend to show us on Tuesday. Entirely new scenery has been painted and built for the whole opera, and the cost of the production will amount to £5,000. . . . (3 March 1910)

And the *Pall Mall Gazette* was intrigued with the elaborate stagecraft that would be involved:

> Five hundred pounds [should be: Five *thousand* pounds] is being spent upon the production of "Ivanhoe" at Covent Garden next Tuesday. From the spectacular point of view it will be the most elaborate performance of the Beecham opera season.
> When the scenery was first tried it was found that it took as long as four hours to set. At this rate the performance, it was realised, would never be over, and one hundred extra hands were engaged.
> In the scene of Cedric's hall, with which the opera opens, it has been the aim of Mr. Henry Emden to give an idea of the rude simplicity of the Saxon period. Huge beams and rafters compose the roof, and on the walls of plaster and stone hang implements of war and of the chase.
> The flare of torches placed at intervals, with a great log fire, in a

huge clumsily constructed fireplace, casts the roof into gloom and unites the lower parts of the hall in a harmony of colour that creates an air of comfort that is wanting in the rude surroundings of the period. The lighting of the scene is said to be very remarkable.

For the first time in the history of Sir Arthur Sullivan's opera the tournament at Ashby will take place in full view of the audience. Twelve horses in full trappings are to appear in the lists, and in the combat between Ivanhoe and the Templar the horses will cross the stage at full gallop. Expert horsemen have been specially engaged for the combat, and they will take the part in this particular scene of the principal singers.

It will be recalled, no doubt, how Sir Arthur Sullivan's music depicts in this scene the clatter of horses at a distance. Now the horses will be seen as well as heard, and twenty-five of the tallest men in the Scots Guards, each over six feet high, have been engaged to act as orderlies and attendants at the tournament. . . .

The scene of the lists has been painted by Mr. Alfred Craven, whose father, Mr. Hawes Craven, is responsible for the original production. Very gorgeous will be the daïs of Prince John, with its Royal colours and heraldic splendours; . . . and opposite will be the tents of the famous Frait-de-Bœuf [i.e. Front-de-Bœuf, who is not listed among the dramatis personae] and the Knights Templar, and over all a forest of flags decorated with the arms of the various knights.

Nor will the spectacular wonders of the opera end here, for Mr. Bruce Smith has designed for the concluding act, at the Castle of Torquilstone, a thrilling burning scene. At the height of the fighting, the castle is stormed and set on fire, and in full view of the audience the background of the scene falls away and discloses the castle burning behind and the soldiers still fighting. . . . (5 March 1910)

Performances had originally been scheduled for March 5th, 8th, and 11th, but the first of these was cancelled either because of the need for extra rehearsal time or because of the management's sudden decision to have an extra performance of Strauss's *Elektra,* which had proven very popular.[30] After the opening performance there were long reviews in all the leading papers. Most of the reviewers were impressed with the elaborate staging of the tournament and of the burning of Torquilstone, as well as with the high quality of the all-British cast, but they had certain reservations about the opera itself. The review in *The Standard* for March 9th is typical criticism:

"Ivanhoe" with its pomp and circumstance, jousts and tourneys, hairbreadth escapes, English atmosphere, tuneful music, and masterly instrumentation, is an excellent entertainment; but, viewed in the light of recent operatic developments, it is more suited to the Coliseum than to Covent Garden. Its numerous ballads, occasional concerted pieces, and weighty choruses are bound together by a form of lyrical declamation that savours of the concert platform rather than of the stage—of the cantata rather than of opera. Indeed, but for the fact that the dialogue is sung, instead of spoken, the music of "Ivanhoe" . . . in no way transcends that of the "Yeomen of the Guard." We have the same full closes, dividing the opera into a series of fixed periods, which impede and hold up the action of the drama, such as it is. There is practically no sense of continuity between the various scenes, and little sense of focus and climax. . . .

Of real dramatic intuition there is little or nothing in the score; of melodramatic conventions, plenty. Melody succeeds melody—and very delightful melodies some of them are—with a persistency that is positively cloying. We feel we are at a ballad concert rather than the Opera, only that we have the scenery and the orchestra to help engage our eyes and ears; and the scenery as provided by Mr. Beecham and the instrumentation as provided by the composer are of the best. For, to give Sullivan his due, the latter throughout is remarkable even for these days of advanced technique. Practically the only dramatic moment is in the scene between Rebecca and The Templar, where the former threatens to hurl herself from the window.

It is not until we reach the scene between Friar Tuck and King Richard that we discover the reasons that made the Savoy operas a joy for ever and "Ivanhoe" the indeterminate thing it is. It is the vein of humour we miss—without which even the "Yeomen," we shrewdly suspect, would not have achieved greatness.

Without question a singularly weak libretto has throughout handicapped the composer, for Mr. Sturgis's book is little more than a series of disconnected tableaux. Still, as has already been said, "Ivanhoe" is brave entertainment. . . .

The performance of March 11th turned out to be the last ever. The opera has not been revived again. Indeed the only other *Ivanhoe* opera that twentieth-century audiences have seen is Marschner's *Templer und Jüdin*. It fared somewhat better in revival than did Sullivan's *Ivanhoe*, but today it too has been put away, and no future revival seems likely.*

---

*Not long after I completed this chapter Sullivan's *Ivanhoe* was revived, for the first time in more than sixty years, by the Beaufort Opera, at the Hurlington School Theatre. The date of the first performance was May 31st, 1973. See the short review by Winton Dean in *The Musical Times* (July 1973), p. 722, and, in anticipation of the event, the interesting articles by Andrew Lamb in *The Musical Times* (May 1973), pp. 475-78, and Nigel Burton in *Music and Musicians* (May 1973), pp. 24-25.

10

§ § §

THE ABBOT

Most of the operas about Mary Stuart, Queen of Scots, owe nothing to *The Abbot* (1820). Pietro Casella's *Maria Stuarda,* with a libretto by Francesco Gonella, obviously does not, since the date of the première in Florence antedates the publication of the novel by seven years. In 1821 the same libretto was revised by Giusti and given a completely new musical setting by Mercadante. A glance at the "personaggi" of the revised printed libretto[1] shows that the story of both operas derives from events in Mary's life that occurred *before* the events of *The Abbot.* The ending is happy. Carlo Coccia's *Maria Stuarda* (1827), with a libretto by Pietro Giannone, is apparently based on Schiller's play: the entire action takes place in England, at Fotheringay Castle, where Mary is Queen Elizabeth's captive.[2] (The part of *The Abbot* in which Mary figures takes place in Scotland, mostly within the confines of the Castle of Lochleven. The novel ends as she hastily departs for England after the total defeat of her forces at Langside.) Donizetti's *Maria Stuarda* (1834), which is still occasionally performed, derives from Schiller; the libretto is by Giuseppe Bardoni.[3]

Théodore Anne did the libretto for Niedermeyer's *Marie Stuart,* which was first performed 6 December 1844 in Paris, at the Opéra.[4] Part of it takes place in France, before Mary goes to Scotland, and thus owes nothing to *The Abbot;* part of it involves Mary's captivity in England and her death—these events occurring after the time of *The Abbot.* The first half of Act IV, however, relates her deposition and thus covers the same ground as chapter xxii. Nevertheless, I doubt that Anne owes anything to Scott. The men who come to force her to sign are Ruthwen (*sic*), Morton, and Murray, with Sir Hamilton, the "gouverneur du château de Loch-Leven," as witness. In the novel we have Ruthven, Lindesay, Melville, and George Douglas, the son of the lord of the castle. Mary's attendants in the operatic version are young Georges Douglas (a coloratura soprano) and Anna Kennedy, rather than Mary Fleming, Catherine Seyton, and Roland Græme. The second part of the act culminates in Mary's escape, but here again I doubt that Anne owes anything to Scott's chapter xxxv. In the opera Bothwell, rather than George Douglas, is instrumental in the success of the enterprise—but in the novel (and in history) he was dead before Mary's confinement at Lochleven.

Constantino Palumbo's *Maria Stuart,* which was first performed at the San Carlo (Naples) in 1874, derives from Schiller; the libretto is by Enrico Golisciani.[5] A work entitled *Marie Stuart,* with "poème" by Julien Goujon and music by Rodolphe Lavello, is cited in Clément and Larousse's *Dictionnaire des Opéras,* but actually it is not an opera: it is a spoken drama with incidental music.[6] First performed in Rouen in 1895, it is avowedly based on Schiller.

Of all the Mary Stuart operas I have seen, the only one that derives from Scott is Fétis' *Marie Stuart en Écosse.*

Marie Stuart en Écosse

The composer of several opéras comiques, Fétis is known today chiefly for his indispensible *Biographie Universelle des Musiciens.* However, his operas did achieve a modest degree of success when they were first produced, all at the Opéra-Comique in Paris. His *Marie Stuart en Écosse; ou, Le Château de Douglas,* with words by F. A. E. de Planard and Roger, had its première on 30 August 1823.[7] It is in three acts. The cast includes Marie Stuart, Clary (young lady attached to the Queen—corresponds roughly with Scott's Catherine Seyton), Lady Fleming (companion to the Queen), Lady Douglas (Scott's Lady of Lochleven), Lord Douglas, Lord Melville, Roland, and Randal. Scott's Lord Douglas, who is the son of the Lady of Lochleven and the father of George Douglas, is mentioned more than once but never appears in the novel's action. The operatic character is Lady Douglas' husband, an old warrior who owes a good bit to Scott's Lord Lindesay. The operatic Melville, Douglas' nephew, is a composite of Scott's Melville plus George Douglas. Roland is simply an officer of the Queen: he does not turn out to be the long-lost son of Julian Avenel. Randal's role is greatly enhanced from what it is in the novel. Here he is the "intendant-concierge du château" rather than a mere boatman. He owes his post to Scott's Dryfesdale, but unlike Dryfesdale he is a comic figure. Notable omissions include Halbert Glendinning, the Lady of Avenel, Edward Glendinning (Father Ambrose), Magdalen Græme, Adam Woodcock, and Young Seyton. In fact the whole first half of the novel is omitted for the obvious reason that Mary Stuart does not figure in it. The story of the opera is a condensed version of just the chapters relating to Mary's captivity, and, as will be observed, there are many bold changes. All the action takes place at the castle, which is called simply the "château de Douglas" (not specified as Lochleven).

Act I opens in a large room next to the Queen's apartment. Two impressive-looking Douglas family portraits are hanging from the paneling. From a balcony one can see the lake and, in the distance, the small town of Kinross. Roland, alone on stage, *speaks* of his boredom. He has fooled concierge Randal and thereby acquired the means of opening the gate (we learn how shortly), but one glance from his beloved Clary has kept him from escaping. (Roland's remarks are suggested by Scott's account of Roland Græme's boredom, at the beginning of chapter xxiv.) In the attractive aria that follows ("Je veux de l'esclavage/M'affranchir en ce jour"), he re-expresses what he has just spoken; his love for Clary has kept him from taking advantage of the means he has of escape, despite his great desire to get away from the confines of the château.[8] After the aria Randal himself enters and scolds Roland for having pushed him playfully into the lake the day before, while they were fishing, thereby causing him to lose the key to the main gate of the château. Afraid of what Lord Douglas might do to him if he should find out, Randal has stolen a similar key from Lady Douglas' chest of drawers and removed the rust from it, so that it looks like the one he lost. He then speaks of Marie Stuart's confinement in the château. When Roland refers to the château as his own prison, Randal accuses him of ingratitude:

> Je ne puis vous comprendre. Orphelin, noble, à la vérité, comme l'épée de vos ancêstres, mais ne possédant pas une tourelle, on vous recommande au Régent; il vous place ice en qualité de premier et unique officier de Marie-Stuart, et vous n'êtes pas content de commencer votre carrière avec une telle protection!

(This is about all we hear of the operatic Roland's past. In the novel it is known at this point that he is an orphan, but not that he is nobly born.) Roland then expresses concern about the Queen's mistrust of him—she evidently believes that he is a spy sent by her enemies (as in the novel). When he speaks of Clary's coldness toward him, Randal replies that unlike his young friend *he* gets along swimmingly with Miss Clary.

Clary now comes out from the Queen's apartment. She tells Roland that the Queen is displeased with him for not having attended to her that morning. She says furthermore that if it were not for the charming company of Randal, she herself would perish. Not wishing to intrude on a tête-à-tête, Roland exits. (Clary is teasing him, as we soon learn. The jealousy motif as here presented has no exact parallel in the novel, but it perhaps owes something to Roland Græme's mistaken notion that George Douglas is in love with Catherine and she with him.) Randal has brought Clary merchandise from Kinross, which he says he has scrupulously examined to catch any communication that might have been smuggled to the Queen along with it. As the *scène* progresses, Clary finds and gets hold of a note that has been hidden in his bonnet. Hearing a bell at the main gate, he departs. (This comic interlude has no exact parallel in the novel, but a message for the Queen is found concealed in the sheath of Roland Græme's sword shortly after his arrival at Lochleven, and the idea of someone going to Kinross for merchandise derives from Roland's mission, later in the story, in behalf of the Lady of Lochleven.) Clary eagerly reads the note and discovers that it is from the Queen's friends, who have made preparations to free her. In the ensuing aria ("De mon zèle et de ma tendresse,/Hélas! j'obtiens enfin le prix!") she implores God to protect the daring enterprise. Then, hearing Lord Douglas approaching, she hastily conceals the note.

Douglas enters, accompanied by Lady Douglas and Lord Melville. The Lady is unhappy that Douglas cannot stay at the château that night, for there is to be a celebration in honor of St. Mary, and as her own name is Marie, the fête will in a sense be hers too. Before he leaves for the Régent's court, Douglas, assuming the role of Scott's Lord Lindesay, insists on seeing "Marie-Stuart," whom Clary insists on referring to as "la Reine." Lady Douglas departs as Marie enters, accompanied by Lady Fleming and Roland. Douglas asks for writing material and orders Roland and the two ladies-in-waiting to leave the room. What follows is based on Scott's account of Mary's abdication (chapters xxi-xxii), but without Lord Ruthven and George Douglas. Some of the spoken dialogue follows the novel closely. When Douglas tells Marie that the "conseil secret" has deemed it best for her to renounce the throne, she asks, *"feignant la surprise,"*

> De la part du conseil secret? Quelle est donc cette autorité, et de qui tient-elle ses pouvoirs?... Mais n'importe; rien de ce qui intéresse la prospérité de l'Écosse ne peut être indifférent à Marie-Stuart. . . .

> "The Secret Council?" said the Queen; "by what powers can it subsist or act, while I, from whom it holds its character, am here detained under unjust restraint? But it matters not—what concerns the welfare of Scotland shall be acceptable to Mary Stewart, come from whatever quarter it will—and for what concerns her own life, she has lived long enough to be weary of it, even at the age of twenty-five. . . ." (chapter xxi)

After he has read the document demanding her abdication, she pretends to be greatly surprised:

> Dois-je croire, mylord, ce que je viens d'entendre? ou dois-je accuser mon oreille d'infidélité? Dites moi que tout ceci n'est qu'un songe; dites-le moi pour votre honneur et pour celui de la noblesse écossaise. Assurez-moi que mes féaux et fidèles cousins, les lords Douglas et Melville, ne sont pas venus voir leur souveraine dans sa prison pour insulter à son malheur.

> "How is this, my lords?" she said: "Are my ears turned rebels, that they deceive me with sounds so extraordinary?—And yet it is no wonder that, having conversed so long with rebellion, they should now force its language upon my understanding. Say I am mistaken, my lords—say, for the honour of yourselves and the Scottish nobil-

ity, that my right trusty cousins of Lindesay and Ruthven, two barons of warlike fame and ancient line, have not sought the prison-house of their kind mistress for such a purpose as these words seem to imply. Say, for the sake of honour and loyalty, that my ears have deceived me." (chapter xxii)

As in the novel, Melville advises her to sign the document. She refuses. The finale begins with an aria for Marie, who solemnly tells Douglas and Melville that she will not give up the throne. Although Fétis' pleasant music usually does not merit particular comment, this one aria does have a passage in which both the imposing, dignified melodic line and the interesting harmony very effectively reinforce the text:

Example 10-1

Roland, Clary, and Lady Fleming now re-enter, and the act ends in a sextet. Unlike her counterpart in the novel, Marie does *not* sign.

The setting is the same in Act II as in Act I. When the curtain rises, Lady Fleming, alone on stage, wonders what will happen now that the Queen has refused to sign. Clary enters and informs her that the Queen is calmly perusing a portfolio which she brought with her from France. In a moment Marie herself enters and sings a *romance* in which she reminisces about her good times in France.[9] Afterwards Roland announces to her that Lord Melville wants to speak with her. When he and the two ladies-in-waiting withdraw, the Queen, left alone for a short while, wonders whether ambition has stifled the noble sentiments she once knew in Melville. Next, in a long *scène* of spoken dialogue, Melville warns her of the dangers which she faces if she does not sign (as in the novel, chapter xxii). But it is not long before her presence reawakens fond memories in his soul. He changes his mind about persuading her to sign, and, behaving like Scott's George Douglas, he agrees to help her. After this about-face, Marie confides to him the hope she has of being freed by friends who are hiding in Kinross. The only problem is to get from the room of her confinement to the shore, where a boat will pick her up. Melville then shows her a secret passageway which will lead her to the shore. Randal interrupts the conversation to inform Melville that Lord Douglas is waiting for him. Melville bids the Queen a hasty adieu and leaves, accompanied by Randal. Marie now calls on Clary and Lady Fleming to rejoin her, and, in the course of the ensuing trio, she joyfully tells them of the secret passage. They all express hope. But when Clary examines the passage more closely, she finds that it goes only so far and then is walled up, as if Marie's captors had half expected her to discover it. Thus escape by this means is impossible. Lady Fleming looks after the disheartened Queen as she retires to her apartment. (The situation here has no exact parallel in the novel, but it was no doubt suggested by the escape-failure that Scott recounts in chapter xxx.)

In a *scène* of spoken dialogue Clary expresses to Roland her bitter disappointment. She wants to believe that he is an honorable young man, that he is not a spy on the side of the Queen's enemies. When she hints at her tender feelings for him, he is overwhelmed. (All this is based loosely on the conversation between Catherine Seyton and Roland Græme in the first half of chapter xxxi.) Roland then says that he himself had once thought of escaping and had even stolen the key to the main gate. He shows it to her, and then, moving toward the balcony, he starts to toss it into the lake. She stops him in the nick of time. She tells him of the plans to free the Queen and of the necessity of having the key that very night, now that the secret passageway has been found unusable. (The key-motif differs from the way it is in the novel, chapters xxxiv-xxxv. Roland Græme forges a set of keys which resemble Lady Lochleven's and eventually succeeds in swapping them for hers. Part of the trick involved making the newly forged keys appear dark and rusty-colored, which Roland managed to do "by the use of salt and water"; this detail probably lies behind the operatic Randal's *removing* the rust from the key which he steals, so that it will look like the one he lost; see above.) Lady Douglas enters and announces that she wants Marie Stuart to attend the fête—her ulterior motive being to lower Marie's pride. When Marie declines to accept the invitation, Lady Douglas perversely orders Randal to let the villagers in. At this point the finale begins. The villagers sing that they have moored their boat and are come to dance at the château. They are impressed with the presence of the Queen, who graciously receives their homage—and thus Lady Douglas' plans to humble her miscarry. When Lady Douglas orders the dancing to commence, the villagers express their reluctance to do anything that might be taken as an insult to the Queen. However, Marie insists that they go ahead and enjoy themselves. All this time Roland is looking out the window for a signal from the rescuers. Clary then sings a slightly risqué *ronde* about a girl named Georgette, who eventually loses her virtue even though she tried very hard not to. (The song ironically and subtly parallels Lady Douglas' situation: she does everything she can to keep the Queen captive, but to no avail, and thus, in a sense, she loses her honor. There is no mention in the libretto of Lady Douglas' having been mistress to James V, Mary's father. The idea of having a song here was no doubt suggested by a line in Mary's discourse at the beginning of ch. xxxv, in which she wonders how the Lady of Lochleven's attention can be diverted so that the keys can be swapped: "Shall my *mignonne* Catherine sing to her one of those touching airs, which draw the very souls out of me and Roland Græme?") As Clary sings, tension begins to build up. The *ronde* has three "couplets." After the first, Roland finally sees a signal which he immediately reports to Lady Fleming, who in turn reports it to the Queen. After the second "couplet" he sees another signal and after the third still another. When Lady Douglas notices a light on the water, Randal tells her that it is no doubt a sign from St. Mary, whom they are celebrating. (In the novel Lady Lochleven looks out the window and sees gleams emanating from the hut of the gardiner Blinkhoolie, in Kinross. She wonders what he is up to so late at night. Roland tries to allay her suspicions by saying that the old man is probably working on his baskets.) Lady Douglas then tells the villagers that a repast has been prepared for them in the garden. The Queen sings, "Adieu, mes bons amis, aimez toujours Marie!" They reply, "Notre cri, toute la vie,/Sera, sera: Vive Marie!" as the act ends. (In the novel no villagers are at the castle on the night of Mary's escape; there is no feast in commemoration of St. Mary. The alteration enables the composer to display his talents in handling large vocal ensembles.)

For Act III the setting changes to the "bord du lac" just outside the walls of the château. Randal and the villagers sing a drinking song, during the course of which Clary and Roland appear from time to time on the balcony to the Queen's apartment. Clary wonders how the escape can be accomplished without the villagers noticing. To get rid of them, she requests that they have their fun at a greater distance from the château, so that the Queen can sleep. They obligingly leave the stage. Randal, somewhat intoxicated, goes into his shelter. When all is quiet, Roland unlocks the gate of the château and comes out, and in a moment Melville appears from the side of the stage where the villagers have just departed. It seems that the rescue-boat from Kinross went to the spot which Melville knew was the termination of the secret passageway. When the Queen was not there waiting, he wondered what went wrong (not realizing that egress from the château by means of the passage was impossible), and, in order to investigate the situation, he detached himself temporarily from the party of rescuers, leaving them at the other spot. As he is talking, the Queen, Clary, and Lady Fleming come out from the château. The problem now is to let the rescuers know that the Queen is here, at the main gate. Melville is sure that the path he had to take in order to avoid being seen by the carousing villagers would be much too dangerous for the ladies. Roland bravely volunteers to traverse the dangerous path to the place where the others are waiting and instruct them to bring the boat around hither. When he has departed, the Queen, Clary, Lady Fleming, and Melville sing a quartet "*à voix basse*" in which they call on heavenly justice to aid their enterprise. Next, hearing someone from a boat call out "Randal!" they soon recognize Lord Douglas, who has just returned to the château. When he disembarks, they step aside out of his sight. Douglas awakens Randal and orders him to inform Lady Douglas that Marie, upon the order of the Régent, is to be conducted immediately to Edinburgh. The two enter the château. Melville then suggests escape by means of Douglas' boat, but the Queen refuses to leave Roland behind. (This situation is somewhat different in the novel. Roland Græme suddenly turns away from the rescuers and their precious charge and rushes back to the castle. Henry Seyton thinks that he has proven false after all. He orders the boatmen to push off from the shore, despite Catherine's protestations of Roland's fidelity and the Queen's express command. Roland returns just in time. He had gone back to the castle to re-lock the gate in order to prevent would-be pursuers from getting out.) The finale begins as Roland re-enters, pursued by two peasants who have noticed his suspicious actions and prevented him from reaching the party of rescuers. The Queen boldly reveals herself to them, and the upshot is that they aid in her escape—by means of Douglas' boat. The alarm bell from the château brings everyone back on stage for the final tableau and ensemble. Douglas, Lady Douglas, Randal, and several valets cry out "O perfide!/O trahison!" but they are powerless to arrest the escape. The villagers, all of whom are sympathetic to Marie's cause, kneel on the shore and call on God to protect her. In the distance the boat begins to disappear from view. "Ah! pour Marie/Plus de prison!" the Queen sings, as the curtain falls.

Obviously a great deal has been changed in this unique operatic rendition of the second half of *The Abbot*. Much more is involved than differences in characters and in details of plot. The predominant change is one of tone. Scott's sober narrative, with its tragic implications and its emphasis on the waste of human endeavor (and life) in a doomed cause, has become an evening of light entertainment.

11

§ § §

KENILWORTH

*K*enilworth (1821) rivals *Ivanhoe* in the number of operas it inspired. They strew the century from Auber's *Leicester,* which appeared less than two years after the publication of the novel, to Isidore de Lara's *Amy Robsart* and Bruno Oskar Klein's *Kenilworth,* both of which were done in the 1890's. Unfortunately I was not able to find any trace of Francesco Vincenzo Schira's *Kenilworth* opera, which was rehearsed at Covent Garden in the fall of 1848, with Sims Reeves in the role of Leicester, but never performed.[1] Nor could I find anything pertaining to Caiani's *Amy Robsart,* which is cited in Clément and Larousse's *Dictionnaire* as having been performed on 29 September 1878, in Foiano, with Brandaglia, Falciai, Vignati, and Colombini in the leading roles.[2]

Leicester

Auber's *Leicester; ou, Le Château de Kenilworth,* with words by Scribe and A. H. J. Duveyrier, was first performed on 25 January 1823 in Paris, at the Opéra-Comique.[3] Later in the year it was produced in Brussels, also in French. It was done in German translation in Pressburg (25 October 1826), Vienna (30 October 1826), Graz (18 October 1827), Hamburg (18 February 1830), Berlin (15 May 1830), and elsewhere. A Russian version, with additional music by Catterino Cavos, opened in St. Petersburg on 14 October 1824. The dramatis personae and the singers who sang the roles on the night of the première include Elisabeth (Mme Lemonnier), Leicester (Huet), Sir Walter Raleigh (Ponchard), Hugues Robsart (Darancourt), Amy Robsart (Mme Pradher), Cicily, lady-in-waiting to Amy (Mme Boulanger), Doboobie, intendant to Leicester (Desessart), and Lords Shrewsbury, Hunsdon, and Stanley. Raleigh is a composite of Scott's Raleigh plus Tressilian and Varney. Cicily fulfills some of the functions of Scott's Janet Foster; she owes her name to Giles Gosling's pretty daughter, Cicely. Doboobie has no exact counterpart in the novel; he owes his name to a name that Scott's astrologer Alasco once had assumed, before the time of the story.

At the end of a formal overture the curtain rises, revealing a Gothic

gallery in the "abbaye de Cumnor." Cicily is alone on stage. She sings a
ballade about a queen and her page which to some extent mirrors the
Elisabeth-Leicester affair. (There is no parallel for this in the novel.)
Afterwards Raleigh enters, whom Cicily immediately recognizes. She
informs him that she has been only five days in employment at Cumnor.
When Raleigh asks her about a young lady who is supposedly concealed
there, she tells him, in the first part of the ensuing duet ("Ce secret-là"),
that she will keep the secret in her heart. He flirts with her. When asked by
her why he has come to Cumnor, he says that like her he will be silent.
Next, in spoken dialogue, he tells her about his unsuccessful love affair
with Amy Robsart. It seems that her father, an old mariner, had left her in
Devonshire under the surveillance of an aunt. One morning Amy disappeared. Her family strongly suspected that Raleigh himself had whisked
her off. He was soon forced into a duel with her brother, whom he
wounded. He has since been denounced as a ravisher by the Star
Chamber and must seek his friend Leicester for protection. (Obviously all
this is quite different from the novel. Scott's Amy has neither brother nor
aunt; her father is not a mariner. She is not wooed by Raleigh at any point
in the story, nor does Raleigh claim Leicester as a friend.) Cicily, who does
not yet know who her employer is, remarks that some say Leicester is
virtually King of England. As the conversation progresses, Raleigh says
that his forced absence from Elisabeth's court is very painful for him. He
speaks of his arrival in the vicinity and of his stay at the Black Bear, where,
like Scott's Tressilian, he heard rumors of a lady supposedly imprisoned
in the abbey. Cicily tells Raleigh that she is well paid to watch after the
person of whom he is speaking. She does not know who she is, but she
describes her as a most attractive young lady. She tells him, moreover, that
he may observe her, if he so desires. In a second duet Raleigh looks out the
window and sees Cicily's mistress, whom he immediately recognizes as
Amy Robsart. After questioning Cicily further about the mysterious lord
of the abbey and after seeing a jewel-box with its coat of arms and its seal,
he begins to realize that the seducer with whom he has to deal is none
other than his friend Leicester. Although he does not reveal his thoughts
to Cicily, she senses from his disturbed demeanor that something is amiss.

When Raleigh has departed, Leicester enters, accompanied by an older
man. Cicily realizes that Leicester must be a lord, but, as I observed above,
she does not yet know who he is. He instructs her to inform the lady of his
arrival and to prepare a room for his guest in another part of the building.
Leicester, whose identity is unknown to his guest (who happens to be
Hugues Robsart), has just saved him from robbers. Not knowing who the
man is, Leicester has brought him to Cumnor to offer him hospitality. He
requests that he not inquire about who the inhabitants of the abbey might
be. During the course of their conversation it comes out that the guest is
no admirer of Leicester, apparently for the reason that he knows him to
be a friend of Raleigh, who he believes has run off with Amy. (Unlike his

counterpart in the novel, seaman Hugues Robsart is a quite prominent character. His arrival at Cumnor, ironically in the company of Leicester, Amy's seducer, is the invention of the librettists.) After the guest has departed to his chamber, Amy enters. Leicester tells her in spoken dialogue that since the court is now at Lemington, only twelve miles away, he decided on the spur of the moment to slip away and visit her. In the ensuing duet Amy makes clear that her love for him means more to her than riches and jewelry; all this she could easily give up. After the duet he assures her that her long-standing desire to go to Kenilworth will some day be possible, but for reasons of which she is not aware he must keep their marriage secret a bit longer. (The *scène* is based loosely on the meeting of Leicester and Amy in chapter vii.) Suddenly Raleigh enters. Amy is understandably surprised, and so too is Leicester, who knows that Raleigh was her former suitor. (The sudden entrance of Raleigh is suggested by the encounter of Tressilian and Amy in chapter iv.) Raleigh says he has sacrificed his personal feelings to tell Leicester that the Queen has decided to go to Kenilworth the next day and to stop en route at Cumnor in order to see the picturesque ruins. (In the novel the Queen does not visit at Cumnor.) Leicester sends Amy away so that he and Raleigh can talk in private.

Raleigh impresses upon Leicester the danger of his position, with Amy on hand, and he tells him that he must choose between Amy Robsart and the crown of England. In reply Leicester informs Raleigh that Amy is his *wife,* the countess of Leicester. As the duologue progresses, Raleigh, assuming the role of Scott's Varney, warns Leicester that he will not have the repose he thinks he will have with Amy, but rather that he will become the laughing stock of his enemies at court and also will bear the brunt of the Queen's wrath. He advises him to continue to keep the marriage secret and to have Amy removed. The old seaman now re-enters and says that he must be on his way. Leicester leads him to believe that Raleigh, whom he does not recognize, is the lord of the abbey. When he offers to do a favor in return for the hospitality he has received, Leicester and Raleigh suddenly come up with the brainstorm of asking him to convey Amy safely to London. Cicily is then told to inform her mistress of the journey she must take. Left alone for a while on stage, Raleigh sings an aria in which he gives voice to the thought that in helping Leicester he will increase his own fortune. Afterwards Cicily re-enters and informs Raleigh what happened when the old seaman saw her mistress: "Auprès de milady,/A peine est-il entré qu'elle pousse un grand cri;/Et lui, courant vers elle,/Quoi! ma fille, a-t-il dit, ma fille dans ces lieux!" "C'est Robsart, justes dieux!" Raleigh exclaims *à part.* He is obviously in quite a dilemma. The sound of trumpets in the distance indicates to him that the Queen and her entourage will soon be at the abbey. He then makes a decision to do something drastic, but he does not tell either Cicily or the audience what he has in mind. The act ends in an atmosphere of excitement and suspense.

For the second act we move to the gardens at Kenilworth. In the first *scène* Doboobie and a chorus of villagers are making the necessary preparations for the arrival of the Queen. When they have departed, Raleigh and Amy enter. He is attempting to escort her to London, but she will not be hurried. She demands to know what has become of her father. Raleigh explains that he gave orders for the elder Robsart to be arrested in Leicester's name and transported back to his château in Devonshire. In the ensuing duet Raleigh tries his best to get her to hurry along, but she dallies, fascinated with the splendor of the Queen's entourage which is approaching. Finally he does succeed in convincing her to hide herself from view. A trumpet fanfare heralds the entrance of Elisabeth, who is accompanied by Leicester, Sussex, Doboobie, and a large number of courtiers. The Queen is impressed and pleased with the warm reception she is given. A contralto, she expresses her feelings in the aira, "Ah! de ces transports éclatants, /J'en conviens, mon âme est charmée." Afterwards, in spoken dialogue, she tells Raleigh that his absence from court has made many a lady unhappy. When he offers "affaires sérieuses" as an excuse, she replies good-humoredly that such is impossible for a person of his disposition and then names him "chambellan du palais" (suggested by the knighting of Raleigh in chapter xxxii). Next she turns to Leicester and questions him about his prisoner, whom she noticed in custody as she was approaching. Since Raleigh had not consulted with Leicester before apprehending Robsart, Leicester is of course baffled by what the Queen is saying. She tells him that she ordered the prisoner to be brought to Kenilworth and demands to know the reason for his arrest. Raleigh fears that all is lost as he beholds Hugues Robsart enter.

Leicester is understandably surprised when he sees that the prisoner is none other than his recent guest at Cumnor. He is even more surprised when the man tells the Queen that he is Hugues Robsart. Robsart now believes that Leicester is involved in the abduction of Amy, and he says so. The Queen then points to Leicester and advises Robsart not to slander him. It is now Robsart's turn to be surprised: he realizes for the first time that his kind host (who had saved him from the robbers) and Leicester are one and the same. When he demands from Leicester an account of his daughter, all are surprised, including the Queen. A large ensemble develops—the Queen singing *à part* that she is troubled, Leicester singing *à part* of his terror, Raleigh softly urging Leicester to control himself, Robsart demanding that the seducer be punished, and the chorus observing that the Queen is deeply moved. Leicester tells everyone present that Amy has by no means been dishonored, that rather she is the glory of her father *and of her husband.* He indicates furthermore that he knows who she has married. When the Queen demands to know the husband's name, Leicester becomes so flustered that he cannot articulate. At this point Raleigh, assuming again the role of Scott's Varney, announces that *he* is Amy's husband. (The *scène* is based loosely on the confrontation of

Elizabeth and Leicester in chapter xvi, at Greenwich Palace rather than Kenilworth.) In the second half of the ensemble all express in one way or another their perplexity: Leicester does not know whether to keep silent or not; Raleigh realizes that his bold action may make Leicester angry. The remainder of the long *scène* is in spoken dialogue. Robsart is very much surprised to learn that the man whom he just recently met at Cumnor is Walter Raleigh and that he is Amy's *husband.* Raleigh insists that his friend Leicester is completely innocent in the affair, that he had simply offered asylum at Cumnor to the newlyweds. When the Queen asks Raleigh if Leicester has ever seen his wife, he resorts to a ruse: "Sur mon honneur, Madame, j'atteste que milord n'a jamais vu ma femme." Elisabeth then apologizes to Leicester for her unwarranted suspicions. Robsart, however, will not be satisfied until he has seen his daughter and knows that everything was done of her own free will. Raleigh replies that he has had her transported to Berkshire because he was afraid that Robsart might cause trouble. Robsart accordingly begs to be excused from the august company to go see about his daughter, and the Queen orders Raleigh to accompany him. Unhappy about the way things have evolved, Leicester asks the Queen for a private audience. He whispers to Raleigh that he is determined to tell her the truth. In reply Raleigh warns him that all will then be irrevocably lost. Nevertheless Leicester requests that arrangements be made for his departure from Kenilworth—with his countess.

In the spoken dialogue that precedes their duet, Elisabeth offers Leicester her hand and the throne. In the duet itself she expresses her desire to marry him at Kenilworth in the presence of all the lords and ladies who are there assembled. Leicester is troubled at the new predicament in which he finds himself. Elisabeth thinks, ironically, that his visible emotional stress is on *her* account. (There is nothing exactly parallel to this in the novel: Scott's Elizabeth would not expose her feelings so openly and uninhibitedly; but the idea of having such a *scène* comes from the opening paragraph of chapter xxxiv, in which we are told of the proposal and are given Elisabeth's mild words of refusal, but no more. "The conversation of Elizabeth and the favourite Earl," Scott explains, "has not reached us in detail.") Raleigh, Doboobie, and the lords and ladies now re-enter. Raleigh tells Leicester *à part* that he has carried out his orders about departure from the château and that the countess awaits him. When Leicester says that he cannot now leave, Raleigh is astonished, but he senses from Leicester's agitation that something has come up. Hugues Robsart enters for the finale, which has no exact parallel in the novel. He tells all present that Raleigh has lied, that Amy is at Kenilworth, and furthermore that he has seen her. Immediately following the ensemble that begins with the words "O sort affreux! ô trouble extrême!" Raleigh asks that if Amy is indeed at Kenilworth, does he not have the right to shield his wife, for private reasons, from indiscreet glances? Elisabeth then orders him to bring Amy forth and introduce her. She tells Leicester *à part* that she wants her to be the first lady of honor at their forthcoming wedding. "Ah! rien n'égale mon malheur," exclaims Leicester, and the act closes in another large ensemble. (The situation as the curtain falls is again one of melodramatic suspense. We in the audience wonder how things will work out.)

The setting for Act III is a gallery of the château that leads out into the gardens. Amy enters *"avec précipitation,"* and, in a long paragraph of spoken dialogue, she wonders why Raleigh has not come to look after her. She is impressed with the grandeur around her. During the course of her aria she sees Leicester with another woman, whom she does not recognize to be the Queen. She cannot believe that Leicester has betrayed her, yet she is very much distressed, and at the end of the aria she sinks dejected into a chair. In a few moments the Queen herself enters. Amy asks who she is and why she was speaking with Leicester. Elisabeth asks in return how she can be so bold as to spy on the actions of her sovereign. When Amy introduces herself as Hugues Robsart's daughter, Elisabeth naturally assumes, from what happened in the previous act, that she is the wife of Raleigh. This Amy denies, as the duet begins, and she goes on to say that Leicester would never allow such infamy. Elisabeth then becomes suspicious and demands to know who her husband might be, but Amy is unwilling to say. (The *scène* is based loosely on the chance meeting of Elizabeth and Amy in the grotto, in chapter xxxiv.) At this point Leicester enters and is of course surprised to find Amy with the Queen. Elisabeth orders him to apprehend Amy because her words have implied that he has betrayed his sovereign. When Leicester asks her whether she really believes he could have done such a thing, she replies, "Non,/Car ma vengeance eût été trop terrible;/L'auteur de cette trahison/Eût payé de sa vie!" Amy immediately realizes the great danger Leicester is in. When Elisabeth demands to know if Raleigh is not indeed her husband, she replies, "Demandez/A milord, qu'il prononce,/Et je souscris d'avance à sa réponse." So far the *scène* has followed loosely events of chapter xxxiv; now comes a significant departure. Elisabeth orders Leicester to have Amy dragged away. This proves to be too much for him, and finally the truth comes out, namely, that Amy is his wife. (In the novel Leicester does not inform the Queen until later, in chapter xl, that Amy and he are married. The revelation takes place in the presence of Tressilian, Burleigh, Walsingham, and Shrewsbury, but not Amy, who has been taken back to Cumnor.) Like her counterpart in the novel, Elisabeth is furious. When she threatens Leicester, he reminds her that he is an Englishman and as such demands to defend himself before his peers (a detail from chapter xxxiv: "My head cannot fall but by the sentence of my peers—to them I will plead, and not to a princess who thus requites my faithful service"). He then departs, taking Amy with him.

At this point in the libretto (but not in either the vocal score or the orchestral score) there is a recitative and aria for Elisabeth, who is alone on stage. She is upset that Leicester has betrayed her feelings, but at least she will be able to reap revenge.[4] After the aria Shrewsbury, Raleigh, and several courtiers enter. Elisabeth calls on Shrewsbury to arrest Leicester as a traitor. Unobserved by the Queen, Raleigh advises him not to hasten to carry out her orders, because she might change her mind, and a pardoned Leicester would prove a dangerous enemy to the person who had arrested him. (The incident is suggested by Elizabeth's actions in chapter xxxiv. There Hunsdon gives her a piece of blunt advice: "And it is like your Grace might order me to the Tower to-morrow, for making too much haste. I do beseech you to be patient.") Shrewsbury then leaves the stage along with all the courtiers except Raleigh.

In spoken dialogue Raleigh tells the Queen that he has learned only that very day the circumstances of Amy's marriage. It is painful for him to discover that she is Leicester's wife, because he once loved her deeply, yet his esteem for his friend Leicester will eventually enable him to forget his sorrow. When Elisabeth says that he can be avenged, Raleigh replies that her chastisement of Leicester would simply show all the world that she loved him, and Leicester is not worthy of such an honor. (Here Raleigh echoes Burleigh's wise words to Elizabeth in chapter xl.) He then sings a *romance* ("Un seul instant, ô ma noble maîtresse") in which he urges her to pardon Leicester's offense. Everyone now re-enters, including Amy and her father. Elisabeth announces that for sundry weighty reasons Leicester's marriage to Amy had to be kept secret; now, at long last, it can be celebrated. She says that on the morrow she must return to London and that Raleigh must accompany her; she will permit Leicester and Amy to remain at Kenilworth. As the court is breaking up, Amy notices that Leicester is in a reverie. "Roi d'Angleterre!" he exlaims *à part*—a phrase used several times during the course of the opera. He then offers her his hand, while in conclusion the chorus sings of Elisabeth's glory.

As anyone can see, the story of the opera is almost a travesty of the original. Such is often the case in French opéras comiques based on Scott. The remarkable happy ending, which brings to mind Nahum Tate's revision of the last act of *King Lear,* occurs also in the Donizetti opera, to which we may now turn.

Elisabetta al Castello di Kenilworth

Known also as *Il Castello di Kenilworth,* this early opera by Donizetti was first performed on 6 July 1829 in Naples, at the San Carlo.[5] The libretto was the work of Andrea Leone Tottola, who ten years earlier had done the libretto for Rossini's highly successful *La Donna del Lago* (see Chapter 2). Although the opera went well in dress rehearsal, on the opening night it was "quasi disapprovata," to quote Donizetti's letter of July 24th to the composer Johann Simon Mayr, his teacher and friend.[6] The reason was that the evening was a formal gala for Queen Isabella Maria, in celebration of her birthday, and as usual on such occasions the audience felt somewhat inhibited. The singers included Adelaide Tosi as Elisabetta, Luigia Boccabadati as Amelia (Scott's Amy Robsart), Eden as Fanny (Janet Foster), Antonio David as Alberto Dudley, Conte di Leicester, Berardo Winter as Warney (*sic*), and Paolo Ambrosini as Lambourne. "The opera was neither very well performed nor very well listened to," Donizetti continued. "Then La Tosi was taken ill, and it was repeated only on the 12th. It was a Sunday, a beautiful day, the theater crowded, the singers happy. . . . I alone trembled. Their Majesties of Piedmont came and applauded. Prince Leopoldo [of Salerno] did as much. The King and Queen of Naples came and did as much. Therefore with the singers animated, an audience that could let itself go—and the result was continuous applause! Everyone was called out, and the evening was very brilliant."[7]

There is no overture. After a short introduction the curtain rises on a setting at Kenilworth. Lambourne and a group of Leicester's retainers sing in anticipation of the Queen's arrival. (The opera, then, begins at a point well past the middle of the novel.) One often repeated musical figure in the orchestra—

Example 11-1

—brings to mind the festive music in *Lucia di Lammermoor,* at the beginning of the scene in which the marriage contract is signed:

Example 11-2

After a while Leicester enters and sings of the predicament he is in. He has reason to believe that the Queen wants to marry him, but, as luck would have it, he is already secretly married to Amelia; hence his soul is lacerated by tyrannical anxiety and anguish. The first musical number ends with Leicester, Lambourne, and the chorus all singing of the Queen's forthcoming visit. Leicester is understandably worried about how Elisabetta would react if she should find out about Amelia.—*Dopo l'Introduzione:* In a passage of orchestra-accompanied recitative, Leicester tells Lambourne that Amelia must be confined to a remote room of the castle, where she will not know about the Queen's visit. (In the novel Amy is confined at Cumnor-Place. Fearing that Varney intends to poison her, she manages to escape, with the aid of Wayland Smith and Janet Foster. She goes to Kenilworth to seek Leicester's protection.) Fanny then enters and urges Leicester to go see Amelia, who has become upset over a presentiment she has had that dire things are about to occur. Leicester replies distractedly that he is unable at the moment to do so. Fanny senses that something is amiss.

Scena e Duo: Greatly agitated, Amelia asks Warney why he is conducting her to a remote, inaccessible room of the castle. Warney replies that it is not for him to interpret his master's will. Amelia then tells him that he must still nourish a grudge against her (presumably because she had once refused his amorous overtures, as in the novel). Vehemently he denies that such is the case—Leicester has simply ordered him to conceal her. Observing how upset she is, he implores her to calm herself ("Calmati, o cara!") and to look on him as her defender. She quickly becomes suspicious of the drift his remarks have taken. When she angrily asks whether it is allowable for him to hope that she would be lacking in her faith to Leicester, he replies that he knows how to get revenge on her for spurning his love. Their heated remarks are momentarily interrupted by the sound of music in the distance, heralding the imminent arrival of the Queen:

Example 11-3

(Donizetti used this same melody a few years later in *L'Elisir d'Amore,* at the first entrance of Dr. Dulcamara.) As the duet concludes, Warney warns Amelia that she herself will be the cause of her future grief.—*Coro, Cavatina e Finale:* At the beginning of this number we hear the sound of trumpets from different towers of the castle and then, once again, the melody we heard in the previous number (see Example 11-3). The people joyfully greet Elisabetta in an impressive, if conventional, choral ensemble. Warney quietly and briefly informs Leicester that Amelia has been put away. "Alfin respire," Leicester replies. In the cavatina that follows, Elisabetta acknowledges the warm reception that her subjects have given her. As she sings, Leicester quietly expresses his uneasiness to Warney, who urges him to get control of himself. Then comes the Queen's cabaletta ("In estasi soave"), at the end of which she is joined by the

jubilant chorus. "Evviva Elisabetta!" they shout.—This part of the opera
was obviously inspired by Scott's colorful account of Elizabeth's arrival at
Kenilworth: "The whole music of the Castle sounded at once, and a round
of artillery, with a salvo of small arms, was discharged from the battlements; but the noise of drums and trumpets, and even of the cannon
themselves, was but faintly heard amidst the roaring and reiterated welcomes of the multitude" (chapter xxx).

The second act begins with a conversation between Leicester and Warney in orchestra-accompanied recitative. Feeling sorry for Amelia, Leicester tells Warney that he will see her and try to calm her restlessness. In
reply Warney advises Leicester to fear the Queen, who will assuredly be
offended should she hear that he is already married. Furthermore he
urges Leicester to have Amelia moved to Cumnor at once. Leicester
agrees to this proposal, and when Warney suggests that Amelia may not
easily be persuaded to go, Leicester says that if she should indeed prove
uncooperative he will formally empower Warney to take her away. Warney remarks *aside,* "L'ingrata è in poter mio," and leaves the stage. We
then hear agitated music in the orchestra as Amelia makes her initial
entrance and confronts her husband. She wonders why her presence
causes him to turn white as a sheet. "Hear me!" he implores her. "No, I
want to speak," she replies; "you listen to me, and be silent!" "Ohimè!" he
exclaims *aside.* She reminds him that he took her away from her father,
that she sacrificed all for love. She agreed to the secret marriage, but now
she finds herself a virtual prisoner of Warney. She wonders why these
things must be. She wonders if this is the faith he once swore to her:

Example 11-4

Touched by her plea, he tells her that he loves her, but he requests that
their marriage be kept secret a while longer. "Elisabetta is in the castle," he
continues, "and does not yet know of our marriage." "But she ought to
know of it," Amelia replies; "further delay is an offense to my dignity."
When she insists on being open about the delicate matter, Leicester
accuses her of vaulting ambition and thanklessness. She accuses him of
having ruthlessly seduced her. As the big duet ends, both sing, "Worries,
sighs, torments, suffering—what heart could stand up to your rigor?"[8]
(The *scena* derives from two separate meetings of Leicester and Amy in
the novel: at Cumnor, chapter vii, and at Kenilworth, chapter xxxv.)

Scena e Aria: At the beginning of this number Lambourne tells a group
of Leicester's followers that Warney is coming soon to speak with them
about a confidential matter of much importance. They assure Lambourne in chorus that he and Warney can rely on their fidelity. Warney

then enters, promising the men generous rewards for the task which he wants to entrust to them. Before explaining what the task is, however, he addresses himself to Lambourne to see whether or not he is still faithful, because now he will require the ultimate proof of his fidelity. He admits to him that he still has a burning desire for the ungrateful Amelia. He goes on to say that he now has the power to destroy her, since Leicester has decided to have her conveyed to Cumnor. In the *larghetto* "Taci, amor!" he hardens himself to the deed that must be done. He then calls on the chorus to aid him. Finally, in the cabaletta, he tells Lambourne that Amelia must die. He gives him a dagger which he is to use in dispatching her after arrival at Cumnor, and he makes him promise to let her know, as she is dying, that Warney is now avenged.—This part of the opera has no exact parallel in the novel, but it owes a little to Varney's machinations with Tony Foster regarding Amy's death. The operatic Lambourne is thus a composite of Lambourne and Foster. The idea of having Amelia murdered by means of a dagger is not in the novel, and interestingly the dagger-motif is a loose end in view of the events of the opera's final scene (see below).

Scena e Quartetto: Determined to claim her rights, Amelia has escaped from the castle by means of a subterranean passage and is now in the park area. Seeing the Queen approaching, she moves aside so that she will not be observed. Elisabetta enters, obviously in a distressed state of mind (owing to her tender feelings toward Leicester). When Amelia overhears her mention Leicester's name, she comes out from concealment. The Queen asks her why she is crying, and she replies that she has been the victim of a traitor. She also tells the Queen that she is the daughter of Ugo Robsart. The Queen then demands to know who the traitor is so that she can punish him. Fully realizing that Leicester will be lost if she names him, Amelia replies, "Warney!"—but in the next breath she says that she has not told the truth and that her fate actually depends on Leicester. The Queen becomes suspicious. (This duet between Amelia and Elisabetta is based on Scott's account of their chance meeting in the grotto, chapter xxxiv. In the novel, however, Elizabeth has already heard of Amy Robsart, and she believes her to be Varney's wife. This Amy vehemently denies, and when Elizabeth demands to know whose wife or paramour she is, she "at length [utters] in despair, 'The Earl of Leicester knows it all.' ") Hunting horns are heard in the orchestra as Leicester enters, accompanied by Warney, with the intention of asking the Queen to join the chase. Both men are greatly surprised to see Amelia with the Queen. As the elaborate quartet begins, Elisabetta cannot but observe that Leicester is distraught: "Freme ondeggia irresoluto. La sua fronte è sbalordita." After the *andante* Elisabetta asks Amelia how it is that her fate depends on Leicester. At this point Warney says that Amelia is *his* wife and that she is mentally deranged. (In the novel Varney claims that Amy is his wife during the confrontation between Elizabeth and Leicester at Greenwich Castle. Tottola has amalgamated the events of chapters xvi and xxxiv.) Amelia protests that what he has said is not true, but to no avail: the Queen peremptorily orders her to be taken away and mewed up. In the final ensemble Amelia, Leicester, and even Warney beg her to show pity, but she is relentless, apparently still motivated by the bitter feeling that Leicester is not altogether innocent.

In recitative at the beginning of Act III Warney tells Leicester that Amelia is confined again to the place whence she escaped. He says furthermore that the Queen has honored his claim as husband to Amelia and has put her completely in his power. "What will become of her?" asks Leicester. "Confide in me," Warney replies; "you will be satisfied." The Queen now enters, and upon her request Warney leaves the stage. She turns to Leicester and tells him that a shadow was cast on his reputation in the preceding act, but now, she pretends, she is thoroughly convinced that Amelia is Warney's wife. (Actually she thinks otherwise and is taking great delight in tormenting him.) As a gift of reconciliation, she offers him Britain and the throne, thoroughly enjoying his confused reaction. When she says specifically that she would like for him to be her consort and reign with her, Leicester finally decides that he can no longer dissimulate: he tells her that he, not Warney, is Amelia's husband. "Punish *me* with death," he cries, "but have pity on *her*." In the remainder of the duet the furious Queen threatens to punish both of them; Leicester again implores her to have pity on Amelia. (The *scena* is based loosely on Leicester's confession to the Queen in chapter xl, but without Tressilian, Burleigh, Shrewsbury, and Walsingham. In the novel the unsuspecting Queen is both angry and surprised. She enjoys tormenting Leicester *after* the confession rather than before.)

The scene now changes to Amelia's place of confinement. In the opening recitative she tells Fanny that Leicester's faithlessness is a torment worse than death. She then sings a conventional aria. First she recalls the happy times of yore: "Par che mi dica ancora,/'Io t'amerò costante!' " But the image flees which once filled her life with joy, and she is left with unbearable sorrow.[9] Immediately after the aria she notices Warney approaching. Fanny hides, and in a few seconds Warney enters, together with Lambourne. Coming quickly to the point he tells Amelia that she must go with him. If she should hesitate, he is empowered by Leicester to take her away by force. Yet, if she will take pity on his unrequited feelings, he will disobey Leicester's orders. Highly incensed, she calls him a monster; she says that she detests him. Warney accordingly resolves to be pitiless in carrying through with his orders, and when Amelia is on the verge of fainting, he offers her a poisoned drink. At this melodramatic moment Fanny bursts forth from hiding, crying out, "Stop! It's poison!" (The poison-motif is taken from the novel, but out of its original context; see chapter xxii.) Warney warns Fanny to look out for herself and again orders Amelia to come with him, while Lambourne vows that Fanny will be Amelia's companion in fate. Suddenly Leicester and a chorus of courtiers enter the room. Leicester is very much surprised at the bold action which Warney has taken. Presently the Queen herself arrives. After pardoning Leicester and Amelia she orders Warney and Lambourne to be taken away (and punished, we can assume). Then, in a formal aria, she admits that she was tempted to take revenge on Leicester, but her deep-seated love for her subjects has resurged triumphant. She commands Leicester to embrace Amelia and honor her as his wife. The opera ends happily, the chorus joining Leicester and Amelia in praise of Elisabetta, "the splendor of the century."

The happy ending and the absence of several of Scott's most memorable characters make *Il Castello di Kenilworth* quite different in overall effect from the novel. Different, but not satisfying. Tottola's libretto is uninspired as well as carelessly put together. All the characters are pasteboard figures in comparison with their originals. The libretto does not exploit to the fullest much that is inherently operatic in the novel. Donizetti's music helps, but although pleasant enough it is not on the same level with his best work. The composer himself did not have a very high opinion of his first Walter Scott opera. "[Between ourselves]," he confided to Mayr at the end of the above-cited letter, "I wouldn't give one piece of *Il Paria* for the whole of *Il Castello di Kenilworth*."[10]

Festen paa Kenilworth

Festen paa Kenilworth, with words by Hans Christian Andersen and music by Christoph Ernst Friedrich Weyse, was first performed on 6 January 1836 in Copenhagen, at the Royal Danish Theater. It was well received on the whole, and it was much discussed in local newspapers and journals.[11] However, it was laid aside the same year, after only seven performances.[12] Despite the happy ending Andersen's libretto [13] follows Scott more closely than do any of the other *Kenilworth* operas. All the main characters are retained except Sir Walter Raleigh, Wayland Smith, and Sir Hugh Robsart, and Robsart is talked about more than once, even though he does not appear among the dramatis personae. Moreover, several of the passages of spoken dialogue are conspicuously close renderings of the original.

The overture begins with a *larghetto*, "fuld af Anstand," one critic wrote, "og—om man saa vil—ridderligt Galanterie, der tyder paa den høie Gjæsts Nærværelse": [14]

Example 11-5

This is followed by a joyful *allegro con brio:*

Example 11-6

We then have a return to the first motiv, with changes in the harmonic structure, and finally a return to the *allegro.* The overture to *Festen* is one of the best known and most often played of Weyse's orchestral compositions.

The opening scene is the tap-room at the Black Bear (see chapters i–ii). To begin with, the guests, who are mostly craftsmen from the town of Cumnor, sing a drinking song, and afterwards Michael Lambourne sings of the wonders of America, where he has spent time during his absence from England.[15] At the end of each stanza Goldthred sings, "Hvor frydeligt!/Gud, hvor det er nydeligt!" and then the rest of the guests sing the refrain: "Skade, at Amerika / Ligge skal saa langt herfra!" The ensuing spoken dialogue follows the novel rather closely. Goldthred thinks of the business opportunities in America, and Lambourne encourages him to be venturesome. As in the novel Lambourne hears of the fates of several of his old comrades. Finally he gets around to asking about Tony Foster. When Bob (Scott's unnamed clerk of the parish) says something about a beautiful lady whom Foster is said to keep at Cumnor-Place, Tressilian eavesdrops on the conversation. Gosling has also heard of the mysterious lady. When Goldthred tells about having once seen her for a brief moment, Lambourne vows that he too will see her. In the quintet (Bob, Goldthred, Gosling, Lambourne, and Tressilian) that concludes the scene, Tressilian decides to accompany Lambourne to Cumnor-Place, despite Gosling's warning that he may get himself into trouble.

The scene now changes to a lavishly redecorated room at Cumnor-Place, where Amy (Emmy in the vocal score) and Jeanette Foster are engaged in conversation, which Andersen has drawn from chapter vi. Amy is delighted with the appearance of the room, and she is thrilled in knowing that her beloved Lei'ster will soon be arriving at Cumnor. When she expresses disapproval of Varney, Jeanette warns her not to cross the man who stands so high in Lei'ster's favor. Amy also says that she does not like the way Tony Foster looks: "Saae han kun ei saa mørk—saa hæslig ud!" Jeanette replies that her father is a better man than Amy thinks, and Amy promises to speak favorably of him to Lei'ster for her sake. She then thinks of her own father and of how unhappy he must be, but one day he will be overjoyed to hear that she is Lei'ster's wife. In the ensuing duet, which is only suggested by the situation in the novel, Amy sings of her happiness and Jeanette wishes her well. Afterwards, when both have left the stage, Tony Foster enters and is presently informed by Morits (Scott's unnamed "aged sour-visaged domestic") that two strangers desire to see him. Tressilian and Lambourne are shown in. The ensuing duologue between Lambourne and Foster, who is not at all pleased to encounter his companion of bygone days, is drawn from chapter iii. After a while Foster asks Tressilian to stay where he is and wait, while he and Lambourne go off to finish their conversation in private. Left alone on stage, Tressilian is given a recitative and aria. The recitative, which is spoken, is a free translation of his soliloquy in the novel, chapter iv ("These are the associates, Amy," etc.). In the aria ("Hvad Hjertet her sig klynger til") he sings first of love's sorrows, but then, breaking out of his despondent mood, he sings of the joy he will have in helping Amy return to her father's breast. Amy now enters and, as in the novel, momentarily mistakes Tressilian for Lei'ster. The ensuing spoken duologue follows the novel closely. Tressilian tells her that her father is ill, and he implores her to leave Cumnor to visit him. She says that she cannot do so at the present time. Becoming overly insistent, he grabs hold of her arm. She cries out for help, and immediately Lambourne and Foster re-enter, accompanied by Varney. (In the novel Tressilian encounters Varney outside, as he is leaving the premises. Andersen's introducing him at this earlier point avoids a change of setting and also heightens the emotional intensity of the situation.) A quintet begins. Tressilian, who is now convinced that Varney is Amy's seducer, begs her once more to follow him, but in vain. In the closing measures Varney and Foster strongly urge him to leave Cumnor at once. He does so, followed by Lambourne, who is not yet in Varney's service.—Briefly, the remainder of the scene at Cumnor consists of spoken duologue between Varney and Foster, drawn from chapter v, in which Varney expresses grave concern about Tressilian's tête-à-tête with Amy; then spoken duologue between Varney and Amy, drawn from chapter vi, in which Varney suggests that Amy not tell Lei'ster of her having seen and spoken with Tressilian; and finally, upon Lei'ster's entrance, a duet for Amy and Lei'ster ("Du kjærlighed, gjør Hjertet glad")—the words suggested by the material of chapter vii.

For the short third scene we move back to the tap-room at the Black Bear. The opening conversation between Gosling and Tressilian is an abridged rendering of their conversation in Scott that takes place in Tressilian's bedchamber (see chapter viii). Tressilian tells the host his suspicion regarding Varney's relationship with Amy, and Gosling advises him to bring the matter to the Queen's attention. Goldthred, Bob, and the other guests come in and sing another drinking song (not in the novel), which serves as the finale to the act. (The act ends lamely. The change of scenery brings only a bit of spoken dialogue and a short, uninteresting, tacked-on chorus.)

The first scene of Act II is the throne-room of the Queen's castle in Greenwich. The opening chorus sung by Lei'ster's faction (the tenors) and Sussex's faction (the baritones and basses) is suggested by the confrontation described by Scott in chapter xvi. The Queen then sings an aria ("Fredens Palme huldt omskygge / Dig, mit elskte Fædreland!"), the opening measures of which are reminiscent of the stately *larghetto* of the overture; at the end she is joined by the chorus. Much of the spoken dialogue that follows is drawn almost verbatim from the novel. The Queen asks Lei'ster if he does not have in his entourage one Richard Varney, who has been accused of having abducted the daughter of Sir Hugh Robsart. When Lei'ster turns pale and becomes so flustered that he can hardly speak, Varney tells the Queen that the lady is *his* wife. As the lengthy conversation progresses, Varney hints to Elisabeth of Lei'ster's romantic interest in her, and she is pleased. As in the novel, she requests that Varney bring his wife to the festivities that are soon to be held at Kenilworth. The scene ends with a choral number, in which all sing the Queen's praises.—We move now to Lei'ster's room in the castle. In spoken dialogue drawn from chapters xviii and xxi, Varney recommends to Lei'ster that Amy actually appear at Kenilworth as Mrs. Varney. Since there seems no other way out of the dilemma arising from the Queen's request, Lei'ster reluctantly agrees to the plan and empowers Varney to carry it out. After Varney has departed for Cumnor, Lei'ster sings a formal aria, suggested by (but not simply translated from) the soliloquies of Scott's Leicester at both the beginning and the end of chapter xxi. Afterwards he opens a door concealed behind the tapestry and summons forth his astronomer, Alasco. The ensuing spoken dialogue is drawn from chapter xviii, with a few changes. The danger, for example, that Alasco foresees as a threat to Lei'ster comes from the North (meaning Kenilworth—hardly the North of England, but northward indeed, as well as westward, from Greenwich) rather than from the West (Cornwall, associated with Tressilian's ancestry, or Devon, the home of Walter Raleigh, who is not among the dramatis personae of the opera). Their conversation leads into a duet, which concludes the scene.

At the beginning of the next scene, Amy's room at Cumnor-Place, Amy sings an aria in which she expresses her happiness, but in her following conversation with Jeanette, drawn from chapter xxii, she wonders what meaning her position and wealth actually have if she must remain a virtual prisoner at Cumnor. Foster then announces the arrival of Varney, who enters forthwith and informs Amy that she must appear at Kenilworth as his wife. As in the novel, she is terribly upset, her lines sometimes following Scott almost word for word:

> . . . Forvovne, bort!
> Bort fra mit Ansigt! jeg foragter Dig!
> Jeg skammer mig, at Du har vakt min Brede.

> "Go, begone, sir—I scorn thee so much, that I am ashamed to have been angry with thee." (chapter xxii)

After Varney and Foster have left the room, Amy implores Jeanette to help her escape. Their conversation is soon interrupted by Foster, who re-enters bearing what he says is Amy's customary evening drink. When Jeanette is on the point of tasting it first, he becomes so upset that he impulsively grabs the glass from her hands. Visibly distraught, he hastens from the room. Jeanette now agrees to help Amy escape, and as the scene ends Amy vows to go to Kenilworth and place herself in Lei'ster's protection. (Except for Amy's aria, everything is in spoken dialogue, either borrowed from or obviously based on Scott's dialogue in chapter xxii.)— For the elaborate finale the setting changes to the countryside. Amy, disguised and wearing a mask, falls in with Schoolmaster Holiday, the dwarf Dickie, and a group of actors and gypsies who are on their way to Kenilworth, where they are to perform. This is a big, colorful scene, suggested by but greatly enhancing the parallel material of chapter xxiv. There is much choral music, a ballet (consisting of dances of gypsies, of shepherds and shepherdesses, and a "Vaabendands af Riddere"), a song by a minstrel, and a general dance. Amy conceals herself when Foster (rather than Lambourne) and Varney suddenly arrive on the scene in search of her. The act ends in a large ensemble, with everyone becoming worked up over the insolence of Varney and Foster, who are forced to leave. (The main alteration in Scott's account is that there is no Wayland Smith who serves as Amy's guide. Moreover Goldthred and Bob, unlike their counterparts in the novel, are among the motley group.[16])

All of Act III takes place at Kenilworth. When the curtain rises, we see a small, vaulted room which is soon entered by Amy, deathly pale, accompanied by Holiday and Dickie. (Much of what follows is based loosely on events of chapters xxvi–xxvii.) Holiday departs after a few moments to make arrangements for the entertainment for which he is responsible. Dickie remains. As Amy pens a letter, he looks out the window and reports to her what he observes regarding the crowd. Upon having completed the letter, she entrusts it to Dickie (who now assumes the role of Wayland Smith) to deliver to Lei'ster. Left alone, she gives vent to her feelings in a soliloquy that is virtually a word-for-word borrowing of the meditation of Scott's Amy at the end of chapter xxv ("I have given him . . . all that a woman has to give," etc.). She then looks out the window and sees Lei'ster at the Queen's side (a detail not in the novel). "Jeg hans ægteviede Hustru!" she exclaims in despair. "Fremmed paa mit eget Slot,/ Glemt, forskudt, forladt af Alle!" We now hear from *without* a "Marche med Chor," which is immediately followed by festive "Harmoni-Musik." Presently Tressilian enters and, as in the novel, is surprised to find Amy in *his* room. The words of the duet they sing are suggested by Scott's dialogue, but omitted is the motif of Amy wresting from her rejected suitor a promise not to interfere with her designs for a period of twenty-four hours. After Tressilian has been gone only a short while, Amy mistakes drunken Mike Lambourne for Lei'ster and opens the door to him. As in the novel (chapter xxxiii), he tries to make love to her, but she frantically detaches herself from his grasp and escapes from the room. (In the novel the Lambourne incident occurs on the morning after Amy's stay in Tressilian's room. Andersen has compressed into this single scene material drawn from at least four chapters.)

The scene now changes to a grotto in the garden. In the background we can see masses of people, some of whom are dancing on the terrasses, others watching the brilliant display of fireworks. The first musical number ("Lystigt afsted! fra Bjerg og Dal / Hoit lader Hornene klinge!") is a conventional chorus of hunters, suggested by the preparations being made for a grand chase at the beginning of chapter xxxiv. Much of what follows is based on the events of this chapter. First, Amy enters the grotto in search of sanctuary. Then Elisabeth enters, deeply moved by Lei'ster's recent proposal of marriage, which she as Queen felt obliged to reject. She does not notice at first that someone besides herself is in the grotto, and when she does, she is surprised that the someone-else falls on her knees before her and implores her for protection. As in the novel, Amy introduces herself as the daughter of Sir Hugh Robsart, and Elisabeth then asks her if she is not Varney's wife. "Nei, høie Frue! nei!" Amy replies emphatically. When Elisabeth demands to know whose wife she is, she replies, "Grev Lei'ster veed det Hele!" As Elisabeth starts to conduct Amy out of the grotto, Lei'ster, Hunsdon, Sussex, Varney, and a group of courtiers appear, and a large ensemble develops. As in the novel, Varney, fearing that the distraught Lei'ster will come out with the truth, manages thoroughly to convince the Queen that Amy is his own wife, and the Queen orders her to be taken away. Afterwards, in spoken dialogue, Varney apprises the Queen of Amy's supposed mental derangement. (Andersen's libretto follows Scott closely on this point. In almost all the other operas the order of events has been changed: Varney tells of Amy's insanity while she is still present.) The chorus sings another number in praise of Elisabeth, and then everyone leaves except Lei'ster and Varney. The spoken duologue that follows is drawn and condensed from chapter xxxvi, Varney attempting to convince Lei'ster that Amy is having a clandestine affair with Tressilian. When Lei'ster virtually empowers Varney to take action as he sees fit ("Jeg overlader Alting til din Omhu!"), Varney leaves the stage. Presently Tressilian enters and is forced by Lei'ster into mortal combat. As in the novel, chapter xxxix, Dickie prevents Lei'ster from killing Tressilian, whom he has defeated, and belatedly presents him with Amy's letter. (No explanation is given for the delay. In the novel Dickie had stolen the letter from Wayland Smith, who was supposed to deliver it.) Lei'ster now realizes Amy's innocence and tells Tressilian that she is his wife. He sends Dickie away in search of Varney.—The scene changes to the Queen's room at Kenilworth. For some reason this part of the opera is not included in the libretto which I used, but the vocal score has a trio for Elisabeth, Lei'ster, and Burleigh. Preceding the trio there is presumably spoken dialogue (not in the score) in which Lei'ster tells Elisabeth that Amy is his wife. Then begins the trio, Elisabeth singing, "Ha! Dudleys Hustru! Din hun er, Forræder!" At first she is angry with Lei'ster for his having willfully deceived her, but upon Burleigh's advice she gives up the childish idea of taking revenge and graciously forgives him. (The scene is based on Leicester's audience with the Queen in chapter xl, but in the opera Tressilian is apparently not present; absent also are Shrewsbury and Walsingham, whom Andersen has omitted from his dramatis personae.)

The final scene is a long, murky gallery *at Kenilworth* (rather than Cumnor). In the background a staircase leads up to a smaller gallery, which leads to the room where Amy has been confined. (The events of the scene follow loosely Scott's final chapter to a point, but then come obvious, significant changes.) When the curtain rises, Varney and Foster come in. Varney tells Foster that Amy must die and shows him a concealed chain that controls an unnoticeable trap-door in the upper gallery. Varney's plan is that he himself will imitate Lei'ster's signal, which will bring Amy forth from her room, while Foster will pull the chain at the right moment—and thus Amy will plunge to her death, which will appear accidental. Foster agrees to enact his part, but first he says that he must go to the chapel to pray. While he is gone, Varney says that the fulfillment of his wishes is close at hand; Amy's death will enable Lei'ster to marry the Queen and become England's King, and Varney himself will rise in the wake of his master's good fortune. He then sings an aria ("En Kraft mig gjennemstrømmer") in which he exults in the revenge he is about to take on Amy and dedicates his life to Fortuna. Afterwards Dickie bursts in and tells Varney that Lei'ster wants to see him at once, and furthermore that Lei'ster loves his wife. Refusing to honor Lei'ster's new orders, Varney rushes up the stairs to the upper gallery—apparently with the intention of going to Amy's room to murder her. (In this episode Dickie assumes the role of Scott's Lambourne, with whom Leicester entrusts an all-important message to be delivered posthaste to Varney which countermands his original orders. Receiving the message but determined to go through with his plans to do away with Amy, Varney murders Lambourne.) In the meanwhile Foster has returned from prayer and has assumed a position at the pillar where the chain is located that controls the trap-door. The finale begins with a passage of "melodrama"—ominous-sounding music in the orchestra alternating with lines *spoken* by Foster. Hearing footsteps on the upper gallery, he pulls the chain. Someone whom he assumes to be Amy plunges to death. At the *allegro molto* Tressilian bursts in and frantically asks Foster where Amy is. Greatly distraught, he replies that she is dead. Dickie then re-enters in great haste and tells Tressilian to come with him at once. At this point Elisabeth, Lei'ster, Hunsdon, and a chorus of courtiers hurry in. Lei'ster looks down into the abyss, sees a mangled corpse, and cries out, "Hun er knust!—o vee mig! vee!" All believe that Amy is dead. But in a few moments Tressilian appears carrying a live Amy in his arms and followed by Dickie. He explains that Varney fell into the trap that had been set for Amy. The opera ends happily, as the Queen gives her good wishes to the Earl and Countess of Lei'ster. Tressilian announces that he will set sail for foreign parts, now that Amy is safe and happy, and in the closing measures all present sing in praise of Queen Elisabeth.

The happy ending fulfills the wish that many a reader no doubt has: If only Amy can somehow be saved! And in this respect the three *Kenilworth* operas discussed thus far are analogous to the *Ivanhoe* operas that end with Ivanhoe being able, after all, to marry Rebecca, who has conveniently turned out to be of noble, Anglo-Saxon, Christian stock. As I observed earlier, however, *Festen paa Kenilworth* on the whole is a close and faithful rendering of Scott's story, at least in comparison with the other *Kenilworth* operas and with other Walter Scott operas in general. The music is of high quality.

Das Fest zu Kenilworth

Eugen Seidelmann's *Fest zu Kenilworth,* a "grosse romantische Oper" in three acts, was first performed on Tuesday, 19 December 1843, at the Stadttheater in Breslau, of which Seidelmann was musical director. A second performance took place on Thursday of the same week. The opera was well received.[17] The composer's wife, a well-known singer in her day,[18] created the role of Queen Elisabeth, and Seidelmann himself did Giles Gosling. Others among the dramatis personae include Robert Dudley, Graf von Leicester (sung by Haimer), Sir Walter Raleigh (Franke), Richard Varney (Prawit), Tressilian (Mertens), Emmy Robsard (Mlle Corabori), Antony Foster (Rieger), Anna, his daughter (Mme Meyer), Michael Lambourne (Wiedermann), Wayland (Brauckmann)—and the Elfenkönigin (Mlle Rose), who has no counterpart in the novel.

The work was never published, but the library of the University of Wroclaw (Breslau) has most of the orchestra score in manuscript—specifically, the overture and Act I (bound up in a single volume), Act II (bound up in another volume), and the "Partitur auf der Bühne" (bound up in a slender third volume). The third act is missing. There is no indication in Acts I and II as to who wrote the libretto, which apparently contained spoken dialogue of which only a small part is included in the score.[19] It is unfortunate that I was not able to come up with a manuscript of a separate libretto, not only for the sake of a complete text but also for more precise stage directions and more detailed descriptions of setting than are to be found in the score. Since I was unable to examine the opera in its entirety, the following discussion is of necessity sketchy. For purposes of convenience I have keyed my remarks to the different musical numbers of the score.

After a formal overture, the curtain rises on a room in Giles Gosling's tavern, the "Wunderbar" (the Black Bear of the novel). The first musical number follows loosely chapters i–ii, with the omission of Goldthred and the clerk of the parish. Michael Lambourne tells the assembled guests that in all his travels he has found no country to match England: " 'Sgeht nirgendsher so flott und bunt / Als hier im lieben Vaterland,/ Im lustigen Engeland." (Scott's Lambourne is more impressed with foreign parts than with his native land.) When he asks about Tony Foster, his one-time companion in mischief, Gosling tells him that Foster has now become a pious man; moreover, he is guarding a lady at Cumnor Schloss. Upon hearing this bit of information, Tressilian wants to know more; and so do Lambourne and the other guests. Gosling accordingly obliges by assuming the role of Scott's Master Goldthred and singing an aria about the mysterious beauty who has been mewed up in the castle. Tressilian is certain that she must be the one for whom he is searching, and when Lambourne determines to go to the castle to catch a glimpse of her, Tressilian says that he will accompany him and share his adventure. Gosling warns them both of the grave danger involved, but to no avail. The number concludes with a reprise of Lambourne's song about merry England.

The scene now changes to Cumnor. No. 2: Emmy sings an aria in which she expresses her fervent desire for Leicester to return: "Noch nicht hier. . . . Robert, komm in meine Arme, press mich in deine Brust!" In the *larghetto,* however, she reminisces about the happy days she spent in Tressilian's company, before she met Leicester. When Leicester came into her life she forgot the whole world.—No. 3 (Elfenchor und Ballet): Emmy falls asleep and dreams what is revealed in the ballet. She awakens much refreshed. (There is nothing comparable to this in the novel.)—No. 4: Emmy sees someone whom she believes to be Leicester, but it is Tressilian (see chapter iv). He tries to persuade her to leave her prison with him and return home to her father. She refuses. He warns her that if she will not follow him willingly, he will use force. She haughtily orders him away. "Des Vaters Willen muss ich erfüllen," he says—and then lays hold of her. "Hülfe! Hülfe!" she cries. "Stille! Stille!" he vehemently urges her: "Es hilft kein Sträuben. . . . Ich rette dich trotz dir."—No. 5: An aria for Varney. He sings that he holds the ladder by which Leicester is ascending to the crown of England. As Leicester moves upward, so too will he; and when Leicester reaches his goal, he will give his trusted right-hand man everything he wants—even Emmy. (The words are suggested by several different monologues for Varney in the novel.)

The scene changes again, this time apparently to Greenwich Castle (the stage directions do not specify). No. 6: Raleigh sings his "Mantelritterlied," in which he tells about the famous overcoat-incident, which Scott relates in chapter xv.—No. 7 (Finale): The number begins with a chorus of people who sing in praise of Queen Elisabeth. Tressilian then makes a formal complaint in the Queen's presence against Varney, whom he believes to be Emmy's seducer. Both Leicester and Varney are taken aback. Tressilian says furthermore that he has actually seen the lady at Cumnor. (In the novel Leicester does not learn about Tressilian's visit at Cumnor until much later, when Varney brings up the matter in order to convince him that Amy has played him false; see chapter xxxvi.) Varney quickly sees the plight Leicester is in, and, as in the novel, he admits to the Queen that Emmy eloped with him against her father's will, but he insists that she is his lawful wife. Leicester is upset at Varney's action but does not contradict him. In an attempt to smoothe over the unpleasant situation that has arisen, the Queen mentions the Fest she will attend the next day at Kenilworth, where she will be Leicester's honored guest. She says emphatically that she will be pleased to see Varney's wife there. Again Leicester and Varney are taken aback. In the final ensemble they do not share with Elisabeth and chorus the general feeling of joyful anticipation. "Vor Kummer mein Herz mir bricht," each sings; "denn Festtags Laune fühle ich nicht." (The finale is based on the events of chapter xvi. Sussex, however, is not among the dramatis personae, and thus Tressilian is more active in the presentation of his suit than is his original.)

At the beginning of Act II we are back at Cumnor. No. 8 (Duet): Emmy is very much upset at Varney's request that she appear at Kenilworth as his wife (see chapter xxii). As the duet develops, he tells her that he loves her. Horrified, she orders him out of her presence. She warns him that he is a lost man if she should decide to reveal his transgression to Leicester. (In the novel Varney's unrequited love for Amy is mentioned as early as chapter vi. No explicit mention is made of it in their encounter of chapter xxii, but it lurks in the background and has bearing on Amy's violent reaction to Varney's plan.)—No. 9: A trio for Emmy, Anna (Scott's Janet Foster), and Wayland. Emmy prays to God to help her in this time of danger; Anna promises to remain true to her "bis in den Tod"; Wayland explains that he will save her and thereby fulfill the request of his master, Tressilian. (The number is suggested by the events of chapter xxiii.)

The rest of the act takes place at Kenilworth. No. 10: Tressilian expresses his sorrow and bitterness in an aria. His wooing of Emmy has been in vain. If death had taken her from him, his memory of her would be beautiful; but she whom he adored has betrayed him. He expresses the desire to retreat from the madding crowd and bury himself in solitude. (The aria's text has no exact parallel in the novel, but it is suggested by Scott's overall characterization of Tressilian.)—No. 11 (Elfenchor): As Emmy sleeps, the elves indicate that they will help out. (Like the "Elfenchor und Ballet" of Act I, this number has no parallel in the novel.)—No. 12: An aria for Lambourne. "Lustig, lustig ist die Welt," he sings.—No. 13: A trio for Emmy, Anna, and Lambourne. Lambourne tries to kiss Emmy, but she will have no part of him: "Fort von mir. Lass mich los! . . . Fort, ungezogener!" Anna is greatly distressed at the plight her mistress is in, but she is powerless to aid her: "Frecher, was erlaubst du dir? Wer hilft uns in dieser Not?" Emmy finally manages to wrest herself from his lascivious clutches and to escape. (The trio is based on Scott's Lambourne's attempted seduction of Amy, whom he finds in Tressilian's room at Kenilworth and whom he believes to be his mistress; see chapter xxxiii. The opera differs from the novel in that Anna is present during the unpleasant encounter; Scott's Janet Foster does not accompany Amy to Kenilworth.)

No. 14 (Finale): The chorus greets Elisabeth as she enters at the head of her entourage. There is a short ballet, and then a trio for Elisabeth, Raleigh, and Leicester. Emotionally disturbed at Leicester's oblique mention of love, Elisabeth excuses herself for a while from the company. In the meantime Emmy, who has escaped her would-be ravisher, finds sanctuary in a grotto. Thither comes Elisabeth also; she fondly meditates on what Leicester has told her, but she ultimately decides, "Ihn lieben darf ich nicht." After a while Emmy reveals herself to Elisabeth, tells her that she is Emmy Robsard, and beseeches her for protection from Varney. When the Queen asks her if she is not Varney's wife, Emmy swears that she is not. The Queen then asks who her husband is, and she replies, "Mylord von Lester." (The finale is based on chapter xxxiv. At this particular point, however, Scott's Amy does not come out and say that Leicester is her husband; instead, she says evasively, "The Earl of Leicester knows it all.") Upon Leicester's re-entrance, Elisabeth points to Emmy and peremptorily demands to know whether she is Varney's wife or not. Leicester is so bewildered upon seeing Emmy at Kenilworth and in the Queen's presence that he does not know what to say. In due course a quintet develops (Elisabeth, Emmy, Raleigh, Leicester, Varney), all singing *sotto voce* sentiments appropriate to the occasion: the Queen notices Leicester's bewilderment; Emmy sings, "Weh, mir!"; Raleigh observes the anger in the Queen's eyes; Leicester sings of broken duty; and Varney expresses his determination to save his master. Varney then tells the Queen for the second time (cf. the finale to Act I) that Emmy is his wife, and he adds that she is mentally deranged ("sie ist von Sinnen"). Emmy is bewildered and dejected when he who should save her remains silent; she begins to wonder whether what is happening is reality or a dream. Unobserved by the others on stage, Varney urges her to be silent: "Schweigt! wenn ihr Lester liebt, es gilt sein Leben./ Euer Widerspruch muss jetzt den Tod ihm geben." The Queen then orders Emmy to be taken away and looked after. The act ends in another large ensemble consisting of the same five principals together with the chorus. Raleigh senses that the truth has not been told.

The "Partitur auf der Bühne" gives evidence that there are five additional musical numbers. No. 18 is a duet for Varney and Foster in which Varney informs Foster that Leicester wants Emmy put to death; but then something miraculous happens, for in the finale (No. 19) soprano voices sing, "Du bist gerettet." The principal review in the *Breslauer Zeitung* (see fn. 17) indicates that Emmy is saved by the elves. Although the ending is happy, the opera in general follows the novel rather closely. The most striking deviation is the introduction of the "Elfenchor und Ballet"—a unique feature of *Das Fest zu Kenilworth* in comparison with other *Kenilworth* operas. The libretto is interesting in that the characters often express their feelings more forthrightly and unabashedly than do their counterparts in the novel. That the work was not published should not be taken as indication that it is inferior to the other *Kenilworth* operas. Many a fine opera that has been performed and enjoyed locally remains in manuscript.

Il Conte di Leicester

Luigi Badia's *Conte di Leicester*, composed to a libretto by Giovanni Battista Canovai, had its première on 20 November 1851 in Florence, at the Pergola. According to Fétis, it was given only one performance. Unfortunately I was able to locate only one musical number,[20] but I did find a copy of the complete libretto (which was published in Florence) in the British Museum. The "personaggi" include Elisabetta (sung at the première by Rosina Penco), Roberto Dudley (sung by Emanuele Sanz), Riccardo Varney (Angelo Baccelli), Edmondo Tressiliano (Achille Rossi), Amy Robsart (Irene Secci Corsi), Foster (Carlo Mariani), Alasco (no name given), and Giles Goslin (Andrea Bigazzi). The opera is in four acts.

The curtain rises on the interior of Giles Goslin's tavern at Cumnor, where a group of comedians, acrobats, and dancers are spending the evening. In the opening chorus they introduce themselves to Goslin and tell him that they are on their way to Kenilworth. They then ask him the name of the cavalier who is sitting by himself, very much wrapt up in his own thoughts. Goslin replies that he does not know, but adds that he pays his bills without quarreling. Realizing that the mysterious stranger is no fit audience for their levity, they ask Goslin whether he would think that the baron of the castello might appreciate what they have to offer. Goslin replies that a beautiful young lady is concealed there who might indeed be grateful for their entertainment. Having overheard the host's remarks, the stranger (Tressiliano) becomes agitated and asks him who the lady is. Goslin replies that he knows not. Tressiliano then asks for the name of the cavalier who loves her. Goslin hesitates to tell, because the man is very powerful, but he finally says, "È Sir Varney." (Scott's Tressilian hears nothing about Varney at the tavern; moreover, Varney is not a knight in the novel until later.) Overjoyed at learning who his rival is, Tressiliano determines to go to the castello. Goslin tells him that access will be easy enough for the entertainers, but not for someone "in sproni, in spada, in guanti," but when Tressiliano gives the entertainers money and convinces them that he is a singer, they readily agree to let him join them. Goslin warns them all that if the cavalier is recognized as such while they are at the castello, he will not be allowed to leave, but the well-meant admonition falls upon deaf ears. (The opening *scena* is based loosely on chapters i–ii, but instead of Lambourne, Goldthred, the parish clerk, and the villagers, we have the entertainers who are to perform at Kenilworth. In the novel they are introduced much later: Amy, having just escaped from Cumnor, and her guide Wayland Smith mingle with them to avoid being noticed by Varney and Lambourne; see chapter xxiv.)

For the second *scena,* which is designed as an aria for Varney, we move to a room in Cumnor-Place. In the opening recitative Varney, with a sardonic smile, muses on the irony of his having been instrumental in bringing Amy and Leicester together, the implication being that he himself had romantic interest in her. He then turns to Foster and demands to know whether Amy's confinement is still a secret. Foster admits that some people know of a lady's presence in the castello and that they suspect she is Varney's mistress. In the first part of his aria Varney sings that Amy must soon be moved from Cumnor; all concerned would be inconvenienced if it should ever be known that she is married to Leicester. He then tells Foster to make sure that no-one ever sees Amy. He even gives him poison to administer to her, should such drastic action ever become necessary.

Foster trembles at the idea, but says he will obey. In the cabaletta Varney points out to him that the path they have taken toward grandeur leaves an abyss behind; it is now too late to turn back. (The *scena* is based loosely on the material of chapter v; however, the poison-motif does not appear in the novel until later.) When Varney and Foster have departed, Amy enters and sings an aria in which she expresses her unhappiness resulting from Dudley's long absence. Next, Foster announces to her that comedians have come to entertain her. Although knowing full well that he is disobeying Varney's command, he has decided to admit them, because he cannot bear to see Amy so unhappy. When the troupe has entered, Amy requests to hear a ballad about love. Tressiliano, disguised as an old minstrel, obliges by singing about a melancholy castle in the midst of the forest, where the sound of the chase is no longer heard. There an old man lives, overwhelmed by sorrow, for the daughter who was his sole joy has left him. At these words Amy becomes very agitated. Tressiliano sings further that the daughter let herself be seduced by a perfidious guest and that the old man weeps alone. Amy now orders Foster to take the chorus away, so that she can speak with the minstrel in private. Foster hesitates, but does as he is told. (In the novel, chapter iv, Tressilian arrives at Cumnor-Place with Michael Lambourne rather than with a troupe of comedians. The ballad, which has no parallel in Scott, is an appropriate operatic touch.)

Amy has seen through Tressiliano's disguise. As their duet begins, he implores her to leave Cumnor at once and return with him to her sorrowing father. When she says that she is unable to do so, he becomes upset. She swears that her love affair has been legitimated, but she is not in a position at the moment to correct his notion that she is Varney's wife. She urges him to go back to her father and comfort him, and she promises that she will return soon and show herself worthy of him. "I understand," he says sarcastically; "when Varney becomes a count and Dudley, King of England." She asks him to explain what he means. He replies that it is obvious to everyone that Dudley is a great favorite of the Queen. Distressed at Tressiliano's words, Amy begins to weep. Again he urges her to return with him to her father. She replies again that she cannot—and sings *aside* of her new sorrow, namely, Dudley's faithlessness. When she persists in refusing, Tressiliano declares that he will reveal everything to the Queen. She implores him to keep silent, but to no avail: he reinstates his determination to inform the Queen of the unwholesome affair. At the end of the duet Amy returns to her room, and Tressiliano departs. (The *scena* is based on the chance encounter of Amy and Tressilian in chapter iv, but with many changes. At this point Scott's Tressilian knows nothing for certain of Varney's connection with Amy. He does not tell her that Leicester is the Queen's favorite—she learns this later, in chapter xx, from Wayland Smith. Moreover, he does not threaten to go to the Queen. His ill-advised insistence upon Amy's immediate departure causes her to cry out for help, and their conversation is terminated when Foster and Lambourne burst in. The operatic duet ends comparatively amicably.)

Act II opens in a small room in one of the towers at Kenilworth. Leicester consults briefly with Alasco, his astronomer, who foresees a crown for him. When Alasco has departed, Leicester sings of the dilemma in which he finds himself: he has a chance to be King, but his conscience does not allow him to abandon Amy. Immediately following the first part of the aria, Varney enters and tells him that he must hasten to meet the Queen, whose approach to the castello is already being heralded by the blast of cannons. In the cabaletta Leicester declares that even though his heart is sore oppressed, he will abandon himself to joy and follow whatever destiny has foreordained. Varney observes *aside* that if his master is destined for the throne, he (Varney) will rise with him. (Leicester's brief conversation with Alasco is suggested by the much longer conversation of the novel, chapter xviii.) The scene now changes to a magnificent garden next to the castello. Foster (rather than Wayland Smith) has conducted Amy hither; he realizes only too well the consequences he may have to suffer for having betrayed his duty. Amy pays him and urges him to flee and save himself. When he has gone, Amy is a bit baffled as to how she should proceed. Noticing the approach of Elisabetta and her entourage, she conceals herself behind a fountain. (The librettist has greatly condensed his source-material. Amy's escape from Cumnor, her peril-fraught journey to Kenilworth, and her misadventures at Kenilworth before encountering the Queen are all omitted.) The Queen enters and is warmly greeted by the chorus. In an aria she thanks everyone, particularly Leicester, for the magnificent reception she has been given. She is noticeably moved when he kneels and kisses her hand.

Suddenly Amy reveals herself and begs the Queen for protection. (The situation differs from that of the novel, chapter xxxiv, in that the two ladies have no initial conversation in the privacy of a grotto.) Varney is surprised at seeing Amy, and Leicester is both surprised and terrified. Amy points to Varney and tells the Queen that she was his prisoner. The Queen then asks Tressiliano if this is the young lady about whom he has informed her; he says that she is. When the Queen speaks of her as if she were Varney's wife, Amy is horrified. "Regina, ah, no!" she cries; "mentirono." Elisabetta then asks Leicester whether he knows the lady, but he is so bewildered he cannot answer. Sensing the danger he is in, Amy declares that he is innocent. A large ensemble develops: Elisabetta singing *aside* of the necessity of her restraining her feelings so that others will not observe how moved she is, Amy expressing *aside* her well-founded suspicion that the Queen is her rival, Leicester fearing *aside* the Queen's wrath, Varney urging Leicester to dissimulate or be forever lost, Tressiliano hoping *aside* that the Queen's wrath will fall on Varney, and the chorus expressing *aside* a sentiment appropriate to the situation. Varney then tells the Queen that Amy is his wife and furthermore that she is mentally deranged. When the Queen asks Tressiliano whether he can show that Varney and Amy are not married, he replies that he cannot. The Queen then takes Amy by the hand and leads her to Varney. "Love her," she tells him, "for she is unfortunate." The *scena* concludes in another ensemble for the same five principals and the chorus. (This, the finale to Act II, is a deft amalgamation of material drawn from chapters xvi and xxxiv. In the former Elizabeth confronts Leicester, at Greenwich Castle, with Tressilian's complaint against Varney, and Varney declares then that he is Amy's husband. In chapter xxxiv the confrontation takes place at Kenilworth, with Amy present—but not Tressilian, who has promised her not to interfere with her actions for twenty-four hours. The Queen is already under the impression that Amy is Varney's wife, and now Varney tells her, in addition, after Amy has been led away, that Amy is demented.)

The entire third act takes place in the chase adjacent to Kenilworth. The opening number is a chorus of hunters, after which Elisabetta and Leicester enter, both dressed in hunting costume. The Queen is tired. She asks Leicester why he is so melancholy and he tells her it is because he stands no longer in her favor. She says that he is mistaken—that on the contrary he is very much in her favor. As their duet progresses, she utters words in an unguarded moment that indicate unmistakably her love for him. She is embarrassed at having said so much and asks him to leave her. He swears that he will be discreet. At the end of the duet *she* leaves the stage, after he has affectionately kissed her hand. (This *scena* is suggested by the tête-à-tête of Elizabeth and Leicester which Scott mentions, but does not relate in detail, at the beginning of chapter xxxiv. It takes place *before* Amy's momentous revelation of herself to the Queen and her plea for protection.)

Varney enters. Leicester forthwith gives him an account of what has just happened. In reply Varney warns him that Amy may cause his downfall—that she is impressed with his name and rank, but that she still loves Tressiliano. As in the novel, chapter xxxvi, Leicester is horrified. Varney then informs him of Foster's part in Amy's escape from Cumnor-Place. "Servo infido!" Leicester exclaims; "sia svenato!" Varney replies that he has anticipated his wishes: Foster is already dead. (The murder of Foster is suggested by Varney's murder of Lambourne in the novel, chapter xl. Scott's Foster shuts himself up in a secret room at Cumnor-Place, when the murder of Amy is discovered, but forgets the key, and thus dies the slow death of starvation.) Varney then shows him one of Amy's gloves, which he says he found in Tressiliano's room. (The novel is more complicated: in addition to the glove there is a packet of jewels which Tressilian attempted to return to Amy but which Varney intercepted.) Leicester is so utterly convinced of Amy's perfidy that he gives Varney permission to do with her as he pleases. As in the novel, chapter xxxvii, he gives him a ring which all will honor as proof that he is acting by his master's authority. Immediately after Varney has departed,

however, Leicester begins to have misgivings; he wonders where jealousy
has led him. Seeing the Queen and the hunters returning, he moves aside
in order to conceal his agitation. There is a brief reprise of the hunting
chorus that opened the act, and the curtain falls.

The setting of the last act is a spacious, brilliantly illuminated room of
the castello. The ladies and gentlemen in the chorus sing of the joy of the
occasion and then exeunt into the adjoining room where a ball is to take
place. (The ball is suggested by the masque that Scott describes in chapter
xxxvii.) In the next *scena* Tressiliano, deep in thought, is accosted by
Leicester, who looks on him as a rival and wants to have his blood.
Leicester shows him the glove belonging to Amy that was found in his
room in the castello. Tressiliano says that he does not understand. "Ospite
non vi sono," he adds; "altrove io scelsi / La mia dimora." In the *romanza*
"Un'infelice veglio" (see fn. 20) he tells Leicester of having found Amy at
Cumnor-Place and of having tried in vain to persuade her to leave and go
home with him to her father. Not satisfied with what he observed there, he
came to Kenilworth to bring the matter to the Queen's attention. Much to
his chagrin he found out that Amy, who had also come to Kenilworth, was
Varney's wife. At this point Leicester announces to Tressiliano that Amy
is *his* wife and countess. Tressiliano is overjoyed. (The *scena* is based on the
confrontation of Scott's Tressilian and Leicester in chapters xxxviii –
xxxix, but there is no duel, and there is no Dickie Sludge to bring in Amy's
letter to Leicester which had miscarried and which shows beyond any
doubt her innocence.)

The Queen now enters, accompanied by a group of ladies and gentlemen whom she dismisses when she sees that Leicester has something
important to say to her. He then tells her, in the presence of Tressiliano,
that Amy is his wife. (In the novel, chapter xl, Burleigh, Shrewsbury, and
Walsingham are also present.) The Queen is furious, and Leicester admits
that he deserves punishment. In the excitement of the occasion, the
Queen speaks so openly of Leicester's having betrayed her that Tressiliano now begins fully to realize Leicester's ambitions and Amy's very
uncertain position. When the ladies and gentlemen re-enter, the Queen
announces to them that Amy Robsart is Leicester's wife. They are duly
surprised. She then requests to have Amy attend her. Leicester says that
she is far away, but the Queen repeats her request in a manner that allows
for no delay or disobedience. Leicester has horrible forebodings in his
heart, but no-one else, not even Tressiliano, suspects that anything is
amiss, and the dancing and gaiety resume. In a few moments Varney
enters. Leicester asks him, "What did you do with Amy?" "I did what you
ordered me to do," he whispers. Leicester suddenly and impulsively
draws a dagger and kills him. "Die, infamous one!" he cries. The Queen
and the whole court are astonished. "What horror!" they exclaim, as the
curtain falls.—The ending is obviously quite different from that of the
novel; it is unique in comparison with the other *Kenilworth* operas. (The

idea of having a murder take place during a ball may have come from Scribe's libretto to Auber's *Gustave III; ou, Le Bal Masqué,* which is the immediate source of Verdi's *Ballo in Maschera* (1859).)

Amy Robsart

Isidore de Lara's *Amy Robsart* was first performed on 20 July 1893 at Covent Garden. The original English text is the work of Sir Augustus Harris, famed manager of the Garden during the 1890's, but for the première a French version by Paul Milliet was used.[21] Emma Calvé sang the title role, and the French tenor Albert Alvarez, Leicester (usually spelled "Lester" in the vocal score; "Leister" in the libretto). Others in the cast included Mlle Armand (Elisabeth), Jean Lassalle (Varney), Charles Bonnard (Tressilian), and Armand Castelmary (Lambourne); the performance was conducted by Enrico Bevignani. De Lara's music was given an unfavorable (and needlessly unkind) review the next day in *The Times,* and the opera was not performed again at Covent Garden. "During the rehearsals . . . ," wrote De Lara thirty-five years later, "I noticed what little interest the British public took in the production of serious operas by native composers, and I came to the conclusion that if an Englishman wanted to follow the career of an operatic composer (and I was determined to do so), he had to seek for fresh fields abroad, and leave the country."[22] The opera did indeed prove more successful on the continent. It was produced in Monte Carlo in 1894, with Marcella Sembrich as Amy, Pierre Emile Engel as Leicester, and Melchissedec as Varney; in 1895 with Lucienne Bréval (Amy), Van Dyck (Leicester), and Kashmann (Varney); in 1896 with Mme Caron as Amy and Francesco Tamagno, the first Otello, as Leicester; in 1897 with Mme Darcléc (Amy) and Tamagno (Leicester). De Lara was justifiably proud that *Amy Robsart* was performed by some of the finest singers in Europe. Other productions in French were staged in the 1890's in Boulogne and Lyons; in Italian in St. Petersburg (29 July 1894) and Florence (26 March 1896). The first night in Florence "was a most brilliant affair, the Prince of Naples, now King of Italy, being present, and the opera was a great success."[23] It was given in the original English by the Carl Rosa Opera Company at the Croydon Grand Theatre (14 May 1920) and elsewhere in England.[24]

After a brief introduction, which begins as a four-voice fugue, the curtain rises on the park adjacent to Cumnor Hall. ("Cumnor Hall," rather than "Cumnor-Place," is the name of the ballad that Scott includes in his Introduction of 1831.) *"Au fond, à droite, on aperçoit le château á travers les arbres. A gauche, un mur avec une petite porte."* Keeping his promise, Lambourne has led Tressilian to the château to see "la belle inconnue" who is confined there. When he reminds Tressilian that he too has a promise to keep, Tressilian tells him to have no fear—that he is a friend of Sir Hugh Robsart, the lady's father, who in fact has sent him to see her. (In the novel Tressilian does not disclose this information to Lambourne.)

Lambourne is not satisfied. He makes clear to him that in bringing him to
see the lady he has acted against the express orders of his master, Richard
Varney, who is master of the château. He urges him not to cause any
disturbance. Then, in a lighter vein, he sings a song about the pleasures of
wine and drunkenness, after which he departs from the stage. (In the
novel Lambourne is not yet in Varney's service. Moreover, Anthony
Foster, rather than Varney, is in charge of Cumnor-Place.) Tressilian is
now left to himself in the courtyard to mull over how he should proceed.
Presently Amy comes out from the château. As in the novel, she momentarily mistakes Tressilian for Leicester, and when she realizes who he is,
she expresses great surprise at seeing him "en ces lieux." He says he has
come to free her. She replies that she *is* free. He then tells her that her
father is dangerously ill and that he wants to see her before he dies. She
replies that she is unable to leave Cumnor at the moment. When he
becomes overly persistent in demanding that she come with him, she cries
out, "A moi! A moi!" and flees. Hearing Amy's cry for help, Varney bursts
in, to the accompaniment of a motiv hereafter associated with him:

Example 11-7

Tressilian believes him to be Amy's cowardly seducer. As in the novel,
they draw their swords and fight, and at the third pass Varney falls. As
Tressilian raises his sword with the intention of dispatching him, Lambourne suddenly appears and prevents him from doing so. Both Lambourne and Varney demand that Tressilian leave the premises at once. As
he is going, Tressilian tells Varney that when they meet the next time, he
will not escape the punishment he deserves. Varney expresses his
gratitude to Lambourne for having saved his life and gives him money to
spend on drink and entertainment. Lambourne exits.

Thus far the action has followed loosely the events of chapters iii and iv.
The content of the aria that Varney now sings is suggested by the conversation between Scott's Varney and Foster, chapter v, and by Varney's
ensuing soliloquy. He sings of his frustration in serving a man who is a
slave to amorous passions, and he looks on Amy as an obstacle in the way
of his making Lester King. After the aria, hearing Lester approach on
horseback, he hastily leaves the stage. The next *scène,* based loosely on
chapter vii, belongs to Lester and Amy. As they rush into each other's
arms, we hear a motiv in the orchestra that recurs elsewhere in the score
and always suggests the intensity of their love:

Example 11-8

"Lester!" "Amy, ma bien aimée!" "Joie immense! Joie immense! De revoir ce qu'on aime!" "O ma femme!" "Ce qu'on aime!" "O mon adorée!" And so forth. During the course of the long love-duet we hear in the background a group of peasants singing as they return home for the night. (There is no parallel for this in the novel; it is a deft musical touch that adds variety, interest, and atmosphere to the duet. The reviewer in *The Times,* however, considered it not only "pointless" but too "strongly suggestive of Gounod.") Lester remarks that the peasants are fortunate in that they can go home each night to their cottages and to those whom they love: such tender repose is not permitted *him.* In short, he must leave Amy again. He tells her that the hour is soon approaching when all the world will know her as his wife, but meanwhile she must remain concealed if she does not want to hurl him to the bottom of a frightful abyss. He then sings of her irresistible charms, and she responds, singing a melody that recurs elsewhere:

Example 11-9

Like the love-duet in *Tristan und Isolde,* this one too goes on and on. There is no Brangäne or Janet Foster "einsam wachend in der Nacht," but later in the duet we hear again from the wings the chorus of peasants, who now sing an aubade heralding the approach of day. Lester tells Amy that he must leave. They fondly bid each other adieu, and Lester exits. Left alone for a few moments, Amy muses on the power of love. Just when she is about to re-enter the château, Varney comes onstage and detains her, as we hear again his leitmotiv in the orchestra (see Example 11-7). After reminding her that his main duty is to guard the château, he says that before Lester's arrival he noticed her engaged in conversation with another man. He asks her whether she has informed Lester of this encounter. Amy is piqued at his asking her about something that she considers none of his business. Varney warns her that Lester might prove jealous, especially if he should find out that the man was none other than Tressilian. (The jealousy-motif comes from the conversation between Varney and Amy in chapter vi, which takes place *before* the arrival of Leicester.) Varney then tells her of the coming festivities at Kenilworth, of the close relationship between Lester and the Queen, and of the rampant rumor that Lester may become King—information that Scott's Amy learns from Wayland Smith at a later point in the story. Visibly shaken, Amy remarks *aside* that doubt and suspicion are beginning to oppress her, while Varney, at the same time, invokes the subtle poison to work which will bring about suspicion in her soul and jealousy in her veins. When he tells her that the only reason for her confinement and anonymity is to facilitate the eventual breaking of her fragile marriage so that Lester will be free to marry the Queen, Amy falls down as if thunderstruck. Varney observes her for a moment and then slowly leaves the stage. At this point Tressilian, who unlike his counterpart in Scott is still lurking "en ces lieux," re-enters and beholds Amy in her plight. She soon revives. "Je t'ai promis de fuir cette demeure," she says. "Je tiens ma promesse. Je pars! Suis-moi!" "Vers ton père, à Lincote?" he asks. "Non!" "Où donc?" "A Kenilworth!"—and the curtain descends rapidly. (In the novel Amy's escape is arranged by Janet Foster and Wayland Smith, and her guide is Wayland, rather than Tressilian. The main reason for her secret depar-ture is her well-founded mortal fear of Varney, whereas the operatic Amy is motivated solely by jealous suspicion.)

The second act begins with an orchestral introduction laden with drum-rolls and trumpet-fanfares, and when the curtain rises we behold the gardens at Kenilworth. Varney approaches Lester, congratulates him on having won the heart of the Queen, and tells him he sees a brilliant future for him. Lester, however, is still in love with Amy. When Varney urges him to forget her, he replies, "Jamais!" Varney then points out to him that if his marriage with Amy should ever be known, he would immediate be surpassed in the Queen's favor by his arch-rival, the Comte de Sussex; moreover, since the Queen obviously loves him, she would be angry at the disclosure, and an angry daughter of Henri Huit would prove a dangerous menace to both himself and Amy. "Amy!" Lester exclaims. "Oh! te livrer, sort affreux! Oh! l'ambition!" He then rushes out, leaving Varney alone on stage for an aria on the subject of ambition. (The conversation between Lester and Varney draws from two different, widely separated conversations in the novel; see chapters xviii and xxxv. The assigning of an aria to Varney was no doubt suggested by his various monologues in the novel.)

The middle section of the act is full of pomp and pageantry. Lester's followers encounter Sussex's, and the two groups sing compliments to each other. There is also a chorus of ladies. When the Queen enters, all present greet her enthusiastically and sing in praise of her. Next comes an elaborate ballet involving groups of Druids, Bretons, Saxons, and Normans (as in the masque of chapter xxxvii) who bring presents to the Dame du Lac and later a pageant in which the Dame du Lac, in the company of an entourage of nymphs, renders homage to the Queen (as in chapter xxx).

The final *scène* is an amalgamation, as in Seidelmann's *Fest zu Kenilworth*, of Leicester's confrontations with the Queen at Greenwich (chapter xvi) and at Kenilworth (chapter xxxiv). Amy suddenly appears, accompanied by Tressilian, and cries out, "Justice! Justice!" Everyone is surprised. Lester sings *aside,* "Amy—C'est fait de moi!" When Amy has advanced and knelt at the Queen's feet, the Queen tells her to speak without fear. Accordingly Amy introduces herself as the daughter of Sir Hugh Robsart, a name which both the Queen and the chorus instantly recognize. Looking hard at Lester, Amy tells the Queen that a cowardly seducer persuaded her to abandon her home and father, and now, having abandoned her, he is about to make a new marriage. (In the novel Amy complains against Varney, not Leicester.) The Queen promises to avenge Amy for the grave injustice she has suffered, even if the wicked one should prove to be an earl or duke, even Sussex or Lester. "C'est à notre bourreau qu'appartiendra sa vie!" she threatens. Not having realized that the Queen would want to take such extreme measures, Amy is horrified, and when the Queen asks for the man's name she hesitates to reveal it. A large ensemble now begins, which eventually includes Amy, Elisabeth, Lester, Tressilian, Varney, and the chorus. The gist of it is that Amy refuses to tell the name of her seducer and false husband because she still loves him, and the chorus admires her for her decision. As the ensemble ends, Amy sings out above all the other voices, "Je l'aime! Je l'aime! Je l'aime!" At this point the Queen has had enough dillydallying around and peremptorily demands that Amy tell who the man is. Inspired by Amy's nobility of character Lester decides to tell the truth, but as he begins his confession Varney interrupts him and declares that Amy is *his* wife—and furthermore that she she has lost her mind. The Queen turns to Amy and asks her if what Varney has said is true. Still fearing for Lester's life, Amy has no choice but to say, "C'est vrai!" The Queen then orders Varney to take his wife away, and in a few moments festive music resumes. As the act closes, the chorus sings, "Dieu sauve Elisabeth!/Daigne la protéger contre tout danger!/Hip! Hip! Hip! Hurrah!"

The third act is divided into two tableaux. When the curtain first rises, a room in the château de Kenilworth is revealed. Lester enters, obviously preoccupied and anxious. *"Il traverse la scène; puis, entendant les échoes lointains de la fête, et les cris de joie du peuple, il s'arrête."* When he hears the people shout "Vive Lester!" he meditates in a recitative and aria on the irony of the situation. All the people must think that he is a royal favorite with unlimited power. How little they know of his precarious position! In seeing his beautiful, beloved Amy before the Queen he experienced for the first time in his life, fear. She made him aware of the baseness of his designs and ambitions. In the final part of the aria he calls on the detestable phantoms of supreme power and ambition to fly away from him. (Lester's aria is not based on any particular passage of the novel, but the sentiment expressed is completely in keeping with his vacillating character, as portrayed by Scott.) Amy now enters, and we have another long love-duet, suggested in part by the conversation of Scott's Leicester with Amy in *her* room at Kenilworth, in the presence of Varney, shortly after the unpleasant confrontation with the Queen. At first she indignantly requests that he have her escorted back to the château of her father, but when he begs for pity, she gives in, pardons him, and tells him she still loves him. Deeply moved, he asks her to go with him to the Queen, but she does not like the idea, because she is still afraid that the Queen will order his execution. (In the novel we have just the opposite: Amy wants to reveal the truth, and Leicester is hesitant about doing so.) In a long monologue she sings that when she fell in love with him, she did not know that he was destined for greater things (i.e. to become the husband of the Queen). She humbly asks his permission to return now to her own family, for she does not want to stand in the way of his career. Again deeply moved, he falls at her feet. "Ange de la miséricorde,/O douce image de devoir!" he sings, as we hear in the orchestra a lovely, saccharine melody played by a solo violin:

Example 11-10

The melody recurs later in the vocal lines, as Amy and Lester sing of the repose they will some day enjoy together at Cumnor, far from the cares of the world. She agrees to go to Cumnor and wait for him, and when she exits, she apparently sets out for Cumnor immediately. Left alone for a few moments, Lester declares that he will undo the wrongs he has done Amy and will live forever united with her in the serenity of infinite love.

When Varney enters, Lester tells him to make preparations for his departure, because he has decided to leave Kenilworth for the calm domain of Cumnor. Varney is displeased with the decision. He says that he gladly served the courtier who aspired to the throne, but that he has no intention of becoming valet to his giddy caprice. Then, as in the conversation between Scott's Varney and Leicester of chapter xxxvi, he tells him of Amy's recent tête-à-tête at Cumnor with Tressilian. Pointing to the window, he says that Tressilian is even now outside in hiding (a detail not in the novel). He says furthermore that he has observed Tressilian wandering around in the immense palace, impudently seeking her whom he adores. "Alors," Lester exclaims, "ce n'est pas la comtesse qu'il va rencontrer, c'est la mort!" Varney withdraws quickly. (We must assume that he sets out immediately for Cumnor, to devise the "accident" by which Amy is killed, but interestingly he has no *carte blanche* from Lester.) No sooner is he gone than Tressilian appears. Lester impetuously challenges him to a duel, gets the better of him, and, placing the point of his sword at Tressilian's throat, demands to know whom he seeks "en ce lieu." (In the novel, chapter xxxix, Leicester intends to kill the fallen Tressilian, but then Dickie Sludge arrives on the scene with Amy's all-important letter, which proves beyond any doubt her and Tressilian's innocence and Varney's criminal treachery.) Tressilian tells Lester on his honor that it was even he whom he was seeking, in order to reveal to him a horrible stratagem that threatens Amy's life. When Lester asks who the criminal is, Tressilian replies, still thinking that Amy is Varney's wife, "Son propre époux Varney." Lester than tells him, "L'époux d'Amy Robsart—c'est moi!" and together they rush out to set forth for Cumnor. (Unlike all the other *Kenilworth* operas, *Amy Robsart* has no scene in which Leicester finally reveals his marriage to the Queen.)

There is a short musical interlude between the first and second tableaux. When the curtain rises again, we are back at Cumnor. To the accompaniment of restless staccato music in the orchestra, we see Amy entering the main tower of the château. When Varney arrives, Lambourne, slightly intoxicated points to the tower and exclaims, "Amy Robsart attend son maître!" Varney tells him that if Lester were King he would raise all his loyal followers to the peerage, but one obstacle stands in his way, namely, Amy. He then explains to Lambourne that there is a "trappe" at the threshold of the door to the tower; it is held in place by a single bolt, which if drawn would release the "trappe," and anyone who tried to cross the threshold would fall into an abyss. Varney suggests to him that he draw the bolt—"hasard" will do the rest. Lambourne is more willing to assist in the project than is Scott's Tony Foster: "Puisque c'est le hasard/Qui lui casse le cou,/Je vais l'aider." As soon as he has departed, Lester arrives in the wings. Amy sees him from her room in the tower: "C'est toi, c'est toi! oh! mon bien aimé!/Comme il est doux, le bonheur du retour!" Lester, still *without,* calls "Amy! Amy!" and Varney exclaims

"Triomphe! Ambition!" as we hear in the orchestra a motiv from the love-duet of Act I (see Example 11-9), but now in ominous-sounding variation:

Example 11-11

Lester rushes on stage, together with Tressilian. "Oui, je viens, ma bien aimée!" he exclaims. Amy, now at the threshold, sings one word, "Lester!"—and suddenly all music stops. In spoken voice Varney shouts, "Lambourne par l'enfer!" and Lambourne, reappearing, exclaims, "C'est fait!" The "trappe" opens, and at the first step Amy takes she disappears into the abyss, to the accompaniment of a loud, rapidly descending chromatic scale in the orchestra—Lester crying, "Amy!" (the first syllable on a high, prolonged B flat). Her death is instantaneous, and in the somber closing measures Lester, completely distraught, sings, "Ciel!... Morte!..."—and then, turning to Tressilian: "Prenez donc mon épée et percez-moi le cœur!" The curtain falls. (The ending obviously differs from that of the novel, where Leicester is not present to witness Amy's "accident." Neither do Tressilian, Wayland Smith, and Sir Walter Raleigh, who arrive at Cumnor-Place just moments too late to save her. At this point Scott's Lambourne is already dead, but in the opera he assumes briefly the role of Tony Foster. For all we know, the operatic Varney and Lambourne live happily ever after.)

De Lara's music is often compared with Massenet's. For the purpose of this study, however, it seems more fitting to recall that in his youth De Lara studied composition at the Milan Conservatory under Alberto Mazzucato, who almost a half century earlier had begun a long, successful career in music by composing a Walter Scott opera (see Chapter 7).

Kenilworth

Bruno Oscar Klein's *Kenilworth*, with a libretto by one Wilhelm Müller (whom I know nothing about), was first performed on 13 February 1895 in Hamburg.[25] The role of Amy Robsart was sung by Hungarian-born Katharina Klafsky, one of the most renowned sopranos in Europe (especially Germany) from about 1880 until her untimely death in 1896. In the cast of characters Amy is described as the daughter of the *Scottish* knight, Sir Hugh Robsart von Lidcotehall; Tressilian, as a *Scottish* nobleman. Indeed, the most striking feature of this opera in comparison with the others I have discussed is the Scottish touch that Müller and Klein have grafted on to Scott's thoroughly English story. The other principals are Queen Elisabeth (sung at the première by Frl. Saak), Janet Foster (sung by Frl. Kornfeld), Lorenz Goldzwirn (Scott's Goldthred; sung by a mezzo-soprano, Frl. Felden), Lord Robert Dudley, Earl of Leicester (sung by Hr. Birrenkoven), Richard Varney (Hr. Hoffmann), Giles Gosling (Hr. Lorent), Michael Lambourne (Hr. Dörwald), Antony Foster (Hr. Waldmann), and the Earl of Sussex (Hr. Hes). The opera was well received at its première, and it was given a quite favorable review the next day in the *Hamburgischer Correspondent*.[26] *Kenilworth* was Klein's first and only opera.[27] To my knowledge, it was not produced anywhere except in Hamburg.

After an orchestral introduction made up in part of themes and motivs that appear here and there during the course of the opera, the curtain opens for the *Vorspiel,* which takes place in a large room in Giles Gosling's tavern "Zur Eule" (rather than the Black Bear; the name perhaps derives from Goldthred's song about the owl at the beginning of chapter ii). A stage direction indicates that many people are in the room in different groups. Some are drinking, some singing, and others playing cards or conversing with the host. Tressilian sits alone at a small table by the chimney and stares pensively into the fire. The opening drinking song owes nothing to Goldthred's song about the owl; it is a song about the tavern itself:

Example 11-12

This is followed by a long monologue for Tressilian, who thinks of Amy and bemoans what she has done; if he should find that she is confined somewhere against her wishes, he will break down the doors of her prison and bring her home to her father. (There is nothing quite comparable to this in Scott's opening scene at the Black Bear; instead, we learn about

Tressilian through the host's surmisings and through the gradual unfold-
ing of the story: see especially Tressilian's short soliloquy at Cumnor-
Place, chapter iv ("These are the associates, Amy," etc.) and his conversation with the host after his return to the tavern, chapter viii.) When
Goldzwirn asks Gosling who the young man is and why he is so melancholy, Gosling replies that he does not know, but that he suspects a lady is
involved. He expresses concern lest Goldzwirn and the others stare at the
guest in rude fashion.

   At this point we hear the voice of Lambourne *without:* "Hallo he, hallo
he! Herrscht denn in Cumnor die Pest?" He violently pushes the door
open and stalks in, and after a few unpleasant exchanges with Gosling and
Goldzwirn, who do not like his lack of manners, he begins his "Landsknechtslied." The introductory measures, which are repeated between
stanzas, give an idea of the rough, masculine character of the piece:

Example 11-13

The text extolls the life of a soldier ("Es lebe der Krieg,/Es lebe die Minne
nach blutigem Sieg") and is more reminiscent of Boieldieu's "Ah! quel
plaisir d'être Soldat" (see Chapter 4) than of anything in the first two
chapters of the novel. At the song's conclusion Gosling finally recognizes
the rowdy newcomer as his long-absent nephew, Michael Lambourne,
and heartily welcomes him home. Tressilian becomes attentive to the
conversation around him when he hears one of the drinkers (*not*
Goldzwirn) tell Lambourne about a beautiful lady confined in the Schloss.
When Lambourne expresses the desire to see her, Gosling tells him that
Tony Foster, the Haushofmeister at Cumnor-Place, guards her like a
dragon from all the world. Nothing daunted, Lambourne replies that
Foster used to be his boon companion and that he is determined to visit
him and see the lady. Tressilian sings *aside* how wonderful it would be if
the lady should prove to be the "Entflohne" whom he seeks, while at the

same time Goldzwirn expresses *aside* the thought that if Lambourne goes to the castle he will see Janet and try to steal her favors. (Goldzwirn is in love with Janet; thus he owes part of his personality to Scott's Wayland Smith, who does not appear in the opera.) Goldzwirn too warns Lambourne that danger may come from the visit, inasmuch as Foster is no person to meddle with. Gosling adds, to the accompaniment of a chorale motiv, that Foster is now a religious man, "und wer auf Cumnor die Andacht stört, den jagt er fort mit Hunden!" "Pah!—Weibergeschwätz, Weibergeschwätz!" Lambourne exclaims and then repeats his determination to go to the castle. In hopes of keeping him from going, Goldzwirn bets him ten ducats that he will not see Foster; he knows that Lambourne, unlike his counterpart in Scott, does not have enough money to make the bet. But unexpectedly Tressilian speaks up and says that he himself wants to go to Cumnor in connection with his pursuit of collecting old legends in England; he will take up the bet for Lambourne if Lambourne will allow him to accompany him. (The terms of the wager differ somewhat from the parallel material in the novel, chapter ii.) Lambourne readily and enthusiastically agrees to Tressilian's proposal. In the ensuing ensemble Goldzwirn expresses concern at the certainty that Lambourne will see Janet, Lambourne vows that he will win the bet, Tressilian expresses his belief that he will see her whom he seeks, Gosling remarks that no sooner has he seen his nephew than the devil leads him off to certain trouble, and the Landleute express concern about the dangerous exploit in which the men are about to engage themselves. Lambourne, Goldzwirn, and Tressilian leave the tavern. As the others are preparing to go, they hear the Abendglocken sound. They listen for a moment and then begin an *Abendlied:*

Das Glocklein der Kapelle
    verkündet süsse Ruh',
Da eilt der Landmann schnelle
    der trauten Hütte zu.

They depart while still singing, and we hear the last strains far in the distance:

Nun geht der Tag zu Ende,
    schon ist der Mond erwacht,
Wir reichen uns die Hände
    und sagen: "Gute Nacht!"

The *Abendlied* is an effective way of closing the *Vorspiel;* there is nothing comparable to it in the novel.[28] A final stage direction indicates that Gosling wakes up a sleeping apprentice with a box on the ear. The boy does his chores, extinguishes the lights, and goes out. Gosling, with a lantern in his hand, looks over the room once more before retiring for the night.

The first act begins with a short orchestral introduction. When the curtain rises, we see a Gothic entrance-hall at Cumnor-Place, with Janet sitting at a table toward the front of the stage. Suddenly Goldzwirn, breathing hard, enters through a window. When he is certain that no one besides Janet is around, he goes up to her and kisses her. In a brief conversation he warns her of the approach of Lambourne and Tressilian. They are interrupted by the sound of a harp from behind the scene and by the voice of Amy singing a *Romanze:*

Example 11-14

The song obviously mirrors Amy's own predicament; strains of it recur later. Hearing someone approaching, Janet anxiously tells Goldzwirn that he must leave at once; he does so, but not before kissing her once more. The beginning of the act has no parallel in the novel, but what follows derives from chapters iii, iv, and vi with a number of interesting changes. As soon as Goldzwirn has gone, Foster leads in Lambourne and Tressilian, who are both dressed as Puritans. Janet withdraws to a corner of the room, from which she can eavesdrop unobserved. Foster tells the two imposters that normally he does not open the gate of the castle to anyone, but he is glad to make an exception for fellow Puritans. As he is singing we hear in the orchestra the chorale motiv that we heard in the *Vorspiel* when Gosling was telling Lambourne of Foster's newly assumed piety. Suddenly Lambourne doffs his drab-colored Puritan mantel, and we hear in the orchestra the opening measures of his "Landsknechtslied" (see Example 11-13). He and Foster converse in a duologue much condensed from the parallel material in chapter iii. Foster is interested in obtaining his services, and they go off together to drink a glass of wine, leaving Tressilian alone on stage. (The ruse of disguise is not used in the novel. Scott's Lambourne simply and deceitfully announces at the door that he wants to see Foster "on pressing business of state." Scott uses the term *precisian* in *Kenilworth* rather than *Puritan*. It may be that Klein's librettist was influenced in his emphasis on Foster's Puritanism by other Waverley novels, such as *Old Mortality.*[29])

Tressilian is marveling at the depressing appearance of the room when Amy enters and, as in the novel, mistakes him for Leicester. When she realizes who he is, she cries "Allmächtiger Gott!" Deathly pale she staggers back and covers her face with both hands. As in the novel, Tressilian tells her that her father is ill and wants to see her. She says that she cannot leave the castle until she is allowed to do so. He pleads with her to go with him, but she insists that her duty forbids it. When he becomes overly persistent, even to the point of grasping her hand, she cries out for help. Varney immediately bursts into the room, and he and Tressilian are soon engaged in mortal combat. Tressilian has just gotten the better of him when they are interrupted by Lambourne, Foster, and Janet. (In the novel Amy's cry brings in Lambourne and Foster rather than Varney, whom Tressilian encounters a bit later, as he is leaving the grounds. The alteration avoids a change of scenery and brings Varney conveniently on stage for what follows in the act; cf. *Festen paa Kenilworth*.) Lambourne and Foster quickly break up the melee, and Lambourne asks to be pardoned for having brought with him so rowdy a companion. Tressilian promises Varney that the next time they meet he shall not escape his sword. As soon as Lambourne and Tressilian have left the room, Varney quietly tells Foster to go after his friend and instruct him to keep an eye on Tressilian. He then turns to Amy and asks her whether she spoke with Tressilian. She considers the matter none of his business and says so. "Hochmüthig Weib, das sollst du büssen!" he remarks *aside,* and we hear in the orchestra two measures of a leitmotiv associated with him:

Example 11-15

In the novel, chapter vi, Varney cleverly advises Amy not to tell Leicester of Tressilian's visit lest he think ill of it. His intention is to put himself in the position of being able to utilize some day her silence to his own advantage. This subtlety is omitted from the opera. Instead, he tells her that the Queen is about to honor Leicester at Kenilworth and that people are saying that she desires to marry him and make him King. (As in De Lara's *Amy Robsart;* in the novel this rumor is told Amy later, in chapter xx, by Wayland Smith.) Regarding herself he tells her that many people believe that she has chosen him (Varney) for a lover and that in the seclusion of Cumnor she has completely dedicated herself to Love. At this remark Amy is beside herself with anger and indignation, and she orders him out of her presence. (The incident is suggested by Amy's emotional reaction in chapter xxii when Varney tells her that Leicester desires her to appear at Kenilworth as Mrs. Varney.) Because of Varney's insult, Amy decides that she must leave Cumnor at once and go to her husband. Janet tells her that next to the balcony there is a ladder by which Goldzwirn visits her and that both she and Amy can easily escape in this way. First, Amy sings a stormy, intensely dramatic monologue ("Zu dir! Gemahl!"), which ends on a high B, and then, with Janet's help, she swings herself over the balustrade. The curtain falls. (Amy's motivation to leave Cumnor is not so well founded as in the novel, where Varney tries to induce her to take a drug prepared by Alasco which, for all she knows, is poisonous; cf. the ending of the first act of De Lara's *Amy Robsart*.)

The second act takes place on a terrace at Kenilworth. *"Im Hintergrunde die Façade des Schlosses. Davor Gruppen von Sträuchern mit Statuen. Man sieht Höflinge und Bewaffnete geschäftig hin und hergehen in Erwartung des Besuches der Königin.—Der grössere Raum der Bühne bildet einen freien Platz. Rechts vorne auf einer Plattform ein Thronsessel mit Baldachin. Links vornen eine Grotte."* Janet opens the act with a song about her fan, which she uses to protect herself from all brash knights and squires. (The song has no parallel in the novel—and serves no especially useful function in the opera. It is in a light vein, much like Holstein's music for Lydia Thompson in *Der Erbe von Morley;* see Chapter 4.) During the last measures Lambourne approaches her and tries to kiss her, but she easily gets rid of him. (This frivolous incident is suggested by the attempt of Scott's Lambourne to make love to Amy in her (i.e. Tressilian's) room in the castle; see chapter xxxiii.) Amy now enters, as we hear in the orchestra two measures of her *Romanze* of Act I (see Example 11-14). She asks Janet whether she has been able to reach the earl. Janet replies that she has not and thus was unable to deliver Amy's letter to him. Amy tells her to guard the letter like a treasure, but almost the next moment Janet inadvertently lets it slip away from her. Suddenly noticing someone coming, they both withdraw into the darkness of the grotto. (In the novel Amy alone withdraws to the grotto, just after her unpleasant encounter with Lambourne. Janet is not with her at Kenilworth. Cf. the parallel material in Seidelmann.) Varney enters, to the accompaniment of his leitmotiv, and discovers the letter, which is obviously from Amy to Leicester, although Leicester's name does not appear anywhere on it. Varney realizes that he will be able to use it to his advantage and make Leicester think that Amy was writing it to someone else. After having pocketed his find, he leaves the stage quickly. (In the novel Wayland Smith was to deliver the letter. It was stolen from him by his prankish friend, Dickie Sludge, who unfortunately did not realize its importance until later. Müller and Klein's handling of the letter-motif makes the story's indebtedness to *Othello* even more obvious than is the novel.) When he has gone, Amy and Janet come out from the grotto, and suddenly they hear Leicester's signal, a musical motiv that recurs often and in many forms:

Example 11-16

When Leicester enters, Amy flies into his arms. (The long love-duet that follows is based on the meeting between Amy and Leicester at Cumnor, chapter vii, and on their meeting at Kenilworth, chapter xxxv, *after* the serious confrontation with the Queen.) He is astonished to see her at Kenilworth. She tells him that she left Cumnor because she was afraid of the ugly rumors which Varney had related to her. Leicester tries to calm her by saying that even the Queen is not immune to rumor. When she mentions her father's illness, he replies that he has heard that the old man has become well again. Amy then suggests that they visit him and that Leicester tell him that she is his wife, but Leicester reminds her that the Queen is his guest and impresses upon her the rashness of her desires. He assures her that the time will soon come when he will be able to recognize her before all the world as his countess. In the meanwhile he urges her to return to Cumnor. The duet ends with Amy singing a high C and Leicester, high A flat.[30]

As soon as Amy has departed, Varney re-enters. He tells Leicester that the Queen has just asked him whether he (Leicester) was the one who abducted Amy Robsart. "Verwünscht!" Leicester exclaims; "und du?" Varney says that like a good servant he directed the blame toward himself, telling her that *he* enjoyed the Fräulein's favor. "O Höllentrug!" is Leicester's initial reaction. Varney is quick to assure him that the ruse worked. Furthermore, when he said to her, "Ihr kennt ja meinen Herrn!/ Für ihn gibt es nur einen Stern!" her eyes gleamed as if she were transfigured. After instructing Varney to take Amy away from Kenilworth, Leicester exits. (The foregoing duologue has no exact parallel in the novel, but it is suggested by the scene at Greenwich Castle, chapter xvi, in which the Queen confronts Leicester with Varney's alleged seduction of Amy.) Alone on stage Varney sings a set piece, his "Lied vom Sturm," in which he compares his own ruthless personality with the murderous fury of a storm. (The piece reminds one of Iago's "Credo," in Verdi's *Otello*; it is in 4/4 time, with triplet 8th notes in the accompaniment. The text does not follow any specific passage in the novel, but it fits rather well Varney's character as depicted by Scott; cf. his aria about "Ambition" in *Amy Robsart*.) When he has departed, Amy and Janet, having lost their way, re-enter and decide to hide for a second time in the grotto.

Stately processional music is heard in the orchestra as the Queen and her entourage enter. The following stage direction gives indication of the grandeur and splendor of the scene:

> *Grosser Aufzug der Königin, des Hofes Leicesters und seines Gefolges. Die Königin, von Juwelen strahlend. Leicester, in weisser Montur mit Juwelen und Goldstoff überdeckt, zur Rechten der Königin. Leicester unbedeckten Hauptes; Varney folgt dicht hinter seinem Herrn und hat dessen schwarzes Sammtbarett mit weisser Feder und diamantenem Knopf in Verwahrung. Der Zug, sowohl Männer als Frauen, die unmittelbar der Königin folgen, besteht aus dem vornehmsten Adel, den Räthen der Regierung und Rittern aller Art. Die Königin nimmt auf dem Throne zur Rechten Platz.—Zuerst ziehen Römer ein, dann celtische Druiden in langen Gewändern mit Harfen. Hierauf sächsische Seekönige: Alle im entsprechenden Kostüm.*

(The pageantry described in the last two lines is suggested in part by the masque in chapter xxxvii; the "sächsische Seekönige" derive presumably from Scott's *Celtic* Lady of the Lake, chapter xxx.) In addition to the Romans, Celts, and Saxons there is a procession of Scottish Highlanders, with appropriate music:

Example 11-17

It is remarkable that Scots folk music should be used in an opera based on *Kenilworth*, which is perhaps the least Scottish of all the Waverley novels. Usually we find one or more Scottish characters in the novels set in parts of the world other than Scotland, but such is not the case with *Kenilworth*. The full chorus now greets Elisabeth in a brief but impressive ensemble,[31] and she graciously acknowledges the warm reception. Noticing Sussex among the noblemen, she is both surprised and pleased. Leicester explains that he has invited him that very day in the hope of patching up their long-standing quarrel. (In the novel it is no surprise to Elizabeth that Sussex is at Kenilworth, inasmuch as she had requested that he be there. His role in the opera is very slight.) When Leicester offers him his hand in reconciliation, he replies that he is prepared for peace *if* Leicester properly and openly acknowledges the shame which his follower Richard Varney has brought on Robsart. Varney then steps forward, kneels before the Queen, and declares that he and Amy are married. (Sussex's complaint and Varney's answer come from the confrontation at Greenwich, chapter xvi; the remainder of the act is based loosely on the memorable confrontation at Kenilworth, chapter xxxiv, which appears in one form or another in every *Kenilworth* opera.) At this point Amy, greatly agitated, comes out from the grotto and vehemently denies that she is Varney's wife. When the Queen begins to question her, she looks at Leicester and says, "Graf Leicester kann Euch alles sagen!" (In the novel Amy becomes upset during the conversation with the Queen *in the grotto* when the Queen refers to her as Varney's wife. They are still there in private conversation when Amy says, "The Earl of Leicester knows it all.") Immediately the Queen becomes angrily suspicious of Leicester, so much so that Amy relents and says that she has accused him falsely. Amy then sings a song about herself, to the accompaniment of a folk melody:

Example 11-18

Amy's vocal line is different, and her words are not to be found in the novel. She sings of having lived peacefully as a child of Nature, much loved by her father. Then a dashing knight came into the picture and won her affection. "Das ist mein Schicksal, Majestät," she concludes. To say that Elizabeth is not particularly moved by her song would be an understatement: she is fed up with the "Räthselspiel" and peremptorily demands to know who her husband is, if not Varney. At this point Varney breaks in and tells the Queen that Amy is mentally deranged. Amy does not deny what he says, and the Queen, feeling pity for her, says that she will put her in the care of her personal physician, Sir Peel (the Dr. Masters of the novel). The final ensemble begins as a quintet for Amy, Elisabeth, Leicester, Sussex, and Varney, all singing words appropriate to the situation. Interestingly, Varney broods on Amy's once having spurned his affections and having threatened to topple him—information that Scott relates much earlier in the story. The chorus joins the principals just before the act closes. Amy, bravely concealing the truth ("Ich trage still mein herbes Leid"), agrees to be led away.

The third act begins with an orchestral introduction. When the curtain rises, we see a dimly lit entrance-hall in Kenilworth; in the background an open balcony. It is night. The opening number is a *Barcarolle*, sung by an offstage chorus:

Example 11-19

After a while Elisabeth and Leicester enter, deeply engrossed in conversation. Noticing that the Queen is in a romantic mood, he decides to take advantage of the situation. He tells her that the desire she has kindled in him now burns with wild force. He pleads his cause passionately ("Elisabeth sei mein!"), even grabbing her hand and trying to draw her to him. She rejects him, but does so gently, reminding him that she must be the mother of her people. A bit flustered, she requests that he leave her alone. When he has gone, she sings a coloratura aria in which she expresses her emotional turmoil ("Wie rollt in den Adern mir stürmisch das Blut!"). Nevertheless she is grateful for his love, and her thrice repeated last line—"Ich weiss mich geliebt, bin nicht mehr allein!"— is overheard by Leicester, who re-enters unobserved by her. At the conclusion of the aria she exits. (The haunting *Barcarolle* has no parallel in the novel. The love-scene is suggested by the tête-à-tête that Scott mentions as having taken place but does not describe in detail. As in *Il Conte di Leicester,* Scott's order of events has been rearranged. In the novel Leicester woos Elizabeth just prior to the big confrontation of chapter xxxiv. Elizabeth retreats to the grotto to be alone in her upset state of mind, and there she meets Amy.)

Varney now enters and tells Leicester that Amy has secretly departed from the castle. He suspects that she has fled to her previous suitor. "Tod und Verdammniss!" Leicester exclaims. (In the novel, chapter xxxvi, Varney suggests that Amy has been unfaithful, but he does not tell the untruth of her having fled from the castle into the arms of Tressilian. The change speeds up the process of Varney's convincing Leicester that Amy has played him false.) Varney then shows him Amy's unaddressed letter, which, it will be recalled, came into his hands earlier, and he easily convinces him that the letter was intended for Tressilian. When he tells him of Tressilian's recent visit to Cumnor, Leicester becomes even more furious: "Sie büsse ihrer Wollust Drang:/ Ich geb' sie ganz in deine Hand!" When Varney requests a token that will prove he is acting according to Leicester's wishes, Leicester gives him the Queen's signet-ring (rather than his own). Varney hurries out, leaving Leicester alone on stage for an aria: "Wie war sie schön! Ein holdes Frauenbild." His initial anger has now changed to a deep sense of personal injury. (The aria has no exact equivalent in the novel. The conversation between Varney and Leicester is greatly condensed from the parallel material of chapters xxxvi-xxxvii.)

Suddenly Tressilian appears and demands justice from Leicester in behalf of Amy. He tells Leicester that even though most people think that Amy was bewitched by his vassal, Richard Varney, he happens to know that she went away with the master himself when she left Lidcote. He begs Leicester to preserve her honor and recognize her as his wife. (In the novel, chapter xxxix, it is a complete surprise to Tressilian when Leicester tells him that Amy is his wife and countess. Like everyone else, Tressilian had thought she was Varney's wife or mistress.) Under the mistaken impression that Tressilian is Amy's lover, Leicester draws his sword and engages him in mortal combat. Suddenly Janet bursts in with the news that Varney has just taken Amy away from the room to which she had been consigned by the Queen. Leicester thinks that Janet is out of her mind, Varney having told him that Amy had fled to Tressilian. Janet insists that Amy has not seen Tressilian at Kenilworth. Leicester then shows her the letter which he thinks Amy wrote to Tressilian. Janet tells him that the letter was not meant for Tressilian but for *him*, and that she lost it in the courtyard, where Varney evidently found it. (In the novel Dickie Sludge breaks up the duel and belatedly delivers Amy's letter, which he had stolen in pique from Wayland Smith, who was supposed to deliver it. As already observed, Scott's Janet does not accompany Amy to Kenilworth.) Now realizing Amy's innocence, but remembering only too well his final instructions to Varney, Leicester is terribly upset. "Dein Wort," he says to Janet, "ruft eine Hölle von Zweifeln mir im Busen wach!" He determines to go to the Queen at once, but at that very moment she enters, as we hear in the orchestra a few measures of music we heard earlier in the act, during her aria:

Example 11-20

Sussex is with her. (What follows is based on Leicester's belated revelation of the truth, chapter xl, but in the novel everything takes place in the Queen's chamber. In avoiding a change of scenery, Müller and Klein avoid a break in the dramatic intensity of the ironic and dangerous situation that is evolving.) Leicester tells her that he loves Amy and that she is his wife. Greatly angered, Elisabeth gives orders for him to be put in chains and conducted to the Tower. Leicester exclaims that she has exceeded the bounds of her authority; he demands the justice that is rightfully his as a peer of the realm (a detail from the confrontation of chapter xxxiv). When Elisabeth furiously vows to crush his pride, Sussex tries to calm her. (In acting as mediator, the operatic Sussex assumes the role of Shrewsbury, chapter xxxiv, and of Burleigh, chapter xl.) Tressilian then says to the Queen that even if Leicester has done a great wrong to her, Amy's life is at stake; he begs her to allow Leicester to hurry to her rescue. Elisabeth agrees to this reasonable proposal, and all leave the stage.

The orchestra plays an interlude during the change of scenery. As the curtain rises, we hear a strain of the Scottish folk melody that has heretofore been associated with Amy (see Example 11-18). Once more we are at Cumnor. Amy is seated at a table. Like Desdemona she is clothed in white and her hair is loose. Completely lost in her thoughts, she hums the opening phrase of her *Romanze* of Act I (see Example 11-14). She then rises from the table and sings briefly of her sadness upon hearing of the death of her father. (In the novel Sir Hugh Robsart dies not long after hearing of Amy's death.) Suddenly Varney enters and declares his burning desire for her. When she repulses his overtures, he exclaims in wild passion that if she does not give him her favor he will drag her to his breast and drink from her chaste lips a nectar of furtive kisses. He clasps her in his arms, but she immediately pushes him back and runs to the open window. With dreadful resoluteness she commands him to leave the room at once; otherwise one jump will free her from his presence and her own shame. (The incident obviously derives from the well-known encounter of Brian de Bois-Guilbert and Rebecca at Torquilstone; see *Ivanhoe*, ch. xxiv, and all the *Ivanhoe* operas.) She shows him the door, and he leaves, deeply impressed with her dignity of character and her resoluteness. When he has gone, Amy sings again of her sadness and expresses the desire for death. All her dreams have turned to sorrow. God is her only consolation. Presently she takes from her bosom a vial and drinks its poisonous contents. She then sinks down in agitation on a settee, singing:

Example 11-21

This is a melody which we have already heard, namely, at the end of the orchestral introduction to the opera; 8th-note triplet figures are in the accompaniment. After the last note Amy falls unconscious to the floor. At this point we hear Leicester's signal behind the scene (see Example 11-16), and immediately Leicester and Tressilian rush in. "Allmächtiger!" Tressilian exclaims; "zu spät, zu spät!" Leicester is beside himself with grief. Again like Desdemona, and in typical operatic fashion, Amy revives for a few parting words with both her husband and the friend of her youth. Then she expires.[32] Leicester cries "Amy!" and falls in inconsolable grief on her lifeless body. Tressilian sings a brief, appropriate tribute to Amy to the melody of her so-called "Verklärung" (see Example 11-21), and the curtain falls slowly.

Amy dies at Cumnor, but virtually all the surrounding circumstances depart markedly from the novel. Müller and Klein were obviously well versed in the trappings and conventions of tragic opera, which are nowhere so evident as in this last scene of the last opera to be based on *Kenilworth*.

* * *

In the early spring of 1977, while this book was in the final stages of proof, there was a revival of Donizetti's *Elisabetta al Castello di Kenilworth* at the Camden Festival (London). The principal roles in this Opera Rara production were sung by Yvonne Kenny (Amelia), Janet Price (Elisabetta), Maurice Arthur (Alberto), and Christian du Plessis (Warney). See William Mann's favorable review in *The Times,* March 31, 1977, p. 9. It seems that the opera had not been performed anywhere since 1835.

12

§ § §

PEVERIL OF THE PEAK

Μy decision to include and discuss the two operas that comprise this chapter is admittedly questionable. Horn's *Peveril of the Peak* is clearly based on Scott's novel, but one might argue that it is a "musical drama" rather than an "opera"; Auber's *Muette de Portici* is clearly an opera, but it is not based primarily on Scott. I have chosen to include the former because, in the first place, Henry Adelbert White has little to say about it in his monograph. Secondly, it is almost everywhere referred to as either a "comic opera" or an "opera"—this fact in itself implying that it somehow stands apart from the average British musical drama. Examination reveals that it contains a somewhat greater amount of music than does the average musical drama and that two of its finales are somewhat more ambitious from a musical standpoint than what one would find, say, in a typical musical drama by Sir Henry Bishop. As for *La Muette de Portici,* it is usually considered Auber's most ambitious and significant achievement. In main outline Scribe's libretto owes nothing to Scott; it is based on the story of the rise and fall of Masaniello, the seventeenth-century fisherman-dictator of Naples. For the intriguing character of Fenella, however, Masaniello's speechless sister, Scribe turned to *Peveril of the Peak.* His incorporation of her into the well-known story makes his version of it unique, so far as I know.

Peveril of the Peak

This "comic opera" is the work of the veteran playwright Isaac Pocock and the English singer and composer Charles E. Horn.[1] It was first performed on 21 October 1826, at Covent Garden. According to White, it was "magnificently mounted and 'tolerably well received.' " It was given nine performances.[2] The published vocal score consists of an overture, six choral ensembles (sometimes with brief solo passages for Sir Geoffrey, Whitaker, Topham, and others), four solo numbers for Alice Bridgenorth (sung by Miss Paton), three solos for Julian Peveril (sung by Mr. Sapio), and three duets for Alice and Julian.[3] The complete text, which White did not see, exists in manuscript in the British Museum.[4]

After the overture the curtain rises on a *"Terrace, with steps, which conduct to the platform of a Turret in Martindale Castle–Beyond the parapet wall a bird's eye view of the distant country, near the peak of Derbyshire—Moultrassie Hall in the low grounds, and the village of Castleton in the distance."* Gatheril, the Peverils' master steward (who corresponds with Scott's Whitaker), and a group of servants sing a glee as they watch for the return of Sir Geoffrey Peveril:

> Look out, look out, 'tis the good old knight:—
> He's kind in the Hall, and he's brave in the fight,
> He ne'er turn'd his back on his friend or his foe,
> As King Charles and the Round Heads very well know—

Seeing a horseman rapidly approaching the castle, all except Gatheril and a boy leave the stage, presumably to greet "the good old knight." Whitaker then enters, along with *"Lance and another, with a Buck slung to a pole, which they carry across their shoulders."* (The operatic Whitaker resembles Scott's Lance Outram, gamekeeper to Sir Geoffrey, while the operatic Lance is a character who appears on stage occasionally but who has no personality and is not important to the story.) In the spoken dialogue that follows, Gatheril tells Whitaker that Sir Geoffrey has just returned from court. Whitaker replies that he is mistaken: two ladies, rather than Sir Geoffrey, have just arrived. Gatheril instructs the boy to impart this information to Lady Peveril, who is "in deep conference" with Bridgenorth. When, in a few moments, the boy re-enters, he says that one of the two ladies will not speak. At this point we hear music in the orchestra (not included in the vocal score) accompanying the entrance of Fenella, who conveys by gestures to those present that she is deaf and dumb. The Countess of Derby then enters. Gatheril recognizes her at once, but she tells him to be silent, inasmuch as she has "especial reasons for privacy." (This portion of the scene is based loosely on the Countess' arrival at Martindale, chapter v, but in Scott's account she is not accompanied by Fenella, who, if born yet, would have been a mere infant at this time.) When Gatheril has dismissed the boy and Whitaker, the Countess asks him whether there is any immediate danger for her. "I trust not, Madam," he replies; "but there has been one Topham in the village, an Officer of the House of Commons, with a warrant to pursue and take certain individuals, accused of being favourers of the plot." (At this early point in the story Scott's Countess is not in trouble resulting from her suspected connection with the Popish Plot; rather, she is out of favor because of her having ordered the execution of William Christian. In the novel Topham is not mentioned until chapter xx.) Fenella is on stage during the whole conversation between Gatheril and the Countess. Despite being supposedly deaf and dumb, she appears to comprehend what they are saying. At the end of the scene Mistress Ellesmere (also a character of the novel) enters to escort the

Countess to Lady Peveril. (One very noticeable omission in the operatic version of the Countess' appearance at Martindale is her memorable encounter with Julian Peveril, age 3, and Alice Bridgenorth, age 18 months. We learn subsequently that both hero and heroine are already young adults and that Julian has already served as page in the Countess' household on the Isle of Man. Pocock has greatly tightened up Scott's sprawling story, which extends over the period 1658–1678.)

For the second scene we move to a room inside the castle. In spoken dialogue Bridgenorth thanks Lady Peveril for the preservation in infancy of his daughter Alice. She in turn thanks him that Sir Geoffrey was spared during the Commonwealth years. She hopes that all civil and religious dissentions may be healed with the restoration of King Charles. Gatheril presently ushers in the Countess and Fenella. *"Bridgenorth turns suddenly at the mention of the name* [Countess of Derby], *and instantly perceives Fenella, who appears to recognize him—They gaze a moment at each other,—Fenella drops her eye, & Bridgenorth averts his head and smiles, saying in a low tone,"* "She here too!—'tis well." (Again, be it noted that Fenella is not present in the corresponding material of the novel, chapter v. In explanation of the action above, we learn subsequently that she is the daughter of Bridgenorth, rather than of Scott's Edward Christian, who does not appear in the opera.) Some of the ensuing conversation follows the novel, but not all. Lady Peveril tells the Countess that son Julian has often spoken of Fenella and has praised her highly. Fenella beams with joy—and thus we suspect already that she is not deaf after all and that she is not altogether indifferent to Julian Peveril. As the conversation develops, the Countess tells Lady Peveril that she stands accused by Titus Oates of participating in the plot. (Interestingly, the plot is never called the Popish Plot in the opera, probably out of respect for English Roman Catholics.) She then rehearses the history of her recent troubles on the Isle of Man—the rebellion, the treachery of William Christian, and his subsequent capture and execution. Upon hearing Christian's fate, Bridgenorth, as in the novel, cannot contain himself any longer. He says that Christian was his brother-in-law and that he had in fact shielded the Countess from the wrath of the Commonwealth. As in the novel, chapter vi, he attempts to arrest her; but at Lady Peveril's command, Gatheril, Whitaker, and Lance enter and take him into their custody. *"Exit the Countess, Lady P. and Fenella, who lingers a moment after their departure, imploring the forbearance of Bridgenorth, and appearing to be influenced by an interest in both parties."* Gatheril restrains Whitaker from using abusive language to Bridgenorth, whom they lead away as the scene closes.

When the curtain rises again, we are at Bridgenorth's home, Moultrassie Hall. Alice opens the new scene with a song, the first stanza of which is a typical example of the "poetic" diction found in most of Pocock's lyrics:

When sorrow speeds the venom'd dart,
And rends the love-lorn maiden's heart,

Soft music, with her silver sound,
Can lull the pain, and heal the wound.
   Then, dwell with me,
     Sweet melody!

Afterwards, Alice expresses wonder as to why her father should find fault
with music. Presently Deborah Debbitch, Alice's governess, enters. She
tells how she managed to cause Major Bridgenorth to relent in his stern
attitude toward dancing: she simply told him it was good for his beloved
daughter's health. Hearing someone approaching, they both enter the
house. *"Julian Peveril appears at the back, equipp'd for angling, in a grey-cloth
Jacket & cap—a rose in his hand."* (In the novel Julian is an angler only when
he is residing on the Isle of Man. This third scene of the opera is based
loosely on Scott's account of the relationship between Julian and Alice,
chapters xi–xiii, but the setting has been shifted from Man to Moultrassie
Hall.) In a short soliloquy Julian voices the thought that if only he and
Alice could marry, all griefs would be forgotten, all dissension end. "As it
is," he continues, "her youth & beauty are wasting in seclusion, and she
will droop and fade, even like this flower." At this point we find Waller's
"Go, lovely rose" in the manuscript, but it has been crossed through and
another lyric put in its place ("This blooming rose is like the Maid," etc.);
neither appears in the published vocal score. After Julian has had a brief
conversation with Deborah (condensed from chapter xi), Alice enters and
requests that Deborah allow her to speak with Julian in private. As in the
novel, Alice tells him that they have done wrong and bids him farewell:
"Farewell, then, farewell! and forget that we have ever seen each other."
"Forget!" he protests. And now we have a duet:

ALICE: Forget me!
JULIAN: Forget thee!
      Ah! never can my heart resign
       Its only hope, its only joy.
     Say, Alice, say, thou wilt be mine,
       And do not with a frown destroy.
       Forget thee—no!
ALICE: Ah! never can our fate combine,
     Then, seek no more my heart to move.
   This willing heart would fain be thine,
     But, ah! it must not, dare not love!
       Forget me—go!
DUO: Forget $\begin{Bmatrix} \text{thee, dearest} \\ \text{me, Julian} \end{Bmatrix}$ ah! forget
   The joy we ne'er again may know,
   Far better had we never met
   Than thus to part—Forget $\begin{Bmatrix} \text{thee, no!} \\ \text{me—go!} \end{Bmatrix}$—

The duet is followed by more spoken dialogue. When Julian says, "He must, Alice, he must, and shall answer me on the subject of my suit," Bridgenorth suddenly appears. "Then, demand that answer now," he says. (In the novel Bridgenorth speaks this line "from without the door"—and then opens the door and enters, repeating his words.) As in the novel, Alice begs her father to do Julian no injury. The remainder of the scene departs from the novel. Hearing someone approaching, Bridgenorth solemnly urges Julian to renounce the Countess of Derby and cleave to the good cause. He then departs, along with Alice and Deborah. No sooner has he gone than Whitaker and Lance enter, in search of him. Whitaker explains to Julian that Bridgenorth had been apprehended at Martindale, but he managed to escape (a detail from chapter vi). When he and Lance have left the stage to continue their search, Julian closes the scene with another song ("Softly o'er the summer sea," according to the libretto; "My fairest, my dearest" in the score).

For the last scene of Act I we are again in a room in Martindale Castle. "We owe Master Bridgenorth some deference, Madam," Lady Peveril tells the Countess, in words lifted virtually verbatim from the novel, chapter vi; "he has served us often, and kindly, in the late troubles; but he shall not insult the Countess of Derby in the house of Sir Geoffrey Peveril." When Sir Geoffrey enters, he learns of Bridgenorth's insolence and Lady Peveril's forced detention of him. (The part of the novel's dialogue in which plans are made to send baby Julian to Man to be a page in the Countess' household is of course omitted, inasmuch as the operatic Julian is already grown up, as we have seen, and has already served as the Countess' page.) Sir Geoffrey exits in order to look into the Bridgenorth affair more closely. Julian then enters—in a departure from the parallel material of the novel. The Countess entrusts him with a packet containing letters of great importance which he must convey for her to London—a motif transposed from Scott's account of Julian's pagehood on the Isle of Man, chapter xviii. *"Fenella enters in great alarm, her action expressive of approaching danger"* (another motif from chapter xviii). Suddenly Sir Geoffrey re-enters with the news that Bridgenorth has escaped (chapter vi again), and almost the next moment he is informed by Gatheril that Bridgenorth "has just entered the house . . . with some strange officers." When Bridgenorth comes on stage, he is accompanied by Topham (who does not appear in the novel until much later). They try to take Sir Geoffrey into custody, but he tears up their warrant. (The corresponding incident in the novel, chapter vii, takes place on a road some distance from the castle.) Bridgenorth then departs, while Topham, who has fallen into the hands of Whitaker, remains at the castle. Whitaker, Julian, Margery (Scott's Cisly Sellok), Mistress Ellesmere, the boy, and others join their voices for the finale: "To horse, to horse—no more delay./To horse, to horse,—mount, mount, and away"—the idea being that the Countess must make her escape quickly and at once.

The first scene of Act II takes place at Whitaker's lodge (see chapter xxv). When the curtain rises, we behold Whitaker, Lance, Ditchley, Roger Raine (who at this point in the novel has been "dead six months and more"), the boy, and other dependents of the Peverils *enjoying themselves over a venison pasty.* Their glee, "Troul, troul, the bonny brown bowl," is one of the most attractive musical numbers in the score.[5] (It has no parallel in the novel.) After a bit of spoken dialogue, Whitaker notices Deborah approaching the lodge. "Something's wrong, I doubt, at the castle," he says. "Sun down, and no light on the Warden's tower!" Deborah enters with news that there is indeed trouble at the castle. "Strike for the house that bred you, and fed you," she tells Whitaker, "—and if you are buried in the ruins, you die a man's death." (These are more or less Mistress Ellesmere's words to Lance Outram in the novel, chapter xxv.) Suddenly Margery rushes in with news that Sir Geoffrey and Lady Peveril have been made prisoners and that Bridgenorth has led Julian away to Moultrassie Hall. Whitaker immediately instructs Deborah to run up to the castle and light up the beacon as a signal, if he is to gather a force of men (cf. the words of Scott's Lance to Cisly Sellok). While she is gone he urges all men present to help him help the Peverils. In a few moments they see the beacon blazing once again, and soon Deborah returns with a message from Lady Peveril, who requests that the men desist from rescuing Sir Geoffrey and herself but try to rescue Julian. The scene ends in a chorus:

> The pale Star of Peveril blazes bright
> An omen of joy to the jolly old knight.
> May it shine on the Peak for a thousand long year!
> So, huzza for the king, and the brave Cavalier!
> Huzza! huzza!
> Huzza for the King, and the brave Cavalier.

The remainder of the act takes place at Moultrassie Hall and culminates in the attempt of Whitaker and other dependents of Sir Geoffrey to rescue Julian (see the last pages of ch. xxv). The material leading up to this final event is borrowed, enlarged, condensed, and altered from various parts of the novel. When the curtain rises, Alice, alone in a room of the hall, expresses the hope that she can see Julian in time to warn him that her father will perhaps try to convert him to the cause of the Puritans (a detail from chapter xvii). She then sings a song entitled "The Young Cavalier":

> O, I never will marry a Puritan lad
> So dull and so formal, so solemn and sad;
> He talks about love while he thinks of your pelf,
> And he cares for no one but him self.[6]

Upon the completion of her song, she leaves the stage. Julian and Bridgenorth then enter, and their conversation about Julian's romantic interest in Alice is condensed from parallel material in chapter xiii. When

Bridgenorth leaves the stage momentarily, Alice re-enters and warns Julian of her father's machinations (chapter xvii again). Apparently at this point they sing the so-called "Battle Duet" ("Surrounded by fear . . .") included in the score, but not the libretto. There follows an argument between Bridgenorth and Deborah; he demands that she leave the hall. (The incident is suggested by Bridgenorth's words about Deborah to Alice, chapter xxiv, when he has learned that she has gone out for a visit: "I will have those . . . and those only, around me, who know to keep within the sober and modest bounds of a Christian family. Who pretends to more freedom, must go out from among us, as not being of us.") After Deborah has departed, Bridgenorth informs Julian that he expects Sir Geoffrey and Lady Peveril to be conducted to Moultrassie (a departure from the novel). Julian tells Bridgenorth that he will not try to escape, inasmuch as he has given his word not to do so. Their ensuing conversation is drawn from the ending of chapter xxiii, as Scott's Bridgenorth is leading Julian away from Martindale Castle, which has just been seized by officers of Parliament. The operatic scene closes with both noticing, as in the novel, that the beacon has been lit.—We move now to another part of the house, where Bridgenorth and Lady Peveril are engrossed in conversation (drawn from their chance nocturnal encounter on the lonely walk near Martindale, at a much earlier point in the story, chapter x). When Topham brings in Sir Geoffrey, the scene then more or less follows Scott's account of the confrontation *at Martindale,* chapter xxiii—a highpoint of the novel. Upon the entrance of Alice and Julian, Lady Peveril exclaims, "My son!—then the misery of our house is full!"—a line lifted almost verbatim from the novel. (Scott's Alice, be it noted, is not on hand at Martindale.) After more dialogue following chapter xxiii, Geoffrey is led off by Topham, and eventually Julian and Bridgenorth find themselves alone on stage. Their ensuing conversation about what part the Peverils allegedly have played in the notorious plot follows the last pages of chapter xxiv. When Julian refuses Bridgenorth's offer of freedom, Bridgenorth exclaims, "Die, then, in thine obstinacy!" (Scott: "Perish, then, in thy obstinacy!") and leaves the stage. Next, in a departure from the novel, Fenella appears. She makes Julian aware that he has lost the Countess' important letters, but a moment later she obligingly produces them for him. She also shows him that his pistols have been tampered with. (In the novel this information is imparted to us not at Moultrassie but at an inn along the London road, as Julian, unobserved, eavesdrops on a conversation between Thomas Chiffinch (*alias* Will Smith) and a courtier; see ch. xxvii.) Julian then sings a song ("Tell me, oh, tell me, thou Maiden dear,/Tell me, without disguise,/Why from thy lady, thou'st wander'd here?"), at the close of which Alice rushes in, exclaiming, "Julian,—Oh Julian, save my father!" (as in the novel, chapter xxv). Whitaker (Scott's Lance Outram) and a group of men have come to set Julian free, but Julian is honor-bound to remain in Bridgenorth's custody. He explains to Sir Geoffrey that he has promised Bridgenorth not to escape, and Sir Geoffrey immediately concedes that the word of a Peveril should not be broken. The would-be rescuers are urged to go home in the final vocal ensemble:

Home, home, good people, home.
    You must no longer stay.
The beacon's light is burning bright
    To guide you on your way.

(The presence of Sir Geoffrey at Moultrassie Hall when it is assaulted is the most striking alteration in the operatic rendition.)

Act III opens in St. James's Park. *"The King is seated—the Duke of Ormond, Arlington & Selby stand beside him. At a little distance, in front of the king, stands Fenella, and behind her, Julian Peveril."* (The scene is based loosely on the events of chapter xxxi, which take place inside the Chiffinch mansion, but the setting is that of chapter xx.) Julian tells King Charles that he is Julian Peveril and that his father is in prison. As he is speaking, *"A shriek is heard, and Alice rushes in, pursued by the Duke of Buckingham."* She begs the protection of the King, as in the novel, and then launches into a recitative ("Monarch & Sire! to thee I lowly bend") and air ("With ruffled wing and plaintive cry/The Dove will from the Falcon fly"). When Charles asks Buckingham to use his influence to protect Sir Geoffrey, Buckingham refuses. Ormond then urges the King himself to act in behalf of Sir Geoffrey, and the King promises to do what he can. (Ormond's plea is suggested by the material of chapter xl.) All then leave the stage except Julian and Alice, who conclude the scene with a duet ("To valley and mountain").—We move now to a room in the Duke of Buckingham's palace. In spoken dialogue drawn and condensed from chapter xxxvii, Buckingham tells his valet Jerningham that Alice Bridgenorth is worth more to him than both the good will of her father and the Kingdom of Man.—Next, in a drawing-room of the palace, Zarah (*alias* Fenella) is revealed. There is a lyric for her in the libretto ("Love in the heart, like dew upon roses") but not in the score. As in the novel, chapter xxxiv, the Duke enters, thinking that he can now satisfy his passion for Alice, but in her stead he finds Zarah. At the end of the scene she leaps through the window, as in the novel, and disappears.—We move now to the *"Inner Hall of Bridgenorth's house in London."* First we see Deborah and Whitaker, who are now married, and obviously Deborah has the upper hand. (In the novel, Lance Outram is a former beau of Deborah; there is talk of the possibility of their marrying, but nothing ever comes of it.) Shouts are heard from *without,* and suddenly Sir Geoffrey and Julian rush in, seeking sanctuary from the rabble who have been heckling them in the aftermath of their trial (see chapter xlii). When Bridgenorth enters, both father and son are duly surprised to learn that he is the proprietor of the house which necessity forced them to enter (see the beginning of chapter xliii). The remainder of the scene departs from the novel. Deborah explains to Sir Geoffrey that she and Whitaker are now man and wife, and after Bridgenorth has led Julian away to see Alice, Sir Geoffrey and the new-lyweds remain on stage for a comic interlude. After a while Julian and Bridgenorth return. When the others have withdrawn, Bridgenorth motions to Alice to come in. He asks Julian to conduct her safely to Lady Peveril and then departs. Julian asks Alice to wait a moment while he goes to apprise Sir Geoffrey of Bridgenorth's plans. While she waits, she sings a song to conclude the scene ("When first he woo'd, and won my love,/How sweetly passed the time away," etc.).[7]

The final scene takes place in the King's Court at Whitehall. It is based loosely on material drawn from chapters xlv: the Countess of Derby pleads before Charles in behalf of the Peverils; xlvi: the treason of Buckingham is told to Charles (but without the dwarf Geoffrey Hudson and the incident of the viol case); xlviii: Buckingham acquits himself of treason; and xlix: Fenella's true identity is revealed; she is *not* deaf and dumb. The most striking difference between this last scene and the ending of the novel is that the operatic Bridgenorth, as already indicated, is a composite of Scott's Bridgenorth plus Edward Christian. Fenella turns out to be his daughter. He thinks that he will be put in the Tower (as does Scott's Edward Christian), but the King is moved by Fenella's plea for her father and banishes him instead (as happens in the case of Christian). As Bridgenorth is about to leave the room, Fenella exclaims,

> Oh! let me see him [i.e. Julian] once again,
>   But once before we part for ever;
> He shall not hear my voice complain,
>   He shall not see me weep—Oh never![8]

But then she decides it is better that she *not* see him. She tells Bridgenorth that she will wander the wide world together with him, and she rushes into his arms. (In the novel there is no such emotion on the part of Fenella for her father, Edward Christian. The altered parting scene recalls to mind the last chapter of *Ivanhoe* and makes all the more obvious Fenella's spiritual kinship with Rebecca.) In a final bit of dialogue plans for the wedding of Julian and Alice are briefly discussed. When Ormond observes that Sir Geoffrey will object, Charles says, as in the novel, "Our royal recommendation shall put that to right. Sir Geoffrey Peveril has not suffered hardships so often at our command, to refuse, at our desire, a match, that will make amends for all his losses." Sir Geoffrey agrees immediately to the King's wish, and the opera ends in a large musical ensemble:

> Long live the King!
> God save the King!
> Thus 'tis we sing of good King Charles.
> Merry may he be!

Ever may we see
Traitors bend the knee to good King Charles.[9]

In a strict sense, of course, Pocock and Horn's *Peveril of the Peak* is "musical drama" rather than "opera." Despite the unusually large amount of music, some of it mildly ambitious, *Peveril* still has its share of the hallmarks of typical English musical drama. Much of the music is uninteresting: the melodic lines, the harmonies, the rhythms are simple to the point of banality. In reshaping Scott's story Pocock does not attempt anything beyond the superficial, inasmuch as light entertainment is his purpose. His Major Bridgenorth (a speaking role) is a pasteboard figure in comparison with the complex, fascinating character of the novel. In defense of this approach, however, both Pocock and Horn might have argued that a serious opera based on *Peveril of the Peak* is not possible, in view of the novel's discursiveness and uneven quality.

La Muette de Portici

Auber's five-act opera, *La Muette de Portici*, with words by Scribe and G. Delavigne, was first performed on 29 February 1828 in Paris, at the theater of the Académie Royale de Musique.[10] The work had a long, distinguished performance history. Here is the story, in brief:

Act I. *Naples, in the gardens of the viceroy.* The viceroy's son Alphonse regrets that he must abandon his mistress Fenella, speechless sister to the Neapolitan fisherman Masaniello, when he marries Elvire. Fenella communicates to Elvire how she was forcibly taken to prison by officer Selva, this procedure having been ordered by the viceroy as a precautionary measure. Later Fenella witnesses the marriage of Alphonse and Elvire, after which she conveys the idea to Elvire that Alphonse was her lover. She escapes in the crowd as the act closes.

Act II. *Portici, along the seacoast between Naples and Mt. Vesuvius.* Masaniello and friends plan revenge on their foreign oppressors. Masaniello swears vengeance on Fenella's seducer, but she will not reveal his name, for she still loves him. All the fishermen swear vengeance in the final choral ensemble.

Act III. *Naples; a public place.* The people prevent Selva from recapturing Fenella. They implore God to aid them in the fearful enterprise which they are about to undertake.

Act IV. *Portici; the house of Masaniello.* Masaniello is now in power, but he is sickened by all the bloodshed and murder. So too is Fenella. Pietro and other friends of Masaniello desire Alphonse's blood. Eluding their pursuers, Alphonse and Elvire arrive on the scene. Elvire implores Fenella to exert her influence to save Alphonse. At first Fenella is reluctant, but she then agrees to try. She causes Masaniello to believe that Alphonse and Elvire are outlaws seeking refuge. Masaniello accepts them in hospitality. When Pietro enters and recognizes Alphonse, Masaniello refuses to give him over.

Act V. *Naples, in the palace of the viceroy.* Masaniello has become mentally deranged. Alphonse raises an army to retake the city. Recalled to his senses, Masaniello fights bravely. As later reported by Alphonse and Elvire, he saved Elvire from the fury of the people, who then turned on him and murdered him. Fenella commits suicide by jumping into the crater of Mt. Vesuvius.

Of the several Masaniello plays I have examined that antedate *La Muette* none includes a speechless young woman in its cast of characters.[11] Well versed in the Waverley Novels, Scribe apparently found Fenella an attractive creation and decided to graft her onto the well-known story of Masaniello as an operatic novelty. His Fenella, in contrast with Scott's, is truly incapable of speech (that is, she is not just pretending). Like the Fenella of the novel she is not deaf, but in contrast she does not pretend to be deaf. Her love for Alphonse, who abandons her for Elvire, is reminiscent of the unrequited love of Scott's Fenella for Julian Peveril. Moreover, her unwillingness to reveal to Masaniello the name of her seducer, for fear of what he would surely do to him, recalls to mind Amy Robsart's unwillingness to tell angry Queen Elizabeth that Leicester is her husband. Scribe knew *Kenilworth* well, having based a libretto on it for Auber's *Leicester* five years previously (see Chapter 11). Masaniello's slight resemblance to Bridgenorth (his religious fervor, for example) is probably coincidental.

The idea of having a mute as a leading character in a grand opera was not well received in all quarters. One biographer of Auber looked on it as a "gageure" rather than as a genuine innovation.[12] Clément and Larousse, on the other hand, state that it was "une inspiration aussi heureuse qu'elle était hardie." Grout too is impressed: "A novelty in the score is that the heroine is a mute personage, who expresses herself only in pantomine to orchestral accompaniment—an interesting and possibly unique use of the melodrama technique."[13] Whatever one might think about the effectiveness of a mute operatic principal, one would have to admit that Scribe and Auber's bold innovation has stimulated much interesting and worthwhile commentary. But most discussions of the opera, Grout's included, lose sight of the point that the original of the operatic heroine in question, Fenella, the dumb girl of Portici, Masaniello's wronged sister, is Sir Walter Scott's Fenella of *Peveril of the Peak*.[14]

13

§ § §

*QUENTIN DURWARD**

One reviewer of the first operatic *Quentin Durward* was of the opinion that the novel presented an impossible task for a librettist:

> Everybody knows Walter Scott's gorgeous and magnificent novel of that name—a work which for variety of character, picturesque description, intense interest, knowledge of the human heart, and beauty of style, is unsurpassed by any production, even of his own pen. But had we been asked what novel of Scott's could less afford to be circumscribed into the limits of an opera, we should have replied, without the least hesitation, "*Quentin Durward.*" The greatest dramatic tactician of the age, Scribe himself, could not, even within the limitation of five acts, have confined one tithe of the incidents which are scattered over Walter Scott's three volumes, every one of which is necessary to the development of the story. Now, Mr. Fitzball is not Scribe; and as he has confined his *libretto* to three acts, the result may readily be imagined.[1]

This caveat notwithstanding, there were two subsequent operatic renditions of *Quentin Durward*, one of which proved modestly successful. All three bear the title *Quentin Durward.*

Laurent's *Quentin Durward*

Henri Laurent's long-expected *Quentin Durward*, with words by Edward Fitzball, was first performed on Wednesday, 6 December 1848, at Convent Garden. It was the young composer's first attempt at opera.[2] "The house was tolerably well attended," the same reviewer wrote, "and the audience left nothing undone to encourage the youthful composer in his

---

**Regarding the accent marks in words such as *Crèvecœur, Maître, Balafré*, etc., I have usually followed the example of the Border Edition. Because of the varied procedure in this matter among the librettos, scores, and editions of the novel which I used, no other solution seemed feasible. For the *Liége* and *Liégeois* of the Border Edition I have written *Liège* and *Liègeois*.

first attempt. A call was made at the end for the principal artists, and afterwards for M. Laurent himself, who appeared and was received with warm applause." Mrs. Donald King sang the role of Isabelle de Croye; Miss Messent sang Princess Joan; Mr. Harrison, Quentin Durward; Mr. Borrani, King Louis XI. The performance was conducted by Francesco Vincenzo Schira, who himself had just recently finished composing a Walter Scott opera.[3] Others among the dramatis personae include the Duke of Burgundy, the Duke of Orleans, Cardinal Balue, the Governor (rather than Bishop) of Liège, Captain Balafré, William de la Marck, Pavilleon (*sic*), Tristran (*sic*), and Martin (Scott's unnamed landlord of the Fleur-de-Lys inn). The British Museum has some of the music [4] and the manuscript of the complete text.[5]

At the conclusion of the overture, the curtain rises on a party of hunters deep in the forest near Plessis-les-Tours. In the opening musical number Tristran and the boar hunters express their grave concern about the King, who, having become separated from the rest of the party, may be in danger. They hasten away in search of him. In a moment the King and Quentin enter. The King thanks the young stranger for having saved his life and asks him his name. First the young man sings a ballad:

> I come frae the land o' the mountain,
>   My footsteps as light as its gale;—
> My heart is as clear as the fountain,
>   That flows thro' my own native vale.—
> My dirk, and my pouch, are my fortune,
>   And gold, tho' the latter may crave;—
> This steel ne'er its hoard shall replenish,
>   But by deeds that are worthy the brave!

In the second stanza he claims that he has left Scotland to seek better fortune, and at the end of both stanzas we hear a Scots tune in the orchestra:

Example 13-1

"And your name?" the King asks. "Is Quentin Durward," he replies. When the King offers to reward him, he replies that what he has done "claims not regard" and that he will "ask no guerdon,—no reward!" The King then asks him to drink a cup of wine with him, and together they sing a drinking duet. In the middle of it Tristran re-enters: "Ah! joy, it is the—" "Hush!—Silence & obey!" the King quickly and quietly orders him.

"My duty understood, promptly, I obey!" The King and Quentin then conclude their duet and leave the stage. When the hunters return, Tristran informs them that the King is safe, and the scene closes with a reprise of the opening chorus. (In the opera the scene of the boar hunt *precedes* the scenes in the inn and at court; thus Quentin does not realize whom he has saved. The idea of a party of hunters searching for a missing king brings immediately to mind the opening scene of *La Donna del Lago;* see Chapter 2.)

The second scene takes place outside the inn and is based mainly on chapters iii-v. When the curtain rises, we see the King and Quentin seated at a table laden with refreshments. Presently the King sings his main solo of the opera—"They call me here,/ They call me there,/ Maître Pierre!"—a piece which the above-quoted reviewer considered "spirited, bold, and ambitiously, although not always clearly, instrumented." Most of the ensuing duologue follows loosely the parallel material in the novel. When Quentin asks Maître Pierre why he is not eating, he replies that he is doing penance. Maître Pierre then asks Quentin the name of his uncle, and Quentin tells him. Maître Pierre says he can well imagine that Quentin would like to be in the same service with his uncle, but Quentin is hesitant about serving the French King and refers to the "acorns" on the King's oak trees (that is, the corpses of men who have been hanged). Maître Pierre tells him to have no fear of such things. He says furthermore that he has "some little interest" at court and might be able to help Quentin out. He offers to convey a message from him to his uncle. At this point "Jacqueline" enters, *"with cup and salver."* "How now, Jacqueline!—Did I not desire that Dame Perette should bring what I wanted?" asks Maître Pierre sternly, in words drawn verbatim from the novel. Greatly agitated she replies that her mother (rather than kinswoman) is ill. We now have a trio—Jacqueline imploring Maître Pierre not to chide her, Quentin requesting him not to chide her, and Maître Pierre promising that he will *not* chide her. Both Jacqueline and Quentin sing of the strange feelings that have come over them, and the King observes what is going on. At the conclusion of the trio Jacqueline exits. "A lovely girl to be the servant at an auberge," says Maître Pierre, as in the novel. He gives Quentin a cup and instructs him to remain where he is until he sees, or hears of, his kinsman. "No reply,—do as you are commanded," he says as he leaves the stage. Quentin learns *after Maître Pierre's departure* (a slight departure from the novel) that the cup contains a purse of gold. As in the novel, he asks innkeeper Martin who Maître Pierre and the "young maiden" really are, but Martin is evasive in answering him. When Martin has left the stage, Jacqueline, with a lute, appears on the balcony. She and Quentin sing the duet "Ye skies of azure!"—this rather than the song about County Guy, which Scott's Jacqueline warbles at this point in the story. "Faded!—Gone!—" Quentin exclaims after she has departed. "It is a phantom which eludes my every step, and every glance!—Yet, she inhabits this old hostelrie, and cannot pass these walls without observation!—I'll penetrate its inmost chamber, but, I'll cast myself at her feet, and—" (here Quentin's words are completely the creation of the librettist). Before he can finish his train of thought, Balafré enters.

As in the novel, chapter v, Quentin does not immediately recognize his uncle, but unlike what we have in the novel, the operatic Balafré announces to Quentin that Maître Pierre has procured for him a commission in the Scottish Archers. (In the novel Quentin was forced into becoming an archer during the course of events that arose from his having cut down the gypsy Zamet Maugrabin, who had just been hanged, in an attempt to save his life.) Again Quentin expresses wonder as to who Maître Pierre really is. Balafré's fellow archers now enter and heartily welcome Quentin into their select group: "Frae the land o' heath and heather,/ Welcome, welcome, bonny Scot!" etc. (In the novel the setting of Quentin's "enrolment" is the Castle of Plessis-les-Tours rather than the hostelry. Scott tells us that the archers sang old Scottish songs, but he does not give us the words.) In the remainder of the scene Fitzball alters the original story with the intention of providing Laurent a text for a musical finale. Jacqueline re-enters.

QUENTIN: Ah! 'tis she!—what sylph-like beauty,
              In that form trans[c]endant beams!—
              Radiant loveliness, surpassing
              All my heart's enchanting dreams!
JACQUELINE: Yes, 'tis he!—what manly beauty
              In his look transcendant beams!—
              Other forms, all—all surpassing!
              Like the image of my dreams!

The King, at the lattice and unobserved by the others, sings,

Yes, they meet,—both,—both enchanted!
   From this land she must depart;—
As her champion he'll prove trusty,
   Prompted by a lover's heart!

(In the next act we learn why Jacqueline must leave: the King has noticed the Duke of Orleans' interest in her and is afraid that this might adversely affect his plans to have him marry Princess Joan. In the novel Louis' motives are much more complicated.) The archers then join the ensemble in chorus:

Fill with wine the sparkling goblet,—
   Quaff around 'ere we depart,—
Here's a toast to bonny Scotland!
   Hand to hand, and heart to heart!

Quentin and Jacqueline are obviously in love, but duty demands that he leave her and go with the archers to the castle.

The second act begins in a gallery of the castle, where a large number of ladies and gentlemen have assembled to greet Princess Joan on this, her "natal day." Balafré explains to Quentin that Joan is affianced to the Duke of Orleans, but not yet wed, and " 'tis murmured that Orleans loveth another." He breaks off his remarks as the King, the Duke, Cardinal Balue, and a group of courtiers enter. Louis expresses to the Cardinal his concern about Orleans' apathy toward Joan. The Cardinal advises him to send Isabel of Croye back to the Duke of Burgundy; he says that from the day she arrived at court he has noticed "the increased coldness of the Duke of Orleans toward Princess Joan." Louis determines rather to send her "to her worthy and near relative, the good Bourbon of Liège." When asked by the Cardinal if he knows about the insurrection there, Louis replies that he has heard it has subsided. Thither she will be sent, and Quentin Durward will protect her along the road. (There is no suggestion of villainy on the part of the King.) When the King calls Quentin to come forward, Quentin discovers to his great surprise that Maître Pierre and the King are one and the same. The King promises to give him an important assignment soon. At this point Joan and Isabel, accompanied by a group of ladies, enter.

CHORUS:	Hail beauteous Joan—etc.
QUENTIN:	What dream is this? 'Tis she! yes she!
ISABEL:	Again we meet—'Tis he—yes he!
KING:	If one he loves, 'tis she—yes she.
ORLEANS:	How beautiful! Ah me—ah me—
CARDINAL:	Your Majesty must see—must see.
JOAN:	Sweet benisons for me—for me.

After Joan has been duly greeted, everyone leaves the stage except the King and Quentin. Louis instructs him to keep watch in the gallery and to allow no one except the ladies to enter. "Farewell," he then says. "Be wary, and thou hast a friend"—words lifted verbatim from the novel. Left alone on stage Quentin sings a "Cavatina and Aria" in which he meditates on the highborn lady with whom he has fallen in love. (In the novel he meditates on the meeting of the King, Cardinal Balue, and Crèvecœur which he has just witnessed; this has been omitted from the opera.) Joan, Isabel, and the ladies re-enter, and in the trio that follows, Joan, Isabel, and Quentin all sing of "unrequited love." Afterwards Joan tells Isabel not to congratulate her on her approaching nuptials, for as much as she loves Orleans, he loves not her. "Sooner than become his bride," she continues, "and a stranger to his heart, the cloister and the veil shall be Joan's welcome refuge." She then sings her ballad, "The merry dance is not for me," which the above-quoted reviewer described as "graceful and characteristic, and treated in the orchestra with much taste and ingenuity." Isabel declares that she will go with Joan to the cloister, inasmuch as she "also loveth unloved." When Joan asks her who "this sudden object of [her] passion" might be, she replies, "A stranger and unknown." Hearing music from *without,* Joan exits. "Gentle cousin," Isabel muses, "—too stern Orleans—if thou kneelest not at *her* pure shrine, at whose feet can we look to behold thee?" (There is no hint of Joan's deformity.) Suddenly Orleans appears, saying, "At thine, beautiful Isabel," in answer to her rhetorical question. Next, in an aria, Isabel tells Orleans that she disdains him; that she would rather perish beneath "galling chains" than give him one jot of encouragement. Upon concluding her aria, she withdraws. Quentin levels his arquebuss and prevents Orleans from following after her. The King then appears and praises Quentin for having faithfully performed his duty. (In the novel he is displeased that Quentin has allowed Orleans to intrude upon the presence of the females.) He now informs Quentin that he will have the task of conducting Isabel safely to her uncle, the Governor of Liège. Orleans is upset that she must depart. Isabel, Joan, the Cardinal, Balafré, ladies, and archers now re-enter for the final "concerted piece," in which all bid farewell to Isabel.—This scene is based loosely on Quentin's first day at court, chapter viii, his watch over the ladies in the Hall of Roland, chapter xi, and other material of the novel. The main alterations are as follows: (a) there is no Lady Hameline; (b) there is no Crèvecœur; (c) the position of Joan is enhanced; (d) there is no suggestion of villainy in the character of the King, who does not plan to have Isabel fall into the hands of William de la Marck; (e) Isabel is given a public farewell—very unlike what we have in the novel, where she leaves in the utmost secrecy.

The second scene takes place before the gates of Liège, with the hall of justice at the right-hand side of the stage. It is a day of festival. Citizens enter in procession and sing in praise of their Governor, who himself soon enters, attended by Pavilleon, ministers, and pages. When the procession has entered the hall of justice, Pavilleon beckons to several of his fellow conspirators, who are all agreed that the Governor must be overthrown. Pavilleon begins reading to them a secret communication from Tristran that has just arrived: " 'I shall send to you with fresh assurances, a trusty minister, under the assumed habit of a Scottish archer. Confide in him and rely on the aid of France.' " He stops when the Governor re-enters along with the procession, but the Governor notices that something mysterious is going on and orders the citizens to disperse. (In the novel there is no such confrontation between the Bishop and the citizens of Liège. Scott suggests that Louis is secretly encouraging the Liègeois to revolt, but there is no specific message from either Louis or Tristan l'Hermite like the one which the operatic Pavilleon receives.) He is then informed by an esquire that "a messenger from his Majesty the King of France, a noble Scottish archer, craves admittance to deliver into [his] safe custody, the Countess of Croye." The Governor welcomes his niece and her "gallant escort." As he leads her off to the palace, Quentin starts to follow in their footsteps, but he is detained by the conspirators, who see in him the secret agent of Tristran's letter. (In the novel, chapter xix, the mere presence of a Scottish archer makes the burghers jump to the conclusion that he has been sent by King Louis as a sign of his interest in the Liègeois and his willingness to send them aid in their struggle against the Bishop.) When Quentin sees the communication from Tristran, he does not know how to respond. Before he joins the others to go to the palace, Pavilleon gives him a document that will give him the details of the plans for insurrection. The scene ends in a brief choral ensemble ("Yes—yes—oppression's reign is past").

We move now to *"an antique Apartment in the Castle—opening at the back by a vestibule."* This final scene of the act is based loosely on Scott's account of the storming and sack of Schonwaldt, chapters xx-xxi. First, Isabel, alone on stage, sings a ballad ("Yes—mem'ry returns to the days of my childhood/When free thro' the halls of my father I stray'd," etc.), after which the Governor enters in the company of a large group of ladies and gentlemen. They all extend cordial welcome to Isabel. Suddenly Quentin rushes in and informs the Governor of the treason that is brewing: "In this habit, mistaken for some traitor—conspirators have unguardedly betrayed to me a plot against your government and your life—Here it is, sir—Read, read—." The finale begins as the Governor reads aloud the treacherous plans outlined in Pavilleon's document. All present vow not to forsake him in his approaching hour of need. The hour soon arrives. Musquetry is heard in the distance. The Governor, Quentin, and many others rush off to arm themselves, while those left on stage sing a prayer ("Powers of pity, hear, oh hear us"). *"Another discharge of musquetry—People appear on the tops of houses, etc. etc. hurling missiles—others contending from below—clashing of swords—musquetry, etc. etc."* The rebels sing, "Down with the tyrant, down!" In a few moments the Governor, mortally wounded, re-enters, *"supported by Quentin and surrounded by Pavilleon—William de la Marck—soldiers."* The ladies implore the assaulters to spare their Governor. "Plead not for me," he sings, "—'twere better die/Than live thus hemm'd in treachery." He expires; and all the adherents to his cause express their awe in a choral ensemble, after which his corpse is carried out. The music *"becomes wild and hurried"* as William de la Marck and his soldiers *"seize the goblets and drink with fierce excitement"*:

Up with the banner and fill fill the bowl—
    To liberty—shout—pass the wine cup around—
The right of the Burgher, who—who shall control—
    Liberty—Liberty echo around.

"Between the pauses of this violent chorus the sacred swell of the prayer is heard. The Soldiers—De la Marck—Pavilleon—People, etc.—form a grand Tableau—waving of Banners–etc. etc." The curtain falls.—The most striking departures from the novel are: (a) the Governor is mortally wounded in combat rather than brutally executed; (b) Pavilleon is depicted both here and in

the preceding scene as something of a villain; (c) there is no attempt on Quentin's part to get Isabel out of the castle after it has fallen to the insurgents.

The first scene of the third act is a square in front of the Duke of Burgundy's palace. The Burgundians sing a chorus of welcome to King Louis, who comes on stage accompanied by the Duke and an entourage of nobles. After the Duke also has welcomed Louis, we have a ballet. Afterwards the Duke of Orleans (rather than Scott's Crèvecœur) enters hastily and informs Burgundy of the insurrection of Liège and the inhuman *murder* of the Governor. (This is a slip in the libretto. As we have just seen, the Governor dies presumably of wounds received in combat.) Orleans says that his information comes "from one who fled for life, and, who affirms, on oath, that an Archer of the King of France's Scottish Guard, was present when the murder was committed." (In the novel, chapter xxvii, Crèvecœur tells Burgundy that he has gotten his information from an Archer (Quentin) who was present.) "Ah!" exclaims Burgundy, "—let no stranger stir from this hall!" Louis replies, "These news, fair cousin, have disturb'd thy reason" (Scott: "These news, fair cousin, have staggered your reason"). In the ensuing "concerted piece" Burgundy accuses Louis of turning the Liègeois away from him, their rightful lord. Louis reminds him that as a vassal of France his present conduct is quite unbecoming. When Burgundy declares that he will make the false King a captive "from this hour," the French soldiers who have accompanied Louis rush to his support. Burgundy then calls on the Burgundians to put down the treacherous guest. The King, as in the novel, urges both groups to suppress their rage. Next, in a slight departure from the novel, he addresses the enraged Duke:

> This is thy hall, 'tis true I am thy guest,
> And that I am thy King thou'lt not disown,
> Deem'st thou one murder can another drown!
> Here, on thy hearth, strike this defenceless breast!
> That future time may tell Burgundian pride,
> How *nobly* thou did'st strike—how calmly Louis died.

Louis' words produce the desired effect. Burgundy becomes reasonable, and he too urges both sides to sheathe their swords. He tells Louis that he can prove he is true by joining forces with the Burgundians and marching toward Liège to put down the rebels. The scene closes with a battle duet for Louis and Burgundy, who are now reconciled. (The action of the novel has been telescoped. Scott's Burgundy does not relent in his negative attitude toward Louis until later, during the events following the cross-examination of William de la Marck's phony herald, Hayraddin Maugrabin; see chapter xxxiii.)

The second scene takes place outside a convent deep in the forest. Quentin and Isabel enter, disguised as peasants, and sing a duet. He has led her safely to her destination, the convent, where she is determined to spend the rest of her days. Near the end of their duet they hear the sound of an organ from *within:*

QUENTIN: They hear us!—and, alas!—they come
        To lead thee to yon living tomb!—
        Oh, lady!—if thou could'st but tell,
        The anguish of this last farewell!
ISABEL: I hear the steps of saintly feet!—
        Soon he and I no more can meet!—
        Ah!—would it were my fun'ral knell,
        Than, thus, to him to say farewell!

Now an abbess, Princess Joan enters, followed by a group of nuns, and welcomes Isabel into the convent. When the doors have been closed, Quentin expresses his anguish in the cavatina "Alone, am I in sorrow." (There is no material comparable to this in the novel, but several times Scott's Isabelle says that she wishes to go into a convent to escape the vexations of the world. Later she actually does find sanctuary in an Ursuline convent, where Quentin talks with her in a private interview.) At this point Tristran enters, in the habit of a Scottish archer; he is accompanied by Pavilleon and several guards. "They mistook thee, for me," he tells Quentin, "there, in Liège,—give me back the paper they to thee confided." When Quentin refuses to do so, the guards drag him to an oak tree and prepare themselves to shoot him, but in the nick of time the King, Burgundy, and a party of soldiers enter. Quentin is saved. The King arrests Tristran for treachery and orders him to be guarded until the Liègeois are chastised—"then cometh his share of the recompense." (This incident is not in the novel. It is suggested by Quentin's bare escape from death by hanging, ch. vi, in the aftermath of Tristan's having caught him trying to save the life of the gypsy Zamet Maugrabin, who had just been hanged. He is rescued just in time by Scottish archers, rather than by the King.) Burgundy now orders Isabel to be brought forth from the convent. In the brief duologue that follows, she tells him that she could never have loved the husband he had chosen for her. "Take all my lands," she says, "and let me die in this nunnery." Burgundy, however, has other plans for her. He announces that whoever brings him the head of William de la Marck shall have her for a bride (a motif from chapter xxxv). "Oh, mercy!—" she exclaims. "Not I,—in,—and let her be with bridal veil adorned, for, as this day yon assassin shall have paid the forfeit of my kinsman's murder, so, be the conqueror whoe'er he may, Isabelle of Croye, with all her rich inheritance, shall him requite." (There is no adorning of the Countess in bridal array in the novel, inasmuch as Scott's Burgundy does not absolutely insist on her marrying the champion: "He that . . . brings us the head of the Wild Boar of Ardennes, shall claim her hand of us; and if she denies his right, we can at least grant him her fiefs, leaving to his generosity to allow her what means he will to retire into a convent.") The scene closes in a large ensemble (Isabel, Joan, Quentin, the King, Burgundy, and soldiers).

The last scene takes place at the ramparts of Liège and is based very loosely on the last two chapters of the novel. The Burgundian and French soldiers, in a brief choral ensemble, invoke the Liègeois to surrender. Quentin then leads a party of Scottish archers into the fray. While the battle is raging, women, children, and old men appear from a breach in the wall and kneel in prayer ("Angel of peace, descend, and hear us!"). *"The walls are blown up,—and De la Marck is seen beneath the sword of Quentin, dead."* (In the novel Quentin temporarily leaves the scene of his mortal combat with De la Marck in order to save Pavillon's daughter Trudchen from would-be rapists. While he is away, Balafré finishes the Wild Boar off, cuts off his head, and is thus technically eligible for the prize, which he magnanimously defers to Quentin.) The King, Burgundy, and soldiers enter. The city has fallen. Quentin comes forth, kneels before Burgundy, and presents him with *"the casque & sword"* of William de la Marck. "Rise, gallant Scot!" Burgundy says, "—the guerdon's yours,—the lady comes!" (Scott's heroine is not present at Liège at this time.) Isabel enters, dressed as a bride and accompanied by nuns. She readily accepts Quentin as her husband-to-be. The opera ends with the chorus singing "Victoria!" and Isabel singing of her ecstasy.

So far as I know, Laurent's *Quentin Durward* has never been revived. The reviewer in *The Musical World* (see fn. 1) found the songs and ballads attractive, but not the concerted pieces and finales (which I have not seen), because in them the composer's immaturity and inexperience were embarrassingly manifest. The musical numbers that I was able to examine are, for the most part, not impressive.

Gevaert's *Quentin Durward*

Quentin Durward, with words by Eugène Cormon and Michel Carré and music by the Belgian composer François Auguste Gevaert,[6] was first performed on 25 March 1858 in Paris, at the Opéra-Comique. It was well received. Subsequent productions in French took place in Brussels (5 October 1858), Ghent (17 December 1858), Antwerp (25 December 1859), Geneva (14 February 1890), and The Hague (December 1891). It was done in Swedish in Stockholm (17 December 1865) and in German in Weimar (20 May 1888). The opera proved very successful in Belgium. It was last revived on 13 October 1930, in Brussels. The cast of characters includes Louis XI (sung at the première by Couderc), Crèvecœur (sung by Faure), Quentin Durward (Jourdan), Lesly le Balafré (Barrière), Tristan l'Ermite (Beckers), Pavillon (Prilleux), the Maugrabin—Scott's Hayraddin Maugrabin (Cabel), Landry—Scott's unnamed proprietor of the Fleur-de-Lys inn (Pallianti), Damien (Coutan), Isabelle de Croye (Mme

Boulard), the Comtesse de Hameline (Mme Révilly), and Rispah (Mme Bélia).[7] Damien, a Burgundian soldier, is not to be found in the novel. The gypsy woman Rispah owes only her name to Scott's Rispah *alias* Marthon. The librettists have handled their subject matter very freely, as we have seen is the case with most opéras comiques deriving from Waverley Novels.[8]

The overture contains several melodies that are heard later in the opera. When the curtain rises, we are at the entrance to the village of Plessis. To the left, there is an "auberge"; to the right, a "pavillon de chasse"; and in the distance, partly visible, the château. *Scènes* i-ii: The first musical number begins with Rispah and a chorus of gypsies making preparations for departure, now that it is daybreak. When the Maugrabin arrives on the scene, the gypsies eagerly ask him to tell what he has been about. He gives them his flask, urging them to drink and not ask questions. As they sing a drinking song, he tells Rispah privately something about the secret mission in which he has been engaged. The number concludes with Rispah and the chorus singing good-naturedly about their relentless persecutor, Tristan l'Ermite ("Messire Tristan/Est un bon ermite,/En tout il imite/Son maître Satan!"). Seeing Tristan approaching, they hastily disperse in all directions. *Scène* iii: In amusing one-word stichomythia Tristan and Landry speak of the two ladies who are concealed in the pavillon de chasse. In addition, Tristan manages to elicit from Landry the information that a stranger from Liège is staying in the auberge. *Scène* iv: When the stranger appears, Tristan realizes at once from his manner that he is a merchant. He has little difficulty getting him to talk about his secret mission, and he offers to take him to the château. (The stranger is none other than Pavillon, the syndic of Liège. Unlike his original, whom we see only in Liège, he turns up already, at this very early point in the story. He plays a larger role than does Scott's Pavillon, and he has been changed by the librettists into an out-and-out comic figure.) *Scène* v: As Quentin makes his first entrance, we hear a motiv that we have already heard in the overture:

Example 13-2

Alone on stage, he sings a recitative and aria. He has just arrived in France from Scotland. After the aria, as he lies down on a bench to sleep, he hears the sound of a lute from the pavillon de chasse and the voice of a young lady singing: "Vole, oiselet, vole au ciel bleu," etc. (this rather than Scott's song about County Guy). When the singing ceases, he goes to sleep. *Scène*

vi: The King, disguised as Maître Pierre, enters together with Tristan l'Ermite. Tristan informs him of the arrival of Pavillon, who has indicated that the Liègeois will rise up against their Bishop just as soon as they have received a signal from France. Suddenly they come upon Quentin sleeping. In the ensuing trio Quentin expresses his vexation with Tristan's rudeness in awakening him ("Chien discourtois," etc.), and Tristan is angered; Maître Pierre tries to pacify both of them. (The situation derives from Quentin's cross words with Tristan in chapter ii, after his difficulty in crossing the ford: "Discourteous dog! why did you not answer when I called to know if the passage was fit to be attempted?") In the spoken dialogue following the trio, Quentin tells Maître Pierre that he looks like a dealer in grain and Tristan resembles rather a dealer in beef, or a butcher—more or less as in the novel. When Maître Pierre asks the young man his name, the dialogue follows Scott closely:

QUENTIN: Quand on m'interroge poliment, je réponds de même: je me nomme Quentin Durward!..
LE ROI: Est-ce un nom de gentilhomme?
QUENTIN: Depuis quinze générations!
LE ROI: Écossais dans l'âme! beaucoup de sang, beaucoup d'orgueil, et grande pénurie de ducats... du moins je le suppose.

At Maître Pierre's request, Tristan goes offstage to tell Landry to set a table for two.

Scènes vii-viii: In spoken dialogue Maître Pierre invites Quentin to partake of his "repas du matin." As their conversation progresses, Quentin, as in the novel, expresses uneasiness about serving under King Louis. When Landry appears, Maître Pierre asks him to have his *niece* (i.e. Isabelle) bring them wine. (In the novel he requests for Dame Perette (i.e. Lady Hameline) and is piqued when Jacqueline (Isabelle) comes instead.) Maître Pierre then asks his guest whether or not he would serve under Guillaume de Lamarck, and Quentin replies that he would not (as in the novel). When he is asked whether he would serve under Charles of Burgundy, he replies that he has little respect for a prince who mistreats women. (In the novel service under the banner of the Duke of Burgundy is out of the question for him, inasmuch as he had recently beaten one of the Duke's foresters, a "rascally schelm," for having shot the falcon he had brought with him from Scotland.) Quentin adds that he has just saved two ladies from Burgundian soldiers—a departure from the novel. The ladies disappeared, but not before the younger one had expressed her gratitude, as he relates to Maître Pierre in the short romance that begins the fourth musical number. (The piece is charming, especially the refrain: "Hélas! qu'elle était belle!") When Jacqueline enters, we have a trio. Quentin recognizes her immediately as the unknown beauty whom he rescued (in the novel he has never before seen her), and Maître Pierre senses their romantic interest in one another. Maître Pierre's ensuing drinking song has special meaning for Jacqueline, for it concerns Burgundians and their forceful actions when they are intoxicated. *Scène* ix: Jacqueline exits as Tristan re-enters. He gives Maître Pierre the secret message that the Maugrabin has brought. When Quentin asks why people are assembling, Maître Pierre tells him that it is "à l'occasion du mariage de Jeanne de France, la fille bien-aimée du roi." (In the novel Louis' not-so-beloved daughter Joan is betrothed to the Duke of Orleans, but their marriage does not materialize.) Quentin then asks about his uncle, Lesly le Balafré. Maître Pierre replies that he knows him slightly. "Et si, comme lui, vous vous décidez à chercher fortune dans ce pays, peut-être pourrai-je vous être utile" (Scott: "And, hark in your ear, I myself have some little interest, and might be of some use to you"; chapter iv). When Quentin asks his benefactor who he is, he replies, as in the novel, that men call him Maître Pierre. (Unlike Laurent, Gevaert does not use the King's pretended identity as the occasion for an aria.) *Scène* x: Quentin having departed, the King informs Tristan that Guillaume de Lamarck, according to the secret message, has sworn allegiance to France. He then mentions to Tristan (rather than to Oliver le Dain) the idea of having Guillaume marry Isabelle.

Scène xi: In the duet "Sonne, sonne" Rispah and the Maugrabin sing of their happiness in receiving money from Tristan. They realize the grave risk they run in being hanged by him, but "qu'importe" so long as he pays well. *Scènes* xii–xiii: Pavillon joins the two gypsies, whose remarks about hanging have frightened him. He expresses his horror at having recently seen hanging from a tree the corpse of a man dressed in a jacket very like his own. (This motif derives from Quentin's observation to Maître Pierre, chapter iii, about "acorns" on the King's trees: "—and on that oak hangs a man in a grey jerkin, such as this which I wear.") Rispah and the Maugrabin then warn him of the man-traps in the vicinity of the château (suggested by Maître Pierre's remarks to Quentin at the end of chapter ii). They warn him also of dangers inside the château. He becomes more and more frightened. At this point Tristan enters, accompanied by Petit-André and Trois-Echelles, and informs Pavillon that the King wants to see him at once in the château. Fearful of what might befall him, Pavillon hesitates—but Tristan insists. (In both *scènes* the librettists present Pavillon's fear in humorous fashion; their conception of him probably owes something to Scribe and Boieldieu's Dikson, the cowardly tenant to the counts of Avenel, in *La Dame Blanche*.) *Scènes* xiv–xvi: A joyful figure in the orchestra accompanies the peasants' chorus which begins the finale:

Example 13-3

Presently Rispah, the Maugrabin, and other gypsies arrive on the scene. As Scottish archers march in, we hear Scottish folk music in the orchestra:

Example 13-4

The archers wonder where Lesly is, and soon he appears, bringing with him Quentin Durward. All present drink a toast to "antique Calédonie." Tristan now ushers Isabelle and Hameline out from the pavillon and introduces them as noble guests of the château. Quentin recognizes one of the ladies as Jacqueline, but now evidently a person of great importance. After quietly urging him to forget her, she disappears behind a cluster of trees. "L'oublier!.." he exclaims aside, "moi!.. jamais!.." and then, addressing himself to the archers: "Je me décide, et dès demain,/Amis, je veux être des vôtres!" [9] (His idea in joining them is to be near Isabelle; in the novel, chapter vi, his decision is forced upon him when he is about to be hanged.) The act concludes in a large ensemble made up of virtually everyone on stage. We hear again the joyful music of Example 13–3. (There is hardly a *scène* in the entire first act that has an exact parallel in Scott. As I have already observed, the librettists have handled their source *ad libitum.* Space does not allow me to explain and discuss at length all the multitudinous divergences, but from my plot-summary they should be reasonably obvious to anyone reasonably familiar with the novel.)

Act II takes place in a large hall inside the château. *Scene* i: Isabelle, alone on stage, sings a recitative and coloratura aria in which she expresses her happiness at having found succor in France. *Scènes* ii–iii: Hameline enters, followed by Rispah. She complains in spoken dialogue of how she and Isabelle have been treated (cf. her remarks to Princess Joan, chapter xi). Isabelle, however, does not share her feelings, for she is genuinely grateful to Louis and joyful that she has escaped the odious marriage to Campo-Basso which Charles of Burgundy had designed for her. Hameline says that Crèvecœur would have aided Isabelle with force, had he not been involved in a war at the other end of Flanders when the matter came up (a motif not in the novel). When Isabelle remarks that she would not want any man to sacrifice his life for her, Hameline retorts that such is all part of the game in chivalric love. (In the novel this idea comes out in conversation during the course of the journey to Liège, chapter xiv.) She confides to Isabelle that she thinks one of the Scottish archers (meaning Quentin) is romantically attracted to her. As Isabelle wishes her good luck, we hear *pianissimo* in the orchestra the march that we heard in the finale to Act I (see Example 13-4). At this point Lesly and Quentin enter. Rispah notices immediately that something is going on between Quentin and Isabelle. Presently Lesly launches into a song about former members of the stalwart Durward family—they are all descended from King Canute—while Isabelle, Hameline, Rispah, and Quentin join him in the refrain: "Ah! c'était le bon temps,/ Pour les héros, pour les amants!" (The idea of the piece owes a little to Lesly's conversation with Quentin about family matters in chapter v.) When Lesly remarks in the ensuing spoken dialogue that Quentin must marry a rich heiress, Quentin is understandably embarrassed. (The *scène* has no exact parallel in the novel.)

The ninth musical number is a "morceau d'ensemble." During the course of the brief orchestral introduction, Rispah cannot help but notice the gallantry that Quentin displays toward Isabelle, and she is now firmly convinced that they love one another. *Scènes* iv–v: The entire court assembles, the chorus singing of the royal marriage that is about to take place. When the King appears, Quentin realizes for the first time the true identity of the man whom he had known as Maître Pierre (as in the novel, chapter viii). Presently Tristan (rather than Scott's Dunois) announces that Charles of Burgundy's envoy, the Comte de Crèvecœur, demands an audience with the King. In the ensuing ensemble Isabelle, Hameline, Quentin, the King, and the chorus express wonder at what Crèvecœur's message might be. As in the novel, Crèvecœur enters with due ceremony and states his master's various complaints, including the demand that Isabelle be sent home forthwith. (In the novel Isabelle is not present on this occasion.) Hearing organ music from the adjoining chapel, the King excuses himself to attend his daughter's wedding—an interesting departure from the novel. Crèvecœur is a bit piqued, but he has no choice but to wait patiently until the King's return. The number ends with a reprise of the opening choral ensemble. (In the novel Crèvecœur does not arrive in the midst of marriage festivities. The alteration gives the composer additional possibilities for colorful music; it also leads to the interesting breaking-up of Scott's Crèvecœur-scene into two parts, separated by the material that comprises *scènes* vi–xiii.)

Scène vi: Alone on stage, Crèvecœur voices in a spoken soliloquy his suspicion of Louis. Then he sings a romance ("Elle était la") in which he expresses his love for Isabelle, whom he has just beheld in Louis' presence. He thinks that it is now time for him to reveal to her his feelings. (In the novel the Duke of Orleans, rather than Crèvecœur, is in love with Isabelle. He appears among the dramatis personae in the operas by Laurent and Maclean, but not in the opera now under consideration. Cormon and Carré have transferred to their Crèvecœur the function that Orleans fulfills in Scott as Quentin's rival for Isabelle's affection.) *Scène* vii: Crèvecœur warns the ever-fearful Pavillon that the Burgundians might hang him, should he fall into their hands. *Scène* viii: When Crèvecœur exits, Tristan enters to inform Pavillon that the King desires to see him in a private interview. He therewith pushes him through a secret door. Rispah then appears and tells Tristan that the young archer loves the young lady, but that the young lady has just written a message to Crèvecœur. *Scène* ix: In an elaborate duet Isabelle asks Crèvecœur for his help, imploring him not to have her sent back to Burgundy. Moved by her entreaty, he agrees to help her and then confesses his love for her. "O ciel!" she exclaims. Crèvecœur is furious when he realizes that there is a rival. Unhappy Isabelle expresses the desire to live out the rest of her life in a convent. Crèvecœur swears *à part* to have vengeance on the rival as soon as he discovers who he is. He exits, as Isabelle sinks down into a chair and weeps. *Scènes* x–xii: The King raises a drapery and appears on the scene, together with Tristan. He quietly tells Tristan that neither Crèvecœur nor the convent is exactly what he has in mind for Isabelle. He then sends him away to fetch Quentin. He admits to Isabelle that he was hiding behind the arras and overheard her entire duet with Crèvecœur. He suggests that she seek protection from the Bishop of Liège. He says that Quentin Durward will be empowered to protect her en route and that Pavillon will go along with them. When Quentin enters, the King urges her to decide quickly between "Crèvecœur ou le couvent, Liège ou Péronne." At this moment Tristan re-enters and informs the King that everything is prepared for the remainder of the wedding festivities.

Scènes xiii–xiv: The chorus sings of the happiness of the occasion, as we hear in the orchestra a melody that appeared first in the overture:

Example 13-5

The King then turns to Quentin and asks him to sing a *lai* of love from his fatherland. He obliges by singing a *ballade* about a faithful servant who gladly loses his life in the service of his beloved queen. This is certainly one of the finest pieces in an opera that has excellent music throughout. At the beginning of the melody to which the queen's words are set—a melody that we have already heard in the overture—there is an effective change from A minor to A major:

Example 13-6

The situation described in the *ballade* and the sentiment expressed mirror to some extent Quentin's relationship with Isabelle. At the entrance of Crèvecœur we hear in the orchestra the restless motiv with which the overture began. Crèvecœur loses no time in presenting his master's demand that Isabelle immediately quit the court of France and return to Burgundy. When the King honors Isabelle's fervent desire to remain, Crèvecœur, in behalf of his liege lord Charles of Burgundy, formally denounces him before the entire assembled court. His words follow Scott's Crèvecœur's memorable speech of chapter viii, but in somewhat condensed form. The words are sung in a monotone that occasionally changes in pitch, while in the accompaniment there is an ostinato pattern that becomes increasingly suspenseful. At the conclusion of the denunciation Crèvecœur throws down his gauntlet, as in the novel. Quentin rushes forth and picks it up, Crèvecœur remarking *aside,* "C'est lui qu'elle aime!" (A departure from the novel. Scott's King Louis instructs Cardinal Balue to pick up the gauntlet and go after Crèvecœur in an effort to pacify him.) The King's followers indignantly sing "Montjoie et Saint-Denis,"[10] while Crèvecœur and his Burgundian followers sing "En guerre, o roi Louis!" (In the novel most of Crèvecœur's followers do not take part in this affair; they wait outside in the antechamber and in the courtyard. In the opera the confrontation between the two factions at this point is reminiscent of what occurs much later in Scott's narrative—namely in chapter xxviii, wherein Charles hears of the murder of the Bishop and furiously accuses house-guest Louis of having had a hand in it.) The King quells the incipient row and tells Crèvecœur that he may leave. There is a reprise of the Montjoie-En guerre ensemble as the act draws to a close. *"Crèvecœur sort par le fond avec ses chevaliers.–Isabelle se precipite aux pieds du roi.— Tableau."* (Once more be it noted that Scott's Isabelle is not present during this memorable confrontation.)

When the curtain rises on Act III, we are in a dilapidated cottage at the entrance to the suburbs of Liège. *Scène* i: Damien and a chorus of Burgundian soldiers sing a drinking song, part of which we have already heard in the overture. Presently Crèvecœur enters and sings first an *adagio cantabile* in which he expresses the idea that glory will compensate him for his lack of success in love. He then sings a drinking song ("Verse le vin"), the chorus joining him in the refrain. The complete musical number closes with a reprise of the initial drinking song. Next, in spoken dialogue, Crèvecœur informs Damien that France and Burgundy are to fight under the same standard against the common enemy. Damien informs Crèvecœur that a Scottish archer wants to see him. In the duologue that constitutes *scène* ii, Crèvecœur and Lesly fill us in on important events that have transpired between the end of Act II and the beginning of Act III—the revolt of the Liègeois, the murder of the Bishop, the captivity of the King at Peronne, and the surface reconciliation between Charles and Louis in alliance against their common enemy, Guillaume de Lamarck. Lesly tells Crèvecœur of the flight of Isabelle and

Hameline from Plessis-les-Tours and of their subsequent disappearance together with their guide, Quentin Durward. The two men almost come to blows over the question of Quentin's worthiness. *Scène* iii: Pavillon, Rispah, and the Maugrabin are brought in as captives by Burgundian soldiers. Ever the comic figure, Pavillon assures Crèvecœur that he is a staunch friend of the Burgundians and an enemy to the rogues of France. He is nonplussed when he hears that the French and the Burgundians are no longer enemies. In the ensuing quintet, composed in the style of a tarentella, Pavillon, Rispah, and the Maugrabin tell conflicting accounts of the events immediately prior to their capture. Rispah and the Maugrabin claim that they were asked by Pavillon for assistance: Pavillon claims that he, Quentin, Isabelle, and Hameline were attacked by "une horde du diable." As each tells his version of what happened, he is constantly interrupted by cries of "Il ment!" from the others. Afterwards, in a bit of spoken dialogue, Crèvecœur expresses anxiety about the safety of the ladies while Lesly expresses concern about Quentin. Rispah manages to escape; Crèvecœur and Lesly exeunt; Pavillon and the Maugrabin remain on stage, in custody. *Scène* iv: The Maugrabin tells Pavillon that the two ladies are now surely in the hands of Guillaume de Lamarck and that Quentin has undoubtedly seen his last battle. Hearing Rispah singing from *without* the song about "Messire Tristan," he takes this as a signal for him to escape, and he does so through a window. Pavillon is afraid to accompany him because of the great height of the window from the ground below; instead, he descends by way of a trapdoor into another chamber.

Scène v: Having eluded their pursuers, Quentin and Isabelle arrive on the scene. Isabelle is exhausted. When she revives they sing a love-duet, which concludes with both of them thanking God for having granted their escape. *Scène* vi: Crèvecœur surprises the lovers and informs Quentin that he is a prisoner (suggested by the events of chapter xxiv, which Scott entitles "The Surrender"). *Scène* vii: When Quentin has departed, Isabelle asks Crèvecœur whether she too is a prisoner. She insists that her flight from Plessis-les-Tours was not voluntary. When she praises Quentin, Crèvecœur becomes cynical. She then sings a *romance* in which she bitterly tells Crèvecœur to go ahead and consign her heart and soul to despair—to go ahead and put Quentin to death for having served her so faithfully. Moved by her nobility of character, Crèvecœur begins to relent. He asks her pardon and agrees to send her to a convent, and he promises to try to save Countess Hameline, who is still in the hands of the enemy. (This is the last mention of Hameline in the opera.) When Isabelle has departed, Crèvecœur sits down for a moment to think. *Scène* viii: Pavillon raises the trap-door, cautiously comes up into the room, and is surprised when he encounters Crèvecœur. He hesitatingly admits that he was in the company of Quentin and the ladies, and he extolls Quentin's courtesy and bravery. Crèvecœur now fully realizes that he cannot obtain his goal of winning Isabelle's affections through violence. He orders Quentin's release. When Pavillon hears that he is to march in the vanguard, in view of his knowledge of the town, he is of course afraid. *Scènes* ix–x: Musical No. 17 begins as a duet. When Crèvecœur tells Quentin that he is free, he replies that he has no intention of departing without Isabelle. Crèvecœur is enraged. Undaunted, Quentin brings forth Crèvecœur's gauntlet and throws it at his feet. Singing in thirds, they vow to fight each other until death. At this moment, however, Lesly enters and announces that Charles and Louis have decided to give Isabelle as bride to whoever brings in "des depouilles du traître" (a motif from chapter xxv, entitled "A Prize for Honour"). Lesly is determined to vie along with Quentin and Crèvecœur for the hand of Isabelle. The number concludes in a trio, as all three sing "Vivent Bourgogne et France,/ Et mort au Sanglier!"[11]

For the final *scène* and number the setting changes to *"une place de Liège.–Au fond, une grande et large rue en escalier."* The chorus jubilantly sings of the great victory. Presently Crèvecœur, accompanied by Quentin and Lesly, brings in the news that Guillaume de Lamarck is dead. The King assumes that Crèvecœur has won Isabelle's hand, but Crèvecœur corrects him and announces to all present that Quentin is the victor. The conquering hero enters, and Isabelle readily agrees to the match. There is a reprise of the *chœur général*, and in the final moments *"Charles le Téméraire paraît au fond suivi de ses chevaliers, portant les bannières de Bourgogne.—Louis XI s'avance à sa rencontre."* (This is Charles' first and only appearance.) The curtain falls. (The material of Scott's last two chapters has been greatly condensed. Gone, for example, as in Laurent's opera, is Quentin's bad luck in having to resign William de la Marck to Lesly when Trudchen Pavillon's predicament demands his immediate attention. Yet the final *scène* is more closely paralleled in the novel than are any of the other *scènes* of the third act.)

Gevaert's score has character. It is full of attractive, memorable melodies; its harmonic texture is fresh and interesting; and it is rhythmically alive. It has much variety, owing in part to the retention of the gypsies (who do not appear in either of the other *Quentin Durward* operas). If one misses Scott's deeply moving depiction of the last encounter between Quentin and Maugrabin (chapter xxxiv: "The Execution"), one must admit that such a scene would be out of keeping with the light approach to their material that the librettists and the composer chose to take.

Maclean's *Quentin Durward*

English conductor and composer Alick Maclean wrote the first version of his operatic *Quentin Durward* in 1892-93, when he was in his early 20's. Sheridan Ross did the libretto. The work was not produced in this form, but a complete vocal score was published in London by E. Ascherberg in

1894.[12] A second version was successfully produced much later, on 13 January 1920, at Newcastle-upon-Tyne. It was produced in London at the Lyceum (English Opera House) on 4 June 1920, with Wynn Reeves conducting. I do not know to what extent Maclean re-worked the original published version, on which my discussion is necessarily based.[13] The cast of characters gives indication in itself that a large amount of Scott's story has been retained. It includes Louis XI, the Duke of Orleans, the Duke of Burgundy, Count Crèvecœur, the Bishop of Liège, Count Dunois, Cardinal Balue, William de la Marck, Ludovic Lesly, Quentin Durward, Oliver Dain, Jacques (Scott's unnamed innkeeper of the Fleur-de-Lys), a messenger from Liège (not in the novel), Princess Joan, Isabelle, and Lady Hameline. Notable omissions include Tristan l'Hermite, Petit-André, Trois-Eschelles, Martius Galeotti, Lord Crawford, Pavillon, and, most notably, Hayraddin Maugrabin.

The opera begins with a lovely, pastoral-like tone-poem for the orchestra. When the curtain rises, we see *"a room in the Fleur-de-Lys inn. It is early morning, and the sun is streaming through a diamond-paved bay-window. A door thrown open at the back shows a path leading through rich foliage."* We see Jacques, the landlord, at his work, and in the distance we hear a chorus of peasants singing "Hie to the vineyards this bright summer day," etc. Their song becomes more and more distant until finally it fades away altogether. *"While the landlord is busying himself with the pewter mugs upon the table, a door opens behind him, and the Countess Hameline, in a peasant's disguise, stands at the threshold and calls to him."* Jacques implores her to go back to her chamber, for the King has left explicit orders that she and her companion not be observed by anyone. Bored with her confinement, Hameline complains about Louis' ungraciousness in not extending to her the hospitality she deems proper. As she withdraws, she angrily tells Jacques that she will not leave her room again "even to wait on the King." (Her displeasure with confinement and lack of attention is suggested by her remarks to Princess Joan, chapter xi, but the encounter between landlord and guest has no parallel in the novel. The added material helps explain how it happens that Isabelle waits on Maître Pierre, even though he had explicitly asked for Hameline.) No sooner has she departed than the King, disguised as Maître Pierre, and Quentin enter. Far in the distance we hear a strain of the peasants' song. "Follow me in, fair Sir," says Maître Pierre to Quentin. "I warrant me thou hast not tasted of the pride of France, of which yon peasants sing, such as shall presently stand before you." "Nay, good Sir! None know better than yourself I have but just arrived in France,/Leaving my Scottish home to seek my fortune, after the custom of my country men." As Quentin is singing, we hear in the orchestra a motiv that is to be associated with him throughout:

Example 13-7

"A gallant custom too, say I," replies Maître Pierre. "And see here! I owe thee a good breakfast/For the wetting my mistake procur'd for thee." Presently Maître Pierre sings a drinking song, which is suggested by Scott's mention in the first paragraph of chapter iv of the "exquisite *vin de Beaulne*" and by Quentin's subsequent observation that "the countenance of his entertainer, which he had at first found so unprepossessing, mended when it was seen under the influence of the *vin de Beaulne*."

The opening scene is based mainly on chapter iv ("The Déjeuner"), but it includes also some of the dialogue between Maître Pierre and Quentin of chapters ii and iii. Librettist Ross follows Scott closely as Quentin inquires about his uncle, expresses hesitation about serving under King Louis, and tells Maître Pierre his name. All the operatic dialogue is sung rather than spoken. When Jacqueline (Isabelle) enters, we hear a saccharine melody in the orchestra:

Example 13-8

(The suggestion of love is obvious. Indeed the story of the opera is mainly the story of Isabelle and Quentin's love-affair. Many other interesting aspects of the novel are either de-emphasized or omitted altogether.) As in the novel, Maître Pierre is irritated that she, rather than Dame Perette (Hameline), has come to serve him. When he makes disparaging remarks about Jacqueline and her "giddy sex," Quentin speaks up in her behalf. At this point, as in Laurent's *Quentin Durward,* we have a trio, Jacqueline expressing wonder as to what makes "this flutt'ring joy" within her breast. Afterwards Maître Pierre asks Jacqueline to withdraw. His ensuing remarks to Quentin about Jacqueline's lowly birth and his repeated inquiry regarding Quentin's birth follow Scott's dialogue of chapter iv. Just before he leaves, he gives Quentin a liberal gift of money, as in the novel. Quentin is reluctant to accept it, but he insists: "Nay, no reply, young man, but do as I have commanded" (Scott: "No reply, young man, but do what you are commanded"). When he has gone, Quentin questions the landlord about Maître Pierre and Jacqueline, but he gets no satisfactory reply. Again the words are very close to Scott's dialogue. After the landlord has departed, Quentin overhears Jacqueline singing from *within* a song about County Guy. Of the three *Quentin Durward* operas here examined, Maclean's alone retains Scott's poem. I think that Scott would have been pleased, for the song of the opera is a perfect realization of his description of it: "The words had neither so much sense, with, or fancy, as to withdraw the attention from the music, nor the music so much of art, as to drown all

feeling of the words. The one seemed fitted to the other; and if the song
had been recited without the notes, or the air played without the words,
neither would have been worth noting."[14] Immediately following the
song, Quentin gives vent to his feelings in a short aria, "Her maiden
grace," which has no parallel in the novel but is suggested by Scott's
remark that Quentin "was engaged in . . . sage reflections." The curtain
falls.

We move now to Louis' court at Plessis-les-Tours. The scene is based on
chapter viii, which is utilized in all the *Quentin Durward* operas and which
indeed is perfectly suited to operatic rendition, with its introduction of
eminent court figures and its account of Crèvecœur's dramatic entry and
denunciation of Louis. The courtiers comment on the various dignitaries
who arrive—Orleans, Dunois, Balue, Oliver. Presently Balafré and Quentin enter (who in the novel are on hand from the beginning). "See, there
you stand, Quentin," observes Balafré, "enroll'd in our honourable corps
of Bodyguard,/And serving 'neath my lance as my esquire;/If thou but
prove as faithful as thou art well-favour'd thou can'st never fail to prove
an honour to thy mother and brave sire of blessed memory." (Ross has
transferred to Balafré the words of Scott's Lord Crawford shortly after
Quentin's official enrolment as a Scottish Archer, chapter vii.) When the
King enters, Quentin is so astonished to see that he and Maître Pierre are
one and the same that he lets his weapon fall. *"The King turns and perceives
him"*: "So, my young Scot, 'tis thou!/Balafré, we hear your nephew is a
brave youth though a somewhat fiery—/We love to cherish such spirits.
Care thou well for him." (Here as elsewhere in the scene the libretto
follows Scott's dialogue rather closely, but in somewhat abridged form.)
At his point Anne of Beaujeau enters and a bit later Princess Joan, both
attended by their ladies-in-waiting. As in the novel, Louis sarcastically
refers to Joan's charms and Orleans' amorous interest in her. Just as he is
about to set forth on a hunt, Dunois interrupts him: "The Burgundian
envoy, sire, is before the castle gates,/And demands an audience." (These
and the words that follow follow Scott very closely.)

LOUIS: And will our ancient vassal prove so masterful,
          Our right dear cousin treat us thus unkindly?
          Nay then, Dunois, we must unfold the Oriflamme
              and cry "Dennis Montjoye!"
DUNOIS: Marry and Amen, my liege!
CHORUS: Amen! Amen! Vive la France! Vive la France! Dennis
              Montjoye!

Louis *"silences them by a movement of his hand,"* at the same time *"suavely"*
remarking, "But God forbid that less than necessity should make us, the
most Christian King, give cause to the effusion of good Christian blood."
He then orders Crèvecœur to be admitted.

"*Crèvecœur enters entirely armed, except his head. A page carries his helmet behind him, and a herald precedes him, bearing the letters of credence which he offers, on his knee, to the king."* We hear for the first time the Crèvecœur-motiv in the orchestra:

Example 13-9

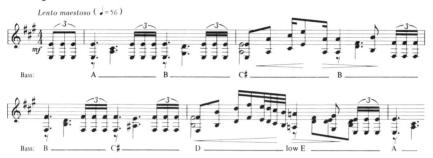

As in the novel Crèvecœur first says that his liege lord, Charles of Burgundy, requests that Louis cease meddling in his towns. Then, reading in spoken voice from a scroll, he says that Burgundy requests furthermore that Louis return the two fugitive ladies. When Louis asks "who [would] presume to say these ladies be in France," he replies that the information was disclosed to Burgundy by someone who saw both them and the king disguised as a burgess at the Fleur-de-Lys. (Who the someone was is not explained in the opera; Zamet Maugrabin and all the other gypsies are omitted from the roster.) "Yon trait'rous knave shall die the death!" exclaims Louis. "And he shall court Death's grinning face full many an hour, ere he come to his relief." (These words are borrowed from the Duke of Burgundy's threat to Quentin, during the course of Louis' trial: ". . . if you palter or double in your answers, I will have thee hung alive in an iron chain from the steeple of the market-house, where thou shalt wish for death for many an hour ere he come to relieve you.") When Louis refuses to honor Burgundy's demands, Crèvecœur denounces him in spoken voice to the accompaniment of a tremolo in the bass on C: "Hearken, Louis of Valois, King of France. I, Philip Crèvecœur of Cordès, in the name of the most puissant lord & prince Charles, Duke of Burgundy, renounce all allegience & fealty towards your crown & dignity—pronounce you false & faithless, & defy you as a prince & as a man." (The passage is much condensed from the corresponding passage in the novel, mainly through the omission of the Duke's long list of titles.) As in the novel Crèvecœur *"plucks the gauntlet off his right hand & flings it on the ground."* The angry French courtiers want to "strike him down," but Louis, forbidding any violence, allows him to depart. Then, again as in the novel (cf. Gevaert's version), Louis urges Cardinal Balue to take up the gauntlet and go after Crèvecœur. While he is gone, the orchestra plays an interlude of agitated music. He returns with a promise from Crèvecœur to stay at Plessis for the next twenty-four hours. The act concludes as the courtiers sing a cheerful, rollicking chorus in anticipation of the hunt in which they are about to engage (see chapter ix, "The Boar-Hunt").

Just before the curtain rises on Act II we hear in the orchestra a motiv which has occurred earlier and which is always associated with Oliver:

Example 13-10

The entire act takes place in Roland's Hall and is based on chapters x–xi. To begin with, *"the tapestry is seen to move,"* and Oliver cautiously conducts Quentin to the post to which he has been assigned: "By his Majesty's commands you are plac'd here, young man./And you will not be long without knowing wherefore you are summon'd./Quit not your weapon. Farewell, and keep good watch." Quentin is alone on stage. The recitative which he now sings follows his soliloquy in Scott ("Good watch! but upon whom, and against whom?" etc.), but in the ensuing aria he muses on the slaughter of his family by "that accursed race of Ogilvies" and on his own upbringing in "the convent's silent walls." (At the corresponding point in the novel he sings "ancient rude ballads." Ross makes this unobtrusive alteration in order to bring in information about Quentin's past life which, in the novel, comes out during his conversation with Balafré at the Fleur-de-Lys, chapter v.) In the final part of the aria Quentin's thoughts turn to her whose image he is unable to tear from his heart. At this point the King enters stealthily by way of a secret door, notices Quentin, approaches him unperceived, and almost succeeds in wresting his weapon from him. He readily overlooks Quentin's unattentiveness in view of the service Quentin rendered to him that very morning "in slaying that fierce boar." (Chapter xi, "The Boar-Hunt," is omitted from the opera; see the closing chorus of Act I.) He then informs Quentin that ladies will enter the hall presently and that he must hearken to what they say. Giving him a present in advance, he says, "If this gold chain should fail to bind thy tongue,/My gossip Tristan hath a necklace tight/Which never fails to cure." With an admonition for him to "be wary," he leaves the stage. (The entire episode in which Quentin guards Louis in his secret conversation with Balue and Crèvecœur has been omitted. The King's words are drawn first from the middle of chapter x, and then from chapter xi. The reference to Tristan is not effective inasmuch as he is not a character of the opera.)

The next part of the act follows the remainder of chapter xi and the beginning of chapter xii: Hameline and Isabelle discuss their lot with Princess Joan; the Duke of Orleans enters and flirts with Isabelle; Joan faints; the King re-enters and is angry with Quentin for allowing Orleans to enter the hall against his express orders. There are a few noteworthy additions, however, in the interest of good opera. The first lady whom Quentin observes is Isabelle rather than Princess Joan. Unaware of his presence she sings an aria ("Ah! my heart is weary") in which she expresses the desire to return to the "peaceful convent" where she was "gently nurtur'd." *"Overcome by his feelings Quentin approaches as if to speak to her when the doors open and the princess Joan enters in conversation with the countess Hameline. Quentin lowers his weapon to them as they pass. Isabelle goes forward to meet Hameline, & bows with dignity to Joan."* (In the novel Joan enters first, accompanied by two ladies-in-waiting; a bit later Isabelle and Hameline enter.) When Hameline makes an observation to Isabelle about yon fair young soldier's "goodly mien," Isabelle sings in an *aside*, "The same I met with in the inn./Lie still my foolish heart./What ails thee thus to beat/Whene'er thou think'st on him?" (Her amorous interest in Quentin is thus much more explicit than it is at the same point in the novel.) Ross and Maclean use Orleans' amorous interest in Isabelle as excuse for the addition of an aria:

Example 13-11

The rest of the act is based on Louis' secret conversation with Oliver in chapter xii. The King plans to allow Isabelle to fall into the hands of William de la Marck. Quentin Durward, who is to be her guard, will probably die trying to protect her, but no matter—he will have served his purpose. (One serious fault with the libretto is that this motif is completely dropped. Quentin does not learn about it from Hayraddin Maugrabin,

who is not in the opera, or indeed from anyone. We hear no more about it
later in the opera.) During the course of this duologue we hear in the
orchestra melodies and motivs which we are familiar with by now. When
Oliver, for example, suggests Orleans as a possible match for Isabelle (not
in the novel, by the way, since Scott's Oliver is well aware of Louis' plan to
marry him off to Joan), we hear strains of his love-song to Isabelle (see
Example 13-11 above). When the ladies of Croye are mentioned, we hear
the melody that we first heard at Isabelle's (Jacqueline's) entrance in Act I
(see Example 13-8). When Crèvecœur is mentioned, we hear his motiv
(see Example 13-9). One new motiv is introduced. At the point where the
King surprises Oliver by suggesting William de la Marck as a possible
match for Isabelle, we hear for the first time a loud, sinister-sounding
descending scale which, as the opera develops, becomes William's leitmotiv:

Example 13-12

Near the end of the act Louis *"places his cap which is surrounded with leaden
images, upon a small table."* He *speaks* the Latin words "Sancte Juliane, Adsis
precibus nostris! Ora, ora, pro nobis!" as *"Oliver looks on with contempt &
almost fear at his hypocrisy."* "He plays the hypocrite with Heav'n itself!"
exclaims Oliver *aside,* as the curtain falls slowly. (The King's Latin words
are drawn verbatim from the novel, chapter xii; but Oliver's reaction
departs from the novel, his final remark deriving from *Quentin's* unex-
pressed thought of chapter viii: "Dares he thus play the hypocrite with
Heaven . . . and sport with God and the Saints, as he may safely do with
men, who dare not search his nature too closely?")

The third act begins with an orchestral tone-poem. After sixteen measures the curtain rises on *"a glade in a forest near Tours."* It is night.
Presently it begins to dawn, as we hear the sounds of birds played by
various highly pitched instruments. At the end of the piece *"the sun has
risen—it is day."*[15] In the distance (and from *backstage*) we now hear a
pastoral-like quartet, made up of Isabelle, Hameline, Quentin, and Bertrand (Scott's Bertrand Guyot, a bass, not listed in the cast of characters at
the beginning of the score). Here are the opening lines:

How softly the breath of morn doth blow
Over each woodland hill.

Sweet echoes awake and linger yet
In glades so calm and still.

At the conclusion of the quartet, which is rather lengthy, *"the ladies of Croye, with their attendant, and two guards headed by Quentin, enter and dismount to rest. All the horses are led away except Isabelle's pony."* (The scene is based loosely on chapter xiv, "The Journey," and the beginning of chapter xv. Notice that there are only two guards, rather than three. Moreover, there is no Petit-André as guide. Nothing is made of the ladies' attendant, who in the novel is the gypsy woman Marthon *alias* Rizpah.) Hameline is bored with the journey and the "endless woods and hills." After a while, thinking that Quentin is interested in her, she asks him to escort her "to yonder brook" so that she can quench her thirst. Left alone on stage, Isabelle sings a short aria, which begins thus:

Example 13-13

Unlike her kinswoman she is impressed with the natural setting: "What a dreamlike glade! Ah! How I love this woodland dell!" Following her aria Quentin re-enters unobserved and watches her decorate her pony with flowers. When she notices his presence, a long duet ensues, during the course of which Quentin tells her that he is conducting her to Liège. She fears "treach'ry by the way," but she is convinced that Quentin does not look like one "to whom a plan of cruelty upon two helpless women might be giv'n" (as in the novel). The duet ends with both singing *aside* of the feelings which they dare not express (suggested by the situation in the novel). The tempo suddenly changes to *allegro non troppo* as they hear, and soon behold, horsemen in the distance. Quentin urges her to flee, but she prefers to brave the danger at his side. Hameline then re-enters, accompanied by her attendant and Bertrand. There is little time for further conversation, for almost the next moment *"Orleans and Dunois enter in armour, with lower'd vizors and drawn swords. Bertrand fights with Dunois, who kills him almost immediately. Quentin wounds Orleans, who falls senseless to the ground. Dunois quickly bestrides the prince to prevent Quentin from raising his vizor."* When Quentin insists on knowing the identity of the knight whom he has felled, Dunois *"deals [him] a blow which makes him stagger back. Quentin quickly recovers himself & attacks Dunois with fury."* So far the confrontation has closely followed Scott's account of it, but the remainder of the scene departs from the novel. Orleans raises his vizor for air, and Quentin, *"aghast,"* now realizes who his adversary was. Suddenly Quentin's other guard rushes in with the news that horsemen are fast approaching. *"Looking in the direction indicated"* Quentin exclaims, "The fellow speaks truth! Mount with ev'ry possible speed!" *"Hameline goes hurriedly out with the guard and attendant. Quentin, after making sure that Bertrand is really dead, follows, bearing Isabelle almost fainting with fear upon his arm. Dunois, who has taken Orleans' helmet off, supports him upon his knee. Orleans' retainers enter, & dismounting, rush to their master's side as the curtain falls."* (In the novel Quentin's mortal conflict with Dunois is broken up by Lord Crawford and a large party of Scottish guard, who conveniently arrive on the scene. There is no reason for Scott's Quentin and his small party to flee.)

For the opera's final scene, which takes place in the banqueting-hall at Schonwaldt, the palace of the Bishop of Liège, the setting and the principal events of chapter xxii ("The Revellers") are boldly spliced together with the principal final events of the novel. The copious material that comes in between—Louis' ill-advised visit to Charles of Burgundy, his house arrest, and his trial—is omitted altogether. When the curtain rises, we see William de la Marck sitting *"at the head of a disordered supper-table"* and *"surrounded by his soldiery and the Citizens of Liège who have joined the insurgents."* William's motiv (see Example 13-12) resounds several times during the boisterous chorus of revellers. Presently *"Quentin enters, holding Isabelle, who is closely veiled, by the hand. They are concealed from De la Marck and his people by a group of men, who also have their backs toward them."* Quentin urges her to have courage. "O plunge your dagger," she replies, "deep within my heart,/ Rather than leave me in these monsters' hands!. . .Ah, if I do but escape this fearful night,/ Ne'er will I forget the one who sav'd me"—lines drawn almost verbatim from the last page of chapter xxi. (Notice that Quentin and Isabelle brave their present danger without the company of Pavillon and his lieutenant, Peterkin Geislaer, both of whom are omitted from the dramatis personae.) At this point De la Marck gives orders for the Bishop to be brought forth. When he appears, having been dragged into the hall by rough hands, he stands *"in silent dignity"* before his captor. *"Quentin draws Isabelle back, and places himself so as to shield her from observation."* While this action is going on, the orchestra plays a doleful motiv associated here and elsewhere with the unfortunate Bishop:

Example 13-14

Lento e maestoso (♩ = 60)

As in the novel, the Bishop denounces De la Marck to his face and then tells him that if he will go barefoot on a pilgrimage to Rome he himself will intercede for the salvation of his miserable soul. "Kill him!" exclaims De la Marck in spoken voice, and *"with one stroke Nikkel fells the Bishop lifeless to the ground."* (In the novel De la Marck glances at Nikkel Blok and raises a finger, "without speaking a word.") *"The body is immediately surrounded and taken unperceived into a small alcove on the left."* When the horrified Liègeois cry out for vengeance, De la Marck orders his followers to attack them, as in the novel, and *"a desperate struggle ensues."* Quentin suddenly seizes young Carl Eberson, William's natural son, and threatens to kill him unless he and *his sister* are allowed to leave the castle safely and immediately. (In the novel Isabelle is introduced to De la Marck as Pavillon's daughter *before* the murder of the Bishop.) Seeing his son in danger, William calls the attack off. When he asks Quentin who he is, Quentin replies, "An envoy of King Louis with matter for your private ear which I will deliver when I've seen my sister safely in Liège." "Ha!" William exclaims, "the wench!—unveil, unveil! No woman calls her beauty her own tonight! Unveil!" Quentin asks him to excuse her, inasmuch as she has made a vow "to Saint Magdalen" (rather than to the Three Blessed Kings) to wear the veil. William says that he will absolve her. (In the novel William's desire to have Isabelle unveil occurs *before* the murder of the Bishop.)

At this climactic point a man rushes in obviously in great excitement. He tells De la Marck that King Louis and Charles of Burgundy have settled their differences and are fast approaching Liège with joint forces. De la Marck, his followers, and the Liègeois all rush out to man the battlements. Left alone together on stage, Quentin and Isabelle sing a duet in which they openly declare their love for one another. (The sentiment owes something to Quentin's private interview with Isabelle at the Ursuline convent, chapter xxxi.) At the end of the duet we hear hasty footsteps *without* and agitated music, and in a few moments the King, Burgundy, Crèvecœur, Dunois, and a few guards burst into the hall. Burgundy orders Quentin to lead them to the Bishop posthaste. *"Quentin goes to the alcove and pulls the curtain aside. As he does so, the dead bishop's head and one arm fall over the step which leads into the room."* All are duly horrified. (In the novel the King and Burgundy know of the Bishop's foul murder *before* coming to Liège.) Burgundy then orders Quentin and the guards to carry the Bishop out and "lay him reverently to rest." While they are away, he expresses to Isabelle his displeasure with her recent course of action. She protests that she could not wed someone whom she did not love. Presently the King intercedes and suggests that Isabelle's hand in marriage be proclaimed as the prize for whoever brings in the Wild Boar's head. Burgundy likes the idea. (In this brief passage the librettist has spliced together two separate conversations between Burgundy and his wayward ward (see chapters xxxii & xxxv). In the latter, when Isabelle flatly refuses to marry Orleans, Charles of Burgundy (rather than the King) decides to offer her as a prize to the slayer of the Wild Boar.) Just as Crèvecœur is about to go forth to issue a formal proclamation regarding Isabelle's future, Balafré and Quentin appear. Balafré announces to all present that his nephew "hath speared a king of swine—/ The great 'Wild Boar' in truth." Burgundy announces in turn that Quentin has won Isabelle's hand in marriage. From backstage we hear the chorus jubilantly singing of the great victory. *"Quentin and Isabelle look towards one another in a bewildered dream of happiness."* The entire chorus comes on stage for the final ensemble: "Victorious! shout the cry in glorious song!" The curtain falls. (The final scene is skillfully contrived. Almost half the novel is effectively telescoped into a time span of about thirty minutes.)

Maclean's score (unlike Laurent's) is interesting in harmonic texture and sensitive and mature in craftsmanship; it has passages of great beauty. Its main fault is a noticeable lack of rhythmic vitality (which is eminently *not* the case in Gevaert's opéra comique, as I have already observed). Sometimes one feels that the opera does not move. The passages of recitative, which often follow the novel faithfully, are ponderous. Interestingly, there is no music of Scottish flavor.[16]

CRÈVECŒUR throws down his glove. A scene from an early production of Gevaert's *Quentin Durward*. From an 1860 issue of *Théâtre Contemporain Illustré*.

14

§ § §

THE TALISMAN

*T*he Talisman, Scott's twenty-first novel, appeared in 1825, forming part of his Tales of the Crusaders. It inspired a musical drama that was staged the next year in London. During the half century that followed came three important operas by well-known composers of different nationalities. The task of the different librettists has been aptly described in particular reference to Arthur Matthison, Balfe's librettist: ". . . his perplexity was the familiar one of superabundant riches; and the selection from the variety of incident offered to him of a just sufficient outline to sustain without strain the interest of an opera to the end; and the adoption of those situations in the story best adapted to illustrate the intention and characteristic spirit of the original, while supplying the widest scope for effect to the musical composer, constituted the by no means inconsiderable difficulties of his undertaking." [1] These remarks describe not unaptly the task of all librettists working from Waverley novels.

The Knights of the Cross

The Knights of the Cross; or, The Hermit's Prophecy was first performed on 29 May 1826 at the Theatre Royal, Drury Lane, and was favorably received. The text was the work of Samuel Beazley,[2] and the music was "composed and selected" by Henry R. Bishop.[3] Most of Scott's characters appear in this musical drama, the only notable omissions being the two dwarfs, Nectabanus and his wife Guenevra. Miss Stephens sang the role of Edith Plantagenet; Mr. Bennett, Sir Kenneth. The role of Blondel, much enhanced from what it is in the novel, was done by Charles E. Horn, the composer of the operatic *Peveril of the Peak* (see Chapter 12).[4] Further performances, sometimes with changes in the cast, took place on May 31st, June 1st, 2nd, and 7th, September 26th, November 7th and 14th, December 12th, 13th, and 21st. Sir Kenneth's noble mastiff-hound Roswal was played by a dog who, according to one reviewer, "seemed to have an intuitive knowledge of the duties imposed, for we never saw an animal assume the appearance of determined ferocity with so much truth or effect."

The first scene of Act I takes place at *"the Cavern of the Hermit of Engaddi"* and is based loosely on chapters iii and iv. Sir Kenneth and the Emir *(alias* El Hakim *alias* Saladin) introduce themselves to each other and speak of the fight they have just had (which is not acted out). When the Emir asks Kenneth whether he is one of King Richard's subjects, he replies, "One of his followers" (as in the novel). Kenneth then speaks of the King's grave illness. The Emir suggests that Richard employ the services of Saladin's physician, who is skilled in the diseases of the East. Kenneth likes the idea and promises that the physician shall have his protection. As the Emir exits, he tells Kenneth that the physician will meet him "on the borders of thy camp." (In the novel we learn somewhat later, chapter viii, that the physician met Kenneth at Engaddi after Kenneth "had tarried a day for him and more.") Later in the scene the Hermit of Engaddi tells Kenneth that he has read in the stars about a marriage between Edith and "Richard's most powerful foe." Kenneth accordingly sees an end to his own "ambitious hopes"—information not introduced until much later in the novel (chapter xiv). The Hermit also tells Kenneth that the Queen and various ladies of the court are at the grotto doing penance for the King's illness. (In the novel, chapter iv, Kenneth does not know why the ladies are present.) The scene concludes with a chorus of nuns ("Ascend, our prayers, on wings of air").—For the second scene we move to Richard's tent. The ailing King is entertained by his favorite minstrel, Blondel, who in the novel is not introduced until almost the very end. In the ensuing dialogue between Richard and Sir Thomas of Gilsland (De Vaux), Richard makes snide remarks about the other leaders of the crusade (as in the novel, chapter vi). Presently Sir Kenneth comes in (see chapter vii) with news about a Moorish physician whom he has brought with him to cure the King. (In the musical drama Kenneth has no ill armor-bearer whom the Moor cures first.) *"Enter, in procession, Saracens, El Hakim, Conrade, Philip, Beau Sceant, Slaves, bearing golden goblets, &c."* Conrade of Montserrat and Beau Sceant, the Grand Master of the Templars, try to dissuade Richard from taking the medicine of an infidel (as in the novel, chapter ix), but Richard defies them, *"drinks the mixture, and sinks back, exhausted, into the arms of his attendants . . . ."*—Scene iii: *"The Camp."* Conrade and Beau Sceant scheme to break up the crusade, their dialogue following in abridged form Scott's dialogue of chapter x. After Beau Sceant has departed, Leopold of Austria arrives on the scene. (In the novel, chapter xi, Conrade visits Leopold the next day in his tent. Beazley has compressed his original, thereby avoiding a change of setting.) Playing upon Leopold's inflated sense of his own importance, Conrade fires him up against Richard, and the act ends with Leopold and his followers leaving the stage to hoist Austria's banner to a position as high as England's. (In the novel this climactic point comes in the middle of chapter xi.)

For the first scene of Act II we return to Richard's tent. Richard awakens from El Hakim's medication, fully recovered. Conrade then enters and tells him what Leopold of Austria is doing. Indignant, Richard hastens away to chastise him.—The second scene takes place at St. George's Mount and begins with a chorus of Austrian crusaders, who have hoisted their banner beside that of England. Suddenly Richard and Conrade enter, accompanied by officers, Templars, and, in a departure from Scott, the Hermit of Engaddi. In the ensuing argument, which follows Scott's dialogue of chapter xi closely, the Hermit (rather than Philip of France) plays the part of peacemaker. Richard entrusts Sir Kenneth with the duty of guarding the Standard of England.—The third scene takes place in the Queen's tent. Queen Berengaria, Edith, Calista, other ladies, and the minstrel Blondel are present. Blondel, assuming the role of Scott's Nectabanus, is to go to Kenneth with Edith's ring and try to lure him from his post. (In the novel we are told all this in a flashback, chapter xiii, *after* Kenneth has succumbed to the shameless trickery.)— Scene iv: *"St. George's Mount."* Sir Kenneth is discovered guarding the standard; his faithful dog Roswal is beside him. Blondel sings an air from *without* ("Oh! listen, listen, gentle knight!"), then enters and succeeds in luring Kenneth from his post.—Scene v: Back at the Queen's pavilion, Edith and the Queen argue about what the latter has done. Piqued that Edith has taken her joke so seriously, the Queen leaves the stage in a huff, accompanied by Calista. (In the novel the Queen flees when a curtain drops, revealing Sir Kenneth: she and her ladies-in-waiting were not fully clothed.) When Kenneth arrives on the scene, Edith urges him to return at once to his post. (Their dialogue follows the novel closely, chapter xiii.)—Scene vi: Back at St. George's Mount, Conrade and his vassals steal the English standard and wound Kenneth's dog. (Scott does not describe this incident as it is actually happening.) When Kenneth returns, he finds the standard gone and his dog dying. El Hakim finds Kenneth in sad plight and promises to cure Roswal. He tries to persuade Kenneth to flee with him (as in the novel, chapter xiv), but Kenneth's sense of honor does not allow him to try to escape his due punishment. El Hakim hastily exits as Richard enters, along with Gilsland, officers, soldiers, gentlemen and others. Richard soon learns what has happened and orders Kenneth to be put to death. (In the novel Kenneth reports to Richard at his pavilion, chapter xv, to apprise him of the loss of the standard. Beazley's minor alteration avoids a change of scenery.) The act ends with a rousing "Chorus and Finale":

Bear him away!
For England's laws declare,
That the traitor this day
His forfeit life must pay.
Bid the headsman prepare.
Bear him away, &c.

The first scene of Act III takes place inside Richard's tent. One by one the Queen, Edith, and the Hermit of Engaddi plead in vain with the King for Kenneth's life (as in the novel, chapter xvii). El Hakim then enters and tells the King that he owes him a life in requital for his recent tent-call and professional services rendered (see chapter xviii). At first Richard is highly incensed, but on second thought he agrees to El Hakim's demands. (El Hakim makes no mention of a talisman either here or anywhere else in the musical drama.)—Scene ii: "*The Camp.*" Conrade and Beau Sceant scheme to have Richard assassinated. (Based on the last two or three pages of chapter xix; Beazley omits Richard's eloquent and memorable oration in the Council Chamber, which comes earlier in the chapter.)—Scene iii: "*The Outside of Richard's Tent.*" A dumb Nubian slave (Kenneth in disguise) brings Richard a message from Saladin (as in the novel, chapter xx). The soldiers have fun tantalizing a Charegite, as in the novel, and they sing a drinking song, suggested by the parallel material of the novel. When the Charegite attempts to kill Richard, the Nubian's dog (Roswal) grabs him by the throat. The Nubian (Kenneth) kills the would-be assassin, but he himself is wounded in the arm in the process. (In the novel, ch. xxi, the dog has nothing to do with this incident. Kenneth prevents the murder by laying hold of the Charegite and scuffling with him. The King himself kills the man as soon as he realizes what is going on.) When Richard sucks the poision from the Nubian's wound, he notices that his black complexion comes off: "So, so, my Scot, thy skin, as well as thy heart, betrays thy noble nature." (In the novel we learn later that Richard suspected at this point the real identity of his saviour. He keeps Kenneth guessing for a long time as to whether or not he sees through the disguise.) Still trying to act out his ruse, Kenneth indicates in writing how the King can discover who stole the standard. He also requests permission to bear privately a message from Saladin to Edith. Richard grants his request, but solemnly warns him not to speak with Edith (see the beginning of chapter xxv).— Scene iv: "*The Queen's Pavilion.*" The Queen and Neville discuss with Edith the black messenger who is about to arrive. (The dialogue follows that of chapter xxv fairly closely, but Edith's words are spoken in the novel by Calista, Scott's Edith being in a separate tent at this point). When Neville, the Queen, and her entourage of ladies depart, Edith receives in private interview the supposed Nubian slave, whom she immediately recognizes as Kenneth. As in the novel, she angrily refuses Saladin's offer of marriage, and she is put out with Kenneth because he will not speak. Suddenly the King enters—a departure from the novel. Edith tells him too in no uncertain terms that she will not wed Saladin. (The dialogue follows the conversation that Scott's Richard has with Edith as he escorts her back to her tent after a song recital given by the newly arrived Blondel in the royal pavilion; see the last pages of chapter xxvi.)—In the final scene, which takes place at the crusaders' camp, Beazley amalgamates events of chapter xxiv (the dog's discovery of Conrade as the thief of the English standard) with events of chapters xxvii and xxviii (the trial by combat). In the novel the latter occurs five days afterwards at the so-called Diamond of the Desert, a part of Saladin's domain. (Notice too Beazley's re-arrangement of Scott's order of events. The material of the previous scene occurs in the novel *after* the discovery of Conrade as thief.) Everyone is on stage for the combat between Kenneth and Conrade. Saladin says that he has come to the crusaders' camp "to see the ceremonial of the standard, and to punish treason." (His remark about punishing treason is a loose end, inasmuch as the operatic Grand Master does not murder the wounded Conrade and is not punished (beheaded) by the operatic Saladin.) As in the novel, Kenneth turns out to be Earl of Huntingdon and Prince of Scotland.

To sum up, the musical drama is a comparatively faithful rendering of the novel. More of the back-biting intrigue appears here than in any of the three operas to be discussed. Interesting aspects of Beazley's workmanship are (1) his enhancement of the role of Blondel, (2) his omission of all reference to the talisman—explanation might have proved tedious, and (3) his clever shaping of the final scene. The music deserves no particular comment.

Il Talismano

Pacini's *Il Talismano; ossia, la Terza Crociata in Palestina* (libretto by the mathematician Gaetano Barbieri) was first performed in the spring of 1829 in Naples, at the San Carlo. Despite Pacini's misgivings about the libretto—misgivings which he was later to express, politely and obliquely, in his memoirs—the opera proved successful.[5] Very shortly after its première it was performed in Milan, at la Scala.[6] The difficult tenor role of the Cavaliere del Leopardo (nowhere called Kenneth) was done by the celebrated Rubini, who enjoyed a triumph equal to that which he had obtained in Bellini's *Il Pirata*.[7] Antonio Tamburini sang Riccardo; his wife Marietta, daughter of the famed choreographer Gioia, sang Berengaria; Emilia Bonini, Edita; and basso buffo Giuseppe Frezzolini, Lord Multon (Scott's De Vaux). Other characters of the opera include a Saracen physician *alias* Saladin (but not *alias* Emir Sheerkohf), the Grand Master of the Templars (a composite of Scott's Grand Master plus Conrade of Montserrat and Leopold of Austria), Berengaria's page Enrico (who corresponds roughly to Scott's Nectabanus), and "un Capo di Marabuti" (Scott's Charegite). Six years after its première the opera was given in Viareggio.[8]

There is no overture. After a short orchestral introduction the curtain rises on a large group of people assembled just outside Riccardo's tent. Among them are Edita, Berengaria, and the Grand Master. All except the Grand Master implore God in the opening *andante sostenuto* to restore health to their indisposed King. After this impressive ensemble Multon enters and gruffly orders everyone to be quiet. He is embarrassed when he notices that the Queen and Edita are in the group. He tells the two ladies that Riccardo is in a deep sleep. "Gran Dio!" they exclaim. "Sarebbe morto?" He assures them that the King is not dead and then tells them about a talisman having been immersed in water from the River Jordan to prepare the draught which finally induced sleep. Already upset at having heard the pagan word *talismano,* the Grand Master now asks Multon whether the King's life is in the hands of a Mussulman. Edita and the Queen express great consternation at the very thought. At this point the Saracen physician comes out from the tent and tells everyone that Riccardo has awakened, and in a few moments Riccardo himself appears. A large ensemble develops. The King is angry when he hears from the Grand Master that the Grand Council of the Crusaders has sent Saladin a message of peace. He asks if all present are prepared to follow him, and they assure him that they are: "Tutti siam col nostro Re." He then instills in everyone except the Grand Master (and of course the Saracen physician *alias* Saladin) the desire to defeat the infidels in battle. The ensemble ends in a sextet with chorus. (Obviously the material of the novel has been rearranged and much altered. Riccardo's operatic address is suggested by his counterpart's eloquent speech in the Council Chamber, which comes at a later point in the story.)

In the recitative that follows, Riccardo asks who bore the message of peace, and Multon tells him that a Scot of unknown origin did so. "Oh sempre a l'Inghilterra/Caledonii fatali in pace e in guerra!" exclaims Riccardo in typical English prejudice against Scots. Berengaria remarks to Edita *sotto voce* that the man in question must be the one whom they encountered at Carmel (rather than Engaddi); Edita implores her to be silent. Multon then tells the King that the Scottish knight wears the sign of a leopard. When he too makes a disparaging quip about Scots, Edita, unable to restrain herself, cries out that he is unfair. Riccardo notices that her cheeks have turned a glowing red. The Saracen wonders what is in her heart, and he observes that the Scot must be the same Scot whom he befriended after having fought with him along the way to Carmel. (Notice that the recitative alludes briefly to material from the early chapters of the novel.) Upon Riccardo's orders, the squires lead the royal ladies and their followers back to their own tents. In the next *scena* the Saracen physician absolutely refuses to take money in recompense for his services (as in the novel, chapter xi). Accordingly the King presents him with a sword as pledge that he will grant him whatsoever he desires and is able to accept, whensoever he should request it. (The motif of the sword as pledge is not to be found in the novel.) After the Saracen has departed, Multon tells Riccardo that he strongly suspects that Edita is in love with the messenger Scot. Riccardo replies that he now has second grounds for detesting him. He dismisses Multon upon the entrance of the Scot, whom he severely upbraids for having been a messenger of peace. The young knight replies that in obeying the leaders of the Council he did not follow his own mind. When Riccardo reprimands him for being a stubborn subject, he replies boldly that he is subject only to the King of Scotland (a remark transferred from the conversation of Scott's Kenneth with the Emir, earlier in the story). Despite the King's request he refuses to divulge his true identity. (At this point in the novel no one suspects that Kenneth is someone else.) Moreover, he refuses to be ruffled by the King's pointed allusion to his affair of the heart. As the duet continues, Riccardo, as in the novel, cannot help admiring the young man's spirit. Suddenly they hear voices from *without* singing that the standard of the Lion of Britain is no longer first among the others. "Che?" exclaims Riccardo, as in the novel (chapter xi). Multon rushes in with the news that the Grand Master is to blame, that he has sworn to leave the crusade, that his followers have lowered the flag of England onto a level with the other flags. Riccardo turns to the Scot and asks him what he thinks about these events. He is just as much enraged as the King and expresses the belief that the incident is a grave insult. Pleased with his reaction, the King entrusts him with defense of the English standard. In the trio that concludes the *scena,* the Scot expresses *aside* the fervent hope that his new duty will be a means of winning favor in the eyes of Edita. (In the opera there is no confrontation between Riccardo and the Gran Mastro, who has here assumed a function of Scott's Leopold of Austria.)

We move now to the pavilion and adjoining garden of the Queen. The ladies of her court are singing as they weave a garland of flowers, and Edita sings with them, musing to herself about the sweet image in her mind of the Scottish knight. Berengaria then enters and proposes to Edita the wager that her knight will leave his post at her (Edita's) command. Edita is reluctant to engage in something so frivolous and potentially harmful to a good knight's career, but Berengaria insists. Edita's ring will be used to lure the knight away. The *scena* ends in an engaging trio for Edita, Berengaria, and the page Enrico (a soprano), who is to approach the knight and thus play the role of Scott's Nectabanus. (Scott does not describe the wager as it is actually taking place. We first learn about it when Sir Kenneth overhears the ladies speak of it *after* he has already left his post and come to the pavilion; see chapter xii.)

The scene now changes to the "Monte degli Stendardi," where the Cavaliere is on duty guarding the English standard, which has been put back in its proper place. In the recitative preceding his aria the Cavaliere sings of the beauties of the night; in the aira he apostrophizes the moon. (The content and mood are suggested by Scott's passage of description at the beginning of chapter xii.) Afterwards, in a bit of recitative, he wonders whether the cloud he sees will perhaps bring destruction to his contentedness. At his point Enrico enters. He shows the Cavaliere Edita's ring and lures him from his post *by saying that Edita is in danger.* (This slight departure from the novel simplifies the operatic hero's decision to leave his post: Sir Kenneth's actions are governed by the complicated ramifications of courtly love.) The Cavaliere rushes off to assist her, while Enrico remains on stage to watch over the standard. (In the novel Nectabanus leads Kenneth to Edith's tent, while the dog Roswal guards the standard.) The finale begins with Enrico repeating *"con ironia"* a fragment from the above-mentioned trio:

Example 14-1

A group of Marabuti and their captain now enter. At the beginning of their brief chorus they make known that they have been hired by the Gran Mastro. They seize Enrico, stifling his cries, and take him with them as they make off with the English standard. When they are gone we hear Edita *without* urging the unlucky Cavaliere to return to his post. (Just the opposite procedure occurs in the novel: we witness Kenneth's interview with Edith and not the theft of the standard.) The Cavaliere returns to find both Enrico and the standard gone. In a poignant ariosa ("Ciel! l'opra hai compiuto/D'immenso rigor") he laments his disgrace: he is no longer worthy of love; death is the only relief that remains for him. Riccardo, Multon, Berengaria, Edita, the Saracen physician, and the entire chorus are on stage for the remainder of the finale. Upon entering, Riccardo sees immediately that the standard is gone. The Cavaliere admits that it has been stolen; he offers neither excuse nor explanation. (As in the Beazley-Bishop musical drama, time has been compressed and there is no change of setting. In the novel Kenneth reports to Richard the next morning in his tent.) When Riccardo condemns the Cavaliere to death, Edita implores Berengaria to reveal the truth. Next comes a fine ensemble ("Tutto lo accusa"), which is composed of Edita, Berengaria, the Cavaliere, the Saracen physician, Riccardo, Multon, and the chorus, most of them singing that although everything points to the Cavaliere's guilt, he does not have the countenance of a traitor. Berengaria and Edita then explain to Riccardo how it came about that the Cavaliere left his post. Riccardo, however, is all the more enraged in learning that the Cavaliere was on such familiar terms with the ladies that they included him in their games. Edita implores him to have pity. "Invan," he replies. At his point the Saracen physician shows Riccardo the sword he gave him earlier and reminds him of his promise. He wants the Scot in recompense for his services. The act ends in a large fugal ensemble, which is made all the more exciting by a storm's having arisen (cf. the Cavaliere's above-mentioned remark about the clouds). Riccardo sings that the storm in Nature is not so great as the tremendous conflict within his own breast.

(To me the finale is the most striking part of the opera. It is conventional, to be sure, but Pacini handles the conventions very skillfully. The motif of the rash promise is not in the novel. El Hakim prevents Richard from having Kenneth put to death when he explains to him something of the magic of the talisman. He must save twelve persons each year. This year he lacks one. Having recently cured an unclean animal (Kenneth's dog) he is now unfit to cure another human being. He persuades Richard to turn Kenneth over to him if the virtue of the talisman is to remain effective with his last patient, namely, Richard himself. See chapter xviii.)

Act II opens in the soldiers' quarters. Feigning drunkenness, the captain of the Marabuti approaches the men as they are cleaning their weapons and relaxing. They rudely tell him to lie down in the back of the room and sleep off his stupor. The Marabuto remarks *aside* that the Grand Master will richly reward him for what he is about to do. Presently Multon arrives and informs the soldiers that they will soon be returning to England. While they are all singing in joyful anticipation of the homeward journey, Riccardo enters. He tells everyone that he has just come from a meeting of the leaders of the crusade, that he inspired them with his words, and that they are all eager to march with him toward Jerusalem. (In the novel, chapter xix, we are present while this memorable meeting is taking place.) Riccardo's remarks are enthusiastically received by the chorus. Suddenly a trumpet is heard from *without*. Multon goes off to investigate the matter, returns in a few moments, and announces that a speechless Nubian has unexpectedly arrived from the court of Saladin. When the Nubian enters, he presents Riccardo with a letter which he has brought from his master. The King reads the message out loud, in spoken voice, to the accompaniment of sustained chords played by the strings—a stock operatic device. Saladin asks for Edita's hand in marriage and indicates that he has entrusted the Nubian with a confidential letter to be delivered to *her*. Riccardo is cool to this idea. As he reads further, Saladin warns him that a coward is plotting to take his life. At that very moment the Marabuto, who has stealthily crept up behind him, attempts to murder him. The quick-thinking Nubian prevents the assassination, and the would-be assassin is apprehended (*not* killed by Riccardo). At this point Enrico enters and announces to all that the Marabuto is a ruffian in the service of the Grand Master. He tells of his having been seized when the standard was stolen and of having been placed in captivity. He has managed to escape by jumping from a balcony. (In the novel, chapter xxiv, Kenneth's dog gives convincing evidence that Conrade of Montserrat stole the standard.) Riccardo immediately orders some of his followers to hasten to the Grand Master and present him with a challenge to combat. Multon and the chorus voice the belief that a duel is not a fitting engagement for Riccardo inasmuch as he is their leader. He replies elliptically: "Si, lo so: ma al novo Sole/Non avrò per me un guerrier?" Then, after giving the supposed Nubian permission to deliver his mes-

sage to Edita, he sings in anticipation of the approaching confrontation
with the Grand Master.

We return now to the Queen's pavilion and garden where we behold
Edita, alone on stage, musing on the fate of her loved one, whom she
believes to be a slave of the Saracens. Multon and Enrico then usher in the
supposed Nubian. Edita is surprised to see Enrico, whom she has not laid
eyes on since his disappearance. He informs her of the forthcoming
combat, which is to be held at the Diamond of the Desert. He explains that
the Grand Master is the defendant, that the King's champion is to be
nominated in due course, and that the King has commanded that all the
ladies of the court be present for the occasion. When he and Multon go
out to bear the news to the Queen, they leave the Nubian in private
interview with Edita, according to the King's wishes. Unlike her counterpart in the novel (chapter xxv), Edita does not see through the Nubian's
disguise. She reads the Sultan's proposal of marriage and declares, to the
great joy of the Nubian, that she will have no part of it. She then asks him if
he by chance has seen in the desert someone who resembles him in all
respects except color. Laying aside his ruse, the Cavaliere replies,
"Quell'infelice sta d'Edita al piede." They sing an elaborate duet, during
the course of which Enrico re-enters unobserved, sees what is going on,
and departs (and presumably reports what he has seen to Riccardo, who
already has suspected the Nubian's real identity—even though the operatic Nubian was not wounded in his scuffle with the Marabuto and thus
there is no incident of Riccardo's sucking poison from his wound and
noticing that his color comes off). The Cavaliere expresses regret that he
had to be the bearer of the unholy proposal from the Sultan. (In the novel,
chapter xxv, the Nubian remains silent throughout the entire interview,
in obedience to the King's express command. The alteration makes possible a duet for hero and heroine—the first in the opera.) In the final part of
the number the Cavaliere is summoned by a chorus of warriors to the
field. He is to be the King's champion. Needless to say, he is overjoyed
with his chance to redeem himself: "Corro al cimento intrepido/Ove
l'onor m'invita;/Meco è l'amor d'Edita;/Chi frena il mio valor?" (Scott's Sir
Kenneth does not receive the King's orders at this time and place.)

The short third act takes place on the field known as the Diamond of the
Desert and is based loosely on chapters xxvii-xxviii. In the opening choral
number we learn that the Grand Master has been killed by his Scottish
adversary. Afterwards, in cembalo-accompanied recitative, Riccardo orders Multon to conduct the champion into his presence. Alluding obviously to Edita, he adds that he is not the only person who awaits him.
Presently Saladino enters in all his pomp, holding by the hand the victorious Cavaliere del Leopardo. It is now clear much to the surprise of
Riccardo, that Saladino and the Saracen physician are one and the same.
The voices of Edita, Berengaria, the Cavaliere, Riccardo, and Saladino
comprise the ensuing quintet ("Oh Ciel! Per pugnar seco"), which is one

of the most impressive numbers in the score. Riccardo indicates that he may have to agree after all to Saladino's wish to wed Edita, inasmuch as Saladino has saved his life. (At the corresponding point in the novel, Richard has already decided against the marriage.) In the final *scena* Multon brings in the news that the Cavaliere is actually the prince royal of Scotland. The last musical number is designed as an aria for the Cavaliere. In the cantabile ("Ah! s'è ver") he gallantly gives up his claim to Edita's hand in the interest of the peace that would be achieved through her marriage to Saladino. But Saladino, not to be topped in chivalry, relinquishes Edita in favor of the deserving Cavaliere. Riccardo readily agrees to the idea, In the florid cabaletta to his aria the Cavaliere expresses his joy: "Ah del mio core il giubilo," etc. Indeed all are pleased with the happy turn of events. The curtain falls.

The opera plot reveals a number of deviations from the original story, although not the drastic changes that one often finds in the Italian and French operas based on Scott. The principals, however, are black-and-white pasteboard figures in comparison with their originals, and there is no sense of the rampant back-biting intrigue which Scott depicts so well. Pacini took more pains with the score than was his want: "Noterò che in questo lavoro feci qualche progresso nel genere declamato, e cercai d'immedesimarmi nell'argomento, onde dare qualche poco di unità allo stile della composizione, cosa non sì facile a conseguirsi: anzi in ciò consiste la maggior difficoltà che incontra un autore d'opere teatrali."[9]

Richard en Palestine

Adam's *Richard en Palestine*, with words by Paul Foucher, was first performed on 7 October 1844 in Paris, at the theater of the Académie Royale de Musique.[10] It is cited in Grove's Dictionary as the most successful of Adam's grand operas. There are only five principals: Richard (sung at the première by Baroilhet), Bérengère (sung by Mme Dorus Gras), Édith (Mme Méquillet), Ismael *alias* Saladin (Levasseur), and Kenneth (Marié). Ismael, who is described as an Arab warrior, corresponds with Scott's El Hakim. Foucher's sharp reduction in the number of characters is indication in itself of the large extent to which he has simplified his source. Examination of the libretto reveals in addition that he has made a number of bold alterations.

Adam's overture is a potpourri of material drawn from the opera proper—the introduction to Kenneth's *romance* of Act III, part of the finale to Act II, Bérengère's song about her fatherland, Act I, an *allegro* in 6/8 time that comes in Act III, and the *allegro marziale* of the finale to Act I. The first act takes place in front of Richard's tent. Kenneth and a chorus of English soldiers, who are praying for God to restore the King's health, are interrupted by the loud, boisterous singing of a chorus of Germans, Leopold's men. When Kenneth asks them to respect the King and be silent, they reply that Richard is not *their* King; moreover, they are jealous that his standard has been placed higher than theirs. Kenneth warns them, "Ne réveillez pas le Lion" (a line borrowed from a different context in the novel), but they reply insolently, "Qu'importe! Il va mourir!" The appearance of Ismael quells an incipient melee. He announces that through his art the King is now resting and that he will live. The Germans express their unhappiness at the positive turn in the King's health and leave the stage. In the following accompanied recitative we learn that Kenneth and Ismael have been acquainted with one another previously. Ismael mentions their having once refreshed themselves at an oasis in the desert (see chapter ii), and he also alludes to Kenneth's having been thrown ashore after a shipwreck (a motif not in the novel). Kenneth then relates some of his recent adventures. He had not been in these parts long before he had the task of saving several ladies from an assault by Moors near the habitation of the Hermit of Engaddi. One of the ladies fainted in fright. How beautiful she appeared while regaining consciousness! Ismael suspects that Kenneth is in love with her. Kenneth then shows him a ring which the unknown beauty left behind when she departed from the place of the assault. (The leaving behind of a ring may have been suggested by the rose-bud episode of chapter iv; otherwise Kenneth's adventure has no resemblance to any incident of the novel. Cf. the *scène* in the first act of Gevaert's *Quentin Durward* in which Quentin tells Maître Pierre of his having recently saved two ladies from Burgundian soldiers.)

When Bérengère and Édith enter, Quentin learns to his sorrow that the unknown beauty whom he loves is beyond his hopes, for she is the cousin of the King. (In the novel Kenneth knows all along who his idol is.) Bérengère thanks Kenneth for defending the ladies and Ismael for curing Richard. When she refers to Kenneth by his Christian name, Ismael is astonished. "Toi, Kenneth... ta patrie?" he asks. "Est l'Écosse," Kenneth replies. "Il suffit," continues Ismael. "Hors du camp des chrétiens la prière m'appelle;/Mais viens me retrouver..." "Quel mystère?" Kenneth asks. "J'ai dit," Ismael replies "*avec autorité.*" (A sense of mystery is created in this brief exchange, which has no parallel in the novel. Explanation comes later.) Ismael leaves the stage as the King, fully recovered, enters in the company of his barons. He sings an aria ("Air pur, qui viens de la patrie"), after which Bérengère presents Kenneth to him as her saviour. Richard briefly thanks Kenneth for his services and then departs along with his barons. Bérengère, having made a sign to Kenneth to remain behind, asks Édith, in his presence, whether she does not have anything to say to her liberator. When she mentions the possibility of Édith's choosing Kenneth as her chevalier, Édith replies that there is little difference between *chevalier* and *fiancé* and that Kenneth is not of high enough station for such an honor. She is grateful to him, but they must bid each other an eternal farewell. When Édith has departed, Kenneth, in a duet with the Queen, sadly gives her the above-mentioned ring and requests that she return it to its owner. Bérengère tells him that she will try to help him in his affair of the heart (see her song, "Dans ma folle patrie"), but Kenneth laments that all is in vain because of his lowly birth: he does not even know who his parents are; he is a "pauvre orphelin." As their duet closes, Bérengère invites Kenneth to give a recital of his unhappy life that very evening in her tent. (The *scène* is an interesting departure from the novel, in which there is nowhere a private conversation between Sir Kenneth and the Queen.) Richard and his entourage re-enter for the finale. The King is angry with the Germans because they disputed his authority during his illness. He has now placed his banner high on Mont Saint-Georges, and, needing someone to defend it, he decides to entrust the task to Kenneth. The act ends in a large ensemble composed of Bérengère, Kenneth, the King, and the full chorus. The music has a martial flavor. (The memorable events of chapter xi—Leopold of Austria's insult to the English standard and Richard's violent reaction—are omitted altogether.)

The second act takes place inside the Queen's tent. The ladies in attendance sing a choral number ("Rive enchanteresse") in which they express their hope for peace. Next comes an elaborate coloratura aria for the Queen (which does not advance the action in any way). In her duet with Édith that follows, she teases Édith with the idea that love and beauty may cause chevaliers to forget their duty. Édith disagrees; she argues that they will always put honor and duty first. At the conclusion of the duet a page comes in and privately communicates something to Bérengère, who then turns to Édith and informs her that she has lost the argument inasmuch as Kenneth happens to be present, having been lured from his duty by the sight of Édith's ring. Édith is horrified: "Vous! ô ciel! exposer la gloire/D'un brave soldat de Richard!" (The *scène* is suggested in part by the conversation among the ladies which Scott's Sir Kenneth overhears just after his arrival at the tent, chapter xiii; the operatic Kenneth overhears nothing.) When Kenneth enters, he is surprised that everything is tranquil, that there is no danger. During the course of the trio that develops, Édith explains to him briefly that he has been the victim of a cruel game, and she urges him to return at once to his post. Kenneth now expresses dismay at having left his post for no good reason. Bérengère likewise urges him to return, assuring him that the King will never know. Suddenly Ismael bursts in. It is too late, he says, for traitors have torn down and trampled on the undefended standard. "Tremblez!..." he then exclaims; "voici Richard, qui ne pardonne pas!" Bérengère, Édith, Ismael, and the chorus of ladies sing "O douleur! nuit déplorable!" as Richard and his entourage of barons and chevaliers enter. The King is about to execute Kenneth on the spot, but Ismael wrests the mace from his hands and throws it aside, saying, "Je t'ai sauvé la vie et t'épargne un remord." (In this action Ismael assumes the role of Scott's De Vaux, chapter xv.) The finale soon develops into a quintet with chorus: Richard

expresses his shame and grief at the treatment his banner has received;
Édith and Bérengère sing of their fright and grief; Kenneth laments that
his glory is no more; Ismael cannot believe that Kenneth would be capable
of such criminal neglect of duty. The King then asks Kenneth what he has
to say for himself in defense. "Rien," he replies; "que la loi me punisse."
"Soit!" exclaims Richard indignantly; "tu seras jugé sur l'heure en
criminel!" The finale concludes with a reprise of the music of the preceding ensemble, with different words: Richard and the barons cry out for
vengeance on the traitor; Kenneth hopes that his punishment may soon
gratify their fury; Bérengère, Édith, and the ladies call on heaven to save
the unfortunate one; Ismael alone hints at the possibility that Kenneth
will somehow have a better fate. Just before the curtain falls, "on vient
prendre à Kenneth son épée." (The finale is based loosely on material from
chapters xv and xvii. Interestingly, the setting is still the Queen's tent. In
the novel Sir Kenneth reports to Richard the next day in *his* tent. In the
musical drama and in Pacini's opera the memorable encounter takes place
at Saint George's Mount. In all three stage versions time has been telescoped and a change of scenery avoided so that there will be no break or
lull in the dramatic intensity of the situation.)

All of Act III takes place inside Richard's tent. The opening *scène* (based
on material from chapter xvi) is designed as a recitative and duet for Édith
and Bérengère. Édith tries to get Bérengère to tell the King the truth
about Kenneth and thereby save his life, but Bérengère is afraid of
Richard's wrath; finally, though, she agrees to do what she can. Édith
withdraws when she sees Richard approaching. As he enters he orders an
officer to have the prisoner brought in and to assemble the Council.
Bérengère approaches her husband timidly. When she expresses wonder
as to why he is so disturbed over the insult to the banner, he becomes
angry. When she suggests that perchance the brave knight was surprised
in a trap, Richard becomes even angrier—so angry, in fact, that Bérengère is afraid to pursue the matter further. Richard declares that his
duty is to see that justice is done; he has but one desire—to be avenged.
Bérengère leaves the stage at a sign from the King, who withdraws into
the recesses of the tent. (The *scène* is based loosely on material from the
beginning of chapter xvii.)

Kenneth is now led in by soldiers, as the orchestra plays a solemn figure
which was heard first in the overture:

Example 14-2

Understandably depressed, he sings a brief *romance* in which he bemoans his lot. Afterwards Ismael enters. He tells Kenneth that he comes not to show pity but rather to perform a duty. "Until now," he continues, "you could not without danger learn of your birth and your name, known to only one man. He served your father; he came to render you the name so much desired." "What prevents him?" asks Kenneth. "He is no more!" Ismael replies. "Dunstan!" Kenneth exclaims, apparently recalling something from his earliest days. Ismael explains that the poor old man, having been cast ashore by a tempest, was brought to his tent for succor. Just before he died, he bequeathed to him a document which reveals Kenneth's parentage. Ismael then hands the said document to Kenneth, who reads it silently and finds out at long last who he really is. (We the audience are left in ignorance for the time being.) He sings a varied second couplet to his foregoing *romance,* at the end of which, unwilling to bring shame upon his parents, he tears the document up. The *scène* ends in a duet. Ismael admires Kenneth's noble spirit and hopes that something can still be done to save his life. (It is not clear whether the tempest in which Dunstan was injured was the same tempest which washed Kenneth ashore. Probably so. We are probably supposed to assume that Dunstan had found out that Kenneth was headed for the Holy Land and that he was trying to overtake him. In the novel Kenneth knows who he is all along. The motif in the opera of a young man finally learning his true identity probably derives from *Guy Mannering* by way of *La Dame Blanche;* the name *Dunstan* recalls to mind Scribe's *Duncan,* who on his deathbed reveals Georges Brown's true identity; see Chapter 4. The idea of a man having secret information about a condemned person's identity which, if revealed, would arrest his execution probably owes something to Rossini's *Ivanhoé,* wherein interestingly the man with the secret is a Mohammedan named Ismael; see Chapter 9.)

The King and his entourage come on stage for the finale, which could be entitled Kenneth's Trial Scene. It begins with a solemn, stately introduction and choral ensemble ("De la justice inexorable / Voici l'instant"). (The material of the finale owes something to chapter xvii, in which Berengaria, Edith, the Hermit of Engaddi, and El Hakim all plead with Richard in Kenneth's behalf; but it owes more in general conception and atmosphere to Rebecca's trial scene as presented in some of the *Ivanhoe* operas.) The King solemnly presents the case against Kenneth, who remains silent. When the King asks him whether he is guilty, he replies that he is. "Qu'espères-tu?" the King asks. "La mort!" is his reply. Richard then sentences him to death. At this moment Édith rushes in, followed by the Queen. She tells Richard that he is deceived, for Kenneth left his post only because he had been ordered to do so by someone dear to Richard himself. Richard thinks that she means the Queen, but Édith, kneeling, immediately explains the momentary confusion: "En ce instant suprême,/ Elle pleure á vos pieds!..." "Grâce, Édith!" exclaims Bérengère in a soft voice. Édith continues: "Mais il faut qu'elle parle et soit, par son courage,/ Digne du noble amour que tout son cœur partage." In short, she loves Kenneth. Now comes a large ensemble composed of the five principals and chorus: Édith declares that she will offer herself to punishment rather than allow Kenneth to perish: Bérengère realizes that Édith is assuming the blame for Kenneth's neglect of duty when she herself is the one really responsible for it; Richard sings that Édith is blemishing his name; Kenneth calls on God to protect his noble protectress; and Ismael observes that both Édith and Kenneth have behaved nobly. Richard, however, believes that she has behaved dishonorably: "Ainsi donc, devant tous, Édith se déshonore!" She replies: "Se déshonore-t-on en sauvant son époux?" All present exclaim, "Son époux!..." Richard is horrified at the thought that she should marry an obscure orphan, but the next moment Ismael comes forward and announces to all that Kenneth is actually David, son of King Malcolm of Scotland. He continues: "Oui, que David retrouve,/ Vivant en moi, l'écrit que Kenneth déchira./ C'est à moi que Dunstan l'a dicté." When Richard asks for proof, Ismael replies that one witness remains whose very name is proof in itself. Suddenly trumpets are heard, signifying the end of the truce, and Ismael reveals himself as the renowned Saladin. *"Pendant ces derniers vers, la tente s'est ouverte et a laissé voir au dehor des écuyers arabes, amenant un cheval richement caparaçonné. Saladin s'elance sur son cheval et disparaît.–Cri général aux armes!–La toile baisse."* (The bold alterations in the original story are too obvious here to require explanation and comment. The last forty percent of the novel has been omitted.)

Richard en Palestine follows Scott's novel least closely of the works examined in this chapter. Sometimes the alterations result in lack of clarity. We are never told, for example, how it came about that Kenneth thinks he is an orphan. What his exact connection had been with the deceased Dunstan is not explained. There is no convincing explanation of the delay on the part of Ismael (Saladin) in revealing Kenneth's real identity. As is often the case in Walter Scott operas, the principals seem very pale replicas of their originals. Interestingly, there is no mention anywhere of a talisman. Adam's tuneful, pleasing music is obviously the work of a well-trained professional, but it is not ambitious nor in any particular way remarkable. Clément and Larousse found it "froide et sans couleur"—too harsh a judgment, in my opinion, but not wholly unfounded.

The Talisman

This, Balfe's last opera, was first performed on 11 June 1874 in London, at Drury Lane, four years after his death.[11] The original English libretto, entitled *The Knight of the Leopard,* was the work of Arthur Matthison. For the première, however, an Italian translation by Giuseppe Zaffira was used in order to suit the fancy of the times.[12] The opera was enthusiastically received and was described the next day in *The Times* as "one of the composer's most carefully-considered and best-balanced works." This same version, *Il Talismano,* was produced shortly thereafter in Dublin (23 September 1874). The original English version, with the title *The Talisman,* was done in New York (10 February 1875) and in Liverpool (15 January 1891). It was given as *King Richard in Palestine* in Monte Carlo (26 March 1918).[13] The famous soprano Christine Nilsson sang the role of Lady Edith at the première; mezzo-soprano Marie Roze did the Queen; tenor Campanini, Sir Kenneth; and baritone Rota, King Richard. Others in the dramatis personae are De Vaux, the Emir, Nectabanus, Philip of France, and Leopold of Austria. The Emir is just an emir: that is, he does not appear also as El Hakim and Saladin. The Hermit of Engaddi is mentioned in the early scenes, but he does not appear as a character. Other notable omissions include the Archbishop of Tyre, the Grand Master, Conrade of Montserrat, Blondel, and the dog Roswal.

The prelude is a potpourri of material from the opera proper.[14] When the curtain opens, we see "the sandy plains in the vicinity of the Dead Sea."[15] The first scene is based loosely on Scott's second chapter, in which Kenneth and the Emir refresh themselves at an oasis, but the opening chorus of Arabs ("Soldiers of Araby, mark what the Koran saith") has no parallel in the novel—Scott's Emir is not accompanied by an entourage of followers. When the Arabs have departed, Sir Kenneth and the Emir come on stage. In the recitative preceding their duet, the Emir refers to their recent combat (which is not acted out) and also to his promise when they made their truce to lead Kenneth to the Hermit of Engaddi. He says that he has heard much about the beauty of the English ladies who are now at Engaddi for prayer and meditation. (In the novel Kenneth does not know beforehand that the ladies are there.) In the ensuing duet Kenneth praises English ladies ("Golden love-locks floating,/ Dancing on the breeze"), while the Emir extolls the beauties of "Saracenic maidens" ("Raven locks o'er clust'ring,/ Brows as ivory white").—The text is only suggested by the discussion of women which Scott's Kenneth and Emir have near the end of chapter ii: Scott is primarily interested in the Emir's difficulty in understanding the concept of courtly love, which renders a Christian knight slave to *one* lady. This scene is our only encounter with the Emir in the opera; as already indicated, he does not reappear later as El Hakim or Saladin.

The second scene takes place in "a corridor of the Chapel of Engaddi" and opens with a recitative and aria for Lady Edith. (In the novel we are not introduced to Edith until later. The text of her *larghetto*—"Solemnly, softly cometh the nightfall," etc.—has no parallel in the novel.) A letter has informed her of Kenneth's imminent arrival at Engaddi as Envoy of the Princes. She knows that Kenneth loves her, and she suspects that he is more than a simple knight, since he has dared to look with affection on Edith Plantagenet. The E-flat major of the *larghetto* changes to minor at the entrance of the comically sinister Nectabanus, who informs Edith that the Queen desires her company and that the Princes' Envoy has arrived. Edith concludes her aria with a passionate cabaletta (in E major) in which she expresses her joy at Kenneth's arrival. After she has departed, Nectabnus, in a recitative, muses on recent events: "Now do I see why yonder smooth tongued Knight did give me the gold to bring him to the Chapel." (In the novel Kenneth has no dealings with Nectabanus prior to encountering him unexpectedly *after* the service.) His aria—"I love the sky when no bright stars shine"—is described in the "pro-em" to the vocal score as "a congenial diatribe of admiration for all that is detestable and mischievous betwixt earth and sky, and of hatred for all that ordinary mortals delight in and hold in the highest esteem." (Nectabanus' role is more prominent in the opera than in the novel.)

We move now to "the rock-hewn gothic Chapel of Engaddi." The action of the scene derives from chapter iv, but much more is made of Edith and Kenneth's mutual recognition. At the same time that Edith and a chorus of ladies are singing the "Salva Regina," Kenneth exclaims, " 'Tis my Edith, she kneels at the shrine./My soul feels her presence. Oh, Edith./Ah! her heart speaks to mine, speaks to mine." During a lull in the chorus Edith exclaims, " 'Tis he! 'tis Sir Kenneth, our spirits unite./My thoughts from pray'r wander to thee, gallant Knight." Edith rejoins the chorus for the conclusion of the "Salve Regina," Kenneth singing at the same time, "My soul feels her presence, her heart speaks to mine." The stage directions in the score are sparse, but the plot summary in the "pro-em" often makes up for this lack: "As the procession winds past the strain subsides; but when Edith finds herself near the kneeling knight she drops a rose-bud at his feet enjoining silence at the same time by an expressive gesture." (Scott's Edith drops one rose-bud and a bit later another. She does not need to enjoin Kenneth to silence because he is more tactful than his operatic counterpart and is not about to speak when speech is obviously out of place.) When all the ladies have gone, Kenneth, now alone on stage, sings an aria described in the "pro-em" as "one of the purest and tenderest inspirations of deep-felt passion that ever breathed in music—a gem of melody destined to a wide popularity, but which in such instances however familiar it renders its object to the ear, never robs it of its undying freshness":

Example 14-3

Flow' - ret I kiss thee, Drink thy sweet breath, Each bloo-my

pe - tal Will che - rish till death, Close to my fond heart

flow' - ret, oh come, Love's gen - tle her-ald, rest rest in thy home.

Strains of the melody are heard at later points in the score. The text is suggested by Scott's sentence: "To grope on the floor for the buds which she had dropped—to press them to his lips—to his bosom—now alternately, now together . . . were but the tokens of passionate love, proper to all ages." At the end of the aria the *"curtain slowly falls; the Knight remains kneeling and kissing the rose."*

The first scene of Act II takes place in Richard's tent. In the opening recitative and aria Richard sings of Berengaria's return from her pilgrimage to Engaddi and of his love for her. (There is no reference to her having gone to Engaddi to pray for his recovery: the operatic Richard is not sick.) When Kenneth enters, Richard alludes to his amorous interest in Edith and tells him that he would have rewarded him earlier, if his aspirations had been humble. "Leopard thou art," he continues, "but beware of my anger!/Tempt not, Sir Knight, the paw of the Lion"— paraphrased from chapter ix, during the course of the conversation in which Richard learns from Kenneth of his mission to Engaddi. De Vaux suddenly enters with the news that the Duke of Austria has abused the English standard. (In the novel, chapter xi, Montserrat is the bearer of these tidings.) Richard, De Vaux, and Kenneth then sing a rousing trio in which they announce their determination to go immediately to St. George's Mount. (The operatic De Vaux is not a well-developed character in comparison with his original. There is virtually nothing of the plain, blunt soldier in his make-up. Indeed, such qualities would be unusual in a role assigned to a tenor.)

We move now to St. George's Mount for a "Concerted Morceau" made up of Richard, Kenneth, De Vaux, the King of France, the Duke of Austria, and choruses of English, French, Austrians, and pages. At the beginning of the scene the action follows the novel, chapter xi, fairly closely. When Richard, pointing to the abused banner, asks, "Who hath done this?" the Duke of Austria replies, " 'Twas I, Duke Leopold of

Austria." The King of France attempts to smoothe things over, but Richard interrupts him: "A truce, oh France, with thy remonstrance. Our brother Austria here hath been a thought too insolent, and Richard hath chastis'd him." He then orders Kenneth to guard the newly hoisted English banner. When the King of France suggests that the Austrian and English forces "should but compete in warring with the Pagan," Richard asks Austria to give him his hand—and he does so, albeit begrudgingly. (In the novel he and his men withdraw after a further insult from Richard.) Richard then urges all present to follow him to Zion. Stimulated by his spirited words, they exclaim,

> Zion, Zion!
> Lead us on, Lion heart! Lead us on, Lion heart!
> Lead us on, to Jerusalem, to Jerusalem . . .
> It is the will of heaven!
> Zion, Zion, Zion, Zion!

In the novel this material comes in chapter xix, just after Richard's eloquent address to the Council of the Crusade. The operatic Richard's ensuing prayer ("Monarch supreme") and war song ("On, valiant squires") have no exact parallels in the novel, but they are *suggested* by the address. Presently everyone leaves the stage except Kenneth, who sings a recitative and aria as he guards the English banner. Again there is no exact parallel in the novel, but both the words and the general atmosphere are suggested by Scott's paragraphs describing Kenneth's feelings at the beginning of chapter xii. Nectabanus' persuasion of Kenneth to leave his post and go to Edith follows more or less the material of chapter xii, although the operatic Kenneth seems more love-sick, that is, less able to control his emotions regarding Edith, than does Scott's hero. In fact throughout the opera Kenneth seems more the sentimental lover than the valiant knight, but, as in the novel, he does not leave his post immediately, for there is a serious conflict in his heart between Love and Honor:

Example 14-4

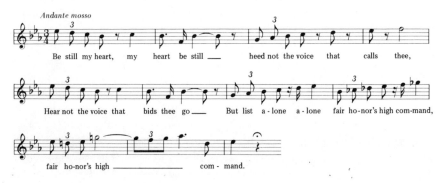

Be still my heart, my heart be still ___ heed not the voice that calls thee,

Hear not the voice that bids thee go___ But list a-lone a-lone fair ho-nor's high com-mand,

fair ho-nor's high _____ com - mand.

(The melody recurs in the finale to the act.) Love wins out when Nectabanus shows Kenneth Edith's ring. Kenneth invokes the "kindly saints"
to guard the banner (because he has no dog) and commands Nectabanus
to lead him "on to yon tent."

The remainder of the act takes place at "the Queen's pavilion, richly
and luxuriously decorated." It opens with a chorus of ladies who sing of
the tedium of waiting until the war is over ("Hours and hours roll slowly
on") and who wonder when they shall return to England. Afterwards the
Queen asks for a harp to accompany herself as she sing a lai of fair
Navarre. This lai ("Beneath a portal") concerns a maiden who sees a monk
recently returned from a pilgrimage and asks for his blessing. She tells
him that her lover is fighting in a war in the very land from which the
monk has just come. It turns out that the monk-pilgrim *is* her lover.
(Berengaria's lai has no parallel in the novel. The idea of having a set piece
like this may have been suggested by Blondel's Song of the Bloody Vest,
which, unlike the lai of Navarre, relates obliquely to the main story.) Upon
Berengaria's request, Edith then sings a song of one Ladye Eveline ("Like
some fair flower by cruel tempest hurt"), who pines away when her lover is
killed in battle. (The song has no parallel in the novel.) In the ensuing
recitative the Queen teases Edith, as in chapter xiii, about the virtual
certainty that she will lose her ring in their wager. In words very close to
Scott's, Edith expresses her disapproval of the Queen's game:

> A world of rubies would I give,
> Ere ring or name of mine had been so used,
> To bring a brave man to disgrace,
> To punishment, perhaps to death.

> "But I would give a bushel of rubies ere ring or name of mine had
> been used to bring a brave man into a fault, and perhaps to disgrace
> and punishment."
>
> (chapter xiii)

Having just returned to the tent, Nectabanus now announces that Kenneth is "behind yon canvas" and has heard everything. As the Queen and
the ladies vacate the stage to Edith and Kenneth, the Queen asks Edith to
ask Kenneth to pardon her. (The operatic Berengaria is a much more
dignified personage than Scott's child-like, spoiled Berengaria, who is
embarrassed that a man should be in her apartment, fears for *her* honor
rather than his, and flees "with a loud shriek." Matthison and Balfe have
considerably elevated her character, as also they have done with Richard.)

The next number is a lengthy recitative and duet for Edith and Kenneth. (The love-story is greatly enhanced from what it is in the novel.
Scott's stance throughout is that Kenneth, in his disguise as the Knight of
the Leopard, is interested in a lady far above him in rank, and therefore
he is strictly limited in what he can do or say—otherwise he would seem
overly presumptuous. In the interest of good opera Matthison and Balfe

disregard the proper etiquette of a courtly-love relationship.) Much of the dialogue in the recitative is close to Scott's. When Edith explains what has happened, Kenneth says humbly,

> One moment I dream'd (oh, what rapture!)
> Love for me in your bosom might live.
> I crave but your pardon, high Lady;
> My daring presumption forgive.

"I wait but for your forgiveness," said the knight, still kneeling, "for my presumption in believing that my poor services could have been required or valued by you."

Edith replies in language less reserved than that of her original:

> Forgive thee, what have I to pardon?
> 'Tis I who have injured thy name,
> And my heart bleeds to see thee debased,
> Yes, my heart bleeds to see thee debased,
> To think of the blot on thy name.
> But fly, gallant Knight, to yon banner,
> Fly, fly, I have nought to forgive.
> I, lo—I esteem thee, would save thee,
> And will cherish thy name while I live.

"I do forgive you. Oh, I have nothing to forgive! I have been the means of injuring you. But oh, begone! I will forgive—I will value you—that is, as I value every brave Crusader—if you will but be-gone!"

Led on by what she has said, Kenneth then exclaims, "Ah! complete the dear word, say thou lov'st me!" (Scott's Kenneth would never have presumed to express himself in such bold fashion.) Edith says that she may say no more. The recitative closes with Kenneth offering to return to her the "fatal, yet if sent by [her], precious ring." Edith begins the duet with language again much less reserved than that of Scott's Edith:

> Keep the ring, yea, keep for ever
> This fond pledge of my regard.
> No command of King or kinsman
> From my heart can thee discard;
> No, no, no, ne'er can thee discard.

"Oh, no, no," she said, declining to receive it. "Keep it—keep it as a mark of my regard—my regret, I would say. Oh, begone—if not for your own sake, for mine!"

The remainder of the duet is Matthison and Balfe's invention. At one point Kenneth apostrophizes the ring thus:

> Charm in peace and shield in battle,

LADY EDITH AND SIR KENNETH, in a scene from Balfe's *Il Talismano*. From the Enthoven Collection, Victoria and Albert Theatre Museum.

SCENE FROM the original production of Balfe's *Il Talismano* at Drury Lane. From *The Illustrated London News*, vol. LXIV, June 20, 1874, p. 581, and by courtesy of the Victoria and Albert Theatre Museum (Enthoven Collection).

Star of promise shining clear,
Precious ring, ah! yes, for ever
Thy bright rays my soul shall cheer.

We are to suppose, then, that to Matthison and Balfe the *ring* is the *talisman* (quite a change from the novel!). Next comes a rousing cabaletta, with Edith and Kenneth both singing, "Away! the voice of honor in lofty tone proclaims./ Away! the flag of England its knightly guard reclaims," etc.

At the close of the duet the King enters. He believes that Kenneth has come to the royal pavilion to tell him of a safe and honorable watch. Kenneth replies that his watch has been neither safe nor honorable. Suddenly De Vaux, assuming the role of Scott's Neville, rushes in with the news that the English banner no longer waves on St. George's Mount. He expresses surprise when he becomes aware of Kenneth's presence: "Sir Kenneth too—Ah, whom see I here?" Richard replies, as in the novel, "A traitor, who by my hand shall die a traitor's death!" Kenneth not only accepts but welcomes his punishment:

Strike, strike, mighty Lion-heart, strike.
Life is as nought now honour's gone.
Strike, oh great King, the unworthy Knight who hath betray'd thee.

(As in Adam's opera, Kenneth's memorable confrontation with Richard takes place in the Queen's pavilion, immediately after the loss of the standard. Unlike the parallel situation in the novel, the ladies are present from the beginning. The scene is based on material from chapters xiii, xv, xvii, and xviii.) The next number is an elaborate sextet with chorus. Edith gets things under way, imploring Richard to spare Kenneth's life:

Example 14-5

As she continues, she openly declares her love for the unfortunate knight (again as in the Adam opera). Berengaria *and De Vaux* (rather than El Hakim or the Hermit of Engaddi) also implore Richard to have mercy. Richard, however, declares that he will show no mercy, and Nectabanus insists that the insult to England can be cleansed but by blood. Kenneth, the last of the principals to join the sextet, expects no mercy: "Come, death; come, grim headsman;/ I fear not, I fear not thy stroke." The people in the chorus now join in, observing Kenneth's bravery. Presently they sing a harmonized rendition of melodic material sung by Kenneth during his duet with Nectabanus at St. George's Mount (see Example 14-4 above), while the principals sing vocal lines which are variations of Edith's initial phrase (Example 14-5 above) and which blend in effectively with the choral ensemble. The total ensemble works up to a huge climax. Then the chorus, singing in unison, begins Edith's phrase, while the principals, also in unison, join in one measure behind in canonic fashion. The ensemble ends with virtually everyone imploring the King to spare the gallant Knight. In the ensuing recitative Edith again begs the King for mercy; she insists that the fault is hers, not Kenneth's. The Queen then confesses that the fault is hers, not Edith's, and begs the King for mercy. Richard finally agrees to spare Kenneth's life, but he will banish him from the Christian camp. (In the novel, chapter xviii, he turns him over to El Hakim.) The act ends in another large ensemble, Kenneth introducing it with the following melody, which is taken up in turn by the other principals and then the chorus:

Example 14-6

Richard and Nectabanus tell Kenneth that he owes his life to Edith and the Queen. The remaining principals and the chorus express heartfelt gratitude to Richard: "Thanks, great monarch, for thy mercy;/ Aye this deed will crown thy glory," etc. The curtain falls.

The first scene of the last act takes place in "an antechamber in Richard's tent." While the orchestra softly plays Kenneth's aria of Act I, "Flow'ret I kiss thee," Richard reads a letter from England in which he learns Kenneth's true identity. De Vaux then informs Richard that the supposed Nubian slave who recently saved his life is none other than Kenneth, who has remained in the camp, despite Richard's orders, for the purpose of punishing Conrade Montserrat, the villain responsible for the loss of the banner. (In this way, then, Matthison and Balfe pass over the material of chapters xix-xxiv.) Richard orders De Vaux to inform Kenneth that all is known and to invite him to attend the high revels that night in the great pavilion. As soon as De Vaux has departed, Edith and the Queen come on stage. In the ensuing trio Edith informs Richard of her desire, owing to her great sorrow, to remain at Engaddi as a nun, while Richard hints that things are perhaps not so bleak as she and Berengaria suppose.

For the final scene we move to the great pavilion. As Richard and the other high personages assume their places, the orchestra plays a rather trite grand march:

Example 14-7

Next we have a part-song entitled "A song to merrie England" (not based on anything in the novel). After receiving warm greetings from the full chorus, Richard orders De Vaux to usher into the royal presence a certain "valiant minstrel Knight," and he urges all "who love the minstrel's gentle art" to listen to him, for he shall sing of love. After a momentary pause, we hear from *without* the voice not of Blondel but of Kenneth singing "Flow'ret I kiss thee." Edith can hardly believe what she hears: "Can I be dreaming? that voice—'Tis he! 'tis Kenneth!" When Kenneth enters, he and Edith join their voices for the remainder of the by now familiar tune. Richard then announces to all present that Kenneth is no traitor but rather the saviour of his life and the Prince of Scotland. He gives Edith's hand to him as all exclaim, "Long live the Prince of Scotland!" Edith expresses her jubilation at this unexpected turn of events in a brilliant coloratura aria ("Radiant splendours, love-lit, sparkling,/ Melt the clouds around me darkling," etc.). Next, "at a beck from the hand of the Lion-Hearted King the curtains closing the back of the pavilion are drawn aside and disclose a view of the sea-shore, with the fleet of the crusading expedition floating in the distance . . . and ready for the embarkation of the allied armies of the red-cross knights . . . ." "And now," sings Richard, addressing the entire assemblage, "our holy mission, nobly, grandly ended,/ Our joyous faces turn we once more home,/ To glorious, merrie England!" All the principals unite with the chorus for the final ensemble, "Glorious England," which is a repetition in vocal arrangement of the grand march:

Homeward yon blue water flows.
Fresh and free the glad wind blows.
Hail, dear England, hail to thee! Hail!

The curtain falls. (The differences between Act III and the last three chapters of the novel are so striking and obvious that no further commentary on my part seems necessary.)

The novel is a multi-faceted work. Richard is sick with a fever, the Soldan displays greater "courtesy" than do the Christians, and the camp is rife with intrigue and petty jealousy; the love story of Kenneth and Edith is only a part of the whole (and not the most interesting part). Matthison and Balfe focus on the love story to an even greater extent than did their predecessors, indeed almost to the exclusion of everything else. At the same time they debase the dignified, courtly-love relationship of the novel into an ordinary, sentimental affair of the heart. But stories of this sort are the heart and soul of much nineteenth-century opera. All in all, their *Talisman* is the most attractive, and perhaps the best, of the various operatic renditions of the novel.

15

§ § §

WOODSTOCK

Several plays based on *Woodstock* are discussed briefly by H. A. White.[1] To my knowledge the novel inspired only one opera. A review in *Le Ménestrel* of the première states that it was "tirée du roman de *Woodstock*,"[2] but this fact has been overlooked everywhere else, no doubt because the title of the opera does not give obvious and immediate indication of its connection with the novel.

Alice

A two-act opéra comique based very loosely on *Woodstock* and entitled *Alice,* with music by Flotow and text by Honoré de Sussy and Gustave Darnay de Laperrière, was first performed early in the spring of 1837, privately, at the Hôtel Castellane.[3] It was well received. Mme de Forges successfully created the title role (Scott's Alice Lee). The Comte de Lucotte, "un ténor fort agréable," sang the role of Charles II. The Vicomte Bordesoulle did the role of Alice's uncle, the Puritan fanatic William Scott (who has little resemblance other than in his hot temper to Walter Scott's old cavalier Sir Henry Lee, *father* of Alice and keeper of the royal lodge of Woodstock; he is a bit reminiscent of Major Ralph Bridgenorth, Puritan fanatic of *Peveril of the Peak* and father of the novel's heroine whose given name, interestingly, is Alice.) The baritone M. Panel sang Daniel, Alice's beau (who has at least *some* resemblance to Scott's tolerant Roundhead, Col. Markham Everard; however, he is a Royalist— ever careful to keep his sympathies subdued so that William Scott will consider him a suitable suitor for the hand of Alice.) Others among the dramatis personae are Sergeant Ruben (not in the novel),[4] the soldier Taff (not in the novel),[5] and Charles' friend Lord Clifford (a role suggested by Scott's Albert Lee, although the librettists apparently had in mind, in addition, Lord Arthur Clifford of the Ancelot-Saintine play, *Têtes Rondes et Cavaliers*—see Chapter 5). As in the novel, the time of the action is 1651; but the setting is "non loin de Brighton" rather than Woodstock.—Some years later the opera was given at the theater of the

Paris Conservatory; the evening was a special occasion arranged for the benefit of people who had suffered in a recent inundation of the Loire. The role of Alice was sung by Mme Anna Thillon, and the other roles were taken by various artists from the Opéra and the Opéra-Comique. The complete text is included in Sussy's *Miscellanées: Essais Dramatiques et Poésies Diverses* (Paris, 1850).[6] The music was not published. According to Flotow's wife, the only manuscript of the score was in the Count of Sussy's possession at the time of his death and was subsequently lost.[7]

The first act takes place inside William Scott's house and begins with a chorus of Cromwell's soldiers ("Parcourons les chemins"), which the reviewer of the première singled out for especial praise. When the soldiers have departed, Alice and Daniel enter *"gaiement"* and ecstatically express their love for one another in a duet. (The Alice and Everard of the novel do not behave so uninhibitedly.) Afterwards William Scott enters, and in spoken dialogue he expresses his disapproval of Daniel's fashionable dress and long hair, both of which make him look too much like a Cavalier. He then tells of the Puritan victory over the Cavaliers at Worcester (as in the novel). The King, however, managed to escape. Anyone who should give aid to him will be punished by death, while 1000 guineas will be given as a reward to the person who delivers him into the hands of the Puritans. When Alice perceives that Daniel is intrigued with the reward, she exclaims, "Je n'en voudrais pas à ce prix!" (The situation here is reminiscent of the proposition that Cromwell makes to Wildrake in chapter viii—namely, that he will give orders to evict the Puritan commissioners from Woodstock Lodge with the tacit understanding that Everard will hand over Charles to the Puritans, should he arrive at the Lodge. Wildrake realizes that these are horrible conditions, and as things turn out, he does not inform Everard of the string attached to Cromwell's seeming generosity.) William Scott remarks that if Daniel had 1000 guineas, he (Scott) would no longer be opposed to Daniel's plans for marriage. Alice cannot refrain from retorting that Scott as a Puritan is supposed to scorn riches. After a bit more conversation Scott and Daniel leave the stage.

Alice, alone, muses that she knows only one fault in Daniel—jealousy. (This is a foreshadowning of what is to come.) Suddenly a stranger (Charles II) enters in great anxiety. He tells Alice that he is an unfortunate adherent to the Stuart party, and in the aria beginning with the words "Le même pays nous vit naître" he implores her to help him. (In the novel, chapter xviii, Alice first encounters Charles at Rosamund's Well; he is disguised as an old woman.) In the ensuing spoken dialogue Alice recalls that Charles I once saved her father from certain death. When the stranger asks her whether the coast is indeed just two miles away, she replies, "Oui." (In the novel the coast is much farther away.) Presently William Scott returns. When he expresses surprise in seeing the strange man, Alice pretends that he is a loyal friend named Dickson from her London days, a good neighbor who helped her take care of her father in his last illness. William Scott believes what she says. (The name *Dickson* was probably suggested by the character of the same name in *La Dame Blanche*.) In reply to William's question about what is going on in London, Dickson says that there is a rumor that Cromwell will be named King. He is understandably moved and upset as William begins to speak of the triumph of Puritanism over the corrupt royal party. When William tells of the joy he experienced in seeing Charles I beheaded, he cannot help exclaiming *à part,* "O mon père!" At this point comes a trio—William singing of his joy in the triumph of Puritanism, Alice imploring God to protect the noble Cavalier, and Dickson (Charles) apostrophizing and praising *à part* his royal martyred father. In the spoken dialogue that follows, Charles can hardly restrain himself from giving himself away. Suddenly all three hear knocking at the door and a voice from *without* demanding that they open up in the name of the Lord Protector. "Je suis perdu!" exclaims Charles *à part.* William notices Alice's troubled look and her hesitation before she finally opens the door. The unexpected visitor is Sergeant Ruben, who leads in a party of soldiers who are tired and thirsty. As they are refreshing themselves he tells William that the son of the tyrant has escaped them. Later in the conversation, when he refers to Alice as "ma belle," William thinks it best that she retire from the room. When she has gone, William reminisces about an important battle in which he hesitated to engage himself, even after the holy standard of Parliament had been raised. But God unexpectedly confronted him, he tells in the musical number beginning with the words "Crétien, éveille-toi," and aroused in him the valor for the holy cause. He is joined by an enthusiastic chorus of soldiers, while Charles, *à part,* prays to God for succor and protection. (The idea of William's hesitation perhaps owes something to Walter Scott's account of Cromwell's hesitation just before the assault on the Lodge, chapter xxxiii.) At the conclusion of the number William and the soldiers depart.

Left alone on stage Charles sings an aria about France, the noble land which sheltered him in his hour of need and to which he now desires to return.[8] Finding her Cavalier melancholy, Alice sympathizes with him in the spoken dialogue that follows. She senses that he is a more important personage than he has indicated and tells him that he can confide in her. Suddenly realizing that he is Charles II, she falls on her knees before him. Charles tells her that he is in quite a predicament, but that fortunately several friends are making preparations for his forthcoming flight to France. One of them, by the name of Clifford, is supposed to bring him word as soon as the time is propitious; but Clifford does not know where he is now to be found, inasmuch as he was forced by circumstances to abandon his former place of refuge in the village. Alice voices the hope that Clifford's intuition will guide him aright. Charles asks her not to disclose his true identity to anyone, not even to Daniel, and he exits when Daniel himself suddenly arrives on the scene. At first unaware of Alice's presence, Daniel sings an aria about how greatly she has charmed him; the pleasures of the soldier and of the gourmet are nothing in comparison with his. He perceives Alice just before he begins the third stanza, in which he sings that the happiness of the seducer in winning new mistresses is nothing beside his own happiness in his love for her. In the spoken dialogue that follows, Daniel senses immediately that something is agitating her, and when he notices a man's mantle, he becomes suspicious. Alice tries to allay his suspicions by telling him that it belongs to Dickson, their house-guest, a friend of the family, but Daniel is incredulous. Sensing from her guilty demeanor that the strange man is in the adjoining room, he opens the door, sees Charles, and orders him to come forth.

The remainder of the act is suggested by Walter Scott's account of the events leading up to the near duel between Everard and Charles (chapter xxviii); Everard believes that the supposed Scotsman Louis Kerneguy (Charles) is his rival for Alice's affection. (In the novel the lover's suspicions are not mere fantasy: Charles actually does try to seduce Alice. Not so in the opera.) Daniel rudely asks Charles who he is. He replies that his name is Dickson and that he is en route to Greenwich to sell his farm. Daniel then comes right out and asks him if he does not in fact love Alice. "Non pas, sur l'honneur!" Charles replies. His words of denial do not convince Daniel, who angrily demands that he choose a weapon and go out to fight with him. When Daniel gets beside himself with jealous anger, Charles has no choice but to draw his dagger. Alice shrieks and throws herself between the two men. Letting the dagger fall, Charles says, "Alice! il vous doit la vie." At his point William, Ruben, and the soldiers come in. William wants to know what the hubbub is all about, and Daniel explains that he has found Alice with a rival lover. Greatly upset, Alice says that she will never marry anyone so jealous as Daniel. (Jealousy is much more prominent in Daniel than in Walter Scott's Everard.) William tells Alice that she has free choice in the dispute; she must decide forthwith which lover she prefers, and the other one must then renounce all claims on her and depart at once. Alice is painfully aware of the dilemma she is in: she must either alienate Daniel or expose the King to danger. (Her situation brings to mind that of Clifford in *Têtes Rondes et Cavaliers,* and of Arturo Talbot in *I Puritani;* see Chapter 5.) The musical finale to the act begins with Alice deciding in favor of Dickson. Daniel and Alice sing farewell to all dreams, hopes, and joys; William expresses pity for Daniel; Charles expresses concern at having damaged the relationship between Alice and Daniel and implores God for help. William then orders Daniel to leave. Daniel, however, is reluctant to do so, because he is still convinced that Alice loves him. When he threatens to wrest her away from Dickson, William determines to have the nuptials that very night. In the final ensemble Daniel gives vent to his fury; William tells him that he does not fear his fury and again orders him to depart; Alice prays to God for succor; Dickson (Charles) observes that his tristful life brings bad luck everywhere. Just before the curtain falls, the soldiers forcibly remove the highly incensed Daniel from the room. (Unlike the parallel situation in the novel, chapter xxviii, the operatic Charles does not reveal his true identity for the sake of Alice and Daniel when clearly their relationship is gravely damaged because of Daniel's ignorance of what the facts are.)

The setting is the same in Act II. At the beginning of the first *scène* we see Lord Clifford, disguised, a captive in the hands of William Scott and the Puritan soldiers, who sing, "Amis, pas de clémence!" When William asks the stranger who he is, he replies mockingly, "Amant de la nature,/Je suis un voyageur/Errant à l'aventure,/Sans argent, mais sans peur." The soldiers then discover that the stranger is in disguise, and they take a paper from him. William realizes that the man must be an adherent to Charles II and threatens him with death if he refuses to talk. In a reprise of the opening ensemble ("Amis, pas de clémence"), Clifford joins in, singing that Providence is watching over him. The musical number continues as Dickson (Charles) enters and inquires about the noise. William explains to him what has happened and shows him the paper. Seeing the words "On vous attend," which he reads out loud, Charles quickly grasps the import of the situation and recognizes Clifford through his disguise. Charles says that he can make the stranger talk if he may converse with him in private. William agrees to this proposal. As Charles is questioning Clifford, William and the soldiers (from the rear of the stage) break in now and then to ask whether the stranger has divulged any information. Between the interruptions Clifford manages to give Charles the information necessary for his escape. When William impatiently asks Dickson what the stranger has said, Clifford himself answers the question by repeating the above-quoted stanza ("Amant de la nature," etc.). In the final ensemble William and the soldiers demand his execution; Charles tells Clifford that in the Puritans' eyes he is culpable, but that in reality he is a hero. (The plot as revealed in this musical number probably owes something to Henry Lee's plans for Charles' escape, chapter xxxii; Albert Lee is to remain behind disguised as Charles and sacrifice his life, if necessary, in diverting the Puritan soldiers from their royal prey.)

After the soldiers have led Clifford away, Alice enters in a melancholy frame of mind. William tells her that he believes she will be happier with Dickson than with the hare-brained Daniel. He then tells Dickson that the two of them should leave Alice to herself, so that she can prepare herself for the wedding. (The motif of the imminent, undesired wedding is not to be found in *Woodstock;* it perhaps derives from *The Bride of Lammermoor.*) The next *scène* is allotted to Alice, who sings an aria about her dilemma: Daniel scorns her because he does not understand the situation. She still loves him, but she has been forced by circumstances to sacrifice her happiness in order to save the King, and for these reasons she feels depressed. At the conclusion of her aria the shadows of evening begin to fall. Suddenly Charles re-enters. He expresses concern about the fate of

Clifford, and also about Alice. She tells him not to trouble himself with thoughts of her, but rather to flee. Realizing that she will be in mortal danger if her part in his escape is discovered, he urges her to come with him. (Nowhere in the libretto is there any indication that he wants her for a mistress.) In a duet she again implores him to flee, and he again implores her to come with him. She does not respond favorably to his proposal, because flight with him would imply that she has been unfaithful to Daniel, whom she still loves. "Un seul espoir vous reste," she sings finally; "Dieu vous sauve, ô mon Roi!" William Scott overhears these words from the wings and rushes in, crying, "Le roi!... le roi!... trahison!" Charles and Alice quickly depart, locking the door behind them (a motif perhaps borrowed from *The Abbot;* see Chapter 10).

Daniel responds to William's cry for help and unlocks the door. Like Everard, he is relieved when he hears that Dickson is not a rival lover but rather Charles Stuart. When William says that he will sound an alarum for everyone to pursue the King, Daniel reminds him that Alice's life will be jeopardized, in view of Cromwell's ordinance that anyone who gives assistance to Charles is to be punished by death. William thinks that Alice's life is of little consequence, so long as the tyrant falls. Daniel is astounded that the old Puritan has so little feeling for his niece, and their conversation becomes more and more heated. Daniel then reminds William of his own vulnerable position in that Charles was given asylum in *his* house; everyone will naturally assume that he assisted in the escape. In reply William suggests to Daniel the possibility that Charles Stuart is Alice's lover. Troubled at this thought, Daniel does not know what to believe. At this point Alice herself enters. When William asks her what has become of Charles, she replies that she has just seen the boat which will transport him to France. Then, hearing the sound of a canon in the distance, she joyfully exclaims, "Charles Stuart est sauvé!" William is incensed: "Malheur! malheur à toi!" Daniel gallantly offers to be her defender, but she is understandably a bit put out with him, and instead of accepting his offer she chastises him for having believed that she was acting in ill faith. She explains that something more sacred than honor compelled her to aid the unfortunate man: she heard the voice of her beloved father calling to her from heaven to save the King. (In this last respect her experience brings to mind William's similar experience, which he related to the soldiers in Act I; see above.) Ruben and the soldiers enter for the final *scène.* Daniel explains that he found himself unable to surrender Alice to Dickson without resistance. "Il fallait," he continues, "que l'un de nous renonçât à Alice, ou mourût;—il a mieux aimé fuir... vous ne le reverrez plus!" Ruben turns to William and asks him what he thinks about these recent developments. Neither Daniel nor Alice knows how William will react or what he will say. Looking fixedly at him, Daniel says that he and Alice hope that he will pardon them for their transgression. "Nous vous aimerons tant!" Alice adds. As if speaking to himself, William says sombrely,

"Mes serments violés!—Ma vieillesse entachée!" Ruben then expresses the wish that they might get on at once with the marriage, even though the bridegroom is not the one whom they had expected.

DANIEL: William!...
ALICE: Mon oncle!...
WILLIAM: Soyez heureux, si Dieu le permet!... (*Bas.*) Pour moi, plus de repos!

In short, William capitulates. The opera closes with the soldiers singing briefly in celebration of the occasion.

Obviously the story of the opera is quite different from the original story. The characters are different too—and simpler. Nothing of Everard's Waverley-like uncertainty as to which side to be on comes out in Daniel, who is clearly a man of Cavalier leanings. The reprehensible side of the personality of Scott's Charles is not evident in the operatic Charles, who is a model of princely virtue and decorum. Scott's hot-tempered old Cavalier, Sir Henry Lee, with his passionate devotion to the Stuart family, is changed into a hot-tempered old Puritan who has an inveterate hatred for the Stuarts. As in *Têtes Rondes et Cavaliers* and *I Puritani*, Cavaliers of the novel become Roundheads in the opera, and vice versa. Alterations of this sort would probably have appeared grotesque to a nineteenth-century English audience, but not to the two French audiences who were so fortunate as to actually see *Alice*. They no doubt were much less knowledgeable about Puritans and Cavaliers in general and probably ignorant altogether of the niceties in the various issues over which so much blood was spilt and so many lives wasted in seventeenth-century England.

16

§ § §

THE HIGHLAND WIDOW

*T*he *Highland Widow* was first published in 1827 as one of the Chronicles of Canongate. To my knowledge, it is the only short work of prose fiction by Scott on which an opera has been based. Interestingly, the one opera in question is a veritable travesty of its original: Scott's deeply moving tragic tale has been metamorphosed into a light, frivolous opéra comique.

Sarah; ou, l'Orpheline de Glencoé

Albert Grisar's *Sarah,* with words by Mélesville (Duveyrier), was first performed in public on 26 April 1836 in Paris, at the Opéra-Comique.[1] The famed Jenny Colon created the title role, which owes something (not much) to Scott's Highland widow, Elspat MacTavish, and something to Scribe's feebleminded Sarah of *La Prison d'Édimbourg* (see Chapter 7). Couderc sang the role of Evan, who is very roughly the operatic counterpart of Scott's ill-starred Hamish Bean. Jansenne sang Evan's commanding officer, Georges Claverhouse, who is a composite of Barcaldine, Sergeant Cameron, and Captain Campbell and who owes his name to the Claverhouse of *Old Mortality.* Deslandes sang the out-and-out comic role of the musician-physician Dougal, who, in recommending Evan for service in the English regiment, performs a function of Scott's wily tacksman Miles MacPhadrick. In other respects, however, Dougal has no resemblance whatever to MacPhadrick or to any other character of the tale. He probably owes his name (and nothing more) to clansman Dougal of *Rob Roy.*[2] The première was given a very favorable review in *Le Ménestrel,*[3] and the production was on the boards several times during the next few months.[4] The orchestral score (without spoken dialogue) was published in Paris by Bernard Latte.[5] M.G. Friedrich translated Mélesville's libretto into German for the vocal score published in Mainz by B. Schott's Sons, who worked in affiliation with Latte.[6] On the whole the opera seems to have been only a partial success. Several commentators have called attention to the triteness of the libretto and to certain deficiencies in the score, particularly with regard to orchestration.[7]

The effervescent overture, with its extended passages of gradual crescendos, is in the style of Rossini. When the curtain rises, we see the interior of Evan's cottage. *"Porte du fond donnant sur les montagnes du Corry-d'Hu et le Loch-Awe."* (Scott has a note on Loch Awe.) *"Une cheminée avec feu de tourbe; à droite un petit cabinet, dont l'entrée est masquée par un mauvais rideau de tartan; du même coté et vers le premier plan, une autre fenêtre, et au-dessous un lit de feuilles de bruyère; plusieurs ustensiles de chasse suspendus aux murs; une table, quelques escabeaux, etc."* As so often in the Walter Scott operas, the opening number is a chorus of hunters. Presently Dougal enters, carrying a bagpipe under his arm, and forthwith launches into a song in praise of his talents as both musician and physician. The men tell him that they are waiting for Evan, who is to join them in their hunt. Dougal observes in reply that Evan is probably in the mountains with Sarah, the feebleminded orphan maiden whom he has brought up. He then sings a *ballade* about Sarah's mysterious origin and her strange compulsion to wander alone through the wild Scottish landscapes. At the conclusion of the *ballade* Evan finally arrives. He tells the hunters that he cannot accompany them, and they depart without him. Dougal then tries to find out, in his clumsy but well-meaning way, the cause of Evan's melancholy. Evan replies that he is worried about Sarah; he is terribly fond of her, and he fears that he will not always be able to provide for her by hunting. Dougal advises him to leave her, but for Evan such recourse is utterly out of the question: "L'abandonner! moi qui ai juré à son père mourant d'être son appui! pauvre vieillard! je le vois encore; c'était le lendemain du massacre de Glencoé, de cette nuit affreuse ou les Anglais, les habits rouges, profitant de notre confiance dans l'amnistrie de Guillaume, égorgèrent trente-huit de nos chefs, jusque dans les bras de leurs femmes, de leurs enfans!" (Evan's account of this shameful, unforgettable incident of the not too distant past is suggested by Scott's *note* on the massacre at Glencoe.) It seems that Evan happened upon Sarah's father, mortally wounded, in the forest. Before he expired, he entrusted to Evan the care and upbringing of his daughter. He also passed on to him a "cachet avec des armes gravées"[8] which he had wrested from one of the English murderers. (Sarah wears this around her neck.) Evan confesses to Dougal that he loves the orphan maiden, despite her apparent mental disorder; unfortunately for him, she loves him only as a brother. To provide for her more adequately he has decided to enlist in a regiment of English soldiers, and he tells of his plans in a moving *romance,* one of the most attractive numbers of the whole opera:

Example 16-1

He asks Dougal, who is acquainted with Colonel Claverhouse, to help him out. He also asks him to look after Sarah during his absence—and even to marry her! Dougal is averse to the idea of marrying "une folle," but he promises Evan that he will speak in his behalf with the colonel.

Not long after Evan has departed, Claverhouse arrives on the scene, and upon Dougal's request he promises to take Evan into his regiment. He then tells of his having been recently saved from death, while he was in the Highlands, by a young lady unknown to him. Dougal informs him that his benefactress was none other than Sarah. After Dougal has departed, Claverhouse muses in spoken recitative on the massacre at Glencoe. It seems that his father had taken part in it and later regretted his actions. His dying request was for his son Georges to seek out any who might have survived (in order to restore to them, we learn later, everything which the English had wrongfully wrested from them). Georges has searched in vain; he fears that he will not be able to fulfill his father's last request. In an aria he sings of his love for his beautiful benefactress. At the conclusion of the number Sarah herself enters, and, momentarily mistaking Claverhouse for Evan, she kisses him. During the course of the dialogue that follows, Claverhouse humorously explains to her what a *husband* is. Suddenly both of them hear the sound of distant trumpets, which indicate to Claverhouse that he must return at once to his regiment. He promises Sarah that he will return that very night. After he has departed, she ponders over what he has taught her. She expresses boredom with her life as a child of Nature ("C'est ennuyeux de courir toujours seule"), and she decides that she wants Evan for her husband. Presently Evan re-enters to tell Sarah of his decision to join Claverhouse's regiment. She is sorrowful at the thought of separation from him, and when he goes out to make final preparations, she deliberates on a means by which she can prevent him from leaving her.

Next, Dougal re-enters to pay Sarah a visit. He is much impressed with her charms, especially when she informs him that she has decided to take on a husband and asks him to teach her how to win one. As the humorous *scène* of spoken dialogue unfolds, Dougal obviously becomes more and more interested in her. Maybe marrying her would not be such a bad idea after all, he muses. Sarah then tells him about her unfortunate friend, "la vieille Meg," who is so ill that she cannot sleep.[9] Before departing, Dougal entrusts Sarah with a sleeping potion to take to Old Meg. We soon learn, however, that she has other ideas about what to do with the potion. When night falls, Evan returns to the cottage, and he and Sarah have their last meal together. She then administers to him a powerful dose of the sleeping potion, which almost immediately takes effect. She sings to him while he sleeps. In the final *scène* other newly enlisted men come to the cottage in search of their friend Evan. They think that he has forgotten his binding agreement, and they do not want to see him undergo the indignity of punishment. (The idea of punishment is in Scott, but the men who seek Hamish Bean do so at a later point in the story, with the purpose of apprehending him for his failure to report to duty.) During the course of the number we hear in the orchestra a melody that was the principal theme of the overture:

Example 16-2

Sarah tells the men that Evan has already departed. She urges them to stop singing their noisy song so that her "sick aunt" lying asleep on the bed will not be disturbed. *"Ils sortent par le fond; et tandis que l'on entend le chœur et la marche, Sarah ferme la porte, revient près d'Evan, souleve un peu le plaid pour le laisser respirer. La musique s'éloigne peu à peu; la toile tombe."*

When the curtain rises on the second act, the setting is exactly the same. Sarah looks at Evan, who is still asleep, and seems to be anxious about his awakening. As in Act I, she sings to him while he sleeps, and afterwards, like Elspat MacTavish, she begins to fear that the dosage was too potent and that he may never awaken. She notices, however, that he is still breathing. Dougal then enters and informs her that he has found her a husband (meaning himself). When she tells him that she has already found someone (meaning the sleeping Evan, whom he does not notice), he thinks that she is coyly referring to himself. He rushes off to find witnesses and entertainers for their wedding, which he wishfully and foolishly thinks is imminent. Finally Evan awakens. When Sarah joyfully tells him that he has overslept, he is astounded and horrified. Soon they hear in the distance a trumpet heralding the reading of an official proclamation. Pointing to the window, Evan says excitedly to Sarah, "Ecoute, et tu vas le savoir."[10] At this climactic moment in the duet we hear the trumpets and strings of the orchestra playing what sounds like a Dead March (no doubt suggested by the Dead March which Scott describes as having been played at Hamish Bean's execution). Sarah listens at the window, hears from afar the voice of the reader, and repeats the individual sentences of the proclamation—to the predictable accompaniment of diminished seventh chords in the orchestra. The upshot of the proclamation is that Evan is condemned to death for having failed to report to duty. (In Scott's tale Hamish Bean is to undergo a severe beating for not reporting to his regiment on time. He is sentenced to death and is executed for having killed one of the soldiers who came to apprehend him.) Sarah slams the window shut in horror. In words suggested by Elspat MacTavish's words to Hamish Bean, she urges him to flee with her into the forests of the Highlands:

> Suis-moi toujours,
> A travers nos campagnes
> Je conduirai tes pas;
> Au fond de nos montagnes
> Ils ne te suivront pas.
> Il n'est rien que ne brave
> Mon courage et mon cœur;
> Je serai ton esclave,
> Ton appui, ton sauveur.

At first he refuses, but then, very unlike Hamish Bean, he *agrees* to her proposal. Suddenly they hear someone knocking at the door. Evan quickly conceals himself.

Enter Claverhouse. He tells Sarah that he is late in coming to her because of recent difficulty with rebels who had to be chastised. He thinks that Sarah is dressed up on his account and that she has set the table for him. Unobserved by Claverhouse, Evan both sees what is going on and overhears the whole comic love-duet, which drips with dramatic irony:

CLAVERHOUSE:	Que peux-tu craindre?
SARAH:	Si l'on venait!
CLAVERHOUSE:	Ton amoureux?
	Rassure-toi, ma chère:
	Il est loin de ces lieux,
	Et n'oserait, j'espère,
	Se montrer à mes yeux!

When at a climactic moment Sarah jumps from Claverhouse's lap, the *cachet* which her father had left her remains in her would-be lover's hands. Claverhouse recognizes it at once as the signet of his own late father, and he is utterly astounded. Suddenly Evan reveals himself. He points a gun in Claverhouse's direction, but he does not have the heart to shoot him; instead he shoots at the window and then casts the gun aside. Evan is not aware that Claverhouse had apprised his men before he entered the cottage that if he needed help he would give a signal. Hearing the gun-shot, the men naturally assume it to be the signal and rush in. Even though Claverhouse tells them that everything is a mistake, they strongly suspect that something is amiss because of the presence of Evan. Just as they are about to take him away to meet his doom, Claverhouse cleverly manages to get him off the hook by telling the overly zealous men that the new recruit who they no doubt supposed had failed to report to duty had actually been all the while under his orders to conduct him safely through the mountains. When he inquires further about the signet, Evan's explanation convinces him that Sarah is the last survivor of the massacre at Glencoe. Carrying out his father's last request, he tells Sarah that she is the inheritor of all the lands and goods of Glencoe: "Dès aujourd'hui, Sarah, le vaste domaine de Glencoé vous appartient." At this point Dougal returns, accompanied by a large group of people. He is surprised to see Evan on hand, and he is even more surprised to learn that Evan, rather than he himself, is to marry Sarah. Claverhouse now announces his decision to take Dougal into his regiment in place of Evan. "Grand merci!" Dougal replies. In conclusion the entire chorus sings in anticipation of the forthcoming festivities:

> Pour fêter si belle noce,
> Sonnez, sonnez à la fois,
> Cornemuses de l'Écosse,
> Fifres, tambours et hautbois.

During the course of the final *scène* we hear in the violins a tune associated with Dougal:

Example 16-3

It appeared first in the accompaniment to his song of Act I about his many talents. Much mention is made of his bagpipe (cornemuse), but the orchestral score has no separate part for one indicated.

Obviously the original story has been profoundly distorted in the operatic rendition. The middle-aged Highland widow, mother of the protagonist, becomes the Glencoe orphan girl, his sweetheart. Elspat MacTavish indicates in chapter iv that she did not know about the slaughter at Glencoe at first hand, for she was not yet born, but she had heard her mother tell of it; Sarah, however, was a small child at the time of the brutal massacre, and she turns out to be the last survivor. Despite the distortions, much of the original story remains. Like Hamish Bean, Evan decides to enlist in military service so that he can provide more adequately for the woman who is dearest to him. On his last night at home she administers to him a strong sleeping potion which effectively disenables him from joining his fellow soldiers in Dunbarton at the designated time. I have already mentioned the place names Loch-Awe and Corry-d'Hu. Glenorquhy, the hometown of Scott's Reverend Mr. Tyre (who has no counterpart in the opera), is once referred to by Dougal as a place where a patient awaits him. One final point: Just before Hamish Bean is executed, he hands to the Reverend Mr. Tyre his golden sleeve buttons—"booty perhaps," Scott writes, "which his father had taken from some English officer during the civil wars"—and asks him to give them to his mother. This incident apparently suggested to Mélesville the *cachet* which, as we have just seen, is so important an item in the unraveling of the operatic plot.

17

§ § §

THE FAIR MAID
OF PERTH

Scott's twemty-third novel, *The Fair Maid of Perth,* was published in 1828, forming in itself the Second Series of the Chronicles of Canongate. It inspired some half dozen plays[1] and one opera, an early work of one of the most important of all operatic composers. Unfortunately the gifted young composer was stuck with a very poor libretto, which in one recent short essay has been aptly described as "the silliest of librettos," "[a ludicrous] travesty of Walter Scott's celebrated novel," and "the worst libretto a cynical old hack ever foisted upon a musician of genius."[2]

La Jolie Fille de Perth

Jules-Henri Vernoy de Saint-Georges and Jules Adenis (but mainly the former) were responsible for the notorious libretto, which Georges Bizet set to music in the summer and fall of 1866. Bizet had no illusions about the quality of his librettists' work. "I shall not use their words for compos-ing," he wrote to his friend Edmond Galabert. "I couldn't dig up a single note if I did."[3] But as a young up-and-coming composer he was scarcely in a position to reject anything from the pen of Saint-Georges, who in his day enjoyed a reputation second only to that of Scribe.[4] The opera was first performed on 26 December 1867 in Paris, at the Théâtre-Lyrique. The famed Christine Nilsson was supposed to have sung the title role, but she broke her contract the last minute in order to undertake the part of Ophelia in the première of Ambroise Thomas' *Hamlet.*[5] The role of Catherine Glover thus fell to Jane Devriès. Mlle Ducasse sang Mab, the Queen of the Gypsies, a role suggested by Scott's glee-maiden Louise.[6] The principal male roles were done by Massy (Henri Smith), Barré (the Duke of Rothsay), Wartel (Simon Glover), and Lutz (Ralph, apprentice to Glover, and on the surface quite unlike Scott's young Conachar, the disguised, cowardly Highland chieftain). The opera was warmly received by the public on the night of the first performance, and it was given an enthusiastically favorable review by Théophile Gautier in *Le Moniteur Universel.* Some of the other reviews were not so kind. When the public's

interest began to wane, the manager of the Théâtre-Lyrique was forced to
drop the new opera—after only eighteen performances.[7] It was produced
with greater success the next year in Brussels. Subsequent productions
took place in Geneva (23 November 1885) and in Paris, at the Opéra-
Comique (3 November 1890). It was given in German translation in
Weimar (8 April 1883) and Vienna (5 May 1883), in Italian in Parma (14
January 1885) and Barcelona (September 1890); in Russian in Kiev (2
January 1887); and in English, by the Beecham Opera Company, in
Manchester (4 May 1917) and London (8 June 1917). It was revived by the
Oxford University Opera Club in 1955. The next year a concert version
(in English) conducted by Sir Thomas Beecham was broadcast by the
BBC.[8] The Wexford Festival presented a successful revival in the fall of
1968.[9]

The prelude is a lovely, quiet tone-poem; its melodies do not recur in
the opera proper.[10] When the curtain rises, we are in the workshop of the
armorer Henri Smith, and we soon realize that the opera, despite its title,
has only superficial resemblance to the novel. The original story has been
both simplified and greatly altered and its cast of characters drastically
reduced. There is virtually no Scottish local color. "The characters, too,"
Curtiss rightly observes, ". . . are stripped of the clear-cut, national
qualities that Scott gave them, and are transformed into operatic
stereotypes."[11] The opening number is an "anvil chorus" sung by the
smiths who work in Henri's shop: "Que notre enclume/Résonne et
fume,/Frappons le fer, frappons!" (There is no exact parallel for this in
the novel.) After the workers have departed to make themselves ready for
the carnival which is to begin that evening (perhaps suggested by the
Fastern's E'en revelry of the novel), Henri takes a moment to meditate on
his relationship with Catherine and on his prospects for marrying her.
Presently Mab enters hastily and asks Henri to shelter her from young
gentlemen who are trying to embrace her. He readily agrees to help her.
In recompense she looks at his palm and tells him that Glover and his
daughter will unexpectedly visit him that evening for supper. No sooner
have the words left her mouth than the visitors' knocks are heard at the
door. Henri conceals Mab in an adjoining room to get her out of the sight
of Catherine, who he knows would jealously suspect that he has another
lady-love. (This incident is suggested by Scott's account of Henry's looking after the gleewoman, upon orders of the Prince, and his taking her
into his home when he learns that she has nowhere to go. He is seen on the
streets with her by Pottingar and Proudfute, and malicious gossip soon
gets back to Catherine, who is peeved about what appears to be her lover's
faithlessness. See chapters xi-xii.)

Catherine and Simon Glover enter, together with Ralph, and sing in
expectation of the carnival which is about to commence. Catherine then
launches into her polonaise, a colorful show-piece for coloratura soprano.[12] Afterwards, when Glover suggests to Ralph that the two of them

leave the lovers to themselves, Ralph, who obviously loves Catherine, expresses reluctance to do so. Heated words then pass between Ralph and Henri, and when Ralph does leave, he menacingly remarks to Henri that a state of war exists between them. (The incident is suggested by Scott's account of the quarrel between Conachar and Smith, chapter ii, in which Conachar pulls out a knife.) Henri reminds Catherine that she will soon be choosing a husband in accordance with the customs of St. Valentine's Day, which is now only two days off. (The novel begins on St. Valentine's Eve. Catherine's choice of Henry as her Valentine in grateful recognition of his having prevented her from being abducted does not signify, at least to her way of thinking, that he is now her fiancé.) During the course of their duet he presents her with "une fleur en or émaillé," which he looks on as a symbol of their love. (In the novel he gives her a finely wrought pair of gloves, which her father had made for her late mother. Unlike the gloves, the flower assumes an important function in the further development of the plot.) Catherine is delighted with the gift, and despite her stereotyped, comic-opera-like coquettishness (see fn. 11), she clearly reveals more interest in Henri Smith as a lover than does Scott's Catherine at this point in the story. Suddenly a stranger appears on the scene. He claims that he has come to have Smith repair his dagger, but his real interest is obviously in Catherine. The orchestral motiv that accompanies his entrance is well suited to his rakish personality:

Example 17-1

In the ensuing trio the stranger begins to flirt with Catherine in the very presence of Henri and soon reveals that he is a duke. Busy at his forge Henri cannot hear all the Duke's words, but he is rightly suspicious of his intentions. Just as Wagner's Hans Sachs hammers away at his shoemaking to disrupt Beckmesser's serenade to Eva, so Henri Smith noisily works away at his forge with the purpose of annoying the impertinent, would-be lover. When Henri sees the Duke grab hold of Catherine's hand, he can no longer restrain himself, but fortunately, just as he is about to deal his rival a hefty blow with his hammer, Mab rushes in from the adjoining room and prevents what would have been a rash action. In the brief quartet that follows, Catherine expresses horror at the idea that Henri apparently has a mistress, while the Duke observes that the strange circumstances may play into his hands. At the beginning of the finale Catherine demands that Henri explain forthwith Mab's presence. When he cannot give her a satisfactory answer, she angrily announces that she intends to leave. At this point we hear from *without* the voice of Glover, singing a popular song:

Example 17-2

Glover enters, accompanied by Ralph, and sees the Duke, whom he immediately recognizes as "notre gouvernour." (In the novel the governor, or rather the provost, of Perth is Sir Patrick Chartaris.) Presently the Duke departs. Catherine then repeats her intention to depart, and she flings to the floor Henri's gift, the gold-enameled rose, which Mab picks up and pockets—an important detail for the subsequent working-out of the plot. In the final ensemble Catherine declares that she will forget Henri, Mab protests that he is innocent, and Henri himself passionately but unsuccessfully pleads his case, while Grover and Ralph sing in the bass part the above-cited song about the good king who followed the law of Bacchus. At the very end, however, Ralph departs from the text of the song and sings, "Je sens que Smith est innocent."

The much admired second act takes place at a public square, at night, and begins with a march and chorus of the night-patrol. This is followed by a large choral ensemble in which all present exuberantly sing of the joys of the carnival. Everyone then joins the Duke in a conventional drinking song (which is perhaps suggested by Scott's account, chapter xvi, of the disguised prince and his lackeys virtually forcing Oliver Proudfute to imbibe more wine than is good for him). Next comes the celebrated *Danse Bohémienne:*

Example 17-3

This is one of the best numbers of the score, and it is certainly the best known, since it is part of the superfluous ballet often interpolated into the last act of *Carmen*. Although one might quibble with Bizet for substituting gypsy for Scottish local color, one cannot find fault with the piece itself, which has been universally admired from the time of the opera's première.[13] The Duke then confides to Mab that he hopes to receive Catherine Glover in his palace, at midnight, and that he is in love with her. Incredulous of the latter remark, Mab sings a charming little song, "Les seigneurs de la cour." When the Duke invites everyone to come with him to his palace, we have a reprise of the choral ensemble about the joys of the carnival. Everyone then leaves the stage except Henri Smith, who places himself just below an upper-story window of Catherine's house and sings his haunting *sérénade*:

Example 17-4

Both the words and the music seem a bit sentimental for Henry Smith as Scott conceived him, but the operatic Henri is not exactly a rough, masculine type, and his *sérénade,* with its beautiful, unforgettable melody, fits his personality perfectly. Interestingly, Scott does make occasional mention of Henry's fame as a singer of ballads. Catherine does not appear at the window, and presently Henri leaves the stage to go into a nearby tavern. It is now midnight. An ominous-sounding motiv is heard in the orchestra as Ralph enters:

Example 17-5

Alone on stage, he gives voice to his heretofore pent-up frustrations in a highly original aria:

Example 17-6

The piece has been frequently singled out by critics for commentary and praise. Klein pointedly observes that Bizet has transformed Saint-Georges' "conventionally jealous apprentice" into "an unforgettable figure—different, maybe, from Scott's self-tormenting Highland chieftain, but in his way no less vivid." He believes that "the great musical dramatist of the future emerges in [this] drinking song, in which a devil-may-care merriment alternates with a sombre anguish." It is a "savage aria." "In all the wide range of opera no scene of drunkenness (and they are legion) surpasses it for poignancy." It is "the promising beginning of a new realism in French opera."[14] After the aria a major-domo enters, walking in front of a litter that is borne by two men. He asks Ralph to show him the dwelling of Miss Catherine Glover. At this point Mab appears in disguise, pretends that she is Catherine, gets into the litter, and is carried away. Scarcely believing what he thinks he has just witnessed, Ralph calls on Henri Smith for help. When he tells him that Catherine has been stealthily carried away, Henri exclaims, "Ah! viens! courons!" and excitedly rushes off. Ralph is about to follow after him, but he suddenly becomes aware of his error: he beholds Catherine herself, who has just opened her window. She sings a section from Henri's *sérénade,* ending it with an ecstatic outburst of feeling. The curtain falls quickly.

Between acts the orchestra plays a minuet—a familiar piece of music because of its inclusion by Ernest Guiraud in the second *Arlésienne* Suite. The curtain then rises on a salon in the Duke of Rothsay's palace, where the Duke is revealed gambling with several of his friends. Presently he makes the remark to one lord that in gambling, just as in love, he has never been a loser. In the wings a small orchestra plays a cheerful tune which brings to mind the gambling scene from *La Traviata:*

Example 17-7

The Duke then sings a recitative and cavatina in which he expresses his love for Catherine. (The number is often omitted.) When Mab enters wearing a mask, he thinks that she is Catherine. The gamblers obligingly withdraw when Mab says that she will unmask herself only in the presence of her lover. All through this strange love-scene the backstage orchestra plays the above-mentioned minuet. Mab keeps her promise about unmasking herself, but first she extinguishes the lamp, and thus the would-be Don Juan remains in the dark as to her real identity. When he becomes overly persistent in his protestations of love, she manages to elude him and withdraw, but in the meantime he has gotten his hands on the gold-enameled flower (Henri's gift to Catherine) which she was wearing. He follows after her. At his point Henri Smith, like countless other operatic tenors, *entre precipitamment, pale les habits en désordre.*" Terribly upset because he thinks Catherine has jilted him, he gives vent to his feelings in an intense broken monologue. He hides himself behind a tapestry as the Duke and the courtiers re-enter. Presently he sees Simon Glover come in, accompanied by Catherine, whom the Duke believes to be the masked lady with whom he has just had a rendezvous. Glover, however, has brought Catherine to the palace to announce before the whole court that she has selected Henri Smith as her Valentine and husband. Hearing these words, Henri comes out from behind the arras and exclaims "Qui moi! votre époux, jamais!" The finale begins. Catherine is horrified that Henri should think that she has been unfaithful to him, and she is unable to convince him of her innocence. She appeals to her father, who of course does believe in her innocence. She then appeals to the Duke, but to no avail, since he still actually believes that he has just been with her. He tells her quietly that he will keep their rendezvous a secret. In the huge Meyerbeer-like ensemble that follows, Catherine exclaims, "C'est être hélas! trop misérable/O mon Dieu quand tout m'accable/Nul ne vient me secourir!" After several moments of loud, impassioned singing on the part of all present, there is a temporary lull, during the course of which Catherine, singing alone, makes a special plea to Henri to believe in her innocence and to recall their former days of happiness. All are deeply moved; the ensemble recommences; Henri weakens and gives in. "Mon Dieu!" Catherine joyfully exclaims in the recitative following the ensemble, "vous avez donc entendu ma prière!" But at that very moment Henri suddenly notices the gold-enameled rose which the Duke is wearing on his jacket. He is beside himself with rage and indignation. Snatching the flower away from the Duke, he holds it before Catherine's eyes and exclaims, in a highly dramatic passage, "Autant je vous aimais,/ Autant je vous méprise!/A present—je vous hais!" The chorus comments appropriately on the "jour de douleur" as Catherine exclaims, "Ah! je meurs!" The curtain falls. (There is no such scene in the novel.)

The setting for the final act is the same as for Act II. When the curtain rises during the brief orchestral introduction, we see Henri Smith seated on a stool in front of his shop. It is early morning of St. Valentine's Day. Soon Ralph and a group of artisans enter, approach Henri, and resolutely tell him that they believe Catherine to be innocent. Henri is not convinced. Ralph then swears that he was mistaken about Catherine's having stealthily left her house in the company of courtiers; in reality she spent the entire night at home. Still Henri is not convinced. When he categorically states that Catherine is the Duke's mistress, Ralph and the artisans are so outraged that they call him a liar. Henri accordingly invokes the judgment of God and says that he will fight in mortal combat with anyone who gainsays what he has said about Catherine and the Duke. Ralph bravely decides that he himself will be Catherine's champion and fight against Henri to prove her innocence. The musical number develops into a formal duet with chorus: Henri and Ralph sing of the ordeal they are about to undergo; the artisans make reference to the shores of the River Tweed (rather than the Tay), where the combat is to take place. (The proposed encounter between Henri and Ralph is suggested by the trial by combat between Scott's Henry Smith and Anthony Bonthron, the assassin of Proudfute, in chapter xxiii, and also by the fight between the two clans, chapter xxxiv, in which Smith at last confronts Conachar, who cowardly escapes by plunging into the River Tay.) When Ralph and the artisans have departed, Henri laments in a recitative that he must fight with Ralph, whom he has nothing against; he wishes that he were fighting instead with the Duke. Suddenly Catherine appears. "O ciel! qu'ai-je vu!" Henri exclaims. "Catherine mourante," she replies dolefully, "qui vent vous voir—pour la dernière fois!" His anger immediately subsides at the sweet sound of her voice, and they sing a poignant duet in which Catherine repeats the notion that she will soon die of her great grief. Hearing a clarion call from *without,* Henri realizes that this is the signal for his forthcoming combat with Ralph. He briefly explains to Catherine how all this has come about. He promises her that Ralph will triumph, that her honor will be preserved, that he himself will die. "Pour toi, pour toi, je vais mourir!" he sings *pianissimo* just before rushing out. Catherine screams, "Henri! Henri! arrêtez! ah!" and falls down "*évanouie.*" Hearing the sound of her voice, Glover rushes in, finds her in this sad state, and carries her into their house.

Young lovers come onstage from all sides during the orchestral introduction to the fine "Chœur de la St. Valentin," a piece that impressed Gautier because of "its fresh color, so loving and springlike."[15] All sing in praise of St. Valentine as the young men present flowers to the girls whom they have chosen to be their fiancées. Suddenly Mab appears in the midst of the crowd. She is searching for Catherine to tell her that through her efforts the Duke came to the spot designated for the ordeal and forbade it to take place; thus Henri Smith is saved. Glover sadly tells her that her good news comes too late, for Catherine has lost her reason. *"Catherine sort de sa maison en chantant, Mab y entre sans être vue de Catherine, tout le monde se retire au fond du théâtre."* Obviously deranged, Catherine sings a short coloratura *ballade*—her "mad scene." Afterwards, as if dreaming, she poignantly expresses her sombre delusion that Henri is dead, that she can never be his Valentine. (The mad scene has no exact parallel in the novel, but it is undoubtedly suggested by Catherine's temporary derangement, chapter xix, just after she has heard the rumor that Smith is dead. She runs through the streets, her hair disheveled, and comes up to Smith's house. When she pounds on the door, he himself lets her in—and she soon regains her sanity.) When Henri re-enters, Glover stops him for a moment and points to Catherine. Henri then moves to a position behind Catherine, without her having seen him, and sings a phrase from his *sérénade*. Hearing his voice, she begins to regain her sanity. When he sings a second phrase, she repeats it perfectly, her sanity having now completely returned. From *within* Mab now opens the window of the Glovers' house and appears wearing a dress just like Catherine's—this action explaining to all how the great misunderstanding came about. Next, singing the melody of the St. Valentine's Chorus, Henri presents flowers to Catherine and asks her to kiss him in recompense. She falls into his arms, Mab comes forth from the house, Glover and the chorus move forward—and all join together for a joyful reprise of the St. Valentine's Chorus, which concludes the opera. (Again, there is no such scene in the novel.)

"As for Walter Scott's novel," Bizet wrote in the above-cited letter to Galabert, "I must confess myself a heretic. I find it loathsome. But let me explain. It is a loathsome novel, but an excellent book."[16] ". . . Bizet's dictum on the work is sound," Curtiss explains. "The book is good because it is permeated with Scott's own virtue, his inborn feeling for his country. But the plot of the novel is tenuously laden with Border feuds and pseudo-Shakespearean royal intrigues, spun out beyond readability."[17] Ironically enough, something similar can be said about *La Jolie Fille de Perth.* It is an unsatisfying *opera* because of its shallow libretto, but an excellent *score* with which Bizet himself, with good reason, was pleased. All things considered, he made the very best of a bad bargain.

18

§ § §

TALES OF A GRANDFATHER, First Series, Chapters VI–IX

T he story of the one opera to be discussed here was inspired by Walter Scott's account of Scotland's struggle for independence at the beginning of the fourteenth century, under the leadership of her brave king, Robert Bruce. Scott wrote and published two versions of his Scottish history. The first comprises Series 1–3 of *Tales of a Grandfather;* it professes "to be only Tales, or Narratives from Scottish Chronicles" and is intended for young readers. The second version, intended for the adult reader, is his *History of Scotland.* In the former the story of Robert Bruce comprises chapter vi–ix of the First Series (chapters vii–xi in the important Revised Edition of 1828); in the latter, chapters viii–xii. The libretto of *Robert Bruce* appears to have been inspired mainly by the popular, simply told earlier version.

Robert Bruce

This last of the Rossini pastiches, with words by Alphonse Royer and Gustave Vaëz, was first performed on 30 December 1846 in Paris, at the Theater of the Royal Academy of Music.[1] The veteran librettists were already acquainted with Scott's work through their having translated and adapted for the French stage, several years earlier, Cammarano's libretto for Donizetti's *Lucia* (see Chapter 8). The Swiss composer Louis Niedermeyer, with the full consent of Rossini himself, carefully put together the score from several of the master's operas, notably and mainly *La Donna del Lago.*[2] Although Niedermeyer had never before written a genuine Walter Scott opera, he was at least familiar with the matter of Scotland: his *Marie Stuart,* with a libretto by Théodore Anne (*not* based on *The Abbot*), had been performed with some degree of success at the Opéra two years previously (see Chapter 10). The lengthy discussion of *Robert Bruce* in Clément and Larousse's *Dictionnaire des Opéras* is highly commendatory. Nevertheless the opera did not prove successful, and it soon disappeared from the musical scene. "The opera failed," according to Grove's entry on Niedermeyer, "but the use of the saxhorn, the eight trumpets in four different keys in the overture and the skill with which various movements from 'Zelmira' and 'Armida' were adapted attracted the attention of musicians." Although obviously *inspired* by Scott, the plot of the opera is for the most part the invention of the librettists. It is not based on any single episode in the life of Robert Bruce but is *suggested* rather by several of the episodes which Scott recounts.[3] The dramatis personae, along with their interpreters at the première and the various voice ranges involved, include Robert Bruce (Baroilhet), baritone; Édouard II (Paulin), tenor—a lover of pleasure but otherwise unlike either the weak king depicted by Scott or the homosexual of the plays by Marlowe and Brecht; Douglas-le-Noir (Anconi), bass; Arthur (Bettini), tenor, officer in Édouard's service—has no counterpart in Scott; Morton (Rommy), bass, English captain—apparently owes his surname to the Henry Morton of *Old Mortality;* Dickson (Bessin), baritone, Highlander in the service of the Count of Stirling—owes his surname perhaps to the Dikson of *La Dame Blanche,* perhaps to the Dickson *alias* Charles II of Flotow's *Alice,* perhaps to Scott's Thomas Dickson, a "strong, faithful and bold man" who was slain in aiding his master Lord Douglas in an assault on English-occupied Douglas Castle; Marie (Mme Stolz), mezzo-soprano, Douglas' daughter—has no counterpart in Scott; Nelly (Mme Nau), soprano, Dickson's daughter—has no counterpart in Scott. The time of the action is 1314.

After the overture, the curtain rises on a setting reminiscent of the first act of *La Donna del Lago:* "Site pittoresque.—Des rochers.—Un lac.—Une chaumière.—Au fond, dans le lointain, le château de Douglas." Scènes i–ii: Wounded Scottish soldiers assemble in the dawn, and Robert Bruce tries to bolster up their sunken spirits. They are soon joined by Douglas, who is accompanied by several warriors. Presently they all hear in the distance the sound of English soldiers on a hunt:

Example 18-1

(The music is the hunting music from *La Donna del Lago,* Act I; cf. Chapter 2, Musical Example 2-4.) Douglas orders the Scottish soldiers to disperse. He and Bruce then go into the cottage to await a boat that will take them safely to his château. Scènes iii–iv: Arthur, Morton, and the English chevaliers enter, to the accompaniment of a familiar "Rossini crescendo" (part of the hunting music from *La Donna del Lago*):

Example 18-2

They sing in choral ensemble of their concern about their King, who has become separated from them during the course of the chase (a motif from Tottola's libretto for *La Donna*). When most of them express fear that he may be in danger, especially if Bruce is still present in the neighborhood, Morton and several others assure them that Bruce was too badly defeated to be much of a menace to anyone; Arthur, moreover, is certain that he has already departed for France. Arthur remains behind when Morton and the chevaliers exeunt to continue their search for the King. In a pensive mood, he sings of his dilemma in a monologue introduced by the orchestral figure that accompanies Uberto's (Giacomo's) entrance in *La Donna del Lago:*

Example 18-3

(Cf. Chapter 2, Musical Example 2–6.) He is in love with Marie, Douglas' daughter, but he is honor-bound to serve the English king. (His dilemma is perhaps suggested by the historical Bruce's feelings of guilt when, in the early part of his career, he fought on the side of the English against his fellow countrymen. Indeed, as one peruses Scott's chapters on Robert Bruce, one finds several examples of Scottish Highlanders who fought at one time or another, for one reason or another, on the side of the English. Interestingly, the man or woman with conflicting loyalties is a character often found in the Waverley Novels—and in the Walter Scott operas.) At the end of his monologue Arthur leaves the stage.

In a few moments Marie and Nelly arrive by boat. Obeying a sign from her mistress, Nelly goes into the cottage (which belongs to Dickson, her father). *Scène* v: Alone on stage, Marie sings in a *cavatine* of her ill-fated love-affair with Arthur. The music is the famous "Oh, mattutini albori" from *La Donna del Lago,* but lowered a major third for mezzo-soprano:

Example 18-4

Calme pensive plage Beau lac miroir des cieux

(Cf. Chapter 2, Musical Example 2–5.) *Scène* vi: Arthur enters suddenly and surprises her. He tells her he has heard that she is engaged to another man. In the ensuing duet she reassures him of her undying love for him, even though marriage at the moment is out of the question. Niedermeyer utilizes here the fine duet between Elena and Uberto in *La Donna del Lago,* Act I, but unlike Rossini he does not always succeed in fitting the music felicitously to the Royer-Vaëz text, as the following example, admittedly extreme and not typical, clearly indicates:

Example 18-5

Ah du ciel arrêt fatal tout m'a-ban-donne et sans re-tour.

(Cf. Chapter 2, Musical Example 2–8.) In the middle of the duet a bell sounds in the distance, and we hear a "chœur de jeunes filles" singing about St. Valentine:

> A la prière
> Viens ce matin,
> Peuple; révère
> Saint Valentin!
> C'est lui qui donne
> Les jours heureux,
> Lui qui pardonne
> Et prie aux cieux.

(The appearance of this ritual connected with St. Valentine no doubt owes something to *The Fair Maid of Perth;* see Chapter 17. In Scott's history not one of the conflicts in which Robert Bruce and his compatriots participate occurs in conjunction with this particular religious festival. However, Douglas' assault on English-occupied Douglas Castle takes place on Palm Sunday, and his assault on the Castle of Roxburgh during Shrovetide.) In the final part of the duet (Rossini's "Cielo in qual'estasi") Marie implores

Arthur to depart, lest her father suddenly appear and see them together.
Scène vii: *Enter* Douglas and Bruce, the latter *"caché sous le tartan d'un
montagnard."* Douglas admits that he once favored Arthur's suit for the
hand of Marie, but in view of present circumstances he insists that Arthur
not see her again. He, Marie, and the disguised Bruce then get into the
boat and push off from shore; Arthur walks away in dejection.

   Scène viii: Nelly, Dickson, and a group of young men and women from
the village come on stage. Nelly and Dickson listen as the young women
sing about St. Valentine (the "D'Inibaca donzella" chorus from *La Donna
del Lago,* Act I). Their song is joyful, but Nelly cannot share their joy
because her mind is on Marie's plight. Dickson remarks *aside,* "Let the
young people have their brief moments of pleasure: sadness will come
only too soon." A short ballet follows; it includes one piece of Scottish
flavor (not from *La Donna del Lago,* which has absolutely no Scottish
music), and it ends with the "Vieni o stella" march from *La Donna* (cf.
Chapter 2, Musical Example 2–9). *Scène* ix: The mirth of the Scots ceases
when King Édouard, Arthur, and the whole entourage of hunters enter.
Édouard sings an aria about pleasure:

Example 18-6

(This is Uberto's aria, "O fiamma soave," which begins Act II of *La Donna;*
again the music is not particularly appropriate for the new text.) When
Édouard mentions the festival to be held that very night at Stirling Castle,
Dickson remarks *aside,* "Scotland will have her turn." *Scène* x: Suddenly
Morton rushes in with news that Douglas is on the other side of the lake.
The King tries to obtain information from the Scots, even offering them
money, but they are silent. In the ensuing ensemble (*not* from *La Donna*)
Édouard and Morton sing of their desire for vengeance, while Nelly,
Arthur, and Dickson call on celestial Providence to help Douglas escape
vengeance. The King then puts Arthur in charge of a party of men whose
sole duty is to capture the Scottish chieftain. "Va," he commands him,
"rapporte-moi sa tête,/ Ou la tienne en répondra!" Thus Arthur finds
himself in even more of a dilemma. The act closes in a large ensemble
consisting of all the principals present together with the entire chorus.

   The first part of Act II takes place in a room in Douglas Castle. *Scènes*
i-iv: When the curtain rises, Marie is revealed *"assise, plongée dans la*

tristesse." Douglas enters immediately from an adjoining room and sings a recitative and aria (borrowed from *Zelmira*). He must leave the castle to join his men, and asks Marie to look after King Robert in his absence. He is sorry that she is unhappy, but there is nothing to be done, inasmuch as her friend Arthur is fighting on the side of King Édouard. At the conclusion of the cabaletta he embraces her and exits. Alone on stage, Marie sings an elaborate recitative and aria (Malcolm Græme's "Elena! oh, tu che chiamo! . . . Oh, quante lagrime"). She realizes that she must sacrifice her love for Arthur, but her soul will fly to him and follow him always. Suddenly Nelly bursts in with the news that the English are upon them. Marie states her determination to save the Scottish king and starts to go to his room to apprise him of the danger, but it is too late—Arthur and the English soldiers enter. Upon Arthur's orders the men leave the stage to continue their march in the gallery. In the ensuing recitative Arthur assures Marie that he can save her father: he tells her of a boat by means of which she and Douglas can stealthily slip away. He exits, not realizing that Douglas has already departed—or that Robert Bruce is in hiding in the castle. *Scène* v: Bruce himself now appears. In the duet that follows, Marie tells him that she will deceive her lover in order to save him; Bruce does not like the idea of her making such a sacrifice, but there seems to be no other choice. (Marie thus finds herself in a dilemma similar to that of Alice Lee, in *Woodstock*, who decides to sacrifice her relationship with Markham Everard in order to save King Charles. See my discussion of Sussy and Flotow's *Alice*, Chapter 15.)

The music for the rest of the act is a re-arrangement of the memorable finale to the first act of *La Donna del Lago*. *Scènes* vi–viii: Arthur enters suddenly and surprises Marie with the disguised Bruce, whom he assumes to be a rival suitor. He expresses anger that she should have been about to escape with the supposed rival, especially in view of his having just taken a grave personal risk in arranging things so that she could escape with her father. When he is on the point of attacking Bruce, Marie throws herself in front of him, offering her body as a shield. (Cf. the similar incident in Flotow's *Alice*.) Her immediate willingness to give up her own life causes Arthur to believe that she sincerely and deeply loves the stranger. Terribly upset, he tells her that he will depart and that she will never see him again. At this climactic moment Robert Bruce, who never liked the idea of so much sacrifice on Marie's part, reveals his true identity to Arthur. (Cf. the very similar incident in *Woodstock*, chapter xxviii. In the parallel *scène* in Flotow's *Alice*, it will be recalled, Charles does *not* reveal himself to Alice's angry beau; see Chapter 15.) Not to be topped in chivalry, Arthur gives Bruce permission to escape by means of the boat, but this plan is thwarted when the English soldiers re-enter, led by Captain Morton, who sees and immediately recognizes Bruce and wants to arrest him. Arthur overrules Morton, they argue, and things are about to get out of hand. Suddenly trumpets are heard backstage, indicating that Douglas and his forces are fast approaching the castle. As Morton and the endangered English soldiers depart, they warn Arthur that Édouard will punish his treason. Douglas then enters, accompanied by several Scottish chieftains. When Bruce tells him that he owes his life to Arthur, Douglas immediately promises Arthur Marie's hand in marriage. Arthur, however, feels honor-bound to return to the English camp, even though Édouard will probably punish him as a traitor. To help prevent misfortune from befalling the man who has just saved his life, Bruce detaches a small oaken branch from a casket and gives it to him as a talisman, to be worn on the crest of his helmet. It will save him from death in the forthcoming battle—the Scots will see it and respect it. A large ensemble develops: all realize the danger that will face Arthur when he returns to the English camp.—The scene now changes to a craggy site near the castle, where bards, warriors, Highlanders, and women have congregated to await the arrival of Robert Bruce. After the bards have sung the familiar "Chorus of Bards," Bruce enters, accompanied by Douglas and Marie. The act ends in a huge ensemble. Robert Bruce and the bards inspire the warriors to perform glorious deeds in the forthcoming battle.

The setting for the first part of Act III is "une gorge de montagnes étroite et sombre dominée par le château de Stirling, bâti sur un rocher à pic.—Il fait nuit." Scènes i–iii: When the curtain rises, Bruce is alone on stage. In a moving romance (borrowed from Zelmira), extremely effective with its unusual harmony and bold modulations, he sadly reminisces about his beloved children, whom the English have executed. (Scott mentions the execution of Bruce's brother Nigel, "a beautiful and brave youth," after the Castle of Kildrummie fell to the English. He also tells of brothers Thomas and Alexander being executed by Edward I.) Douglas enters, followed by Dickson and a band of gypsies and jongleurs. Strategy calls for Dickson to enter the castle openly, in the company of these motley entertainers, while Bruce, Douglas, and their followers will slip in through a secret, subterranean passage. When the time of assault is ripe, Dickson is to give them a signal by means of a kindled branch—a detail suggested by Scott's account of Bruce's landing in Carrick. As soon as Dickson and the bohémiens have departed, Bruce and Douglas are joined by a large chorus of chevaliers, Highlanders, and Scottish soldiers, who sing in subdued voices of the now imminent battle.

The setting changes to a festively decorated hall inside Stirling Castle, where Édouard and a group of English chevaliers (scène iv) sing a conventional drinking song. This is followed by a ballet. (The historical account is quite different: an effective Scottish blockade of the English in Stirling Castle leads to Edward's amassing a huge army to come to their rescue, and the Scots rout the superior English forces in the resulting Battle of Bannockburn.) Scènes v–vi: Morton interrupts the ballet with news that the Scots are in arms. Édouard's composure is not ruffled at this turn of events. "De les vaincre demain il sera temps encor," he says. But when

Arthur enters and is accused by Morton of treason, Édouard seethes with rage. He gives orders for Arthur to be executed at once: "Que sous la hache à l'instant il périsse!" Suddenly Marie and Nelly burst in. Marie announces to all that she is Arthur's accomplice, and she intimates to Arthur that she has come to die with him. A fine ensemble begins (the quartet from *Bianca e Faliero,* often used at the end of *La Donna del Lago* instead of Elena's "Tanti affetti"—see Chapter 2, fn. 12):

Example 18-7

When Édouard again expresses his determination to have Arthur put to death, Marie warns him that he must then fear the tempest which she will call down on his head. Enraged, Édouard orders his soldiers to execute both the traitor and his accomplice. *"Les soldats entraînent Arthur. Marie se précipite dans ses bras."* Suddenly trumpets are heard from without. Marie tells Édouard to tremble, for Robert Bruce is now master of the castle. *Scène* vii: The backdrop opens and reveals the castle's ramparts, which are overrun by Scottish soldiers. "Victoire!" Bruce exclaims. Several Scottish soldiers call for the execution of Édouard, but Arthur manages to protect and save him by revealing the talisman. (This bit of action is in the libretto, but not in either the full score or the vocal score.) "Écosse, a toi l'indépendance!" exclaims Bruce; "A Robert l'immortalité!" exclaims Marie; "A Robert l'immortalité!" exclaim all. The opera concludes with a reprise of the "Chorus of Bards."

My examination of the individual Walter Scott operas began with a Rossini opera. It has ended with a Rossini pastiche which draws mainly on that selfsame opera.

19
§ § §
CONCLUSION

The foregoing study shows that the influence of Sir Walter Scott on nineteenth-century opera was immense. Many more operas are either based on Waverley Novels or indebted to them in some way than has heretofore been realized. As we have seen, some of them were performed frequently and widely throughout the nineteenth century; some are the work of important librettists and composers; a few are among the finest operatic achievements of the century. Why this vogue for Scott? What is there about his work that is conducive to good opera? Several answers to these questions have evolved in the preceding chapters. A summary seems in order.

First, there is the static pictorial element—battlements of castles, grand and festively decorated rooms, picturesque ruins, dark forests, bleak, craggy landscapes, or the "wild and lonely loch" which made such a profound impression on Stendhal at the première of *La Donna del Lago*. (Interestingly, dark forests and bleak, craggy landscapes are important visual aspects of Wagner's Ring operas.) Some of Scott's large broad-canvas scenes involving multitudes of people and lots of movement can readily be turned into effective operatic stage spectacles. The burning of Torquilstone, the storming of the Tolbooth, and Elizabeth's arrival at Kenilworth come immediately to mind. Moreover, his skillfully and memorably drawn black-and-white, two-dimensional characters (that is, his less complex characters), whose actions are normally governed by one or two dominant passions, can be converted into operatic roles much more easily than could a Hamlet or a Stephen Dedalus. There is also great variety in types of people in each novel. Some of Scott's most memorable pages are scenes in which his sharply defined characters come into intense personal conflict with one another. A scene like this is often excellent material for an ensemble. Notable examples are the unexpected, forced entrance of Edgar of Ravenswood into the presence of Lady Ashton, Sir William, Lucy, Sholto, Craigengelt, Bucklaw, and Bide-the-Bent, just after Lucy has signed the marriage contract; or the unpleasant confrontation at Kenilworth of Queen Elizabeth with the Earl of Leicester, Amy

Robsart, and Richard Varney; or the pleas of Berengaria, Edith, the Saracen, and the Hermit of Engaddi to dissuade King Richard from having Sir Kenneth put to death. Sometimes the intense conflict involves only two persons, such as Brian de Bois-Guilbert's attempt to seduce Rebecca in the tower room and her threat to jump from the balcony if he should approach one step nearer—an unforgettable encounter that is utilized in *all* the *Ivanhoe* operas. I have repeatedly called attention to Scott's theatrical direct discourse and to the frequent soliloquies in which his leading characters lay bare their thoughts. Sometimes the librettist has really very little to do in converting a Scott soliloquy into an effective vehicle for an operatic aria, because the chosen soliloquy already possesses a structure quite similar to that of the conventional recitative, cavatina, and cabaletta.

Many a situation in Scott is either eminently operatic in itself or easily alterable into something operatic. Rebecca's trial scene, with her eloquent plea before the relentless Templars, is perfect material for opera. Some of the operatic renditions of it are certainly as impressive as the fine trial scene, better known today, in Giordano's *Andrea Chénier*. In the novel's last chapter Rebecca is about to be burned at the stake, but through Ivanhoe's timely arrival and espousal of her cause she is saved—in the nick of time and in the manner of the romantic "rescue" operas. In the final act of *Jeanie Deans* MacCunn's librettist, Sheridan Ross, alters Scott's material to make it more suitable and more effective as rescue opera: Effie is actually conducted to the gallows and is about to be executed; at the very last moment, when all hope seems gone, Jeanie arrives from London, bearing with her a pardon from the king. The situation is close to that of the final act of Puccini's *Fanciulla del West.* Earlier in *Jeanie Deans,* Scott's depiction of David Deans's abhorrence at what Effie has done becomes, with slight modification, material for an effective operatic cursing scene—in this case, an embittered father cursing his wayward daughter. The Waverley Novels are indeed full of inherently operatic situations, examples of which are countless.

In almost everything Scott wrote one can find at its emotional core a large, significant, and essentially unresolvable conflict between two opposing cultures, or ideals, or fanaticisms, or life-styles. It comes in many different forms: Scottish vs. English, Highland vs. Lowland, Cavalier vs. Roundhead, Saxon vs. Norman, Jewish vs. Christian, Saracen vs. Christian, gypsy vs. Christian, country vs. court, and so forth. Normally there is a leading character who finds himself caught in the middle; he cannot wholeheartedly, or fanatically, support either side because he has ties on both sides; he *wavers* between one side and the other. The story is primarily concerned with his destiny evolving, or working itself out, in the context of the given conflict; he himself has little control over what happens to him. This is what *Waverley* is all about. Interestingly, this also is what one finds in Bizet's *Carmen,* the Waverley-like character being Don

José. José is of the conventional world of Spain; he has strong ties to his regiment, his fiancée, his mother. On the other hand he is irresistibly attracted toward Carmen and the mysterious, unconventional world of the gypsies. He first enters their world at the inn of Lillas Pastia. During the course of Carmen's castanet dance he hears a distant bugle summoning him back to his quarters, just as Waverley, while a guest in the home of the pedantic old Jacobite, Baron Cosmo Comyne Bradwardine of Bradwardine, receives a summons to return to his regiment. Like Waverley he becomes a victim of circumstances which virtually force him to change sides. After he has done so, again like Waverley, he experiences a feeling of revulsion toward the people whom he had formerly found attractive—whom he had romanticized. When Micaëla arrives at the smugglers' camp with news of his mother's illness, he decides to return to the conventional world; but unlike Waverley, who learns to accept the fact that Flora Mac-Ivor does not love him, he is unable to forget Carmen, and the final tragedy occurs when he returns to her. The conflict between gypsydom and conventional Spain resembles the conflict between Scottish and English in the Waverley Novels. I do not mean to imply that Bizet's librettists, Henri Meilhac and Ludovic Halévy, or the author of the original story, Prosper Mérimée, either borrowed from Scott or were directly influenced by him, but similarities in story material do exist, and they are striking. Like the Scottish Highlanders, Bizet's gypsies are rugged, able to endure physical hardship, superstitious, of dark complexion, passionate; his world of Spain, like England, is just the opposite. Both *Carmen* and *Waverley* have the dark-lady vs. light-lady types: Carmen and Micaëla; Flora Mac-Ivor and Rose Bradwardine. The smugglers' camp of Act III—"a wild desolate spot in the heart of the mountains"—resembles the bleak, craggy, Scottish Highland landscape which we have observed in many Walter Scott operas. This is the line of thinking that prompted me to suggest, in Chapter 1, that *Carmen* is closer than *La Jolie Fille de Perth* to the real essence of Scott. One cannot help but wonder whether Bizet's having read Scott's *Fair Maid* critically, having struggled in setting to music a bad libretto based on it, and having curiously substituted gypsy for Scottish local color might have had bearing on his being attracted, just a few years later, to the Carmen story.

A similar conflict between two strong opposing forces, with the hero caught in the middle, is the basic subject matter of Wagner's *Tannhäuser*. In many respects Venus and Elisabeth are to Tannhäuser what Carmen and Micaëla are to Don José. During the wild, uninhibited bacchanale *auf dem Venusberg* Wagner's musical texture is chromatic and exotic-sounding; not so in Elisabeth's two arias (cf. Carmen's "Habanera" and Micaëla's aria). He uses a sophisticated development of the same technique in *Tristan und Isolde*, wherein the subtle alternation between chromatic and diatonic texture underscores penetratingly and most effectively the conflict between the private world of hero and heroine on one hand and the conventional world on the other. (He might have gotten the idea of this technique from Rebecca's trial scene in Marschner's *Templer und Jüdin;* see Chapter 9.) The conflict between two opposing forces, then, whatever they might be, with leading characters caught in a dilemma, is effective subject matter for opera because it opens up a wide range of musical as well as dramatic possibilities. In the form of a culture conflict it lies at the heart of *Norma, Lakmé,* and especially *Madame Butterfly;* in each case the character for whom the opera is named finds herself in an intolerable dilemma, and the opera ends with her inevitable death.

Throughout this study I have called attention to material in the Walter Scott operas which apparently derives from or is indebted to previous operas, some of them Scott operas and some of them not. No further commentary is necessary. However, it seems fitting to conclude with observation of a few specific borrowings from Walter Scott operas that lurk in well-known operas of the current standard repertoire. The fine *Danse Bohémienne* from *La Jolie Fille de Perth,* as I have already noted, appears in the superfluous ballet music which directors sometimes graft onto the last act of *Carmen* (see Chapter 17, Musical Example 17-3).[1] Although *Il Castello di Kenilworth* is never performed today, the music that accompanies Elisabetta's grand arrival at Kenilworth is familiar because of Donizetti's own re-usage of it, several years later, in his ever-popular *L'Elisir d'Amore* (see Chapter 11, Musical Example 11-3). Grout and others have called attention to Wagner's indebtedness in *Lohengrin* to *Der Templer und die Jüdin.* His handling of the Gotteskampf of Act I brings to mind the final scene of *Templer und Jüdin,* and his conception of Telramund—a brave, basically noble-spirited man who in succumbing to his passions loses his priceless honor—obviously owes much to Marschner's Bois-Guilbert. There is at least one striking musical echo. In his angry, intensely emotional outburst of despair at the beginning of Act II, Telramund exclaims at one point:

Example 19-1

The melody is built on a descending diminished seventh chord. Almost
the same thing, in a somewhat similar situation, occurs at the beginning of
Guilbert's important "Scene und Arie" (*Templer,* Act II):

Example 19-2

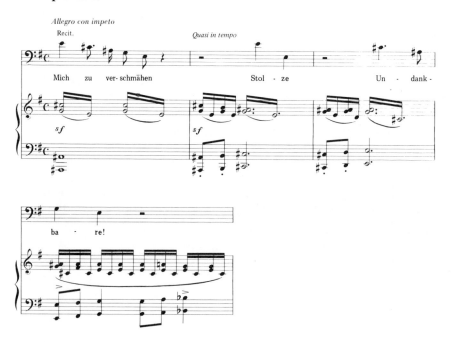

Telramund's situation here is actually much closer to that of another
operatic Bois-Guilbert. When we first behold Nicolai's "templario" (Act I,
scene ii) he too has just lost a battle to an unknown knight and has been
shamed in front of a crowd of people. The sombre orchestral introduction to Briano's impassioned recitative ends wtih two descending diminished seventh chords followed immediately by a descending scale in
the bass. The passage sounds Wagnerian:[2]

Example 19-3

Furthermore, it may be that in the well-known opening measures of *Tristan und Isolde* Wagner has unconsciously echoed a curious figure that appears near the end of the overture to *Il Templario:*

Example 19-4

I would not want to push this point, for it certainly *looks* more convincing than it sounds, Nicolai's tempo being *allegro* rather than *lento.* My next example, however, is indeed striking. In the love-duet of Act II Wagner has consciously or unconsciously borrowed from Nicolai's finale to Act I the brief, quiet passage that immediately follows Vilfredo's revelation of his true identity:

Example 19-5

The echoes in Wagner from *Il Templario* come as no startling surprise in view of the well-known echo from *Die lustigen Weiber von Windsor* in the second act of *Die Meistersinger*.[3] To turn for a moment to *La Dame Blanche*, a Scott opera which Wagner deeply admired, I suspect that the false notes which Siegfried blows during the forest scene in *Siegfried*, first with the reed and then with his horn, owe something to Georges Brown's mistake in recalling the Scottish anthem which he had known as a small child:

Example 19-6

Moreover, the jolting 5/4 rhythm that Wagner uses in depicting Tristan's final delirium as he excitedly awaits Isolde's imminent appearance—

Example 19-7

—may have been prompted by the remarkable 5/4 passage which Georges Brown sings in "Viens, gentille dame" as he excitedly awaits the appearance of the mysterious White Lady, whom he has just summoned:

Example 19-8

So much for Richard Wagner's connection with Sir Walter Scott—an obscure, indirect connection altogether different from his open and manifest indebtedness to Shakespeare's *Measure for Measure* in *Das Liebesverbot* and to Bulwer-Lytton for *Rienzi.*

Of all the Walter Scott operas which I have examined, only *Lucia di Lammermoor* is a permanent fixture in the standard repertoire. *La Donna del Lago, La Dame Blanche, I Puritani, La Jolie Fille de Perth,* and Sullivan's *Ivanhoe* are still performed occasionally. *Jeanie Deans, Der Templer und die Jüdin,* De Lara's *Amy Robsart,* Gevaert's *Quentin Durward,* Maclean's *Quentin Durward,* and Balfe's *Talisman* have been performed in the present century, but not in recent years. A number of the Scott operas achieved a respectable degree of success in the nineteenth century but did not survive into the twentieth; others were only moderately successful; and some were not performed anywhere except locally. Several failed; a few never reached the public at all. Scott concluded *The Bride of Lammermoor* with comments on Lady Ashton, the unforgettable personage who dominates the novel's course of events. It seems fitting for me to conclude with one last reference to *Lucia di Lammermoor.* Of the whole large and significant group of operas which were inspired by the works of one writer, Sir Walter Scott, and which well-nigh dominated the operatic scene in the nineteenth century, Donizetti's *Lucia* is the grand and glorious vestige. Its permanent place in the standard operatic repertoire keeps alive a fascinating chapter in the history of modern European culture.

APPENDIX

The Quartet "Appena il vidi" from Mazzucato's *La Fidanzata di Lammermoor*. Reproduced photographically from the copy in the Biblioteca del Conservatorio "Giuseppe Verdi".

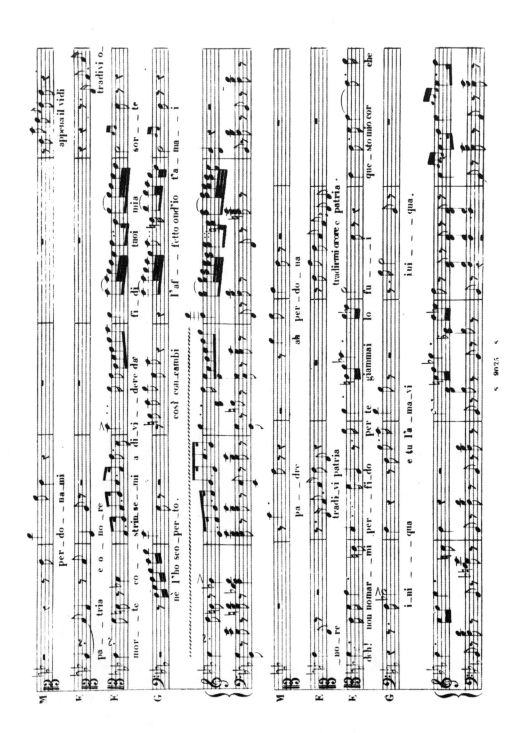

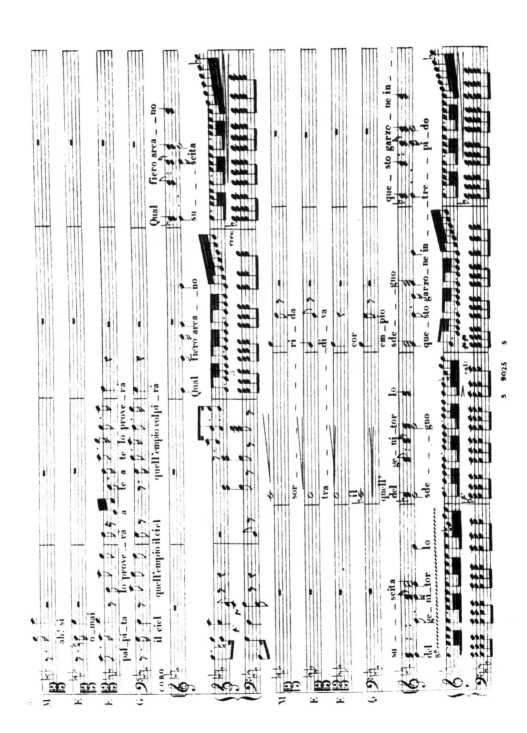

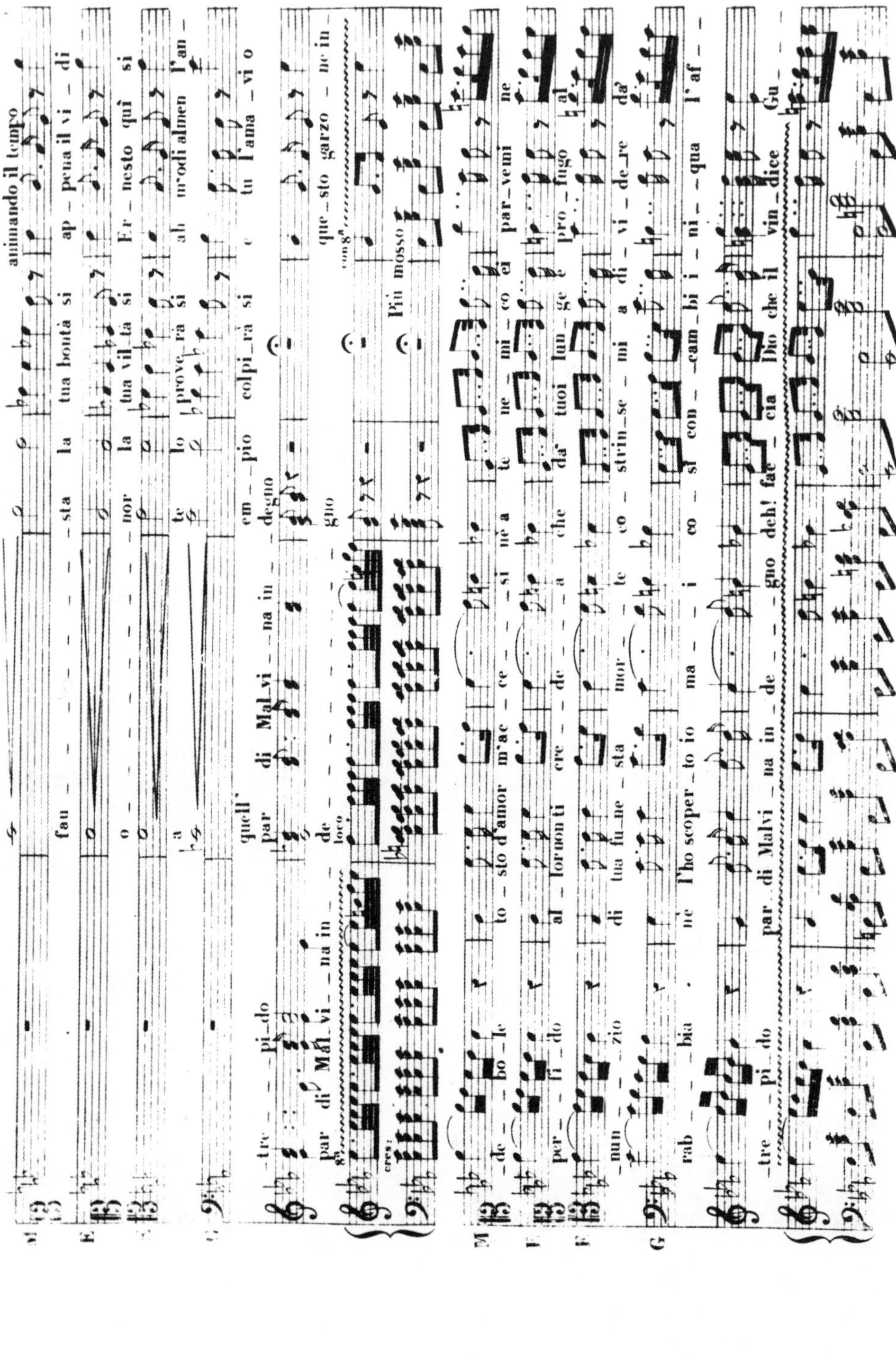
animando il tempo
Più mosso
cresc.
S 9025 6

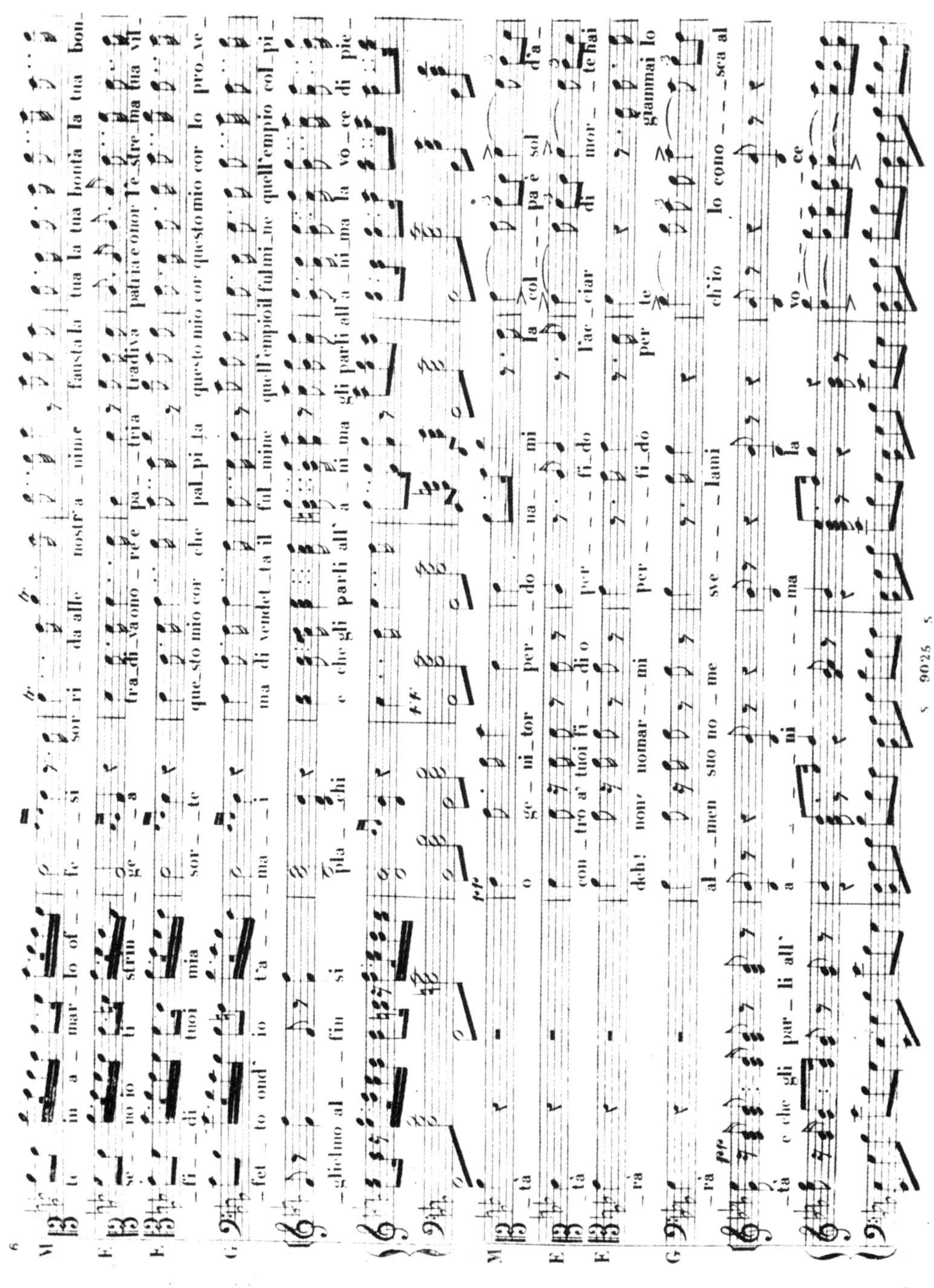

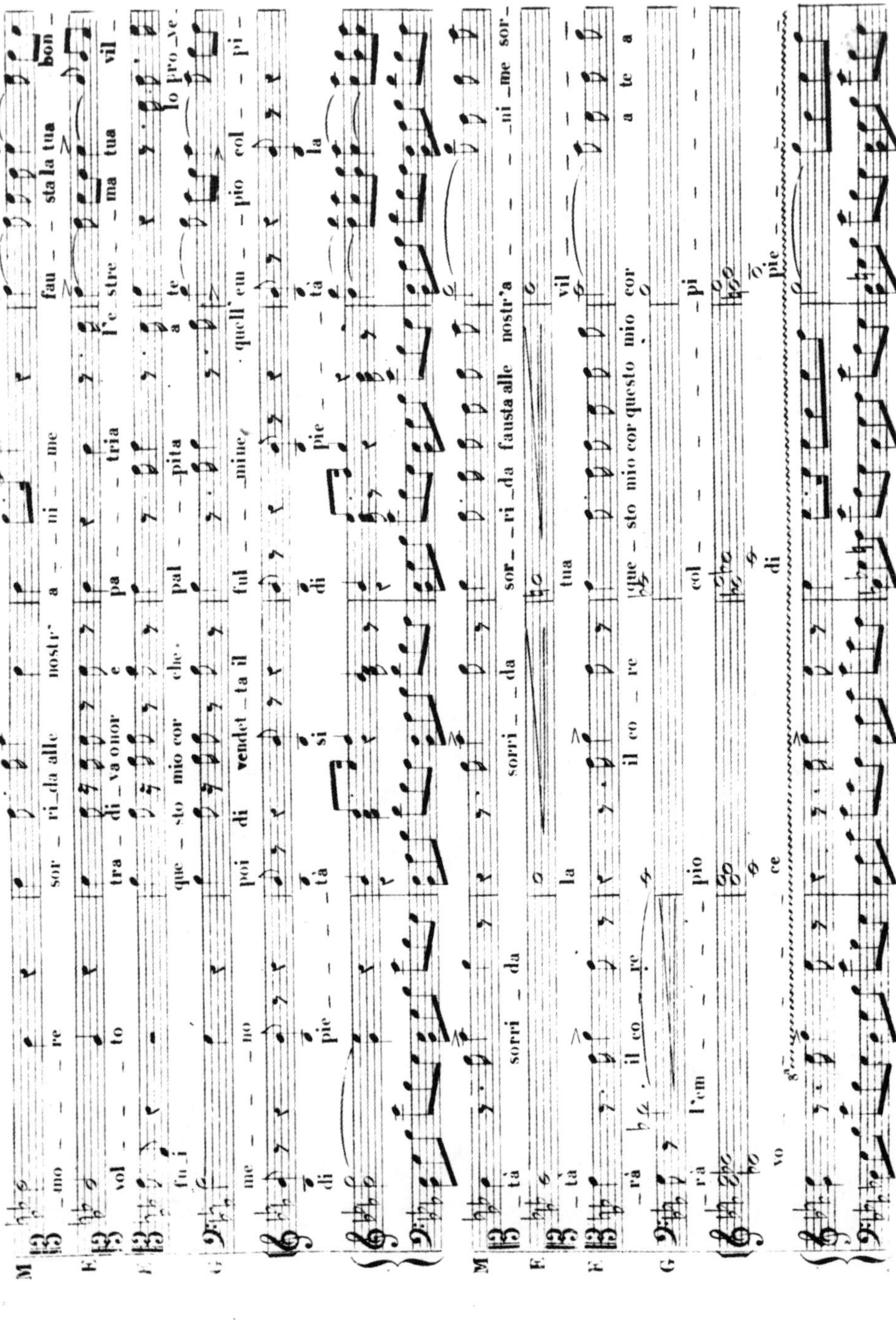
M
F
F
G
_mo - - - re sor - ri_da alle nostr' a - - ni - - me fau - - sta la tua bon -
vol - - - to tra - di_va onor e pa - - - tria l'e_stre - - ma tua vil -
fu_i que - sto mio cor che. pal - - - pita a te lo pro_ve -
me - - - no poi di vendet_ta il ful - - - mine, quell'em - - pio col - - - pi -
di pie - - ta si di pie - - tà la
tà sorri _ da sorri _ _ da sor_ _ri_da fausta alle nostr'a - - - - - - ni_me sor -
ta la tua vil -
rà il co - re il co - re que - sto mio cor questo mio cor a te a
rà l'em - - - - pio col - - - - pi -
vo ce di pie -
pp
S 9025 S

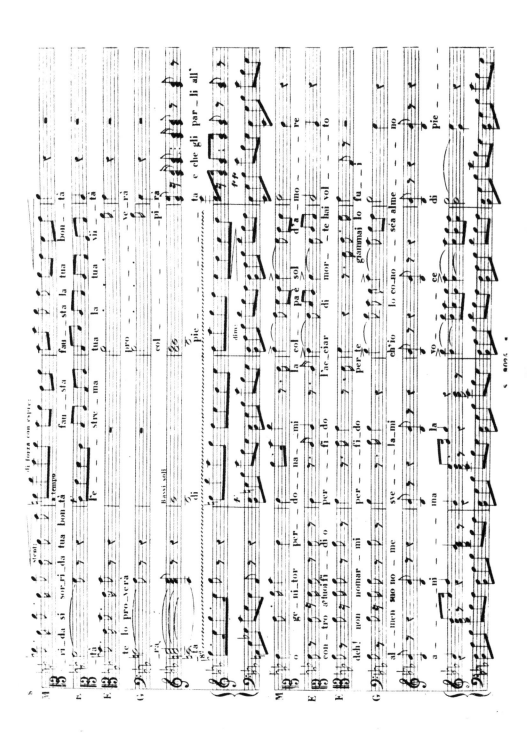

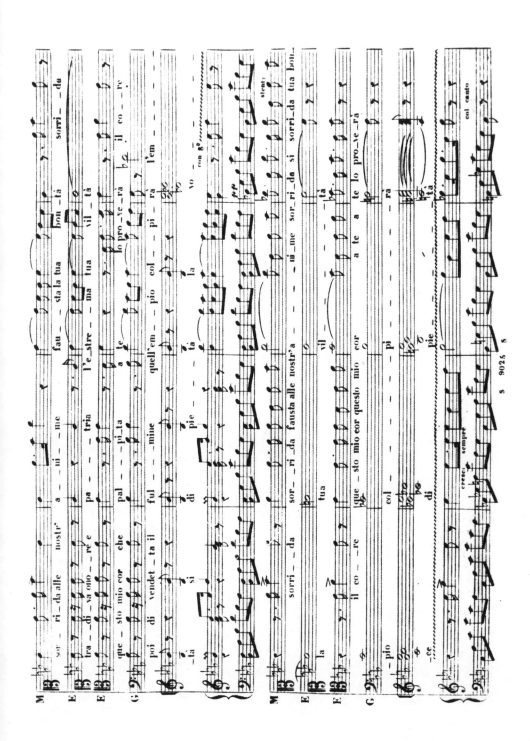

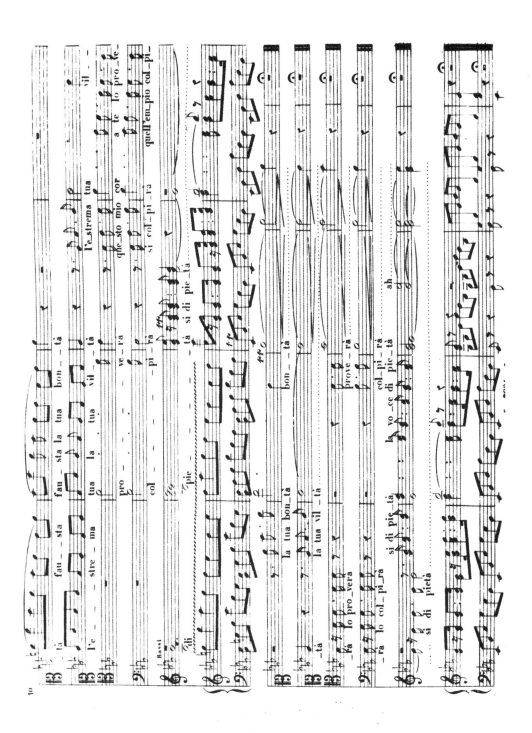

NOTES

CHAPTER 1

1. "Walter Scott e la Musica," *La Rassegna Musicale,* V (1932), 318-334.

2. "Walter Scott et les Musiciens," *Le Ménestrel,* XCIV (1932), 389-390.

3. "Sir Walter Scott and Opera," *Opera,* XIX (1968), 872–878.

4. Miss Forbes' article is quite short. Thus there is little space for her to reveal any real knowledge, beyond external matters, of either the music to an opera cited, its libretto, or its relation to the Scott novel from which it derives. The same can be said about Martin Cooper's recent newspaper article, "The Tartan Curtain Rises," *The Daily Telegraph* (18 September 1971), p. 9.

5. *Franz von Holstein: Ein Dichterkomponist des 19. Jahrhunderts* (Leipzig, 1931). (See Chapter 3 of the present study.)

6. The important musical dramas are discussed quite adequately by White.

7. Winton Dean alludes to a *Love's Labour's Lost* by Mozart and a *Twelfth Night* by Schubert; "these are quaint attempts to fit new librettos to the music of 'Cosi fan tutte' and 'Die Zauberharfe' "—*Shakespeare and Opera,* p. 91, included in *Shakespeare in Music,* ed. Phyllis Hartnoll (London, 1964).

8. For further information see Chapter 10.

9. A vocal score is in the British Museum.

10. *Op. cit.,* p. 96.

11. I would be very grateful to anyone for information about material which I failed to locate.

12. C. Hutchins Lewis' *Ivanhoe* (1907); it is better classified as a "school operetta."

13. See Winton Dean, *op. cit.,* p. 92.

14. E.g. in *Masterplots; The Oxford Companion to English Literature;* and J. Walker McSpadden, *Waverley Synopses: A Guide to the Plots and Characters of Scott's "Waverley Novels"* (New York, 1909).

15. I have borrowed this phrase from Francis R. Hart, *Scott's Novels: The Plotting of Historic Survival* (Charlottesville, Va., 1966).

16. *The Journal of Sir Walter Scott* (New York, 1890), I, 289.

17. Besides the *Journal* passage just cited, see A. Hedley, "Was Sir Walter Scott Musical?" *Music and Letters,* XVII (1936), 151–153.

18. For an extended study of Scott's reputation through the ages, see James T. Hillhouse, *The Waverley Novels and Their Critics* (Minneapolis, 1936). In the past few years there has been a noticeable awakening of interest in Scott.

CHAPTER 2

1. See *Cumberland's Minor Theatre*, vol. III.

2. A single number does exist in autograph manuscript—the recitative and duet for Elena and Malcolm ("Ah! nel fatal conflitto di amore e di dover") which opens the second act. (In the Rossini opera this is normally replaced by Uberto's aria, "O fiamma soave.") See Helmut Schultz, *Johann Vesque von Püttlingen: 1803–1883* (Regensburg, 1930), pp. 50, 276, 278. Vesque's opera was entitled *Elena; ossia, La Donna del Lago.*

3. A note by Bishop prefixed to the overture as it appears in the vocal score. I have used the copy in the British Museum, which, like all vocal scores to "musical dramas," does not contain the spoken dialogue. Morton's complete text was published separately in 1811. This too can be found in the BM.

3b. Schubert did set to music German translations of three songs from *The Lady of the Lake:* "Raste, Krieger! Krieg ist aus" ("Soldier, rest! thy warfare o'er") (I.xxxi); "Jäger, ruhe von der Jagd!" ("Huntsman, rest! thy chase is done") (also I.xxxi, and designated by Scott as a continuation of the above); and the well-known "Ave Maria! Jungfrau mild" ("Ave Maria! maiden mild!") (III.xxix).

4. See Stendhal's *Life of Rossini*, trans. by Richard N. Coe (London, 1956), pp. 377–379, and Francis Toye's *Rossini: A Study in Tragi-Comedy* (New York, 1934), pp. 88–89.

5. See the very full entry in Loewenberg.

6. This production was taped during performance and later made available on discs to the members of Edward J. Smith's private record club. The singing is magnificent.—To my knowledge the opera has never been recorded commercially.

7. See Alan Blyth's review in *Opera*, XX (1969), 638–639. This production also was taped and later issued privately on discs by Sidney Grey. The opera was well done, but vocally it was not quite so satisfying as was the Florence revival.

8. I have used the Breitkopf & Härtel edition of the vocal score (Leipzig, [1825?]) and have compared it with a Ricordi edition (Milan, 1840) and with an edition in Italian published by Marquerie Frères (Paris, 1852). All three are in the BM.

9. See the vocal score, pp. 47–48.

10. At the première Malcolm was sung by Rosamunda Pisaroni—"one of the ugliest actresses imaginable," wrote Stendhal (p. 413)—she had been disfigured by an attack of small-pox. But he admitted that she "rose to the front rank as a singer as a result of the reputation which she made by her performance in this opera" (p. 380).

11. The translation is the one in Davidson's Musical Opera-Books, vol. LVII (London, [1876]). The Italian text is on the left-hand side of each page and the English translation on the right. The vocal lines of several arias, duets, and choruses are also given.

12. The 1958 revival in Florence omitted "Tanti affetti" and ended instead with the quartet from *Bianca e Faliero* followed by a reprise of the duet for Elena and Uberto near the beginning of Act I. This standard alteration was sanctioned by Rossini himself. It makes for a more effective ending musically, in my opinion, but as Alan Blyth notes, it "[leaves] poor Malcolm out in the cold" (*op. cit.*, p. 638). The 1969 revival at Camden Town Hall preserved the original ending. (In recent years Marilyn Horne has been using "Tanti affetti" in the music lesson scene of

The Barber of Seville. She received a standing ovation for her performance of the aria in an unforgettable recital at Emory University, March 2nd, 1971.)

CHAPTER 3

1. The holograph orchestral score can be found in the music archives of Karl Marx University, Leipzig; and also a separate libretto, in the hand of the poet-composer himself.

2. The BM has a copy of the vocal score (Offenbach and Frankfurt: André, [1876]), and also the full score.

3. See Gerhard Glaser, *Franz von Holstein: Ein Dichterkomponist des 19. Jahrhunderts* (diss. Leipzig, 1930), pp. 87–88. Glaser goes on to point out several inconsistencies in plot that are evident in *Hochländer* as compared with *Gastfreunde*. They arose when Holstein attempted to make the romantic elements of the story more realistic.

4. The earlier version, however, is closer to Scott in one particular—the account of Reginald's earliest past, especially his abduction by gypsies (a detail not in the later version). Cf. Harry Bertram, of *Guy Mannering.*

5. Bredal used the same tune in *Bruden fra Lammermoor,* but for a quite different purpose. See Chapter 8.

6. See Glaser, *op. cit.,* p. 11.

7. Cf. Glaser, p. 91.

8. This motif recalls to *my* mind the episode from Morton and Bishop's *Knight of Snowdoun* in which Roderick gives himself up to Earl Mar (who will order his immediate execution) in order to receive reward money that will enable him to free Douglas. Holstein almost certainly would not have known the musical drama.

CHAPTER 4

1. The musical drama (1816) by Thomas Attwood and Sir Henry R. Bishop is discussed thoroughly by White, pp. 9–26. In his bibliography White lists as an opera *La Sorcière; ou, l'Orphelin Écossais* (1821), by Victor (J. H. Brahain-Ducange) and Frédéric (Dupetit-Méré). A text is in the BM; it is a play rather than an opera or musical drama.

2. Her next opera, *Le Loup Garou,* was written to a libretto by Scribe and first performed at the Opéra-Comique. See the entry on her in Fétis.

3. My guess is that she wrote the text too. The Bibliothèque Nationale has copies of her later, published operas, but Mlle Wallon (see my preface) and I could find no entry whatever for *Guy Mannering* in any of the various card catalogues at our disposal. The MS may yet exist somewhere.

4. For detailed information about Scott's reputation in France, see Louis Maigron, *Le Roman Historique a l'Époque Romantique: Essai sur l'Influence de Walter Scott* (Paris, 1898), pp. 99–133.

5. This was taped and later made available on discs by Edward J. Smith to the members of his private record club. Gedda's interpretation of his difficult role is stylish, musically intelligent, and superb vocally.

6. See Dieter Schnabel's interesting review in the *Bonner General-Anzeiger* (21 July 1971), p. 9.

7. It stars Michel Senechal (Georges Brown), Françoise Louvay (Anna), Adrien Legros (Gaveston), Aimé Doniat (Dikson), Jane Berbié (Jenny), and Geneviève

Baudoz (Marguerite). The orchestra and chorus of Raymond Saint-Paul are under the direction of Pierre Stoll. Unfortunately this fine recording can no longer be bought, since Vega (a French company) has folded. I have heard the copy in the University of Illinois Music Library. (A single Vega disc of excerpts [30 LT. 13024] can still occasionally be found in major West European record stores, such as Lido Musique, in Paris.)

8. All musical quotations are from the Peters edition (#741) of the vocal score, *Die weisse Dame,* with the French text dubbed in from the old Launer vocal score. For the complete text I used the libretto included in the *Œuvres Complètes de Scribe.* (There is no spoken dialogue in the Launer score; in the German score it is abridged.)

9. The phrase is Grove's.

10. The tenor's name was König. Others in the Munich cast included Frl. Gottlieb (Eveline), Frl. Radecke (Lydia), Frl. Schefzky (Lady Sarah), Herr Schlosser (William Seyton), Herr Bausewein (Godolphin), and Herr Mayer (Allan); according to the favorable review in the *Allgemeine Musikalische Zeitung,* X, no. 6 (10 Feb. 1875), 88–89.

11. S. Bagge, "Franz von Holstein's dreiactige Oper 'Der Erbe von Morley'," pt. 1, *AMZ,* X, no. 26 (30 June 1875), 402.

12. All quotations, music and text, are from the Breitkopf & Härtel vocal score, which can be found in the Newberry Library.

13. In spirit this scene is reminiscent of the trio of Lady Harriet, Nancy, and Tristan near the beginning of Flotow's *Martha.*

14. The introduction to her Lied is the music we have already heard in the Vorspiel (see Example 4–7).

15. *Op. cit.,* pt. 2, *AMZ,* X, no. 27 (7 July 1875), 419.

16. This is excellent "melodramatic" comedy. There is a similar incident in Augustin Daly's *Under the Gaslight.*

17. Perhaps suggested to Holstein by the famous Gute Nacht quartet from *Martha.*

18. *Franz von Holstein: Ein Dichterkomponist des 19. Jahrhunderts* (diss. Leipzig, 1931), p. 77.

19. *Op. cit.,* pt. 3, *AMZ,* X, no. 28 (14 July 1875), 440.

20. Some of these points are noted also by Glaser, p. 78.

21. *AMZ,* X, no. 6 (10 Feb. 1875), 88.

22. *Op. cit.,* pt. 1, *AMZ,* X, no. 26 (30 June 1875), 404–405.

CHAPTER 5

1. A copy is in the Library of Congress. It was published in London, in 1820.

2. It is published in the form of a vocal score, a copy of which is in the BM.

3. See the full entry in Loewenberg.

4. One commercial recording of the complete opera stars Maria Callas as Elvira; another, Joan Sutherland.

5. The play was published in Paris, in 1833. It can be found in the BM.

6. For the surname Talbot cf. Col. Philip Talbot, of *Waverley.*

7. The old Novello vocal score has a convenient English translation by Natalia Macfarren.

8. Gerhart von Westerman, *Opera Guide*, trans. Anne Ross (New York, 1965), p. 133. The opera is summarized in detail, pp. 133–135.

9. *Ibid.*, p. 135.

1. The Pocock-Davy musical drama is discussed by White, pp. 34–52.

2. In the issue of 7 May 1837.

3. I searched in vain at the Bibliothèque Nationale, the Bibliothèque de l'Opéra, and the Bibliothèque de l'Arsenal.

4. Not in Scott. She is apparently Jarvie's wife in the opera.

5. *Friedrich von Flotow's Leben: Von seiner Witwe* (Leipzig, 1892), p. 87. She writes further that the opera "hiess ursprünglich *Rob le barbe* und gelangte im Hôtel des Grafen Castellane zu Paris von illustren Dilettanten mit grossem Erfolge zur Aufführung."

6. They are in the BN (voice with piano accompaniment). The title page of each number lists all seven, including the opening words.

7. (New York, 1926), pp. 174–175.

8. *Ibid.*, pp. 175–176.

9. Cecil Smith, *Musical Comedy in America* (New York, 1950), p. 175.

10. I have chosen to reproduce this since the score is out of print and seldom to be found in libraries. I used copies at Duke University, the Newberry Library, and the Chattanooga Public Library.

11. Quoted in Cecil Smith, pp. 78–79.

12. *The Canterbury Pilgrims* (performed at the Metropolitan) and *Rip van Winkle*.

1. The complete text, published by William Stockdale (London, 1819), is in the BM.

2. The vocal score is in the BM.

3. See White, pp. 62–64.

4. Usually sung to the words, "Oh where, and oh where . . . ."

5. The words are close to Scott's "Good even, good fair moon, good even to thee" (chapter xvii).

6. Again the lyrics are Scott's, with one minor change.

7. Perhaps suggested by Madge's threatening to "rive every dud off [Jeanie's] back" in chapter xxxi, when Jeanie tries to get out of entering the church in her company.

8. The words to the song in the vocal score are different; the first line reads, "The Skylark springing to the dawn."

9. I used the libretto in the BM, included in *La France Dramatique au Dix-Neuvième Siècle*.

10. Apparently no vocal score was ever published. An orchestral score is in the BM.

11. Is the name intentional irony on the part of the librettists? Most people would have known about Goethe's Marguerite, who murdered her baby.

12. I used the Edmond Mayand vocal score in the Newberry Library.

13. The BM has several editions of the libretto. I used the one printed in Florence (1838) by Giuseppe Galetti. This is a more complete text than what is to

be found in the Mayand vocal score, which sometimes condenses passages of recitative.

14. The information about the performance history comes mostly from Loewenberg.

15. This piece was sung by Mattiwilda Dobbs in Freemasons' Hall, Edinburgh, 1 September 1971, in an interesting recital entitled "Walter Scott in Music and Song," which formed part of the official program of the 25th Edinburgh International Festival.

16. The Stichting Toonkunst-Bibliotheek (Amsterdam) has two MSS of the text. I used Ms/Ber/23 and compared it with Ms/Ber/17. Ms/Ber/23 includes an interesting letter from Lavry to the composer in which he suggests certain changes in the first two scenes of Act II, so that the act will be rendered "plus comique et plus piquant." The letter was written in May, 1846. Berlijn's orchestral score (also in the Toonkunst-Bibliotheek) reveals that the changes were made; the original words have been deleted and new words put in their place. The large manuscript is bound up in two volumes, one for each act: Ms/Ber/29 and Ms/Ber/30. The overture is not included, but Berlijn did write an overture, and it was printed in Amsterdam by Brix von Wahlberg (a conductor's score and orchestral parts). The score has no date on its title-page, but it was apparently printed late in the century, probably after Berlijn's death (January 1870). It can be found in the Municipal Museum of The Hague.—There is some confusion with regard to Berlijn's name, which appears variously as A. Berlijn, Anton Berlijn, A. W. Berlijn, Aron Wolff Berlijn, and Aaron Wolf Berlijn.

17. Except for this phrase the letter is in Dutch. It is inserted in the second volume of the orchestral score, immediately following selection #12.

18. A glance at the score shows that the director's remark is well-taken. There is much florid coloratura work in unusually high tessitura for both the leading soprano and the first tenor.

19. For further information about Berlijn see the obituary notice in *Caecilia: Algemeen Muziekaal Tijdschrift van Nederland,* XXVII, No. 5 (1 March 1870), 39–40.

20. I would translate "gentil Lutin" as "amiable sprite."

21. Berlijn did not complete the orchestration for this number.

22. The orchestration is far from complete.

23. I have compared Jeannie's words with Lucie's in Royer and Vaëz's French version of Cammarano's libretto. There are no remarkable echoes in diction, but in sentiment and design the two scenes are quite similar.

24. The orchestration is not complete.

25. This trio (No. 12) of the Chevalier, Patrice, and Bolbury, which lacks complete orchestration, marks the end of the composer's efforts. If the opera had been accepted, Berlijn would no doubt have written music for the final scenes and filled out the orchestration for Tom's aria, the mad scene, the Chevalier's aria, and the trio.

26. According to the lengthy and not altogether favorable review in *The Scotsman* (16 November 1894). Unfortunately the reviewer's critical judgment is marred by his dogged insistence that the "domestic" story of Jeanie Deans is not suitable material for opera and by his preconceived notion that successful operatic music must be tuneful and simple.

27. See the enthusiastically favorable review in *The Scotsman* (11 April 1934). The cast included Miss Kirsty Anderson (Jeanie), Neil Forsyth (Dumbiedykes),

Andrew Simpson (George Staunton), Miss Naysmith Young (Effie), Miss Mildred Grant (Madge Wildfire), Frank Brady (Deans), Miss M. P. Greig (Queen Caroline), Philip Powell (Argyle), Miss J. R. Rae (Janet Balcristie), and Miss M. Taylor (Lady Suffolk). Additional performances took place on April 12th and 13th.

27b. The cast included Patricia Hay (Jeanie), Ronald Morrison (Dumbiedykes), John Robertson (George Staunton), Patricia McMann (Effie), Joan Alexander (Madge), William McCue (Deans), and others; the conductor was James Louchran.

28. I have used the vocal score published in 1904 by Augener, which is simply a reprint of the vocal score published in 1894 by Mathias & Strickland; copies can be found in the Newberry Library and in the BM. (I have compared all quoted textual material with the separate libretto published by Phipps and Connor; this too is in the BM.)

29. The dying Valentine's cursing of Marguerite in the presence of all the townsfolk (Gounod's *Faust*) is one obvious analogue; so also is Edgardo's cursing of Lucia (see Chapter 8).

30. Interestingly, the general mood and the sustained chords in low register in the orchestra bring to mind Dick Johnson's monologue in the last act of *La Fanciulla del West,* just before his famous aria.

31. The resemblance in situation to the final scene of *La Fanciulla del West* is striking.

CHAPTER 8

1. Typical is the following excerpt from E. Irenæus Stevenson's "Essay on the Story of the Opera," prefixed to the Schirmer vocal score of *Lucia:* "It was not the first time that Scott's touching romance had been turned into opera. But the scores by Donizetti's contemporaries—Carafa (1829), Ricci, by Mazzucato (1834), and Bredal (1832)—are long ago forgotten, with their thin contents." I have found no other reference to a *Bride of Lammermoor* opera by either Federico or Luigi Ricci. I suspect that Stevenson was confused by Federico's having done an opera based on *The Heart of Mid-Lothian* (see Chapter 7). The essay is full of mistakes and questionable opinions.

2. I used the BM copy of the text included in *La France Dramatique au Dix-Neuvième Siècle,* XVIII, 311–327. It is dated 1837. An earlier edition (Paris, 1828) is also in the BM.

3. Adam's music was not published. The autograph orchestral score is in the Bibliothèque Nationale. It includes only the music *he* wrote, not the borrowed numbers.

4. The original cast included Bouffé as Caleb, Derval (Henri), Armand (Édouard), Mᵐᵉ Génot (Clara), Preval (Jaket), Guenée (Krik), Mᵐᵉ Albert (Emmy), and Fleury (the Registrar).

5. The libretto indicates that the words are sung to the "Air du Petit Dragon," evidently a well-known tune of the times.

6. The libretto indicates that the words are sung to the air "On dit que je suis sans malice."

7. A trio, sung to the air "Mon cœur à l'espoir s'abandonne."

8. As pointed out earlier, Adam helped Boieldieu with the overture (see Chapter 4).

9. During the course of this summary, which is based on the printed text (see fn. 2), I have indicated which musical numbers are by Adam. Three additional pieces in the MS of the orchestral score are not to be found in the libretto:

(a) Folios 9–13: Emmy sings to Krik and Jaket about "la Fiancée de Lammermoor." At first the melody is more or less the same as that of her *ballade* in *scène* xvi, but the second half is quite different. The number would have come in *scène* iii. Adam apparently cancelled it when he decided to use the *ballade,* and replaced it with two borrowed *airs* for Emmy.

(b) Folios 14-19: This is a song for Clara in which she tells about saving Henri's life during the storm at sea. It would come in *scène* viii.

(c) Folios 39-43: An extra song for Henri.

10. This was published separately (Paris, 1829), with a parallel French translation in prose. I used the copy in the Bibliothèque Nationale.

11. I say "presumably" because the vocal score (published in Paris probably about the time of the première) does not include the recitatives, the words to which can be found in the libretto (see fn. 10). I cannot say for certain that these words were sung rather than spoken, but such was normally the case in Italian opera of this period, and older vocal scores do not always include recitatives. Copies of the vocal score can be found in the BM and in the Newberry Library.

12. At the première these roles were sung, respectively, by Zuchelli, Sig^ra Pisaroni, Sig^na Sontag, Sig^na Amigo, Donzelli, Santini, Graziani, Sig^ra Rossi, Profeti, and Giovanola.

13. "Lammermoor" is used interchangeably with "Ravenswood."

14. It can be found in the Bibliothèque de l'Opéra.

15. I have been unable to find any information about Rieschi (Riesck, Rieski) other than the brief notice in the Fétis Supplement, where mention is made of his *Bianca di Belmonte,* which was a complete fiasco at la Scala.

16. Sometimes referred to as *Ida di Lammermoor.* The libretto is listed under Bornaccini in the Bologna Catalogue of Librettos.

17. "Sognai ch'errante e profuga," etc. (arranged for voice & piano and published in Milan by Artaria). (The text of the cavatina is the same as that which Rieschi's Ida sings in *Fidanzata* I.v. The cabaletta's text is different.)

18. The Bibliothèque de l'Opéra has two copies of the printed libretto. One of them has a brief hand-written note on the blank page facing the title-page: "Opera espressamente composta per queste scene, esito infelice."

19. The libretto indicates that these roles were sung, respectively, by Giuseppe Binaghi, Sig^ra Eugenia Sant'Angelo, Giovanni David, Agostino Sant'Angelo, Giovanni Battista Placi, and Sig^ra Giacinta Moriondi.

20. Appended to the libretto is an extra *scena* for Bucklaw, to be inserted at the beginning of Act II. He gives voice to the suspicion that Guglielmo is not being honest with him. He and his followers sing that they will be avenged if indeed Guglielmo has double-crossed them. (It may be that the singer who played Bucklaw found his part too small and wanted it enhanced. If this *scena* is included, Guglielmo's words to Ida in II.ii are in part truthful.)

21. At the première these roles were sung, respectively, by Vincenzo Prattico, Eufrosina Marcolini, Atanasio Pozzolini, Luigi Alessandrini, Giacomo Radaelli, and Linda Fiorio.

22. Some of my observations are perhaps of no consequence, since it is conceivable that the printed libretto of *Ida* has been cut. I do not know whether Bassi himself did the revision, or someone else. Nor do I know how the music of *Ida* compares with that of *Fidanzata*.

23. *Bruden fra Lammermoor: Originalt romantisk Syngestykke i fire Acter* (Copenhagen, 1832). This is not included in the editions I have seen of Andersen's collected works. I used a microfilm of the copy in the Kongelige Bibliotek. It can also be found in the BM. For a brief, rather uncomplimentary review of Andersen's workmanship, see the *Allernyeste Skilderie af Kjöbenhavn*, No. 94 (23 November 1832), p. 1497. For a detailed negative evaluation see the *Maanedsskrift for Litteratur*, IX (1833), 191–195. The second reviewer takes Andersen to task for claiming that his work was "original," when in fact he lifted almost verbatim many a line from the novel (or, more precisely, from the Danish translation that was at his disposal).

24. They included (1) Ailsie's Hexesang, "Fuldmaanen skinner paa Busk og Krat," (2) Edgar's Recit. og Cavatine, "Mandens dybe, bittre Sorg," (3) Ailsie's Vise, "Et Dyb og dog Guds Himmel," (4) Bucklaw's Recit. og Cavatine, "Ingen kan sin Skjæbne kjende," (5) Bucklaw's Vise, "Penge, Penge! tro mit Ord," (6) Edgar's Romance, "Du som kjender hver en Tanke," (7) Lucy and Edgar's Duet, "Vi skilles maae, o bittre Smerte," (8) the Jægerchor, "Glade Lyst! hör Hornet toner!" (9) Lord and Lady Ashton's Duet, "Let knækker Stormens Kast," and (10) Ailsie's Skotsk Vise, "Der sidde to Ravne paa Træet hist." The publisher was C. C. Lose. They can be found in the Kongelige Bibliotek. In addition, Lose published the overture in an arrangement for piano done by Bredal himself and a potpourri of favorite themes from the opera, also arranged by the composer.

25. The copy in the Kongelige Bibliotek is not an autograph MS, according to Dr. Sven Lunn, but rather the work of a professional copyist.

26. For a brief, convenient summary of critical opinion, see the article on Bredal in the *Dansk Biografisk Leksikon*, IV.

27. The musical illustrations from the overture follow the printed arrangement for piano. Other illustrations in this section follow the printed material, unless otherwise indicated.

28. In his foreword Andersen mentions having found this with a German text, "Jung Karl ist mein Liebling." Some forty years later Holstein used the same tune, with the original words in German translation, in *Die Hochländer* (see Chapter 3).

29. Andersen's version of Thomas the Rhymer's ominous prophecy regarding the last Laird of Ravenswood:

> When the last Laird of Ravenswood to Ravenswood shall ride,
> And woo a dead maiden to be his bride,
> He shall stable his steed in the Kelpie's flow,
> And his name shall be lost for evermoe!

Caleb repeats these words to Edgar in chapter xviii, just before Edgar leaves Wolf's Crag to visit the Ashtons at Ravenswood.

30. The illustration is from the orchestral score.

31. All my musical illustrations to Act III come from the orchestral score.

32. See Andersen's remarks about the ballad in his foreword.

33. The illustration is from the orchestral score.

34. From the orchestral score. Cf. Donizetti's use in Lucia's mad scene of fragments from the fountain-scene duet.

35. According to Schmidl's *Dizionario Universale dei Musicisti.*

36. The Bibliothèque de l'Opéra has two copies of this. In the foreword Beltrame refers to an earlier printing in conjunction with the première, in Padova.

37. The single number is the fine quartet with chorus, "Appena il vidi," which comes at the end of Act I (see below). It was published in Florence and Milan by Ricordi. Since it is both interesting and rare, I have reproduced it photographically in the Appendix, from the copy in the Biblioteca del Conservatorio "Giuseppe Verdi." (Apparently neither the orchestral score nor a vocal score was ever published; the autograph MS of the former may still exist, hidden away in some archive in Italy and long since forgotten.)

38. These roles were sung, respectively, by Gaetano Maspes, Sig^{ra} Carolina Patteri, Giuseppe Zoboli, Sig^{ra} Marianna Hazon, and Sig^{ra} Teresa Rossetti in the Milan production.

39. I have used the Schirmer vocal score (It.-Eng.) and compared it here and there with the Peters edition (It.-Ger.). The French version, *Lucie de Lammermoor,* with words by Alphonse Royer and Gustave Vaëz, differs from the original in several respects. For an interesting comparison see William Ashbrook, *Donizetti* (London, 1965), pp. 424–425.

40. In a recent production of *Lucia* Alisa appeared as a blind old woman. This conception of the role cannot be justified by either text or music. It was purely a gimmick on the part of the stage director (but an intriguing one, I will have to admit). See the review in *Opera* (January 1969), p. 35.

CHAPTER 9

1. Printed in London, 1820, by W. Smith. It can be found in the BM, but not under Beazley's name.

2. "*The mere utterance of Sounds, without the distinct articulation of Words,* does not deserve to be called SINGING: it is merely playing upon the Voice—*a Concerto on the Larynx.* . . . The *chef d'œuvre* of difficulty is, a PLAIN ENGLISH BALLAD, which, 'when unadorned, is adorned the most,' and, indeed, will hardly admit of any ornament beyond an *apogiatura* [spelled thus]. This style of Song is less understood than any; and though apparently, from its simplicity, it is very easy, yet, to warble it with graceful expression requires a great deal of real judgment, and a most attentive consideration of every note and every syllable, because it is an appeal to the heart. Decorated Ditties merely play about the ear, and seldom excite any sensation beyond."

3. For further information see White, pp. 108–110.

4. Published separately in Paris, 1826. A copy is in the BM.

5. The orchestral score was published in Paris, a copy of which is in the Bibliothèque Nationale. (Although excerpts for voice and piano do exist, apparently no complete vocal score was ever published.)

6. Included in *Cumberland's British Theatre,* Vol. XXV (1829). See also BM MS. Addit. 42894, fols. 299–348. Joseph Wood sang Ivanhoe; Mary Ann Paton (later Mrs. Wood), Rebecca; Henry Phillips, Cedric.

7. The Popish Plot is not designated as such in the operatic *Peveril of the Peak,* probably out of respect for British Roman Catholics (see Chapter 12).

8. The situation is reminiscent of the choral number in *La Prigione d'Edimburgo*, Act II, in which the women show pity for Ida (Effie) while the men demand her immediate death (see Chapter 7).

9. I have used the vocal score published in Leipzig by Friedrich Hofmeister. It has presumably the complete text, together with an Italian translation. I have touched up my quotations from the text, after collation with two separately printed librettos included in Breitkopf & Härtel's Textbibliothek (Nos. 183 & 226).

10. Other parallels between Marschner's *Templer und Jüdin* and Richard Wagner are pointed out in Chapter 19.

11. A vocal score was published in Milan, by Ricordi. A copy is in the Newberry Library.

12. *Le Mie Memorie Artistiche: Autobiografia del Maestro Cav. Giovanni Pacini*, ed. Ferdinando Magnani (Florence, 1875), p. 66.

13. A complete libretto was published in conjunction with this production (Milan, 1834). I used the copy in the BM.

14. A musical number preceding a warrior's departure for battle is an operatic convention. Cf. the first scene of Verdi's *Aida*, where the very same words— "ritorna vincitor"—are used. (There are no musical echoes, I hasten to add.)

15. From the vocal score. The words to the cabaletta are different in the libretto.

16. The complete vocal score, with Italian text, was published by Schlesinger in Paris ca. 1850; it can be found in the Newberry Library and in the BM. The Bibliothèque Nationale has Danglas' French version, *Le Templier*, which contains ballet music not in the original. An Italian libretto, with a parallel French translation in prose (*not* Danglas' version), was published in conjunction with the Paris production of 1868; the BM has a copy.

17. Danglas' version has five acts.

18. This scene was evidently omitted from the Paris production of 1868. It is not included in the above-cited libretto.

19. The suspenseful, hushed atmosphere of this number reminds one of the chorus of murderers in Verdi's *Macbeth* or the "Zitti, zitti" chorus in *Rigoletto*, Act II.

20. In the Paris production of 1868 this *scena* began the third act; see the above-cited libretto.

21. It is in the Bibliothèque de l'Opéra.

22. Neither the vocal score nor the two librettos are dated. I have supplied the dates suggested in the BM Catalogues.

23. The setting is given a detailed description in the 1882 libretto. Remarkable features of this libretto are its elaborate descriptions of setting, its lengthy stage directions, and, at the end, its detailed information about the costumes that the singers wear in each act.

24. On the relationship between voice and character, see Charles Hamm, *Opera* (Boston, 1966), pp. 11–17.

25. From the dedication-page of the vocal score, published by Chappell & Co. The music was arranged for pianoforte by Ernest Ford, who conducted many of the performances. Copies can be found in the Sibley Music Library (Eastman School of Music), the University of London Library, the BM, and elsewhere. I have used the vocal score for all musical and textual quotations, but I have touched

up the latter after collation with the separate libretto, published also by Chappell.

26. The shift in mood makes for highly dramatic opera, as Sullivan well knew. Cf. the ending of the third act of *Il Trovatore,* when word is unexpectedly brought to Manrico that his mother, Azucena, has been taken prisoner by the Count di Luna; he vows vengeance in the famous aria, "Di quella pira." Or cf. the change of mood in the last act of *La Bohème:* the horseplay in Rodolpho's garret stops when Musetta enters with news that Mimi, desperately ill, has returned.

27. I had always thought the incident of the novel a bit far-fetched until I heard the late German actress Katharina Kivernagel recall a similar incident in which she herself, many years ago in Berlin, had been involved. She was telling the story to a small group of friends one night in the Contra-Kreis Theater, in Bonn. As she spoke, the famous chapter in *Ivanhoe* came immediately to my mind. "Einen Schritt weiter und ich springe aus dem Fenster!" were her very words. When I asked her whether she had ever read *Ivanhoe,* she replied that she had not, nor had she ever so much as heard of the novel and its author.

28. The subtlety of the novel is lost. Brian at first refuses to do battle with a wounded man. Ivanhoe replies:

> "Ha! proud Templar, . . . hast thou forgotten that twice didst thou fall before this lance? . . . I will proclaim thee, Templar, a coward in every court in Europe—in every Preceptory of thine Order—unless thou do battle without farther delay."

> Bois-Guilbert turned his countenance irresolutely towards Rebecca, and then exclaimed, looking fiercely at Ivanhoe, "Dog of a Saxon! take thy lance, and prepare for the death thou hast drawn upon thee!" (chapter xliii)

The situation is especially effective in that Ivanhoe has unwittingly aggravated Brian's emotional turmoil by using almost the same words that Rebecca used in defying him during the course of the temptation scene at Torquilstone:

> "But I will proclaim thy villainy, Templar, from one end of Europe to the other. . . . Each Preceptory—each Chapter of thy Order, shall learn, that, like a heretic, thou hast sinned with a Jewess." (chapter xxiv)

29. For much of my information about the 1910 revival, I am indebted to Miss Margaret L. Nicholson, archivist at Covent Garden, who very graciously loaned me a typed copy of a talk entitled "Sullivan at the 'Garden' " which she gave at a meeting of the Gilbert and Sullivan Society, 24 November 1969, in London.

30. As Miss Nicholson pointed out, the newspapers differed as to the reason for the cancellation.

CHAPTER 10

1. *Maria Stuarda: Regina di Scozia* (Bologna, 1821). A copy is in the Bibliothèque de l'Opéra.

2. The BM has a complete Italian-English libretto, and also four of the eight musical numbers that were published. The opera was first performed in London, at the Haymarket. For reference to Coccia's *Edoardo in Iscozia,* see Chapter 1.

3. The time is 1587, and the action takes place at Westminster and at Fotheringay Castle. (The BM has a vocal score and a separate libretto.)

4. The BM has the vocal score. For Niedermeyer's connection with Rossini's *Robert Bruce,* see Chapter 18.

5. The Bibliothèque Nationale has the complete vocal score, which was published in Milan by E. Lucca (n.d.).

6. An autograph MS of the music (scored for piano alone) is in the Bibliothèque Nationale.

7. The complete text (listed under Planard) is in the BM. The various musical numbers were published with piano accompaniment (Paris, n.d.); most of them can be found in the Bibliothèque Nationale. The librettist De Planard also had a hand in Carafa's *Prison d'Édimbourg* (see Chapter 7) and in Adam's *Caleb de Walter Scott* (see Chapter 8).

8. In spirit the music is reminiscent of Georges Brown's "Quel plaisir d'être soldat," from *La Dame Blanche*.

9. Cf. the formerly well-known *romance*, "Adieu donc, belle France," in Niedermeyer's *Marie Stuart*.

CHAPTER 11

1. Schira was a veteran conductor at the Garden. "Eine höchst pittoreske Persönlichkeit, war er ein heftiger Gegner Wagners, Boitos und selbst Gounods; das Ungestüm, mit dem er seine Meinungen kundtat, brachte ihm den Spitznamen *'the firebrand Schira'* ein" (*MGG*). I do not know who did the libretto. It may be that all MSS relating to the work were destroyed in the fire that devastated the old opera house in 1856.

2. Rossini's *Elisabetta, Regina d'Inghilterra* owes nothing to Scott, since it antedates *Kenilworth* by several years.

3. The Newberry Library has a copy of the vocal score published in Paris by A. Brullé (n.d.). Like most vocal scores of opéras comiques, it does not have the spoken dialogue. The complete text can be found among the *Œuvres Complètes de Scribe*. The BM has the orchestral score. Duveyrier used the pen name Mélesville.

4. I can only speculate on the reason why Auber might have decided not to set this number to music, since the sentiment expressed certainly has musical possibilities. Perhaps he felt that an additional aria for Elisabeth would give her unwarranted prominence in view of the fact that Amy is the real heroine.

5. A vocal score was published by Schonenberger in Paris [1855?], a copy of which can be found in the Bibliothèque Nationale. (The BN also has an earlier vocal score, published in Naples, but some of the musical numbers are lacking.) I did not run across a separately printed libretto, but the vocal score presumably has the complete text. The autograph orchestral score is in the library of the Naples Conservatory.

6. See Herbert Weinstock, *Donizetti and the World of Opera in Italy, Paris, and Vienna in the First Half of the Nineteenth Century* (New York, 1963), p. 66. See also William Ashbrook, *Donizetti* (London, 1965), p. 108.

7. As translated and quoted in Weinstock, pp. 66–67.

8. The English paraphrases in this paragraph are mine.

9. The aria minus the cabaletta was sung by Mattiwilda Dobbs in Freemasons' Hall, Edinburgh, 1 September 1971, in a recital entitled "Walter Scott in Music and Song," which formed part of the official program of the 25th Edinburgh International Festival. Her rendition of this number was singled out by Conrad Wilson for especial praise in his favorable review which appeared the next day in *The Scotsman*. (Cf. Chapter 7, fn. 15.)

10. As translated in Ashbrook, p. 108. Ashbrook's contention that Tottola's

libretto derives from Scribe's *Leicester* is over-stated. (The happy ending can be found also in Gaetano Barbieri's five-act play, *Elisabetta al Castello di Kenilworth,* which was first performed on 5 April 1823, in Milan.)

11. See *Dagen,* No. 6 (7 Jan. 1836), No. 22 (26 Jan.), No. 23 (27 Jan.); *Söndagen,* No. 6 (7 Feb. 1836); *Iris* (1836), pp. 16, 20, 22–24; *Musikalsk Tidende* (1836), pp. 41–44, 49–61, 78–80. These I have seen. For other references see entry #285 of Birger Frank Nielsen's *H. C. Andersen Bibliografi* (H. Hagerup-København, 1942).

12. According to Sven Lunn's article on Weyse in the *Dansk Biografisk Leksikon,* Vol. XXV. Dr. Lunn told me in 1968 that Weyse discusses *Festen* in his Letters.

13. Included in his *Samlede Skrifter,* 2nd ed. (Copenhagen, 1878), IX, 69–167.

14. . . . a *larghetto,* "full of dignity, and, if you will, chivalric courtesy, which suggests the presence of the illustrious guest"—*Musikalsk Tidende* (1836), p. 51. All musical quotations are from the vocal score, published in Copenhagen in 1877 by the Samfundet til Udgivelse af Dansk Musik (without the spoken dialogue). Copies can be found in the BM and in the Kongelige Bibliothek. The latter also has two MSS of the full score, one of which is Weyse's autograph.

15. At the première Hr. Phister sang the role of Lambourne. Other principal roles were done by Jfr. Zirza (Elisabeth), Hr. Sahlers (Lei'ster), Hr. Kirchheiner (Varney), Mme Kragh (Amy), Hr. Schwartzen (Tressilian), Hr. Schneider (Foster), Jfr. Kofod (Jeanette), and Hr. Waltz (Dickie).

16. According to the vocal score, but not the libretto.

17. See the short entry in the *Breslauer Zeitung,* Beilage zu No. 299 (21 Dec. 1843), p. 2399, and the review in the Erste Beilage zu No. 301 (23 Dec. 1843), p. 2415.

18. Known professionally at first as Marie Deckmann, she made her debut in Koenigstadt, 1837, in Bellini's *I Capuleti ed i Montecchi.* Later she sang at the Royal Theater in Hannover, and in February 1840 she was engaged for leading roles at the theater in Breslau. She married Seidelmann on 27 September 1841.— According to Fétis.

19. According to the review in the *Breslauer Zeitung* (see fn. 17), it was the work of "several" authors, whose identities were not disclosed.

20. Tressiliano's *romanza* of Act IV, "Un'infelice veglio," in an arrangement for voice and piano. It is in MS and can be found in Livorno, at the Biblioteca Comunale Labronica. I have not seen it.

21. A vocal score, with the French text, was published in Paris (1894) by Choudens. A copy is in the Newberry Library. Choudens also published a separate libretto (1894)—which can be found in the BM.

22. *Many Tales of Many Cities* (London, [1928]), p. 104.

23. *Ibid.,* p. 113.

24. Croydon is now part of London. See *The Croydon Times* of May 8th, 1920, for a flowery announcement about the forthcoming performance there of *Amy Robsart.* Kate Campion was scheduled to sing the title-role; Gladys Seager, Elizabeth; Parry Jones, Leicester; Lewys James, Varney; Lovat Crossley, Tressilian.

25. A vocal score was published in Leipzig, 1894, by Friedrich Hofmeister. A copy is in the Newberry Library.

26. In the Mittags-Ausgabe. "Die gestern zum Benefiz unserer ersten dramatischen Sängerin Frau Klafsky aufgeführte Novität ist ein Werk, das volle Beachtung verdient. Mag man sich zu dem Ganzen stellen, wie man will, auf jeden Fall ist die Oper "Kenilworth" die Schöpfung eines intelligenten, geschmachvol-

len und vornehm empfindenden Musikers, der jeden Gemeinplatz vermeidet
und einem hohen Ziele nachstrebt. . . . Die Oper hat uns lebhaft interessirt [*sic*],
und wenn ihr auch der eigentliche dramatische Nerv fehlt, so ist sie immerhin die
Schöpfung eines begabten, lebhaft empfindenden Musikers, der eine ideale
Anschauung von seiner Kunst hat." The evening was a great triumph for Mme
Klafsky: "Dass Frau Klafsky zu ihrem Benefiz eine neue Oper eines bislang
unbekannten deutschen Componisten wählte, ehrt sie und das Werk. Aus der
Partie der Amy schuf sie eine lebensvolle Gestalt, die sie mit der ganzen Inner-
lichkeit, die ihr in so hohem Grade eigen ist, beseelte und die sie im letzten Akt zur
erschütternden Darstellung brachte. Der genialen Künstlerin wurden namentlich
am Schluss begeisterte Ovationen zu Theil."

27. Klein was born in Osnabrück in 1858. He studied first under his father, who
was organist at the Osnabrück Cathedral, and later at the Munich Conservatory.
He immigrated to the United States in 1878, and from 1884 until his death in 1911
he was head of the piano department at the Convent of the Sacred Heart, in New
York. (See the short entry in Baker.)

28. It recalls the offstage chorus of peasants, returning home for the night, that
De Lara's Amy and Lester hear during the course of their long love-duet at
Cumnor, Act I.

29. Indeed, the relationship between Goldzwirn and Janet Foster brings vaguely to mind Cuddie Headrigg and Jenny Dennison. Note also Goldzwirn's stealthy
coming into the castle by way of a window, and cf. Cuddie's amusing incursion into
the kitchen of Tillietudlem. (See Chapter 5.)

30. Several passages in the duet are reminiscent of the love music in *Tristan und
Isolde,* Act II. For that matter, much of the opera sounds very Wagnerian.

31. It is in the key of B flat and is slightly reminiscent of the *Lohengrin* Wedding
March, which, in fact, could easily be sung to Müller's text: "Tugend und rein im
Tugendschein/Naht die Gebiet'rin voll Majestät," etc.

32. Cf. the ending of Carafa's *Nozze di Lammermoor* (Chapter 8).

CHAPTER 12

1. Horn came to the United States in 1847 and lived in Boston, where he served
as conductor of the Handel and Haydn Society until his death two years later. I
have not seen the music he composed for Samuel James Arnold's *The Wizard; or,
The Brown Man of the Moor* (1817), based on *The Black Dwarf,* nor do I know where it
can be found.

2. See White, pp. 175–176, 242. White indicates in a footnote that "the musical
score and copy of the lyrics, in manuscript form, are a part of the Brown Collection, Boston Public Library."

3. A copy is in the BM.

4. Included in *Plays from the Lord Chamberlain's Office,* Vol. XV, MS. Addit.
42,879, folios 398–507. It is entitled *Fenella; or, Peveril of the Peak.* In the quoted
material that follows I have occasionally had to touch up the punctuation.

5. Not in the MS of the libretto. Instead, there is a piece in Scots dialect ("O,
Willie brew'd a peck o' maut"). The change may have been prompted by the
belated realization of the absurdity of having a Scottish song in an opera based on
a thoroughly *English* Waverley novel. (But cf. Klein's *Kenilworth,* Chapter 11.)

6. Not in the MS of the libretto. Instead, there is the lyric, "Why was I doom'd to love,/And doom'd to love in vain," etc.

7. A song for Julian entitled "The Shepherd's reed," not in the libretto, comes just before Alice's song in the score. Apparently it is intended for this scene.

8. Not in the score.

9. Not in the MS of the libretto. Instead:

> Merrily, cheerily, here we sue,
> Kind and fair ones, now to you;
> Cheerily, merrily, would you deign
> To let the "Dumb Girl" talk again.

There is an indication that this is to be sung to Horn's well-known tune, "Cherry ripe."

10. The opera is often listed under the title *Masaniello*. While at the BM I examined a Fr.-Eng. vocal score (London: Novello [1873]); an It.-Eng. vocal score (London and New York: Boosey & Co., [1872]); the separate libretto included in *La France Dramatique au Dix-Neuvième Siècle*, Vol. XVII (Paris, 1841); and a Ger.-Eng. libretto (London, 1843).

11. Specifically, I have examined the following items: (a) T.B., *The Rebellion of Naples, or the Tragedy of Massenello* (London, 1651); (b) Bertholdus Feind, *Masagniello Furioso, oder die Neapolitanische Fischer-Empörung* (Hamburg, 1727); (c) J.F.E. Albrecht, *Masaniello von Neapel: Original-Trauerspiel in fünf Aufzügen* (Berlin, 1789); (d) George Soane, *Masaniello, the Fisherman of Naples* (London, 1825)—first performed on 17 February 1825 at Drury Lane, with incidental music by Bishop (see Chapter 14, fn. 3); (e) Carafa's *Masaniello, ou Le Pêcheur Napolitain* (libretto by Moreau and Lafortelle), first performed on 27 December 1827 at the Opéra-Comique. (Only items d and e could have owed anything to *Peveril of the Peak*, which was published in January, 1823.) The libretto for Stefano Pavesi's *Fenella, o La Muta di Portici*, first performed on 5 February 1831 at the Fenice (in Venice), is probably a translation of Scribe's libretto; I have not seen it.

12. B. Jouvin, *D.F.E. Auber: Sa Vie et Ses Œuvres* (Paris, 1864), p. 38.

13. *A Short History of Opera*, 2nd ed. (New York, 1965), p. 317. (The MS libretto of Horn's *Peveril* indicates that music is to accompany Fenella's pantomimes, but none of it appears in the published vocal score.)

14. No commercial recording of the complete opera exists, but a private recording of a performance in Paris (June, 1971) was recently released by Edward J. Smith. It stars Monique de Pondeau (Elvire), Pierre Lanni (Masaniello), André Mallabrera (Alphonse), Yves Bisson (Pietro), Bernard Demigny (Borella), and Claude Gentry (Selva); the conductor is Jean Doussard.—For further information about Auber and *La Muette* see John W. Klein, "*Daniel-François Auber (1782-1871)*," *Opera*, XXII (1971), 684–690. This interesting article appeared after I had already written the section above. Klein is one of the few commentators who do express awareness of the muette's origin. He also emphasizes the high esteem which Richard Wagner had for the opera.

CHAPTER 13

1. *The Musical World*, Vol. XXIII, No. 50 (9 Dec. 1848), p. 790.

2. There is no entry for Laurent in any of the standard reference works. According to the above-cited review, he had formerly been "a pupil of the Royal

Academy of Music, and while prosecuting his studies at that institution displayed
. . . a talent for composition which augured well for his future."

    3. See my introductory paragraph to Chapter 11.

    4. Specifically, the following published selections, bound up in one volume:

        1. The Overture . . . Composed and Arranged for the Piano Forte . . .

        2. Grand March . . . Composed for the Piano Forte . . .

        3. Favorite Airs . . . Composed & Arranged for the Piano Forte . . .

           a. The Archers' Chorus

           b. "I come from the land of the mountain"

           c. "Ah! 'tis she"

           d. "And dare I dream when far away?"

           e. "Yes, mem'ry returns to the days of my childhood"

           f. Rondo Finale: "Like crystal streams"

        4. "Alone am I in sorrow" (ballad for Quentin)

        5. "I come from the land of the mountain" (ballad for Quentin)

        6. "Is she a spirit?" (ballad for Quentin)

        7. "The halls of my fathers" (ballad for Isabelle)

        8. "The merry dance is not for me, or the vesper bell" (ballad for Princess Joan)

        9. "They call me here, they call me there, Maître Pierre" (song for King Louis)

      10. "Ye skies of azure" (duet for Isabelle and Quentin)

Nos. 4–10 are arranged for voice and piano. No complete score, vocal or orchestral, seems to have been published. I do not know whether any material in MS still exists.

    5. Included in *Plays from the Lord Chamberlain's Office,* Vol. CLI (MS. Addit. 43,015), folios 308–345. I have made a few corrections and emendations in my quotations from this MS. The 2nd act is in a different hand from that of the 1st and 3rd acts, and not so carefully penned.

    6. A fine musicologist, Gevaert is still remembered for his treatise on instrumentation, which, according to Grove, is "2nd in importance only to that by Berlioz." In 1871 he went to Brussels, where he succeeded Fétis as director of the Conservatoire. Shortly before his death (1908) he wrote a national anthem for the Congo.—The list of librettos that Cormon and Carré wrote in collaboration includes, besides *Quentin Durward, Les Pêcheurs de Perles* (Bizet). Carré collaborated with Jules Barbier in the libretto for Gounod's *Faust,* which was first performed one year after the première of *Quentin Durward.* See fn. 11.

    7. Petit-André, Trois-Echelles, (spelled thus), and Charles le Téméraire appear on stage briefly, but they neither sing nor speak.

    8. I used the complete libretto as it appears in *Théâtre Contemporain Illustré* and the vocal score (which does not include the spoken dialogue) published in Paris by Alexandre Grus. Both can be found in the BM, and elsewhere.

    9. This is a wonderful moment in the score. Indeed, the entire finale is most attractive.

    10. Cf. Louis' words when Dunois has apprised him of the reason for Charles' having sent Crèvecoeur to him: "Ay . . . is it even so?—will our ancient vassal prove so masterful—our dear cousin treat us thus unkindly?—Nay then, Dunois, we must unfold the *Oriflamme,* and cry *Dennis Montjoye!"*

    11. The trio brings to mind the trio in Gounod's *Faust,* Act IV (Faust, Valentin,

Mephistopheles) both in rhythmical texture and in the three registers of voices used (Quentin: tenor—Crèvecœur: baritone—Lesly: bass). See fn. 6.

12. A copy is in the BM.

13. The opera as given at the Lyceum was apparently somewhat abridged. See the review in *The Times* of 5 June 1920.

14. See also his overt hints to Sir Henry Bishop and Catherine Stephens, as he continues: "It is, therefore, scarcely fair to put upon record lines intended not to be said or read, but only to be sung. But such scraps of old poetry have always had a sort of fascination for us; and as the tune is lost for ever—unless Bishop happens to find the notes, or some lark teaches Stephens to warble the air—we will risk our credit, and the taste of the Lady of the Lute, by preserving the verses, simple and even rude as they are."

15. Cf. the orchestral introduction to the third act of *Tosca*.

16. The reviewer in *The Times* (see fn. 13) expressed his reservations thus: "Mr. Maclean finds plenty of occasion for the use of telling tunes and bright orchestration, but he never seems quite to make up his mind as to any definite style of treatment or any principle of coherence between the parts. The music all seems a little haphazard."

CHAPTER 14

1. From the "pro-em" (introduction) to the vocal score of Balfe's *Talisman* (see fn. 14 below).

2. A printed edition is included in *Cumberland's British Theatre*, Vol. XXXIV. (See also Brit. Mus. MS. Addit. 42878, folios 117–184.)

3. The autograph score is in the BM—Addit. MS. 27719 (which contains also the autograph of Bishop's music for George Soane's *Masaniello, the Fisherman of Naples;* see Chapter 12, fn. 11). Bishop "selected" music from Boieldieu, from the overture to Beethoven's *Fidelio,* and from *The Humorous Lieutenant* and *The Beacon of Liberty* (two of his own earlier musical dramas). (See also Brit. Mus. MS. Addit. 36965 for five musical numbers, chiefly choruses.)

4. As a singer Horn was most highly acclaimed for his interpretation of the role of Caspar, in *Der Freischütz.*

5. *Le Mie Memorie Artistiche: Autobiografia del Maestro Cav. Giovanni Pacini,* ed. Ferdinando Magnani (Florence, 1875), p. 57. Of Barbieri, Pacini writes that he was a man "di singolare ingegno, molto ameno nel conversare, e di una onestà scrupolosa; ma le formole algebriche e le figure geometriche mal si confanno colla poesia. Nelle prime sta il calcolo, nella seconda l'ispirazione."

6. A separate libretto was published in Milan, 1829, by Antonio Fontana; the BM has a copy. Ricordi published a vocal score (Milan, 1829); this too is in the BM.

7. *Le Mie Memorie Artistiche,* p. 57.

8. *Ibid.,* p. 74.

9. *Ibid.,* p. 57.

10. A vocal score published by the Bureau Central de Musique can be found in the Bibliothèque Nationale. Inasmuch as *Richard* is opéra rather than opéra comique, the score contains the complete text. A separate libretto was published in Paris, 1844, by C. Tresse. (This too can be found in the BN.)

11. George Alexander Macfarren put finishing touches on the score.

12. Cf. Isidore de Lara's *Amy Robsart,* which, as I observed in Chapter 11, was

first produced in French translation. Unlike the Balfe opera under discussion here, *Amy Robsart* was given more often in translation than in the original English.

13. The performance data comes from Loewenberg. See also White, p. 186.

14. I have used the It.-Eng. vocal score published in London by Duff & Stewart; a copy can be found in the Newberry Library. (My discussion is geared to the original English text, and in quotations I have sometimes emended the punctuation.)

15. Quoted from the plot summary given in the "pro-em" to the vocal score.

CHAPTER 15

1. Pages 186–188.

2. In the issue for Sunday, 7 May 1837. All my information about the première comes from this review.

3. For further information on opera at the Hôtel Castellane, see the first paragraph of my discussion of Flotow's *Rob-Roy,* Chapter 6.

4. The name *Ruben* was perhaps suggested by *Reuben* Butler, of *The Heart of Mid-Lothian.*

5. The name *Taff* perhaps derives from *Taffril,* a lieutenant in *The Antiquary.*

6. Pages 1–61. My information about the performance at the Paris Conservatory comes from the note on page 3.

7. *Friedrich von Flotow's Leben: Von seiner Witwe* (Leipzig, 1892), p. 88. "Nur einige Nummern," she continues, "deren Erhaltung der Komponist der Sorgfalt eines Freundes zu verdanken hatte, wurden aus dem Schiffbruche gerettet. (I do not know whether these numbers still exist.)

8. The French audiences that heard *Alice* no doubt found this number especially attractive; it owes little, if anything, to the novel.

CHAPTER 16

1. Some weeks earlier, Grisar's publisher arranged a soirée at the home of M. Mélesville in which all the music was performed. See Arthur Pougin, *Albert Grisar: Étude Artistique* (Paris and Brussels, 1870), pp. 40–41.

2. White mentions a play entitled *Dougal the Piper; or, The Highland Widow,* which he says was first performed on 20 September 1836 in Edinburgh, at the Adelphi, and "ran for nine nights . . . with a successful revival in 1852" (pp. 192 and 237). This information is misleading. Apparently two different plays are involved: (1) *The Highland Widow,* first performed at the Adelphi on 17 (*not* 20) September 1836 (White repeated the erroneous date which he found in James C. Dibdin's *Annals of the Edinburgh Stage*), with Mrs. Fisher in the title-role and Mr. Murray as Dick Heartless (a character not in Scott's story); and (2) *Dougal the Piper; or, The Orphan of Glencoe,* performed at the Theatre-Royal on 2 & 3 January 1852, with Bruce Norton as Dougal and Fanny Vining as *Effie,* the orphan of Glencoe. It may be that the latter play derives from Grisar's opera. Unfortunately I have little further information about it. The notices and short reviews in Edinburgh newspapers and journals give no indication as to the play's author, and playbills for the Theatre-Royal are lacking for January 1852 in both the Scottish National Library and the Edinburgh Public Library.

3. In the issue for Sunday, 1 May 1836.

4. According to Pougin, p. 45, fn. 1.

5. A copy is in the BM.

6. This too is in the BM. The complete German text is printed on ten triple-columned pages that precede the vocal score proper, which consists of the over-ture and thirteen numbers (with Fr.-Ger. text). The vocal score does not always dovetail with the orchestral score: some of the numbers come to a rounded-off conclusion instead of leading, as in the orchestral score, into the next number in the fashion of through-composed opera. My discussion is geared to the French text (published by Marchant in Paris, 1836), which I have compared in all particulars with the German text. (Mélesville's real name was Anne Honoré Joseph Duveyrier.)

7. Pougin, pp. 43–45. See also Fétis' comments on *Sarah* in his entry on Grisar.

8. *Wappensiegel* in the German version.

9. There is no Meg in *The Highland Widow*. Mélesville may have borrowed the motif of an offstage sick old woman from *La Prison d'Édimbourg* (cf. the account given by Scribe's Sarah of her mother's last illness), and he no doubt named the woman after Meg Merrilies of *Guy Mannering*.

10. In the German version: "Höre nur! Du wirst mich bald verstehen!"

CHAPTER 17

1. See H. A. White, pp. 189–190, 235.

2. John W. Klein, "Bizet's 'Scottish' Opera," *Opera*, XIX (1968), 786–793.

3. As quoted by Mina Curtiss in *Bizet and His World* (London, 1959), p. 174.

4. Saint-Georges "was responsible, either singly or with a collaborator, for the books of nine of Fromental Halévy's most successful operas, three of Auber's, four of Clapisson's, Balfe's *The Bohemian Girl*, Donizetti's *La Fille du Régiment*, Flotow's *Martha,* and dozens of others"—Curtiss, p. 172.

5. *Ibid.,* p. 196.

6. A few years later Mlle Ducasse created the role of Frasquita in *Carmen.*

7. For further information about the opera's reception, see Curtiss, pp. 211–215.

8. The date was 5 October 1956. The cast included Mattiwilda Dobbs (Catherine), Anna Pollack (Mab), Alexander Young (Henry Smith), Niven Miller (the Duke of Rothsay), David Ward (Ralph), and Owen Brannigan (Simon Glover). A private recording of this performance was released a few years ago by Edward J. Smith.

9. October 26, 30; November 1, 3. See William Mann's review in *The Times* (29 October 1968), p. 11.

10. I have used the Choudens vocal score, first published in 1868. (The orchestral score was not published until after Bizet's death.)

11. *Op. cit.,* p. 175. "In the novel," she continues, "the heroine, Catherine, is not unlike Micaëla in *Carmen.* On stage she becomes the familiar comic-opera flirt, a transformation that makes her mad scene in the last act doubly unconvincing. Smith, her suitor, a very upstanding man, well drawn by Scott, is reduced to a foolish, lovelorn simulacrum of a man. The Duke of Rothsay, potentially a Scottish Don Juan or Rigoletto type of duke, merely attempts unsuccessfully the most banal operatic seductions. Louise, the glee-maiden or female wandering

minstrel, one of the most original and colorful figures in the novel, is unrecognizably changed into a conventional gypsy, Mab."

12. An alternative for this number is a lovely *rêverie*, totally different in musical character and much more in keeping with Catherine's personality as conceived by Scott; the words, moreover, obliquely foreshadow subsequent events of the opera.

13. "In the second act," wrote the critic Gautier (see above), "we noted . . . particularly the bacchanale of the gypsies, which recalls with unusual felicity those strangely passionate songs with their mad verve, harsh, savage, yet so sadly tender and melancholy, so nostalgically reminiscent of the *Zigeuner*" (as translated and quoted in Curtiss, *op. cit.*, pp. 211–212). More recently the *danse* has been described as "one of the first triumphs in opera of a vivid and picturesque exoticism" (Klein, *op. cit.*, p. 788).

14. *Op. cit.*, p. 790.

15. As translated and quoted in Curtiss, p. 212.

16. As translated and quoted in Curtiss, p. 174.

17. *Ibid.*, pp. 174–175.

CHAPTER 18

1. A separately printed libretto can be found in the *Bibliothèque Dramatique*, Vol. III; a copy is in the BM.

2. The BM has the full score, which was published in Paris by Troupenas, and also an Italian vocal score published in Milan by Giovanni Ricordi and dedicated by him to the celebrated tenor, Giovanni Battista Rubini. Neither has any indication whatever that Rossini's music was arranged by Niedermeyer. The Italian translation was the work of Calisto Bassi, who wrote the libretto for Rieschi's *Fidanzata di Lammermoor* some fifteen years earlier (see Chapter 8).

3. The last sentence of the preface to the libretto (see fn. 1 above) is inaccurate: "L'argument du présent *libretto* est un simple épisode de cette mémorable guerre."

CHAPTER 19

1. Camille Saint-Saëns rightly deplored this unnecessary, unorganic addition, which Bizet himself would no doubt have deplored; see Mina Curtiss, *Bizet and His World* (London, 1959), p. 462.

2. It brings vaguely to mind the Gotteskampf-Motiv as well as the leitmotiv associated with Wotan's spear.

3. Discussed by Robert M. Rayner in *Wagner and "Die Meistersinger"* (London, 1940), p. 229.

While this book was in the final stage of proof, my colleague John Dowling brought to my attention the opera *Le Revenant*, based on "Wandering Willie's Tale" (in *Redgauntlet*), with words by Albert de Calvimont and music by José Melchor Gomis. It was first performed in Paris, at the Opéra-Comique, on December 31, 1833. Professor Dowling discusses this work in his recent book, *José Melchor Gomis: Compositor Romántico* (Madrid, 1973), pp. 51–58. Included in his appendix are excerpts reproduced photographically from the orchestral score, which can be found in the BN and in the library of Texas Tech University. In a future study I intend to show the relationship between *Le Revenant* and other Walter Scott operas.

INDEX